THE LEGACY OF AD HOC TRIBUNALS IN INTERNATIONAL CRIMINAL LAW

In the post-Nuremberg era, two of the most important developments in international criminal law are the International Criminal Tribunal for Yugoslavia (ICTY) and the International Criminal Tribunal for Rwanda (ICTR). Created through UN Security Council resolutions, with specific mandates to prosecute those responsible for serious violations of international humanitarian law, the ICTY and the ICTR played crucial roles in the development of international criminal law. Through a series of chapters written by leading authorities in the field, *The Legacy of Ad Hoc Tribunals in International Criminal Law* addresses the history of the ICTY and the ICTR and the important aspects of the tribunals' accomplishments. From examining the groundwork laid by the ICTY and the ICTR for greater international attention to crimes against humanity to the establishment of the International Criminal Court, this volume provides a comprehensive overview of the impact and lasting roles of these tribunals.

MILENA STERIO is Associate Dean and Professor of Law at Cleveland-Marshall College of Law, Cleveland State University. She has published numerous law review articles in this field and is the author of four books including *Domestic Solutions to International Crime* (Cambridge University Press 2015).

MICHAEL P. SCHARF is Dean of the Law School and the Joseph C. Hostetler – Baker Hostetler Professor of Law at Case Western Reserve University School of Law. Scharf, who previously served as Attorney Adviser for UN Affairs at the US Department of State, is the author of over 100 scholarly articles and eighteen books, three of which have garnered national book of the year honors.

The Legacy of Ad Hoc Tribunals in International Criminal Law

ASSESSING THE ICTY'S AND THE ICTR'S MOST SIGNIFICANT LEGAL ACCOMPLISHMENTS

Edited by

MILENA STERIO

Cleveland-Marshall College of Law

MICHAEL P. SCHARF

Case Western Reserve University School of Law

CAMBRIDGE
UNIVERSITY PRESS

CAMBRIDGE
UNIVERSITY PRESS

University Printing House, Cambridge CB2 8BS, United Kingdom

One Liberty Plaza, 20th Floor, New York, NY 10006, USA

477 Williamstown Road, Port Melbourne, VIC 3207, Australia

314–321, 3rd Floor, Plot 3, Splendor Forum, Jasola District Centre, New Delhi – 110025, India

79 Anson Road, #06–04/06, Singapore 079906

Cambridge University Press is part of the University of Cambridge.

It furthers the University's mission by disseminating knowledge in the pursuit of education, learning, and research at the highest international levels of excellence.

www.cambridge.org
Information on this title: www.cambridge.org/9781108417389
DOI: 10.1017/9781108277525

© Cambridge University Press 2019

First published 2019

A catalogue record for this publication is available from the British Library.

Library of Congress Cataloging-in-Publication Data
NAMES: Sterio, Milena, editor. | Scharf, Michael P., 1963– editor.
TITLE: The legacy of ad hoc tribunals in international criminal law: assessing the ICTY's and the ICTR's most significant legal accomplishments / edited by Milena Sterio, Cleveland-Marshall College of Law; Michael P. Scharf, Case Western Reserve University.
DESCRIPTION: Cambridge, United Kingdom; New York, NY, USA: Cambridge University Press, 2019. | Includes index.
IDENTIFIERS: LCCN 2018037700 | ISBN 9781108417389
SUBJECTS: LCSH: International criminal courts – History. | International Criminal Tribunal for Rwanda – Influence. | International Tribunal for the Prosecution of Persons Responsible for Serious Violations of International Humanitarian Law Committed in the Territory of the Former Yugoslavia since 1991 – Influence.
CLASSIFICATION: LCC KZ7230 .L437 2019 | DDC 345/.01–dc23
LC record available at https://lccn.loc.gov/2018037700

ISBN 978-1-108-41738-9 Hardback

Contents

Contributors

Margaret M. deGuzman, Associate Professor at Temple University Beasley School of Law, Philadelphia. Professor deGuzman's scholarship focuses on the role of international criminal law in the global legal order, with a particular emphasis on the work of the International Criminal Court (ICC). She is currently participating in an international expert group studying the proposed addition of criminal jurisdiction to the mandate of the African Court on Human and People's Rights.

Before joining the Temple faculty, Professor deGuzman was an Adjunct Professor at Georgetown University, where she taught graduate courses in international human rights law. She also clerked on the Ninth Circuit Court of Appeals and practiced law in San Francisco for six years, specializing in criminal defense. Professor deGuzman also served as a legal advisor to the Senegal delegation at the Rome Conference where the ICC was created and as a law clerk in the Office of the Prosecutor of the International Criminal Tribunal for Former Yugoslavia. She was a Fulbright Scholar in Darou N'diar, Senegal.

Professor deGuzman received her PhD in 2015, from the Irish Center for Human Rights, National University of Ireland; her JD from Yale Law School in 1999; her MALD from Fletcher School of Law and Diplomacy, Tufts University; and BScFS from Georgetown University School of Foreign Service.

Yvonne M. Dutton, Associate Professor of Law, Dean's Fellow and Grimes Fellow at Indiana University Robert H. McKinney School of Law. Professor Dutton graduated from Columbia Law School in 1991, where she served on the *Columbia Law Review* and was a Harlan Fiske Stone Scholar. After graduation, Professor Dutton clerked for the Honorable William C. Conner, United States District Judge for the Southern District of New York. Dutton has practiced law as a federal prosecutor in the US Attorney's Office for the Southern District of New York, where she tried narcotics trafficking and organized crime cases. She has also practiced as a civil litigator in law firms in New York and California.

Professor Dutton's research interests include international criminal law, international human rights law, and maritime piracy. She has published her research in a variety of law reviews. In 2013, she published her book entitled *Rules, Politics, and the International Criminal Court: Committing to the Court*. In 2011, Professor Dutton was a fellow in Columbia Law School's Careers in Law Teaching Program.

Stuart Ford, Associate Professor of Law, John Marshall Law School, Chicago. Professor Ford has published articles on the International Criminal Court, the International Criminal Tribunal for the Former Yugoslavia, the Special Court for Sierra Leone, the responsibility to protect doctrine, crimes against humanity, and genocide. In 2015, Professor Ford received John Marshall's Faculty Scholarly Achievement Award. His current research explores the effectiveness of international criminal tribunals, with the goal of improving their success. He is currently Co-Chair of the American Society of International Law's International Courts and Tribunals Interest Group and is a past Chair of the American Association of Law Schools' Section on International Human Rights. He spent the summer of 2015 as a Visiting Professor at the International Criminal Court where he helped the Office of the Prosecutor develop performance metrics for its investigations and prosecutions.

Prior to joining John Marshall, Professor Ford worked as an Assistant Prosecutor at the Extraordinary Chambers in the Courts of Cambodia, to prosecute senior leaders of the Khmer Rouge. Before moving to Cambodia, he was an associate at Fulbright & Jaworski in Minneapolis and Howrey Simon Arnold & White in Washington DC.

Professor Ford received an LLM in Public International Law and Armed Conflict, with Distinction, from the University of Nottingham. He received his JD, with honors, from the University of Texas School of Law, where he was a member of the Texas Law Review and Order of the Coif. He was also a recipient of the Robert S. Strauss Endowed Presidential Scholarship in Law.

Gregory S. Gordon, Associate Professor at the Chinese University of Hong Kong Faculty of Law. Professor Gordon formerly served as Associate Dean (Development/ External Affair) and Director, Research Postgraduates Programme. Before joining the faculty, Professor Gordon taught at the University of North Dakota School of Law, where he was a Director of the school's Center for Human Rights and Genocide Studies. He earned his BA (summa cum laude) and JD at the University of California at Berkley. He then served as law clerk to US District Court Judge Martin Pence. Professor Gordon went on to work with the Office of the Prosecutor for the International Criminal Tribunal for Rwanda, where he served as Legal Officer and Deputy Team Leader for the landmark "media" cases, the first international post-Nuremberg prosecutions of radio and print media executives for incitement to genocide. For this work, Professor Gordon received a commendation from Attorney General Janet Reno for "Service to the United States and International Justice."

In 2003, Professor Gordon joined the US Department of Justice Criminal Division's Office of Special Investigations, where he helped investigate and prosecute Nazi war criminals and modern human rights violators.

Professor Gordon has trained high-level federal prosecutors in Addis Ababa at the request of the Ethiopian government, as well as prepared prosecutors for the Khmer Rouge leadership trial at the Extraordinary Chambers in the Courts of Cambodia in Phnom Penh and trained lawyers and judges at the War Crimes Chamber for the Court of Bosnia and Herzegovina. He is one of the world's foremost authorities on incitement to genocide, and his book *Atrocity Speech Law: Foundation, Fragmentation, Fruition*, proposing a new paradigm for international hate speech law, was published by Oxford University Press in 2017.

Professor Gordon co-wrote the US Supreme Court amicus brief on Holocaust and Darfur Genocide survivors in the case of *Yousuf* v. *Samantar*. He also represented the International League for Human Rights at the International Criminal Court Conference in Kampala, Uganda. He serves as a consultant for the International Nuremberg Principles Academy and is an adviser on hate speech issues for the Sentinel Project on Genocide Prevention's Advisory Council. Professor Gordon is also on the Council of Advisors for the Global Institute for the Prevention of Aggression.

Kimberly Larkin, Associate, Three Crowns, LLP, Washington office. Ms. Larking specializes in international arbitration and public international law. Prior to joining Three Crowns, Ms. Larkin worked at the US Department of State in the Office of the Legal Adviser where she advised on US and international legal matters before regional and international organizations, including advising Rwandan officials on rule of law and transitional justice matters. She has also worked for a global pro bono law firm advising government clients on international law and in the New York and Hong Kong offices of a leading international arbitration firm.

Ms. Larkin received her JD from Stanford Law School in 2016, where she served as president of the Stanford International Law Society, submissions chair of the Stanford Journal of International Law, and coach of the Stanford Vis International Arbitration team.

Ms. Larkin received an MA degree *avec grande distinction* from the Université Libre de Bruxelles, 2013. She also received a BA degree *magna cum laude* from Davidson College in 2011.

Dr. Yvonne McDermott Rees, Associate Professor of Law, Swansea University, Wales, UK. She joined the College of Law and Criminology at Swansea in 2017.

She was previously a Senior Lecturer in Law at Bangor University, Wales. She has also worked in the Irish Department of Foreign Affairs, and as a consultant to the United Nations High Commissioner for Refugees, United Nations Office of Internal Oversight Services, and the Organization for Security and Co-operation in Europe. Professor McDermott Rees holds undergraduate law degrees from the National University of Ireland, Galway, an LLM in Public International Law from Leiden University, and a PhD from the Irish Centre for Human Rights. Her doctoral thesis was awarded the Special Mention of Rene Cassin Thesis Prize 2014. She is an Academic Fellow of the Honourable Society of the Inner Temple and a Door Tenant at Invictus Chambers, London.

Professor McDermott Rees's research interests are primarily in the fields of human rights and international criminal law. Her research has been published in leading journals, including the *American Journal of International Law*, *Leiden Journal of International Law*, *Journal of International Criminal Justice*, *International Criminal Law Preview*, and *Law, Probability, and Risk*. Her monograph, *Fairness in International Criminal Trials*, was published by Oxford University Press in 2016. Her work has been cited as legal authority by numerous leading international and national courts, including the International Criminal Court and the Supreme Court of India.

Valerie Oosterveld is an Associate Dean at the University of Western Ontario, Canada. Her research and writing focus on gender issues within international criminal justice. She is a member of the Royal Society of Canada's College of New Scholars, Artists, and Scientists. She teaches courses in the field of international law. She is the Deputy Director of Western University's Centre for Transitional Justice and Post-Conviction Reconstruction, and is affiliated with the Department of Women's Studies and Feminist Research. Professor Oosterveld is the co-author of one of Canada's leading texts on public international law – *International Law: Doctrine, Practice, and Theory* (Irwin Law). This text has twice been cited by the Supreme Court of Canada.

Before joining Western Law in July 2005, Professor Oosterveld served in the Legal Affairs Bureau of Canada's Department of Foreign Affairs and International Trade. In this role, she provided legal advice on international criminal accountability for genocide, crimes against humanity and war crimes, especially with respect to the International Criminal Court, the International Criminal Tribunals for the Former Yugoslavia and Rwanda, the Sierra Leone Special Court, and other transitional justice mechanisms. She was a member of the Canadian delegation to the International Criminal Court negotiations and subsequent Assembly of State Parties. She also served on the Canadian delegation to the 2010 Review Conference of the Rome Statute of the International Criminal Court in Kampala, Uganda.

Michael P. Scharf, Dean of the Law School, Case Western Reserve University. He is also the Director of the Frederick K. Cox International Law Center and Joseph C. Hostetler – BakerHostetler Professor of Law. He is the host of "Talking Foreign Policy," a radio program broadcast on WCPN 90.3 FM. In addition, Dean Scharf serves as Managing Director of the Public International Law and Policy Group, a Nobel Peace Prize-nominated NGO that provides pro bono legal assistance to developing states and states in transition. In 2013, Scharf headed the Blue Ribbon Committee that drafted a statute for a War Crimes Tribunal for Syrian atrocities.

During a sabbatical in 2008, Dean Scharf served as Special Assistant to the Prosecutor of the Cambodia Genocide Tribunal. In 2004, Dean Scharf served as a member of the international team of experts that provided training to the judges of the Iraqi High Tribunal, and in 2006 he led the first training session for the investigative judges and prosecutors of the newly established UN Cambodia Genocide Tribunal.

During the first Bush and Clinton Administrations, Scharf served in the Office of the Legal Adviser of the US Department of State, where he held the positions of Attorney-Adviser for Law Enforcement and Intelligence, Attorney-Adviser for United Nations Affairs, and delegate to the United Nations Human Rights Commission. In 1993, he was awarded the State Department's Meritorious Honor Award "in recognition of superb performance and exemplary leadership" in relation to his role in the establishment of the International Criminal Tribunal for the former Yugoslavia.

Dean Scharf graduated from Duke University School of Law, with Order of the Coif and High Honors. He was a judicial clerk to Judge Gerald Bard Tjoflat on the Eleventh Circuit Federal Court of Appeals. He is the author of over 100 scholarly articles and 18 books, including *The International Criminal Tribunal for Rwanda*, which was awarded the American Society of International Law's Certificate of Merit for outstanding book in 1999, and *Enemy of the State: The Trial and Execution of Saddam Hussein* which won the International Association of Penal Law's book of the year award for 2009. His last four books have been published by Cambridge University Press. Dean Scharf continues to teach International Law and was ranked as 17th most cited author in the field since 2010 by the Lieter study, issued in June 2016.

Milena Sterio, Associate Dean for Faculty Enrichment and Professor of Law at Cleveland Marshall College of Law, Cleveland State University.

Professor Sterio earned her law degree, *magna cum laude*, from Cornell Law School in 2002. At Cornell, she was Order of the Coif, general editor of the *Cornell International Law Journal*, and a member of Phi Beta Kappa. In 2003, she earned an LLM, *cum laude*, in Private International Law from the University Paris

I-Pantheon-Sorbonne; in 2002, she earned a Maitrise en droit franco-americain, *cum laude*, in Political Science and French Literature from Rutgers College, New Brunswick, New Jersey. Before joining the faculty of Cleveland Marshall, she was an associate in the New York City firm of Cleary, Gottlieb, Steen, & Hamilton and an Adjunct Law Professor at Cornell, where she taught in the International War Crimes Clinic. Her research interests are in the field of international law, international criminal law, international human rights, law of the seas, and in particular maritime piracy, as well as private international law. She has published numerous law review articles and several books. Professor Sterio's academic work has been cited by United States federal courts. She has participated in the meetings of the United Nations Contact Group on Piracy off the Coast of Somalia and has been a member of the Piracy Expert Group, an academic think tank functioning within the auspices of the Public International Law and Policy Group. In addition, Professor Sterio is a member of the Board of Directors of the Public International Law and Policy Group, Co-Chair of the Women in International Law Interest Group and of the International Criminal Law Interest Group at the American Society of International Law, and Chair of the International Law Section of the American Association of Law Schools.

Professor Sterio is one of six permanent editors of the prestigious IntLawGrrls blog. In the spring of 2013, Professor Sterio was a Fulbright Scholar in Baku, Azerbaijan, at Baku State University.

Jennifer Trahan, Associate Clinical Professor of Global Affairs at NYU. Professor Trahan has served as counsel and of counsel to the International Justice Program of Human Rights Watch; she has served as Iraq Prosecutions Consultant to the International Center of Transitional Justice; and she has worked on cases before the Special Court for Sierra Leone and the International Criminal Tribunal for Rwanda. Professor Trahan is the author of *Genocide, War Crimes, and Crimes against Humanity: A Digest of the Case Law of the International Criminal Tribunal for Rwanda* (HRW 2010), and *Genocide, War Crimes, and Crimes against Humanity: A Topical Digest of the Case Law of the International Criminal Tribunal for the Former Yugoslavia* (HRW 2006).

Professor Trahan attended the International Criminal Court's Special Working Group on the Crime of Aggression and the International Criminal Court's Review Conference in Kampala, Uganda. She is the Chairperson of the American Branch of the International Law Association's International Criminal Court Committee, and a member of the Association of the bar of the City of New York's Task Force on National Security and the Rule of Law, as well as the International Law Association's Committee on Use of Force. She has also taught at Columbia University, Fordham Law School, Brooklyn Law School, The New York School, and lectures at Salzburg Law School's Summer Institute on International Criminal Law.

Prior to entering the field of international law, Professor Trahan spent ten years in private practice as a litigator at the New York City law firm Schulte Roth & Zabel LLP. She holds an AB from Amherst College, a JD from NYU School of Law, and an LLM from Columbia Law School, specializing in international law.

Paul R. Williams, Rebecca I. Grazier Professor of Law and International Relations at the American University, Washington College of Law. He is also the director of the joint JD/MA program in International Relations. Professor Williams is the co-founder of the Public International Law & Policy Group, a nonprofit group that provides pro bono legal assistance to states and governments involved in peace negotiations, post-conflict constitution drafting, and war crimes prosecutions. Professor Williams has assisted over two dozen peace negotiations and post-conflict constitutions. Professor Williams has advised governments across Europe, Asia, as well as North and sub-Saharan Africa on state recognition, self-determination, and state succession issues. Professor Williams has authored five books on a variety of topics such as international human rights, international environmental law, and international norms of justice. Additionally, Professor Williams has testified before congressional committees concerning peace strategy in Kosovo and holding war criminals accountable. Prior to his arrival at American University, Professor Williams spent time as a Senior Associate with the Carnegie Endowment for International Peace and as a Fulbright Research Scholar at the University of Cambridge. Professor Williams has also served as an Attorney-adviser for European and Canadian affairs at the US Department of State, Office of the Legal Adviser. Professor Williams holds a PhD from the University of Cambridge, 1998; a JD from Stanford Law School, 1990; and a BA from University of California at Davis, 1987.

Jonathan Witmer-Rich, Associate Professor at Cleveland Marshall College of Law, Cleveland State University. Professor Witmer-Rich's research focuses on criminal procedure and criminal law theory. His articles have appeared in Florida Law Review and in Criminal Law and Philosophy. He teaches courses in criminal law, criminal procedure, and law and terrorism. He currently serves as counsel to the Criminal Rules Committee of the Ohio Commission on the Rules of Practice and Procedure. Following law school, Professor Witmer-Rich clerked for Judge M. Blane Michael on the Fourth Circuit Court of Appeals, and for Judge Joseph R. Goodwin on the US District Court for the Southern District of West Virginia. He then worked as a litigator associate for three years at Jones Day in Cleveland. Before joining the faculty at Cleveland Marshall in 2009, Professor Witmer-Rich practiced at the Federal Public Defender's Office in Cleveland. He also represented several detainees at the Guantanamo Bay detention facility in habeas corpus proceedings.

Foreword

by Richard J. Goldstone
Founding Chief Prosecutor of the ICTY and the ICTR

The first half of the 1990s was a period of wide support for international law and international courts, both criminal and civil. In May of 1993, the United Nations International Criminal Tribunal for the former Yugoslavia (ICTY) was established as a minimal response from the United Nations Security Council to the egregious war crimes and crimes against humanity that were being committed in the former Yugoslavia. The United Nations International Criminal Tribunal for Rwanda (ICTR) and hybrid tribunals followed and ultimately, in the middle of 1998, the Rome Statute for the International Criminal Court (ICC). In 1994, the United Nations Convention on the Law of the Sea came into operation and established the International Tribunal for the Law of the Sea. In 1995, the World Trade Organization established its Appellate Body as a court of final instance to entertain appeals from reports issued by panels in disputes between WTO members.

The ICTY enjoyed the fullest support from the United States and received its crucial economic and political assistance. That support continued when the Security Council, in 1994, established the ICTR. Significantly, the United States did not object when the ICTY's exercise of jurisdiction included Kosovo at a time, during 1999, when NATO forces, under the leadership of the United States, used military force against the Serb Army of Slobodan Milosevic in order to protect the Albanian population.

The support for international law and international courts during the 1990s did not continue. With regard to the ICC, in 2001 the United States, among other measures, "unsigned" the Rome Statute. In more recent times that Court has been under relentless attack by the African Union and increasingly criticized by governments that were among its traditional supporters. That change is particularly apparent with regard to my own country, South Africa, where a withdrawal from the Rome Statute remains an open question. In recent months there have been attacks on the WTO by the Trump Administration, which is preventing vacancies on the Appellate Body from being filled. China, India, Russia, and the United States continue to remain outside the ICC. The United States remains the only large nation that has failed to ratify the United Nations Convention on the Law of the Sea.

It is in that context that this book could not be more timely. It contains an impressive analysis of the legacy of the ICTY and ICTR. While no one can expect a perfect record from any human endeavor, the fourteen chapters provide an exhaustive and careful analysis of just about every aspect of the work of the ad hoc tribunals. They include the important development and recognition of gender-related crimes, superior responsibility, fair trial standards, incitement as a war crime, and rules of evidence and procedure. There is an impressive analysis of the jurisprudence of the ad hoc tribunals and its contribution to the advance of international criminal law. There is an evaluation of the roles the ad hoc tribunals played in the target countries and, at the same time, recognition that in the area of reconciliation the tribunals appear to have enjoyed little success.

There are many allusions to the relationship between politics and the work and legacy of the ad hoc tribunals. This includes the political platform that the ICTY inadvertently gave to Milosevic and Seselj, who insisted on self-representation, and the problems that disruptive defendants create for the presiding judges. Other chapters consider sentencing issues and the difficulties they present for courts that have to consider massive crimes that frequently include thousands of victims.

There are legitimate and helpful criticisms of aspects of the work of the tribunals. They include the inaccessibility and undue length of many of the judgments and inadequacy of the steps taken, to ameliorate the unavoidable distance of the tribunals from the scenes of the crimes and the homes of the victims.

In the concluding chapters, Michael Scarf and Milena Sterio state that "it is this book's conclusion that overall, the tribunals have contributed significantly to the development of international criminal law and international humanitarian law, and that they will continue to influence future prosecutions at the International Criminal Court, as well as future efforts to instill international justice." That conclusion is amply justified by the excellent analyses contained in the book.

This work will be enjoyed by all interested in the history of modern international criminal law and it will be an indispensable resource and reference for all students of the subject.

Introduction

Michael P. Scharf and Milena Sterio

The International Criminal Tribunal for the Former Yugoslavia (ICTY) and the International Criminal Tribunal for Rwanda (ICTR) were the first modern-day ad hoc international criminal tribunals. Both were created through United Nations Security Council resolutions, with specific mandates to prosecute those responsible for serious violations of international humanitarian law in the former Yugoslavia and in Rwanda, respectively. The tribunals were not meant to exist forever, and after two decades, the ICTR has completed its work and has shut its doors completely, while the ICTY is concluding its last two cases. With the closing of these ad hoc tribunals, an important chapter in international criminal law has come to an end. The ICTY and the ICTR played crucial roles in the development of international criminal law five decades post-Nuremberg. They reignited the development of this field of law, and their case law contributed toward the fine-tuning of complex legal doctrines, such as genocide, accomplice liability, the definition of international armed conflict, the prosecution of crimes of sexual violence. This book addresses the legacy of the ICTY and the ICTR through a series of chapters written by leading authorities in the field that each discuss an important aspect of the tribunals' accomplishments. It is this book's aim to provide a comprehensive overview of the impact and lasting role of these ad hoc tribunals within the field of international criminal law.

BACKGROUND: THE CREATION OF THE AD HOC TRIBUNALS

History's first international criminal tribunal was the Nuremberg Tribunal, set up by the victorious allies after World War II to prosecute Nazi atrocities. Although many States and commentators hoped there would be a permanent war crimes tribunal created in the aftermath of the Nuremberg trial, it would be nearly fifty years before events on the ground and international political currents would align to enable the international community to establish another international war crimes tribunal. Just a few months after the break-up of the Soviet Union, genocide returned to Europe for the first time since Nazi Germany. The location was Bosnia-Herzegovina, which had recently declared its independence from what was left of the former Yugoslavia (Serbia and Montenegro).

Prior to its dissolution in 1991–92, Yugoslavia was not so much an ethnic melting pot as a boiling cauldron of ethnic tension with deep historic roots. The assent of a hardline Serbian nationalist government in Serbia headed by Slobodan Milosevic prompted Croatia and Slovenia to declare their independence on June 25, 1991, with Bosnia following suit on March 1, 1992. The Bosnian Serbs, under the leadership of their self-styled president, Radovan Karadzic, and military leader, Ratko Mladic, immediately launched attacks against the Croatian and Muslim populations in northeast and southern Bosnia, with the goal of connecting Serb-populated regions in north and west Bosnia to Serbia in the east. Within a few months, the Serbs had expelled, killed, or imprisoned 90 percent of the 1.7 million non-Serbs who once lived in Serbian-held areas of Bosnia.[1]

With Russia's assumption of the permanent seat and veto of the Soviet Union in the Security Council in December 1991,[2] the Security Council emerged from the Cold War paralysis of the previous forty years and was experiencing a rare (though short-lived) era of cooperation. The first test for the reinvigorated Council was the deepening crisis in the Balkans. The Security Council adopted a series of measures aimed at restoring peace and halting the bloodshed, including imposing economic sanctions on Serbia, establishing a no-fly zone, creating safe areas, authorizing force to ensure the delivery of humanitarian aid, and excluding Serbia from participating in the General Assembly.[3] Finally, on May 25, 1993, the Security Council adopted Resolution 827, establishing "an international tribunal for the sole purpose of prosecuting persons responsible for serious violations of international humanitarian law committed in the territory of the former Yugoslavia since January 1, 1991."[4] Within two years, the Tribunal had been set up at The Hague, its eleven judges had been elected by the General Assembly, its Chief Prosecutor had been selected by the Security Council, and its first trial was ready to begin.

While the ICTY was preparing its first case, a genocidal conflagration was ignited in the small African nation of Rwanda by the death of its Hutu president when his plane was shot down by a surface-to-air missile on April 6, 1994.[5] Nearly 800,000 people (mostly of the minority Tutsi tribe) were slaughtered during the next hundred days at a rate nearly three times greater than the rate of the loss of Jewish lives during the Holocaust.[6] When the massacres began in Rwanda, the Security

---

[1] Michael P. Scharf, Balkan Justice, The Story Behind The First International War Crimes Trial Since Nuremberg 21–8 (1997).

[2] Michael P. Scharf, *Musical Chairs: The Dissolution of States and Membership in the United Nations*, 28 Cornell International Law Journal 29, 46–7 (1995).

[3] Scharf, *supra* note 1, at 33–5.

[4] SC Res. 827, U.N. SCOR, 48th Sess., 3217th mtg., UN Doc. S/RES/827 (May 25, 1993).

[5] Virginia Morris & Michael P. Scharf, The International Criminal Tribunal For Rwanda 47 (1998).

[6] *Id.*

Council's first reaction was to withdraw nearly all the United Nations peacekeeping troops from the country for their safety. In July 1994, the Security Council established a Commission of Experts, which issued a report on October 2, 1994, confirming that genocide had been committed by the Hutus against the Tutsis and recommending the establishment of an International Criminal Tribunal to prosecute the perpetrators. A month later, on November 8, 1994, the Security Council adopted Resolution 955, providing for the establishment of a second ad hoc tribunal for Rwanda, which would have its own trial chambers to be headquartered in Arusha, Tanzania, but share the Prosecutor and the Appeals Chamber of the ICTY.[7]

Since their establishment, the ICTY has indicted 161 individuals (ranging from common soldiers to generals all the way to prime ministers), of whom 83 were ultimately convicted; and the ICTR has indicted 95 individuals (ranging from media personalities to heads of corporations to high level officials), of whom 61 were convicted. But the legacy of these unique institutions cannot be measured simply in the number of defendants or conviction rates.

ASSESSING THE LEGACY OF THE TRIBUNALS

In the context of international criminal tribunals, scholars have defined "legacy" to mean a lasting impact, most notably on bolstering the rule of law in a particular society by conducting effective trials while also strengthening domestic capacity to do so. Legacy, in this context, implies the extent to which a particular court has had a significant effect by modeling best practices in handling the individual cases and compiling a historical record of the conflict. Legacy also means laying the groundwork for future efforts to prevent a recurrence of crimes by offering precedents for legal reform, building faith in judicial processes, and promoting greater civic engagement on issues of accountability and justice. This type of legacy is supposed to be long-lasting and continue to have an impact even after the work of the tribunal is completed. A 2008 United Nations High Commissioner's Report on maximizing the legacy of hybrid courts asserted that the need for such tribunals to leave a legacy is firmly accepted as part of United Nations policy.[8]

In addition to the above view of legal legacy and impact, tribunals can have other types of roles which can meaningfully affect the pursuit of justice and human rights. Professors King and Meernik have described the core missions of the ICTY's mandate (to bring to justice those responsible for serious violations of international humanitarian law) as follows: (1) developing the Tribunals' functional and institutional capacities; (2) interpreting, applying, and developing international humanitarian and criminal law; (3) attending to and interacting with the various

---

[7] *Id.* at 72.
[8] Office of the UN High Comm'r for Hum. Rts., Rule-of-Law Tools for Post-Conflict States: Maximizing the Legacy of Hybrid Courts, at 4–5, UN Doc. HR/PUB/08/2, UN Doc. No. E.08.XIV.2 (2008).

stakeholders who have vested interests; and (4) promoting deterrence and fostering peace-building to prevent future aggression and conflict.[9] This framework is also applicable to the ICTR, as this tribunal was charged with the same mandate as the ICTY, with the addition of promoting national reconciliation in Rwanda. In light of the above, "legacy" can be defined more broadly as the enduring influence of the tribunals' work and processes on the ideals, conceptions, and instrumentalities of international criminal law, justice, and human rights. This book takes on a more specific approach to discussing legacy issues regarding the ad hoc tribunals (ICTY and ICTR): it assesses the legacy in the field of international criminal law. While the tribunals' legacy is equally important in the development of domestic justice as well as human rights more broadly, this book adopts a more singular approach and focuses on the field of international criminal law. In this manner, this book aims to provide a comprehensive overview of the significance, impact, and legacy of the ad hoc tribunals through the lens of international criminal law. In addition to its value to scholars, this book serves as a guide and tool to practitioners in the area, as well as to those considering the creation and establishment of new ad hoc tribunals in the future, such as government officials, United Nations specialists, NGOs, and academics. In addition, this book may be of use to those who work with the International Criminal Court (ICC), as much of the ad hoc tribunals' case law has served and will serve as important precedent within the ICC, and as the ICC will most likely continue to enhance the same international criminal law principles and doctrines which the ad hoc tribunals have developed.

Other studies of the ad hoc tribunals' legacy thus far have addressed other issues, such as the effect and impact of tribunals on the people in the affected areas (i.e., Yugoslavia and Rwanda), the role that the tribunals have played in establishing restorative justice, the obstacles and challenges that the tribunals have faced, the role that the tribunals have played in ending domestic/regional cultures of impunity, the tribunals' deterrence effects, and their potential contributions to building lasting peace. This book tangentially addresses some of these issues, but it does so through an international criminal law focus and specific discussion of some of the key legal developments and contributions of the ICTY and the ICTR.

This book focuses on three different aspects of "legacy." In Part I, it discusses legacy in the general sense, by focusing on the overall legacy of the ICTY and ICTR on the development of international criminal law and their contribution to the field of human rights law, as well as on benchmarks necessary in order to determine the existence of such a legacy. In Part II, this book focuses on the most important aspects of the tribunals' normative and operational legacy. In Part III, the book looks forward

---

[9]　Kimi L. King & James D. Meernik, Assessing the Impact of the International Criminal Tribunal for the Former Yugoslavia: Balancing International and Local Interests While Doing Justice, *in* The Legacy of the International Criminal Tribunal for the Former Yugoslavia 7, 8 (Bert Swart et al. eds., 2011).

to the impact of the ICTY and the ICTR on the International Criminal Court and on the future of global peace and justice.

In Part I, Milena Sterio's Chapter 1 on "The Yugoslavia and Rwanda Tribunals: A Legacy of Human Rights Protection and Contribution to International Criminal Justice" assesses the legacy and impact of the ICTY and the ICTR in the development of human rights norms, as well as their contribution to the field of international criminal justice. According to Sterio, "the ICTY and the ICTR have significantly contributed toward the development of the field of international criminal law and toward the protection of human rights, by sending a message of impunity and holding those responsible for serious human rights violations criminally accountable, as well as by protecting defense rights on an individual level."[10] Jennifer Trahan's Chapter 2 on "Examining the Benchmarks by Which to Evaluate the ICTY's Legacy" distinguishes between the ICTY's legacy in the judicial and prosecutorial sense, where the tribunal has achieved significant successes, and the ICTY's contribution toward broader socio-transformative goals, where the tribunal has been much less impactful. Trahan concludes that "[w]hile tribunals may be able to make certain contributions to broader transformative goals (and the ICTY has arguably made inroads here as well), such work is often better done by other actors and should not be expected of tribunals."[11]

In Part II, authors discuss various normative and operational legacies of the ICTY and ICTR. Michael Scharf's Chapter 3 on "How the *Tadic* Appeals Chamber Decision Fundamentally Altered Customary International Law" discusses the landmark *Tadic* decision of the ICTY Appeals Chamber, which held that the same principles of liability which apply to international armed conflict also pertain to internal armed conflict, and thus contributed to the normative legacy of the Yugoslavia tribunal. According to Scharf, the *Tadic* decision was not only transformative, but it also constituted a "Grotian Moment" – a period of accelerated formation of customary law norms. The *Tadic* decision thus resulted in a significant change in international criminal law, as "much of the conduct prohibited by treaties governing international armed conflicts now constitutes prosecutable war crimes when committed in internal armed conflicts."[12] Chapter 4, which is a transcript of a roundtable discussion held at International Law Weekend 2016, featuring Milena Sterio, Michael Scharf, Margaret deGuzman, Jenia Iontcheva Turner, Beth Van Schaack, and Paul Williams as panelists, focuses on the *Karadzic* case in the ICTY, and the tribunal's decision to convict a defendant on genocide charges. This chapter discusses the Yugoslavia tribunal's contribution to

---

[10] Milena Sterio, The Yugoslavia and Rwanda Tribunals: A Legacy of Human Rights Protection and Contribution to International Criminal Justice [11].

[11] Jennifer Trahan, Examining the Benchmarks by Which to Evaluate the ICTY's Legacy [25].

[12] Michael P. Scharf, How the Tadic Appeals Chamber Decision Fundamentally Altered Customary International Law [59].

the development of jurisprudence on genocide in the normative sense, as well as in the operational sense – the Karadzic case may serve as prosecutorial and operational precedent to future tribunals handling complex genocide prosecutions.[13] In Chapter 5, "Atrocity Speech Law Comes of Age: The Good, the Bad and the Ugly of the International Speech Crimes Jurisprudence at the Ad Hoc Tribunals," Gregory Gordon discusses the development of the "speech crimes" jurisprudence at the ICTY and the ICTR. Gordon concludes that although this type of jurisprudence will likely necessitate future elaboration and development, the tribunals have contributed significantly to its initiation. "[D]evelopment [of speech crimes jurisprudence] at the ad hoc tribunals will be looked on by history as likely its most formative phase – the period when atrocity speech law came of age."[14] In Chapter 6, Michael Scharf addresses "The Once and Future Doctrine of Joint Criminal Enterprise." In this chapter, Scharf focuses on the development of the joint criminal enterprise mode of liability at the ICTY and ICTR, as well as at other ad hoc tribunals, including the Special Court for Sierra Leone and the Extraordinary Chambers in the Courts of Cambodia. Scharf concludes that through the case law of these ad hoc tribunals, more aggressive forms of joint criminal enterprise, such as "JCE III," "had fully ripened into a customary international law doctrine, and will undoubtedly be applied by many tribunals and domestic courts in the future."[15] In Chapter 7, Yvonne McDermott discusses "The Tribunals' Fact-Finding Legacy." McDermott argues that the Yugoslavia and Rwanda tribunals have left behind an important fact-finding legacy regarding the standard of proof in evidentiary as well as conviction matters, regarding the role of witness testimony, as well as regarding the length and accessibility of judgments.[16] In Chapter 8, entitled "The Legacy of the ICTY and ICTR on Sexual and Gender-Based Violence," Valerie Oosterveld explains how the ICTY and the ICTR have contributed to the prosecution of sexual and gender-based violence crimes.[17] According to Oosterveld, the ICTY and the ICTR's work was "pioneering," in light of the fact that prior tribunals had paid very little attention to the investigation and prosecution of sexual and gender-based violence crimes. Oosterveld thus concludes that the ICTY and the ICTR have been "courts of 'firsts.'" Chapter 9, entitled "The Defense of Duress to Killing Innocents: Assessing the Mixed Legacy of the ICTY and the ICTR," focuses on defense-based legacies of the ICTY and the ICTR. Jonathan Witmer-Rich argues in this chapter that the case law

---

[13] A Roundtable on the Legacy of the Karadzic Trial at the International Criminal Tribunal for the Former Yugoslavia (International Law Weekend 2016 Panel, featuring Milena Sterio, Michael P. Scharf, Margaret deGuzman, Jenia Iontcheva Turner, Beth Van Schaack, and Paul Williams) [73].

[14] Gregory S. Gordon, Atrocity Speech Law Comes of Age: The Good, the Bad and the Ugly of the International Speech Crimes Jurisprudence at the Ad Hoc Tribunals [104].

[15] Michael P. Scharf, The Once and Future Doctrine of Joint Criminal Enterprise [161].

[16] Yvonne McDermott, The Tribunals' Fact-Finding Legacy [180].

[17] Valerie Oosterveld, The Legacy of the ICTY and ICTR on Sexual and Gender-Based Violence [197].

of the ICTY and ICTR, and in particular the *Erdemovic* case in the ICTY, contributed significantly to the development of duress as a defense to charges of war crimes and crimes against. In addition, Witmer-Rich criticizes the *Erdemovic* decision and proposes a novel way to conceptualize the defense of duress in international criminal law.[18] Chapters 10 and 11 focus on the sentencing legacy of the Yugoslavia and Rwanda tribunals. Yvonne Dutton, in Chapter 10, discusses "Sentencing Policies of the Ad Hoc Tribunals." Dutton concludes that the ICTY and the ICTR have "contributed a legacy toward a uniform and coherent sentencing approach in the field of international criminal law."[19] Moreover, Dutton argues that although the length of particular sentences may vary from one tribunal to the other, both the ICTY and the ICTR have applied a consistent sentencing framework in light of the gravity of the offense which they sought to punish. In Chapter 11, "Mixed Messages: The Sentencing Legacy of the Ad Hoc Tribunals," Margaret deGuzman approaches the tribunals' sentencing legacy from a different aspect. deGuzman argues that a particular aspect of the tribunals' sentencing practice "undermined their normative and sociological legacies: their failure to clarify whether and when the tribunals apply and ought to apply global sentencing norms and when the application of local norms is more appropriate."[20] deGuzman thus concludes that the tribunals' sentencing legacy contributes less than it could have to international criminal law, because of the tribunals' mixed sentencing messages, which did not appropriately reconcile global and local sentencing norms. In Chapter 12, on "Combatting Chaos in the Courtroom: Lessons from the ICTY and ICTR for the Control of Future War Crimes Trials," Michael Scharf addresses one of the operational legacies of the ICTY and ICTR – the management of cases within courtrooms at international criminal tribunals.[21] Scharf examines how the ICTY, ICTR, and other modern war crimes trials have grappled with the challenges of maintaining control of the courtroom, especially in the context of self-represented defendants. Scharf considers various ways of limiting the defendant's right to self-representation in the context of international criminal trials, while balancing such limitations both with the defendant's due process rights and with global interests of justice, necessitating open, expeditious, and fair trials.

Part III of the book focuses on the future. In this part, authors discuss the impact of the ICTY and ICTR on future international criminal trials, as well as on the International Criminal Court, and the tribunals' contribution to the future of international peace and justice. In Chapter 13, Stuart Ford discusses "The Impact of the Ad Hoc Tribunals on the International Criminal Court." Ford focuses on two

---

[18] Jonathan Witmer-Rich, The Defense of Duress to Killing Innocents: Assessing the Mixed Legacy of the ICTY and the ICTR [221].

[19] Yvonne M. Dutton, The Sentencing Legacies of the Ad Hoc Tribunals [249].

[20] Margaret M. deGuzman, Mixed Messages: The Sentencing Legacy of the Ad Hoc Tribunals [269].

[21] Michael P. Scharf, Combatting Chaos in the Courtroom: Lessons from the ICTY and ICTR for the Control of Future War Crimes Trials [286].

ideas: how the International Criminal Court has been "indebted" to the ICTY and the ICTR, and how the International Criminal Court has been a reaction to the ad hoc tribunals. Ford thus concludes that an important legacy of the ICTY and the ICTR has been their contribution to the very formation of the International Criminal Court, but that, at the same time, "the ICC was also an opportunity for the drafters to fix some of the perceived flaws in the ad hoc tribunals."[22] In Chapter 14, entitled "Twenty-Four Years On: The Yugoslavia and Rwanda Tribunals' Contributions to Durable Peace," Paul Williams and Kimberly Larkin discuss the ICTY's and the ICTR's contributions to global peace and justice. Williams and Larkin argue that the ICTY and the ICTR have inspired a culture of international criminal justice, by professionalizing atrocity documentation and prosecution while creating a near-universal expectation of justice-based accountability for crimes against humanity.[23] According to Williams and Larkin, this contribution by the ICTY and the ICTR has been particularly valuable, because it has enabled current regional and international mechanisms to address crimes against humanity more agilely and assertively than their predecessors.

In sum, this book will address the ICTY's and ICTR's normative and operational legacy by discussing the tribunals' legacy on a general level, and by focusing on their specific contribution to the development of the field of international criminal law. In addition, this book will assess the tribunals' legacy on future international criminal justice and peace efforts, including on the International Criminal Court. While the ad hoc tribunals' legacy, as discussed throughout this book, is comprised of both negative and positive aspects, it is this book's overall theme and ultimate conclusion that the ICTY and the ICTR have had a positive impact on the development of international criminal law, and that their legacy will contribute toward the advancement of this field.

---

[22] Stuart Ford, The Impact of the Ad Hoc Tribunals on the International Criminal Court [307].
[23] Paul R. Williams & Kimberly Larkin, Twenty-Four Years On: The Yugoslavia and Rwanda Tribunals' Contributions to Durable Peace [326].

PART I

The Legacy of the Yugoslavia and Rwanda Tribunals

The Yugoslavia and Rwanda Tribunals: A Legacy of Human Rights Protection and Contribution to International Criminal Justice

Milena Sterio[*]

1.1 INTRODUCTION

... violations of human rights cannot stand as legitimate acts of state. Therefore, they must be considered as criminal acts, committed by individuals who can and should be prosecuted in criminal proceedings.[1]

The Nuremberg and Tokyo tribunals, in the wake of World War II, created the precedent that individuals, including state leaders, could be held criminally accountable for war crimes and crimes against humanity. The Nuremberg experience in particular set in motion the idea that individuals responsible for massive human rights violations should face criminal responsibility. This idea remained somewhat dormant until the early 1990s, when two new ad hoc tribunals for the former Yugoslavia and for Rwanda were created by the United Nations Security Council. Over the past two decades, the international community has witnessed a proliferation of international and hybrid tribunals tasked with prosecuting those responsible for human rights violations: the International Criminal Court was created in the late 1990s and began its work in 2002; and several ad hoc tribunals have been created to investigate and prosecute cases in East Timor, Cambodia, Sierra Leone, Lebanon, Kosovo, and Bosnia.[2] Most recently, the United Nations General Assembly established a Mechanism for Syria, tasked with collecting and storing evidence of massive human rights violations in Syria, such as genocide, crimes against humanity, and war crimes. The Mechanism is expected to share this type of evidence and

---

[*] Associate Dean for Academic Enrichment and Professor of Law, Cleveland-Marshall College of Law.

[1] *Human Rights Advocacy and the History of International Human Rights Standards, Individual Criminal Accountability*, available at http://humanrightshistory.umich.edu/accountability/individual-criminal-accountability/.

[2] For background on the International Criminal Court, *see* Laura Barnett, *The International Criminal Court: History and Role*, Background Paper, Library of Parliament (Canada) (2013), at 5–6, available at https://lop.parl.ca/Content/LOP/ResearchPublications/2002-11-e.pdf. For background on hybrid tribunals, *see* Sterio M., *The Future of Ad Hoc Tribunals: An Assessment of Their Utility Post-ICC*, 19 ILSA J. INT'L & COMP. L. 237 (2013).

information with future tribunals prosecuting those responsible for such violations of human rights in Syria – with national jurisdictions as well as with a future ad hoc tribunal for Syria (should one be established).[3] These tribunals, starting with the Yugoslavia and Rwanda courts and leading to the Syrian Mechanism, have significantly contributed toward the protection of human rights and toward international criminal justice in general, by fine-tuning existing substantive human rights norms and by developing elaborate procedures aimed at protecting defense rights and the impartiality and fairness of judicial processes.

This chapter will examine the human rights legacy and contribution to international criminal justice of the Yugoslavia and Rwanda Tribunals. For each of these ad hoc tribunals, this chapter will analyze their substantive and procedural focus on the protection of human rights. This chapter will conclude that it is likely that current and future ad hoc tribunals will continue to build upon the Yugoslavia and the Rwanda tribunals' legacy in the field of human rights, and that they will continue to contribute toward the elaboration of human rights norms and toward enhancing the goals of international criminal justice.

1.2 THE YUGOSLAVIA AND RWANDA TRIBUNALS' LEGACY: THE GENERAL FRAMEWORK

The International Criminal Tribunal for Rwanda (ICTR) officially closed, having completed all of its trial and appellate-level work, at the end of 2015.[4] The International Criminal Tribunal for Yugoslavia (ICTY) issued its final judgment in November 2017, and the tribunal formally ceased to exist on December 31, 2017. Remaining proceedings in the cases of Ngirabatware, Karadžić, Šešelj, and Stanišić and Simatović are under the jurisdiction of the so-called Mechanism for International Criminal Tribunals (Mechanism or the Mechanism).[5] The Mechanism has been mandated to perform a number of essential functions previously carried out by the ICTY and the ICTR, and has assumed responsibility for, inter alia, the enforcement of sentences, administrative review, assignment of cases and counsel, review, contempt, and appellate proceedings, issues regarding the referral of cases to national jurisdictions, witness protection measures, as well as various evidentiary and documentary issues.[6] In carrying out these multiple functions, the Mechanism maintains the legacies of these two pioneering ad hoc

---

[3] United Nations Mechanism for International Criminal Tribunals, *A Compendium on the Legacy of the ICTR and the Development of International Law*, available at http://unictr.unmict.org/en/compen dium-legacy-ictr-and-development-international-law.

[4] *Id.*

[5] United Nations Mechanism for International Criminal Tribunals, *Cases*, available at www.unmict.org/en/cases.

[6] United Nations Mechanism for International Criminal Tribunals, *Functions*, available at www.unmict.org/en/about/functions.

international criminal courts and strives to reflect best practices in the field of international criminal justice and international human rights.

With the closing of the ICTR and of the ICTY, an important chapter in international human rights law has come to an end. The ICTY and the ICTR played crucial roles in the development of international criminal law five decades post-Nuremberg, and they contributed toward the solidification of several human rights norms. They reignited the development of international human rights law in general, and their case law contributed toward the fine-tuning of complex legal doctrines, such as genocide, superior or command responsibility, the definition of international armed conflict, the prosecution of crimes of sexual violence, as well as toward the crystallization of norms protecting human rights.

In the context of international criminal tribunals, scholars have defined "legacy" to mean a lasting impact, most notably on bolstering the rule of law in a particular society by conducting effective trials while also strengthening domestic capacity to do so. Legacy, in this context, implies the extent to which a particular court has had a significant effect by modeling best practices in handling the individual cases and compiling a historical record of the conflict.[7] Legacy also means laying the ground-work for future efforts to prevent a recurrence of crimes by offering precedents for legal reform, building faith in judicial processes, and promoting greater civic engagement on issues of accountability and justice. This type of legacy is supposed to be long-lasting and continue to have an impact even after the work of the tribunal is completed. According to the United Nations Office of the High Commissioner for Human Rights, "legacy" signifies the lasting impact of an ad hoc tribunal on promoting the rule of law in a particular society, which can be achieved by conducting effective trials in order to end impunity while also strengthening domes-tic judicial capacity.[8] In addition to the above view of legal legacy and impact, tribunals can have other types of roles which can meaningfully affect the pursuit of justice and human rights. Professors King and Meernik have described the core missions of the ICTY's mandate (to bring to justice those responsible for serious violations of international humanitarian law) as follows: 1) developing the Tribunals' functional and institutional capacities; 2) interpreting, applying, and developing international humanitarian and criminal law; 3) attending to and interacting with the various stakeholders who have vested interests; and 4) promoting deterrence and

---

7   Pocar F., (2008), *Completion or Continuation Strategy? Appraising Problems and Possible Developments in Building the Legacy of the ICTY*, 6 J. INT'L CRIM. JUSTICE 6: 655; O'KEEFE R., INTERNATIONAL CRIMINAL LAW 483–91 (2015).

8   A report on maximizing the legacy of hybrid courts asserted that the need for such tribunals to leave a legacy is firmly accepted as part of United Nations policy (Office of the UN High Commissioner for Human Rights, *Rule of Law Tools for Postconflict States, Maximizing the Legacy of Hybrid Courts*, at 4–5, UN Sales No. HR/PUB/08/2 [2008]).

fostering peace-building to prevent future aggression and conflict.[9] This framework is also applicable to the ICTR, as this tribunal was charged with the same mandate as the ICTY, with the addition of promoting national reconciliation in Rwanda. In light of the above, "legacy" can be defined more broadly as the enduring influence of the tribunals' work and processes on the ideals, conceptions, and instrumentalities of international criminal law, justice, and human rights.

1.3 THE YUGOSLAVIA AND RWANDA TRIBUNALS' LEGACY IN THE FIELD OF INTERNATIONAL HUMAN RIGHTS AND INTERNATIONAL CRIMINAL JUSTICE

While the tribunals' legacy is equally important in the development of domestic justice and international criminal law more broadly, the focus of this chapter is on the field of international human rights and international criminal justice – what is the significance, impact, and legacy of the ad hoc tribunals through this particular lens? It is this author's hope that the legacy of ad hoc tribunals in the fields of international human rights and international criminal justice will be of particular assistance to those who work with the International Criminal Court (ICC), as much of the ad hoc tribunals' case law has served and will serve as important precedent within the ICC, and as the ICC will most likely continue to enhance the same international law principles and doctrines which the ad hoc tribunals have developed. It is also this author's hope that the ICTY and the ICTR will serve as models for future ad hoc tribunals, and that such future tribunals will continue to build upon the ICTY's and the ICTR's legacy in the field of human rights law and international criminal justice.

1.3.1 *Prosecuting Genocide*

First, the ad hoc tribunals have contributed to the protection of universal human rights by successfully charging and convicting defendants of genocidal offenses, and by establishing that the violation of the most basic human rights standard – the protection of human life – should never remain unpunished.[10]

The ICTR in the Akayesu case became the first international tribunal to enter a judgment for genocide as well as the first to interpret the definition of genocide set forth in the 1948 Geneva Conventions. In the Kambanda case, also before the Rwanda tribunal, the defendant pled guilty to genocide, marking the first time in the history of international criminal law that an accused person admitted

---

9   King Kimi L. & Meernik James D., *Assessing the Impact of the International Criminal Tribunal for the Former Yugoslavia: Balancing International and Local Interests While Doing Justice*, in THE LEGACY OF THE INTERNATIONAL CRIMINAL TRIBUNAL FOR THE FORMER YUGOSLAVIA 7–8 (Swart B. et al. eds., 2011).

10 Robinson D. & MacNeil G., *The Tribunals and the Renaissance of International Criminal Law: Three Themes*, AMERICAN J. INT'L L. 110: 191, 193–6 (2016).

responsibility for genocide and conspiracy to commit genocide. And by accepting this guilty plea in the Kambanda case, the Rwanda tribunal became the first international tribunal since Nuremberg to issue a judgment against a former head of state. In another case (Bosco Barayagwiza, Nahimana, and Ngeze), the ICTR convicted members of the Rwandan media by holding them responsible for broadcasts intended to inflame the public to commit acts of genocide.[11]

The ICTY was the first international criminal tribunal to enter a genocide conviction in Europe. In April 2004, in the case of Radislav Krstić, the Appeals Chamber determined that genocide was committed in Srebrenica in 1995, through the execution of more than 7,000 Bosnian Muslim men and boys following the takeover of the town by Bosnian Serb forces.[12] Several other completed ICTY cases relating to the Srebrenica events have ensured that the genocide has been well-documented and, in the words of ICTY President Theodor Meron, "consigned to infamy."[13] And according to the appellate judgment in the Krstic case (2004), "those who devise and implement genocide seek to deprive humanity of the manifold richness its nationalities, races, ethnicities and religions provide. This is a crime against all humankind, its harm being felt not only by the group targeted for destruction, but by all of humanity."[14] In one of its most prominent judgments, the ICTY trial chamber convicted the former Bosnian Serb leader, Radovan Karadzic, of genocide with respect to the Srebrenica massacre and sentenced him to forty years of imprisonment.[15] In this case, which is currently on appeal with the appeals chamber, the ICTY trial chamber indicated its willingness to infer the defendant's requisite mens rea of intent, necessary for of a conviction of genocide, based on an inference of the defendant's knowledge of the events taking place at Srebrenica, and based on his failure to do anything to stop such events from unfolding.[16] While some have criticized this type of more inventive judicial reasoning regarding the finding of genocidal intent,[17] it remains undisputed that through the Karadzic case, the Yugoslavia tribunal has contributed toward its own legacy of

---

[11] Kendall S. & Nouwen S. M. H., *Speaking of Legacy: Toward an Ethos of Modesty at the International Criminal Tribunal for Rwanda*, AMERICAN J. INT'L L. 110: 212, 219; United Nations Mechanism for International Criminal Tribunals, *ICTR Milestones*, available at http://unictr.unmict.org/en/ictr-milestones.

[12] Prosecutor v. Krstic, Case No. IT-98–33-A, Appeals Judgment (Apr. 19, 2004).

[13] International Criminal Tribunal for the Former Yugoslavia, *Address by ICTY President Theodor Meron* (June 23, 2004), available at www.icty.org/en/press/address-icty-president-theodor-meron-poto cari-memorial-cemetery.

[14] Prosecutor v. Krstic, Case No. IT-98–33-A, Appeals Judgment, para. 36 (Apr. 19, 2004).

[15] Prosecutor v. Karadžić, Case No. IT-95–5/18-T, Judgment, para. 6070–2 (Int'l Crim. Trib. for the Former Yugoslavia) (Mar. 24, 2016), available at www.icty.org/x/cases/Karadžić/tjug/en/160324_judge ment.pdf.

[16] *See generally* Sterio M., *The Karadzic Genocide Conviction: Inferences, Intent, and the Necessity to Redefine Genocide*, 31 EMORY INTERNATIONAL LAW REVIEW 271 (2017).

[17] *Id.*

convicting defendants of genocide and of signaling to the international community that genocide will no longer go unpunished.

In sum, the ICTY and the ICTR have significantly contributed toward the prosecution of the crime of genocide and toward the notion that genocide is a crime against all that will never again be tolerated by the international community. According to Robinson and MacNeil, "[t]he Tribunals have done much to make the law of genocide workable."[18] By focusing on the crime of genocide, which entails the intentional destruction of a specific group within a larger population, the ICTY and the ICTR have established that violations of basic human rights norms, such as the right to life, impose individual criminal responsibility on the offenders (an outcome which human rights tribunals are unable to reach because of their nonpenal nature).

1.3.2 *Prosecuting Crimes of Sexual Violence*

Second, the ICTY and the ICTR have contributed to the development of international human rights law by developing case law on crimes of sexual violence and by focusing on specific gender issues. In the Akayesu case, the Rwanda tribunal for the first time defined the crime of rape in international criminal law and recognized rape as a means of perpetrating genocide.[19] The Rwanda tribunal created a special unit for gender issues and assistance to victims of genocide, choosing to focus on gender issues and to provide support and care to the victims of genocide. In this manner, the tribunals have, in addition to developing case law on crimes of sexual violence, created a participatory legacy – the idea that victims of serious crimes have a voice within international criminal prosecutions of such crimes.[20] This idea, for better or for worse, is squarely present within the Rome Statute of the ICC. This idea contributes toward the overall protection of human rights by creating a specific participatory role for victims of human rights violations, and by placing an emphasis on victims within international criminal law.

The ICTY has also played a historic role in the prosecution of wartime sexual violence in the former Yugoslavia and has paved the way for a more robust adjudication of such crimes worldwide. From the first days of the Tribunal's mandate, investigations were conducted into reports of systematic detention and rape of women, men, and children. More than a third of those convicted by the ICTY have been found guilty of crimes involving sexual violence. Such convictions are one of the Tribunal's pioneering achievements. They have ensured that treaties and conventions which have existed on paper throughout the twentieth century have

---

[18]   Robinson & MacNeil, *Three Themes*, 196.
[19]   Prosecutor v. Akayesu, Case No. ICTR-96-4-T, Trial Judgment, paras. 732–3.
[20]   United Nations Mechanism for International Criminal Tribunals, *ICTR Milestones*, available at http://unictr.unmict.org/en/ictr-milestones.

finally been put in practice, and violations punished.[21] The ICTY took groundbreaking steps to respond to the imperative of prosecuting wartime sexual violence. Together with its sister tribunal for Rwanda, the Tribunal was among the first courts of its kind to bring explicit charges of wartime sexual violence, and to define gender crimes such as rape and sexual enslavement under customary law.[22]

The ICTY was also the first international criminal tribunal to enter convictions for rape as a form of torture and for sexual enslavement as a crime against humanity, as well as the first international tribunal based in Europe to pass convictions for rape as a crime against humanity, following a previous case adjudicated by the ICTR. The ICTY proved that effective prosecution of wartime sexual violence is feasible, and provided a platform for the survivors to talk about their suffering. That ultimately helped to break the silence and the culture of impunity surrounding these terrible acts. According to Robinson and MacNeil, "the Tribunals have recognized many other forms of sexual and gender-based violence, including sexual slavery, enforced prostitution, enforced sterilization, sexual mutilation, and public humiliation of a sexual nature. Related significant developments lie not in the definition of crimes but in the much-needed judicial interventions to ensure that sexual violence is suitably prioritized, properly investigated, and responsibly handled."[23]

In addition, the ICTY established a robust Victims and Witnesses Section (VWS), which provided witnesses with assistance prior to, during, and after their testimony, ranging from practical issues to psychological counseling during their stay in The Hague.[24] In this manner, the Yugoslavia Tribunal, like the Rwanda Tribunal, has contributed significantly to the legacy of developing and prosecuting gender-specific crimes and crimes of sexual violence, and to ensuring meaningful victim participation in the adjudication process. The two tribunals have thus contributed toward the protection of human rights norms by ensuring that those who violate such norms, including specific norms on women's rights, will face criminal accountability.

1.3.3 *Doctrine of Superior Responsibility*

Third, both ad hoc tribunals have contributed toward the development of the doctrine of superior responsibility, by holding that superior responsibility applies to civilians in leadership positions, and that it is not confined to purely military leaders.[25] In the so-called Celebici case, the ICTY established the modern-day

---

21 *Sexual Violence and the Triumph of Justice*, documentary, available at www.icty.org/en/in-focus/timeline.
22 International Criminal Tribunal for the Former Yugoslavia, *ICTY Timeline*, available at www.icty.org/en/in-focus/timeline.
23 Robinson & MacNeil, *Three Themes*, 202.
24 International Criminal Tribunal for the Former Yugoslavia, *Witnesses*, available at www.icty.org/en/about/registry/witnesses.
25 Robinson & MacNeil, *Three Themes*, 204–9; Prosecutor v. Delalic, Case No. IT-96–21-A, Appeals Judgment, paras. 56–84 (Feb. 20, 2001).

understanding of the doctrine of command or superior responsibility by laying "the groundwork and underlying principle of this doctrine."[26] Through this case, the ICTY established that nonmilitary commanders may also be prosecuted for the crimes committed by their subordinates, so long as a superior-subordinate relationship can be established, as well as the superior's requisite mens rea of "knowing or having reason to know" (that subordinates were committing atrocities).[27] Subsequent ICTY case law established that superiors may be punished for inactivity – for a failure to act after the superior has been informed of the subordinates' atrocities, in a "post-crime scenario of superior responsibility."[28] In the Blagojevic case, the ICTY further broadened the scope of command responsibility by interpreting the word "commission" in Article 7(3) of the ICTY Statute to encompass all modes of participation listed in Article 7(1) (planning, ordering, instigating, and aiding and abetting crimes).[29] And in Oric, the ICTY appellate judges held that a superior can be held criminally liable for his subordinates' planning, instigating, ordering, committing, or aiding and abetting a crime.[30] This position – that superior responsibility covers all the different modes of the subordinates' criminal conduct falling under Article 7(1) – has been subsequently adopted by the ICTR as well.[31] The Oric appellate judgment also broadened the scope of superior responsibility by holding that superiors can be liable for the acts of more remote subordinates, even if "intermediary" subordinates are involved, so long as the superior had effective control over the situation.[32] According to the Oric appellate judgment, "[t]he direct perpetrators of a crime punishable under the Statute do not need to be identical to the subordinates of a superior. It is only required that the relevant subordinates, by their own acts or omissions, be criminally responsible for the acts and omissions of the direct perpetrators."[33] Finally, according to the Oric precedent, a superior can be held liable for crimes committed by anonymous subordinates if the perpetrators can be identified by their affiliation to a group or unit, if the superior has effective control over the subordinates, and if it is clear that such anonymous subordinates are responsible for the committed offenses.[34]

The ICTY, and the ICTR to a somewhat lesser extent, has thus contributed toward the development of the superior or command responsibility doctrine by establishing that nonmilitary commanders face liability for the acts of their subordinates in a similar manner that military commanders do. This contribution by

---

[26] van Siledregt E., *Command Responsibility at the ICTY – Three Generations of Case-law and still Ambiguity, in* THE LEGACY OF THE INTERNATIONAL CRIMINAL TRIBUNAL FOR THE FORMER YUGOSLAVIA 377, 379 (Swart B., Zahaqr A. & Sluiter G. eds., 2011).

[27] *Id.* at 378.

[28] Hadzihasanovic & Kubura (IT-01–47-AR72), Appeals Chamber (July 16, 2003), para. 51.

[29] Blagojevic (IT-02–60-A), Judgment, Appeals Chamber (May 9, 2007), paras. 277–85.

[30] Oric (IT-03–68-A), Judgment, Appeals Chamber (July 3, 2008), para. 21.

[31] *See* Nahimana et al. (ICTR-96–11), Judgment, Trial Chamber (Dec. 3, 2003), paras. 485 ff.

[32] Oric (IT-03/68-A) Trial Chamber (June 30, 2006), para. 478.

[33] *Id.*

[34] *Id.*

the ad hoc tribunals is particularly relevant in light of modern-day warfare, where conflicts are often fought outside of well-defined militaries and where orders and policies are often crafted by nonmilitary leaders. In addition, the ICTY and the ICTR have contributed toward the development of the doctrine of superior responsibility by broadening the scope of such responsibility to include commander liability for various modes of participation by subordinates, and to include commander liability in cases of inaction or omission, as well as in cases of so-called intermediary subordinates. In this manner, the tribunals have contributed toward upholding and protecting basic human rights norms of protection of life and protection from torture and violence, by holding all leaders, including nonmilitary ones, responsible for possible violations of such norms.

1.3.4 *Cooperation with National Jurisdictions and Authorities*

Fourth, the ad hoc tribunals have established a legacy of cooperation and impact on domestic jurisdictions between international tribunals and national authorities. Multiple countries have signed agreements on the enforcement of the ICTR's sentences (Mali, Benin, France, Italy, Mali, Rwanda, Senegal, Swaziland, and Sweden). "These agreements illustrate the important role national authorities play in ensuring that those convicted of serious violations of international law serve their sentences in compliance with international detention standards."[35] In addition, the Rwanda Tribunal upheld the first referral of an international criminal indictment to Rwandan national authorities for trial, in the case against Jean-Bosco Uwinkindi. A total of eight ICTR cases have now been referred to Rwanda. Two additional cases have been referred to France for trial. Monitoring in all referred cases is presently being conducted by the Mechanism.[36] By establishing lasting cooperation between the ICTR and national authorities, as well as by providing monitoring schemes, this tribunal has contributed toward ensuring that national jurisdictions and authorities protect and respect human rights in their own ongoing and future trials and proceedings. According to Kendall and Nouwen, "[it] has been widely claimed that the ICTR has shaped the Rwandan criminal justice system," by influencing national authorities to abolish the death penalty, to ensure better witness protection programs, and to improve prison conditions.[37]

Throughout its existence, the ICTY Office of the Prosecutor (OTP) has worked closely with the new states and territories that emerged from the former Yugoslavia on their domestic prosecutions. In the aftermath of the war in Bosnia and Herzegovina (BiH), returning displaced persons and refugees voiced fears about arbitrary arrests on suspicion of war crimes. To protect against this, the OTP agreed

---

[35] United Nations Mechanism for International Criminal Tribunals, *ICTR Milestones*, available at http://unictr.unmict.org/en/ictr-milestones.

[36] *Id.*

[37] Kendall S. & Nouwen S. M. H., *Speaking of Legacy*, 212.

to operate a "Rules of the Road" scheme under which local prosecutors were obliged to submit case files to The Hague for review. The Rules of the Road procedure, established under the Rome Agreement of February 18, 1996, regulated the arrest and indictment of alleged perpetrators of war crimes by national authorities. As part of the Tribunal's contribution to the re-establishment of peace and security in the region, the ICTY prosecutor agreed to provide an independent review of all local war crimes cases. If a person was already indicted by the OTP, he could be arrested by the national police. If the national police wished to make an arrest where there was no prior indictment, they had to send their evidence to the OTP. Under the Rome Agreement, decisions of the OTP became binding on local prosecutors. In this manner, the ICTY OTP ensured that national authorities within the former Yugoslavia engaged in legitimate prosecutions only without harassing individuals who had not committed any wrongdoing (for political or other nonlegal purposes).[38] Thus, the ICTY OTP contributed toward the protection of basic human rights norms of individuals living in the former Yugoslavia, by ensuring that they were free of arbitrary arrest and unwarranted legal proceedings.

To ensure that as many persons as possible suspected of war crimes are brought to justice, the OTP has provided assistance to national bodies in the region by passing on evidence that may have been of use in local investigations and by transferring whole cases for prosecution locally. A dedicated transition team within the OTP was tasked with handing over to national courts cases involving intermediate- and lower-ranking accused. Such cases have included case files of suspects investigated by the OTP but where no indictments were ever issued, which has resulted in the referral of some files with investigative material to authorities in Serbia, Croatia, and Bosnia, which have then pursued these cases. Secondly, despite indictments issued by the ICTY, a total of eight cases involving thirteen accused have been referred to courts in the former Yugoslavia, mostly to Bosnia and Herzegovina, pursuant to Rule 11bis of the Rules of Procedure and Evidence. On the basis of an ICTY indictment and the supporting evidence provided by the Tribunal's prosecution, these cases are then tried in accordance with the national laws of the state in question.[39] Thus, the ICTY has contributed toward the protection of human rights norms by ensuring that many of those accused of horrific human rights violations are brought to justice – within national jurisdictions – and by ensuring that national jurisdictions have the tools necessary in order to conduct successful prosecutions while respecting the defendants' rights.

Finally, the OTP has promoted regional cooperation among national prosecutors. The ICTY prosecution has strongly supported efforts to enhance cooperation in criminal matters between states of the former Yugoslavia, as it is an essential step toward rebuilding trust and justice in the region. Successful trials before national

---

[38] International Criminal Tribunal for the Former Yugoslavia, *Working with the Region*, available at www.icty.org/en/about/office-of-the-prosecutor/working-with-the-region.

[39] *Id.*

courts require that prosecutors in the neighboring countries can collaborate in the collection of evidence and securing witnesses. OTP officials have taken part in several regional meetings, facilitating the creation of good working relationships between the prosecutors in the different states.[40] Thus, the Rwanda and the Yugoslavia tribunals have created a significant legacy of cooperation with national authorities and have developed specific models of cooperation that have contributed toward the rebuilding of national justice systems. In this manner, the tribunals have contributed toward the protection of human rights by ensuring that many defendants are prosecuted by the ad hoc tribunals and by national jurisdictions, and by promoting adequate due process and judicial standards within national jurisdictions.

1.3.5 *Operational and Procedural Legacy*

Fifth, the ad hoc tribunals have created a significant legacy in the operational sense – by establishing specific case management strategies for the prosecution of complex international crimes and by establishing particular evidentiary procedures resulting in the long-term preservation of evidence, which will enable national jurisdictions to prosecute additional cases in the future. For example, the ICTR has held special deposition proceedings in the case of Félicien Kabuga to preserve evidence for use at trial once he is arrested. Similar proceedings were later held in the cases of two other fugitives: Augustin Bizimana and Protais Mpiranya.[41] By holding these proceedings, the ICTR has ensured that the passage of time does not jeopardize the international community's ability to bring these suspects to trial when they are finally apprehended. And the ICTY has established specific evidentiary standards regarding victims of crimes of sexual violence, by allowing them to testify anonymously – witnesses have been able to testify under a pseudonym, with face and voice distortion in video feeds, or in closed session. Through the development of its rules of procedure, the ICTY has also sought to protect the victims of sexual violence from abusive lines of questioning during testimony. "These efforts have led to improved procedural rules, improved protection of victims and witnesses, and the inclusion of relevant advisers on the Tribunals' staffs."[42] The ad hoc tribunals have thus left behind an operational legacy, which will undoubtedly serve as a model for future international criminal prosecutions. They have contributed toward the protection of the human rights of people victimized in crimes of sexual violence and have ensured, in at least three cases, that future tribunals will be able to prosecute perpetrators of human rights violations (by preserving evidence for potential future prosecutorial use).

---

[40] *Id.*
[41] United Nations Mechanism for International Criminal Tribunals, *ICTR Milestones*, available at http://unictr.unmict.org/en/ictr-milestones.
[42] Robinson & MacNeil, *Three Themes*, 202.

1.3.6 *Defense Rights*

Sixth, the ICTR and the ICTY have established a significant legacy regarding due process rights for the accused. According to Michael Karnavas, former President of the Association of Defence Counsel Practicing before the ICTY, "[t]he results at the end of a trial will be meaningless unless a robust defence is afforded to the accused."[43] Despite some shortcomings, it may be argued that the ICTY and the ICTR have established a powerful legacy of the protection of defendants' rights.

The ICTY Statute established that every defendant had the right to counsel of his or her own choosing, and that indigent defendants would be provided with defense counsel. In accordance with Article 21 of the ICTY Statute, an accused person may elect to represent himself in person.[44] While this right is not unlimited, several ICTY cases have recognized the right to self-representation and allowed the accused to conduct their own defense. Slobodan Milosevic was allowed to conduct his own defense and to self-represent, and defendants Radovan Karadzic and Vojislav Seselj also conducted their defense pro se.[45] In Krajisnik, the ICTY Appeals Chamber held that the defendant "nonetheless has a 'cornerstone' right to make his own case to the Tribunal."[46] In such cases of self-representation, the Tribunal, through the Registrar, has ensured the provision of adequate facilities to the self-represented accused, including the assignment of legal advisers and other support staff to assist the self-represented accused in the preparation of his case, privileged communication with certain categories of defense team members, photocopying and storage facilities. Furthermore, the ICTY Registrar adopted a special Remuneration Scheme for persons assisting indigent self-represented accused. A provision was also made for the assignment of an investigator, a case manager, and a language assistant where necessary, to assist with translation.[47] It should be noted that, while many have criticized the ICTY's struggle with the right to self-representation and have highlighted the tribunal's ambiguous approach to this issue, the fact remains that the ICTY did allow several high-profile defendants to represent themselves and did establish this general defense right.[48] The ICTR, however, has granted the right

---

43 International Criminal Tribunal for the Former Yugoslavia, *Defence*, available at www.icty.org/en/about/defence.

44 *Updated Statute of the International Criminal Tribunal for the Former Yugoslavia*, Article 21, available at www.icty.org/x/file/Legal%20Library/Statute/statute_septo9_en.pdf.

45 Temminck Tuinstra J., *The ICTY's Continuing Struggle with the Right to Self-representation, in* THE LEGACY OF THE INTERNATIONAL CRIMINAL TRIBUNAL FOR THE FORMER YUGOSLAVIA 346, 353 (Swart B., Zaharand A. & Sluiter G. eds., 2011).

46 Decision on Mocilo Krajisnik's Request to Self-represent, on Counsel's Motions in relation to Appointment of Amicus Curiae, and on the Prosecution Motion of 16 February 2007, Krajisnik, IT-00–39-A (May 11, 2007), ICTY App Ch.

47 Trechsel S., *Rights in Criminal Proceedings under the ECHR and the ICTY Statute – A Precarious Comparison, in* THE LEGACY OF THE INTERNATIONAL CRIMINAL TRIBUNAL FOR THE FORMER YUGOSLAVIA 182–3 (Swart B., Zaharand A. & Sluiter G. eds., 2011).

48 Temminck Tuinstra J., *The ICTY's Continuing Struggle*, 346.

to self-representation to only one accused, Akayesu, and solely during the sentencing phase of his trial.[49]

In addition to the defendant's right to self-represent, the ICTY established other important rights for the defendant, such as the right to obtain information upon arrest, the right to be brought before a judge, as well as the right to be tried within a reasonable time.[50] Although the ICTR has been criticized on some of these accounts, it adopted virtually identical Rules of Procedure and Evidence as the ICTY, and its judges demonstrated a willingness to protect some of these defense rights. For example, in the case of Jean-Bosco Barayagwiza, the ICTR Appeals Chamber found such fundamental violations of the right to be brought promptly before a judge and to habeas corpus proceedings that it dismissed the indictment and ordered that the defendant be immediately released.[51] Thus, both tribunals have contributed toward the legacy of defense rights – by establishing, through case law as well as through elaborate Rules of Procedure and Evidence, that even those accused of the most serious crimes are entitled to the protection of their due process rights.[52]

1.4 CONCLUSION

As discussed throughout this chapter, the ICTY and the ICTR have contributed significantly toward the elaboration of human rights norms on both the substantive and procedural levels. These ad hoc tribunals have contributed toward the development of specific international criminal law norms, aimed at imposing liability on those most responsible for heinous human rights violations. As discussed above, the ICTY and the ICTR were the first tribunals ever to prosecute and convict individuals of genocide; they were pioneers in terms of prosecuting crimes of sexual violence; they confirmed the idea that civilian leaders can face criminal responsibility in almost the same manner as military commanders; they established specific protective procedures for victims, in order to ensure their safe participation within criminal proceedings involving their aggressors. In addition, these ad hoc tribunals have solidified due process rights for all defendants, including those accused of the most serious crimes and human rights violations. Finally, these ad hoc tribunals have developed extensive procedural and evidentiary rules, which have contributed

---

[49] *Id.* at 345.

[50] Trechsel S., *Rights in Criminal Proceedings under the ECHR and the ICTY Statute – A Precarious Comparison, in* Swart B., Zaharand A. & Sluiter G. (eds.), THE LEGACY OF THE INTERNATIONAL CRIMINAL TRIBUNAL FOR THE FORMER YUGOSLAVIA 160–73 (2011).

[51] Jean-Bosco Barayagwiza v. The Prosecutor, Case No ICTR-97-19-AR73, Decision of the Appeals Chamber (Nov. 3, 1999).

[52] Some authors have criticized the Yugoslavia and Rwanda tribunals about their failure to adequately protect some defense rights. Despite such shortcomings, it is this author's conclusion that the tribunals have succeeded in establishing a general legacy regarding the importance of defense rights, and it is this author's hope that future tribunals will build on the legacy of the ICTY and ICTR in this respect.

further toward safeguarding defendants' due process rights and toward protecting the fairness and impartiality of international judicial processes.

In sum, the ICTY and the ICTR have significantly contributed toward the development of the field of international criminal law and toward the protection of human rights, by holding those responsible for serious human rights violations criminally accountable, as well as by protecting defense rights on an individual level. The general protection of human rights can be perceived as part of the tribunals' legacy, and future ad hoc tribunals will undoubtedly continue to examine the ICTY and ICTR case law and procedures as relevant models. "The solutions implemented after the ICTY's and ICTR's closure will undoubtedly become part and parcel of the international criminal justice landscape, shaping the normative environment of other ad hoc tribunals and similar experiences in the decades to come."[53]

---

[53] Guido Acquaviva G., *"Best Before Date Shown": Residual Mechanisms at the ICTY, in* THE LEGACY OF THE INTERNATIONAL CRIMINAL TRIBUNAL FOR THE FORMER YUGOSLAVIA 536 (Swart B., Zaharand A. & Sluiter G. eds., 2011).

2

Examining the Benchmarks by Which to Evaluate the ICTY's Legacy

Jennifer Trahan[*]

How one evaluates the legacy of the International Criminal Tribunal for the former Yugoslavia (ICTY)[1] depends on the benchmarks used to measure its accomplishments. While there appears to be no precise unanimity on what it is that international tribunals are expected to achieve, first and foremost, clearly, they are judicial institutions. When measured by judicial or prosecutorial goals, the ICTY has clearly achieved significant successes. One might even argue it has been the most successful international tribunal to date, at least in terms of its capacity to pursue high-level prosecutions, render generally well-reasoned jurisprudence on key areas of international criminal law, and establish a solid evidence-based record as to the crimes committed. A complicating factor, however, is that survey results show populations in the former Yugoslavia do not share this positive assessment. This raises the question of how these survey results impact on evaluating the ICTY's accomplishments.

If one expects a tribunal will achieve broader, socially transformative goals, it is in such areas the ICTY has had a mixed record of success (and this is linked to the poor survey results). Yet, one could argue it was never reasonable to expect a tribunal would play such a transformative role, and, to the extent such a role was suggested, it may have unduly raised expectations. Even examining such broader, transformative goals, however – such as contributing to peace and security, and restoration of the rule of law (through its own work and assistance to national war crimes prosecutions) – the ICTY appears to have made contributions. A limited contribution has also been shown in the area of deterrence, but only in the later years of the tribunal's work. Where one sees really no success is in the area of reconciliation – if that was

---

[*] Clinical Professor, The Center for Global Affairs, NYU-SPS. Erin Lovall provided research assistance. The views in this chapter expand on a book chapter jointly co-authored by Jennifer Trahan & Iva Vukušić, *The ICTY and the Three-Tiered Approach to Justice in Bosnia and Herzegovina*, in LEGACIES OF THE INTERNATIONAL CRIMINAL TRIBUNAL FOR THE FORMER YUGOSLAVIA: A MULTIDISCIPLINARY ACCOUNT (Oxford University Press, forthcoming 2019).
[1] The full name of the tribunal is The International Tribunal for the Prosecution of Persons Responsible for Serious Violations of International Humanitarian Law Committed in the Territory of the Former Yugoslavia since 1991.

ever an intended goal of the ICTY. The Tribunal has also neither created a single accepted narrative of the past nor silenced denial of crimes, although neither was probably reasonable to expect, and both, along with any reconciliation, must await future transitional justice work in the region and perhaps eventual changes in political leadership.

Under the resolution that created the ICTY, the UN Security Council held out that the ICTY would bring "justice," "contribute to the restoration and maintenance of peace," and "contribute to ensuring that ... violations are halted" (i.e., deterrence).[2] The UN Security Council resolution that created the International Criminal Tribunal for Rwanda (ICTR) also cited that it would create "reconciliation,"[3] with ICTY officials sometimes claiming the ICTY would do likewise.[4] Certainly, asking the ICTY (and other tribunals) to render "justice" (for example, adjudicate individual criminal responsibility after trials adhering to international standards of due process) is a reasonable goal.[5] Expecting that tribunals will "contribute to the restoration and maintenance of peace," or create deterrence, seem more tenuous propositions. Furthermore, more than two decades after the creation of the ICTY and ICTR, perhaps the international community should not claim tribunals will achieve reconciliation; this may simply not be an appropriate goal to foist on the shoulders of a judicial institution.[6]

In Section 2.1, this chapter examines the ICTY's accomplishments using more traditional criteria related to judicial or prosecutorial accomplishments, and argues

---

[2]   SC Res. 827, UN Doc. S/RES/827 (May 25, 1993).

[3]   SC Res. 955, UN Doc. S/RES/955 (Nov. 8, 1994) ("*Convinced* that in the particular circumstances of Rwanda, the prosecution of persons responsible for serious violations of international humanitarian law would ... contribute to the process of national reconciliation.")

[4]   *See, e.g.*, Seventh Annual Report of the President of the ICTY to the UN Security Council, UN Doc. AI55/273-S/20001777, Aug. 7, 2000, para. 217 ("The Tribunal works as an agency of reconciliation in southeastern Europe"); Annual Rep. of the Int'l Tribunal for the Prosecution of Persons Responsible for Serious Violations of Int'l Humanitarian Law Committed in the Territory of the Former Yugoslavia, para. 16, UN Doc. A/49/342, S/1994/1007 (Aug. 29, 1994), www.icty.org/x/file/About/Reports%20and%20Publications/AnnualReports/annual_report_1994_en.pdf (Anthony Cassese, first President of the Tribunal, writing that the ICTY "is a tool for promoting reconciliation"); Gabrielle Kirk McDonald, then-President of the ICTY, Remarks at the US Supreme Court (Apr. 5, 1999) ("The ICTY was created to assist with efforts to bring peace, justice, and reconciliation to the Balkans.")

[5]   Hannah Arendt famously claimed the sole purpose of criminal trials is "to render justice, and nothing else." Hannah Arendt, Eichmann in Jerusalem: A Report on the Banality of Evil 254 (1963). While tribunals certainly can make additional contributions, "justice" is no doubt their most significant purpose.

[6]   Later, in 2003, when looking for the ICTY to conclude its work, the UN Security Council: (1) reaffirmed that the ICTY should concentrate on prosecuting "the most senior leaders suspected of being most responsible for crimes within the ICTY's jurisdiction and transferring cases involving those who many not bear this level of responsibility to national jurisdictions"; (2) called on the international community to assist national jurisdictions in improving their capacity to try war crimes cases transferred from the ICTY; and (3) called on the donor community to create a special chamber within the State Court of Bosnia Herzegovina to prosecute war crimes. SC Res. 1503, UN Doc. S/RES/1503 (Aug. 29, 2003).

that, measured against these criteria, the ICTY has proven quite a successful institution. A complicating factor, as mentioned above, is that many in the region do not share this positive assessment. In Section 2.2, the chapter examines more society-wide transformative goals, where it appears the ICTY did make certain contributions – although perhaps it is not reasonable to expect a tribunal will always make such contributions. In other areas, such as reconciliation, we see distinctly less success (perhaps none at all). Ultimately, it is the lack of a shared narrative and denial of crimes that seem the greatest challenges – but these will have to await future progress by other transitional justice actors and/or new generations of political leaders. The experience of the ICTY thus presents an important lesson for the future on managing expectations as to what tribunals can reasonably be asked to accomplish.

2.1 BENCHMARKS FOR MEASURING JUDICIAL OR PROSECUTORIAL ACCOMPLISHMENTS

There is not necessarily unanimity as to what it is that one expects international or hybrid tribunals to achieve.[7] The lack of agreed benchmarks or goals is somewhat troubling (and some might argue there is not one set of criteria to be used for all tribunals).[8] Yet, one means of evaluation is certainly using the goals set by the UN Security Council, the ICTY's "mandate-provider."[9] That said, are all the goals the Security Council mentioned necessarily goals that tribunals must achieve in order to be considered successful? Even assuming one agrees with the goals, how does one evaluate whether they have been met? Must evaluation be subject to rigorous analytic testing or objective measurement? Can contributions be made even if they cannot be quantified?[10] And, through whose eyes does one conduct the inquiry – from the perspective of the international community or perspectives from the region?

---

[7] *See* Yuval Shany, *Assessing the Effectiveness of International Courts: A Goal-based Approach*, EUROPEAN YEARBOOK OF INTERNATIONAL ECONOMIC LAW 423 (2015) (calling for "a richer understanding of the concept of international court effectiveness," and for developing a "more sophisticated evaluative methodology"); Birju Kotecha, *The ICC: What Counts as a Success?*, JUSTICE IN CONFLICT (Sept. 13, 2013), https://justiceinconflict.org/2013/09/13/the-icc-what-counts-as-a-success/ (accessed on August 8, 2017) (calling for the development of performance criteria by which to evaluate the ICC's performance).

[8] Shany suggests "specific goals" should be "set for each and every court." Shany, Assessing the Effectiveness of International Courts, *supra* note 7. It is unclear whether he means each international and hybrid tribunal should have its own goals. The author would hope more standardization could be agreed on – that one would have agreed justice-related benchmarks, while recognizing that some tribunals, in their unique circumstances, might accomplish broader transformative goals.

[9] Shany uses the term "mandate-provider." *Id.*

[10] Shany suggests: "Future research projects ought to attempt to develop a mythology for identifying, where possibly, quantitative and qualitative means for assessing the degree to which relevant goals [of international courts] are attained (including, the evaluation of outcome indicators) in ways that would meet valid statistical and analytical standards." *Id.* Yet, he admits that some goals such as whether "national reconciliation" has been advanced "could be very hard to capture, and almost impossible to quantify." *Id.*

The UN Security Council's goal that the ICTY would contribute to "justice" seems the most reasonable proposition – that, first and foremost, tribunals are courts, and therefore, their central mandate must be prosecutions.[11] Recognizing that there may be differing understandings of the word "justice"[12] – for example, victims might have a broad understanding[13] – this chapter will utilize a narrower construction: adjudicating individual criminal responsibility through trials that adhere to internationally recognized standards of due process.

This chapter suggests that the ICTY has proven quite a successful institution considering: (a) the ICTY's conducting high-level prosecutions pursuant to internationally recognized fair trial standards; (b) the ICTY's success in having all indictees apprehended; (c) the ICTY's creation of an extensive body of generally well-reasoned jurisprudence; (d) the ICTY's focus on previously under-reported and under-documented crimes such as sexual and gender based violence (SGBV); (e) the ICTY's having nearly 5,000 victims and witnesses testify, allowing their voices to be heard; (f) the ICTY's establishing a solid historical record and extensive documentary archive; and (g) the ICTY's contributing to rule of law through its own work, capacity-building in the region, and more globally.[14]

Finally, this section grapples with the complicating factor that, despite these significant accomplishments, many in the region do not share these views. Disappointing survey results do not minimize the ICTY's actual accomplishments, but they do lead one to ask: in whose name is a tribunal rendering "justice"? Certainly, its audience cannot solely be the international community. And, is it not then

---

[11] *See, e.g.,* Marko Milanović, *Courting Failure: When Are International Criminal Courts Likely to be Believed by Local Audiences?, in* The Oxford Handbook of International Criminal Law (Kevin Jon Heller, Frédéric Mégret, Sarah Nouwen, Jens Ohlin & Darryl Robinson eds., forthcoming 2018) ("The primary role of international criminal courts and tribunals is to punish those deserving of punishment.")

[12] In Yuval Shany's terminology, there may be problems of "goal ambiguity." Shany, Assessing the Effectiveness of International Courts, *supra* note 7.

[13] "In many ways, justice is in the eye of the beholder. Whether an individual believes that justice has been achieved often depends upon a person's role in a conflict, the harm suffered, who is in charge of creating and operating a given justice mechanism, and many other factors. However, most everyone can agree what constitutes the lack of justice, and that is impunity for those who have committed grave crimes." Erin K. Lovall & June E. Vutrano, *Seeking Truth in the Balkans: Analysis of Whether the International Criminal Tribunal for the Former Yugoslavia Has Contributed to Peace, Reconciliation, Justice, or Truth in the Region and the Tribunal's Overall Enduring Legacy* 5 Law Journal for Social Justice 252 (2015); Janine N. Clark, *Peace, Justice and the International Criminal Court: Limitations and Possibilities,* 9 Journal of International Criminal Justice 521, 523 (2011) (justice "is in many ways a deeply subjective notion; 'delivering justice usually means different things to different people'"); *Id.* at 543 ("'Justice' is a multi-dimensional concept that encompasses judicial and nonjudicial forms, retributive and restorative elements.")

[14] The author's list of accomplishments fairly closely corresponds to the ICTY's own list, although the author's list is slightly broader. The ICTY lists its achievements as: holding leaders accountable, bringing justice to victims and giving them a voice, establishing the facts, developing international law, and strengthening the rule of law. *See Achievements,* ICTY, www.icty.org/en/about/tribunal/achievements (accessed on August 8, 2017). Interestingly, neither list corresponds that closely with the goals originally set out by the UN Security Council. *See* text accompanying note 2 *supra.*

problematic when positive assessments are not shared by those in the region, who one would think ought to be the tribunal's primary audience? As discussed below: maybe, and maybe not.

2.1.1 High-Level Prosecutions Conducted Pursuant to Internationally Recognized Fair Trial Standards

The ICTY indicted 161 individuals, most of whom faced prosecution,[15] with many higher- and mid-level accused. The resolution creating the ICTY did not mandate that it prosecute only those who bore the "greatest responsibility" for the crimes perpetrated, and, indeed, the ICTY commenced with the lower-level prosecution of Omarska and Keraterm camp guard Duško Tadić.[16] Yet, the ICTY's prosecutions ultimately included: former President of Serbia, and later, the Federal Republic of Yugoslavia, Slobodan Milošević; former Republika Srpska President and Supreme Commander of its armed forces, Radovan Karadžić; former Colonel General of the VRS (Army of Republika Srpska) Ratko Mladić; former Croatian General Ante Gotovina; and commander of the Kosovo Liberation Army (KLA) and former (and current) Prime Minister Ramush Haradinaj. Probably the most prominent Bosnian Muslim prosecuted was Naser Orić.[17] The ICTY also accepted the guilty plea of former Republika Srpska President Biljana Plavšić, reminding one that women can be perpetrators as well.[18] In total, the ICTY sentenced ninety individuals to a total of more than 1,121 years in prison, as well as six life sentences.[19]

It is true that the Milošević case ended with the accused's death midway through trial, and the Gotovina[20] and Haradinaj[21] cases ended in acquittals, yet other tribunals too have had prosecutions terminate after the deaths of the

---

[15]   Ninety were sentenced; thirty-seven had proceedings terminated after indictments were withdrawn; nineteen were acquitted; thirteen had their cases transferred to national jurisdictions; and two are in retrial before the MICT. *Infographic: ICTY Facts & Figures*, ICTY, www.icty.org/en/content/info graphic-icty-facts-figures (accessed on Sept. 30, 2018).

[16]   Prosecutor v. Tadić, Case No. IT-94-1-I (Int'l Crim. Trib. for the Former Yugoslavia).

[17]   Orić commanded Army of the Republic of Bosnia and Herzegovina (ARBiH) forces around Srebrenica. He was sentenced to two years at trial, but acquitted on appeal. He was later arrested in Switzerland, and while Serbia requested his extradition, he was returned to Bosnia. *See* Denis Dzidic, *Srebrenica Commander Naser Orić Charged With War Crimes*, BALKAN INVESTIGATIVE REPORTING NETWORK (BIRN) (Aug. 27, 2015), www.balkaninsight.com/en/article/srebrenica-commander-oric-charged-with-war-crimes-08-27-2015 (accessed on July 26, 2017).

[18]   Prosecutor v. Plavšić, Case No. IT-0039 & 40/1, Trial Chamber Judgment (Int'l Crim. Trib. for the Former Yugoslavia, February 27, 2003) (case not appealed).

[19]   *Key Figures of the Cases*, ICTY, www.icty.org/x/file/Cases/keyfigures/key_figures_en.pdf (accessed on Aug. 8, 2017); *Judgement List*, ICTY, www.icty.org/en/cases/judgement-list (accessed on Sept. 6, 2017).

[20]   The case was originally brought against Ante Gotovina, Mladen Markač, and Ivan Čermak, with Čermak acquitted after trial, and Gotovina and Markač originally sentenced to eighteen and twenty-four years respectively, but acquitted on appeal.

[21]   The case was originally brought against Ramush Haradinaj, Idriz Balaj, and Lahi Brahimaj, with Brahimaj sentenced to six years' imprisonment, but acquitted after partial retrial, and Haradinaj and Balaj acquitted after retrial.

accused,[22] and cases end in acquittal.[23] While the ICTY was roundly criticized for prosecuting Milošević on too many counts – a total of 66 counts covering crimes in Bosnia, Croatia, and Kosovo,[24] which lengthened his trial[25] – that is an easy criticism to present in hindsight. If the ICTY had pursued a truncated indictment with only representative charging, it would no doubt have faced the opposite criticism of not prosecuting on sufficiently comprehensive charges, and disappointing victims of the crimes omitted.[26]

Less understandable is the result reached in the Gotovina case, which ended in acquittal when the Appeals Chamber in part could not determine the proper legal rule to apply to collateral damage – the radius around a military target within which artillery projectiles would need to strike to constitute permissible "collateral damage."[27] The Appeals Chamber judges could have entertained additional expert submissions or remanded the issue to the Trial Chamber for further consideration. Acquittal seems a puzzling result in the face of legal uncertainty that presumably could have been resolved. Moreover, the acquittal actually had significant consequences in the region, helping nationalistic Croatians perpetuate a false narrative that, because there were no ICTY convictions regarding Operation Storm, there were no crimes committed,[28] when in fact there were significant Serb civilian fatalities and widespread civilian displacement when Croatian Army (HV) forces retook Croatia's Krajina region.[29] The initial Haradinaj trial collapsed amidst

---

[22] Several of the Special Court for Sierra Leone's original thirteen indictees died prior to trial, and Hinga Norman died after trial but prior to judgment. One of the ECCC indictees in Case 2 died (and one was found not competent to stand trial). One of the STL indictees died midway through trial.

[23] The ICC case against Mathieu Ngudjolo Chui ended in acquittal, Prosecutor v. Chui, Case No. ICC-01/04-02/12, as has the ICC case against Jean-Pierre Bemba Gombo, Prosecutor v. Jean-Pierre Bemba Gombo, Case No. ICC-01/05-01/08. Fourteen were acquitted by the ICTR. United Nations Mechanism for International Criminal Tribunals, *The ICTR in Brief*, http://unictr.unmict.org/en/tribunal (accessed on Sept. 3, 2017).

[24] Prosecutor v. Milošević, Case Nos. IT-99-37-AR73, IT-01-50-AR73, IT-01-51-AR73, Decision on Prosecution Interlocutory Appeal from Refusal to Order Joinder (Int'l Crim. Trib. for the Former Yugoslavia, Feb. 1, 2002) (considering the three indictments joined).

[25] Milošević died four years into his trial, just weeks short of its scheduled conclusion. *Slobodan Milošević Trial – The Prosecution's Case*, ICTY, http://www.icty.org/en/content/slobodan-milo%C5%A1evi%C4%87-trial-prosecutions-case (accessed on Mar. 9, 2017).

[26] For more on the Milošević trial, *see* GIDEON BOAS, THE MILOŠEVIĆ TRIAL: LESSONS FOR THE CONDUCT OF COMPLEX INTERNATIONAL CRIMINAL PROCEEDINGS (Cambridge, 2007).

[27] Prosecutor v. Gotovina, Case No. IT-06-90-A, Appeals Chamber Judgment (Int'l Crim. Trib. for the Former Yugoslavia, Nov. 16, 2012) (Judges Agius and Pocar dissenting). The Trial Chamber determined that a 200-meter margin of error was permissible, but the Appeals Chamber rejected the standard as arbitrary and overturned the convictions.

[28] *See* Marko Milanović, *The Impact of the ICTY on The Former Yugoslavia: An Anticipatory Postmortem*, 110 AMERICAN JOURNAL OF INTERNATIONAL LAW 233, 251 (2016) (only 26.1 percent of Croatian respondents believed crimes were committed against Croatian Serbs during Operation Storm).

[29] Estimates are over 500 civilian fatalities and 200,000 displaced. For background on Operation Storm, *see* generally, *Storm in The Hague*, SENSE NEWS, https://snv.hr/oluja-u-haagu/oluja-en.html (accessed on Sept. 3, 2017).

accusations of witness intimidation – a problem that has also plagued other tribunals;[30] the retrial also ended in acquittal for lack of sufficient evidence.[31]

Thus, while not all the ICTY's high-level prosecutions ended successfully from an OTP vantage point, certainly bringing the cases – against high-level perpetrators from multiple sides in the wars[32] – was an extremely significant accomplishment. "[I]t is exceptionally unlikely that any of the high-ranking political and military leaders that have been tried by the ICTY would ever have been (successfully) prosecuted before domestic courts."[33]

2.1.2 *Success in Having All Indictees Apprehended*

It is well-known that the ICTY was also successful in having all its original indictees apprehended.[34] (That Karadžić and Mladić were apprehended late in the life of the ICTY, as was lesser-known accused Goran Hadžić, partly explains why the ICTY's trials took so many years.)[35] While the record of arrests is indeed impressive, the arrests were conducted, of course, not by the ICTY, but by various military and police forces.[36] The arrests also occurred only after the United States placed conditions on financial assistance to counties in the region on their cooperation with the ICTY,[37] and the European Union conditioned

---

[30] *See Kenya – ICC Starts Investigation into Witness Tampering in Kenyatta, Ruto and Sang Cases,* Africa Sustainable Conservation News (Jan. 30, 2017), https://africasustainableconservation.com/ 2017/01/30/kenya-icc-starts-investigation-into-witness-tampering-in-kenyatta-ruto-and-sang-cases/ (accessed on Sept. 1, 2017).

[31] *See* Marija Ristic, *Can the New Kosovo Court Keep Witnesses Safe?*, Balkan Transitional Justice (Jan. 20, 2016), www.balkaninsight.com/en/article/can-the-new-kosovo-court-keep-witnesses-safe-01-20-2016 ("In her memoirs, as well as in her many reports to the UN Security Council, [former ICTY Prosecutor Carla] Del Ponte said that she believes the intimidation of witnesses seriously affected the verdicts in the cases against senior KLA officials Fatmir Limaj and Ramush Haradinaj – both of whom were acquitted.")

[32] *See, e.g.,* Victor Peskin, *Beyond Victor's Justice? The Challenge of Prosecuting the Winners at the International Criminal Tribunals for the Former Yugoslavia and Rwanda,* 4 Journal of Human Rights (2005) (the importance of prosecuting on all sides).

[33] Milanović, The Impact of the ICTY on The Former Yugoslavia, *supra* note 28, at 233; Mirko Klarin, *The Impact of the ICTY Trials on Public Opinion in the Former Yugoslavia,* 7 International Criminal Justice 89, 90 (while Bosnian Muslims are critical of the ICTY, "they know that had it not been for the ICTY, there would have been no accused, no trials and no convictions").

[34] For a detailed account of various key arrests, *see* Julian Borger, The Butcher's Trail: How the Search for Balkan War Criminals Became the World's Most Successful Manhunt (New York, 2016).

[35] Karadžić was apprehended thirteen years after his indictment, and Mladić apprehended fifteen years after his indictment. Dan Bilefsky & Doreen Carvajal, *Serbia Says Jailed Mladic Will Face War Crimes Trial,* New York Times (May 26, 2011), www.nytimes.com/2011/05/27/world/europe/27ratko-mladic.html?pagewanted=all&_r=0; *Serbia Captures Fugitive Karadzic,* BBC News (July 22, 2008), http://news.bbc.co.uk/2/hi/europe/7518543.stm.

[36] *See* Borger, The Butcher's Trail, *supra* note 34.

[37] *See, e.g.,* Julie Kim, *Balkan Cooperation on War Crimes Issues,* US Cong. Research Serv., RS 22097, 2008; Steven Woehrel, *Conditions on U.S. Aid to Serbia,* Cong. Research Serv., RS 21686, 2008.

progress in EU accession talks.[38] Thus, while the ICTY was the beneficiary of this significant track record of apprehensions, multiple divergent actors were responsible.[39] (Still, this author will list success in apprehensions as a "benchmark" by which to judge the ICTY, as other tribunals have had far less success with arrests, and that may prove a negative factor in assessing their accomplishments.)[40]

2.1.3 *Creating an Extensive Body of Well-Reasoned Jurisprudence*

The ICTY, through its trial and appeals chamber judgments, also created an extremely comprehensive body of jurisprudence on the elements of genocide, war crimes, and crimes against humanity, as well as modes of individual and command responsibility, and other aspects of international criminal law.[41] The ICTY, complemented by its sister tribunal, the ICTR, is thus the first modern international criminal tribunal to create such a wealth of law, which can serve as a body of precedent both to national courts pursuing war crimes cases in the region, as well as international, hybrid, and national chambers elsewhere.[42]

While this author would suggest there were isolated, disappointing low points in the ICTY's jurisprudence – such as the Perišić,[43] Gotovina,[44] and initial

---

[38] *The Hague Tribunal: Substantial Progress, Key Arrests Expected*, US Institute of Peace (June 27, 2005), www.usip.org/publications/2005/06/hague-tribunal-substantial-progress-key-arrests-expected (accessed on Sept. 3, 2017).

[39] This track record was put in slight jeopardy as there were two former ICTY fugitives in Serbia wanted on charges of witness tampering. *Interpol Issues Red Notices for Serbians Wanted in UN Case*, AFP, The New Indian Express (Mar. 31, 2017), www.newindianexpress.com/world/2017/mar/31/interpol-issues-red-notices-for-serbians-wanted-in-un-case-1588193.html (accessed on Sept. 7, 2017).

[40] The International Criminal Court currently has fifteen outstanding arrest warrants. *Situations and Cases, Defendants at Large*, ICC, at www.icc-cpi.int/defendants?k=At%20large (accessed on Aug. 21, 2017).

[41] For a compilation of the jurisprudence, *see* Jennifer Trahan, Genocide, War Crimes and Crimes Against Humanity: A Topical Digest of the Caselaw of the International Criminal Tribunal for the Former Yugoslavia (New York, 2006).

[42] It is disappointing the ICC is not more closely following this jurisprudence, which, while not binding, could still be persuasive. *See, e.g.*, Prosecutor v. Ongwen, Case No. ICC-02/04-01/15, Decision on the Prosecutor's Position on the Decision of Pre-Trial Chamber II to Redact Factual Descriptions of Crimes from the Warrants of Arrest, Motion for Reconsideration, and Motion for Clarification, para. 19 (Int'l Crim. Ct., Oct. 28, 2005) ("the rules and practice of other jurisdictions, whether national or international, are not as such 'applicable law' before the Court . . . [s]pecifically, the law and practice of the ad hoc tribunals.")

[43] In the Perišić case, after nearly twenty years of jurisprudence otherwise, the ICTY Appeals Chamber suddenly added a third prong to the test for "aiding and abetting" – insisting on a showing that the aiding and abetting was "specifically directed" toward the accomplishment of a crime. That standard has since been repudiated. *See* Jennifer Trahan & Erin Lovall, *The ICTY Appellate Chamber's Acquittal of Momčilo Perišić: The Specific Direction Element of Aiding and Abetting Should Be Rejected or Modified to Explicitly Include a 'Reasonable Person' Due Diligence Standard*, 40 Brooklyn Journal of International Law 171 (2015).

[44] *See supra* note 27 and accompanying text.

Šešelj[45] acquittals – that does not diminish the significant output of otherwise well-reasoned jurisprudence in the vast majority of cases. There were also important high points in the ICTY's adjudications: that individual criminal responsibility exists for war crimes committed in internal armed conflict,[46] and the adjudication that the crimes in and around Srebrenica constituted genocide.[47] The Milošević indictment was also the first indictment by an international tribunal against a sitting head of state,[48] and his trial was the first trial of a leader for crimes committed while the person was head of state.

By criticizing specific acquittals, the author does not imply that international or hybrid tribunals must always convict. Tribunals must ensure their prosecutions adhere to internationally respected fair trial standards, and reach well-reasoned results on both the law and facts, regardless of whether that results in conviction or acquittal.[49] (And, while the acquittals mentioned had unfortunate impact in the region, the author will disagree with the suggestion that judges should consider such impact;[50] in the author's view, the judges must adjudicate solely based on the facts and law presented to them.)

2.1.4 *Prosecuting Under-Reported and Under-Prosecuted Crimes (SGBV)*

The perpetration of SGBV, including but not limited to rape, was, unfortunately a dominant feature of both the Rwandan genocide and crimes in the former Yugoslavia, with an estimated 250,000–500,000 rape victims in Rwanda,[51] and an

---

45   The trial-level acquittal of Vojislav Šešelj, the leader of the Serbian Radical Party, was heavily criticized as going against twenty years of ICTY conclusions, but recently changed to a conviction on appeal. Prosecutor v. Šešelj, Case No. IT-03-67-T, Trial Chamber Judgment (Int'l Crim. Trib. for the Former Yugoslavia, Mar. 31, 2016) (dissenting opinion by Judge Flavia Lattanzi); Marko Milanović, *The Sorry Acquittal of Vojislavi Seslj*, EJIL: Talk! (Apr. 4, 2016), www .ejiltalk.org/the-sorry-acquittal-of-vojislav-seselj/comment-page- (accessed on Aug. 14, 2017); Prosecutor v. Šešelj, Case No. MICT-16-99, Appeals Chamber Judgment (Mechanism for International Criminal Tribunals, Apr. 11, 2018).

46   Prosecutor v. Tadić, Case No. IT-94-1-AR72, Decision on the Defence Motion for Interlocutory Appeal on Jurisdiction (Int'l Crim. Trib. for the Former Yugoslavia, Oct. 2, 1995).

47   Prosecutor v. Krstić, Case No. IT-98-33-A, Appeals Judgment (Int'l Crim. Trib. for the Former Yugoslavia, Apr. 19, 2004); Prosecutor v. Blagojević and Jokić, Case No. IT-02-60-A, Appeals Judgment (Int'l Crim. Trib. for the Former Yugoslavia, May 9, 2007); Prosecutor v. Popović, Case No. IT-05-88-A, Appeals Judgment (Int'l Crim. Trib. for the Former Yugoslavia, Jan. 30, 2015).

48   *Milosevic Indictment Makes History*, CNN.COM (May 27, 1999), www.cnn.com/WORLD/europe/ 9905/27/kosovo.milosevic.04/ (accessed on Aug. 8, 2017).

49   It is also possible there were weaknesses in some of the cases of which the author is not aware.

50   *See* Iva Vukušić, *Judging their Hero: Perceptions of the International Criminal Tribunal for the Former Yugoslavia in Croatia*, in PROSECUTING WAR CRIMES: LESSONS AND LEGACIES OF THE INTERNATIONAL CRIMINAL TRIBUNAL FOR THE FORMER YUGOSLAVIA (James Gow, Rachel Kerr, and Zoran Pajic eds., New York, 2014), 172 ("It is the professional duty of everyone involved in these trials and the deliberations to keep in mind the evidence and arguments, but also the impact that their work has on the populations they allegedly serve.")

51   Nancy Sai, *Women Under Siege*, Conflict Profile Rwanda (Feb. 8, 2012), www.womensmediacenter.com/ women-under-siege/conflicts/rwanda (citing estimates of UN Special Rapporteur on Rwanda Rene Degni-Segui) (accessed on Sept. 3, 2017).

estimated 20,000–50,000 rape victims from the former Yugoslavia.[52] In the former Yugoslavia, for example, Bosnian Serb forces ran an infamous "rape camp" in Foča, with women held in various locations in sexual and domestic servitude.[53] While it is a sad testament to what happened that this jurisprudence had to be developed, it is now extremely significant that, for the first time, rape has been recognized (in the jurisprudence of the ICTR) as a form of genocide,[54] and (in the jurisprudence of the ICTY) as both a crime against humanity[55] and a war crime.[56] Rape has also been acknowledged to constitute torture.[57] In total, "more than seventy individuals have been charged [by the ICTY] with crimes of sexual violence."[58]

Additional ICTY jurisprudence facilitated the tribunal's prosecution of SGBV cases, including holdings that: (1) in circumstances where war crimes and crimes against humanity are occurring, true consent is not possible;[59] (2) no corroborating evidence is require to prove rape;[60] and (3) a woman's past history of conduct is irrelevant to rape prosecutions.[61] In various cases, the ICTY also rendered findings as

---

[52] European Union estimate of 20,000; Bosnian Interior Ministry estimate of 50,000. KEN BOOTH, THE KOSOVO TRAGEDY: THE HUMAN RIGHTS DIMENSIONS 73 (New York, 2012); *see also* Sue Turton, *Bosnian War Rape Survivors Speak of Their Suffering 25 Years On*, THE INDEPENDENT (July 21, 2017), www.independent.co.uk/news/long_reads/bosnia-war-rape-survivors-speak-serbian-soldiers-balkans-women-justice-suffering-a7846546.html.

[53] Prosecutor v. Kunarac, Case No. IT-96-23 & 23/1, Trial Chamber Judgment (Int'l Crim. Trib. For the Former Yugoslavia, Feb. 22, 2001).

[54] Prosecutor v. Akayesu, Case No. ICTR-96-4-T, Trial Chamber Judgment (Int'l Crim. Trib. for Rwanda, Sept. 2, 1998), *aff'd on appeal*, Appeals Chamber Judgment, June 1, 2001.

[55] Prosecutor v. Kunarac, Case No. IT-96-23 & 23/1A, Appeals Chamber Judgment, paras. 127–9 (Int'l Crim. Trib. for the Former Yugoslavia, June 12, 2002) (hereinafter "Kunarac Appeals Chamber Judgment"); Prosecutor v. Kvočka, Case No. IT-98-30/1, Trial Chamber Judgment, paras. 175, 180–3 (Int'l Crim. Trib. for the Former Yugoslavia, Nov. 2, 2001), *aff'd on appeal*, Appeals Chamber Judgment, Feb. 28, 2005.

[56] Prosecutor v. Kvočka, Case No. IT-98-30/1A, Appeals Chamber Judgment, para. 395 (Int'l Crim. Trib. for the Former Yugoslavia, Feb. 28, 2005) (hereinafter "Kvočka Appeals Chamber Judgment"); Kunarac Appeals Chamber Judgment, *supra* note 55, paras. 127–9.

[57] Kunarac Appeals Chamber Judgment, *supra* note 55, paras. 150–1.

[58] *Landmark Cases*, ICTY, www.icty.org/en/in-focus/crimes-sexual-violence/landmark-cases (accessed on Sept. 3, 2017).

[59] The ICTY Appeals Chamber in Kunarac emphasized that "the circumstances giving rise to the instant appeal and that prevail in most cases charged as either war crimes or crimes against humanity will be almost universally coercive. That is to say, true consent [of a rape victim] will not be possible." Kunarac Appeals Chamber Judgment, *supra* note 55, para. 130.

[60] Prosecutor v. Delalić, Case No. IT-96-21-T, Trial Judgment, para. 936 (Int'l Crim. Trib. for the Former Yugoslavia, Nov. 16, 1998) ("The Trial Chamber notes that sub-Rule 96(i) of the Rules provides that no corroboration of the testimony of a victim of sexual assault shall be required.")

[61] Prosecutor v. Delalić, Case No. IT-96-21-T, Trial Judgment, para. 70 (Int'l Crim. Trib. for the Former Yugoslavia, Nov. 16, 1998) (rule 96(iv) provides that prior sexual conduct of the victim shall not be admitted in evidence). *See also* Kunarac Appeals Chamber Judgment, *supra* note 55, paras. 128–9 ("Resistance" is not a requirement. "Force or threat of force provides clear evidence of nonconsent, but force is not an element per se of rape."); Kvočka Appeals Chamber Judgment, *supra* note 56, para. 396 ("The Trial Chamber determined that 'in cases of sexual assault a status of detention will normally vitiate consent in such circumstances.'")

to SGBV crimes committed against men,[62] which are often under-reported and under-prosecuted crimes.[63]

2.1.5 Giving Nearly 5,000 Victims the Ability to Be Heard through Their Testimony

Nearly 5,000 victims and witnesses testified at the ICTY.[64] While some percentage did so through protective measures, the vast majority testified in open court.[65] Under the ICTY's procedures, victims and witnesses testified only when called as witnesses, and did not have independent standing to appear, as they do at the Extraordinary Chambers in the Court of Cambodia (ECCC), the Special Tribunal for Lebanon (STL), and the ICC.

While tribunals are sometimes criticized as "perpetrator focused" (in that they focus on convicting perpetrators) and not generally "victim centric" (as, for example, a truth commission would be), in the former Yugoslavia, there has been no comprehensive truth commission.[66]

Admittedly, the experience of testifying potentially risks both re-traumatization when witnesses recount harrowing events and do so in the presence of the accused,[67] and involves cross-examination (which can be intimidating, as it essentially aims to question the witnesses' veracity). Yet, isolated victim voices suggest that testifying can also prove an empowering experience.[68]

While permitting victims independent standing to appear at trial suggests it would provide them more of a voice, this has not necessarily proven the case. At the ICC,

---

[62] *Tadić* was the first case to consider sexual violence against men during war. *Landmark Cases*, ICTY, *supra* note 58. Sexual violence against men was also examined in other ICTY cases, including *Češić*, *Mucić*, *Todorović*, and *Simić*.

[63] Maite Vermeulen, *Hidden Victims: The Story of Sexual Violence against Men in Armed Conflict* (2011), www.e-ir.info/2011/09/04/hidden-victims-the-story-of-sexual-violence-against-men-in-armed-conflict/ (accessed on Sept. 3, 2017).

[64] *Witness Statistics*, ICTY, www.icty.org/en/about/registry/witnesses/statistics (accessed on Mar. 12, 2017).

[65] Even where voice distortion was used as a protective measure, the testimony was still heard, even if not through the victim's original voice.

[66] *See* Coalition for RECOM, at www.recom.link/ (proposal for a regional truth commission).

[67] The ICTY's website states that the Victims and Witnesses Section (VWS) provides "witnesses with assistance prior to, during and after their testimony, ranging from practical issues to psychological counselling during their stay in The Hague." *Crimes of Sexual Violence*, ICTY, www.icty.org/en/in-focus/crimes-sexual-violence (accessed on 9/3/2017). *See also* KIMI KING & JAMES MEERNIK, ECHOES OF TESTIMONIES: A PILOT STUDY INTO THE LONG-TERM IMPACT OF BEARING WITNESS BEFORE THE ICTY (2016) (lessons learned from the ICTY's experiences with witnesses).

[68] *See* KING & MEERNIK, ECHOES OF TESTIMONIES, *supra* note 67, at 130 (67 percent of ICTY witnesses surveyed believed their testimony contributed to providing justice, and 70.7 percent believed it contributed to discovering the truth about the wars in the former Yugoslavia). "In addition to being given the opportunity to publicly tell their stories, witnesses [were] pleased when their contribution [was] acknowledge by the Tribunal and when they [saw] their testimony . . . relied upon in the final judgment." *Id.*

for example, due to the massive numbers of victims in each case, victims are generally only heard through their common legal representative, with only a few testifying in person.[69] Many fill out a form to qualify as a "victim of the case," but their voices are not heard beyond that, and limited individualized reparations have been awarded.[70] Ironically, the ICTY, which does not grant victims independent standing, has actually had far more victims and witnesses testify before it.[71]

There are many additional ways that victims in the region could have their voices heard in addition to providing testimony (either at the ICTY or local courts in the region). Victim testimony could, for example, be facilitated by the creation of a regional truth commission, such as RECOM,[72] which has garnered a fair amount of public support but not been enacted. Other potential tools include: informal documentation projects such the Humanitarian Law Center's "Kosovo Memory Book";[73] granting further collective reparations to victims;[74] allowing victims greater say in memorialization projects; and facilitating recovery in individual reparations cases.[75] In short, there is significantly more that can be done to give voice to victims, but these tasks are more traditionally the province of other transitional justice mechanisms.

Thus, while the ICTY was not particularly designed as a forum to give voice to victims, through its cases, nearly 5,000 primarily victims and witnesses have had their voices heard.[76]

---

[69]   Author's Aug. 10, 2017 meeting with staff of ICC VPRS.

[70]   Author's Aug. 10, 2017 meeting with staff of ICC VPRS.

[71]   For instance, in the ICC's *Bemba* case, there were 5,229 victims authorized to participate, but only twenty-three were involved in person at trial. *Situation in the Central African Republic in the Case of the Prosecutor v. Jean-Pierre Bemba Gombo*, ICC-01/05-01/08-3343, Judgment Pursuant to Article 74 of the Statute (Int'l Crim. Ct., Mar. 21, 2016). An additional two victims participated at the sentencing phase. Decision on Sentence Pursuant to Article 76 of the Statute, (June 21, 2016), www.icc-cpi.int/Pages/record.aspx?docNo=ICC-01/05-01/08-T-371-ENG (accessed on Sept. 12, 2017).

[72]   Regional Commission Tasked with Establishing the Facts about All Victims of War Crimes and Other Serious Human Rights Violations Committed on the Territory of the Former Yugoslavia in the period from 1991–2001. Coalition for RECOM, at www.recom.link/. Vukušić explains that RECOM is a "victim-focused initiative consisting of some 1,800 nongovernmental organizations, human rights groups and victims' associations, as well as individuals – that advocates for the establishing of a regional commission that would be tasked with establishing facts about the mass human rights violations that were committed and the victims [who] suffered the consequences of those brutalities." Vukušić, Judging their Hero, *supra* note 50, at 163.

[73]   *See Kosovo Memory Book*, HUMANITARIAN LAW CENTER, www.hlc-rdc.org/?p=12831&lang=de (accessed on Aug. 9, 2017).

[74]   In Bosnia, only a small pension is granted if a person is recognized as a "civilian victim of war." *Compensating Survivors in Criminal Proceedings: Perspectives from the Field*, TRIAL INTERNATIONAL (2016), at 41.

[75]   The nongovernmental organization TRIAL International has facilitated SGBV victims in Bosnia obtaining reparations, and has had limited success in having reparations awarded in criminal cases. *Id.* at 14.

[76]   Some who testified were called by the defense, and included perpetrators and other defense witnesses.

2.1.6 Establishing a Solid Historical Record and Extensive Documentary Archive

Through evidence presented at trial,[77] the ICTY has also constructed a solid evidentiary record as to the crimes committed during the wars in the former Yugoslavia. This record includes: testimony of victims, witnesses, and the accused; video footage; expert reports (such as DNA or ballistics reports); artifacts (such as hand ligature and blindfolds); recordings of intercepted conversations; forensic evidence (as to mass graves and re-burials of mass graves); and aerial surveillance images.[78] This evidence is analyzed in the Tribunal's judgments, and trial proceedings can be viewed in documentation centers, such as the one established by Sense News at the Srebrenica-Potočari Memorial. There also exists a vast, searchable electronic database of evidentiary materials that can be utilized by historians, academics, and NGOs, as well as local war crimes prosecutors, or even individual citizens who want to learn of the crimes committed.[79] "The Tribunal and the material it gathers have already contributed immensely to our understanding of the history of that part of the world and we must continue using everything the ICTY acquired through the years to understand how these events took place and why."[80]

While, as discussed below, creating this record[81] has unfortunately not silenced denial of crimes in the region, nor has it resulted in acceptance of one narrative as to the war or crimes committed, it was perhaps not reasonable to think a tribunal could accomplish either goal. Yet, having this vast historical record based on documentary evidence certainly lessens the space for denial.[82] As former ICTY Prosecutor and

---

[77] According to the ICTY's website, there have been 10,800 days of trial, creating 2.5 million pages of transcripts. *Infographic: ICTY Facts & Figures*, ICTY, www.icty.org/en/content/infographic-icty-facts-figures (accessed on Aug. 8, 2017).

[78] *See, e.g.*, Iva Vukušić, *The Archives of the International Criminal Tribunal for the Former Yugoslavia*, 98 JOURNAL OF THE HISTORICAL ASSOCIATION 623, 626 (2013).

[79] *ICTY Court Records*, UN, http://icr.icty.org/default.aspx (accessed on Sept. 3, 2017). The ICTY is in fact the only criminal tribunal that allows the public to search evidence in this way. Author e-mail with Iva Vukušić. Commenting on the value of a tribunal's archives, former ECCC International Co-Prosecutor Robert Petit observed:

> I think one of the lessons from Cambodia . . . is that the impact of the court is not only the judgment, but what happens after. The archives of the court, making findings available, opening up the results of the whole institution, I think can also have a major impact because it might allow people to find answers to their own questions . . . If the court does it right, it will have its impact with its judgments, but it will also leave . . . a legacy of information, of evidence available. I think it can help rebuild the country.

Trahan interview of Robert Petit, Sept. 29, 2016, at 3. Interviews are on file with the author.

[80] Vukušić, The Archives of the ICTY, *supra* note 78, at 635.

[81] The record is not necessarily a full historical record, as judgments reflect the evidence admitted, and will not necessarily cover events during the war but not criminal, nor the roles of lower- and mid-level perpetrators not tried by the ICTY.

[82] *See* Diane F. Orentlicher, *Shrinking the Space for Denial: The Impact of the ICTY in Serbia*, OPEN SOCIETY JUSTICE INITIATIVE, May 2008; Vukušić, The Archives of the ICTY, *supra* note 78, at 625; *but see* Marko Milanović, *Establishing the Facts About Mass Atrocities: Accounting for the Failure of the*

Prosecutor for the Mechanism for International Criminal Tribunals (MICT) Serge Brammertz explains: "[T]he underlying evidence is a very strong record which can always be put in front of those who still think that they have to deny those crimes and who are refusing to accept that perhaps people from their own community have been involved in massive crimes."[83] Additionally helpful to potentially combatting denial are guilty pleas received by the ICTY, such as that of Dražen Erdemović, the first person openly to admit taking part in the Srebrenica massacre.[84]

2.1.7 Contributing to Rule of Law, through Its Own Work and Capacity-Building in the Region

The ICTY has also contributed to rule of law development by showing rule of law at work through its own prosecutions, and by assisting with capacity-building in the region. The ICTY likely also played a role in setting precedent for creation of the International Criminal Court.

The commission of mass crimes of course indicates that rule of law has broken down – that rather than recourse to law, there is recourse to armed force and the perpetration of atrocity crimes. Thus, the ICTY's work has importantly demonstrated rule of law at work. However, the location of the tribunal in The Hague, Netherlands – necessary as its creation occurred while war was still ongoing in the region[85] – has minimized the number of individuals from the region able to experience the trials first-hand. An active exchange program to have interns from the region work at the Tribunal has helped somewhat in bridging this gap, as have broadcasts and news reports about the Tribunal's work by Sense News,[86] as well as the work of the ICTY's Outreach Program.[87]

ICTY to Persuade Target Audiences, 47 GEORGETOWN JOURNAL OF INTERNATIONAL LAW 1321 (2016) ("'shrinking the space for denial' [has] been negligible at best").

[83] Lovall and Vutrano, Seeking Truth in the Balkans, *supra* note 13, at 303 (quoting interview of Serge Brammertz).

[84] Prosecutor v. Erdemović, Case No. IT-96-22, Appeals Chamber Judgment (Int'l Crim. Trib. for the Former Yugoslavia, Oct. 7, 1997) (hereinafter "Erdemović Appeals Judgment"). Similarly significant in trying to silence denial was discovery of the so-called Scorpions video of Serbian paramilitary conducting executions in the village of Trnovo, near Srebrenica. *Srebrenica Executions Trnovo*, YOUTUBE, www.youtube.com/watch?v=7UMH6VKgKKo. While it could have proven a much more transformative moment, the video's release basically only caused the nationalistic narrative to switch from full denial (crimes at Srebrenica never occurred) to partial denial (crimes occurred, but not genocide). And, notwithstanding release of the video, survey results still suggest significant denial of the crimes at Srebrenica. *See* text accompanying note 101 *infra*.

[85] The ICTY was created in 1993.

[86] Sense News has had an office, run by Mirko Klarin, located in the ICTY's building for the last two decades. Sense News has covered all ICTY trials, reporting on them daily in Bosnian-Croatian-Serbian and English, producing over 10,000 daily or weekly reports, over 700 television programs, and several documentary films. *See generally* SENSE NEWS, www.sense-agency.com/home/home.4.html?verz=2 (accessed on Aug. 14, 2017).

[87] *See Outreach*, ICTY, www.icty.org/en/outreach/home (accessed on Aug. 14, 2017).

The ICTY has also assisted capacity-building in the region. Because the ICTY's "completion strategy"[88] envisioned that certain lower-level cases or files would be transferred back to courts in the region,[89] focus needed to be given to domestic capacity-building. This has taken the form of providing evidence, sharing knowledge, and contributing jurisprudence to the War Crimes Chamber of the State Court in Bosnia, the War Crimes Chamber of the Belgrade District Court, and the Croatian judiciary.[90] The ICTY's massive archive of evidence has also been, and will continue to be, available to such national court prosecutions.[91] Despite this assistance, however, there are still concerns that, in the region, "the [domestic] judicial systems continue to operate under the persistent political influence of their respective governments."[92]

Finally, by its successful functioning, the ICTY likely also contributed to the momentum that helped establish the ICC – itself a "rule of law" development on a macro-level. Creation of the ICTY (and, later, the ICTR) basically resurrected the field of international justice, which had lain dormant since the work of the International Military Tribunals after World War II.[93] In the words of ICTY and later MICT President, Judge Theodor Meron:

---

[88] Dates were set for both the ICTY and ICTR to (1) finish issuing indictments (by 2004), (2) complete trials, and (3) complete appeals. While the first date was met, dates for finishing trials and appeals were adjusted several times, with final work of the ICTY concluding on Dec. 31, 2017, and remaining work to be done by the MICT. The MICT is the residual mechanism of both the ICTY and ICTR. *See United Nations Mechanism for International Criminal Tribunals*, at www.unmict.org/en/about (accessed on Aug. 12, 2017).

[89] Thirteen cases were transferred back to counties in the former Yugoslavia for trial. *Infographic: ICTY Facts & Figures*, ICTY, *supra* note 15. Transfers were made pursuant to rule 11bis of the ICTY's Rules of Procedures and Evidence.

[90] *Achievements*, ICTY, *supra* note 14.

[91] Vukušić, Archives of the ICTY, *supra* note 78, at 629.

[92] Milanović, The Impact of the ICTY on The Former Yugoslavia, *supra* note 28, at 234, citing 2015 *Serbia Progress Report*, EUROPEAN COMMISSION 11, http://ec.europa.edu/enlargement/pdf/key_docu ments/2015/20151110_report_serbia.pdf ("[J]udicial independence is not assured in practice. There is scope for political interference in the recruitment and appointment of judges and prosecutors."); *2014 Bosnia Progress Report*, EUROPEAN COMMISSION 12, http://ec.europa.eu/enlargement/pdf/key_docu ments/2014/20141008-bosna-and-herzegovina-progress-report_en.pdf ("There are persistent flaws in the independence and impartiality of the judiciary. Political interference has continued.") Milanović also characterizes the ICTY's capacity-building as "modest." Milanović, The Impact of the ICTY on The Former Yugoslavia, *supra* note 28, at 234. A recent report suggests the State Court in Sarajevo is facing difficulties and is far off the National Strategy for Processing of War Crimes Cases. *See* Judge Joanna Korner, *Processing of War Crimes at the State Level in Bosnia and Herzegovina*, OSCE (2016), www.osce.org/bih/247221?download=true. While there are war crimes prosecutions occurring in Belgrade, they are criticized as not targeting mid- or higher-level perpetrators. Trahan, July 17, 2017 meeting with Budimir Ivanišević, Executive Director, Humanitarian Law Center; *War Crimes Proceedings in Serbia (2003–2014)* OSCE MISSION TO SERBIA (2015), p. 17, www.osce.org/serbia/ 194461?download=true (accessed on Sept. 8, 2017).

[93] Charter of the International Military Tribunal, Aug. 8, 1945, 85 UNTS 251, at http://avalon .law.yale.edu/imt/imtconst.asp; International Military Tribunal for the Far East Charter, Jan. 19, 1946, TIAS No. 1587, at www.jus.uio.no/english/services/library/treaties/04/4-06/military-tribunal-far-east.xml (accessed on Aug. 8, 2017).

The apogee of this golden age of international criminal law was the creation of a permanent judicial mechanism for international crimes, the International Criminal Court, which fulfilled a long-held dream of many generations of academics and lawyers. These achievements, however, were only made possible because of the success of the ICTY, which proved the erstwhile unthinkable – that the international community can reach consensus and act in the face of mass atrocities and that a day of reckoning will befall those who perpetrate them.[94]

2.1.8 Assessment of the ICTY by the Public in the Former Yugoslavia

2.1.8.1 Reckoning with Dismal Survey Results

Finally, when evaluating the ICTY's judicial and prosecutorial accomplishments, one might ask: through whose eyes does one conduct the evaluation? The above analysis is from an international perspective (and, no doubt, not every member of the international community would necessarily agree with all points). Survey results from the former Yugoslavia, however, show that such an optimistic assessment of the ICTY is not shared in the region.

In his article, "The Impact of the ICTY on The Former Yugoslavia: An Anticipatory Postmortem," Marko Milanović compiled findings of public opinion surveys commissioned by the Belgrade Center for Human Rights (BCHR) and sponsored by the Organization for Security and Cooperation in Europe (OSCE).[95] They reveal a generally dismal picture of views of the ICTY among segments of the public in Bosnia, Serbia, Croatia, and Kosovo.

Only public surveys from Bosnia (the Federation) and Kosovo (the Albanian population) show a positive assessment of the ICTY.[96] Surveys in Bosnia have negative results in Republika Srpska (the predominantly Serb entity),[97] and in Kosovo, with Kosovo Serb respondents.[98] Additionally, the public in both Serbia

---

[94] Judge Theodor Meron, *Foreword, in* 20 Years of the ICTY, Anniversary Events and Legacy Conference Proceedings 7 (ICTY Outreach Programme, 2013); *see also* Milanović, The Impact of the ICTY, *supra* note 28, at 234 ("without the tribunals for Yugoslavia and Rwanda, there might never have been a permanent International Criminal Court"); Shany, Assessing the Effectiveness of International Courts, *supra* note 7 ("The ICC and ICTR have been modeled after the ICTY, which in turn, was modeled on the International Military Tribunal at Nuremberg.")

[95] Milanović, The Impact of the ICTY, *supra* note 28. For details of survey methodology, *see id.* at 236. Surveys were conducted in Serbia in 2003, 2004, 2005, 2006, 2009, and 2011; in Bosnia in 2010 and 2011; in Croatia in 2010 and 2011; and in Kosovo in 2007 and 2012. *Id.* at 237–9.

[96] In Bosnia (Federation) in 2012, 59 percent viewed the ICTY positively. *Id.* at 240, citing 2012 BCHR Bosnia Survey. In 2012, 82 percent of Kosovo Albanians were satisfied with the ICTY. *Id.* at 240, citing UNSP 2012 Kosovo Survey.

[97] In Republika Srpska, 84 percent viewed the ICTY negatively in 2012. *Id.* at 240, citing 2012 BCHR Bosnia Survey.

[98] In 2012, 87 percent of Kosovo Serb respondents were not satisfied with the ICTY. *Id.* at 240, citing UNSP 2012 Kosovo Survey.

and Croatia hold quite negative views,[99] generally dismissing the ICTY as ethnically biased.[100]

Survey results about whether the public believes that crimes adjudicated by the ICTY actually occurred also reveal poor results, with an ethnic component to the findings. For example, as to whether crimes were committed in Srebrenica, "barely one-fifth of the Bosnian Serb population believe that any crime (let alone genocide) happened in Srebrenica, while two-fifths say that they had never even heard of any such crime."[101] One sees similar negative results when examining whether individuals from Republika Srpska believe that crimes in other locations were committed, compared to respondents from the Federation, who were much more likely to have heard of the crimes and believe them to be true.[102]

Milanović concludes that "each ethnic group in the former Yugoslavia is still firmly attached to its own version of reality."[103] He also ponders whether some survey respondents were lying in the surveys, or "lying to themselves" when they gave certain responses.[104]

Even within Bosnia (the Federation), while there is support for the work of the ICTY, there is also disappointment that there were not more convictions, that there were acquittals in particular cases (Perišić and Gotovina),[105] and that ICTY sentences were too low.[106] Nevertheless, the predominant view here of the ICTY is positive.

Survey results improved somewhat when focusing on youths (aged 16–23) and those with a university education.[107] Thus, older and less educated respondents were

---

[99]   In Serbia, 71 percent viewed the ICTY negatively in 2011, and in Croatia 64 percent viewed it negatively in 2011. *Id.* at 240, citing 2011 BCHR Serbia Survey and 2011 BCHR Croatia Survey.

[100]   "Croats dislike the ICTY because they think the ICTY is biased against Croats, while Serbs dislike it because they think it is biased against Serbs." *Id.* at 242. There is, of course, a minority in both Serbia and Croatia who do not share these views.

[101]   *Id.* at 235. For further details of views as to whether crimes occurred in Srebrenica, and/or whether they constituted genocide, *see id.* at 246–9. Milanović concludes: "It is hard to escape the impression that a significant portion of the Republika Srpska respondents who say they never even heard of thousands of dead or injured civilians in the siege of Sarajevo are actually being (consciously) deceptive. They are lying – to themselves and/or to others – in order to protect their sense of identity, which is threatened by the question." *Id.* at 254.

[102]   *See id.* at 249 (chart of survey results, showing widespread denial in Republika Srpska of crimes in Bijelina, Zvornik, Sarajevo, Prijedor, Travnik, and Celebici – the latter two involving Croat and Serb civilian victims, and Serb civilians).

[103]   *Id.* at 257.

[104]   *Id.* at 254.

[105]   *See* notes 43, 27 *supra.*

[106]   Klarin, The Impact of the ICTY Trials, *supra* note 33, at 90 (Bosnian Muslims "are disappointed by the small number of accused, the lengthy trials, and prison sentences they see as too low."); *see also* Vukušić, Judging their Hero, *supra* note 50, at 159 ("we frequently see Croats given short sentences for crimes, as gruesome as torture, committed against Serbs"); *id.* at 157 (criticizing the ten-year sentence of Veselin Sljivančanin for crimes in Ovčara, where around 200 people were killed).

[107]   Milanović, The Impact of the ICTY, *supra* note 28, at 241.

the ones more likely to deny crimes had occurred and hold negative views of the ICTY.[108]

Unfortunately, the survey findings do not seem out of line with views one generally encounters in the region.[109]

2.1.8.2 How Much Do Dismal Survey Results Matter?

The broader question is what to make of such views when evaluating the ICTY's legacy. Is it not problematic that these views exist? Wouldn't the public in the former Yugoslavia be the main target audience for the ICTY's work – in whose name justice is purportedly being done?[110] Do negative survey results impact on the ICTY's actual accomplishments? Trying to answer these questions warrants extensive analysis,[111] but the author will at least offer some initial thoughts.

First, survey results are not an indicator of the ICTY's *actual* accomplishments; rather, they reflect *views* of its accomplishments. Revisiting the old adage "justice must be done and seen to be done," survey results do not go to *whether* justice was done, but where it was *seen* to be done. Accordingly, that the public in the former Yugoslavia might not concur with the author's points about the ICTY's accomplishments (articulated above) does not mean the accomplishments were not achieved. For example, most people in the former Yugoslavia would not know whether the ICTY had rendered groundbreaking jurisprudence on SGBV or not, but that does not mean that the ICTY did not do so. Thus, views from the region are certainly not the only way to measure the ICTY's accomplishments.

Second, survey results are conducted at a point in time and subject to change. For example, the surveys in Croatia, which were quite negative, were conducted in 2010 and 2011. Now that General Gotovina has been acquitted, would they be more positive? Quite possibly.

Third, one might consider how susceptible to whim such results are.[112] Ponder whether we would really think more of the ICTY (that it had a greater "impact") if

---

[108]   *Id.*

[109]   Author's own observations. *See also* Vukušić, *Judging their Hero, supra* note 50 (discussing nationalistic views dominantly held in Croatia).

[110]   A cynical view by Refik Hodžić is that the ICTY never saw itself as committed to the public in the former Yugoslavia, but only to the international community. Refik Hodžić, *Accepting a Difficult Truth: ICTY is Not Our Court,* Justice Report (Mar. 8, 2013), at www.justice-report.com/en/articles/ comment-accepting-a-difficult-truth-icty-is-not-our-court.

[111]   One such analysis is by Marko Milanović, who appears to conclude that because of poor survey results, the ICTY has failed in its impact. *See, e.g.,* Milanović, The Failure of the ICTY to Persuade, *supra* note 82 ("the Tribunal was from the outset doomed to fail"). To this author, the surveys are *one* measure of impact, but not the only measure, and do not indicate the ICTY has failed, but it has not made sufficient inroads with what should be a key target audience. *See* Neil J. Kritz, *Where We Are and How We Got Here: An Overview of Developments in the Search for Justice and Reconciliation, in* The Legacy of Abuse: Confronting the Past, Facing the Future (Alice H. Henkin ed., 2002), 27 (the "primary audience" of an international tribunal should be "the population of the country in question").

[112]   Author e-mail with Iva Vukušić, Aug. 7, 2017.

Croatians took a more positive view after Gotovina's acquittal? What if one could analyze that the shift in view occurred, not because the public had any under-standing of the merits of the case, but were reacting reflexively that acquittal of a high-level Croatian must be good? What if the shift in views could be linked to a false view that Croatian forces committed no crimes during Operation Storm?[113] (Indeed, because the Croatian military operation was a defensive one, segments of the Croatian public appear to mistakenly dismiss that war crimes could have occurred.)[114]

Fourth, it is possible that to reach more mature survey conclusions, one would need to wait a much longer period of time and that future surveys will be needed.[115] Initially, views may still shift slightly depending on the final outcomes of the Karadžić and Mladić cases, and possibly further ICTY Outreach, if continued under the MICT.[116] But, probably, more significantly, future events (not of the ICTY's making) – e.g., whether added countries in the region join the European Union and their economies improve, and/or whether there are new political lea-ders – might eventually cause a more positive reassessment of the work of the ICTY. The implementation of additional transitional justice tools, such as a regional truth commission, RECOM, might also improve views of the ICTY.

Fifth, as will be discussed in Section 2.2.4, poor survey results appear to stem from nationalistic views encouraged by leaders during the 1990s (and even held pre-1990s), and still accepted by certain populations in the region today, perpetuated by political leadership. As discussed further below, it was probably never reasonable to think the ICTY's work (even given its Outreach Program) could have helped transform the political landscape.[117] That lack of political transformation also helps explain why "reconciliation" has made little progress.

---

[113] "In the minds of many Croats, individuals in the Croatian forces cannot be guilty of committing crimes against ethnic Serbs from Croatia." Vukušić, Judging their Hero, *supra* note 50, at 152.

[114] *Id.* at 152.

[115] *See, e.g.,* Shany, Assessing the Effectiveness of International Courts, *supra* note 7 (suggesting the importance of timing of any study of international court effectiveness); *see, e.g.,* Milanović, Courting Failure, *supra* note 11 (noting that surveys from 1950 as to German views about the IMT were also poor, and only later – and as a result of other events – did views on the IMT improve).

[116] Shifts, however, might be modest, as a majority of Serbians already view the ICTY as anti-Serb, so final convictions of Karadžić and Mladić would only solidify that narrative. As noted, the Bosniak population already generally holds a positive assessment.

[117] While voices are often critical that Outreach was only created six years into the life of the Tribunal, as Marko Milanović points out, at the time of the Tribunal's creation, nationalistic narratives of the war and crimes committed had already been formed – indeed, different narratives existed already as to the events of World Wars I and II. *See* Milanović, Courting Failure, *supra* note 11 ("By the time the ICTY was created the wars in Bosnia and Croatia were in full swing, and some of the worst crimes already having been committed . . . Whole belief systems were already in place."); Milanović, The Failure of the ICTY to Persuade, *supra* note 82, at 1345 (noting different narratives as to World Wars I and II).

2.2 BENCHMARKS FOR MEASURING SOCIALLY TRANSFORMATIVE
GOALS (OR MAYBE NOT)

As noted above, the Security Council, in addition to holding out that the ICTY would bring "justice," also stated that the ICTY would contribute to international peace and security, and "contribute to ensuring that . . . violations are halted" (which suggests deterrence).[118] While the initial resolution did not claim the ICTY would contribute to "reconciliation" (although the parallel ICTR resolution made this claim),[119] ICTY officials later took this position.[120]

Judged by such broader, socially transformative goals, the ICTY had a mixed record of success, with: (a) contributions made to international peace and security by marginalizing key perpetrators through their indictments; (b) some indications of deterrence late in the life of the ICTY, although none shown in the early years; but (c) probably no evidence that the ICTY's work caused reconciliation. As discussed below, there is also no single accepted shared narrative in the region regarding the war or crimes committed,[121] and denial of crimes continues – although these can hardly be blamed on the ICTY, as both would likely require transformation of the political environment, which is not a task one should expect of a tribunal.

First, one might ask: are any of the above even appropriate benchmarks for evaluating the successes or failures of tribunals? If a tribunal cannot claim to have advanced international peace and security or deterrence, has it failed in its mandate? If it did not advance reconciliation, has it failed? The author would argue resoundingly in the negative. Tribunals are at heart judicial institutions, and it is as such that they primarily should be evaluated (using criteria such as those discussed in Section 2.1). Nonetheless, as shown below, the ICTY did have some limited successes when viewed against some of these broader benchmarks, although the author contends these generally should *not* be considered benchmarks for judging the efficacy of international or hybrid tribunals.

2.2.1 *Contributing to International Peace and Security*

As to contributing to international peace and security, firstly, the language stating that the ICTY would do so was likely put in the Security Council's resolution to denote that the UN Security Council was acting under Chapter VII of the UN

---

[118] SC Res. 827, UN Doc. S/RES/827 (May 25, 1993).
[119] SC Res. 955, UN Doc. S/RES/955 (Nov. 8, 1994).
[120] *See* note 4 *supra.*
[121] By "single shared narrative," the author does not mean literally that all historians will narrate the past the same way. Of course there will be differences in how history is told. The term is used here as shorthand for moving away from the divisive, nationalistic narratives that have existed and continue to exist, in which an ethnic group's victimhood is overstated and crimes committed by group members are minimized.

Charter when it created the ICTY.[122] In the Tadić case, the ICTY clarified that it was not required that the ICTY actually succeed in restoring peace to the former Yugoslavia for the UN Security Council to have acted properly under Chapter VII, only that the ICTY's creation was one measure adopted toward that end.[123]

Sometimes tribunals may be able to contribute to peace, particularly in the immediate aftermath of mass atrocities, when indicting and apprehending key perpetrators may have a helpful stabilizing effect by removing them from power.[124] Yet, tribunals are clearly not always able to do so. For example, prosecuting former Khmer Rouge leaders who are in their eighties, when their crimes occurred decades ago, probably has had little impact on peace in Cambodia; yet one would hardly deem the ECCC unsuccessful for this reason.[125] Thus, whether a tribunal can actually contribute to peace and security would seem entirely context-specific, and should not be a benchmark for judging a tribunal's success.[126]

That said, it is generally acknowledged that the ICTY *did* contribute to international peace and security by indicting high-level accused (such as Karadžić and Mladić), which eventually drove them off the political and military stages, respectively, while they lived for many years in fear of apprehension and were eventually arrested.[127] In addition, "former ICTY Prosecutor Justice Richard Goldstone has argued that the [indictment of Karadžić and Mladić] was essential to peace because their subsequent exclusion from the negotiations of the historic Dayton peace accords facilitated the participation of Bosnia's Muslim-led government in those talks."[128] It is also possible that indictment of high-level alleged perpetrators (and

---

[122] See SC Res. 827, *supra* note 2 (the ICTY will "contribute to the restoration and maintenance of peace").

[123] Prosecutor v. Tadić, Case No. IT-94-1, Decision on the Defense Motion for Interlocutory Appeal on Jurisdiction, paras. 39–40 (Int'l Crim. Trib. for the Former Yugoslavia, Oct. 2, 1995).

[124] See, e.g., Clark, Peace, Justice and the International Criminal Court, *supra* note 13, at 542 ("Removal [of people like Lord's Resistance Army commander Joseph Kony] by the fact that they are now under indictment may initially be seen as an obstacle to peace but further down the road it may be exactly what is needed to get a stable peace in Northern Uganda.")

[125] The ECCC has faced separate difficulties stemming from lack of independence from Cambodian Government executive interference. *See* Laura McGrew, *Performance and Perception: The Impact of the Extraordinary Chambers in the Courts of Cambodia*, OPEN SOCIETY JUSTICE INITIATIVE (2016).

[126] Extensive scholarship exists on the so-called "peace versus justice" debate, particularly in the context of the ICC, and whether the ICC's work has impeded peace or can advance it. *See, e.g.*, Clark, Peace, Justice and the International Criminal Court, *supra* note 13 (also noting the relationship between criminal trials and peace remains empirically under-researched); Bartlomiej Krzan, *International Criminal Court Facing the Peace vs. Justice Dilemma*, 2 INTERNATIONAL COMPARATIVE JURISPRUDENCE 81 (2016). The author will not attempt to rearticulate the debate here.

[127] Karadžić was living under an assumed name of Dragan Dabić, posing as a new-age healer, while Mladić was in hiding. Julian Borger, *The Hunt for Radovan Karadžić, Ruthless Warlord Turned 'Spiritual Healer,'* THE GUARDIAN, Mar. 22, 2016, www.theguardian.com/world/2016/mar/22/the-hunt-for-radovan-karadzic-ruthless-warlord-turned-spiritual-healer (accessed on Aug. 7, 2017).

[128] *Pursuing Justice in Ongoing Conflict: A discussion of current practice*, ICTJ (June 2007) (paper prepared for Nuremberg conference), http://ictj.org/sites/default/files/ICTJ-Global-Justice-Conflict-2007-English.pdf (at 3). *See also* Milanović, The Impact of the ICTY, *supra* note 28, at 255 ("It is

their eventual trials) also may have "diminished the perceived need for *other* individuals to engage in acts of revenge."[129]

One study concludes there was no peace dividend from the ICTY's work, based on measuring impact on peace and human rights in countries with and without international or hybrid tribunals.[130] Yet, the study contains an important caveat that "conditions might have deteriorated even further in these states had such [tribunal] efforts not been made."[131] The study thus appears quite inconclusive given that caveat. Of course, one will never quite know, because we cannot know what the Balkans would look like today had Karadžić, Mladić, or Milošević, for instance, never been indicted.

This illustrates the problem that, even when a tribunal does contribute to international peace and security, it is extremely difficult to prove that or precisely quantify the extent of the benefit. Were years of peacekeeping expenditures possibly avoided, or the cost of more years of armed conflict (lost lives and economic destruction), by marginalizing key actors who had led the campaign to build a "Greater Serbia" through ethnic cleansing? They might have been, yet that would seem nearly impossible to prove or quantify. Certainly, if one could somehow make this type of calculation, it might assuage skeptical donor countries who complain about the high cost of tribunals,[132] since tribunal costs pale in comparison to peacekeeping expenditures.[133]

a matter of historical record that (at US insistence) the ICTY's indictment of Bosnian Serb political and military leaders Radovan Karadžić and Ratko Mladić meant that they could not participate in the Dayton peace process, in which the Bosnian Serb side was represented by Slobodan Milošević, while ICTY indictees were subsequently excluded from holding public office in Bosnia, pending trial.")

[129] James D. Meernik, Angela Nichols and Kimi L. King, *The Impact of International Tribunal and Domestic Trials on Peace and Human Rights After Civil War*, 11 INTERNATIONAL STUDIES PERSPECTIVES 309, 315 (2010) (noting that possibility, but concluding "that there does not appear to be any substantial and positive effects stemming from the utilization of trials in post-conflict states in terms of preventing conflict recurrence").

[130] *Id.*

[131] *Id.* at 322.

[132] International and hybrid tribunals have proven quite expensive. If one were to evaluate them on the basis of efficiency and cost-effectiveness, for instance, measured by cost per prosecution, the results would no doubt be poor. But cost per prosecution measures none of the other benefits tribunals can achieve, which are often very difficult to quantify. Former Prosecutor of the Special Court for Sierra Leone and Prosecutor of the Residual Special Court for Sierra Leone Brenda Hollis suggests that one might alternatively measure the number of crimes covered in each prosecution over the cost of the trial, and then the numbers would come out much more favorably. Trahan, Sept. 29, 2016, interview of Brenda Hollis, at 4. Former ICTY and ICTR Prosecutor Richard Goldstone also warned that speedy resolution of cases may sacrifice transparency for the sake of expeditiousness. Richard Goldstone, *Evaluating the Performance of International Courts and Tribunals*, 2016 Brandeis Institute for International Judges (summarizing his remarks), at www.brandeis.edu/ethics/pdfs/internationaljustice/biij/Performance_BIIJ2016.pdf (accessed on Aug. 22, 2017).

[133] Trahan, Oct. 1, 2016, interview of ICTY and MICT Prosecutor Serge Brammertz, at 3; Trahan, Oct. 5, 2016, interview of Special Tribunal for Lebanon Registrar Daryl Mundis, at 5–6; Trahan, Oct. 3, 2016, interview of Chief of the Court Support Services Section, ICTY Registry, Gregory Townsend, at 6 (all noting the minimal cost of tribunals compared to the cost of ongoing armed conflict); Kritz, Where We Are and How We Got Here, *supra* note 111, at 28–9 (ICTY costs are a small fraction of the cost of NATO peacekeeping operations).

There is a recent trend of trying to conduct data-driven empirical research to assess accomplishments of international criminal tribunals.[134] Empirical analysis can be helpful. However, there may be tribunal accomplishments that cannot be quantitatively analyzed. How would one measure the value of having indicted and/ or tried high-level perpetrators? How would one measure the value of rendering new and significant jurisprudence in the field of international criminal law? How would one measure the value of having established a massive documentary-based record of crimes that can be analyzed by historians and future generations? How would one measure (or even know) what would have happened without high-level indictments? It seems facially obvious that there are certain contributions that tribunals make that will escape quantification or empirical testing, yet that does not mean they have not rendered these benefits.

2.2.2 Deterrence

As to the claim that the ICTY would "contribute to ensuring that . . . violations are halted"[135] (which suggests deterrence), what brought the war in Bosnia to a halt was, most directly, negotiation and implementation of the Dayton Peace Accords,[136] enforced by an international peacekeeping presence and the Office of the High Representatives. Atrocities in Kosovo were brought to an eventual halt by NATO aerial bombardments, and Serbia and Kosovo resolving matters in a manner similar to the attempted Rambouillet Accords,[137] with Kosovo then policed by The Kosovo Force (KFOR). Thus, most directly, it was other events that brought the violations to a halt, not the ICTY's work.

In terms of deterrence, it is very hard to make any claim, particularly in the ICTY's early years, that crimes were deterred. Indeed, the worst single atrocity of the war – the Srebrenica massacre (which commenced on July 11, 1995) – occurred well after the ICTY had been created. Clearly, the Tribunal's existence did not deter that tragedy, nor many others.

On the other hand, the lack of initial deterrence is quite understandable because the ICTY commenced operations only gradually.[138] Indeed, in the start-up phase, it was unclear whether it would even become an operating tribunal. Even when the ICTY commenced its first case against one lower-level perpetrator, that still hardly suggested it would eventually try high-level perpetrators. It did not help that prior to

---

[134] *See, e.g.,* Meernik, Nichols, and King, The Impact of International Tribunal and Domestic Trials, *supra* note 129.

[135] SC Res. 827, *supra* note 2.

[136] General Framework Agreement, UN GAOR, 50th Sess., annex 4, UN Doc. A/50/790 (Nov. 30, 1995).

[137] Rambouillet Agreement – Interim Agreement for Peace and Self-Government of Kosovo, March 1999.

[138] For an account of the difficult early years of operations, *see* GARY JONATHAN BASS, STAY THE HAND OF VENGEANCE: THE POLITICS OF INTERNATIONAL WAR CRIMES TRIBUNALS (Princeton University Press, 2000).

the ICTY, the last similar tribunals had been the IMTs at Nuremberg and Tokyo.[139] If high-level perpetrators were initially not deterred, there is good reason. A recent study suggests that only in later years did some deterrence occur with respect to Montenegro.[140]

But, again, does this limited showing in terms of deterrence mean the ICTY was not an effective tribunal? Again, the author would argue in the negative. Whether any single tribunal can cause deterrence would seem to hinge on a variety of factors, such as whether there is anticipation of high-level apprehensions and trials (if one expects to deter high-level perpetrators), whether there is jurisdiction over the crimes in question, and whether the tribunal is seen as an effective institution. Thus, while the field of international justice hopes to deter atrocity crimes so that tribunals are someday no longer required, if the jurisdiction of international and hybrid tribunals and number of individuals prosecuted remain as limited as they currently are (with sometimes no prosecutions at all), it is rather understandable that there is not yet a more significant general deterrent effect.[141]

2.2.3 *Reconciliation*

Probably the greatest fallacy – for those who believed this proposition[142] – was that the ICTY's work would bring about reconciliation in the region. Perhaps the international community should simply stop claiming that trials reconcile formerly warring or antagonistic groups. This author would argue that reconciliation is simply *not* an appropriate benchmark by which to evaluate the ICTY's, or any tribunal's, work.

To begin with, academic literature reveals disagreement: (1) on what reconciliation is (there is not one single accepted definition); (2) as to whether it is a process (being reconciled) or the end state that matters (achieving reconciliation); and (3) whether reconciliation is something that can be mandated by the state ("top-down"), or has to be created at the grassroots or interpersonal level ("bottom-up"), or whether

---

[139] *See* note 93 *supra* (Nuremberg and Tokyo Charters).

[140] Jacqueline R. McAllister, *The Justice Gambit: Lessons from the International Criminal Tribunal for the former Yugoslavia on Deterring Atrocities*, presented at the International Studies Association Annual Convention 2017, Baltimore, MD (concluding, based on over 200 interviews, that "the ICTY played a key role in deterring select rebel and government forces' use of violence against civilians, particularly in the 2001 Macedonian conflict").

[141] One study concludes whether the ICC can have deterrent effect hinges on a state's commitment to the rule of law, and willingness to grant the ICC necessary powers to carry out its mission. James Meernik, *The International Criminal Court and the Deterrence of Human Rights Atrocities*, 17 JOURNAL OF CIVIL WARS 318–9 (2015). The ICTY probably did contribute to *specific* deterrence, in that the individuals indicted and apprehended were prevented from committing further crimes. Again, however, this would seem impossible to prove: how would one prove that because Perpetrator X was in custody, he never committed additional crimes that he would have committed had he not been in custody?

[142] *See* note 4 *supra* (ICTY officials making this claim).

it must be both "top-down" and "bottom-up."[143] Others argue that, because reconciliation has connotations of "forgive thy killer," it should not even be a goal, and one should instead settle for peaceful coexistence of formerly antagonistic groups.[144]

For victims to witness trials may exacerbate tensions in the short term; there is nothing to suggest that witnessing a trial and even seeing a guilty verdict renders former perpetrators and their victims "reconciled."[145] Moreover, those on trial at the ICTY were often fairly high-level accused, whereas those in the region may have been victimized by their neighbors or local police, who did not attract the ICTY's attention. Seeing Milošević tried, then, would probably *not* reconcile someone in Brčko who was held at a detention camp and tortured by a former neighbor; expecting reconciliation in such circumstances (especially if the former neighbor was never prosecuted locally) seems, to put it mildly, a disconnect.

In the words of former ICTY prosecutor Sir Geoffrey Nice:

> Criminal trials have nothing to do with reconciliation. The trial of the rapist is not intended to reconcile the rapist or the victim. The trial of the burglar is not intended to reconcile the household to the burglar. Trials have entirely different purposes. Their principle is actually to separate people, not reconcile them, and to punish one side. If you look again at the documents after the foundation documents [of the ICTY] you will find that reconciliation disappears from the reporting to the UN, because a certain degree of reality crept in.[146]

While it is an extremely complex question whether reconciliation could occur without trials, one view is that the justice that tribunals render sets the foundation on which reconciliation may later be built.[147] Yet, it seems hard to envision reconciliation occurring absent a conducive political climate ("top-down" leadership endorsing, or at least not impeding, it), and grassroots organizations facilitating it ("bottom-up" work).

The most famous example of reconciliation was the South African Truth and Reconciliation Commission. There, the process was led by two extraordinarily charismatic leaders – former political prisoner turned president, Nelson Mandela,

---

[143]   *See, e.g.,* David Bloomfield, *On Good Terms: Clarifying Reconciliation,* BERGHOF REPORT No. 14 (October 2006).

[144]   *Id.* at 10–11, citing Charles Villa-Vicencio, *Reconciliation, in* PIECES OF THE PUZZLE: KEYWORDS ON RECONCILIATION AND TRANSITIONAL JUSTICE 6 (Charles Villa-Vicencio and Erik Doxtader eds., Cape Town: Institute for Justice and Reconciliation, 2005); Bloomfield, On Good Terms, *supra* note 143, at 13 ("[c]oexistence is a less loaded term ... [and] carries none of the religious overtones").

[145]   If a perpetrator pleads guilty and confesses, that might be different; yet, if the sentence is then short (because the plea counts toward mitigation), victims still might be dissatisfied. *See, e.g., Erdemović,* Appeals Judgment, *supra* note 84 (after entering a guilty plea, Erdemović was originally sentenced to ten years, later reduced to five years, for participation in the murder of an estimated seventy individuals).

[146]   Lovall and Vutrano, Seeking Truth in the Balkans, *supra* note 13, at 269 (quoting interview with Sir Geoffrey Nice).

[147]   *Id.* at 269 (quoting Serge Brammertz: "As much as I am convinced that prosecution alone will never lead to reconciliation ... I am also convinced that without accountability, without prosecuting and punishing those who are responsible for the crimes committed, no reconciliation is possible.")

and Archbishop Desmond Tutu.[148] It is quite an understatement to say that the former Yugoslavia has had no such comparable leadership to urge reconciliation or create a political climate conducive to it. Thus, whereas there is grassroots work on reconciliation being conducted by NGOs in the region, such as Youth Initiative for Human Rights[149] and the Post-Conflict Research Center in Sarajevo,[150] absent also having a more conducive political climate, it is unclear whether reconciliation will come about.

The lack of reconciliation[151] is not the fault of the ICTY, but will have to be achieved (if at all) by future actors in the region, using additional transitional justice tools over and above prosecutions. While tribunals play a critical role in setting the foundation upon which reconciliation may be built, both empirical and anecdotal evidence is lacking that trials create reconciliation. Reconciliation thus should not be a benchmark for measuring the effectiveness of tribunals.[152]

2.2.4 *Creating a Single, Shared Narrative of Facts and Silencing Denial of Crimes*

While neither the UN Security Council nor the ICTY itself claimed it would create a single, shared narrative of the events in the former Yugoslavia nor silence denial of crimes,[153] the lack of either appears the greatest impediment to local and transitional

---

[148]   Even in South Africa, widely touted as a success story with its Truth and Reconciliation Commission, there is so much income disparity along racial lines that it is hardly clear it should be, or whether "reconciliation" was actually achieved.

[149]   YIHR facilitates youth exchanges in the region. *See* website of Youth Initiative for Human Rights, at http://democratic-youth.net/yihr (accessed on Mar. 6, 2017).

[150]   *See* website of PCRC, at www.p-crc.org/ (accessed on Aug. 10, 2017). Important work on youth outreach was also conducted by the ICTY's Outreach Program. *See Youth Outreach*, ICTY, at www .icty.org/en/outreach/youth-outreach (accessed on Aug. 8, 2017).

[151]   Milanović, The Failure of the ICTY to Persuade, *supra* note 82, at 1359 ("the post-Yugoslav societies are today nowhere near a joint truth that could potentially lead to reconciliation").

[152]   Whether the ICTR caused or contributed to reconciliation in Rwanda is an extremely complex question. The official Rwandan narrative – that there are no Hutus and Tutsis – does not necessarily mean those groups are reconciled, nor that individuals have in fact lost their group identities. For a study attempting to measure reconciliation in Rwanda, *see* Republic of Rwanda, *National Unity and Reconciliation Commission* (NURC), Rwanda Reconciliation Barometer (October 2010), www .nurc.gov.rw/index.php?id=70&no_cache=1&tx_drblob_pi1%5BdownloadUid%5D=16.

[153]   The ICTY comes perilously close to overselling its accomplishments when it states: "The Tribunal's judgements have contributed to ... *preventing attempts at revisionism* ..." *Achievements*, ICTY, *supra* note 14 (emphasis added). While the wealth of ICTY evidence helps contribute to preventing attempts at revisionism, revisionism has not been prevented, as revisionism occurs each time crimes are denied.
As Marko Milanović points out, the ICTY also oversells itself when it states: "The detail in which the ICTY's judgements describe the crimes and the involvement of those convicted *make it impossible for anyone to dispute* the reality of the horrors that took place in and around Bratunac, Brčko, Čelebići, Dubrovnik, Foča, Prijedor, Sarajevo, Srebrenica and Zvornik, to name but a few." Milanović, The Impact of the ICTY, *supra* note 28, at 235, quoting ICTY website. In fact, survey results show that people in the region deny these very crimes. *See id.* at 249 (denial of crimes including at Zvornik, Čelebići, Sarajevo, and Srebrenica).

justice initiatives in the region, and, ultimately, a better perception of the work of the ICTY. Unfortunately, to make inroads in either area might require political trans-formation – something the ICTY was never designed to even attempt.

Milanović's compilation of survey results suggests some of the disparaging views of the ICTY result from the populace holding nationalist narratives of the past, which are then reinforced by political leadership. These narratives tend to reinforce in each group their own sense of victimhood (e.g., the Serbs as victims, the Croats as victims), and denial about crimes having been committed by nationals of the same group.[154]

When Serbs in Republika Srpska or Serbia are told that Ratko Mladić is a national hero,[155] and certain segments of the population uncritically accept this narrative, is it any wonder that – particularly with much of the news media under state control[156] – large segments of that population do not look approvingly at the ICTY's work? Similarly nationalistic rhetoric of course inflamed the wars in the 1990s, and instances can still be found in parts of the former Yugoslavia today.[157]

It is the role of Outreach to communicate the tribunal's work to its constituent population. But here, the ICTY's Outreach Program – which conducted a variety of initiatives[158] – should not be faulted, because it faced a tremendously difficult political climate within which to perform its work. "[F]rom the moment it appeared on the stage, the ICTY has been the object of intense, vilifying propaganda by

---

[154] Milanović discusses survey results revealing that each group sees itself primarily as "victims," and the "other" primarily as perpetrator. *Id.* at 242–3. One exception was in the Federation, where "virtually all the Federation respondents who say they heard of a crime also say that they believe it happened, *even when the perpetrators were Bosniaks." Id.* at 250 (emphasis added). *See also* Vukušić, Judging their Hero, *supra* note 50, at 161 (discussing false narratives of "the heroism, victimhood and right-eousness of 'us' and the aggression and brutality of 'them'").

[155] When the author was in Belgrade in summer 2017, vendors sold t-shirts with Mladić's image on them.

[156] *See, e.g.,* Milanović, The Failure of the ICTY to Persuade, *supra* note 82, at 1336 & n. 43 (citing low rankings by Freedom House of press freedom in Croatia, Serbia, Kosovo, and Bosnia); Vukušić, Judging their Hero, *supra* note 50, at 161 (discussing the media in Croatia perpetuating a "simplistic, one-sided perception of the past"); Klarin, The Impact of the ICTY Trials, *supra* note 33, at 90 (discussing the media, in the early years of the Tribunal's existence, as "under government control").

[157] *See, e.g.,* Milanović, The Failure of the ICTY to Persuade, *supra* note 82, at 1354–5 (citing an anniversary party for Operation Storm, with nationalistic singers performing to a crowd of 80,000, chanting "kill a Serb"); Guy Delauney, *Serbian Elections: Radical Šešelj Back in Parliament*, BBC News (Apr. 25, 2016) www.bbc.com/news/world-europe-36128489 (referring to Vojislav Šešelj: "On his return to the political scene, his rhetoric was as fiery as ever. The EU and NATO are one and the same, he says; those who support them are traitors to Serbia.") (accessed on Dec. 9, 2017); Republika Srpska President Milorad Dodik has called the Srebrenica genocide "the greatest decep-tion of the twentieth century." *See Bosnian Serb Leader: Srebrenica Was 20th Century's 'Greatest Deception,'* Reuters (June 25, 2015), www.reuters.com/article/us-bosnia-serbia-arrest-idUSKBN0P51OL20150625 (accessed on Aug. 14, 2017).

[158] One was titled "Bridging the Gap." It consisted of "one-day events, held in the towns where some of the most serious crimes took place, [and] included candid and comprehensive presentations from panels of Tribunal staff who were directly involved in the investigation, prosecution and adjudication of alleged crimes." *See Outreach, Bridging the Gap with Local Communities,* ICTY, http://www.icty.org/en/outreach/bridging-the-gap-with-local-communities (accessed Sept. 9, 2017).

dominant elites, especially in the Croat and Serb ethnic communities, through nationalist-controlled media which marginalized competing viewpoints."[159] Furthermore, as Milanović points out, there has been a fair amount of "elite continuity" in the former Yugoslavia – it is not a situation in which one side ousted the other, nor has there been significant transformation of the political landscape.[160]

Commenting on the challenges faced by the ICTY's Outreach Program, Prosecutor Brammertz admitted the ICTY could have used more emphasis on outreach (and most agree it started late, in 1999, several years into the life of the Tribunal),[161] but he blames the real difficulties on political leadership:

> As long as the new political leadership has not the courage to accept that there were wrongdoings by the predecessors in the past, as long as you don't have this attitude by the political leadership, it is very, very difficult to convince people. We see this every day with the hate speech which is still very, very present, with the denial of the genocide in Srebrenica, or denial of crimes in general where today some parts like Republika Srpska or others are calling experts to rewrite the history of the conflict and to rewrite expert reports on cases on which we have already a final judgment in The Hague. So there is for sure place for a *mea culpa* at the tribunal to explain better, but I think the major problem is that many politicians in the former Yugoslavia are still very nationalistic in their approach and are still thinking that by dividing, they have more chances to be reelected than by moving together towards a common future, and this is extremely disappointing ... [N]ow, nine years in the office, I would say that's the most disappointing to see – a number of members in the political leadership having this kind of destructive attitude where it should be the opposite.[162]

It was arguably not the ICTY's role to create a shared narrative of the past; that would more appropriately be done by a regional truth commission, such as RECOM. It could also be accomplished by a new generation of political leaders moving beyond divisive narratives. (And maybe RECOM can only occur once there is a new generation of political leadership – as governments currently do not appear to be enacting RECOM.) A similarly honest appraisal of the past also has to

---

[159] Milanović, The Impact of the ICTY, *supra* note 28, at 258. *See also* Klarin, The Impact of the ICTY Trials, *supra* note 33, at 96 ("It is illusory to expect the Outreach Programme ... to fight effectively the powerful propaganda machines at the disposal of the political elites dictating the public attitude towards the ICTY in the Balkans.")

[160] *See* Milanović, Courting Failure, *supra* note 11 (analyzing the extent of elite continuity in the former Yugoslavia); Klarin, The Impact of the ICTY Trials, *supra* note 33, at 90 ("In the first seven years of the Tribunal's existence ... Serbia, Croatia and Bosnia were ruled by the individuals and members of the political and military elites who were themselves suspected of involvement in the war crimes then being investigated by the OTP.") Milanović suggests that whereas opinion polls of the work of the ECCC and Special Court for Sierra Leone are more favorable, this may not indicate better outreach, but that the work they were able to do did not threaten the political elites. Milanović, Courting Failure, *supra* note 11.

[161] Outreach commenced only in 1999.

[162] Trahan, Oct. 1, 2016, interview of Serge Brammertz, at 4.

eventually permeate school curriculums, which have also proven tainted by nationalism.[163]

Denial of crimes could also be addressed at the legal level. There has been proposed legislation in Bosnia to criminalize denial of the Srebrenica genocide.[164] While the United States does not adopt this type of legislation for reasons of free speech, Europeans generally take a different approach, for example, criminalizing denial of the Holocaust.[165] While a law might prove helpful in silencing denial of Srebrenica as a genocide, forcing a narrative is not necessarily the same as having it really accepted.[166] Furthermore, survey results suggest it is not only denial of Srebrenica that is at issue, but many more crimes are denied as well.[167]

Selective use of memorialization (to memorialize only victims from one's "own" ethnic group) is also a prominent form of denial that is visible in many parts of the former Yugoslavia. For instance, Republika Srpska builds only memorials to Serbs who died in and around Srebrenica,[168] or in Prijedor, where many of the camps were located. In the words of activist and former ICTY spokesperson Refik Hodžić: "You cannot have, in Prijedor, ten, literally, monuments to Serb soldiers who have died in the war – which is perfectly fine with me, I fully understand the need to memorialize that loss – while at the same time not to have a mention in any way of 3,500 citizens of Prijedor – civilians who were killed."[169] This is also a way of whitewashing the past.

---

[163] Milanović, The Failure of the ICTY to Persuade, *supra* note 82, at 1346; Denis Dzidic, *Bosnia's Segregated Schools Maintain Educational Divide*, BALKAN INSIGHT, Feb. 13, 2015, www .balkaninsight.com/en/article/bosnia-s-segregated-schools-maintain-educational-divide (accessed on Aug. 14, 2017).

[164] Danijel Kovacevic, *Bosnian Genocide Denial Punishment Law Angers Serbs*, BIRN, Balkan Transitional Justice (June 14, 2017), www.balkaninsight.com/en/article/bosnian-genocide-denial-pun ishment-law-angers-serbs-06-14-2017 (accessed on Sept. 3, 2017).

[165] *Expanding Holocaust Denial and Legislation against It*, JERUSALEM CENTER FOR PUBLIC AFFAIRS (Apr. 27, 2008), http://jcpa.org/article/expanding-holocaust-denial-and-legislation-against-it/ ("Over half the states of Europe now criminalize Holocaust denial.") (accessed on Sept. 3, 2017).

[166] The same double-edged sword existed with the US and EU's conditionality policy, which greatly facilitated ICTY arrests. *See* text accompanying note 38 *supra*. "Even when the government coop- erated [with the ICTY], there was always a sense that this was done because it was pressured into it, not because of any genuine concern." Vukušić, Judging their Hero, *supra* note 50, at 173; *see also* Klarin, The Impact of the ICTY Trials, *supra* note 33, 93 (in one survey, 54 percent of Serbs believed Serbia should cooperate with the ICTY but "only to the extent sufficient to avoid sanctions or because it is a prerequisite for getting financial aid and for being reintegrated into the international community").

[167] *See* note 102 *supra* and accompanying text. Some denial could be actual dispute whether "genocide" occurred because the massacre of over 8,300 was not, for example, as massive as the death toll in Rwanda. While there is no numerical threshold over which killing of members of a protected group constitutes "genocide," the law requires a "substantial" part of the protected group be targeted. Prosecutor v. Krstić, Case No. IT-98-33-A, Appeals Judgment (Int'l Crim. Trib. for the Former Yugoslavia, Apr. 19, 2004), paras. 8–9. The ICTY held this requirement met by the killings in and around Srebrenica. *Id.*, paras. 15–18, 673. Most denial, however, is probably not based on such legalistic distinctions.

[168] The Srebrenica–Potočari Memorial was mandated and built by the international community.

[169] Lovall and Vutrano, Seeking Truth in the Balkans, *supra* note 13, at 308 (interview of Refik Hodžić).

That nationalistic narratives continue, along with denial of crimes, does not diminish the ICTY's actual accomplishments. The ICTY *did* create a significant historical record of the crimes that occurred and *did* render extremely significant convictions. It may simply take time and more of a transition away from the nationalistic politics of the past for the public in the region to accept the ICTY's accomplishments. In the meanwhile, NGOs, media, and intellectuals who are often in the minority when they strive to combat these narratives, at least have the important achievements of the ICTY to assist them.

2.3 CONCLUSION

Tribunals are, at heart, only judicial institutions, and their work should be primarily assessed as such. When viewed in this light, the ICTY was quite a successful institution. While tribunals may be able to make certain contributions to broader transformative goals (and the ICTY has arguably made inroads here as well), such work is often better done by other actors and should not be expected of tribunals.

While negative public views in the former Yugoslavia about the ICTY's work are disheartening, they do not impact on what the ICTY *actually* accomplished, but how it is *seen*. Clearly, there is much more transitional justice work remaining, but this will now have to be achieved (or not) by other actors. Unfortunately, there may be limits on what NGOs in the region can accomplish under current political leadership. Perhaps when more transitional justice work is completed, and/or a new generation of political leaders is in place, there may eventually be a much more positive assessment of the ICTY.

The European Union could also play a positive role assisting transitional justice in the region as to countries still pursuing EU accession, for instance, by: urging the implementation of RECOM; urging additional reparations for victims; insisting that local war crimes prosecutions continue with more vigor than they currently manifest;[170] and suggesting that politicians keep their nationalistic rhetoric in

---

[170] The National Strategy for Processing of War Crimes Cases in Bosnia is years off its target. *Bosnian War Crimes Case Strategy 'Failing,'* BIRN, Balkan Transitional Justice (Jan. 29, 2016) ("A new analysis shows that the Bosnian strategy for war crimes cases has failed to meet its targets because hundreds of complex cases remain unfinished and the others will not be completed on time.") Furthermore, the War Crimes Prosecutor's Office in Belgrade recently lacked a prosecutor for a year and half, and now had a key case dismissed due to vacancy of the post, with other cases in similar jeopardy. Trahan July 17, 2017 meeting with Budimir Ivanišević, Executive Director, Humanitarian Law Center; *see also* Filip Rudic, *Serbia Selects New Chief War Crimes Prosecutor*, BIRN, Balkan Transitional Justice, www.balkaninsight.com/en/article/serbia-chooses-new-chief-war-crimes-prose cutor-05-15-2017-1 (concerned that Serbia's new chief war crimes prosecutor, Snežana Stanojković, looks "likely to make crimes committed against Serbs – rather than by them – her priority in the post") (accessed on Sept. 8, 2017). "Further pressure must be applied in order for countries in the region to realize that prosecuting war crimes suspects fairly, impartially and efficiently without a political agenda is, ultimately, in everyone's best interests." Vukušić, Judging their Hero, *supra* note 50, at 161.

check. There would have clearly still been a role for the ICTY's Outreach Program to continue its important work, which it could have done as part of the MICT.[171]

Finally, the experiences of the ICTY can also provide an important learning lesson as to establishing reasonable benchmarks for what it is that tribunals can accomplish. As new tribunals are being established – such as a hybrid tribunal in the Central African Republic,[172] the hybrid tribunal for Kosovo,[173] and possibly one for South Sudan[174] – neither their staff nor the international community should oversell what it is that a tribunal is capable of achieving, so their work can be evaluated by realistic benchmarks.

To close with the words of Refik Hodžić: "For better or worse, the lasting peace is not up to the ICTY: it is up to us, and it has always been."[175]

---

[171] Milanović suggests there was basically nothing Outreach could have done to achieve better results in the region because it was fighting the narratives of the dominant political elite. Milanović, The Impact of the ICTY, *supra* note 28, at 258. To this author, that does not suggest there never should have been Outreach, nor that the ICTY (in its MICT phase) should stop trying to have impact.

[172] Peter Snyder, *Central African Republic Government Establishes Special Criminal Court*, JURIST (Apr. 23, 2015), www.jurist.org/paperchase/2015/04/central-african-republic-government-establishes-special-criminal-court.php.

[173] Website of the Kosovo Specialist Chambers & Specialist Prosecutor's Office, www.scp-ks.org/en/specialist-chambers/background (accessed on Dec. 1, 2016).

[174] *UN Rights Chief Urges Establishment of Hybrid Court for Atrocities in South Sudan*, UN NEWS CENTRE (Dec. 14, 2016), http://www.un.org/apps/news/story.asp?NewsID=55801#.WHA4OlzKtfo

[175] Hodžić, Accepting a Difficult Truth, *supra* note 110.

PART II

Normative and Operational Legacy of the Yugoslavia and Rwanda Tribunals

3

How the *Tadic* Appeals Chamber Decision Fundamentally Altered Customary International Law

Michael P. Scharf

3.1 INTRODUCTION

On the eve of the establishment of the International Criminal Tribunal for the Former Yugoslavia in 1993, the International Committee of the Red Cross "underlined the fact that according to international humanitarian law as it stands today, the notion of war crimes is limited to situations of international armed conflict."[1] Yet, in its first decision, on October 2, 1995, the Appeals Chamber of the Yugoslavia Tribunal held that the same principles of liability that apply to international armed conflict apply to internal armed conflicts. Despite dubious provenance, this sweeping decision has been affirmed by the Rwanda Tribunal and the Special Court for Sierra Leone; it has been codified in the military manuals of several governments; it has been enshrined in the 1998 Statute of the International Criminal Court; and is now recognized as customary international law despite the dearth of state practice or prolonged period of development. This chapter examines how the return of genocide to Europe for the first time since World War II and the creation of the first international criminal tribunal since Nuremberg sowed the seeds for rapid recognition of this expanded area of international criminal liability.

3.2 THE CONCEPT OF ACCELERATED FORMATION OF CUSTOMARY INTERNATIONAL LAW

Normally, customary international law, which is just as binding on States as treaty law,[2] arises out of the slow accretion of widespread State practice evincing a sense of legal

---

[1] *Some Preliminary Remarks by the International Committee of the Red Cross on the Setting-Up of an International Tribunal for the Prosecution of Persons Responsible for Serious Violations of International Humanitarian Law Committed on the Territory of the Former Yugoslavia*, DDM/JUR/422b (Mar. 25, 1993), at 2, *reprinted in* 2 Virginia Morris & Michael P. Scharf, An Insider's Guide to the International Criminal Tribunal for the Former Yugoslavia 391–2 (Transnational Publishers, 1995).

[2] While customary international law is binding on States internationally, not all States accord customary international law equal domestic effect. A growing number of States' constitutions automatically

obligation (*opinio juris*).[3] Consistent with the traditional approach, the US Supreme Court has recognized that the process of establishing customary international law can take several decades, or even centuries.[4] Not so long ago, France took the position that thirty years is the minimum amount required, while the United Kingdom has said nothing less than forty years would be sufficient.[5] The International Law Commission, at the beginning of its work, demanded State practice "over a considerable period of time" for a customary norm to emerge.[6] In the 1969 *North Sea Continental Shelf Cases*, however, the International Court of Justice observed that customary norms can sometimes ripen quite rapidly, and that a short period of time is not a bar to finding the existence of a new rule of customary international law, binding on all the countries of the world, save those that persistently objected during its formation.[7]

As the *Max Planck Encyclopedia of Public International Law* has observed, "recent developments show that customary rules may come into existence rapidly."[8] The venerable publication goes on to explain:

> This can be due to the urgency of coping with new developments of technology, such as, for instance, drilling technology as regards the rules on the continental

incorporate customary law as part of the law of the land, and even accord it a ranking higher than domestic statutes. BRUNO SIMMA, International Human Rights and General International Law: A Comparative Analysis 165, 213 (1995). In the United States, customary international law is deemed incorporated into the federal common law of the United States. Some courts, however, consider it controlling only where there is no contradictory treaty, statute, or executive act. *See* Garcia-Mir v. Meese, 788 F.2d 1446 (11th Circ. 1986) (holding that the Attorney General's decision to detain Mariel Cuban refugees indefinitely without a hearing trumped any contrary rules of customary international law).

[3] For the definition of customary international law, *see North Sea Continental Shelf* (Federal Republic of Germany v. Denmark; Federal Republic of Germany v. Netherlands), Merits (Feb. 20, 1969), ICJ Rep. 3, para. 77.

[4] *The Paquete Habana*, 175 U.S. 677, 700 (1900).

[5] Franscesco Parisi, *The Formation of Customary Law*, paper presented at the 96th Annual Conference of the American Political Science Association (Aug. 31, 2000), at 5.

[6] *See Working Paper by Special Rapporteur Manley O. Hudson on Article 24 of the Statute of the International Law Commission* 2 Y.B. INTERNATIONAL LAW COMMISSION 24, 26, UN Doc. A/CN.4/16 (1950).

[7] *North Sea Continental Shelf* (Federal Republic of Germany v. Denmark; Federal Republic of Germany v. Netherlands), Merits (Feb. 20, 1969), ICJ Rep. 3, paras. 71, 73, 74. The Court stated:

> Although the passage of only a short period of time is not necessarily. . . a bar to the formation of a new rule of customary international law. . . an indispensable requirement would be that within the period in question, short though it might be, State practice, including that of States whose interests are specially affected, should have been both extensive and virtually uniform in the sense of the provision invoked; and should moreover have occurred in such a way as to show a general recognition that a rule of law or legal obligation is involved.

Id. at para. 74. While recognizing that some norms can quickly become customary international law, the ICJ held that the equidistance principle contained in Article 6 of the 1958 Convention on the Continental Shelf had not done so as of 1969 because so few States recognized and applied the principle. At the same time, the Court did find that that Articles 1 and 3 of the Convention (concerning the regime of the continental shelf) did have the status of established customary law. *Id.* at 24–7, paras. 25–33.

[8] Treves, *supra*, para. 24; *accord* INT'L LAW ASS'N, *supra* note 16, at 20.

shelf, or space technology as regards the rule on the freedom of extra-atmospheric space. Or it may be due to the urgency of coping with widespread sentiments of moral outrage regarding crimes committed in conflicts such as those in Rwanda and Yugoslavia that brought about the rapid formation of a set of customary rules concerning crimes committed in internal conflicts.[9]

Drawing from the writings of Professor Bruce Ackerman, who used the phrase "constitutional moment" to describe the New Deal transformation in American constitutional law,[10] some international law scholars have used the phrase "international constitutional moment" to convey the concept of accelerated formation of customary international law.[11] But since these changes occur largely outside a constitution or treaty framework, elsewhere I have made the case that a more apt term for this phenomenon is "Grotian Moment," named for Hugo Grotius, the fifteenth-century Dutch scholar and diplomat whose masterpiece *De Jure Belli ac Pacis* helped marshal in the modern system of international law.[12]

How does accelerated formation of international law occur? Professor Myers McDougle of Yale Law School famously described the customary international law formation process as one of continuous claim and response.[13] To illustrate this process, consider the question of whether international law permits a State to use force to arrest a terrorist leader in another State without the latter's consent – a question that recently arose when the United States kidnapped an al-Qaeda leader from Libya in October 2013.[14] The claim may be express, such as demanding that its special forces be allowed to enter the territorial State to

[9] *Id.*

[10] BRUCE ACKERMAN, Reconstructing American Law (1984).

[11] Bardo Fassbender, *The United Nations Charter as Constitution of the International Community*, 36 COLUM. J. TRANSNAT'L L. 529 (1998); Jenny S. Martinez, *Towards an International Judicial System*, 56 STAN. L. REV. 429, 463 (2003); Leila Nadya Sadat, *Enemy Combatants After Hamdan v. Rumsfeld: Extraordinary Rendition, Torture, and Other Nightmares from the War on Terror*, 75 GEO. WASH. L. REV. 1200, 1206–7 (2007); Anne-Marie Slaughter & William Bureke-White, *An International Constitutional Moment*, 43 HARV. INT'L. L. J. 1, 2 (2002); Ian Johnstone, *The Plea of "Necessity" in International Legal Discourse: Humanitarian Intervention and Counter-Terrorism*, 43 COLUM. J. TRANSNAT'L L. 337, 370 (2005).

[12] *See generally*, MICHAEL P. SCHARF, Customary International Law in Times of Fundamental Change: Recognizing Grotian Moments (2014). The term "Grotian Moment" was first coined by Princeton Professor Richard Falk. *See* International Law and World Order 1265–86 (Burns H. Weston et al. eds., Thomson/West 4th edn. 2006). Grotius (1583–1645) is widely considered to have laid the intellectual architecture for the Peace of Westphalia, which launched the basic rules of modern international law. Hedley Bull ET AL., Hugo Grotius and International Relations 1, 9 (1992). While the results of Westphalia may have been simplified by the lens of history, and Grotius' role may have been exaggerated, Westphalia has unquestionably emerged as a symbolic marker and Grotius as an emblematic figure of changing historical thought. "Grotian Moment" is thus an apt label for transformational events in customary international law.

[13] *See generally* M. S. McDougal & N. A. Schlei, *The Hydrogen Bomb Tests in Perspective: Lawful Measures for Security*, 64 YALE L. J. 648 (1955).

[14] Ernesto Londoño, *Capture of Bombing Suspect in Libya Represents Rare 'Rendition' by U.S. Military*, WASHINGTON POST (Oct. 6, 2013), available at http://articles.washingtonpost.com/2013–10-06/world/ 42771116_1_kerry-terrorism-suspects-libyan-government (last accessed Feb. 22, 2014).

arrest the terrorist, or implicit, such as sending its special forces into the territorial State without its permission to apprehend the terrorist. The response to the claim may in turn be favorable, such as consenting to the operation or refraining from protesting the extraterritorial apprehension. In such case, the claim and response will begin the process of generating a new rule of customary international law. Some States may imitate the practice and others may passively acquiesce in it.

"Custom pioneers" (the first State or international organization to initiate a new practice) have no guarantee that their action will lead to the formation of a binding custom. Indeed, the response may be a repudiation of the claim, as in the case of Libya's protest of the un-consented apprehension of the al-Qaeda operative.[15] In such case, the repudiation could constitute a reaffirmation of existing law, which is strengthened by the protest. Or, the claim and repudiation could constitute a stalemate, which could decelerate the formation of new customary international law. The reaction of Third States is also relevant. Out of this process of claim and response, and third-party acquiescence or repudiation, rules emerge or are super-seded. Just "as pearls are produced by the irritant of a piece of grit entering an oyster's shell, so the interactions and mutual accommodations of States produce the pearl – so to speak – of customary law."[16] As mentioned above, usually, this process of customary international law formation takes decades or centuries. But sometimes, as with the *Tadic* decision, world events are such that customary international law develops quite rapidly.[17]

3.3 THE *TADIC* DECISION

3.3.1 *Events Leading to the* Tadic *Decision*

Articles 2 through 5 of the ICTY Statute appended to Resolution 827, which had been drafted by the UN Office of Legal Affairs based on proposals submitted by

---

[15] *Id.*

[16] MENDELSON, *supra*, at 190.

[17] *North Sea Continental Shelf* (Federal Republic of Germany v. Denmark; Federal Republic of Germany v. Netherlands), Merits (Feb. 20, 1969), ICJ Rep. 3, paras. 71, 73–4 (hereinafter *North Sea Continental Shelf*) (2012). The Court stated: "Although the passage of only a short period of time is not necessarily ... a bar to the formation of a new rule of customary international law ... an indispensable requirement would be that within the period in question, short though it might be, State practice, including that of States whose interests are specially affected, should have been both extensive and virtually uniform in the sense of the provision invoked; and should moreover have occurred in such a way as to show a general recognition that a rule of law or legal obligation is involved." *Id.* para. 74. While recognizing that some norms can quickly become customary international law, the ICJ held that the equidistance principle contained in Article 6 of the 1958 Convention on the Continental Shelf had not done so as of 1969 because so few States recognized and applied the principle. At the same time, the Court did find that that Articles 1 and 3 of the Convention (concerning the regime of the continental shelf) did have the status of established customary law.

various governments and NGOs, set forth the subject-matter jurisdiction of the Yugoslavia Tribunal. Article 2 provides that the Tribunal has jurisdiction over Grave Breaches of the four Geneva Conventions of 1949. Article 3, which is the focus of this chapter, confers power on the Tribunal to prosecute persons "violating the laws or customs of war," including but not limited to a list of violations culled from the Regulations annexed to the 1907 Hague Convention (IV), "Respecting the Law and Customs of War on Land." Article 4 provides jurisdiction over acts of genocide, and Article 5 covers crimes against humanity. Notably, the Yugoslavia Tribunal's Statute did not specify whether the fighting in Yugoslavia constituted international conflict or a civil war (internal armed conflict) – "a question pivotal to the application of the laws of war."[18]

The Tribunal's first case, *Prosecutor v. Tadic*, concerned a Bosnian Serb café owner and part-time karate instructor, who lived in the Prijedor district in northwest Bosnia. Dusko Tadic was charged with thirty-one counts of Grave Breaches of the Geneva Conventions, violations of the laws and customs of war, and crimes against humanity. The charges stemmed from the torture and murder of Muslims at the Serb-run Omarska, Karaterm, and Trnopolje prison camps and the nearby villages of Kozarac, Jaksici, and Sivci during the summer of 1992. In most instances, the indictment assigned three counts to each separate act charged: the first count was charged under Article 2 of the Tribunal's Statute, the second count was charged under Article 3, and the third was charged under Article 5.[19]

On June 23, 1995, Tadic's attorneys filed a preliminary motion to dismiss the charges for lack of jurisdiction, arguing in part that the Tribunal lacked subject-matter jurisdiction because its Statute applies only to crimes committed in connection with an international (as opposed to an internal) armed conflict. On August 10, 1995, the Trial Chamber denied the defense's motion to dismiss, and via interlocutory appeal, the Appeals Chamber of the Tribunal affirmed the ruling of the Trial Chamber on October 2, 1995.[20]

3.3.2 An Analysis of the Tadic Appeals Chamber Decision

In an *amicus* brief filed in *Tadic*, the United States argued that the conflict in Yugoslavia was clearly an international one, and that the members on the Security Council viewed it as such when they established the Tribunal.[21] The Appeals

---

[18]   Allison Marston Danner, *When Courts Make Law: How the International Criminal Tribunals Recast the Laws of War*, 49 VANDERBILT LAW REVIEW 1, 23 (2006).

[19]   Michael P. Scharf, *Trial and Error: An Assessment of the First Judgment of the Yugoslavia War Crimes Tribunal*, 30 NEW YORK UNIVERSITY JOURNAL OF INTERNATIONAL LAW AND POLITICS 167, 167 (1998).

[20]   Prosecutor v. Tadic, Appeals Chamber, Decision on the Defense Motion for Interlocutory Appeal on Jurisdiction, Case No. IT-94-1-AR72 (Oct. 2, 1995), reprinted in 35 I.L.M. 32 (1996).

[21]   *Submission of the Government of the United States of America Concerning Certain Arguments Made by Counsel for the Accused in the Case of The Prosecutor of the Tribunal v. Dusan Tadic*, at 22 (July 17, 1995).

Chamber refused to classify the fighting in Bosnia as an international armed conflict, but at the same time it upheld its jurisdiction on the ground that Article 3 of the Tribunal's Statute applies in both international and internal armed conflict. While recognizing that the Article was intended to "reference" the 1907 Hague Convention (IV), "Respecting the Laws and Customs of War on Land," which applied only in international armed conflicts, the Chamber reasoned that Article 3 was not limited to Hague law because the list of offenses in Article 3 is merely illustrative, not exhaustive.[22] Rather, the Appeals Chamber asserted that Article 3 includes "all violations of international humanitarian law other than the Grave Breaches of the four Geneva Conventions" (which were covered in Article 2 of the Tribunal's Statute).[23] In particular, the Appeals Chamber concluded that Article 3 encompasses violations of Hague law, infringements of Geneva law other than Grave Breaches, and most importantly, violations of Common Article 3 of the Geneva Conventions and Additional Protocol II to the Geneva Conventions, which cover certain conduct committed in internal armed conflict.[24] In the view of the Appeals Chamber, Article 3 of the Tribunal's Statute "functions as a residual clause designed to ensure that no serious violation of international humanitarian law"[25] whether in internal or international armed conflict escapes the Tribunal's jurisdiction, thus making "such jurisdiction watertight and inescapable."[26]

One commentator has stated that "[t]he Tribunal's holding that Article 3 extends to civil war is as bold as it is ill-founded."[27] The text of Article 3 empowers the Tribunal to prosecute persons for violations of the "laws or customs of war," which the Tribunal itself acknowledged was "a term of art used in the past" to make reference to the 1907 Hague Convention, a treaty that applies only to international armed conflicts.[28] Yet the Chamber opined that the provision was also intended to incorporate a more modern customary humanitarian law, of which the Hague Convention was only an "important segment."[29]

The Appeals Chamber availed itself of the negotiating record of the Tribunal's Statute to support its position. However, it disregarded the most important part of that record, namely the UN Secretary-General's report that accompanied the Statute, despite the fact that the Statute and Report were drafted by the UN Office of Legal Affairs, and the Security Council had adopted the Statute without revision. The Secretary-General's report stressed that the Tribunal's jurisdiction should be confined to rules of international humanitarian law "which are beyond any doubt

---

[22] Prosecutor v. Tadic, *supra*, at para. 87.

[23] *Id.* at para. 87.

[24] *Id.* 89.

[25] *Id.* at para. 91.

[26] *Id.* at para. 91.

[27] Geoffrey Watson, *The Humanitarian Law of the Yugoslavia War Crimes Tribunal: Jurisdiction in Prosecutor v. Tadic*, 36 VIRGINIA JOURNAL OF INTERNATIONAL LAW 687, 709 (1996).

[28] Prosecutor v. Tadic, *supra*, at para. 87.

[29] *Id.* at para. 87.

part of customary law."[30] Yet, the Secretary-General's list of instruments that had "beyond any doubt" become part of customary international law included the Geneva and Hague Conventions, the Genocide Convention, and the Nuremberg Charter, but not Additional Protocol II to the Geneva Conventions.[31]

The Appeals Chamber placed a great deal of emphasis on the interpretive statements made by the Security Council delegations at the time the Resolution was adopted. The US delegate, in particular, declared that Article 3 of the draft Statute "includes all obligations under humanitarian law agreements in force in the territory of the former Yugoslavia at the time the acts were committed, including Common Article 3 of the 1949 Geneva Conventions, and the 1977 Additional Protocols to those Conventions."[32] It is of note that the United States' position was that Common Article 3 and Additional Protocol II should apply, not because they formed part of customary law with individual criminal responsibility, but rather because the parties to the conflict had specifically agreed early on that they would apply these provisions of international humanitarian law.[33] The other two statements that the Chamber relied on were far more ambiguous. Thus, the British delegate said that Article 3 is "broad enough to include applicable international conventions," without specifying which conventions were "applicable."[34] And the French delegate said Article 3 covered "all the obligations that flow" from humanitarian conventions in force at the relevant time, but did not specify whether France believed obligations under Protocol II did so.[35]

The Chamber decision tries to minimize the fact that most of the members of the Council took no position on the scope of Article 3. Stressing that "no delegate contested these declarations," the Appeals Chamber concluded that they provided an "authoritative interpretation" of Article 3.[36] But, as Professor Geoffrey Watson, who was present in the Council Chamber when Resolution 827 was adopted, has observed: "The reality is that every State's delegate read a statement prepared or at least vetted in advance by that State's government. No delegate was authorized to jump up and 'object' when it heard the final version of the US or French remarks.

---

[30]   *Report of the Secretary-General Pursuant to Paragraph 2 of Security Council Resolution 808*, UN SCOR, 48th Sess., 3175th mtg., UN Doc. S/RES/808 (1993), reprinted in 32 International Legal Materials (1993), at para. 34.

[31]   *Id.* at para. 34.

[32]   *See Provisional Verbatim Record of the 3217th Mtg. of the Security Council* (May 25, 1993) at 11, UN Doc. S/PV.3217, *reprinted in* 2 VIRGINIA MORRIS & MICHAEL P. SCHARF, AN INSIDER'S GUIDE TO THE INTERNATIONAL CRIMINAL TRIBUNAL FOR THE FORMER YUGOSLAVIA 179 (Transnational Publishers, 1995).

[33]   *See Suggestions Made by the Government of the United States of America, Rules of Procedure and Evidence for the International Tribunal for the Prosecution of Persons Responsible for Serious Violations of International Humanitarian Law Committed in the Former Yugoslavia*, IT/14 (Nov. 17, 1993), *reprinted in* 2 Virginia Morris & Michael P. Scharf, AN INSIDER'S GUIDE TO THE INTERNATIONAL CRIMINAL TRIBUNAL FOR THE FORMER YUGOSLAVIA 516 (Transnational Publishers, 1995).

[34]   *See Provisional Verbatim Record of the 3217th Mtg. of the Security Council, supra,* at 19.

[35]   *Id.*

[36]   Prosecutor v. Tadic, *supra* note, at para. 88.

Moreover, the declarations . . . were made after the delegations had already voted on the resolution."[37]

Meanwhile, the Appeals Chamber conveniently overlooked the fact that an equal number of States expressed qualms about the breadth of the Tribunal's subject matter jurisdiction as supporting a broad interpretation. The Japanese delegate, for example, suggested that "more extensive legal studies could have been undertaken on various aspects of the Statute, such as the question of the principle of *nullum crimen sine lege*" – a question raised by a broad interpretation of Article 3.[38] The Spanish delegate noted that the Statute could have benefited from improvements, "especially in determining the substantive subject matter and temporal jurisdiction" of the Tribunal,[39] and the Brazilian delegate said that many unspecified but important "legal difficulties" were not resolved to his government's satisfaction.[40]

Professor Watson further observes that the State practice relied upon by the Appeals Chamber "is no more compelling than the prepared declarations of a minority of the Security Council."[41] Professor Christopher Greenwood, who was later elected to a judgship on the International Court of Justice, has similarly concluded that "it is also doubtful whether the practice discussed in this part of the [Appeals Chamber] decision really sustains some of the inferences drawn from it."[42]

The Appeals Chamber conceded that traditional international humanitarian law distinguished sharply between international and internal armed conflict, but it asserted with very little evidence of State practice that the distinction has gradually disintegrated as civil strife has become more vicious and large scale.[43] The Chamber cited few examples of actual war crimes trials arising out of internal conflict, and no examples whatsoever of a war crimes trial involving violations of Additional Protocol II. Instead, the Tribunal put much emphasis on the fact that the UN General Assembly has twice (in 1968 and in 1970) declared that humanitarian law applies to "all types of armed conflicts."[44] Yet these UN General Assembly resolutions are a questionable source of authority for the Chamber's position. The two Resolutions predate Additional Protocol II, and while they speak in terms of applying humanitarian law to "all armed conflicts," they do not specifically mention internal armed conflict, and they nowhere address the question of individual criminal responsibility for war crimes.[45]

---

[37] Watson, *supra*, at 709.
[38] See *Provisional Verbatim Record of the 3217th Mtg. of the Security Council, supra.*
[39] *Id.*
[40] *Id.*
[41] Watson, *supra* note 27, at 713.
[42] Christopher Greenwood, *International Humanitarian Law and the Tadic Case,* 7 EUROPEAN JOURNAL OF INTERNATIONAL LAW 265, 278 (1996).
[43] Prosecutor v. Tadic, *supra*, at para. 97.
[44] *Id.* at paras. 110 and 111.
[45] See *Declaration on Respect for Human Rights in Armed Conflicts,* GA Res. 2444, UN GAOR, 23rd Sess., Supp. No. 18, UN Doc. A/7218 (1968), available at http://www1.umn.edu/humanrts/instree/1968c.htm; *Basic Principles for the Protection of Civilian Populations in Armed Conflict,* GA Res. 2675, UN GAOR,

3.3.3 *Was the* Tadic *Decision a Grotian Moment?*

Notwithstanding the Appeals Chambers' assertion that it was simply "declaring" customary international law, the great weight of authority at the time of the *Tadic* decision viewed war crimes liability as applicable only to international armed conflict. Thus, in its 1993 comments to the United Nations on the establishment of the Tribunal, the International Committee of the Red Cross, the organization charged with the application of the laws of war, stated: "according to International Humanitarian Law as it stands today, the notion of war crimes is limited to situations of international armed conflict."[46] A similar view was expressed in the 1993 Report of the UN Commission of Experts on War Crimes in the Former Yugoslavia, which stated: "the content of customary law applicable to internal armed conflict is debatable. As a result, in general, unless the parties to an internal armed conflict agree otherwise, the only offences committed in internal armed conflict for which universal jurisdiction exists are crimes against humanity and genocide, which apply irrespective of the conflict's classification."[47]

When the Security Council established the International Criminal Tribunal for Rwanda in 1994 (a year before the *Tadic* Appeals Chamber decision was issued), the Council expressly conferred jurisdiction over individuals accused of violating Common Article 3 and Additional Protocol II. In describing this development, the Secretary-General left little doubt that this was a departure from existing customary international law. Thus, the Secretary-General reported to the United Nations that

> [T]he Security Council has elected to take a more expansive approach to the choice of the applicable law than the one underlying the statute of the Yugoslav Tribunal, and included within the subject-matter jurisdiction of the Rwanda Tribunal international instruments, regardless of whether they were considered part of customary international law or whether they have customarily entailed the individual criminal responsibility of the perpetrator of the crime. Article 4 of the statute, accordingly, includes violations of Additional Protocol II, which, as a whole, has not yet been universally recognized as part of customary international law, and for the first time criminalizes common article 3 of the four Geneva Conventions.[48]

25th Sess. Supp. No. 28, UN Doc. A/8028 (1970), available at: http://daccess-dds-ny.un.org/doc/RESOLUTION/GEN/NR0/349/40/IMG/NR034940.pdf?OpenElement.

[46] *Some Preliminary Remarks by the International Committee of the Red Cross on the Setting-Up of an International Tribunal for the Prosecution of Persons Responsible for Serious Violations of International Humanitarian Law Committed on the Territory of the Former Yugoslavia*, DDM/JUR/422b (Mar. 25, 1993), at 2, *reprinted in* 2 Virginia Morris & Michael P. Scharf, An Insider's Guide to the International Criminal Tribunal for the Former Yugoslavia 391–392 (Transnational Publishers, 1995).

[47] UN Commission of Experts Established pursuant to Security Council Resolution 780 (1992), *Final report*, UN Doc. S/1994/674 (May 27, 1994) at para. 52, available at http://ess.uwe.ac.uk/comexpert/REPORT_TOC.HTM.

[48] *Report of the Secretary-General Pursuant to Paragraph 5 of Security Council Resolution 955* (Feb. 13, 1995) UN Doc. S/1995/134, at para. 12.

Professor Alison Danner of Vanderbilt University has observed that the end of great wars frequently bring a radical transformation of the law of war in their wake.[49] The end of World War I witnessed the drafting of the 1925 Geneva Protocol banning use of poisonous gas, and the 1929 Geneva Conventions to protect wounded soldiers and prisoners of war. The end of World War II saw the negotiation of the 1949 Geneva Conventions, granting further protections to soldiers, sailors, prisoners of war, and civilians. But "the hostility to extending the rules to civil wars is manifest in the records from the 1949 and 1974–77 Diplomatic Conferences" which drafted the Geneva Conventions and their Additional Protocols.[50] With its end point the breakup of the Soviet Union in 1991, the Cold War saw its own revolution in the laws of war, marked by the creation of the Yugoslavia Tribunal and the issuance of the *Tadic* Appeals Chamber decision. Professor Danner has called the *Tadic* decision "revolutionary."[51] Professor William Schabas of Middlesex University has written that, with the *Tadic* decision, the Appeals Chamber "stunned international lawyers by issuing a broad and innovative reading of the two war crimes of the ICTY Statute."[52]

Like other Grotian Moments, the Yugoslavia Tribunal was established at a historically unique moment, where the politics of the Security Council had undergone a short-lived makeover due to the dissolution of the Soviet Union. The Appeals Chamber's *Tadic* decision, moreover, was issued at a point where "the relevant underlying treaties were old, where underlying conditions had changed, and where there was little prospect for the treaties' revision."[53] As former President of the Yugoslavia Tribunal, Theodor Meron, explained shortly after the *Tadic* case, "in many other fields of international law, treaty making is faster than the evolution of customary law. In international humanitarian law, change through the formation of custom might be faster."[54] In justifying its bold judicial action, the Appeals Chamber rhetorically asked: "Why protect civilians from belligerent violence, or ban rape, torture or the wanton destruction of hospitals ... when two sovereign States are engaged in war, and yet refrain from enacting the same bans or providing the same protection when armed violence has erupted 'only' within the territory of a sovereign State?"[55]

Though it would be a stretch to conclude that the *Tadic* decision was in fact a codification of existing customary international law, it did serve as a powerful

---

[49] Allison Marston Danner, *When Courts Make Law: How the International Criminal Tribunals Recast the Laws of War*, 49 VANDERBILT LAW REVIEW 1, 2 (2006).

[50] *Id.* at 45.

[51] *Id.* at 23.

[52] WILLIAM SCHABAS, An Introduction to the International Criminal Court 42 (Cambridge University Press, 2001).

[53] Danner, *supra*, at 5.

[54] Theodor Meron, *The Continuing Role of Custom in the Formation of International Humanitarian Law*, 90 AMERICAN JOURNAL OF INTERNATIONAL LAW 238, 247 (1996).

[55] Prosecutor v. Tadic, *supra*, at para. 97.

catalyst for a variety of State actions and statements that rapidly crystallized the new law. Just three years after the Appeals Chamber's decision, the *Tadic* precedent had a powerful effect on the outcome of the Rome Diplomatic Conference to establish an International Criminal Court (ICC). During the negotiations in Rome, the question of whether the ICC's jurisdiction should extend to atrocities committed in civil war was a source of contention. The United States, France, Japan, and the United Kingdom supported the inclusion of civil wars within the jurisdiction of the ICC, while China, India, Indonesia, Pakistan, Russia, and Turkey opposed the application of war crimes to civil wars.[56] The delegates were able to break the deadlock by the unifying force of the Yugoslavia Tribunal's *Tadic* decision. Thus, declaring that they were following customary international law, the negotiators codified the *Tadic* approach of distinguishing the rules governing international and noninternational conflicts, with a distinct provision in the ICC Statute devoted to each.[57] At the time this book went to press, there were 123 States Parties to the ICC Statute,[58] and many of them had enacted domestic statutes enabling their courts to prosecute war crimes in internal as well as international armed conflict.[59] Even nonparties, including China, India, Russia, and the United States, implicitly embraced the *Tadic* decision when they voted in the Security Council on February 26, 2011, to refer the matter of war crimes and crimes against humanity in Libya's civil war to the ICC's jurisdiction.[60]

Subsequently, when the Special Court for Sierra Leone was established in 2002, the drafters followed *Tadic*, giving the hybrid Tribunal jurisdiction over war crimes in internal armed conflict.[61] Within a few years of the *Tadic* decision, the Yugoslavia Tribunal, Rwanda Tribunal, and Special Court for Sierra Leone had convicted dozens of defendants for war crimes committed in civil wars. There are no examples of States publicly criticizing the Tribunals' jurisprudence regarding culpability for atrocities in internal armed conflict.[62] Professor Danner suggests that is because the developing countries, who long opposed war crimes liability in civil wars, "may not

---

[56] Danner, *supra*, at 45.
[57] Rome Statute of the International Criminal Court, Article 8 (July 17, 1998) 2187 UNTS 90 (distinguishing between "international armed conflict" in paragraph 2(b) and "armed conflict not of an international character" in paragraphs 2(c)–(f)).
[58] For an up-to-date list of ratifications of the ICC Statute, *see* www.coalitionfortheicc.org/? mod=download&doc=4352.
[59] Amnesty International, *Universal Jurisdiction: A Preliminary Survey of Legislation Around the World* (October 2011) at 1; *Report of the Secretary-General Prepared on the Basis of Comments and Observations of Governments on The Scope and Application of the Principle of Universal Jurisdiction*, UN Doc. a/65/181 (July 29, 2010) at 11, 12.
[60] Security Council Resolution 770, UN Doc. SC/10187/Rev.1** (Feb. 26, 2011) available at: www.un.org/ News/Press/docs/2011/sc10187.doc.htm
[61] Statute of the Special Court for Sierra Leone, Article 3 (Jan. 16, 2002), available at: www.sc-sl.org/ LinkClick.aspx?fileticket=uClnd1MJeEw%3d&tabid=176.
[62] Danner, *supra*, at 5.

wish to pick a fight with an institution established by the powerful Security Council."[63]

Meanwhile, a growing number of States have incorporated the Tribunals' jurisprudence into their military manuals and training materials on the laws of war. The *Manual on the Law of Armed Conflict* issued in 2004 by the United Kingdom, for example, includes references to the case law of the Tribunals, including on the definition of armed conflict.[64] The *Tadic* decision was also specifically cited in the handbook for law-of-war training for members of the US Judge Advocate Generals' Corps.[65] The *Tadic* decision has also been cited as persuasive authority by domestic courts, by international organizations, by NGOs, and by scholars.[66] Within a year of the *Tadic* decision, the International Law Commission, noting "that the principle of individual criminal responsibility for violations of the law applicable in internal armed conflicts had been reaffirmed by the International Criminal Tribunal for the former Yugoslavia," codified this legal development in the 1996 Draft Code of Crimes against the Peace and Security of Mankind.[67]

3.4 CONSEQUENCES ARISING OUT OF THE *TADIC* PRECEDENT

One of the principal failings of the codified laws of war had been their inapplicability to internal armed conflicts. The *Tadic* decision effectively transformed the rules negotiated in 1949 and 1977 to make them more relevant to modern conflicts, which frequently involve civil wars rooted in ethnic tension. In essence, with respect to "serious offenses," the *Tadic* decision blurred the line between international and internal armed conflict so that some of the most important rules of customary law applicable to international armed conflict would now apply to civil wars as well. According to the Appeals Chamber, these rules would include "protection of civilians from hostilities, in particular from indiscriminate attacks, protection of civilian objects, in particular cultural property, protection of all those who do not (or no longer) take active part in the hostilities, as well as prohibition of means of warfare proscribed in international armed conflicts and ban of certain methods of conducting hostilities."[68]

As a result of the *Tadic* decision, much of the conduct prohibited by treaties governing international armed conflicts now constitutes prosecutable war crimes

---

[63]   *Id.* at 44.

[64]   UK Ministry of Defense, *The Manual of the Law of Armed Conflict* 29 (2004).

[65]   International & Operational Law Department, The Judge Advocate General's Legal Center & School, US Army, *Law of War Handbook* 82, 144, 209–12 (2004).

[66]   Danner, *supra*, at 49.

[67]   Draft Code of Crimes against the Peace and Security of Mankind, art. 20(f) and commentary thereto, *Report of the International Law Commission to the General Assembly*, 51 UN GAOR Supp. (No. 10) at 112 and 119, U.N. Doc. A/51/10 (1996), *reprinted in* [1996] 2 YEAR BOOK OF THE INTERNATIONAL LAW COMMISSION, UN Doc. A/CN.4/SER.A/1996/Add.1 (Part 2).

[68]   Prosecutor v. Tadic, *supra*, at para. 127.

when committed in internal armed conflicts. Former ICJ Judge Christopher Greenwood has concluded that customary international law growing out of the *Tadic* decision "regarding internal armed conflicts is of the greatest importance and is likely to be seen in the future as a major contribution to the development of international humanitarian law."[69] The logical outcome of this development is that war crimes other than Grave Breaches of the Geneva Conventions, whether committed in international or internal armed conflict, will now be subject to universal jurisdiction, and possibly the requirement of *aut dedere aut judicate* (the duty to prosecute or extradite) in the same way that Grave Breaches are.[70] In addition, such war crimes will not be subject to statutes of limitations and may constitute an exception to Head of State immunity for former leaders for acts done while in office.[71] Today, the worst violations of international humanitarian law are occurring in an internal armed conflict in Syria. On December 21, 2016, the United Nations General Assembly established a mechanism to pave the way for trials of those responsible for such atrocities[72] – something that would never have been viewed as consistent with customary international law before *Tadic*.

While the jurisprudence of the ad hoc international criminal tribunals has facilitated the accelerated formation of customary international law with respect to other matters, such as application of the joint criminal enterprise concept of liability by international tribunals,[73] recognition of recruitment and use of child soldiers as a

---

[69] Greenwood, *supra*, at 279.

[70] *Cf. Questions Related to the Obligation to Prosecute or Extradite* (Belgium v. Senegal) (July 20, 1012) available at: www.icj-cij.org/docket/files/144/17064.pdf.

[71] Jing Guan, *The ICC's Jurisdiction Over War Crimes in Internal Armed Conflicts: An Insurmountable Obstacle for China's Accession?*, 28 Pennsylvania State International Law Review 703, 715 (2010).

[72] UN GA Res. A/RES/71/248 (Dec. 21, 2016), UN Doc. A/71/L.48 (Sep. 21, 2017) available at: www.un.org/ga/search/view_doc.asp?symbol=A/71/L.48

[73] Prosecutor v. Tadic, Judgment, Case No. IT-94-1-A, ICTY Appeals Chamber, 15 July 1999; Prosecutor v. Milutinovic, Decision on Dragoljub Ojdanic's Motion Challenging Jurisdiction – Joint Criminal Enterprise Liability, Case No. IT-99-37-AR72, ICTY Appeals Chamber (May 21, 2003); Prosecutor v. Krnojelac, Judgment, Case No. IT-97-25-A, ICTY Appeals Chamber (Sep. 17, 2003), para. 96; Prosecutor v. Simic, Judgment, ICTY Trial Chamber, Case No. IT-95-9-T (Oct. 17, 2003), para. 149; Prosecutor v. Kvocka, Judgment, Case No. IT-98-30/1-A (Feb. 28, 2005), paras. 105, 309; Prosecutor v. Krnojelac, Judgment, Case No. IT-97-25-A (Sep. 17, 2003), paras. 96, 100; Prosecutor v. Brdjanin, Judgment, Case No. IT-99-36-A (Apr 3, 2007), para. 395; Prosecutor v. Brdjanin, Decision on Interlocutory Appeal, Case No.IT-99-36-A (Mar. 19, 2004); Prosecutor v. Stakic, Case No. IT-97-24-A, Judgment (Mar. 22, 2006), paras. 101–4; Prosecutor v. Krjaisnik, Judgment, Case No. IT-00-39-T (Sep. 27, 2006), para. 1082; Prosecutor v. Milosevic, Decision on Motion for Judgment of Acquittal, Case No. IT-02-54-T (June 16, 2004), para. 291; Prosecutor v. Krstic, Judgment, Case No. IT-98-33-A, ICTY Appeals Chamber (Apr. 19, 2004), para. 144; Prosecutor v. Ntakirutimana, Judgment, Case Nos. ICTR-96-10-A and ICTR-96-17-A, ICTR Appeals Chamber (Dec. 13, 2004), paras. 461–84; Prosecutor v. Rwamakuba, Decision on Interlocutory Appeal Regarding Application of Joint Criminal Enterprise to the Crime of Genocide, Case No. ICTR-98-44-AR72.4 (Oct. 22, 2004), paras. 14–30; Prosecutor v. Kayishema and Ruzindanda, Judgment, Case No. ICTR-95-1-A, ICTR Appeals Chamber (June 1, 2001), para 193; Prosecutor v. Nchamihigo, Decision on Defence Motion on Defects in the Form of the Indictment, Case No. ICTR-2001063oR50 (Sep. 27, 2006), paras 14, 21; Prosecutor v. Brima, Kamara and Kanue (AFRC Case), Decision on Motions for Judgment of Acquittal Pursuant to Rule

war crime,[74] and of forced marriage as a crime against humanity,[75] none of the other decisions has had the pervasive transformative effect of the *Tadic* decision. This Grotian Moment has even had a significant effect on US policies in its "war on terrorism." Thus, in the 2006 landmark case of *Hamdan* v. *Rumsfeld*, an Al Qaeda detainee held at Guantanamo Bay argued that the Military Commission established by President Bush's Executive Order did not comply with the minimum requirements of Common Article 3 of the Geneva Conventions. The Bush Administration responded in part that Common Article 3 applied only to internal armed conflicts, and that the war against Al Qaeda was international in scope. In ruling that the Military Commission was invalid, the US Supreme Court cited the Yugoslavia Tribunal Appeals Chamber decision in *Tadic* for the proposition that "the character of the conflict is irrelevant" in deciding whether Common Article 3 applies.[76]

98, Case No. SCSL-04-16-T (Mar. 31, 2006), paras. 308–26; Prosecutor v. Norman, Fofana and Kondewa (CDF Case), Decision on Motions for Judgment of Acquittal Pursuant to Rule 98, Case No. 04-14-T (Oct. 21, 2005), para. 130.

[74] Prosecutor v. Alex Tamba Brima (AFRC Trial Judgment), SCSL-04-16-T, Judgment (June 20, 2007) (SCSL, Trial Chamber II); Prosecutor v. Alex Tamba Brima (AFRC Appeals Judgment), SCSL-04-16-A, Judgment (Feb. 22, 2008) (SCSL, Appeals Chamber); Prosecutor v. Moinina Fofona (CDF Trial Judgment), SCSL-04-14-T, Judgment (Aug. 2, 2007) (SCSL, Trial Chamber I); Prosecutor v. Moinina Fofona (CDF Appeals Judgment), SCSL-04-14-A, Judgment (May 28, 2008) (SCSL, Appeals Chamber); Prosecutor v. Sesay (RUF Trial Judgment), SCSL-04-15-T, Judgment (Mar. 2, 2009) (SCSL, Trial Chamber I); Prosecutor v. Sesay (RUF Appeals Judgment), SCSL-04-15-A, Judgment (Oct. 26, 2009) (SCSL, Appeals Chamber); The Prosecutor v. Thomas Lubanga Dyilo, ICC-01/04-01/06, Decision on the Confirmation of the Charges (Jan. 29, 2007) (ICC, Pre-Trial Chamber I).

[75] Judgment, Prosecutor v. Brima, Kamara, and Kanu, SCSL, Appeals Chamber (Feb. 22, 2008), para. 195.

[76] Hamdan v. Rumsfeld, 126 S.Ct. 2749, 2774 n.63 (2006).

4

A Roundtable on the Legacy of the *Karadzic* Trial at the International Criminal Tribunal for the Former Yugoslavia[1]

Milena Sterio: I am sure that all of you are familiar with the fact that on March 24, 2016, the International Criminal Tribunal for the Former Yugoslavia ("ICTY" or "Yugoslavia Tribunal") trial chamber found Radovan Karadzic guilty of one count of genocide, multiple counts of crimes against humanity, and multiple counts of war crimes.[2] He was sentenced to forty years in prison, which, in light of his age – he is seventy-one now – basically amounts to a life sentence. He was actually acquitted of one count of genocide. He had been accused of two different sets of crimes: genocide at Srebrenica and also genocide in various other Bosnian municipalities. The ICTY Trial Chamber convicted him of the one count of genocide at Srebrenica, but acquitted him of the other count of genocide that took place in the other Bosnian municipalities. Our panel today will focus on the genocide conviction, and we will talk about the definition of genocide, and then the ICTY interpretation of the definition of genocide.

Before we begin our discussion, let me just briefly introduce the panelists. Reading their entire bios would take up all of our time, so in the interest of time I will just highlight some of their most distinguished accomplishments.

Professor Meg deGuzman is a professor of law at Temple Law School, where she teaches criminal law, international criminal law, and transitional justice. Her scholarship focuses on the role of international criminal law in the global legal order, with a particular emphasis on the work of the International Criminal Court (ICC). Professor deGuzman holds a PhD from the Irish Centre for Human Rights at the National University of Ireland and a JD from Yale Law School. Before joining the

---

[1] This chapter contains the edited transcript of the International Law Weekend Panel, the Legacy of the Karadzic Case, which was held in New York City in October 2016, shortly after the Karadzic Trial Court decision was issued. The panel was transcribed and edited, and footnotes were added by the following Cox International Law Center Fellows: Lauren Stuy, Celena Krause, Manal Nizam, Benjamin Boggs, Kevin J. Vogel, and Michael Silverstein.

[2] *See* Julian Borger & Owen Bowcott, *Radovan Karadzic Sentenced to 40 Years for Srebrenica Genocide*, THE GUARDIAN (Mar. 24, 2016), www.theguardian.com/world/2016/mar/24/radovan-karadzic-crimin ally-responsible-for-genocide-at-srebenica.

Temple faculty, she had clerked on the Ninth Circuit and practiced law in San Francisco for several years, specializing in criminal defense. She was a legal advisor to the Senegal delegation at the Rome Conference for the ICC, and also a law clerk in the Office of the Prosecutor of the ICTY.

Professor Paul Williams is the Rebecca I. Grazier Professor of Law and International Relations at American University, where he teaches both at the law school and the School of International Service. He, along with Michael Scharf, co-founded the nongovernmental organization Public International Law and Policy Group, which is a Nobel Peace Prize-nominated NGO based out of Washington, DC. Professor Williams has assisted more than two dozen peace negotiations and post-conflict constitutions, and has advised governments across Europe, Asia, and North and Sub-Saharan Africa on state recognition, self-determination, and state succession issues, as well as drafting constitutions. He holds a PhD from Cambridge University and a JD from Stanford Law School.

Dean Michael Scharf is Dean and professor at the Case Western University School of Law. He is also the director of the Frederick K. Cox International Law Center. He, with Professor Williams, co-founded the Public International Law and Policy Group. He is the author of more than one hundred scholarly articles and seventeen books, including a book specifically on the Yugoslavia Tribunal and Slobodan Milosevic, and he is one of the most cited authors in the fields of international law and international criminal law. He holds JD and undergraduate degrees from Duke Law School and Duke University.

Professor Jenia Turner is a professor at the Southern Methodist University Dedman School of Law, where she teaches criminal procedure, comparative criminal procedure, international criminal law, European Union law, and international organizations. Before joining the SMU Dedman School of Law, she served as a Bigelow Fellow at the University of Chicago Law School. She has a JD from Yale Law School and has worked at the Yugoslavia Tribunal.

Professor Beth Van Schaack is currently the Leah Kaplan Visiting Professor in Human Rights at Stanford Law School and also a visiting scholar at the Center for International Security and Cooperation at Stanford University. Before that, she worked as Deputy Chief to the Ambassador-at-Large for War Crimes Issues in the Office of Global Criminal Justice at the US Department of State. In that capacity, she helped to advise the Secretary of State, as well as the Undersecretary for Civilian Security, Democracy, and Human Rights, on the formulation of US policy regarding the prevention of and accountability for mass atrocities such as war crimes, crimes against humanity, and genocide. Before that, Professor Van Schaack was a professor of law at Santa Clara University School of Law, where she taught and researched in the fields of international law, international criminal law, and international human rights. She is a graduate of Stanford University and Yale Law School.

Let's begin our discussion by focusing on the definition of genocide. So, Michael, can you tell us about the definition of genocide? The definition itself is fairly narrow, and there might be situations that *look like* genocide, but do not constitute genocide because of the narrowness of the definition itself.

Michael Scharf: I should start briefly with the history that explains how we came to this definition. It starts in 1945, at the end of World War II, with Adolf Hitler's "Final Solution," when a professor by the name of Raphael Lemkin came up with the term "genocide." In 1945, the Nuremberg Charter was negotiated, and it does not include the crime of genocide, although it does include crimes against humanity. In 1946 – about seventy years ago to this day – the judgment of the Nuremberg Trial came out, also with no reference to genocide.[3] In 1947, at the Einsatzgruppen Case, somebody who many of us know in the room – the last surviving prosecutor at Nuremberg, Ben Ferencz – used the word "genocide" for the first time in a courtroom to describe the mass murders that this special death squad had committed. In 1948, finally, at the height of the Cold War, the Genocide Convention is negotiated. I should mention that it was controversial in the United States – it took thirty years for the US Senate to finally ratify it.

It was thought that the Convention was something that had to be widely ratified to be accepted, and so, in order to get the Convention to be acceptable to all the countries in the world – and this is a time when the world was really divided between the East and West, and the proxies of the Soviet Union and the United States – they watered down the concept of genocide, so it is a very narrow definition with a specific intent. Basically, genocide is the mass murder or sterilization of an ethnic, racial, national, or religious group with the intent to destroy the group.[4] That's my paraphrase. This was purposely narrow because at the time Stalin was doing purges, where almost 30 million Soviet citizens were killed for political opposition to the regime. That could have been defined as genocide, but they specifically wrote it so that Stalin's purges would not be included.[5] There were also things going on in the United States that were specifically excluded, like the United States' treatment of African Americans during the pre-Civil Rights era, and also what had happened previously with Native Americans.[6]

There are situations around the world that we think of, in general terms, as genocide, but which are actually excluded from this definition. The biggest one – which is a real pain in the butt for the Extraordinary Chambers in the Courts of

---

3   Lemkin coined the term "genocide" in a book he wrote in 1944. *E.g.,* United States Holocaust Memorial Museum, *What Is Genocide?*, www.ushmm.org/wlc/en/article.php?ModuleId=10007043 (last visited Oct. 14, 2017).

4   Convention on the Prevention and Punishment for the Crime of Genocide art. 2, Dec. 9, 1948, 78 UNTS 277.

5   Milena Sterio, *The Karadžić Genocide Conviction: Inferences, Intent, and the Necessity to Redefine Genocide*, 31 EMORY INT'L L. REV. 271, 274 (2017).

6   *See* William A. Schabas, *Origins of the Genocide Convention: From Nuremberg to Paris*, 40 CASE W. RES. J. INT'L L. 35, 45–50 (2007).

Cambodia (ECCC), the Cambodia genocide tribunal – is the situation in Cambodia.[7] We all call it "the killing fields genocide." The only way really to prosecute the Khmer Rouge for genocide is to stretch the definition into something known as "auto-genocide," which most commentators don't believe. Because of that, the only genocide counts that the ECCC are prosecuting are against the Cham and the Vietnamese who were killed in Cambodia, and not for the million people who were slaughtered in the killing fields.[8] There are other situations as well. So, what we have to understand about the Genocide Convention – which applies to all the international tribunals – is that it was a product of its time, which was a very divisive time. There were compromises made in order to get the Eastern Bloc to join it and, because of those compromises, genocide is not as broad a crime as we convention-ally think.

Milena Sterio: Now, it is important to note that the statutes of the Yugoslavia and Rwanda tribunals essentially copy the definition of genocide verbatim from the Genocide Convention. So, defendants that are prosecuted for genocide are prose-cuted under the individual statutes, but the statutes embrace the Convention's genocide definition.

Beth, let me ask you: why do you think it's important for a tribunal – like the Rwanda tribunal or the Yugoslavia tribunal – to charge a defendant with genocide? When it comes to Karadzic, some people have asked, "Why not just charge him with crimes against humanity? Why go the genocide route when you know that that is going to be a more difficult conviction to obtain?"

Beth Van Schaack: It's a great question. There have been conversations about the fact that crimes against humanity, as a sort of genus crime, would in many respects encompass situations that would also rise to the level of genocide. Crimes against humanity requires a showing of a widespread or systematic attack against a civilian population. That population does not need to be defined as a protected group, as Michael said. It does not have to be a racial group or a homogeneously ethnic group. It can be any group of civilians.[9] That's the sort of defining characteristic. You need a widespread or systematic attack, but you don't need to show proof of an intent to destroy the group in whole or in part. You just have to show the existence of an attack. So, many genocidal situations would also fall under crimes against humanity.

Now, why do we need the two crimes? Why not sort of fold them into each other? One argument that has been made is that genocide can be committed even without mass violence. It's not an effects-based crime or an outcome crime; it's a crime of

---

[7]   *See* Adam Taylor, *Why the World Should Not Forget Khmer Rouge and the Killing Fields of Cambodia*, WASH. POST (Aug. 7, 2014), www.washingtonpost.com/news/worldviews/wp/2014/08/07/why-the-world-should-not-forget-khmer-rouge-and-the-killing-fields-of-cambodia.

[8]   *See First Genocide Charges to be Heard at ECCC*, EXTRAORDINARY CHAMBERS IN THE COURTS OF CAMBODIA (Sept. 4, 2015), www.eccc.gov.kh/en/articles/first-genocide-charges-be-heard-eccc.

[9]   Rome Statute of the International Criminal Court art. 7, Jul. 17, 1998, 2187 UNTS. 3.

intent. So, theoretically, the killing of a handful of individuals, if done with the requisite specific intent, could constitute genocide. And there is one case arising out of the ICTY that often does not get remembered when we think about where the ICTY has gone on genocide, and that's the *Jelisic* case. Jelisic was an individual who called himself the "Serb Adolf," and he articulated a genocidal intent. At the trial chamber level, he was actually acquitted of the genocide count but convicted of crimes against humanity for the same underlying conduct. Somewhat controversially, the prosecutor decided to appeal, in part to make law around genocide as a distinct crime separate and apart from crimes against humanity. On appeal, the appeals chamber reinstated those genocide counts and, in fact, found him guilty.[10] Even though he had only been associated with the injury and harm to, say, a dozen or so individuals, the Court found that you could convict someone of genocide under those circumstances. So, that's one argument.

The second argument that gets made for why we should retain genocide as a separate concept is that it somehow does capture something differently than crimes against humanity. With genocide, we are targeting a group based upon what many people would consider – or at least what was considered at the time the Genocide Convention was drafted – to be immutable characteristics, like your race, ethnicity, et cetera. With religion, things start to get fuzzy, because of course we all can change our religion potentially. But one of the reasons it works with this idea of immutability is that the tribunals have satisfied themselves with a subjective interpretation. If the perpetrators and the victims saw themselves as being part of different ethnic groups, even if some sort of an objective analysis would not necessarily agree with that, they found genocide. I think Rwanda is a great example of that. You have the Hutus and the Tutsis, who are really more economic groups, or maybe social groups – a legacy of colonialism. They all carried identity cards, but spoke the same language, practiced the same religion, intermarried, and did not have vastly different social customs of any sort. Nonetheless, the tribunal found genocide there. So, there is this idea of targeting individuals based upon immutable characteristics, and therefore genocide in a way sits a little bit at the apex of international criminal law because it has that extra, superfluous intent.

Margaret deGuzman: The last comment Beth made is a good jumping-off point. In terms of genocide as the apex of international crimes, I think it's a little bit unfortunate that often people say things like, "Genocide is the crime of crimes" or "It's the worst of crimes." I think it's unfortunate because it in some way sort of dilutes crimes against humanity. And it's just not accurate, either. As Beth said, the

---

[10] The Appeals Chamber actually declined to reverse the acquittal, even though it found that the Prosecutor's evidence would have been sufficient to support a conviction for genocide. Prosecutor v. Goran Jelisic, Case No. IT-95-10-A, Appeals Chamber Judgment (July 5, 2001). In its judgment, the Appeals Chamber noted that there was evidence that Jelisic believed that he was following a plan set down by superiors, but there was also evidence that he acted as a "one-man genocide mission, intent upon personally wiping out the protected group in whole or in part." *Id.* at para. 66.

Jelisic case involved one individual with a heinous intent, but without the context of an overall attack that was aimed at destroying a group (at least this was the holding). In comparison, crimes against humanity sometimes can be crimes that affect many more people much more deeply. This gets into a broader discussion that I focus on in my scholarship about what it means to say that international crimes are especially serious crimes. I'll leave that to the side, but my point for the purposes of this discussion is that I think it is unfortunate that we've ended up with this rhetoric around genocide that leads people to feel very strongly about getting genocide convictions, which didn't have to be the case. As Milena said, I was at the Rome Conference when the Rome Statute was negotiated – as were a number of people in the room – and there was some very brief discussion about maybe just subsuming genocide within crimes against humanity, or making it a form of crime against humanity, or in some circumstances a sort of aggravating circumstance at sentencing like we have hate crimes as aggravating circumstances domestically. It just didn't go anywhere, largely for political reasons. People sort of didn't want to touch the Genocide Convention. There was enough messiness around trying to define all the other crimes. So, it was the briefest of conversations. People said, "Look, we have got the Genocide Convention's definition. We can't open that Pandora's box." It's contributed to an unfortunate situation where there's this rhetoric that doesn't actually match the legal realities very well.

Paul Williams: I would agree one hundred percent with Meg. It has put us in an odd situation where, in order for transitional justice to be effective at impacting the political process – and I don't mean the political process impacting the transitional justice process, but vice-versa – it has to be genocide. We're in a situation of post-caring. People think, "War crimes happen everywhere, crimes against humanity happen everywhere." There's plenty of space for special envoys, peace negotiators, and mediators to accommodate and appease those who are responsible for these crimes because it's all very complicated. But if something is labeled as genocide, that creates moral clarity. And all of a sudden, the mediators have less room to accommodate, appease, and negotiate with those who are responsible for genocide. I think that's a good thing. This is transitional justice being used to constrain the bad decisions that are made in the political arena and in the political environment. It's also something that's pursued by victims. And, like Meg pointed out, they've conflated genocide and crimes against humanity, but there's this notion that if you're a victim of war crimes or crimes against humanity, you're a victim of bad things. But if you're a victim of genocide, you are a victim of the highest of crimes – the apex of crimes – and that contributes to the victim catharsis, the victim healing.

I think we've been very unfair to the victims by, in a sense, continuing this momentum. There's a sense that, because other situations have been labeled "genocide," if you really have been victimized then you want your situation to be labeled genocide as well. And if you haven't been officially subjected to "genocide," you feel like you've just been subjected to other types of crimes like everyone else, so there's less of the healing. There's also a historical record. A number of entities have been or are in the process of being created through crimes against humanity and possibly genocide. Three of the four signatories of the Dayton Accords, which currently govern the political environment in Bosnia, were indicted or were deemed indictable by the Tribunal for crimes against humanity and genocide.[11] And that should be taken into consideration as we continue to interact with the state of Bosnia and think about how its political situation might be reformed. By locking something into the historical record, I think that helps to guide even ongoing political interaction with states.

Milena Sterio: I know that Jenia here wants to weigh in, and then Michael does, and then we will talk about the *Karadzic* case.

Jenia Turner: Just very briefly, I think this is going to be relevant to the case later. One strategic point, from the prosecutor's point of view, to charge genocide – in addition to the symbolic meaning, which informs this choice – is for sentencing purposes. The courts have actually treated genocide more seriously and have imposed harsher sentences.[12] So just from a very strategic standpoint, prosecutors would want to charge genocide, in addition to the symbolic meaning. Whether that's good or bad, that's a separate question.

Michael Scharf: I just wanted to add two points, one about political pressure and political will, and the other about modes of liability. In respect to the first, political pressure, if you call something genocide officially, there's a lot of political pressure to intervene and to act. For that reason, the United States – which was not in the mood to intervene into Bosnia on the ground – really struggled to ignore the fact that what was going on was genocide and to avoid at all costs using the "g word." And compare that to what the United States did about ten years later in the Sudan, where the United States was the first country to say it was genocide. In Sudan, the United States had the political will to agree with the Security Council's referral of the Al Bashir case to the International Criminal Court. The term genocide is very powerful in the diplomatic arena.

The other thing that's unique to genocide we haven't talked about, but it's worth mentioning, is that it has unique modes of liability. Written into the Convention – and this has been duplicated in each of the international criminal courts' statutes – is that genocide has the mode of liability of *conspiracy*. It's the only crime in international law that has conspiracy. Second, there's *incitement* to commit genocide. That's unique. Third, there's *attempt* to commit

[11]   *See* Julian Borger, *Bosnia's Bitter, Flawed Peace Deal, 20 Years On*, THE GUARDIAN (Nov. 10, 2015), www.theguardian.com/global/2015/nov/10/bosnia-bitter-flawed-peace-deal-dayton-agreement-20-years-on.

[12]   *See* 3 GIDEON BOAS ET AL., International Criminal Law Practitioner Library Series 397 (2011).

genocide.[13] I'm curious actually, Beth, if Jelisic was convicted of attempt or whether it was the full genocide, because normally you would have to have massive killing – if not by him, then by somebody – in order to have the completed crime of genocide, but not necessarily attempt.[14] Finally, on top of all of that – and this does lead to the *Karadzic* case – is that the Yugoslavia tribunal was the first tribunal to apply what was really a brand new mode of liability: joint criminal enterprise liability (JCE). One of the versions of that mode is actually a negligence-based form of liability, and commentators have argued that JCE should not apply to genocide, because genocide is a specific-intent crime, and JCE applies to people who are even negligent or just have knowledge. Under JCE, if you join a criminal group that is committing atrocities, with knowledge of what the group is doing, then you are responsible for what every member of that group does, when it was reasonably foreseeable that they would do that.[15] That's a negligence standard.

Milena Sterio: Now I want to focus on the actual case, and I want to talk about how the tribunal reached its conclusion that Karadzic had participated in this joint criminal enterprise and had the specific intent to commit genocide. The trial lasted for several years, hundreds of witnesses were heard, and hundreds of documents were admitted into evidence. However, the prosecution really did not have any type of smoking-gun evidence to establish that Karadzic really displayed the specific intent to commit genocide at Srebrenica. The tribunal focused on two specific conversations that Karadzic had with another civilian administrator in the region. However, the tribunal's trial chamber really had no substantive knowledge of the content of those conversations. Some people have argued that this is a genocide conviction where the tribunal's trial chamber inferred knowledge, and then, based on that inference of knowledge, the trial chamber inferred genocidal intent.[16]

So, Beth, let me go to you. What do you think of this type of judicial reasoning? Is this just a reality now because – unlike the Holocaust paradigm where the Germans kept meticulous records of everything – when it comes to Rwanda or Yugoslavia we don't have records of people explicitly saying, "I'm going to destroy this ethnic group," or "I'm going to do x, y, and z," so we have to infer and deduce and rely on circumstantial evidence?

---

[13] Convention on the Prevention and Punishment for the Crime of Genocide art. 3, Dec. 9, 1948, 78 UNTS 277.

[14] Jelisic was charged with what Michael Scharf calls "full genocide," that is to say, killing members of a protected group with the specific intent to destroy the group in whole or in part. Prosecutor v. Jelisic, Case No. IT-95-10, Second Amended Indictment, available at www.icty.org/x/cases/jelisic/ind/en/jel-2ai981019e.pdf.

[15] *See* 14 Guilla Bigi, Joint Criminal Enterprise in the Jurisprudence of the International Criminal Tribunal for the Former Yugoslavia and the Prosecution of Senior Political and Military Leaders: The Krajisnik Case, Max Planck Yearbook of United Nations Law 52–4 (A. von Bogdandy & R. Wolfrum, eds., 2010).

[16] Sterio, *supra* note 5, at 285–6.

Beth Van Schaack: We do. And the tribunal is very self-conscious about the fact that they are making an inference, and the standard that they have set under those circumstances is that it must be the *only reasonable inference*. They were not able to find, when it came to the municipalities, that the only reasonable inference was that Karadzic was acting with genocidal intent.[17] Michael mentioned the importance of JCE to this case: there were nested joint criminal enterprises that were alleged within the indictment. Some of them had to do with attacks, sniping attacks and shelling attacks on Sarajevo. Those were sort of law-of-war counts. There was the hostage taking of the UN peacekeepers, that was a separate JCE. There was Srebrenica as a JCE. And then there was what they called the "overarching JCE," which was the JCE to commit genocide writ large throughout a number of municipalities within Bosnia, and that was the count that ended up in acquittal on genocide.[18] The court looked at statements he had made, at meetings that had been had, using sort of an effects-based reasoning, working from the effects on the ground backward, that you would only act with genocidal intent to create these outcomes and they would not otherwise have acted that way. And based upon all of this mess, sort of, of circumstances, the tribunal could not reach the conclusion that he was acting with genocidal intent vis-a-vis those municipalities. Now, there was a very different result with respect to Srebrenica, which I think would have been a hard outcome not to reach, given that Srebrenica has been the subject of multiple cases – multiple prosecutions – and Karadzic's involvement has come out in those other proceedings. It would have been a very odd state of affairs indeed if he'd been acquitted with respect to Srebrenica.

We still have *Mladic*, so there's some possibility that we could reach a conclusion that there was a larger genocidal plan within Bosnia, but so far the results at the ICTY have not reached that, and they've ended up being relatively consistent with what the International Court of Justice found in a case brought by Bosnia against Serbia for state responsibility for genocide. In that case, the ICJ also concluded that they could not determine with whatever the standard of proof they were operating under – and they're quite mushy about articulating what that standard is, but it seems to rise to somewhat of an almost criminal-law standard – that they could show a Serbian policy.[19] So, the result is many Bosniaks felt that Serbia as a nation was created by virtue of a genocide, because there was this massive effort at ethnic cleansing, and the borders that exist now are the result of a genocidal act, and so far the jurisprudence has not necessarily supported that narrative.

Margaret deGuzman: With regard to whether the specific intent was proven, you mention the conversations with the civilian administrator. Those conversations,

---

[17] *Id.* at 284.
[18] *Trial Judgement Summary for Radovan Karadžić*, International Criminal Tribunal for the Former Yugoslavia (2016), www.icty.org/x/cases/karadzic/tjug/en/160324_judgement_summary.pdf.
[19] *Application of the Convention on the Prevention and Punishment of the Crime of Genocide (Bosnia and Herzegovina v. Serbia and Montenegro)*, Judgment, ICJ Reports 2007, at 43.

some of them were conducted in code and the tribunal drew inferences from that.[20] That does not strike me, as someone who has practiced and teaches criminal law, as an unusual or reprehensible thing to do. I think the judgment has been criticized with regard to whether the intent was really proven, and at least coming from the perspective of criminal law, I'm not sure how warranted those criticisms really are.

The other point I wanted to make is regarding this idea about the "only reasonable inference." I think it's actually quite a high standard that does not comport with, at least in the United States, jurisprudence and the ideas we have about "beyond a reasonable doubt." Judges will typically say that "beyond a reasonable doubt" is the kind of certainty you would have when making an important decision concerning your own most important affairs, or something like that. The "only reasonable inference," to me, seems to be higher than that. I think the tribunal set a very high standard. Whether they met that standard, maybe we could debate, but I think that – from at least where I'm sitting – the evidence seems to have met the "beyond a reasonable doubt" standard.

Milena Sterio: Just to clarify, the detail of what we're discussing is really about whether one could reasonably infer that Karadzic had agreed with this other person that their common plan was simply to eliminate Bosnian Muslims from the area. I think almost anyone would agree that that was their original plan. But then at some point, that plan in July 1995 morphed into, "Let's just kill them," as opposed to busing them somewhere else. So, part of what the tribunal had to struggle with was this idea: Did Karadzic know that the plan had changed and was now to bring them all to Srebrenica and gun them down? And then, if he knew, did he share the special intent with everybody else, to do that? I think that's part of the struggle the tribunal has here. Michael?

Michael Scharf: So, our chair is a real expert at this, and being the chair she can generally only ask questions but I'm going to put her on the spot. The defense counsel, Peter Robinson – who is actually a wonderful man and he tries very hard to uphold the sanctity of the trial and appeals process – has a brief and he sent us a copy. Everybody here has one and I want to quote from it. He says,

> Milena Sterio of Cleveland Marshall Law School, commenting on the judgment, noted that, if one accepts the idea that one of the most fundamental goals of international criminal justice is to secure the highest level of convictions against those who commit atrocities, and that the most significant conviction is that of genocide, then one would support the argument that the definition of genocide should be interpreted more loosely to allow the inferences of the sort used against Karadzic by the trial court.

---

[20]   Sterio, *supra* note 5, at 285.

Then here's the key part: "But if one thinks, on the other hand, that the rule of law is the most important thing, and that legal definitions should be interpreted strictly, then one may take issue with the trial chamber's liberal approach to finding a genocidal intent based on inferences." And I want to ask Milena if she stands by that.

Milena Sterio: Well, since I'm not Donald Trump, I'm going to say I do. [laughter]. No, I do, and part of the argument I've made in another article is that I think that the Genocide Convention definition is too narrow for today's modern-day conflict, such as the Rwanda conflict or the Yugoslavia conflict, and the type of evidence needed – like we had from World War II – we're simply never going to have.[21] So, I think that trial chambers, as a consequence, are really left having to infer and deduce. Obviously, I think that Karadzic must have had the knowledge and intent that the plan was to eliminate, bus out groups of Bosnian Muslims, but I don't know if it was the only reasonable inference. I don't disagree with Meg that perhaps the standard is too high. I don't know that that standard really has been met, that the only reasonable inference based on these conversations that we have no substantive knowledge about – these are closed room conversations. Now, there is somebody who apparently was like next door who was eavesdropping, and he was able to testify that, "yeah I overheard them say XYZ," but we really don't know. So, I don't really know that the only reasonable inference, by that legal standard, is that Karadzic must have shared this intent to change the plan from eliminating to killing. I'm not really sympathetic to the defendant at all. I just think that, by very strict legal standards, I'm not sure that this is the soundest judicial reasoning.

Michael Scharf: By the way, that guy you were referring to in the next room, this is one of the problems with this case. His name is Nikolic. He was under a plea deal, where he himself was accused of all sorts of things, and his sentence and judgment were lowered significantly for his cooperation in this case.[22] The trial court, uniquely, did not mention that in its decision, and so the defense council says, "Yes, this does happen all the time, but you have to bring it to the appeals court's and the world's attention so that they understand how to appropriately put it in its perspective."

Milena Sterio: This is actually the perfect moment, I think, to bring Jenia in. I know you're an expert on sentencing issues. So, weigh in with your comment and then we'll talk about sentencing.

Jenia Turner: Just one issue, and this relates to your earlier question and sort of the realities of these prosecutions and how we adjust to those. So, it's true that Nikolic's sentence was reduced, so perhaps that casts some doubts about his credibility. But

---

[21] *Id.* at 292–3.

[22] *Momir Nikolic*, Trial International (2016), https://trialinternational.org/latest-post/momir-nikolic/.

then, on the other hand, if you're not going to have intercepts of every conversation then you kind of have to rely on insider witnesses, and the other insider witnesses when testifying before the tribunal, of course, had an interest in diminishing their own responsibility for what happened. Unless you give a deal to someone, they're not going to incriminate themselves by saying, "Yes, that was our special intent." That's just something to keep in mind, and I don't know how we get around it other than through coming out and recognizing it, and I think they did recognize, sort of, that there were some credibility issues, but maybe not as much as the defense attorney would have liked. As far as the sentencing goes, if you want me to . . . ?

Milena Sterio: Yeah, so the prosecution was actually very unhappy with this sentence – forty years – even though functionally it is a life sentence.[23] Karadzic is seventy-one now, so even if he were to get out after having served two-thirds of his sentence, most likely he will die in prison. Do you think that that sentence is consistent with the other tribunal sentences in previous cases? Do you share some of the prosecution concerns that it is too lenient?

Jenia Turner: Yeah, so, there are two questions. One is, is it functionally equivalent to a life sentence? If we take into account the time he has spent in detention, plus the release after two-thirds of his sentence, it's nineteen years I think it comes out to. So, he may actually not serve life in prison, depending on how long he lives.

But apart from that, I think there is a symbolic issue. You know, you oppose sentences for symbolic purposes: What is the just sentence for purposes of retribution, or purposes of deterrence, and so forth? There have been a couple of empirical studies of sentencing at the ICTY and the ICTR, and they have studied the factors that aggravate and mitigate sentences. And basically, if you look at the factors that aggravate sentences, just about all of them were present in this case, so Karadzic's high position, high rank, that's a big one that increases the sentence, and the fact that he was convicted of genocide. Even though courts will say, "Oh, there's no hierarchy of crimes," if you look at the empirical studies, genocide has been punished more harshly.[24] Even within the crimes against humanity that he was convicted for, crimes like extermination and persecution, just the discriminatory grounds crimes which can come closer to genocide, those have been punished more harshly. Also, the number of counts. He was convicted on ten counts, which is also higher than normal.[25] I think it's not consistent. I think the prosecution has something to complain about. This is if we look at the average sentence. On the other hand, if you will, look at a couple of other people who have been sentenced, high-level defendants like Plavsic and Krajisnik. Plavsic, because of a guilty plea, ended up getting eleven years, and Krajisnik on the appeal ended up getting, I think, like

---

[23] See Trial Judgement Summary for Radovan Karadžić, supra note 18.
[24] See, e.g., Barbora Holá, Catrien Bijleveld & Alette Smeulers, Consistency of International Sentencing: ICTY and ICTR Case Study, 9 EUR. J. OF CRIMINOLOGY 539 (2012).
[25] See Trial Judgement Summary for Radovan Karadžić, supra note 18.

twenty.[26] They were high-level political leaders in Republika Srpska. From that perspective, one could say maybe it was warranted. But I think that's the issue. There was a lot of disappointment with those sentences, that they were out of step with other sentences that were rendered by the tribunal. So, yes, I think the prosecution has something to complain about.

Paul Williams: To be slightly diplomatic about this, these sentences by the Yugoslav Tribunal are utterly outrageous. We're talking twenty-seven years, thirty years, thirty-five years, forty years.[27] "Well, he's an old guy, he's seventy-one, he's not feeling so well, so let's give him forty. It's effectively a life sentence." We are talking about *crimes against humanity* – rape camps, torture, mass murder, genocide. One of the mitigating factors was that he stepped aside from political office. He stepped aside from political office because he was indicted for crimes against humanity! The Dayton Accords said you cannot stand for political office if you've been indicted for crimes against humanity.[28] And the reason why is because this is perpetrator-centered justice. This is one of these key areas where the tribunal has rampantly failed to grasp and understand its role in the process of transitional justice. There are prosecutors doing the things that prosecutors do. Now this afflicts us as well – with the FBI and emails and stuff like that – sort of prosecutors operating in a very narrow mindset and a very narrow box. But the prosecutors should be thinking about – and the tribunals should be thinking about – the role that they're playing in victim healing, victim catharsis, deterrence, and signaling that these crimes are the most outrageous of outrageous crimes. If someone in about thirty states of the United States kills an individual and it's premeditated, they face the death penalty or life imprisonment. Many places, like New York, have gotten rid of it. But there's real incompatibility between a domestic crime and these, what are supposed to be the most heinous crimes. There's also a real disconnect between elite justice. So, if you're contemplating being a war criminal, be in charge, because then you're going to be tried in The Hague, or maybe in Arusha, and you'll get this type of considera-tion and you'll get this type of justice. But if you're a low-level perpetrator, you'll probably be tried by the domestic courts and you'll receive much more harsh justice. I think that's one reason we're having a blowback against the international tribunals from the victims. You're getting blowback from the perpetrators as well from certain countries, but you're getting it from the victims because they're not seeing it as

---

[26] Deirdre Montgomery, *ICTY Update: Cermak Defence Case – Sainovic et al. Appeal – Hartmann Conviction – Plavsic Early Release*, International Criminal Law Bureau (Sept. 23, 2009), www .internationallawbureau.com/index.php/icty-update-cermak-defence-case-sainovic-et-al-appeal-hart mann-conviction-plavsic-early-release/.

[27] *Judgement List*, International Criminal Tribunal for the Former Yugoslavia, www.icty.org/en/ cases/judgement-list (last visited Oct. 15, 2017).

[28] Raymond Bonner, *In Reversal, Serbs of Bosnia Accept Peace Agreement*, N.Y. Times (Nov. 24, 1995), www.nytimes.com/1995/11/24/world/in-reversal-serbs-of-bosnia-accept-peace-agreement.html.

justice they are familiar with, and that feeds into their need for victim healing, victim catharsis, and an accurate historical record.

Margaret deGuzman: I'm going to have to diplomatically disagree with my friend Paul. I think that, first of all, the Yugoslav tribunal judges in the statute were instructed to have recourse to the general practice in the former Yugoslavia in sentencing. In the former Yugoslavia, the maximum sentence for, I believe, any crime, was twenty years, so forty years is double that.[29] And they had the death penalty. So, twenty years or the death penalty. The Yugoslav tribunal is obviously not going to impose the death penalty, which violates human rights. So, I think that double the maximum sentence – other than the death penalty – in terms of sending a message to the local population, is quite in sync with local norms, in terms of punishment. It's not in sync with US norms, I completely agree with you there, but US norms are completely out of whack. I mean, they violate human rights. So, if you look at the rest of the world, we're outrageous. So, comparing, I really don't want anyone to think that the Yugoslav tribunal – or any of these international tribunals – should and in any way try and mimic US sentences.

I think the real question becomes how to think about these sentences in terms of the goals of the tribunal, and there I think we're on the same page. But to me, because this is a hybrid court – it has both transitional justice goals and global justice goals – and with regard to the transitional justice goals, I think looking at the domestic sentencing practices is appropriate and, as I said, I think it reflects those adequately. And then if you think about the global justice goals, I think that sentencing framework invokes human rights norms. I don't think that in sentencing, international tribunals – including the ICC, which has also started to sentence and has been criticized by some folks for sentences that don't appear as serious as they expect – but if we think about this in terms of human rights norms, I think that changes the way that we analyze these sentences.

Jenia Turner: To the question about the goals of the tribunals and how those sentences relate to the goals. To the extent that it's inconsistent with previous sentences of the tribunal – which I think it is – when you have lower-level offenders, or offenders who have committed fewer crimes and less serious crimes, being sentenced to life imprisonment or to forty years for less than what Karadzic did, I think that flies in the face of any norm, including human rights norms, whether it's retribution, or deterrence, rule of law, you name it. So, even if you take the human rights norm, I think that sentence was concerning.

Margaret deGuzman: Can I just respond to that? I'm not sure I agree with that either, because I think that kind of assumes retributive justice, ordinal proportionality analysis. It assumes that we should be ranking defendants according to their desert and punishing more those who deserve more, which I think for many people

---

[29] MARK A. DRUMBL, Atrocity, Punishment, and International Law 158 (2007).

that's easy to accept. I question that because I think that it's very hard, if not impossible, to determine what anybody deserves. I certainly wouldn't want to be the judge trying to do that, and I think if judges take a more utilitarian approach – rehabilitation, how much cost to the society, to this individual, do we have to incur to accomplish the nonretributive goals – it's a much more productive way to go.

Jenia Turner: Okay, real quick, I think you need to take the utilitarian perspective, the sentence has to be predictable. Utilitarianism doesn't work unless the sentence is predictable. So, I think it's strange to start worrying about rehabilitation when Karadzic's case comes around.

Milena Sterio: Actually, that's the perfect segue. I would like us to talk about the role of the tribunal, and this case in particular, on the region. What do we think? And this really goes back to the main function of these tribunals. When you go back to 1992–3, when you think of the Security Council resolution establishing the tribunal, I mean, we know that the threshold the Security Council needs to meet in order to act is that there is a breach of international peace and security.[30] But, you know, I think it goes well beyond that, and I was on this panel earlier this morning on Syria, and we were talking about this, and I said something that many people probably disagree with. I said that I'm not really sure how much the Yugoslavia tribunal – I don't know about Rwanda – but I'm not sure how much the Yugoslavia tribunal really contributed towards peace in the region. I think it maybe accomplished other goals, but I'm not really sure that it did much towards conflict resolution. And if you look at surveys today, there is actually an article that just came out in the American Journal of International Law by my colleague Marko Milanovich, who is a professor at Nottingham in the United Kingdom, where he talks about this, and all these surveys that he did in the region basically show you that, to this day, people in the region perceive the tribunals and perceive international justice very differently, and really based on their ethnic belonging.[31] So, unsurprisingly the Serbs still view the tribunal as this awful thing, and victor's justice, and "we're not the only blameworthy ones." So, I'm not sure what kind of long-lasting role the tribunal has had. Michael, why don't you start, and then Beth, if you want to weigh in on this.

Michael Scharf: So, I have a personal stake in this because twenty-some odd years ago, David Scheffer and I co-wrote the Security Council resolution and Madeline Albright's explanation of the vote on the creation of the Yugoslavia tribunal.

Milena Sterio: Do you stand by that?

---

[30] *See* Fausto Pocar, *Statute of the International Criminal Tribunal for the former Yugoslavia*, AUDIOVISUAL LIB. OF INT'L L., http://legal.un.org/avl/ha/icty/icty.html (last accessed Oct. 15, 2017).

[31] Marko Milanovich, *The Impact of the ICTY on the Former Yugoslavia: An Anticipatory Response*, 110 AM. J. OF INT'L L. 233 (2016).

Michael Scharf: I do not, and I'll tell you why. We stuck a clause into the Security Council resolution that said that this creation of the tribunal, and the trials it would have, would significantly foster peace and reconciliation in the region.[32] We did that based on what we believed was the Nuremberg experience. And that's because everybody at that time believed that Nuremberg had been responsible for the discrediting of the Nazi ideology and bringing the German people into a different mindset, so that they could join NATO and be supporters of international justice and all these international tribunals. A few years ago, the State Department declassified a document that they had been keeping secret. When this was published, I was one of the first people to cite it because it's really important. It was a document that indicated that the State Department had created a fiction – on purpose – about the role of Nuremberg. They had actually done opinion polls, like Gallup polls, in Germany at the time of Nuremberg and in the years subsequent, that found out that ninety-five percent of the German people did not believe that Nuremberg was fair and did not think that Hermann Goring and the other Nazis were guilty.[33] So, the idea that Nuremberg actually led to reconciliation and changed the minds of the German people was a fiction purposely perpetrated and hidden for fifty years by the US State Department – which we at the State Department didn't even know about – and therefore, we made a mistake, I think, in putting this in the Security Council resolution.

The reason it is a mistake is because it creates a heightened expectation for what the tribunal is going to accomplish. What happened, in fact, is when Milosevic was on trial, he did the same thing that Hermann Goering had done sixty years earlier, and that is he re-propagandized the population who were watching his trial day-by-day on television. And the polls indicated in Serbia that as the trial went along, there was a greater and greater wedge, rather than bringing people together.[34] Now, I think, in fact, that if you look at almost every international tribunal – Rwanda, Special Court for Sierra Leone, Cambodia, Lebanon, you name it – they've all had the short-term effect of wedging people apart rather than bringing people together. In the long run, however, they do create a historic record. But it might take generations before that historic record is embraced, and it takes other things. At Nuremberg, one of the things that happened was that the United States was an occupying power. For twenty years we wrote the history books that little German kids read, and so the narrative that they learned through our propaganda was to discredit the Nazis. That probably had more effect than the Nuremberg judgment itself. And what I believe strongly is that these international tribunals, in the end game, have to

---

[32] SC Res. 827 (May 25, 1993).

[33] Polls taken "from 1946 through 1958 indicated that over eighty percent of the West German people did not believe the findings of the Nuremberg tribunal and considered the Nuremberg proceedings to be nothing but 'acts of political retribution without firm legal basis.'" Michael P. Scharf, *Lessons from the Saddam Trial*, 39 CASE W. RES. J. INT'L L. 1, 4 (2007).

[34] KLAUS BACHMANN & Aleksandar Fatić, The UN International Criminal Tribunals: Transition Without Justice? 100–2 (2015).

come out with documentaries and other ways to have a public relations approach to make sure that whatever the historic lessons are, that it permeates the population. And even with that, I do think it takes generations for those effects to come through. And, so, as you said, there are other good reasons to have international tribunals and mechanisms, but we were wrong to stick that in the Security Council resolution because that was based on a myth.

Beth Van Schaack: I think Michael's absolutely right that some of the goals that motivated the creation of the early ad hoc tribunals were overly ambitious. We talked about reconciling communities, healing relationships. We talked about retribution, which we can argue about with the sentencing conversation. The creation of an accurate historical record so you could prevent the emergence of revisionist histories. We talked about deterrence, both specific deterrence with respect to particular perpetrators – neutralizing those individuals, taking them off the battlefield by virtue of a criminal process – and also more general deterrence, sort of sending a message of a reasonable expectation of accountability in the event that you breach international norms. And then there is always this other goal of expressivism, which Meg and others have written quite a bit about, which is the idea of articulating the international community's program around a particular set of acts.[35] So, if we look at those goals, I think it's pretty clear that reconciliation and healing have not been brought about by the tribunal, and may have, in fact – as Michael mentioned – been worsened. A lot of social science research now about counter-messaging shows that it is not just about what the message is; it's who the messenger is and how receptive the recipient is.[36] And so, if the messenger is illegitimate, the articulation of a counter-message will actually serve to reinforce the original belief rather than undermine or replace the original belief. And that may have been, a little bit, based upon the comments we heard today, what was happening in this particular region. It's very hard to test the deterrence questions. Even looking at deterrence in the immediate region, what we now know to be a genocide at Srebrenica happened after the tribunal had been established.[37] The goal was that the creation of the tribunal would cause individuals to stop and think before they joined campaigns of crimes against humanity, war crimes, or genocide. Would things have been worse had there not been a tribunal? Would things have been better had we established a tribunal earlier on, before individuals had already been associated with abuses? So, it was a sort of, "Well, I'm going to be

---

35 Margaret M. deGuzman, *Choosing to Prosecute: Expressive Selection at the International Criminal Court*, 33 MICH. J. INT'L L. 265 (2012).

36 *See, e.g.*, *ICSR Insight – The Power of the Swarm: Where Next for Counter-Messaging?*, INT'L CTR. FOR THE STUDY OF RADICALISATION AND POLITICAL VIOLENCE (July 12, 2016), http://icsr.info/2016/07/icsr-insight-power-swarm-next-counter-messaging/.

37 *See, e.g.*, *Aftermath*, UNITED STATES HOLOCAUST MEMORIAL MUSEUM, www.ushmm.org/confront-genocide/cases/bosnia-herzegovina/bosnia-aftermath ("On May 25, 1993, while the conflict in Bosnia continued – and a full year before the genocide at Srebrenica – the UN Security Council created the International Criminal Tribunal for the Former Yugoslavia (ICTY) to prosecute the perpetrators of the atrocities.")

prosecuted either way, I might as well go for the win," in this case. We can never test these things. There has been, though, some emergent empirical research coming out of the ICC by Beth Simmons and others that does suggest that the creation of the ICC, ratification, and movement on cases may be bringing about some sort of a deterrent effect within ICC situation countries.[38] That's still really recent research. It's really hard to test a negative, in a way, how things might have been different. We can't operate in parallel universes. So, what we come back to is what good was the tribunal if it doesn't bring about reconciliation, et cetera. We have the retributive goal, that individuals who committed crimes were subjected to penalties, and we have this expressivism, this idea that the international community, or an entity of the international community, articulating the fact that these norms are important and that they were breached in this particular situation. How that impacts things in the long term, I think we're still waiting to see.

Paul Williams: But for the Yugoslav tribunal, you would not have had short-term nor long-term peace in Bosnia or the former Yugoslavia. What the tribunal did is what diplomats couldn't do. It went into the political fabric of the former Yugoslavia and extracted those individuals who were responsible for war crimes, crimes against humanity, and denied them the ability to continue either furthering the conflict or furthering destabilization in the region. The tribunal indicted Karadzic and Mladic before the Dayton peace negotiations.[39] There is no way they could go to Dayton under an indictment, not that Dayton was a perfect agreement, but you got an agreement. Most commentators would acknowledge that that would not have happened if they were there. Biljana Plavsic served as the president of the Republika Srpska after the Dayton agreement. She was plucked out of Bosnia and sent to The Hague. Krajisnik served as one of the three rotating presidents of Bosnia-Herzegovina after the Dayton accords, happily continuing what he was trying to accomplish during the war. He was plucked out of Bosnia and served time for crimes against humanity. Prlic was the foreign minister of Bosnia after Dayton. He was plucked out of Bosnia and political society and sent to The Hague. President Milosevic of Serbia was plucked from Serbia, was sent from Serbia by Serbians after he served his term and presidency, and removed from the scene. You would not have the democratic Serbia that you have today – regardless of people's perspectives in Serbia of the tribunal – if Milosevic had not been indicted and if he had remained on the political scene in Serbia in order to continue his consolidation of power and his totalitarian regime.[40] In Kosovo, you have the leading negotiator and the deputy

---

[38] *See* Hyeran Jo & Beth Simmons, *Can the International Court Deter Atrocity?*, 70 INT'L ORG. 443 (2016).

[39] *See, e.g.*, Diane F. Orentlicher, *That Someone Guilty Be Punished*, INT'L CTR. FOR TRANSNATIONAL JUST., 26–7 (2010), www.ictj.org/sites/default/files/ICTJ-FormerYugoslavia-Someone-Guilty-2010-English.pdf.

[40] *See* SABRINA P. RAMET & VJERAN PAVLAKOVIC, Serbia Since 1989: POLITICS AND SOCIETY UNDER MILOSEVIC AND AFTER (2005).

negotiator, Milutinovic and Sainovic, both plucked from the political scene and sent to The Hague to serve time.

Now, what happens when you don't have a tribunal and you don't pluck people from the political scene? Well, you have the Gulf Cooperation Council Agreement in Yemen, where the very first paragraph of the agreement says that President Saleh has immunity, in 2011.[41] How'd that work out in Yemen? Saleh is one of the two primary protagonists at the moment of the brutal war that is occurring in Yemen. If we had a tribunal that had jurisdiction over the current conflict in Yemen, Saudi Arabia might actually employ better targeting practices, stop blowing up hospitals, stop blowing up schools. If we had had jurisdiction in Sri Lanka, you might have had a government that felt more constrained in the way in which it carried out its war against the LTTE and appear to be carried out against the Tamil population. Syria – if there was some type of jurisdiction over Syria, you might have at least thought before using chemical weapons, using barrel bombs, using atrocities as a means of conducting war by the Syrian government and the Syrian regime. I think one looks at the very practical aspects of building the peace process, and I emphasize this because there is a lot of, "Well, let's have justice later, let's do peace. Let the diplomats negotiate the agreements. We're saving lives. Don't clutter this with justice. Justice can't be politicized." No, justice plays a very practical role in removing individuals who make death camps, who do mass torture, who do mass killings, from the political environment so that you can have a healing process and you can have short-term as well as long-term political transformation.[42] And if we ignore it, we end up with our Yemens, and with our Syrias.

Michael Scharf: Just briefly, so students of criminal law know there are two types of deterrence: specific deterrence, which is what Paul was talking about – and I think he is absolutely right – and general deterrence, which is what Beth had alluded to. And I do want to mention one historic thing that we should all keep in mind. And that is what happens when you don't have any accountability. So, remember that in 1939, on the eve of Germany's invasion of Poland, when Hitler was telling his generals, "I want you to do total war and kill lots and lots of civilians and others." And the generals said, "We are not comfortable doing that, that's not what professional soldiers are trained to do." And he said, "What are you afraid of?" He said, "Who, after all, today remembers the fate of the Armenians?"[43] What he was telling them is that during World War I, when a million Armenians were killed by the Turks in what arguably was the first modern genocide, there was a treaty after the war – the

[41] *See* Agreement on the Implementation Mechanism for the Transition Process in Yemen in Accordance with the Initiative of the Gulf Cooperation Council (GCC) (May 12, 2011) UNTS.

[42] James Meernik & Kimi Lynn King, *The Effectiveness of International Law and the ICTY–Preliminary Results of an Empirical Study*, 1 INT'L. CRIM. L. REV. 343, 3–4 (2001).

[43] KEVORK B. BARDAKJIAN, Hitler and the Armenian Genocide (1985). This paraphrase is the English version of the German document handed to Louis P. Lochner in Berlin. For the German original *see Akten zur Deutschen Auswartigen Politik 1918–1945*, Serie D, Band VII, 171–2 (Baden-Baden, 1956).

Treaty of Lausanne – that gave complete amnesty to the Turks. Nobody was held responsible, and Hitler could focus on that and say, "Nobody is ever held responsible for these things, so you don't have anything to worry about."

And what is true is that *nobody* today can say, "Who remembers the fate of the Bosnians?" Because these crimes were proven in a court of law. There is a historic record. There is a video record. And, hopefully, this means that they cannot be used by the next Adolf Hitler as an excuse for ordering atrocities. I do think that's right, that there is now an age of accountability. And generals in particular – not necessarily dictators, because dictators are kind of crazy, they don't have good cost-benefit analysis and they don't think they are going to be caught – but the generals are the reasonable ones. They talk about these international courts. They have discussions about, "If we do that, we may be held to account in The Hague." I think that is what's changing.[44]

Jenia Turner: Something very brief – I actually want to second what Michael said earlier about the tribunals making documentaries. The *Karadzic* judgment is almost 3,000 pages long, and as important as that is for the historical record, I think if you're going to want to have an impact on the ground, you really need some other medium. I think documentaries are a great one. Just seconding what you said.

Milena Sterio: Now, in light of all that, we were just discussing the purpose and the rules of the tribunals in the region, let me ask the panelists: What do you think, how central is the genocide conviction? Would the tribunal play a different role in the region if we didn't have genocide convictions, even assuming that it does play an important role? Specifically focusing on transitional justice issues, how important do you think the genocide conviction itself is? Beth, do you want to start?

Beth Van Schaack: I'm not from the region, and I don't study it particularly, so it's hard to know. But I think Meg is right that it becomes about the genocide acquittal rather than the conviction of ten counts of war crimes, and crimes against humanity, and one count of genocide. And, so, the headline is always, "Karadzic acquitted of genocide." It's not, "Karadzic convicted of this." I think Cambodia will be very similar when those outcomes are – it's about the genocide. That's all the victims seem to care about.[45] So, I do worry a little bit that that will color the way in which this gets articulated. My sense in the region, though, is the individuals that were supportive of him or who may be associated with the group that he was associated with will feel that this is just another example of anti-Serb bias, whereas the victims'

---

[44] See, e.g., Aghavni Yeghiazaryan, *Nicholas Koumjian: "International Justice Prevents Atrocities,"* Aurora Prize, https://auroraprize.com/en/aurora/article/interview/9522/nicholas-koumjian-interna tional-justice-prevents-atrocities/2017.

[45] Harriet Fitch Little, *Forty Years After Genocide, Cambodia Finds Complicated Truth Hard to Bear,* The Guardian (Apr. 16, 2015), www.theguardian.com/world/2015/apr/16/forty-years-after-genocide-cambodia-finds-complicated-truth-hard-to-bear.

groups will say that this is just another example of why the tribunals are completely out of touch with our experience of victimhood. Sort of a pox on both houses.

Milena Sterio: That's exactly what the perception of the judgment itself was, where it was really criticized heavily on both sides.

Jenia Turner: I agree with that, and I was going to make the same comment. My sense of the reactions is that it just depends on who is interpreting it.

Michael Scharf: Let me ask a poll, this will be interesting, an unscientific poll. How many people in the room think that genocide is a more powerful, more important, or worse crime than crimes against humanity? Raise your hand.

Milena Sterio: We should have done this before and after. [laughter].

Margaret deGuzman: I think you have to clarify whether you mean: they think it's more powerful as a sociological phenomenon or they actually think it's a more serious crime.

Michael Scharf: Shall I divide it up?

Margaret deGuzman: Yeah, divide it up.

Michael Scharf: Okay. You ask it, Meg.

Margaret deGuzman: Okay. How many people think that, sociologically, that actually people in the world generally think that genocide is more serious than all the other crimes? [most raised their hands] Now, how many people think that genocide is in fact normatively a more serious crime? Most of you, okay. A few of you have not bought the argument, but most have.

Michael Scharf: The answer to number one, I think, explains why it is going to be seen as important that there was a partial acquittal, and why if the appeals court overturns the other part of genocide, there's going to be an outcry.

Margaret deGuzman: Wait, I'll say just one thing about that, and I was going to pick up on your point about long-term and short-term from before. I mean, I think we're talking right now about the short-term effect. But I don't think we should lose sight of the long-term as well. The effect on the region, just like Nuremberg, short-term it was rejected by a lot of folks. Long-term, it has had a tremendous effect in Germany and around the world.[46] I think that the ICTY and this conviction will have the same long-term effect.

Milena Sterio: I think that some of it is already happening, when you talk to the people in the region. I think it's generational. I think the newer generations don't

---

[46] Christian Tomuschat, *The Legacy of Nuremberg*, 4 J. INT'L CRIM JUST. 830, 830–44 (2006).

care about the conflict as much as their parents or their grandparents did. So, I do think this question of long-term effect is a very important one.

The tribunal in the *Karadzic* case, and some other cases, has been criticized for certain things. For example, the prosecutor's failure to disclose potentially exculpatory evidence in a timely fashion.[47] Maybe this is just details, maybe it wouldn't have affected the Karadzic conviction, but do you perceive those procedural failures as undermining the overall legacy of the tribunal? Paul, do you want to start?

Paul Williams: Yeah, just briefly. I think the defense attorney has a whole long list of ways in which Karadzic might not have received a fair trial.[48] But I think one has to acknowledge that these trials are exceedingly complex because the crimes with which these individuals are charged are exceedingly complex, and there is a process of indictment, *prima facie*. There's other pretrial hearings and things along those lines. And there's oftentimes this, "Let's apply the American standard of sentencing to the tribunal." I think there's also this notion of, "Let's apply the American standard of all of that due process, and all of that disclosure, to these out-of-the-ordinary, complex tribunals." So, I think that presumably there were various missteps along the way and information that wasn't shared early enough – X, Y, or Z. But in the context of the overwhelming evidence and the overwhelming testimony that was brought to bear, I think they are exceedingly minor.

Milena Sterio: Meg, do you agree?

Margaret deGuzman: Yeah, you're grinning because I'm a defense attorney. [laughter]. Yes, I do think – I mean, I didn't follow the procedural irregularities enough to speak with authority on this question. But my general sense is that the evidence is sufficiently strong to overcome whatever those procedural irregularities were. And just to sort of bolster the idea, the standard is the human rights standard. I do think that it is very important that these tribunals express – one of the things they are expressing, in addition to the condemnation of the crimes – is the importance of defendants' rights and adhering to due process standards. So, when those issues come up, I think it's very important to pay close attention to them. And at the same time, I think in this particular case there was significant evidence that made that balance.

---

[47] *See* Prosecutor v. Karadzic, Case No. MICT-13-55R90.3, *Prosecution Response to Karadzic's Request to Designate Single Judge to Consider Appointing an Amicus Curiae Prosecutor*, Int'l Crim. Trib. for the Former Yugoslavia (Jun. 2, 2014).

[48] *See, e.g.,* Radosa Milutinovic, *Radovan Karadzic Appeals against Genocide Conviction*, BALKAN TRANSNATIONAL INSIGHT (Jul. 22, 2016), www.balkaninsight.com/en/article/karadzic-files-appeal-notice-07-22-2016 ("The trial chamber considered him guilty in advance and then constructed the verdict to justify its presumption," Robinson added. Karadzic insisted that the presumption of innocence was "violated" even before the beginning of his trial because the judges failed to "limit the amorphous indictment and make sure the prosecution would respect its obligation to disclose its evidence to the defence.")

Jenia Turner: On the disclosure issue. There were a number of motions by the defense – a number of which were sustained – on delayed disclosure of material, and in some cases, potentially exculpatory evidence. So, the chamber did look at those motions, they gave time to the defense, they gave extra time to defense to catch up. And I can understand the problems that the prosecution had because I think they turned over two million, close to three million, pages of documents. Anyone who has been on a complex civil litigation case knows what that means. That said, the defense, for the most part, and perhaps not in the *Karadzic* case, but in general, the defense has to rely on disclosure extensively because the defense does not have the same resources, and oftentimes is facing a hostile state when it's trying to investigate these cases. Disclosure is extremely important to a fair trial, so I think that it is an issue, and it's an issue that has faced the ICC as well. And that's an issue that we all need to be thinking about – how to manage disclosure with these millions of documents in a way that doesn't impact the fair trial of the accused.

Milena Sterio: Sure, and we all know how long these cases have taken and how frustrated many were that Milosevic, that his case was never completed. But is there a way around it, really? Beth?

Beth Van Schaack: Just to point out one other procedural innovation that might be of interest to people in the audience and that is sort of emerging within international criminal law as somewhat of a standard practice. And that is this idea of taking judicial notice of adjudicated facts.[49] The prosecutor in some respects did a pyramidal approach to these cases, as we would expect from a domestic prosecutor, starting with lower-level individuals and sort of working their way up to the leaders, the architects, individuals who were exercising command authority over the actual, physical perpetrators. And what we saw in the ICTY, and that has been raised in the appellate papers by the defendant, is an overwhelming reliance upon previously adjudicated facts. So, in the old days, we had to argue about whether there was an armed conflict, when the armed conflict began, how to classify that armed conflict, which crimes were adjudicatable emerging out of that armed conflict. None of that went forward. Was there a widespread or systematic attack against a civilian population? None of that had to be re-adjudicated because it had already been adjudicated with respect to these particular geographic localities and subordinates under the defendant. And so, on the one hand, there's efficiency gains, of course, to doing that. Why should we have to fight about whether this was a noninternational armed conflict or not? Of course, it's been established three or

---

[49] E.g., Prosecutor v. Popovic, Case No. IT-05–88-A, Judgment, Int'l Crim. Trib. for the Former Yugoslavia (Jan. 30, 2015) ("The Appeals Chamber considers that a trial chamber may exercise its discretionary power to determine whether to take judicial notice of an adjudicated fact, even if the fact may have been less central to the charges in the previous proceedings of the Tribunal than in the current proceedings, so long as the adjudicated fact has been 'established by the Trial Chamber [in the previous proceedings] on the basis of evidence.'")

four times that it was, and eventually became an international armed conflict. Nonetheless, Karadzic himself didn't get to make the arguments he would have liked to have been able to make, because it was so well established at that point. And so, there's the risk, of course, is that we start having these trials go fully on the papers, potentially to the detriment of defendants, who want to be able to make their own best arguments and are not capable of doing so because a court takes judicial notice.

Milena Sterio: Now, I have one last question for our panelists and then we'll open it up to your questions. I want to talk about the appellate process really briefly. The case is currently on appeal. Both Karadzic and the prosecution have appealed. The appeal is now within the residual mechanism because the ICTY itself is supposed to complete the *Mladic* trial and then shut down. I was hoping at the time that I proposed this panel that we would be farther along in that appellate process, however, as of now we don't really have a clear indication of how long that will take. The briefs are now due on December 5 of this year, and then we'll see what the residual mechanism does with those. I want to ask each of our panelists – and you're on tape, Michael has this vintage recorder [laughter] – what is your best prediction regarding the appeal? If you had to guess and say what you think will happen. Beth, let's start with you. What do you think?

Beth Van Schaack: I think it's going to be largely affirmed. I can't imagine there's going to be much innovation either on the facts or the law. I don't know if others disagree with me.

Jenia Turner: I agree with that. Sentencing might change, that is my prediction, one possibility. The other thing I would say is, even if the appellate chamber does reverse the conviction on genocide – which I wouldn't place a serious bet on it, but it's possible – even if they do that, there's still the command responsibility. So, even if they change the mode of liability, I think there's certainly a lot more on the command responsibility side of things.

Milena Sterio: And on the sentencing, do you think the sentence is likely to go up or down?

Jenia Turner: Oh, I think it might go up.

Beth Van Schaack: Just to weigh in on the point here, which I think is important, this point on command responsibility. The use of forms of responsibility here that Michael sort of outlined for us really helpfully was really interesting. The trial chamber was very careful to often make findings on multiple and potentially redundant grounds – JCE I, where the individual shares the intent of the group of individuals who are trying to implement a criminal enterprise; JCE III, where the crimes that occurred were maybe not part of the original plan of this group of confederates, but were nonetheless foreseeable to that group.[50] And then also command responsibility, which says even if Karadzic didn't share the intent, or even if the crimes themselves were not foreseeable at the time the JCE was formed, if he knew or should have known that subordinates were committing offenses, either failed to prevent them *ex ante* or failed to punish them *ex post*, he can still be held liable. The tribunal, the trial chamber, made findings and rulings on those. So, as Jenia mentioned, you could imagine the appeals chamber tinkering with which counts fell under which form of responsibility, but you might end up with the same outcome.

Michael Scharf: The president of the Appeals Mechanism is Ted Meron, a former Israeli legal advisor, then an American advisor to the State Department, a professor at NYU. He's known as being very tough in both sentencing and tends to be pro-prosecution in his decisions. I think that if he's the president of the tribunal, we're going to probably see a more pro-prosecution outcome. [on September 27, 2017, Judge Meron withdrew from the Karadzic Appeal after the defense accused him of bias].

Paul Williams: I think, even in light of Mike's comments, the trial chamber got it right. The appeals court will either be tough or conservative, and will affirm. Despite my hopes for an increased sentence, I'm guessing they'll probably stick with the forty years.

Margaret deGuzman: Yeah, I don't think I disagree with what's been said. I would just add that with regard to the genocide conviction, and the intent issue, I think it's too wrapped up in issues of the fact finder evaluating credibility of witnesses for the appeals chamber to really change that.

Milena Sterio: Well, we have at least fifteen minutes or so for your questions. So, raise your hand and, if you can, keep your questions brief. Why don't we take three questions?

Audience Member: I'm wondering what you think of the notion that perhaps there's an argument to be made that, when you're invoking past genocidal acts in committing new genocidal acts, that may give rise to harsher sentencing in the case. For example, in the Balkan wars, there were echoes and invocations of the acts that were committed during World War II by the Chetniks on the Serb side and by the Ustashe on the Croat side. And as a second, separate question, I'm curious what the panel thinks of the rhetoric going on right now with Native American groups here in the United States

---

[50] *See, e.g.,* Attila Bogdan, *Individual Criminal Responsibility in the Execution of a "Joint Criminal Enterprise" in the Jurisprudence of the ad hoc International Tribunal for the Former Yugoslavia*, 6 INT'L CRIM. LAW REV. 63 (2006).

using the term "genocide" with regard to things like the Dakota Access Pipeline.[51]

Milena Sterio: Another question?

Audience Member: Thank you to the panel for a fascinating discussion. Using the Armenian example as something that we can learn from what happens when you don't have a tribunal. In the 1940s, Armenians and Jews had a wealth tax imposed on them. Armenians to this day and Kurds to this day are persecuted in Turkey. You have a Turkey that has, up until recently, been playing "footsie" with ISIS, and ISIS is committing genocidal attacks. How can the international community address this lack of accountability for the Armenian genocide today, and does the international community, or nations subject to the Genocide Convention, have a duty to prevent genocide, and as part of that duty, do they have a duty to confront genocide denial rather than aid and abet it, as the United States has been doing by opposing congressional efforts to condemn the Armenian genocide?

Milena Sterio: We'll take one more question. There's somebody up here.

Audience Member: So, the panel talked a bit about a high, or mushy, burden of proof within the court as well as procedural errors within the tribunal. So, I just wanted to ask if anyone on the panel had insights into how these factors played into the acquittal of Seselj and any insights into how that could progress in the future with an appeal.[52]

Moderator: Sure. Beth, do you want to start? And feel free to answer one, or all, of the questions.

Beth Van Schaack: Well, those are tough questions. So, the history question is an interesting one, because if you remember reading some of the first opinions that came out of the tribunal and then the press around these events, they almost always go back in history, right? They always start with, in the Bosnian situation, in the 1300s. There were events there that got invoked by perpetrators as, "We're finally getting justice, we're finally turning the tables." And a lot of the press around the work of the ICTY talked about "long-standing ethnic animosities" and "deep-seated historical hatreds," and created a sort of image of inevitability about this, that this was just a repeat of the past rather than, I think, really focusing on the role that political leaders were playing in fomenting groups and bringing people together based upon what are, in many respects, arbitrary ethnic grounds, and creating this system of

---

[51] *See, e.g., "This Nation Was Founded on Genocide": MSNBC's Lawrence O'Donnell on Dakota Access,* INDIAN COUNTRY TODAY (Aug. 26, 2016), https://indiancountrymedianetwork.com/news/politics/this-nation-was-founded-on-genocide-msnbcs-lawrence-odonnell-on-dakota-access/.

[52] *See* Marlise Simons, *Vojislav Seselj, Serbian Nationalist, Is Acquitted of War Crimes by Hague Tribunal,* N.Y. TIMES (Mar. 31, 2016), www.nytimes.com/2016/04/01/world/europe/vojislav-seselj-war-crimes.html.

fear.[53] Basically, you had something to fear from this other group – that they were going to seize power, or resources, or your property, or your daughters, or whatever it is. And I think that's really a nefarious kind of narrative, but we do see it repeating. And so, this idea of the past predicting the future, I think, was very much present in that phenomenon.

Jenia Turner: Just following up on that, the judgment does talk about that narrative a lot, explaining and talking about this notion of how they created the narrative of, "We can't live with Bosnian Muslims and we have to have our own territory. Oil and water don't mix because there has been this historical grievance and there will be genocide against us otherwise." So, this very much comes out in the judgment. Now as to your question about should it influence sentencing, I am not sure that it should influence sentencing as such, but I think it does help explain how these conflicts are created, number one, and number two, it helps us understand what the mechanism was to create this plan. I mean, a lot of judgment is about the creation of this plan of displacing, ethnic cleansing, displacing Bosnian Muslims. So, I think it definitely plays a lot in that narrative and the judgment really does address it quite a bit.

On the Armenian genocide, I am not sure that judicially you can address it at this point, simply because there's not any people who are alive that could be prosecuted. You know, as far as truth commission or some historical record creation, I think that's a different question. And Europe, of course, has been sort of a battleground for these Armenian genocide denial laws. I think countries have taken very different views on it in large part because of different notions of free speech. The United Kingdom and some of the Scandinavian countries are much more kind of concerned about possibly – just like they are generally with hate speech – concerned about where the line is, and countries like France and Germany are more open to it. It's just a very different view on what the line on hate speech is. That's all I can say about that.

Michael Scharf: So, on the first question about past genocidal acts and also what Beth said about how, because of the need for efficiency, these tribunals are starting to take judicial notice of the proof of genocide in previous cases. I was at the Rwanda tribunal when an American defense counsel named Peter Erlinder argued that it was unfair for the court not to allow him to argue that the genocide didn't occur just because in a previous case they had found that it did occur, because the previous lawyer, he said, was completely incompetent, and he was going to do a much better job of disproving it, and he should have that ability and that chance.[54] He was not

---

[53] *See, e.g.*, James Meernik & Jose Raul Guerrero, *Can International Criminal Justice Advance Ethnic Reconciliation? The ICTY and Ethnic Relations in Bosnia-Herzegovina*, 14 Se. Eur. and Black Sea Stud. 383 (2014).

[54] *See, e.g.*, Peter Erlinder, *"Genocide Denial" in Rwanda: Questioning the Official View of History*, Global Research (Oct. 27, 2014), www.globalresearch.ca/genocide-denial-in-rwanda-questioning-the-official-view-of-history/5410169.

given that chance. And I was a little sympathetic to that argument, even though the story in Rwanda is fairly one-sided and compelling.

The second thing I wanted to mention is, when I speak, I often do that quote about Adolf Hitler and "who remembers the Armenians," and I always get a bunch of people afterwards who are pro-Turkey coming in and saying, "There was no genocide, it was never proven." And I think that is what happens when you don't have a judicially-created historic record. We didn't have one, as Milena mentioned, about the full genocide, the scope of the genocide in Bosnia, because the Milosevic trial – which set out to prove that – ended with his death, and they decided they weren't going to have a judgment. They temporarily erased history. So, one of the most important things about the *Karadzic* case is that in 1,100 pages they are telling a story through judicial decision-making that was not able to be told because of the death of Milosevic, and hopefully will change people's minds down the road.

The final thing I want to mention about the *Seselj* case. Paul and I were at Nuremberg a month ago when Serg Brammertz was asked at a panel, "What do you think about the *Seselj* decision?" He says, "Listen, I've never done this before. The appeal is pending, but I've got to tell you this was the worst decision ever. It is totally unfounded, and if they don't change it on appeal, I'm going to be going around telling everybody that there was a travesty of justice, which you normally don't see your former prosecutors doing." And so, I think we have to wait and see what happens on appeal. He was pretty confident that things would be changed on appeal. [the Appeals Chamber ultimately reversed the acquittal]

Paul Williams: Okay, I feel like we are playing panel Jeopardy. And so, if I look at the board, the only question remaining is that Native American Dakota access, so I'll go with Dakota Access for 200. [laughter]. I'm glad you asked that question, it gets to the point about a narrative of which we were talking about earlier about genocide. If you're looking at the history of genocide against the Native Americans in the United States, it is really quite clear. But the current situation with the Dakota Access is one of Native American lands, sacred lands, burial sites, running an oil pipeline under the only source of drinking water, but they threw out the word "genocide." And folks will be like, "Genocide? It's a pipeline. And it's sacred sites. And it's water pollution. It's not really genocide. And so what are they all worked up about?" And they lose, it distracts. They put the term in there, but it distracts from the fact that you're running a pipeline through their sacred land. And you're running it through their only source of water. There's environmental issues. There's religious issues. There's cultural heritage issues. Those things people should be excited and dynamic about and that should be the conversation, which would probably go further towards, you know, finding a way to redirect this pipeline. But because they feel that in our sort of post-caring environment, where even domestically unless it's genocide, "well whatever, we don't really care, it's okay not to care." They feel that they have to grasp for the genocide. They're not going to get it, and folks are going to shrug their shoulders and everyone will forget about it four months from now.

Margaret deGuzman: I'm going to go for double Jeopardy and see what the next question is. [Laughter.]

Milena Sterio: We'll take two more questions.

Audience Member: I worked with the ECCC in Cambodia and that's how I'm going to frame my question. So, I actually thought of posing this question in terms of "food for thought" in terms of how we think about such criminal tribunals. On one hand, there is an international perspective, and on the other hand is the truth-seeking for locals. So, my experience with the ECCC was that the long, complicated trials were not what the Cambodians were looking for. A lot of times they participated in it. A lot of things got lost in translation and half the time there were arguments over things like "is this a leading question or not," which is not relevant to them. All they wanted was someone to hold accountable and someone to say, "I'm sorry." And I guess that's what the decision did for them. But, on the international side, you always have this whole paradigm about due process. And I mean, even before this court, in 1998, the Cambodians actually tried Pol Pot in absentia and sentenced him to death. And the international community looked at it and said, "Look, you can't try someone in absentia. He needs his due process." But to the Cambodians, I think that was something more of what they wanted. And then, my last question is on acquittals. Are acquittals necessarily bad? Because in the ECCC, the whole track record has just been convictions so far. And one of the questions was, if this is not a rigged tribunal, if there is due process and there is defense, surely at some point in time there would be acquittals. And instead of saying that acquittals denied them legitimacy, the truth, perhaps acquittals together with convictions could lead to a sphere in which, you know, the truth has really been out there because of the difference in the narratives.

Milena Sterio: Okay, one last question.

Audience Member: Hi, thank you very much for giving me a chance to ask my question. I'm from Turkey but I'm not one of those Turks. [laughter].

Milena Sterio: Not a genocide denier. [laughter].

Audience Member: My question is about the transitional justice in the area of the former Yugoslavia. So, I'm aware of a lot of arguments ongoing against the ICTY, saying that it's biased, and it's biased against Serbia and Serbians.[55] In 2013, there was

---

[55]   *See, e.g.,* Evan Bruning et al., *Partial Impartiality: A Review of Alleged Bias in the International Criminal Tribunal for the Former Yugoslavia,* Ne. U. Pol. Rev. (Apr. 15, 2016), www .nupoliticalreview.com/2016/04/25/partial-impartiality-a-review-of-alleged-bias-in-the-international-criminal-tribunal-for-the-former-yugoslavia/.

a judge, a Danish judge, who was disqualified, saying that ICTY is biased and I think he also mentioned that ICTY didn't address NATO bombings and all this stuff. I wonder what you think about this issue. And do you also think that these events hampered transitional justice and decreased the reliability of the courts?

Milena Sterio: I'm going to ask our panelists to respond in a minute each. And maybe, Meg, would you like to start?

Margaret deGuzman: So, I'll just say one quick thing about the legitimacy of the ICTY, transitional justice, and NATO bombings. I think that international justice is not perfect. This is a hybrid court and, as I said before, I think that this means that it has both local and global justice objectives. And it's not perfect, and it has not been and will not be perfect on either one. I think if we take a long-term view, we can be much more sanguine about its effects on transitional justice, local justice, than if we take a short-term view. And I think the same can be said at the global justice level. It's true, there was no accountability for – or even a full investigation of – some of the NATO actions in the region. And that's too bad. Power politics behind that are unfortunate. But I don't think we should strongly condemn the legitimacy of the ICTY too strongly according to that, because we know that's power politics, that's the reality going into these things.

Paul Williams: I think acquittals are a good thing if there is insufficient evidence to prove the guilt of those that have been charged. Tribunals are timid, and they are tardy, and they do make mistakes. And you do want to guard against victor's justice. And so, in the case of *Seselj,* "Oops." The court of appeals will fix that. But on other acquittals, I think the tribunal, at least the Yugoslavia tribunal, has been very clear-eyed and has demanded a high standard of proof.

Michael Scharf: So, about the Cambodia tribunal. I was, on my sabbatical, a special assistant to Robert Petit, when he was the chief prosecutor.[56] And I would say they are long trials, but they've had short, historic moments that everybody in Cambodia is going to remember, which will make them effective. In the *Duch* trial, the Defendant confessed. He was the camp commander of Tuol Sleng, and he confessed. Nobody's going to forget that. There's no denying that that occurred. And in the case of brother number one, there's a video of him playing chess and confessing. And the question he asked in this video was extraordinary. The partner said, "Do you feel bad about all the people you killed that were innocent?" And he says, "Look, it's like being a doctor. You remove the cancer, you've got to remove some skin that's noncancerous around it. And so we did that. Yes, lots of innocent people were killed, but I had to do this for my country." Boom! The people are going to remember that. He was guilty. He admitted it. So, I do think the Cambodia tribunal in some ways is

---

[56] See, e.g., Robert Petit, *Lawfare and International Tribunals: A Question of Definition: A Reflection on the Creation of the "Khmer Rouge Tribunal,"* 43 CASE W. RES. J. INT'L L. 189 (2010).

more effective than other tribunals because you have the defendants acknowledging their guilt.

Beth Van Schaack: Just a short theme that ran though both of those questions, and that is this relationship between transitional justice and international justice, in other words, criminal trials. Yesterday, or the day before, there was a really interesting panel at the New York Bar Association run by Elena Baylis on this question of what is the interaction between those two.[57] The idea of the truth commission, which was invoked with respect to Cambodia, emerged in Latin America, where trials were foreclosed because there was a general amnesty that had been imposed on the situation that essentially extinguished any civil claims and prevented the ability to bring criminal claims on the part of the state. So, the truth commission emerged as a sort of consolation prize – "We can't have real accountability, and so we'll give victims an opportunity to bear witness, and we'll create a sort of historical record and write a report and put in some recommendations in there in terms of reform." And what we've learned is, that what started out as sort of a consolation prize actually has a lot of merit in and of itself. There are things that truth commissions and other transitional justice mechanisms can accomplish that now we know – bringing us full circle to the first question of the day – trials just cannot do and are not good at that. Trials are good at certain things, but they are not good at other things. I think as an international community, we need to think a lot more creatively about how to layer and how to sequence these different transitional justice mechanisms so that you have criminal trials, perhaps for those most responsible, and for some emblematic criminal acts that happened in a conflict. Maybe you can't have criminal justice for everything. Then you also have a truth commission, where you give victims a chance to really bear witness, to tell their full story, and not just that little slice of the story that's necessary to convict an individual. But let them start at the beginning and tell their story. And then you create another historical record, but one that can maybe lay the groundwork for reform, reconciliation, et cetera, moving forward. So, I think both of those questions really touched on this idea of the limitations at trials and other ways we can accomplish those very lofty goals that we hope to accomplish with this system of international justice.

Milena Sterio: Well, we will end our panel on that note. Please join me in thanking our panelists.

---

[57] *See, e.g.*, Elena A. Baylis, *Reassessing the Role of International Criminal Law: Rebuilding National Courts through Transnational Networks*, 50 B.C. L. Rev. 1 (2009).

5

Atrocity Speech Law Comes of Age

The Good, the Bad and the Ugly of the International Speech Crimes Jurisprudence at the Ad Hoc Tribunals

Gregory S. Gordon*

5.1 INTRODUCTION

Resuscitated amidst the explosion of early-1990s mass internecine violence in the Balkans and Rwanda, the post-Cold War international criminal law project, which had begun at Nuremberg, faced daunting challenges. Apart from harnessing the tremendous resources and goodwill needed to create a from-scratch judicial infrastructure, an intricate international cooperation regime and a culture-clash legal cadre, there was a distinct dearth of doctrine. Jurisprudence on war crimes and crimes against humanity had been frozen in a World War II-era time warp, and the offense of genocide had never been adjudicated before an international court. Thus, apart from its historic revival of the global-prosecution ethos and its meting out punishment to the atrocity architects, the case law of the ad hoc tribunal experiment may be its most important legacy. Many have rightfully expressed gratitude for its stitching from whole cloth a comprehensive corpus of law in reference to genocide, or its breakthroughs in assigning liability to sexual violence, among other accomplishments. But one of the signal ad hoc tribunal achievements often omitted in the encomia is the body of law developed governing the relationship between speech and atrocity.

This Chapter is devoted to analyzing that achievement. While much ink has been spilt in other contexts dissecting the offense of incitement to genocide, the International Criminal Tribunal for Rwanda (ICTR) and the International Criminal Tribunal for the former Yugoslavia (ICTY) have gone well beyond that

* Professor of law and former associate dean (Development/External Relations) and director, Research Postgraduates Programme, The Chinese University of Hong Kong Faculty of Law. Professor Gordon has previously worked with the Office of the Prosecutor for the International Criminal Tribunal for Rwanda, where he served as Legal Officer and Deputy Team Leader for the landmark "Media Cases," the first international post-Nuremberg prosecutions of radio and print media executives for international speech crimes. He is one of the world's foremost authorities on incitement to genocide, and his book *Atrocity Speech Law: Foundation, Fragmentation, Fruition*, proposing a new paradigm for hate speech in international criminal law, was published by Oxford University Press in 2017. In 2018, Professor Gordon received the university's Research Excellence Award.

offense in developing the jurisprudence. Hate speech as the crime against humanity of persecution, instigation and ordering have also loomed large in the calculus of individual criminal responsibility for rhetoric that foments or fuels mass violence. In that sense, the work of the ad hoc tribunals represents a significant growth phase, when atrocity speech law realized its essential form and came of age, perhaps before achieving its final flowering. Thus, if Nuremberg represented the birth of this legal corpus, then the ad hoc tribunals might be said to represent its adolescence.

But while adolescence is a period of growth, it is also a period of awkward transition. And the atrocity speech jurisprudence of the ICTR and the ICTY reflects that. Confronting the International Criminal Court, as well as any other future ad hoc or municipal adjudicators, will be a slew of problems created or left unresolved by the ICTR and ICTY. These include, *inter alia*, issues of causation in respect of incitement, noninciting hate speech in reference to persecution, the degree of a speech's contribution to violence as regards instigation and the prospect of inchoate liability for the offense of ordering. But in deciding these issues, courts in coming years will greatly benefit from the important elemental groundwork and policy insights shared over the span of more than two decades by ICTY/ICTR jurists from around the world.

In considering that contribution, as well as some of its problematic aspects, this Chapter proceeds in four parts. After this introduction, Section 5.2 provides a background into the atrocities perpetrated in the former Yugoslavia during that country's early 1990s disintegration and in Rwanda during the 1994 genocide against the Tutsis. In addition to exploring the role speech played in sparking and fueling those atrocities, this section examines the establishment of the ICTY and ICTR and provides an overview of the key atrocity speech law cases decided by those tribunals. Section 5.3 then considers the atrocity speech law jurisprudence developed by the ad hoc tribunals. Analysis of this case law is divided according to the key speech offenses, beginning with incitement to genocide, and then moving on to persecution, instigation and ordering. Section 5.4 then considers the legacy of this jurisprudence – its key contributions as well as some of the thornier issues it has created or questions it has left unresolved. The Chapter then concludes with some final reflections in Section 5.5 on needed areas of development in this body of law as well as prospects for future justice.

5.2 BACKGROUND: POST-COLD WAR ETHNIC SLAUGHTER AND THE ADVENT OF THE AD HOC TRIBUNALS

5.2.1 *Atrocities in the Balkans*

5.2.1.1 Disintegration and Ethnic Cleansing

Under the leadership of resistance hero Josip Broz Tito, the post-World War II confederation of Yugoslav states became the Social Federal Republic of Yugoslavia

(SFRY), a cohesive joining in one nation of Serbs, Croats, Muslims, Slovenes, Albanians, Macedonians and Montenegrins.[1] In the fuller light of history, though, Tito appears to have been the personal glue that held the union together.[2] With his death in 1980, followed by a decline in the country's economic fortunes and the gradual collapse of communism (coextensive with the rest of Eastern Europe), Yugoslavia's ethnic and political cohesion began to fray.[3] By May 1991, Croatian and Slovenian declarations of secession from the Serbian-dominated central government in Belgrade meant the state was coming apart.[4]

The most ethnically diverse of SFRY's six federal units, with a population that was 44 percent Muslim, 31 percent Serb and 17 percent Croatian, Bosnia-Herzegovina also began making noise about breaking away from the mother country. One year later it did, having declared independence in March 1992.[5] This did not please Bosnia's extremist Serb contingent, led by Radovan Karadžić, head of the Serb Democratic Party (SDS). In October 1991, as Bosnian independence loomed large on the horizon, Karadžić had issued a candid genocidal warning to Bosnian Muslims considering an independence vote: "This might lead Bosnia into a hell and [cause] one people to disappear."[6] The Bosnian choice to secede triggered the prophesied SDS response. With backing from the neighboring Serbian army, they launched an armed conflict with the goal of seizing control of the state and subjecting its non-Serb citizens to a campaign of murderous ethnic cleansing.[7]

The forces at Karadžić's disposal, led by Bosnian Serb General Radko Mladić and aided by various paramilitary groups, captured close to seventy percent of the would-be country's territory.[8] By then, the ethnic cleansing campaign had begun. The territory's Muslim and Croatian population were brutalized through waves of murder, torture, rape and other inhuman treatment meant to drive them over the frontiers so as to "purify" the country.[9] All of this "ethnic cleansing" culminated

---

[1] ROBERT J. DONIA, Radovan Karadzic: Architect of the Bosnian Genocide 11 (2015).

[2] *Id.* at 17.

[3] *Id. See also* Branka Magas, The Destruction of Yugoslavia: Tracking the Break-Up 1980–1992, Introduction, xii–xiii (1993).

[4] Roger P. Alford, *The Self-Judging WTO Security Exception*, 2011 UTAH L. Rev. 697, 716 (2011).

[5] Paul Williams & Jennifer Harris, *State Succession to Debts and Assets: The Modern Law and Policy*, 42 HARV. INT'L L.J. 355, 385 (2001) (chronicling the date of Bosnia-Herzegovina's withdrawal from SFRY); Patrick Robinson, *The Interaction of Legal Systems in the Work of the International Criminal Tribunal for the Former Yugoslavia*, 16 ILSA J. INT'L & COMP. L. 5, 13 (2009) (detailing the ethnic breakdown in Bosnia-Herzegovina).

[6] KEMAL KURSPAHIC, Prime Time Crime: Balkan Media in War and Peace 97 (2003).

[7] David Binder, *C.I.A. Doubtful on Serbian Sanctions*, N.Y. TIMES, Dec. 22, 1993, at A3 (reporting that the Serbian Government supplied the Serbian forces which took control of more than two-thirds of Bosnia).

[8] *Id.*

[9] Lindsay Peterson, *Shared Dilemmas: Justice for Rape Victims under International Law and Protection for Rape Victims Seeking Asylum*, 31 HASTINGS INT'L & COMP. L. REV. 509, 512 (2008) ("In the late 1980s and early 1990s, Croatia, Slovenia, and Bosnia declared independence and Bosnian Serbs initiated a policy of ethnic cleansing to rid the nation of Croats and Muslims.")

infamously at the Srebrenica massacre in July 1995, the worst slaughter of civilians in Europe since World War II – and later declared to be a genocide.[10]

5.2.1.2 The Role of Hate Speech

An integral part of the Bosnian Serb ethnic cleansing campaign was the pervasive use of hate speech. This virulent anti-Muslim/Croat propaganda stirred up mutual fear and hatred that incited the Bosnian Serb population against the other ethnicities.[11]

In order to disseminate the propaganda, the SDS planned the takeover of the Bosnian radio media infrastructure, which was television-focused at that time.[12] At the beginning of August 1991, as part of war preparations, an SDS/Yugoslav-backed militia called the "Wolves of Vučjak" wrested control of the TV transmitter on Kozara Mountain between Banjaluka and Prijedor.[13] Other Bosnian Serb militia groups then hijacked transmitters in the enclaves of Plješevica, Doboj, Trovrh, Velež and Vlašić, and thereby handed over the country's television airwaves to the SDS.[14] Bosnian Muslim and Bosnian Croat TV station employees were subsequently sacked and supplanted by Bosnian Serbs.[15] Nontelevision broadcast and print media were also seized. In effect, all of Bosnia's Fourth Estate was purged of Muslim and Croat journalists, only to be replaced by their Bosnian Serb counterparts.[16]

5.2.1.3 The Substance of Bosnian Serb Propaganda

In this way, citizens of the fledgling country had no access to Bosnia's previously irenic broadcast discourse that "had one constant line in the months leading to the war . . . their opposition to the war."[17] In contrast, the toxic SDS message of "all Serbs in a single state" (supplementing that of Serbian president Slobodan Milošević) saturated the headlines and airwaves in ethnically mixed towns throughout Bosnia.[18] Noel Malcolm explains that "it was as if all the TV stations in the USA had been taken over by the Ku Klux Klan."[19]

---

[10]   *Id. See also* Aleksandar Marsavelski, *The Crime of Terrorism and the Right of Revolution in International Law*, 28 CONN. J. INT'L L. 243, 264 n.123 (2013) ("Perhaps the most notable example is the genocide in Srebrenica, which was committed in 1995 by the Bosnian Serbs . . .")

[11]   Prosecutor v. Brđanin, Case No. IT-99–36-T, para. 80 (Int'l Crim. Tribunal for the former Yugoslavia Sept. 1, 2004).

[12]   *Id.* at 98.

[13]   *Id. See also Brđanin*, Case No. IT-99–36-T, para. 81.

[14]   KURSPAHIC, *supra* note 6, at 98.

[15]   *Brđanin*, Case No. IT-99–36-T, para. 81.

[16]   *Id.*

[17]   KURSPAHIC, *supra* note 6, at 97.

[18]   *Id.*

[19]   Noel Malcolm, Bosnia: A Short History 252 (1996).

SDS politicians then threw even more fuel on the fire through malicious orations specifically aimed at creating "fear and hatred amongst the ethnic groups and inciting the Bosnian Serbs against other ethnic groups."[20] Over time, this noxious discourse was ratcheted up. Warnings of Muslim/Croat designs to exterminate Bosnian Serbs were accompanied by exhortations to eliminate those groups before they could make good on their supposed plans.[21] These prophesies of genocide were graphically enhanced by images of maimed combatants and tales of Muslim criminality against Bosnian Serbs dating back to the region's Ottoman occupation in the fourteenth century.[22] As this dangerous discourse crescendoed, Muslims and Croats were implicitly threatened with murder and other horrible consequences if they did not leave. And, by the time of its genocidal end-phases, Bosnian Serb propaganda "openly incited people to kill non-Serbs."[23]

5.2.1.4 The Impact of the Propaganda

As noted, the Bosnian Serb propaganda campaign was launched in support of a massive ethnic cleansing operation. The ICTY Trial Chamber in *Prosecutor* v. *Brđanin* explained how it realized its ultimate objective:

> The propaganda campaign achieved its goals with respect to both the Bosnian Serb and the [non-Serbs]. While influencing the Bosnian Serb population to perceive and treat the non-Serb inhabitants as enemies and preparing the Bosnian Serb population for the crimes that were committed later, it also instilled fear among the non-Serb population and created an atmosphere of terror, which contributed to the subsequent mass exodus of non-Serbs.[24]

Quite appallingly, the campaign "culminated in the massacre of as many as 8,000 Bosniak men and boys at the town of Srebrenica in July 1995."[25] And "the attempt to eradicate the male Muslim population following the capture of Srebrenica represents the gravest and most obvious example of genocide during the wars in the former Yugoslavia."[26]

---

[20]   *Brđanin*, Case No. IT-99–36-T, para. 82
[21]   *Id.*
[22]   *Id.*
[23]   *Id.*
[24]   *Id.* at 83.
[25]   *Ethnic Cleansing*, HISTORY.COM, www.history.com/topics/ethnic-cleansing (last visited July 31, 2015). *See also* Noreen L. Hertzfield, *Lessons from Srebrenica: The Danger of Religious Nationalism*, KRIPKE CENTRE JOURNAL OF RELIGION & SOCIETY, Supplement Series 2 (2007), http://digitalcommons.csbsju. edu/cgi/viewcontent.cgi?article=1003&context=theology_pubs (referring to "the ethnic cleansing that culminated in the massacre of Srebrenica …")
[26]   Helga Brunborg, Torkild Hovde Lyngstad & Henrik Urdal, *Accounting for Genocide: How Many Were Killed in Srebrenica?*, 19 EUROPEAN J. POPULATION 229, 232 (2003).

5.2.1.5 Other Propaganda Connected to the Balkan Atrocities

THE VOJISLAV ŠEŠELJ CASE. Bosnian Serbs were not the only disseminators of ethnic cleansing propaganda during that period. A prominent example in this regard is Vojislav Šešelj, an extremist anti-Muslim/Croatian politician operating in Serbia.[27] Founder of the Serbian Radical Party and organizer and leader of the Serb militia group known as the "Šešelj's Men," he was indicted by the ICTY in connection with rousing Serb paramilitaries to ethnically cleanse large swathes of the region of Muslims and Croats. Thus, the targeted ethnic cleansing spanned Croatian territory, as well as areas in Bosnia and Herzegovina and the ethnically mixed Vojvodina region of Serbia.[28] The ICTY indicted Šešelj in connection with this hate speech and related violence against Muslims and Croats. The charges included involvement in a joint criminal enterprise, as well as instigation and persecution as a crime against humanity.[29] On March 31, 2016, an ICTY Trial Chamber acquitted him, but that verdict was appealed by the prosecution.[30]

A little over a year later, an Appeals Chamber of the International Residual Mechanism for Criminal Tribunals entered convictions against Šešelj under Counts 1, 10, and 11 of the Indictment for instigating deportation, persecution (forcible displacement), and other inhumane acts (forcible transfer) as crimes against humanity, as well as for committing persecution, based on a violation of the right to security, as a crime against humanity.[31] In particular, the Appeals Chamber found that the Trial Chamber erred in not holding Šešelj responsible for a speech he gave in Hrtkovci, Vojvodina (Serbia), on May 6, 1992, calling for the expulsion of the non-Serbian population.[32] Other than agreeing with the prosecution that the Trial Chamber erred in finding that there was no widespread or systematic attack against the non-Serbian civilian population in Croatia and Bosnia and Herzegovina, the remainder of the prosecution appeal was dismissed.[33]

THE DARIO KORDIĆ CASE. Another prominent ethnic-cleansing-propaganda case emanated from the Bosnian Croat community. The ICTY defendant in that matter, politician Dario Kordić, allegedly targeted his Muslim neighbors in the area of Lašva

---

[27] Bernard A. Cook, *Vojislav Šešelj*, *in* 2 EUROPE SINCE 1945: AN ENCYCLOPEDIA 1135 (Bernard A. Cook ed., 2001).

[28] Prosecutor v. Šešelj, Case No. IT-03–67-PT, Third Amended Indictment, paras. 4–10 (Dec. 7, 2007).

[29] *Id.* paras. 15–34; Gregory S. Gordon, *Šešelj's Provisional Release: Hate Speech, International Criminal Procedure and Transitional Justice*, JURIST, Feb. 7, 2015, http://jurist.org/forum/2015/02/gregory-gordon-seselj-release.php.

[30] Marlise Simons, *Tribunal Acquits Serbian Nationalist of War Crimes*, N.Y. TIMES, March 31, 2016, at A9.

[31] International Residual Mechanism for Criminal Tribunals (MICT), *Appeals Chamber Reverses Šešelj's Acquittal, in part, and Convicts him of Crimes against Humanity*, MICT Press Release, Apr. 11, 2018, www.irmct.org/en/news/appeals-chamber-reverses-%C5%A1e%C5%A1elj%E2%80%99s-acquittal-part-and-convicts-him-crimes-against-humanity (hereinafter "MICT Press Release").

[32] *Id.*

[33] *Id.*

Valley. He was indicted for persecution as a crime against humanity for "encouraging, instigating and promoting hatred, distrust and strife on political, racial, ethnic or religious grounds, by propaganda, speeches and otherwise."[34] For this speech activity, he was charged with persecution as a crime against humanity.[35] As we will see below, Kordić was convicted on various counts connected to the ethnic cleansing campaign, but not for persecution. Nevertheless, the case establishes that Muslims were the object of a Bosnian Croat ethnic cleansing-focused hate speech campaign in this region.

5.2.2 *The Rwandan Genocide*

5.2.2.1 Prelude to the Apocalypse

Taking over from the Germans as colonizers, Belgium governed Rwanda from 1916 through 1962 and used the Tutsi ethnic group (composed of roughly 15 percent of the population) to manage the territory, which consisted of the majority Hutus (74 percent) and Twa (1 percent).[36] After harboring decades of resentment born of a sense of disenfranchisement exacerbated by extreme Tutsi privilege, the Hutus, on seizing majoritarian power toward the end of Belgian rule, subjected the Tutsis to successive waves of violence.[37] Beginning in 1959 (a year reverently dubbed by Hutu extremists as the "1959 Revolution") and continuing for the next few years, thousands of Tutsis were slaughtered and many thousands more fled, creating pockets of large refugee communities throughout central Africa.[38] One of those exile groups, located in Uganda, founded the Rwandan Patriotic Front in 1987 and launched a 1990 invasion of the homeland.[39]

Encountering Zairean and French resistance in aid of the Rwandan government, the incursion soon stalled. But the threat fueled the rise of a fledgling "hate media" industry in Rwanda.[40] Of these early extremist Hutu mouthpieces, the best known was *Kangura* ("Wake Them Up" or "Wake It Up"). Founded by Hassan Ngeze in 1990 and described as "one of the most virulent voices of hate,"[41] it "became a

---

[34] Prosecutor v. Kordić & Čerkez, Case No. IT-95-14/2-T, Judgment, para. 37 (Int'l Crim. Trib. for the Former Yugoslavia Feb. 26, 2001).

[35] *Id.*

[36] George Stanley, Genocide, Airpower and Intervention: Rwanda 1994, *in* STOPPING MASS KILLINGS IN AFRICA: GENOCIDE, AIRPOWER AND INTERVENTION (Douglas C. Peifer ed., 2008).

[37] JAVAID REHMAN, The Weaknesses in the International Protection of Minority Rights 66 (2003) (referring to the post-independence "massacre of approximately 20,000 Tutsi men, women and children").

[38] Frank K. Rusagara, The Spread of "Genocide Ideology" within the Great Lakes Region: Challenges for Rwanda, *in* RWANDA FAST FORWARD: SOCIAL, ECONOMIC, MILITARY AND RECONCILIATION PROSPECTS 218 (Maddalena Campione & Patrick Noac eds., 2004) (referring to the "Tutsi diaspora" in the region).

[39] JOHN SHATTUCK, Freedom on Fire: Human Rights Wars and America's Response 30 (2003).

[40] *Id.*

[41] ALISON DES FORGES, Leave None to Tell the Story: Genocide in Rwanda 77 (1999).

primary instrument in the preparation of the Hutu population of Rwanda for the genocide of the Tutsi population . . ."[42] Within months of the RPF invasion, Ngeze published in *Kangura* No. 6 "The Hutu Ten Commandments," a "venomous tract" that was "widely circulated throughout the country."[43] Its Eighth Commandment read: "The Bahutu [Hutus] should stop having mercy on the Batutsi [Tutsis]." One Hutu hardliner publicly interpreted this commandment as meaning: "We the people are obliged to take responsibility to wipe out this scum."[44]

The years that followed brought more instability. The Rwandan economy was weakening, and there was pressure from international donors on President Juvénal Habyarimana to give up his party's political monopoly and institute democratic reforms.[45] At the same time, the RPF continued its military incursions from Uganda, gaining the upper hand in the first part of 1993, driving within nineteen miles of the capital and then declaring a ceasefire.[46] To resolve the differences between the Rwandan government and the RPF, the United Nations helped broker the "Arusha Accords," which established a power-sharing arrangement between the two sides and deployment of the United Nations Assistance Mission to Rwanda (UNAMIR) to monitor the ceasefire and implementation of the Accords.[47] Hutu extremists, especially the close circle around Habyarimana known as the *Akazu*, felt as if everything was closing in on them.[48] They were recruiting militia from the ranks of the unemployed Hutu youth and arming them with guns and machetes.[49] More and more ethnic violence was being visited upon Tutsi civilians.

This bloodshed was being fanned by the burgeoning hate media, whose influence was spreading as its messages were becoming more virulent. Its most popular outlet

---

[42] Samuel Totten & Paul Robert Bartrop, 2 Dictionary of Genocide: M-Z 306 (2008).

[43] SHATTUCK, *supra* note 36, at 30. The Ten Commandments were, in fact, a call for comprehensive exclusion of Tutsis from society and are as follows: (1) Hutu males must not have close personal or work relations with Tutsi women; (2) Hutu women are superior to Tutsi women; (3) Hutu women must fraternize only with Hutu men; (4) Tutsis are dishonest and no Hutu should conduct business with them; (5) all high-level positions in society should be occupied by Hutus only; (6) the education sector should be majority Hutu; (7) the military must be exclusively Hutu; (8) The Hutu should stop having mercy on the Tutsi; (9) all Hutus must have unity and solidarity; and (10) the ideology of the 1959 and 1961 revolution (when many Tutsis were disenfranchised, forced to leave Rwanda or massacred) must be taught to Hutu at all levels. TOTTEN & BARTROP, *supra* note 39.

[44] SHATTUCK, *supra* note 37, at 30.

[45] Michael Renner, Fighting for Survival: Environmental Decline, Social Conflict, and the New Age of Insecurity 120 (1997) (describing the economic decline based, in part, on the drop in world market prices for tea); Roland Paris, At War's End: Building Peace After Civil Conflict 70 (noting the pressure on Habyarimana to liberalize the country's political system).

[46] GEORGINA HOLMES, Women and War in Rwanda: Gender, Media and the Representation of Genocide 22 (2014).

[47] John James Quinn, The Nexus of the Domestic and Regional within an International Context: The Rwandan Genocide and Mobutu's Ouster, *in* THE INTERNATIONALIZATION OF INTERNAL CONFLICTS: THREATENING THE STATE 54 (Amy L. Freedman ed., 2014).

[48] BARBARA F. WALTER, Committing to Peace: The Successful Settlement of Civil Wars 146 (2002).

[49] JAMES E. WALLER, Becoming Evil: How Ordinary People Commit Genocide and Mass Killing 223 (2007).

was a radio station known as RTLM – an acronym for Radio Télévision Libre des Milles Collines. Its founder was Ferdinand Nahimana, an extremist Hutu history professor who had been appointed by Habyarimana to run the national Rwandan media office (known as ORINFOR).[50] He had been sacked from that job when he had Radio Rwanda broadcast a false communiqué warning of a supposed Tutsi assassination plot.[51] The communiqué broadcast, in conjunction with militia being sent to an exclusive Tutsi enclave, led to a massacre and served as a dress rehearsal for the Rwandan Genocide.[52] Out of a job and contemplating the dreaded Arusha Accords power-sharing arrangement with the RPF, Nahimana used his extremist network to launch RTLM as the voice of Hutu power.[53] He was supported by Habyarimana and members of the *Akazu*. And one of his key collaborators, attorney Jean-Bosco Barayagwiza, was a founder of the most extreme of the hardline Hutu parties – the Coalition for the Defence of the Republic (CDR).[54]

In contrast to the stodgy programming of Radio Rwanda, RTLM announcers were colorful, colloquial, flippant and edgy. And they were very effective at stirring up ethnic hatred. As described by Rwanda expert Linda Melvern:

> In the street markets hundreds of cheap portable radios suddenly became available and the new station was immediately popular. It appealed to the young people with its disc-jockeys, pop music, and phone-ins. The announcers, unlike those who worked for Radio Rwanda, used street language. Using the FM frequency, RTLM carried no factual reports but there were commentaries and lengthy interviews and it soon became obvious that the new radio station was part of a campaign to promote extremist Hutu propaganda.[55]

In effect, RTLM was being integrated into an overall extremist Hutu plan to rid the country of the RPF and the perceived "fifth-column" Tutsis supposedly helping them within the country.[56] They were preparing for genocide. On the evening of April 6, 1994, on Habyarimana's return from Arusha for regional talks on implementation of the Accords, two surface-to-air missiles were fired in the direction of his airplane, one of which struck, blowing it up as it approached the airport.[57] Within hours, an interim government was in place led by Colonel Théoneste Bagosora, who had warned during the negotiation of the Arusha Accords that he would be preparing for the "apocalypse."[58] Throughout the murder operations of that long night, Bagosora's vision was being realized – the genocide of the Tutsis had begun.

---

[50] Dina Temple-Raston, Justice on the Grass: Three Rwandan Journalists, Their Trial for War Crimes, and a Nation's Quest for Redemption 26 (2005).

[51] *Id.* at 27.

[52] *Id.* at 27–8.

[53] *Id.* at 30–1.

[54] *Id.* at 31–2.

[55] Linda Melvern, Conspiracy to Murder: The Rwandan Genocide 53 (2004).

[56] Sangkul Kim, A Collective Theory of Genocidal Intent 115 n.79 (2016).

[57] Linda Melvern, A People Betrayed: The Role of the West in Rwanda's Genocide 115 (2000).

[58] *Id.* at 54.

5.2.2.2 The Messages of *Kangura*, RTLM and Extremist Government Officials

In the last part of 1993, in the lead-up to the genocide, Rwanda's Ministry of Information, having monitored the country's growing anti-Tutsi press, described *Kangura* as "the most extremist paper."[59] The crude rag routinely vilified Tutsis as "wicked" thieves and killers, "using women and money against the vulnerable Hutu."[60] This kind of slander degraded to the point of dehumanizing Tutsis. *Kangura* routinely referred to Tutsis as *Inyenzi*, or cockroaches, as prominently announced in the article titled "A Cockroach Cannot Give Birth to a Butterfly."[61] Jolyon Mitchell notes that *Kangura* "regularly employed the word *Inyenzi* to describe the Tutsi people, as the Nazis use the term 'vermin' to describe Jews."[62]

A natural, and inevitable, extension of this message was calls for the extermination of the Tutsis. Dehumanization laid the groundwork; but invoking past wrongs and current threats served as direct catalysts. Regarding the former, Jolyon Mitchell points out that "history was repeatedly used to demonize Tutsis and to underline how Hutus have been victims of their oppression in the past."[63] For example, an infamous cover of a *Kangura* December 1993 issue stands out.[64] Juxtaposed with the ironic words "Tutsi, Race of God" a machete was depicted along with the question: "What weapons can we use to defeat the *Inyenzi* once and for all?" Tying it all back to Belgian-era enmity, a follow-up question then asked, "What if someone brought back the Hutu Revolution of 1959 to finish off these Tutsi cockroaches?"[65] To underscore the long lineage of hate, the cover also depicted Grégoire Kayibanda, the leader of the so-called "1959 Revolution."[66]

Kangura's other method of incitement was grounded in fabricating contemporaneous existential threats. According to Joylon Mitchell:

> At the same time the RPF or Tutsis were accused of atrocities, which were in fact being perpetrated by Hutu groups. These "accusations in a mirror" were intended to instill fear that the minority Tutsi were planning and attempting to exterminate the Hutu majority.[67]

RTLM availed itself of many of the same stratagems but with the added power of vocalization. Pre-genocide, there was negative stereotyping of Tutsis (referring to them as devious, disproportionately wealthy, violent and bloodthirsty, among other

---

[59] JOLYON P. MITCHELL, Promoting Peace, Inciting Violence: The Role of Religion and Media 88 (2012).
[60] *Id.*
[61] *Id.*
[62] *Id.*
[63] *Id.*
[64] ALISON DES FORGES, "Leave None to Tell the Story": Genocide in Rwanda 87 (1999).
[65] *Id.*
[66] *Id.*
[67] MITCHELL, *supra* note 56, at 88.

things), and dehumanization (via animal/insect metaphors, such as *Inyenzi*).[68] But RTLM went beyond *Kangura* in terms of incitement techniques. In particular, it employed verbal attacks directed at particular individuals (those individuals were often physically harmed afterwards – for example, an April 1994 broadcast denounced a doctor in Cyangugu, who was burnt alive in front of his house three days later).[69] During the genocide, this sort of rhetoric continued, but was made more potent by direct calls for Tutsi extirpation as well as retrospective extolling of large-scale liquidation actions and petitions to RTLM listeners to cover up the incriminating traces of genocide.[70]

With regard to explicit pleas to exterminate the Tutsis, the most chilling example was a broadcast of announcer Kantano Habimana on June 4, 1994:

> One hundred thousand young men must be recruited rapidly. They should all stand up so that we kill the *Inkotanyi* [Tutsi] and exterminate them . . . The reason we will exterminate them is that they belong to one ethnic group. Look at the person's height and his physical appearance. Just look at his small nose and then break it.[71]

Contemporaneous with these toxic media messages, politicians at both the local and national level were also ramping up the anti-Tutsi rhetoric. Officials as highly placed as Prime Minister Jean Kambanda, along with figures at the lower rung, such as mayor Jean-Paul Akayesu, were making speeches to the public imploring them to attack the Tutsis.[72]

5.2.2.3 The Impact of the Anti-Tutsi Rhetoric and the Subsequent ICTR Cases

Despite relatively low literacy rates in Rwanda at that time, *Kangura* had a strong impact in terms of persuading the majority group to commit genocide. This was so because of the country's strong oral tradition. In fact, Ngeze's newspaper was the object of discussion throughout the nation.[73] Literate supporters of the paper would discuss its content with illiterate ones. According to one Rwandan: "Because *Kangura* was extremist in nature, everyone spoke of it, in buses and everywhere [so] the news would spread like fire; it was sensational news."[74] Per Jolyon Mitchell: "These popular discussions of the paper and the exposure on RTLM ensured that,

---

[68]   Gregory S. Gordon, *"A War of Media Words, Newspapers and Television Stations": The ICTR Media Trial Verdict and a New Chapter in the International Law of Hate Speech*, 45 Va. J. Int'l L. 139, 161 (2004) (hereinafter "A War of Media").

[69]   *Id.*

[70]   *Id.* at 162.

[71]   Prosecutor v. Nahimana, Barayagwiza, & Ngeze, Judgment and Sentence, ICTR Case No. 99–52-T para. 396 (Dec. 3, 2003).

[72]   William A. Schabas, *Hate Speech in Rwanda: The Road to Genocide*, 46 McGill L.J. 141 157 (2000).

[73]   Mitchell, *supra* note 56, at 89.

[74]   *Id.*

while *Kangura* had a comparatively small print run ... both its Kinyarwanda and French editions attracted wide public attention."[75]

Of course, RTLM's impact was even more ubiquitous and pernicious. Pre-genocide, many were describing RTLM as "Radio Rutswitsi," in other words, in the native Kinyarwanda, the radio that "burns," implying that "this was a station that fanned the flames of hatred."[76] Once the genocide began on April 6, many began to refer to it as "Radio Machete," with some even going further and calling it "Vampire Radio," as it was "calling for blood and massacres."[77]

RTLM's direct role in fomenting the murder of up to 800,000 Tutsis in one hundred days was described powerfully by ICTR judge Naventhem Pillay:

> The Chamber accepts that this moment in time [the downing of the airplane on April 6] served as a trigger for the events that followed. That is evident. But if the downing of the plane was the trigger, then RTLM and *Kangura* were the bullets in the gun. The trigger had such a deadly impact because the gun was loaded. The Chamber therefore considers the killing of Tutsi civilians can be said to have resulted, at least in part, from the message of ethnic targeting for death that was clearly and effectively disseminated through RTLM and *Kangura* before and after 6 April 1994.[78]

5.2.3 Relevant Statutory Instruments and Judgments in the Key Cases

5.2.3.1 The Genocide Convention and Incitement

As a starting point for the law of incitement, we must turn to the 1948 Convention on the Prevention and Punishment of the Crime of Genocide. Article II of the Convention defines "genocide" as a series of acts (including, for example, killing and causing serious bodily or mental harm) committed with the intent to destroy, in whole or in part, a national, ethnic, racial or religious group, as such.[79] Article III then states that a number of related acts committed in furtherance of Article II shall also be punishable. This includes, at Article III(b), "direct and public incitement to commit genocide."[80] As Articles 2(3)(c) of the ICTR Statute[81] and 4(3)(c) of the

---

75 *Id.*
76 *Id.* at 89.
77 *Id.*
78 *Nahimana*, et al., ICTR Case No. 99–52-T para. 953.
79 Convention on the Prevention and Punishment of the Crime of Genocide, GA Res. 260 (III) A, 78 UNTS 277 (Dec. 9, 1948) (hereinafter "Genocide Convention").
80 *Id.*
81 Statute of the International Criminal Tribunal for the Prosecution of Persons Responsible for Genocide and Other Serious Violations of Humanitarian Law Committed in the Territory of Rwanda and Rwandan Citizens Responsible for Genocide and Other Such Violations Committed in the Territory of Neighboring States, Between 1 January 1994 and 31 December 1994, SC Res. 955 (hereinafter "ICTR Statute").

ICTY Statute[82] are identical to Article III(c) of the Genocide Convention, the ad hoc tribunals could use the latter as their jurisprudential point of reference.[83]

5.2.3.2 Creation of the Tribunals

The ICTY was established within the context of certain United Nations Security Council initiatives taken in 1992 and 1993 as ethnic cleansing was being perpetrated in the territories of the former Yugoslavia, particularly in Bosnia and Herzegovina. In August 1992, with the global community aware of the atrocities but doing nothing to help, the Security Council issued Resolution 771, outlining and censuring breaches of international law, including "ethnic cleansing," that were taking place in the former Yugoslavia.[84] The Council then established a Commission of Experts to analyze the crimes referred to in Resolution 771 via Resolution 780 of October 6, 1992.[85] The Commission's investigation yielded a February 1993 recommendation to set up an ad hoc war crimes tribunal,[86] which the Security Council established via Resolution 827, on May 25, 1993.

The Security Council's resolution had the effect of creating "an international tribunal for the sole purpose of prosecuting persons responsible for serious violations of international humanitarian law committed in the territory of the former Yugoslavia between 1 January 1991 and a date to be determined by the Security Council upon restoration of peace."[87] The Statute of the Tribunal, along with a report from the Secretary-General, was incorporated as an annex into the Resolution.[88]

[82] Statute of the International Tribunal for the Prosecution of Persons Responsible for Serious Violations of International Humanitarian Law Committed in the Former Yugoslavia Since 1991, UN SCOR, 48th Sess., Annex, UN Doc. s/25704 (1993), reprinted in 32 ILM 1159, 1169–1201 (1994) (hereinafter "ICTY Statute").

[83] It should also be mentioned that the Rome Statute of the International Criminal Court criminalizes incitement to genocide at Article 25(3)(e): "In accordance with this Statute, a person shall be criminally responsible and liable for punishment for a crime within the jurisdiction of the Court if that person ... in respect of the crime of genocide, directly and publicly incites others to commit genocide." Rome Statute of the International Criminal Court, art. 25, July 17, 1998, 2187 UNTS 3, reprinted in 1 United Nations Diplomatic Conference of Plenipotentiaries on the Establishment of an International Criminal Court, Official Records (1998) (hereinafter "Rome Statute").

[84] SC Res. 771, U.N. SCOR, 47th Sess., 3106th mtg. at 2, UN Doc. S/RES/771 (1992).

[85] SC Res. 780, P6, U.N. SCOR, 47th Sess., 3119th mtg. at 2, UN Doc. S/RES/780 (Oct. 6, 1992) ("Requests the Secretary-General to establish, as a matter of urgency, an impartial Commission of Experts to examine and analyse the information submitted pursuant to resolution 771 [1992] and the present resolution, together with such further information as the Commission of Experts may obtain through its own investigations or efforts, of other persons or bodies pursuant to resolution 771 [1992], with a view to providing the Secretary-General with its conclusions on the evidence of grave breaches of the Geneva Conventions and other violations of international humanitarian law committed in the territory of the former Yugoslavia.")

[86] UN Security Council, Commission of Experts, Interim Report of the Commission of Experts Established Pursuant to Security Council Resolution 780 (1992), para. 55, UN Doc. S/35374 (Feb. 10, 1993).

[87] SC Res. 827, UN SCOR, 48th Sess., 3217th mtg., UN Doc. S/RES/827 (1993).

[88] ICTY Statute, *supra* note 79.

As the Security Council was debating the establishment of the ICTY, extremist Hutus were planning the April-July Rwandan Genocide. And, as with the Balkan atrocities, the international community stood idly by while hundreds of thousands of innocent Tutsis were being hacked to death with machetes. Nevertheless, the world did take cognizance of the slaughter via reports of the Special Rapporteur for Rwanda,[89] and the preliminary report of a Commission of Experts that was set up in circumstances similar to the one established for the former Yugoslavia.[90]

The Expert Commission issued its report in October 1994. Parallel to its Yugoslav predecessor, it advised justice measures via the creation of an international criminal tribunal.[91] As before, the Security Council acted in accordance with that advice. On November 8, 1994, it adopted Resolution 955 establishing an "international tribunal to prosecute those responsible for genocide and other serious violations of international humanitarian law committed in Rwanda between 1 January 1994 and 31 December 1994."[92] Practically identical to its ICTY predecessor, the ICTR Statute had different war crimes provisions, as the atrocities in Rwanda took place within the context of a strictly noninternational armed conflict.

5.2.3.3 The Relevant Statutory Provisions

The relevant provisions of the ICTR and ICTY Statutes, for the purposes of this Chapter, cover instigation, ordering, genocide and crimes against humanity (persecution). And those parts of the respective statutes are identical. Concerning instigation and ordering, ICTR Statute Article 6(1), under the rubric of "Individual Criminal Responsibility," provides that a person "who planned, *instigated, ordered,* committed or otherwise aided and abetted in the planning, preparation or execution of a crime referred to in articles 2 to 4 [i.e., genocide, crimes against humanity and war crimes] of the present Statute, shall be individually responsible for the crime."[93] Article 7(1) of the ICTR Statute is nearly a clone of ICTR Article 6(1) (with the sole difference that it makes reference to "articles 2 to 5," as the ICTY Statute has two separate articles criminalizing war crimes, but the ICTR only has one).[94]

Genocide is covered in Article 2 of the ICTR Statute and Article 4 of the ICTY Statute. ICTR Statute Article 2 declares:

---

[89] UN Doc. S/1994/1157, annex I and annex II.

[90] WILLIAM A. SCHABAS, Genocide in International Law: The Crime of Crimes 100 (2000); Preliminary Report of the Commission of Experts Established Pursuant to Security Council Resolution 935 (1994), UN Doc. S/1994/1125; Final Report of the Commission of Experts Established Pursuant to Security Council Resolution 935 (1994), UN Doc. S/1994/1405.

[91] *Id.*

[92] ICTR Statute, *supra* note 78.

[93] *Id.* art. 6(1) (emphasis added).

[94] ICTY Statute, *supra* note 79, art. 7(1).

1. The International Tribunal shall have the power to prosecute persons committing genocide as defined in paragraph 2 of this article or of committing any of the other acts enumerated in paragraph 3 of this article.
2. Genocide means any of the following acts committed with intent to destroy, in whole or in part, a national, ethnical, racial or religious group, as such:
    (a) killing members of the group;
    (b) causing serious bodily or mental harm to members of the group;
    (c) deliberately inflicting on the group conditions of life calculated to bring about its physical destruction in whole or in part;
    (d) imposing measures intended to prevent births within the group;
    (e) forcibly transferring children of the group to another group.
3. The following acts shall be punishable:
    (a) genocide;
    (b) conspiracy to commit genocide;
    (c) direct and public incitement to commit genocide;
    (d) attempt to commit genocide;
    (e) complicity in genocide.[95]

As for crimes against humanity (persecution), the relevant provisions are found in Article 3 of the ICTR Statute and Article 5 of the ICTY Statute. ICTR Statute Article 3 declares:

> The International Tribunal for Rwanda shall have the power to prosecute persons responsible for the following crimes when committed as part of a widespread or systematic attack against any civilian population on national, political, ethnic, racial or religious grounds:
>
> (a) murder;
> (b) extermination;
> (c) enslavement;
> (d) deportation;
> (e) imprisonment;
> (f) torture;
> (g) rape;
> (h) persecutions on political, racial, and religious grounds;
> (i) other inhumane acts.[96]

Despite divergences in the chapeau section of each crimes against humanity formulation – the ICTY appends an armed conflict nexus (more on this later) and

---

[95] ICTR Statute, *supra* note 78, art. 2; ICTY Statute, *supra* note 79, art. 4.
[96] ICTR Statute, *supra* note 78, art. 3. The ICTY Statute is different save certain elements of the chapeau, which reads: "The International Tribunal shall have the power to prosecute persons responsible for the following crimes when committed in armed conflict, whether international or internal in character, and directed against any civilian population." ICTY Statute, *supra* note 79, art. 5.

the ICTR includes a widespread attack on discriminatory grounds – each provision has more or less the same *structure*. Each begins with the foundational premise of an attack against a civilian population, and then follows with the same enumerated set of offenses. Most significantly, each formulation treats "persecution" as a separate crime. Avitus Agbor has observed that "the ICTY and ICTR have treated the definitions of crimes against humanity in the respective Statutes as synonymous."[97]

5.2.3.4 The Key Decisions

The ICTY jurisprudence has been less focused on hate speech per se than the ICTR. Still, we have seen that, specifically with respect to hate speech, two significant ICTY decisions have been handed down – *Prosecutor v. Kordić* (2001) (Bosnian Croat accused of directing ethnic cleansing campaign charged with related hate speech as CAH-persecution) and *Prosecutor v. Šešelj* (2016) (extremist Serb politician charged with CAH-persecution regarding anti-Muslim/Croat hate speech to militias linked to ethnic cleansing operations).[98] Moreover, regarding the elements of persecution as a crime against humanity (not necessarily connected to hate speech), the following ICTY cases make important contributions: *Prosecutor v. Tadić* (1997) (in a case against lower-level politician/paramilitary leader, the Trial Chamber provides the foundational elements of persecution); *Prosecutor v. Kupreškić* (2000) (Lašva Valley ethnic cleansing case wherein the *actus reus* of persecution is detailed); and *Prosecutor v. Brđanin* (2004) (underlying acts of persecution should not be considered in isolation, but in context, looking at their cumulative effect).

The easily demonstrable connection between hate speech and genocide in Rwanda transformed the ICTR into a virtual laboratory for the development of international speech crimes law. Its work is encapsulated in a string of groundbreaking decisions: *Prosecutor v. Akayesu* (1998) (the ICTR's first incitement decision finding liability based on defendant's urging Hutu militia to slaughter town's Tutsi population); *Prosecutor v. Kambanda* (1998) (incitement conviction against Prime Minister of rump genocide regime); *Prosecutor v. Ruggiu* (2000) (Belgian RTLM announcer's incitement conviction included a count of crimes against humanity [persecution] based on hate speech); *Prosecutor v. Niyitegeka* (2003) (incitement

---

[97] Avitus A. Agbor, Instigation to Crimes against Humanity: The Flawed Jurisprudence of the Trial and Appeals Chamber of the International Criminal Tribunal for Rwanda, *Forward*, xxiv (2013).

[98] Prosecutor v. Dario Kordić, Case No. IT-95-14/2-T, Judgment (Int'l Crim. Trib. for the Former Yugoslavia Feb. 26, 2001); Prosecutor v. Šešelj, Case No. IT-03-67-T, Judgment (Int'l Crim. Trib. For the Former Yugoslavia March 31, 2016). See also Prosecutor v. Šešelj, Case No. MICT-16-99-A, (Mechanism for International Criminal Tribunals April 11, 2018) (reversing, in part, the Trial Chamber's decision and convicting Šešelj pursuant to Counts 1, 10 and 11 of the indictment for instigating deportation, persecution [forcible displacement], and other inhumane acts [forcible transfers] as crimes against humanity, as well as for committing persecution, based on a violation of the right to security, as a crime against humanity).

charges based on Rwandan minister's use of bullhorn directly after massacre to thank killers for "good work"); *Prosecutor v. Nahimana, Barayagwiza & Ngeze* (2003) (finding radio and print media executives guilty of incitement in connection with the establishment of RTLM and dissemination of its genocidal broadcasts as well as founding and publishing of anti-Tutsi newspaper *Kangura*); *Prosecutor v. Bikindi* (2008) (extremist Hutu tunesmith's liability based on code-word calls for murder directly before massacre, not on hate songs written before the genocide and disseminated by others). Those decisions, and others, will be considered in greater detail in the pages that follow.

5.3 THE JURISPRUDENCE DEVELOPED BY THE AD HOC TRIBUNALS

The framing of the ad hoc tribunal statutes described the offenses that would be charged by prosecutors related to the 1990s ethnic bloodbaths in the former Yugoslavia and Rwanda. But the shape and criteria of those transgressions were yet to be determined. By decade's end, however, the tribunals had begun rendering landmark decisions and offering crucial insights regarding the core international crimes. Those insights, as they continued into the new millennium, led to the maturation of an entire body of jurisprudence – what I have referred to in my scholarship as "atrocity speech law." In particular, by the time of the final phases of the tribunal completion strategies, those judgments had constructed a full doctrinal matrix of elements with respect to each of the speech-related offenses, including direct and public incitement to commit genocide, crimes against humanity (persecution), instigation and ordering. Each of these modalities will now be considered in turn.

5.3.1 *Direct and Public Incitement to Commit Genocide*

The prominent role of the ICTR in connection with speech-related crimes has already been mentioned. And as Rwanda's 1994 mass criminality centered around a genocide campaign, the offense of direct and public incitement to commit genocide would feature prominently in Tribunal judgments. Having been first codified after Nuremberg, the crime was at last applied in an international criminal proceeding as the bloody twentieth century finally neared its end.

5.3.1.1 *Prosecutor v. Akayesu*

On September 2, 1998, an ICTR Trial Chamber convicted former Taba commune mayor Jean-Paul Akayesu of various charges, including genocide, direct and public incitement to commit genocide and crimes against humanity.[99] As "the first

---

[99] Prosecutor v. Akayesu, Case No. ICTR-96-4-T, Judgment (Sept. 2, 1998) (hereinafter "Akayesu Judgment"). Akayesu was charged with incitement in Count 4 of the Indictment. *Id.* para. 1.2.

conviction for genocide following the signing of the Genocide Convention in 1948," it is an epochal precedent.[100] But it is also significant as the first post-1948 finding of guilt for incitement to genocide.[101] Thus, it is a foundational doctrinal decision and needs to be examined closely.

Akayesu, a former school teacher, was elected mayor of Taba in April 1993 and served in that position until June 1994. Although initially protecting the commune's Tutsis, Akayesu had a change of heart after an April 18 meeting with members of the genocidal interim government.[102] The basis of the incitement count was a speech Akayesu made the following day. At a large meeting conducted around the corpse of a young Hutu, Akayesu pled with the population to unite in order to eliminate what he referred to as the sole enemy: the accomplices of the *"Inkotanyi"*– a pejorative reference to Tutsis.[103]

The Trial Chamber's analysis of Akayesu's incitement liability started with Article 91 of the Rwandan Penal Code, which defined incitement as "directly provoking another to commit genocide through speeches at public gatherings, or through the sale or dissemination of written or audiovisual communication."[104] Straight away, the bench opined that the crime would have been committed even had the incitement not precipitated violence.[105] That said, in the factual portion of the decision, the judges found there was a link between Akayesu's speech and resultant violence.[106] And the Chamber even went so far as to say that "it is not sufficient to simply establish a possible coincidence between the Gishyeshye meeting and the beginning of the killing of Tutsi in Taba, but that *there must be proof of a possible causal link* between the statement made by the Accused during the said meeting and the beginning of the killings."[107]

The Chamber also considered the crime's *mens rea*. It found that element comprises the intent directly to prompt or provoke another to commit genocide. Put another way, she who incites others to commit genocide must herself have the specific intent to commit genocide, *viz.*, the intent to destroy, in whole or in part, a

[100] Fred Grünfeld & Anke Huijboom, The Failure to Prevent Genocide in Rwanda: The Role of Bystanders 20 (2007).
[101] *See* Charity Kagwi-Ndungu, The Challenges in Prosecuting Print Media for Incitement to Genocide, *in* The Media and the Rwanda Genocide 338 (Alan Thompson ed., 2007) ("In the first conviction of the ICTR, for direct and public incitement to commit genocide, the Trial Chamber described the essential elements of the crime.")
[102] Dianne Williams, Race, Ethnicity and Crime: Alternative Perspectives 184 (2012).
[103] Akayesu Judgment, ICTR Case No. 96–4-T para. 673. *See also* Gordon, A War of Media, *supra* note 65, at 139, 150.
[104] *Id.* para. 553.
[105] *Id.*
[106] *Id.* paras. 673–5. The judgment read: "The Chamber is of the opinion that there is a causal relationship between Akayesu's speeches at the gathering of 19 April 1994 and the ensuing widespread massacres of Tutsi in Taba." *Id.* para. 673.
[107] *Id.* para. 349.

national, ethnic, racial or religious group, as such.[108] On the facts before it, the *Akayesu* bench found the *mens rea* element had been satisfied.[109]

The "public" criterion was analyzed too. The Trial Chamber quoted the International Law Commission, which defined public incitement as "a call for criminal action to a number of individuals in a public place" or to "members of the general public at large by such means as the mass media, for example, radio or television."[110]

Next, the Chamber looked at the "direct" element. It held that, per this criterion, the speech "should be viewed in the light of its cultural and linguistic content."[111] The implication is that a speech found to be "direct" in one locale might not be in another, in light of the listeners' cultural and linguistic mindset.[112] In other words, an individualized factual inquiry is necessary in each case. And "incitement may be direct, and nonetheless implicit."[113]

In the end, it boils down to "whether the persons for whom the message was intended immediately grasped the implication thereof."[114] Thus, directness would seem to be decided as a function of witness testimony, either fact or expert witness. In *Akayesu*, the Trial Chamber considered both. In particular, expert analysis of several publications and broadcasts by a linguistics expert confirmed that the term "*Inkotanyi*" would be comprehended by Kinyarwanda speakers in the April-July 1994 period to mean "RPF sympathizer" or "Tutsi."[115] And several fact witnesses corroborated the linguist. They gave evidence to the effect that when a speaker urged his listener to "eliminate" the "*Inkotanyi*," it was grasped as a call to kill all Tutsis.[116] The expert and lay testimony allowed the Chamber to infer that in the context of the time, place and circumstances of Akayesu's oration, "*Inkotanyi*" generally denoted "Tutsi."[117] Thus, each criterion having been met, the Tribunal could conclude that Akayesu was guilty of incitement.

5.3.1.2 Cases between *Akayesu* and *Nahimana*

Two days after Akayesu's epochal conviction, in *Prosecutor v. Kambanda* (1998), the ICTR made history again by becoming the first international court to convict a head of government for commission of atrocity crimes.[118] The guilty plea of Jean

---

[108] *Id.* para. 560.
[109] *Id.*
[110] *Id.*
[111] *Akayesu*, ICTR Case No. 96-4-T para. 557.
[112] *Id.*
[113] *Id.*
[114] *Id.* para. 558.
[115] *Id.* paras. 147, 340.
[116] *Id.* paras. 333-47.
[117] *Id.* paras. 361, 709.
[118] Kingsley Chiedu Moghalu, *Image and Reality of War Crimes Justice: External Perceptions of the International Criminal Tribunal for Rwanda*, 26 Fletcher F. World Aff. 21, 37 n.40 (2002).

Kambanda, the genocide-government's prime minister, was based on a count of incitement to genocide, among others.[119] The factual basis for the incitement charge was predicated on Kambanda's announcement on RTLM air waves that the media outlet should continue to encourage the elimination of the Tutsi civilian population, specifically stating that the station was "an indispensable weapon in the fight against the enemy."[120] The former prime minister also admitted traveling to various prefectures to inspire the population to kill.[121] This included congratulating those who had already murdered Tutsis. Kambanda's incitement also included use of an infamous metaphor, combined with accusation in a mirror, which was repeatedly broadcast: "[Y]ou refuse to give your blood to your country and the dogs drink it for nothing."[122]

Not quite two years after Kambanda's historic conviction, a guilty plea in the case of *Prosecutor* v. *Ruggiu* (2000) gave the Tribunal another occasion to consider the scope of the incitement crime.[123] The ICTR's only white European defendant, Belgian RTLM announcer Georges Ruggiu, verbally attacked Tutsis, moderate Hutus, and Belgians in the period leading up to and during the Rwandan Genocide.[124] And he relied extensively on euphemisms to persuade his listeners to commit genocide against the Tutsis. For instance, broadcasting in his native French tongue, he urged the population to "finish off the 1959 revolution."[125] Although this term might seem genocidally neutral on its surface, given the widespread Tutsi massacres of 1959, it was 1994 code for destroying that ethnic minority. Similarly, the term *Inyenzi*, within the socio-political context of 1994 Rwanda, meant "persons to be killed."[126] Ruggiu admitted to using this term extensively during his genocide-period radio utterances. Also as part of the factual basis of his plea, Ruggiu acknowledged telling his listeners to "go work" as part of encouraging "civil defense."[127] Again, given Rwanda's socio-political realities at that time, the average citizen would have perceived the term "go to work" as signifying "go kill the Tutsis and Hutu political opponents of the interim government."[128] Another component of his incitement liability was Ruggiu's congratulating Tutsi mass executioners for their genocidal efforts.[129] Finally, Ruggiu also availed himself of the "accusation in a

---

[119] Prosecutor v. Kambanda, Case No. ICTR 97–23-S, Judgement and Sentence (Sept. 4, 1998).

[120] *Id.* para. 39(vii).

[121] *Id.* para. 39(viii).

[122] *Id.* para. 39(x).

[123] Prosecutor v. Ruggiu, Case No. ICTR 97–32-I, Judgement and Sentence (June 1, 2000).

[124] *See* PAUL R. BARTROP, A Biographical Encyclopedia of Genocide 280 (2012) (hereinafter "Biographical Encyclopedia") ("[Ruggiu's] programs consistently incited his listeners to commit murder or serious attacks against the physical or mental well-being of the Tutsis and constituted acts of persecution against Tutsis, moderate Hutus, and Belgian citizens.")

[125] *Ruggiu*, Case No. ICTR 97–32-I, paras. 44(iii), 50.

[126] *Id.* para. 44(iii).

[127] *Id.* para. 44(iv).

[128] *Id.*

[129] *Id.* para. 50.

mirror" incitement technique (although this terminology was not used by the Trial Chamber) – warning his listeners that the Hutu population needed to be vigilant against attacks by Tutsi infiltrators.[130]

The Tribunal's next significant incitement decision was *Prosecutor v. Niyitegeka* (2003).[131] The defendant there had been a Radio Rwanda journalist and was sworn in as the genocidal rump government's Minister of Information on April 9, 1994.[132] His guilt was predicated on a series of meetings during which he told militias to "to go back to work." And, right after a massacre, he thanked the paramilitaries for "good work" and encouraged them to 'return the next day to continue the "work."[133] The Trial Chamber ruled that Niyitegeka's exhorting the militias to "go to work" was "understood by his audience as a call to kill the Tutsi, and that the Accused knew his words would be interpreted as such."[134] The judges also wrote that in "thanking, encouraging and commending [the militia] for the "work" they had done, "work" was "a reference to killing Tutsi."[135] According to the bench, then, retrospective applause for past genocidal murder in the context of ongoing genocidal operations constituted an implicit form of incitement.[136]

Based on these judgments,[137] certain conclusions can be drawn regarding the nature and scope of incitement: (1) it can be effected via warnings that violence will be visited upon the audience by the intended victims unless the audience acts first and eliminates the intended victims (i.e., "accusation in a mirror") (2) congratulating genocidal killers after they have killed (and implicitly may kill again) falls within the scope of incitement; (3) metaphors (such as "go to work"), even if not phrased in the imperative (e.g., Kambanda's law-of-the-jungle allusion to drinking blood) can constitute incitement; and (4) encouraging incitement within the context of ongoing incitement in a context of mass violence can itself amount to an independent act of incitement (e.g., Kambanda's encouragement of RTLM on the RTLM air waves). Unfortunately, as described below, the ICTR decisions never explicitly analyze the scope of incitement, or its various techniques, across the different cases.

---

[130] *Id.* para. 44(v).

[131] Prosecutor v. Niyitegeka, Case No. ICTR 96–14-T, Judgment and Sentence (May 16, 2003).

[132] *Id.* paras. 5, 6.

[133] *Id.* paras. 432, 433.

[134] *Niyitegeka*, Case No. ICTR 96–14-T para. 435.

[135] *Id.* para. 436.

[136] *Id.* The Trial Chamber did not explicitly so hold but the text permits drawing this inference. *See* Gregory S. Gordon, *Music and Genocide: Harmonizing Coherence, Freedom and Nonviolence in Incitement Law*, 50 SANTA CLARA L. REV. 607, 612 (2010) (hereinafter "Music and Genocide") (noting that the ICTR found that thanking genocide perpetrators for their "good work" was "in part, the basis of the incitement conviction").

[137] Soon after *Niyitegeka*, and right before the *Nahimana* judgment that will be discussed below, the ICTR issued an incitement-focused decision in Prosecutor v. Kajelijeli, Case No. ICTR 98-44A-T, Judgment and Sentence (Dec. 1, 2003). As that case involved explicit calls to genocide, the decision did not contain an analysis of the scope or nature of incitement. Therefore it is not highlighted here.

This is responsible for one of the key deficits in the jurisprudence that will be dealt with in Section IV of this Chapter.

5.3.1.3 *Prosecutor* v. *Nahimana* (the *Media Case*)

While the ICTR cases decided through the first half of 2003 provided guidance as to the nature and scope of the incitement offense, and fleshed out certain key criteria, one element remained entirely unexamined – "incitement" itself. But that aspect of the offense was extensively considered in the landmark decision of *Prosecutor* v. *Nahimana et al.*, otherwise known as the *Media Case.*[138] The three defendants in that case, RTLM founders Ferdinand Nahimana and Jean Bosco Barayagwiza, and *Kangura* editor-in-chief Hassan Ngeze, were found guilty of, among other offenses, direct and public incitement to commit genocide.

To this point, as we have seen, the jurisprudence had already defined the elements of "direct" and "public." But what about the element of "incitement" itself? To put on the element's necessary judicial gloss, the Trial Chamber would have to determine whether, in transmitting the content of the messages at issue, the relevant media outlets had engaged in the permissible exercise of free speech or in nonprotected hate advocacy. This entailed scrutinizing existing international case law. And, in doing so, the chamber distilled four criteria through which speech content regarding protected group characteristics (such as race or ethnicity) could be classified as either legitimate expression or criminal advocacy: (1) purpose; (2) text; (3) context; and (4) the relationship between speaker and subject.[139]

Regarding the purpose criterion, the Trial Chamber furnished examples of certain legitimate undertakings: historical research, dissemination of news and information and public accountability of government authorities.[140] At the opposite end of the spectrum, overt appeals for carnage would evince a patently illegitimate purpose.

The Chamber indicated the "text" criterion, for its part, would further assist in edifying the objective of the discourse. To illustrate, it cited to *Robert Faurisson* v. *France.*[141] In that case, the United Nations Human Rights Committee (HRC) had to resolve the tension between Article 19 of the International Covenant for Civil and

---

[138] Prosecutor v. Nahimana, Barayagwiza & Ngeze, Case No. ICTR 99–52-T, Judgement and Sentence (Dec. 3, 2003).

[139] The first two criteria, purpose and text, are lumped together by the Trial Chamber, but I have argued elsewhere that they should be considered separately. *See* Gordon, A War of Media, *supra* note 65, at 172. Moreover, the Tribunal did not explicitly characterize as a separate criterion the relationship between the speaker and the subject. I have also demonstrated that this should be considered as a distinct point of analysis given a close reading of the *Nahimana* judgment. *See id.* at 173–4; *see also* Robert H. Snyder, *"Disillusioned Words Like Bullets Bark": Incitement to Genocide, Music, and the Trial of Simon Bikindi*, 35 GA. J. INT'L & COMP. L. 645, 666 (2007) (adopting this analysis).

[140] *Nahimana*, Case No. ICTR 99–52-T, paras. 1000–06.

[141] International Covenant on Civil and Political Rights, Communication No. 550/1993: France (Jurisprudence) P 7.5, UN Doc. CCPR/C/58/D/550/1993 (1996) (Robert Faurisson v. France).

Political Rights (ICCPR), guarding liberty of expression, with Article 20, proscribing incitement to national, racial or religious discrimination.[142] Faurisson was challenging his French conviction for publishing his opinion questioning the existence of gas chambers at Nazi concentration camps (describing them as "magic gas chambers" in the Complaint). The ICTR Trial Chamber centered its analysis on the HRC's finding that the expression "magic gas chamber" implied Faurisson's inquiry was driven more by anti-Semitism than the quest for historical truth.[143] The Trial Chamber found that this differed from *Jersild* v. *Denmark*, a case decided under the European Convention on Human Rights (ECHR). In *Jersild*, the European Court of Human Rights reversed the Danish incitement conviction of a television reporter who interviewed members of a racist youth group but did not explicitly condemn them.[144] The ICTR Trial Chamber found that the journalist in *Jersild* distanced himself from the group's ethnic hatred message by referring to the group members as "racist" and "extremist youths."[145] This textual analysis, the Trial Chamber found, allowed the *Jersild* court to find that the program's objective was news dissemination, not propagation of racist views.[146]

Perhaps of greatest importance in the analysis was the "context" criterion – i.e., circumstances exogenous to and surrounding the text and necessary to discern its significance. The Trial Chamber again turned to the *Faurisson* case, where the HRC had noted that, in context, disputing the well-established historicity of Holocaust gas chambers would foster anti-Semitism. Then the chamber considered the European Court of Human Rights case *Zana* v. *Turkey*.[147] That case involved a former regional mayor's statement, seemingly condoning Kurdish massacres, by saying "anyone can make mistakes."[148] The statement was made in the context of violent clashes between government and Kurdish separatist forces. The *Nahimana* judges found that the European Court had sustained the underlying conviction since, in light of the massacres occurring at the time, the mayor's statement was "likely to exacerbate an already explosive situation."[149] The ICTR panel further fleshed out the context criterion by explaining that the adjudicator should also evaluate the tone of the speaker in vocalizing the words at issue.[150]

---

[142]   *Id.* para. 1001.

[143]   *Nahimana*, Case No. ICTR 99–52-T, para. 1001.

[144]   Jersild v. Denmark, 19 Eur. Ct. H.R. 1, 27 (1994). The European Court of Human Rights has calibrated its statutory interpretation to accommodate the right to free speech, Article 10(1) of the Convention, with the right to constrain speech for national security or protection of the rights and reputations of others, Article 10(2) of the Convention. *See* Gordon, A War of Media, *supra* note 65, at 146.

[145]   *Nahimana*, Case No. ICTR 99–52-T, paras. 993, 1001.

[146]   *Id.*

[147]   Zana v. Turkey, 27 Eur. Ct. H.R. 667, 670 (1997).

[148]   *Id.*

[149]   *Nahimana*, Case No. ICTR 99–52-T, para. 1091.

[150]   *Id.* para. 1022.

Finally, the Trial Chamber added one more criterion for evaluation of the "incitement" element – the relationship between the speaker and the subject of the speech.[151] Reference to this criterion is rather straightforward. In particular, the analysis should be more speech-protective when the speaker is part of a minority criticizing either the government or the country's majority population. The contrary will apply (i.e., less speech-protective) if the situation is reversed and the speaker is part of the majority, and the speech attacks the minority group – the situation that pertained during the Rwandan Genocide.

The Trial Chamber then applied these criteria. And doing so allowed it to "distinguish between permissible speech and illegal incitement in the cases of *Kangura* and RTLM."[152] In particular, the judges noted "that some of the articles and broadcasts offered into evidence ... conveyed historical information, political analysis, or advocacy of ethnic consciousness regarding the inequitable distribution of privilege [between Hutus and Tutsis] in Rwanda."[153]

For instance, the Chamber considered a December 1993 broadcast made by defendant Barayagwiza wherein he spoke of discrimination he experienced as a Hutu child.[154] According to the first criterion in the "incitement" analysis, the purpose of Barayagwiza's account appeared to be raising ethnic awareness. The text itself alluded to historical inequities but did not call for violence. Further, the context then was not that of fully realized genocide, as would be the case after April 6, 1994, but rather social volatility and political discord. Finally, the speaker related his experience as a member of the politically dispossessed condemning the establishment of that era. In distinguishing Barayagwiza's transmission as an acceptable instance of free speech, the Trial Chamber described it as "a moving personal account of his experience of discrimination as a Hutu."[155]

Held up in contrast to this was the June 4, 1994, broadcast by Kantano Habimana (seen previously) where he implored the audience to exterminate the "*Inkotanyi,*" or Tutsis, "who would be known by height and physical appearance."[156] Habimana finished: "Just look at his small nose and then break it."[157] The purpose and text of this rhetoric leave no doubt – this was unadulterated promotion of ethnic violence – the radio personality "in no way attempted to distance himself from his message."[158] The context was genocide taking place at the time of the broadcast. And the speaker was part of the majority Hutu ethnic group, supporting a government campaign

---

[151] *Id.* para. 1006.
[152] Gordon, A War of Media, *supra* note 65, at 174.
[153] *Id.*
[154] *Nahimana,* Case No. ICTR 99–52-T, para. 368.
[155] *Nahimana,* Case No. ICTR 99–52-T, para. 1019.
[156] *Id.* para. 396.
[157] *Id.*
[158] *Id.* para. 1024.

directed at exterminating the minority Tutsis. This is not speech that should have been accorded any presumption of free expression protection.[159]

The judgment also took on the issue of causation, emphasizing again that incitement did not require a showing of violence occasioned by the charged speech. "The Chamber notes that this causal relationship is not requisite to a finding of incitement. It is the potential of the communication to cause genocide that makes it incitement."[160] Nevertheless, inconsistent with this, the Chamber once again made factual findings regarding causation, ascribing to "the media" the role of genocide catalyst at the macro level – while the downing of President Habyarimana's plane may have triggered the genocide, "RTLM, *Kangura*, and CDR were the bullets in the gun."[161] Moreover, as alluded to previously, the Chamber devoted a portion of its analysis establishing the micro-level link between the murder of individual Tutsis and their being specifically mentioned by name in broadcasts, both before and after the commencement of the Rwandan Genocide on April 6, 1994.[162] If causation is irrelevant to proving the crime, why devote so much to chronicling it?[163]

On November 28, 2007, the ICTR Appeals Chamber issued its decision in the *Media Case* and upheld those portions of the judgment analyzing the elements of direct and public incitement to commit genocide.[164] That section of the judgment most relevant for purposes of this paper generally affirmed the approach taken by trial judges regarding incitement:

> The Appeals Chamber considers that the Trial Chamber did not alter the constituent elements of the crime of direct and public incitement to commit genocide in the media context (which would have constituted an error) ... Furthermore, the Appeals Chamber notes that several extracts from the [Trial Chamber] Judgment demonstrate that the Trial Chamber did a good job of distinguishing between hate speech and direct and public incitement to commit genocide ... The Appeals

[159]   Gordon, A War of Media, *supra* note 65, at 175–6.
[160]   *Nahimana*, Case No. ICTR 99–52-T, para. 1015.
[161]   *Id.* para. 953.
[162]   *Id.* para. 478.
[163]   Richard Wilson speculates the preoccupation with causation stems from the Tribunal wanting a degree of comfort in certifying compliance with genocide's draconian *mens rea* requirement. *See* Richard Wilson, *Inciting Genocide with Words*, 36 MICH. J. INT'L L. 295–8 (2015). Susan Benesch questions whether the causation analysis is meant to compensate for a poorly developed test for determining incitement. *See* Susan Benesch, The Ghost of Causation in International Speech Crime Cases, *in* PROPAGANDA, WAR CRIMES TRIALS AND INTERNATIONAL LAW 257 (Predrag Dojcinovic ed., 2012) (examining the relevance of causation in the ICTR judgments) (hereinafter "The Ghost of Causation").
[164]   Prosecutor v. Nahimana, Barayagwiza & Ngeze, Case No. ICTR-99–52-A, Judgment, paras. 695–7 (Nov. 28, 2007). Of note, given the beyond a reasonable doubt standard, the Appeals Chamber did rule that certain pre-genocide speech that had factored into the Trial Chamber's verdict could not be deemed incitement. *See id.* paras. 740–51. It also found that the defendants' pre-1994 conduct, which had also factored into the Trial Chamber's finding of liability for incitement, was beyond the ICTR's temporal jurisdiction. This, in turn, resulted in a reduction of the defendants' respective sentences. *See, e.g., id.* para. 314.

Chamber will now turn to the Appellants' submissions that the Trial Chamber erred (1) in considering that a speech in ambiguous terms, open to a variety of interpretations, can constitute direct incitement to commit genocide, and (2) in relying on the presumed intent of the author of the speech, on its potential dangers, and on the author's political and community affiliation, in order to determine whether it was of a criminal nature. The Appellants' position is in effect that incitement to commit genocide is direct only when it is explicit and that under no circumstances can the Chamber consider contextual elements in determining whether a speech constitutes direct incitement to commit genocide. For the reasons given below, the Appeals Chamber considers this approach overly restrictive.[165]

5.3.1.4 *Prosecutor* v. *Bikindi*

Simon Bikindi was a prominent pre-genocide pop composer and musician in Rwanda.[166] He was also involved in Rwandan politics, having been a member of Habyarimana's MRND party as well as having served in the Ministry of Youth and Sports.[167] As an artist, he sought to inject his extremist Hutu political views into his music. He was known for his infamous standard *Njyewe nanga Abahutu* (*I Hate the Hutu*), as well as other jingles, including *Bene Sebahinzi* (*Descendants of the Father of Farmers*) and *Twasezereye ingoma ya cyami* (*We Said Goodbye to the Monarchy*).[168] These recordings supposedly demonized Tutsis as "Hutu enslavers, enemies or enemy accomplices by blaming the enemy for the problems of Rwanda, by continuously making references to the 1959 Revolution and its gains by the *rubanda ngamwinshi* [Hutu] and by supporting the Bahutu Ten Commandments, and inciting ethnic hatred and people to attack and kill Tutsi."[169]

During the genocide, "many of the killers sang Bikindi's songs as they hacked or beat to death hundreds of thousands of Tutsis with government-issued machetes and homemade nail-studded clubs."[170] Bikindi was out of Rwanda when the genocide began (he was in Europe arranging for a tour).[171] But he returned before the orgy of killing was over, and allegedly, while traveling through some of the killing sites, urged *Interahamwe* militia to slaughter Tutsis.[172]

---

[165] *Id.* paras. 695–7. Susan Benesch has written that the Appeals Chamber "rebuked" the Trial Chamber for "not drawing a clear line between hate speech and incitement to genocide." Susan Benesch, *Vile Crime or Inalienable Right: Defining Incitement to Genocide*, 48 Va. J. Int'l L. 485, 489 (2008) (hereinafter "Vile Crime"). As indicated clearly by paras. 696–7, however, her assertion is simply not backed up by the actual text of the judgment.

[166] Donald G. McNeil Jr., *Killer Songs*, NY Times, Mar. 17, 2002, www.nytimes.com/2002/03/17/magazine/killer-songs.html.

[167] *Id.*

[168] *Id.*; Prosecutor v. Bikindi, Case No. ICTR-01–72-T, Judgment, para. 187 (Dec. 2, 2008).

[169] *Id.*

[170] McNeil, *supra* note 163.

[171] *Id.*

[172] Bartrop, A Biographical Encyclopedia, *supra* note 121, at 38 (2012).

On June 15, 2005, the ICTR indicted Bikindi on six counts for crimes perpetrated in 1994, including one count of direct and public incitement to commit genocide pursuant to Articles 2(3)(c) and 6(1) of the ICTR Statute.[173] The incitement charge was based on the playing and dissemination of Bikindi's extremist Hutu songs (at political rallies, during radio broadcasts and at pre-killing meetings), and his speeches exhorting extremist Hutu party activists and militia to exterminate the Tutsi population.[174]

In the media buzz and academic discourse surrounding the case, much attention was focused on the songs.[175] But the Trial Chamber's conviction of Bikindi on incitement grounds was not based on the defendant's music. The Chamber did rule that Bikindi's songs "advocated Hutu unity against a common foe and incited ethnic hatred."[176] And it held that his music was "deployed in a propaganda campaign in 1994 in Rwanda to incite people to attack and kill Tutsi" – implicitly finding it could have constituted incitement to genocide.[177] But the judges ruled there was insufficient evidence to conclude beyond a reasonable doubt "that Bikindi composed these songs with the specific intention to incite such attacks and killings, even if they were used to that effect in 1994."[178] Similarly, the bench held there was insufficient evidence proving Bikindi "played a role in the dissemination or deployment of his ... songs in 1994."[179]

Instead, the Trial Chamber premised Bikindi's guilt for incitement solely on speech uttered while he traveled on a road between the Rwandan towns of Kivumu and Kayove in late June 1994. Tutsis were being massacred in the vicinity. And testimony established that, during his outbound travel to Kivumu, Bikindi, riding in a truck with a loudspeaker, said to the militias: "You sons of *Sebahinzi*, who are the majority, I am speaking to you, you know that the Tutsi are minority. Rise up and look everywhere possible and do not spare anybody."[180] This was interpreted to mean that although some Tutsi had already been killed, others were hiding and Bikindi was calling on people to do all that was necessary to eliminate any remaining Tutsis.[181]

Evidence at trial also confirmed that, returning from Kayove, Bikindi stopped at a roadblock and met with leaders of the local *Interahamwe*, where he insisted, "you

---

[173] *Bikindi*, Case No. ICTR-01–72-T, para. 5.

[174] Prosecutor v. Bikindi, Case No. ICTR-01–72-T, Amended Indictment, paras. 31–41 (June 15, 2005) (hereinafter "Bikindi Indictment").

[175] *See, e.g.*, Benesch, *supra* note 163, at 491 ("The ICTR is now set to sail further into uncharted waters, since it is conducting the trial of a Hutu pop star, Simon Bikindi, whose elliptical lyrics and catchy tunes – officially banned in Rwanda since 1994 – incited genocide, according to the ICTR prosecutors.")

[176] Prosecutor v. Bikindi, Case No. ICTR-01–72-T, Judgment and Sentence, para. 249.

[177] *Id.* para. 255.

[178] *Id.*

[179] *Id.* para. 263.

[180] *Id.*

[181] *Id.* para. 268.

see, when you hide a snake in your house, you can expect to face the consequences."[182] After Bikindi left the roadblock, members of the surrounding population and the *Interahamwe* intensified their search for Tutsi, using the assistance of
dogs and going into homes to flush out those still hiding.[183] Per additional trial
testimony, a number of people were subsequently killed.[184]

One witness testified that, on Bikindi's coming back from Kayove, he heard him
ask over a truck loudspeaker "[h]ave you killed the Tutsis here?" and he further
demanded whether they had killed the "snakes."[185] He also heard Bikindi's songs
being played as the vehicles moved on.[186]

Based on these statements, the Trial Chamber held:

> Bikindi's call on "the majority" to "rise up and look everywhere possible" and not to
> "spare anybody" immediately referring to the Tutsi as the minority unequivocally
> constitutes a direct call to destroy the Tutsi ethnic group. Similarly, the Chamber
> considers that Bikindi's address to the population on his way back from Kayove,
> asking "Have you killed the Tutsis here?" and whether they had killed the "snakes"
> is a direct call to kill Tutsi, pejoratively referred to as snakes. In the Chamber's view,
> it is inconceivable that, in the context of widespread killings of the Tutsi population
> that prevailed in June 1994 in Rwanda, the audience to whom the message was
> directed, namely those standing on the road, could not have immediately under-
> stood its meaning and implication. The Chamber therefore finds that Bikindi's
> statements through loudspeakers on the main road between Kivumu and Kayove
> constitute direct and public incitement to commit genocide.[187]

5.3.1.5 Cases After *Bikindi*

In *Prosecutor v. Kalimanzira* (2009),[188] the Trial Chamber convicted the genocide
rump government's Minister of Interior, Calixte Kalimanzira, of, among other
charges, direct and public incitement to commit genocide in connection with a
speech made to militia manning a certain roadblock. Such speech was found to
satisfy the "public" element because the "incitement to kill Tutsis was clear, direct,
and in a *public place*, to an *indeterminate group of persons*."[189] Nevertheless, the
Appeals Chamber, interpreting the speech's milieu quite differently from the Trial
Chamber, overturned this portion of the conviction because the speech was not
directed toward a sufficiently "large" audience (despite the number being unknown)

---

[182] *Id.*
[183] *Id.*
[184] *Id.*
[185] *Id.* para. 269.
[186] *Id.*
[187] *Id.* para. 423.
[188] Prosecutor v. Kalimanzira, Case No. ICTR-05–88-T.
[189] *Id.* paras. 560–1.

or via mass media or via electronic volume enhancement (such as a loudspeaker system or bullhorn – as in *Bikindi*).[190]

Similarly, three years later, another ICTR Trial Chamber convicted the rump government Minister of Planning Augustin Ngirabatware of, *inter alia*, direct and public incitement to commit genocide in connection with a speech made to as many as 150–250 persons at a roadblock.[191] The Trial Chamber found this to be "public" because the number of listeners indicated were not all manning the road-block.[192] The Appeals Chamber affirmed that reasoning[193] and, via reference to the prosecution's arguments, alluded to the "publicly accessible location at which Ngirabatware made the inciting statement."[194]

5.3.1.6 Failure to Apply the Framework

Unfortunately, in all the post-*Media Case* (Trial Chamber) decisions, in varying degrees, the various Trial and Appeals Chambers failed to apply, in a consistent or systematic manner, the incitement framework constructed by the early cases. Thus, only parts of the framework have been consulted, resulting in inconsistent and uneven jurisprudence. *See, e.g., Prosecutor* v. *Serugendo* (no reference to the crime's "incitement" criterion and only cursory acknowledgment of its other criteria);[195] and *Prosecutor* v. *Muvunyi* (conflating the "direct" and "incitement" elements and only considering the "context" criterion of the latter).[196]

5.3.2 *Hate Speech as the Crime against Humanity of Persecution*

5.3.2.1 Background: The Armenian Genocide and the Nuremberg Cases

In modern times, the term "crimes against humanity" appears to have been coined by the Entente Powers during World War I. On May 28, 1915, France, Great Britain and Russia issued a joint declaration to Turkish officials noting that "[i]n view of these crimes of Turkey against humanity and civilization," the Allies would "hold personally responsible [for] these crimes all members of the Ottoman government and those of their agents who are implicated in such massacres."[197] But the Allies failed to follow through, and Ottoman perpetrators never stood in the dock on crimes against humanity charges.

---

[190] Prosecutor v. Kalimanzira, Case No. ICTR-05–88-A, para. 156 (Oct. 20, 2010).
[191] Prosecutor v. Ngirabatware, Case No. ICTR-99–54-T, Judgment and Sentence (Dec. 20, 2012).
[192] *Id.* para. 1367.
[193] Prosecutor v. Ngirabatware, Case No. MICT-12–29-A, Judgment paras. 53–54 (Dec. 18, 2014).
[194] *Id.* para. 51.
[195] Prosecutor v. Serugendo, Case No. ICTR-2005–84-I, Judgment and Sentence (June 12, 2006).
[196] Prosecutor v. Muvunyi, Case No. ICTR-2000-55A-T, Judgment and Sentence (Sept. 12, 2006).
[197] Timothy L. H. McCormack & Gerry J. Simpson, The Law of War Crimes: National and International Approaches 45 (1997)(alteration in original).

But Nazi war criminals were treated differently after World War II. Before the International Military Tribunal (IMT) at Nuremberg, several officials from the Hitler regime were charged with crimes against humanity (CAH) pursuant to Article 6(c) of the Nuremberg Charter, which criminalized "murder, extermination, enslavement, deportation and other inhumane acts committed against any civilian population before or during the war, or *persecutions on political, racial or religious grounds* in execution of or in connection with any crime within the jurisdiction of the Tribunal."[198] (This required link with the Charter's other substantive crimes, i. e., crimes against peace/war crimes (the so-called "war nexus"), was dropped in the subsequent statute (Control Council Law No. 10) governing Allied prosecutions in the individual German zones.)[199]

In its jurisprudence, the Nuremberg tribunals interpreted persecution as a crime against humanity quite broadly. One expert has observed that in its general finding of Nazi persecution of the Jews, the IMT focused on "the passing of discriminatory laws; the exclusion of members of an ethnic or religious group from aspects of social, political, and economic life; and the creation of ghettos."[200] The Tribunal also convicted various Nazi leaders of persecution vis-à-vis an expansive scale of conduct. For instance, the gravamen of the persecution count against Hitler's chief lieutenant, Hermann Goering, were the economic harms he inflicted on the Jews, particularly his imposing on them a one-billion-mark penalty after *Kristallnacht*, a 1938 anti-Jewish pogrom initiated and conducted by the Nazis.[201] Baldur von Schirach's CAH-persecution conviction was based principally on his deportation of Jews from Vienna in his capacity as that city's *Gauleiter* (regional branch Nazi leader).[202]

Of particular interest for the purposes of this Chapter were the Nuremberg CAH-persecution cases against top Nazi media figures. Before the IMT, crimes against humanity (CAH) charges were brought against Julius Streicher, publisher of the weekly anti-Semitic newspaper *Der Stürmer*, and Hans Fritzsche, head of the Radio Section of the Nazi Propaganda Ministry.[203] The IMT convicted Streicher of CAH-

---

[198] Nuremberg Rules, in Agreement for the Prosecution and Punishment of the Major War Criminals of the European Axis art. 6(c), Aug. 8, 1945, 59 Stat. 1544, 1547, 82 UNTS 279 (emphasis added) (hereinafter "Nuremberg Charter").

[199] *See* Beth Van Schaack, *The Definition of Crimes against Humanity: Resolving the Incoherence*, 37 COLUM. J. TRANSNAT'L L. 787, 791, 797–8 (1999) (describing the "war nexus" and its being deleted in Control Council Law No. 10 and explaining that it was included in the Nuremberg Charter to blunt accusations of using an *ex post facto* law given that CAH had never previously been codified or charged).

[200] Mohamed Elewa Badar, *From the Nuremberg Charter to the Rome Statute: Defining the Elements of Crimes against Humanity*, 5 SAN DIEGO INT'L L.J. 73, 128 (2004).

[201] *See* United States v. Goering, Judgment (Int'l Mil. Trib. Sept. 30, 1946), *reprinted in* 6 FRD 69, 148–9 (1946) (describing how Goering's interest in raising the billion-mark fine was "primarily economic – how to get their property and how to force them out of the economic life of Europe").

[202] *Goering*, Judgment, von Schirach, 6 FRD at 172–3.

[203] Gordon, A War of Media, *supra* note 65, at 143.

persecution in connection with his vicious newspaper harangues against the Jews. The judgment against Streicher, often referred to as "Jew-Baiter Number 1,"[204] did not posit a direct causal link between Streicher's communications and any particular instances of killing. Rather, it characterized his brand of journalism as a poison "injected in to the minds of thousands of Germans which caused them to follow the [Nazi] policy of Jewish persecution and extermination."[205] At the same time, the Tribunal found that, given his knowledge of the Nazis' executing the Final Solution, "Streicher's incitement to murder and extermination at the time when Jews in the East were being killed under the most horrible conditions clearly constitutes persecution on political and racial grounds in connection with War Crimes as defined by the [IMT] Charter, and constitutes a Crime against Humanity."[206]

As head of the Radio Division of the Propaganda Ministry and host of the daily radio program "Hans Fritzsche Speaks," Fritzsche espoused the general policies of the Nazi regime, which "aroused in the German people those passions which led them to the commission of atrocities."[207] But the IMT acquitted Fritzsche on the ground that his discourse was less incendiary than Streicher's, and that he had not exercised control over the formulation of propaganda policies. The IMT took him at his word that he had resisted promoting the most radical Nazi views and had been a mere conduit of directives passed down to him.[208] With regard to the charge that he had incited the commission of war crimes by deliberately falsifying news to arouse passions in the German people, the IMT found no evidence Fritzsche knew any such information was false.[209]

A third propaganda defendant, Otto Dietrich, was charged by the American zonal Nuremberg Military Tribunal (NMT) with CAH-persecution pursuant to CCL No. 10 as part of the *Ministries Case* (the *Dietrich Judgment*).[210] As Reich Press Chief from 1937–45, Dietrich exercised ideological oversight and control over all of Germany's newspaper editors and was in a position to select the newspaper content Hitler reviewed on a daily basis.[211] Based on his management of Germany's virulently anti-Semitic print media content in the period leading up to and during the

---

[204]   EARLE RICE, Nazi War Criminals 34 (1998).
[205]   *Goering*, Judgment, Streicher, 6 FRD at 161–3.
[206]   *Id.*
[207]   *Goering*, Judgment, Fritzsche, 6 FRD at 186–7.
[208]   Transcript of IMT Proceedings, June 26, 1946, reprinted in 17 *The Trial of German Major War Criminals: Proceedings of the International Military Tribunal Sitting at Nuremberg Germany* 243, 245, 256 (1948).
[209]   *Goering*, Judgment, Fritzsche, 6 FRD at 186–7. This decision has been roundly criticized as being at odds with the Nuremberg Principles as embodied in the IMT Judgment and Nuremberg Charter. See Gordon, A War of Media, *supra* note 65, at 144 n.17.
[210]   United States v. von Weizsaecker (*Ministries Case*), Judgment, *in* 14 TRIALS OF WAR CRIMINALS BEFORE THE NUREMBERG MILITARY TRIBUNALS: "THE MINISTRIES CASE" 308, 565–76 (1951) (hereinafter "14 Trials of War Criminals: The Ministries Case").
[211]   Ralf Georg Reuth, Goebbels 176 (1993).

Holocaust, Dietrich was found guilty of CAH-persecution. In the words of the *Ministries* NMT:

> It is thus clear that a well thought-out, oft-repeated, persistent campaign to arouse the hatred of the German people against Jews was fostered and directed by the press department and its press chief, Dietrich ... The only reason for this campaign was to blunt the sensibilities of the people regarding the campaign of persecution and murder which was being carried out ... [The] clear and expressed purpose [of these press and periodical directives] was to enrage Germans against the Jews, to justify the measures taken and to be taken against them, and to subdue any doubts which might arise as to the justice of measures of racial persecution to which Jews were to be subjected ... By them Dietrich consciously implemented, and by furnishing the excuses and justifications, participated in, the crimes against humanity regarding Jews.[212]

5.3.2.2 The ICTY Foundational Persecution Judgments

Interestingly, despite providing important guidance regarding the general outlines of CAH-persecution, none of the post-World War II jurisprudence enumerated its precise elements. As explained by Robert Cryer:

> It remains controversial whether the Nuremberg Charter created new law, or whether it recognized an existing crime. Among those concluding that it was a new crime, many argued that the principle of non-retroactivity had to give way to the overriding need for accountability for large-scale murder and atrocities recognized as criminal by all nations. Perhaps because of this uncertainty in the status of crimes against humanity, the Nuremberg judgment tended to blur discussion of crimes against humanity and war crimes and provided very little guidance on the particular elements of the crime.[213]

Moreover, it was still not even clear if the IMT "war nexus" applied to crimes against humanity. The chapeau of ICTY Statute Article 5, which empowered the Tribunal to prosecute CAH offenses only "when committed in armed conflict," might have led some to conclude it was still a requirement.[214] But the global community was quickly disabused of that notion when the Security Council adopted the ICTR Statute without such a requirement in the CAH chapeau (Article 3 – only requiring the enumerated crimes be committed "as part of a widespread or systematic attack against any civilian population on national, political, ethnic, racial or religious grounds").[215] Moreover, subsequent ICTY case law

---

[212]   14 Trials of War Criminals: "The Ministries Case," *supra* note 207, at 565–76 (1950).
[213]   Robert Cryer et al., An Introduction to International Criminal Law and Procedure 230–1 (3rd edn. 2014).
[214]   ICTY Statute, *supra* note 79, art. 5.
[215]   ICTR Statute, *supra* note 78, art. 3.

confirmed that this limitation in the Statute was jurisdictional rather than definitional. For example, in *Prosecutor* v. *Kunarac, et al.*, the Appeals Chamber held: "[T]
he requirement [committed in armed conflict] contained in Article 5 of the Statute
is a purely jurisdictional prerequisite which is satisfied by proof that there was an
armed conflict and that objectively the acts of the accused are linked geographically
as well as temporally with the armed conflict."[216]

Further, thanks to the issuance of other ICTY CAH decisions, a test for persecution began to take shape. In *Prosecutor* v. *Tadić*, an ICTY Trial Chamber laid out
three foundational requirements: (1) the occurrence of a discriminatory act or
omission; (2) a discriminatory basis for that act or omission on one of the listed
grounds, specifically race, religion or politics; and (3) the intent to cause and a
resulting infringement of an individual's enjoyment of a basic or fundamental
right.[217]

In *Prosecutor* v. *Kupreškić*, another ICTY Trial Chamber articulated a four-part
test for ascertaining whether conduct can satisfy a CAH-persecution's *actus reus*
requirement: (1) a gross or blatant denial; (2) on discriminatory grounds; (3) of a
fundamental right, laid down in international customary or treaty law; and (4)
reaching the same level of gravity as the other crimes against humanity enumerated
in Article 5 of the ICTY Statute.[218]

In setting forth this new *actus reus* test, and by way of clarifying it, the *Kupreškić*
Chamber offered some important insights concerning the character and extent of
persecution: (a) "a narrow definition of persecution is not supported in customary
international law,"[219] and was understood by the IMT to "include a wide spectrum of
acts ... ranging from discriminatory acts targeting ... general political, social and
economic rights, to attacks on [the] person";[220] (b) persecution also includes acts
such as murder and other serious acts on the person; (c) it is "commonly used to
describe a series of acts rather than a single act," as "[a]cts of persecution will usually
form part of ... a patterned practice, and must be regarded in their context"; and (d)
"[a]s a corollary to [(c)], discriminatory acts charged as persecution must not be
considered in isolation" and "may not, in and of themselves, be so serious as to
constitute a crime against humanity" – for example, curtailing rights to participate in
social life (such as visits to public parks, theaters or libraries) must not be considered
in isolation but examined in their context and weighed for their cumulative effect.[221]

---

[216]   Prosecutor v. Kunarac, et al., Case Nos. IT-96–23 & IT-96–23/1-A, Judgment, para. 83 (Int'l Crim.
        Trib. For the Former Yugoslavia June 12, 2002).
[217]   Prosecutor v. Tadić, Case No. IT-94–1-T, Opinion and Judgment, para. 715 (Int'l Crim. Trib. for the
        Former Yugoslavia May 7, 1997).
[218]   Prosecutor v. Kupreškić, Case No. IT-95–16-T, Judgment, para. 621 (Int'l Crim. Trib. for the Former
        Yugoslavia Jan. 14, 2000).
[219]   *Id.* para. 615.
[220]   *Id.* para. 597.
[221]   *Id.* para. 615.

Applying this precedent, the Trial Chamber in *Prosecutor* v. *Brđanin* found that "'the denial of fundamental rights to Bosnian Muslims and Bosnian Croats, including the ... right to proper judicial process, or right to proper medical care' [constitute] persecutions."[222] Significantly, the Trial Chamber rejected the defense argument that "any conviction [for a violation of any of these four rights] violates the principle of legality."[223] It found that, "the Accused is obviously confusing the underlying acts or violations with the actual crime charged, namely that of persecution."[224] And it concluded: "Any possible conviction would be for this crime and not for the underlying acts or violations [which] should not be considered in isolation, but in context, looking at their cumulative effect."[225]

5.3.2.3 The ICTR Hate Speech as Persecution Cases

PROSECUTOR V. RUGGIU. In general, the ICTR took the position that hate speech could be the *actus reus* for CAH-persecution. The first case to so hold was *Prosecutor* v. *Ruggiu*, which we previously considered in connection with the offense of incitement to commit genocide.[226] It will be recalled that both before and during the Rwandan Genocide, Georges Ruggiu, a Belgian national who worked as an RTLM announcer, let loose a torrent of venomous invective against Tutsis, moderate Hutus and Belgians.[227]

In taking his guilty plea, the Trial Chamber described Ruggiu as playing "a crucial role in the incitement of ethnic hatred and violence" against both Tutsis and Belgian residents in Rwanda.[228] Apart from incitement, his admission of guilt was also predicated on committing the crime of CAH-persecution.[229] In sentencing him, the Trial Chamber had occasion to review the Nuremberg jurisprudence regarding this delict. It began with the *Streicher* judgment, observing that the IMT in that case "held that the publisher of a private, anti-Semitic weekly newspaper 'Der Stürmer' incited the German population to actively persecute the Jewish people."[230] The Trial Chamber then held that "[t]he *Streicher* Judgement is particularly relevant to the present case since the accused, like Streicher, infected peoples' minds with ethnic hatred and persecution."[231]

Citing *Kupreškić*,[232] the ICTR Trial Chamber then laid out the specific elements of CAH-persecution: "(a) those elements required for all crimes against humanity

---

[222] Prosecutor v. Brđanin, Case No. IT-99-36-T, Judgment, paras. 1029–1031 (Int'l Crim. Trib. for the Former Yugoslavia Sept. 1, 2004).

[223] *Id.* para. 1030.

[224] *Id.* para. 1030.

[225] *Id.* paras. 1030–1031.

[226] *Prosecutor* v. *Ruggiu*, Case No. ICTR 97–32-I, Judgment and Sentence (June 1, 2000).

[227] Bartrop, Biographical Encyclopedia, *supra* note 121, at 127.

[228] *Ruggiu*, Case No. ICTR 97–32-I, Judgment and Sentence, para. 50.

[229] *Id.* paras. 10, 42–5.

[230] *Id.* para. 19.

[231] *Id.*

[232] *Kupreškić*, Case No. IT-95-16-T, Judgment, para. 627.

under the ICTR statute, (b) a gross or blatant denial of a fundamental right reaching the same level of gravity as the other acts prohibited under Article 5, and (c) discriminatory grounds."[233] Concerning element (a), the Chamber reviewed the CAH *mens rea*, which it held to be the *intent* to commit the target crime (murder, rape, etc.), along with the *knowledge* of the broader context (i.e., the widespread or systematic attack against the civilian population) in which that enumerated crime occurs.[234] Regarding the latter, the Chamber noted:

> The perpetrator must knowingly commit crimes against humanity in the sense that he must understand the overall context of his act ... Part of what transforms an individual's act(s) into a crime against humanity is the inclusion of the act within a greater dimension of criminal conduct; therefore an accused should be aware of this greater dimension in order to be culpable thereof. Accordingly, actual or constructive knowledge of the broader context of the attack, meaning that the accused must know that his act(s) is part of a widespread or systematic attack on a civilian population and pursuant to some kind of policy or plan, is necessary to satisfy the requisite *mens rea* element of the accused.[235]

In respect of the latter two elements, the judges opined:

> The Trial Chamber considers that when examining the acts of persecution which have been admitted by the accused, it is possible to discern a common element. Those acts were [direct and public radio broadcasts all aimed at singling out and attacking the Tutsi ethnic group and Belgians] on discriminatory grounds, by depriving them of the fundamental rights to life, liberty and basic humanity enjoyed by members of wider society. The deprivation of these rights can be said to have as its aim the death and removal of those persons from the society in which they live alongside the perpetrators, or eventually even from humanity itself.[236]

There are two key takeaways from these extracts. First, the offense of CAH-persecution can be consummated without the speaker explicitly urging violence. By invoking *Streicher*, the *Ruggiu* panel focused on the *Stürmer* editor's goading the German public to "persecute" the Jews. But "persecution" does not ineludibly denote physical violence. As defined by Oxford Dictionaries, "persecution" is "hostility and ill treatment, especially because of race or political or religious beliefs; oppression."[237] This point is reinforced by the Trial Chamber's stress on Streicher's infecting "peoples' minds with ethnic *hatred* and persecution."[238] The analogy is clear given the Chamber's describing Ruggiu's persecution liability as arising from

---

[233] *Ruggiu*, Case No. ICTR 97–32-I, Judgment and Sentence, para. 21.
[234] *Id.* para. 20.
[235] *Id.* (alteration in original) (internal quotation marks omitted) (quoting Prosecutor v. Kayishema, Case No. ICTR-95–1-T, Judgment, para. 133–134, May 21, 1999).
[236] *Id.* para. 22.
[237] *Definition of Persecution*, OXFORD DICTIONARIES, http://oxforddictionaries.com/definition/english/persecution (last visited Oct. 7, 2017).
[238] *Ruggiu*, Case No. ICTR 97–32-I, Judgment and Sentence, para. 19 (emphasis added).

radio broadcasts that "singled out" and "attacked" Tutsis and Belgians. Put another way, the radio harangues themselves attacked the victims – they were not merely a means by which the defendant urged others to perpetrate violence. Within the legal meaning of "persecution," the words themselves can effect a deprivation of rights, including security and liberty itself.

Second, given the chapeau's *mens rea*, of necessity, the speaker will utter her words mindful that they are part of a widespread or systematic attack directed against a civilian population. As a result, the rhetoric in question cannot be an exceptional expression of contempt that merely sullies the reputation of the target. Rather, it will be toxic speechifying consciously in chorus with physical violence or inhumane treatment. This is not mere "bad speech" in a garden-variety social setting; these are weaponized words in service of a massive or meticulously planned assault on civilians.

THE MEDIA CASE. Along with liability for direct and public incitement to commit genocide, the ICTR also evaluated the guilt of Ferdinand Nahimana, Jean-Bosco Barayagwiza and Hassan Ngeze in reference to CAH-persecution. Consistent with the *Ruggiu* Trial Chamber, the *Media Case* judges began by considering *Kupreškić's* prerequisite of a "gross or blatant denial of a fundamental right reaching the same level of gravity" as the other acts enumerated as "crimes against humanity under the Statute."[239] It then concluded that "hate speech targeting a population on the basis of ethnicity, or other discriminatory grounds, reaches this level of gravity and constitutes persecution under Article 3(h) of its Statute."[240] The judges expounded further:

> In *Ruggiu*, the Tribunal so held, finding that the radio broadcasts of RTLM, in singling out and attacking the Tutsi ethnic minority, constituted a deprivation of "the fundamental rights to life, liberty and basic humanity enjoyed by members of the wider society." Hate speech is a discriminatory form of aggression that destroys the dignity of those in the group under attack. It creates a lesser status not only in the eyes of the group members themselves but also in the eyes of others who perceive and treat them as less than human. The denigration of persons on the basis of their ethnic identity or other group membership in and of itself, as well as in its other consequences, can be an irreversible harm ... Unlike the crime of incitement, which is defined in terms of intent, the crime of persecution is defined also in terms of impact. It is not a provocation to cause harm. It is itself the harm. Accordingly, there need not be a call to action in communications that constitute persecution.[241]

---

[239] Prosecutor v. Nahimana, Barayagwiza, & Ngeze, Judgment and Sentence, ICTR Case No. 99–52-T para. 1072 (Dec. 3, 2003) (quoting Prosecutor v. Kupreskic, Case No. IT-95–16-T, Judgment, para. 627 [Int'l Crim. Trib. for the Former Yugoslavia Jan. 14, 2000]).

[240] *Id.*

[241] *Id.* para. 1072–3.

Of note, the Trial Chamber implicitly, and unqualifiedly, placed hate speech on the same gravity level as the other listed CAH offenses. This position was rooted in international law's general sanctioning of hate speech. Thus, parties to the widely adopted International Covenant on Civil and Political Rights (ICCPR) and Convention on the Elimination of all Forms of Racial Discrimination (CERD) must proscribe advocacy that promotes and incites discrimination against protected groups.[242] Consensus about hate speech among municipal jurisdictions, the Chamber noted, further bolstered this ratio as similar prohibitions could be found in the domestic criminal codes of a large swath of nations, including Rwanda, Vietnam, Russia, Finland, Ireland, Ukraine, Iceland, Monaco, Slovenia and China.[243]

The Chamber also pointed out that its holding was on all fours with *Streicher*. In that case, the Nuremberg IMT found the tabloid editor guilty of CAH-persecution "for anti-Semitic writings that significantly predated the extermination of Jews in the 1940s."[244] And Streicher's gutter-journalism was perceived, the *Media Case* Chamber emphasized, "to be a ... poison that infected the minds of the German people and conditioned them to follow the lead of National Socialists in persecuting the Jewish people."[245] In light of all this authority, then, the *Media Case* bench ruled that "hate speech that expresses ethnic or other forms of discrimination violates the norm of customary international law prohibiting discrimination."[246]

With these principles in mind, the Chamber then evaluated the conduct of the media defendants in the dock. And it found liability:

> In Rwanda, the virulent writings of *Kangura* and the incendiary broadcasts of RTLM functioned in the same way, conditioning the Hutu population and creating a climate of harm, as evidenced in part by the extermination and genocide that followed. Similarly, the activities of the CDR [of which Barayagwiza was a founding member], a Hutu political party that demonized the Tutsi population as the enemy, generated fear and hatred that created the conditions for extermination and genocide in Rwanda.[247]

The Chamber's finding was linked to specific instances of hate speech as persecution.[248] For instance, the decision referenced a pre-genocide (February 1993) *Kangura* piece carrying the headline "A Cockroach Cannot Give Birth to a

---

[242] *Id.* para. 1074.
[243] *Id.* para. 1075. Although I am sympathetic to the Trial Chamber's holding, I do not share its view on the importance of the consensus on international and municipal prohibitions on hate speech. I believe that the speech is criminal in the special CAH context because it must be moored to a widespread or systematic attack against a civilian population, not because it is typically criminalized in the garden-variety domestic setting.
[244] *Id.* para. 1073.
[245] *Id.*
[246] *Id.* para. 1076.
[247] *Id.* para. 1073.
[248] *Id.* para. 1078.

Butterfly."[249] The judges noted that the piece was "brimming with ethnic hatred" but "did not call on readers to take action against the Tutsi population."[250]

The judgment also made reference to an "RTLM interview broadcast in June 1994, in which Simbona, interviewed by Gaspard Gahigi, talked of the cunning and trickery of the Tutsi." Per the Chamber, this also constituted persecution."[251] Such persecutory hate speech was also directed at women, the Chamber observed. "The portrayal of the Tutsi woman as a *femme fatale*, and the message that Tutsi women were seductive agents of the enemy, was conveyed repeatedly by RTLM and *Kangura*."[252]

This section of the judgment was fittingly put into perspective by a trial witness, who testified that the defendants' persecutory speech "spread petrol throughout the country little by little, so that one day it would be able to set fire to the whole country."[253] This, the Chamber added, "is the poison described in the *Streicher* judgment."[254]

5.3.2.4 The ICTY Hate Speech as Persecution Cases

PROSECUTOR V. KORDIĆ. The decision in *Prosecutor v. Kordić* (2001) is the ICTY's sole indication of its position on whether hate speech can constitute the *actus reus* for CAH-persecution.[255] As will be recalled, Dario Kordić was a prominent Bosnian Croat politician, who was accused of helping spearhead Bosnian Croat efforts to ethnically cleanse an area of central Bosnia-Herzegovina of Muslims so as to integrate it into greater Croatia.

Count One of the indictment accused Kordić and others of perpetrating the ethnic cleansing campaign by, *inter alia*, "encouraging, instigating and promoting hatred, distrust and strife on political, racial, ethnic or religious grounds, by propaganda, speeches and otherwise."[256] For unknown reasons, and inconsistent with mainstream judicial writing craft, the judgment failed to identify the speeches that are the subject of the persecution count. Nor does it examine the text of any such speeches.[257] Similarly, nowhere in the written decision can one find reference to any prosecution characterization of the allegedly persecutory speech.[258] It is difficult to explain this significant information vacuum.

---

[249] *Id.*
[250] *Id.* para. 1037.
[251] *Id.* para. 1078.
[252] *Id.* para. 1079.
[253] *Id.* para. 1078 (internal quotation marks omitted).
[254] *Id.*
[255] Prosecutor v. Kordić, Case No. IT-95–14/2-T, Judgment, para. 209 (Int'l Crim. Trib. for the Former Yugoslavia Feb. 26, 2001).
[256] *Kordić*, Case No. IT-95–14/2-T, Annex V, para. 37.
[257] Gregory S. Gordon, *Hate Speech and Persecution: A Contextual Approach*, 46 VAND. J. TRANSNAT'L L. 303, 326 (2013) (hereinafter "Contextual Approach").
[258] One paragraph in the judgment, 523, does set forth the *defense* arguments regarding Kordić's statements. *Kordić*, Case No. IT-95–14/2-T, Judgment, para. 523. That paragraph merely asserts that

Nonetheless, despite the factual lacunae, the Trial Chamber engaged in what can only be described as an academic analysis of hate speech as persecution in the abstract. In order to determine whether the nominally charged hate speech at issue could constitute the *actus reus* of the persecution count, the panel applied the four-prong test formulated in *Kupreškić*: "(1) a gross or blatant denial; (2) on discriminatory grounds; (3) of a fundamental right, laid down in international customary or treaty law; (4) reaching the same level of gravity as the other crimes against humanity enumerated in Article 5 of the [ICTY] Statute."[259]

Before applying the test, the Chamber made a couple of preliminary observations. First, it held that "acts which meet the four criteria set out above, as well as the general requirements applicable to all crimes against humanity, may qualify as persecution without violating [the *nullum crimen* principle]."[260] The Chamber also noted that in previous ICTY persecution convictions, the conduct in question consisted of physical assaults on the victims and their property.[261] Nevertheless, the judges observed that the persecution offense "encompasses both bodily and mental harm and infringements upon individual freedom."[262]

Applying *Kupreškić*, though, the *Kordić* Chamber did not find the supposed hate speech could satisfy the *actus reus* test and thus amount to persecution. Its analysis was contained in paragraph 209, whose initial text did not augur well for the prosecution: "[The] indictment against Dario Kordić is the first indictment in the history of the International Tribunal to allege this act [encouraging and promoting hatred on political, racial, ethnic or religious grounds]."[263] The rest of the paragraph was then devoted to rendering a decision on the merits. It found that, given an inferior gravity level in relation to other CAH enumerated acts, as well as a lack of customary international law status, hate speech could not serve as the *actus reus* for CAH-persecution. In the words of paragraph 209:

> The Trial Chamber, however, finds that this act [hate speech], as alleged in the Indictment, does not by itself constitute persecution as a crime against humanity. It is not enumerated as a crime elsewhere in the International Tribunal Statute, but most importantly, it does not rise to the same level of gravity as the other acts enumerated in Article 5. Furthermore, the criminal prohibition of this act has not attained the status of customary international law. Thus to convict the

---

the defendant's statements were not "racially inflammatory" or intended to foment hatred of Bosnian Muslims by Bosnian Croats. *Id.* This paragraph stands alone – there is no commentary on it by the Chamber. The prosecution's response to it is not provided either. Gordon, Contextual Approach, *supra* note 254, at 327.

[259] *Kordić*, Case No. IT-95–14/2-T, Judgment, para. 195.

[260] *Id.*

[261] *Id.* para. 198.

[262] *Id.*

[263] *Id.* para. 209. Curiously, however, the Chamber neglected to mention that several other judicial opinions had grappled with this issue outside of the ICTY.

accused for such an act as is alleged as persecution would violate the principle of legality.[264]

A footnote number 272 is dropped in support of paragraph 209.[265] It claimed that "criminal prosecution of speech acts falling short of incitement finds *scant* support in international case law"[266] (suggesting, of course, that there is *some* support for such prosecutions – notwithstanding the *Kordić* panel's omitting to define the vital term "*incitement*"). Based on the text that immediately follows, the implied small modicum of support would appear to come from *Streicher*, whose reach the Chamber attempted to limit. In that case, the *Kordić* Chamber noted, "the International Military Tribunal convicted the accused of persecution because he 'incited the German people to active persecution,'" which amounted to "*incitement* to murder and extermination."[267]

The footnote then cited to the ICTR judgment in *Prosecutor v. Akayesu* for the proposition that legitimate speech crimes prosecutions at the ad hoc tribunals had been limited to incitement, implying that hate speech as persecution was not a viable charge. The reference to *Akayesu* seems meant to emphasize the paucity of speech-focused CAH-persecution charges in atrocity cases. But liability was only collaterally connected to speech in that case. As we have seen, Jean-Paul Akayesu was not a journalist or major politician, but a small-town mayor whose liability was based on the fact that he happened to make one speech that led to an incitement conviction; the portion of the *Akayesu* decision cited by the ICTY Trial Chamber was in reference to incitement, not CAH-persecution. And so it was inapposite.

Remarkably, however, the judgment omitted all reference to the *Ruggiu* precedent, which was entirely on point. That decision had been handed down the previous year and involved a defendant convicted of CAH-persecution. On a related note, the *Kordić* Chamber also asserted without further elaboration that "the only speech act explicitly criminalised under the statutes of the International Military Tribunal, Control Council Law No. 10, the ICTY, ICTR and ICC Statute, is the direct and public incitement to commit genocide."[268]

The *Kordić* panel also tried to cast doubt on the ICCPR/CERD-anti-incitement-justification of the ICTR hate-speech-as-persecution jurisprudence. The judges asserted that certain countries have signed on to the ICCPR and CERD with reservations regarding the hate speech provisions.[269] Given this supposed "split,"

---

[264] *Id.* (footnotes omitted).

[265] *Id.* para. 209 n.272.

[266] *Id.*

[267] *Id.* (emphasis added). Of course, the *Kordić* Chamber ignored *Streicher's* key language about the defendant's having "infected the German mind with the virus of anti-Semitism." And the incitement referenced by the Chamber is to "persecution" – not violence.

[268] *Id.* Apart from being flawed grammatically, that observation is erroneous given that, as seen previously in this paper, "instigating" and "ordering" are other speech acts explicitly criminalized in the ICTY and ICTR Statutes.

[269] *Id.*

the *Kordić* Chamber found, "[T]here is no international consensus on the criminalisation of this act [incitement] that rises to the level of customary international law."[270] But only the United States, a radically speech-protective jurisdiction, is ever specified as a reserving state. Thus, the Chamber's asserted "split" in the world on this issue is never backed up.

PROSECUTOR V. ŠEŠELJ. The other ICTY case centering on hate speech as persecution was *Prosecutor v. Vojislav Šešelj* (2016).[271] As we saw previously, Šešelj's early-1990s orations urged Serb ultranationalist militias to kill and ethnically cleanse non-Serbs in portions of Croatia, Bosnia and the Serbian province of Vojvodina. As a result, the ICTY charged him with individual (via direct commission, instigation and aiding and abetting) and joint criminal enterprise (JCE) responsibility for commission of war crimes and crimes against humanity, including persecution.[272]

On March 31, 2016, two of the Šešelj Trial Chamber judges, over the strong dissent of a third, acquitted the defendant of all charges against him in a case that had dragged on for nearly nine years.[273] Elsewhere I have described the judgment as flawed.[274] Its key deficiency in reference to the crimes against humanity charges lay in its baseline analysis of the situation in the former Yugoslavia. In stark contrast to well-settled ICTY precedent, the two majority judges found that extremist Serbs did not carry out a widespread or systematic attack against non-Serb civilians in relevant areas during the time in question.[275] Rather, they opined, the milieu was strictly one of garden-variety armed conflict where civilians from all ethnic groups participated in "street fighting" over contested territory, but no criminal actions were directed toward civilians.[276] Thus, rather than engaging in ethnic cleansing, the two judges found that the Serb militias were merely providing safe convoy.[277]

---

[270] *Id.*

[271] Prosecutor v. Vojislav Šešelj, Case No. IT-03–67-T, Judgment (Int'l Crim. Trib. for the Former Yugoslavia March 31, 2016).

[272] Prosecutor v. Šešelj, Case No. IT-03–67, Third Amended Indictment, paras. 5, 10(b), 17(k) (Int'l Crim. Trib. for the Former Yugoslavia Dec. 7, 2007). The speeches, including some characterized as "instigation," were also relevant in the indictment insofar as they constituted part of Šešelj's contribution to the JCE to commit war crimes and crimes against humanity.

[273] Marlise Simons, *Tribunal Acquits Serbian Nationalist of War Crimes*, N.Y. TIMES, Mar. 31, 2016, at A9.

[274] Gregory S. Gordon, *Vojislav Šešelj's Acquittal at the ICTY: Law in an Alternate Universe*, Jurist, Apr. 11, 2016, www.jurist.org/forum/2016/04/gregory-gordon-seselj-acquittal.php.

[275] *Šešelj*, Case No. IT-03–67-T, para. 192 ("The majority considers that insufficient evidence was offered to establish irrefutably that a widespread or systematic attack was directed against civilian populations.")

[276] *Id.* ("[Rather than a widespread or systematic attack against a civilian population] the evidence proffered and examined reveals an armed conflict between opposing military factions with some civilian elements involved.") The Trial Chamber added: "The presence of an indeterminate portion of civilian combatants, within the context of confrontations that many witnesses described as street fights wherein every square inch of territory, every house was fought over, provides a perspective that forecloses the view that an attack was directed against a civilian population." *Id.*

[277] *Id.* para. 193.

Thus, the panel majority concluded that armed Serb extremists were, in effect, running a kind of charitable Greyhound bus service for non-Serb residents of the areas they attacked. Of course, this meant that they could not have committed a widespread or systematic attack against those civilians. Consequently, with a core CAH chapeau element entirely missing, the majority obviated the necessity to analyze Šešelj's liability for CAH-persecution.[278]

5.3.2.5 The *Media Case* Appeals Chamber Decision

By the end of 2001, as we have seen, there was an apparent split between the ICTR and ICTY regarding extremist rhetoric and persecution. The Rwanda tribunal found that hate speech not calling for action, on its own, could satisfy the offense's *actus reus*. The Yugoslav tribunal found otherwise. The split might have been resolved by the Appeals Chamber in the ICTR *Media Case*, whose defendants challenged their convictions for, *inter alia*, hate speech as CAH-persecution.[279] But it was not.

As might have been expected, Nahimana, Barayagwiza and Ngeze relied on *Kordić* to argue that mere hate speech could not be the basis of a CAH-persecution conviction.[280] This contention was supported by an *amicus curiae* brief from the Open Society Institute (OSI), an American nongovernmental organization. In arguing that the defendants' persecution convictions should be reversed, the brief stressed that Streicher's persecution conviction was solely based on his "prompting 'to murder and extermination at the time when Jews in the East were being killed under the most horrible conditions.'"[281] OSI developed further this line of reasoning by also citing the IMT's acquittal of Hans Fritzsche "on grounds that his hate speeches did not seek 'to incite the Germans to commit atrocities against the conquered people.'"[282]

In sustaining the findings of guilt, the Appeals Chamber found that hate speech, in the context of other conduct comprising a persecutory campaign against a victim group, could be the basis for a CAH-persecution conviction.[283] But it refused to decide whether hate speech, on its own, could be the predicate for a charge of persecution as a crime against humanity: "The Appeals Chamber is of the view that

---

[278] *Id.* para. 293. In the words of the majority: "As a threshold matter, given that the majority has not affirmed the existence of crimes against humanity, the analysis that follows will be limited to determining whether the accused is liable for instigating commission of violations of the laws or customs of war." *Id.* As noted previously, this portion of the Trial Chamber's judgment – finding that there was no widespread or systematic attack against a civilian population – was overturned on appeal. MICT Press Release, *supra* note 31.

[279] Prosecutor v. Nahimana, Barayagwiza, & Ngeze, Case No. ICTR 99–52-A, Judgment (Nov. 28, 2007).

[280] *Id.* para. 970.

[281] *Id.* para. 979.

[282] *Id.* The brief also criticized the *Media Case* Trial Chamber for failing to follow the *Kordić* judgment, which had found that mere hate speech could not constitute persecution. *Id.*

[283] *Id.* paras. 985–6.

it is not necessary to decide here whether, in themselves, mere hate speeches not inciting violence against the members of the group are of a level of gravity equivalent to that for other crimes against humanity."[284] Thus, the issue was left unresolved.

5.3.3 *Instigation*

In considering the establishment of the ad hoc tribunal statutes, we saw previously that ICTY Statute Article 7 and ICTR Statute Article 6 both assign liability to persons who "planned, *instigated*, ordered, committed or otherwise aided and abetted in the planning, preparation or execution of [genocide, crimes against humanity and war crimes]."[285] Instigation, the second enumerated mode of liability in these articles, has been an important charge in terms of establishing guilt in relation to atrocity at both tribunals. As a result, cases issued by ICTR/ICTY panels have gone a long way toward fleshing out the elements of this offense. This section will now consider those elements.

5.3.3.1 Actus Reus

The first ad hoc tribunal case to shed light on instigation's elements was *Prosecutor* v. *Dusko Tadić* (1997). The *Tadić* Trial Chamber took a broad view of Article 7(1) for purposes of outlining general culpability and ruled:

> [The] accused will be found criminally culpable for any conduct where it is determined that he knowingly participated in the commission of an offence that violates international humanitarian law and his participation directly and *substantially affected the commission of that offence* through supporting the actual commission before, during, or after the incident.[286]

The following year, the *Akayesu* Trial Chamber offered more gloss on the actual conduct portion of the offense. It found that instigation "involves prompting another to commit an offence; but this is different from incitement in that it is punishable only where it leads to the actual commission of an offence desired by the instigator."[287] In *Prosecutor* v. *Semanza* (2003), a different ICTR bench probed further the potential scope of conduct that could satisfy the offense. And it concluded that its *actus reus* also encompassed "urging" or "encouraging."[288] And yet another ICTR panel, in *Prosecutor* v. *Ndindabahizi* (2004), specified that such conduct cold be effected "verbally or by other means of communication."[289] The *Prosecutor* v. *Blaškić* Trial Chamber elaborated further in this regard: "Instigation can be performed by any means, both by express or

---

[284] *Id.* para. 987.
[285] ICTR Statute, *supra* note 78, art. 2; ICTY Statute, *supra* note 79, art. 4. The substantive crimes are found in Articles 2–4 of the ICTR Statute and 2–5 of the ICTY Statute.
[286] Prosecutor v. Tadić, No. IT-94-1-T, Judgment, para. 692 (May 7, 1997) (emphasis added).
[287] Prosecutor v. Jean-Paul Akayesu, Case No. ICTR-96-4-T, Judgment para. 482 (Sept. 2, 1998).
[288] Prosecutor v. Semanza, Case No. ICTR-97-20-T, Judgment and Sentence, para. 555 (May 15, 2003).
[289] Prosecutor v. Ndindabahizi, Case No. ICTR-2001-71-I, Judgment and Sentence, para. 456 (July 15, 2004).

implied conduct."[290] Still, the instigation need be "specific enough to constitute instructions ... to the physical perpetrators to commit" the target offense.[291]

But instigation, according to the ad hoc tribunals, is not limited to affirmative acts. The *Blaškić* Chamber held that Article 7(1)'s wording "is sufficiently broad to allow for the inference that both acts and omissions may constitute instigating" and that "this notion covers both express and implied conduct."[292] If the charged conduct consists of an omission, the burden falls on the prosecution to prove the instigator was "under a duty to prevent the [target] crime from being brought about."[293] Further, if the duty is found to exist, omissions "amount to instigation in circumstances where a commander has created an environment permissive of criminal behavior by subordinates."[294]

But there are limits. In *Prosecutor v. Orić* (2006), the Trial Chamber set out the full spectrum of instigation's *actus reus*. At one end of the gamut, instigation's "prompting" must be more than simply facilitating the principal crime's commission, which may suffice for aiding and abetting (for instance, in situations where the defendant had already resolved to commit the target crime, before utterance of the charged speech).[295] At the other end of the continuum, though, despite "a certain capability to impress others," instigation is different from "ordering."[296] The latter "implies at least a factual superior-subordinate relationship," while the former "does not presuppose any kind of superiority."[297]

5.3.3.2 Mens Rea

Not at first the object of consensus between the two ad hoc tribunals, a *mens rea* standard for instigation eventually materialized. Along the way, terms such as "knowledge," "intent," "indirect intent" and "intent with awareness" were utilized by different ICTR/ICTY Trial Chambers. In *Prosecutor v. Kamuhanda* (2004), for instance, the judges ruled that the instigator's "knowledge" that that his acts assisted in the commission of the offense could fulfill the *mens rea* element.[298] That differed from *Prosecutor v. Bagilishema* (2001), which held that

---

[290]   Prosecutor v. Blaškić, Case No. IT-95–14, Trial Chamber Judgment, para. 280 (Mar. 3, 2000).
[291]   Prosecutor v. Brđanin, Case No. IT-99–36-T, Judgment, paras. 468, 527, and 662 (Sept. 1, 2004).
[292]   Prosecutor v. Blaškić, Case No. IT-95–14-T, Judgment, para. 280 (Mar. 3, 2000). Presumably, this would mean instigation could be effectuated via images or nonverbal movements. *See* Jerry Kang, Trojan Horses of Race, 118 Harv. L. Rev. 1489, 1524 (2005) (noting that "nonverbal behavior can instigate retaliatory responses").
[293]   Prosecutor v. Orić, Case No. IT-03–68-T, Judgment, para. 273 (Int'l Crim. Trib. for the Former Yugoslavia June 30, 2006).
[294]   Prosecutor v. Galić, Case No. IT-98–29-T, Judgment, para. 168 (Int'l Crim. Trib. for the Former Yugoslavia Dec. 5, 2003).
[295]   *Orić*, Case No. IT-03–68-T, Judgment, para. 271.
[296]   *Id.* para. 272.
[297]   *Id.*
[298]   Prosecutor v. Kamuhanda, Case No. ICTR 95-54A-T, Judgment and Sentence, para. 599 (Jan. 1, 2004).

that the instigator must "intend" that the offense be perpetrated. At the same time, *Prosecutor v. Kordić & Čerkez* (2001) required that the instigator "directly intended" to elicit the commission of the offense.[299]

Then, in *Prosecutor v. Orić* (2006), the Trial Chamber, having reviewed the existing set of schizophrenic benchmarks, as well as the general doctrinal contours of the crime, embraced an "intent" standard for instigation.[300] In particular, the Trial Chamber found that the instigator must have a "double intent" – the intent to utter the speech and the intent for the target crime to be committed (in other words, two layers of intent).[301]

5.3.3.3 Contribution

Instigation becomes criminal only if the offending speech is followed by associated felonious conduct.[302] In other words, the prosecutor must establish a link between the exhortation and consummation of the target offense.[303] In principle, this should not be tantamount to saddling the crime with a "but-for" causation requirement. Thus, the jurisprudence establishes that "it is not necessary to prove that the crime would not have been perpetrated without the accused's involvement."[304] Rather, the prosecution must only establish "that the contribution of the accused in fact had an effect on the commission of the crime."[305]

In different judgments, this "contribution" requirement has been articulated in various ways. Certain ad hoc tribunal judges have found, for instance, that prosecutors must produce proof that the charged conduct amounted to "a clear contributing factor"[306] or "substantially contributed"[307] to the acts of the principal perpetrator. And separate ICTR panels have held that, on top of "substantial," the instigator's contribution need be "direct."[308] Not surprisingly, this smorgasbord of different iterations of the standard has created a certain amount of confusion in the jurisprudence.[309]

---

[299]   Prosecutor v. Bagilishema, Case No. ICTR-95-1A-T, Judgment of Trial Chamber I, para. 31 (June 7, 2001); *Kordić*, Case No. IT-95-14/2-T, para. 387.

[300]   *Orić*, Case No. IT-03-68-T, Judgment, para. 279.

[301]   *See* WIBKE TIMMERMANN, Incitement in International Law 242 (2014) ("The intention has to be 'present with respect to both the participant's own conduct and the principal crime he is participating in,' that is, the instigator must have a 'double intent.'")

[302]   *Akayesu*, Case No. ICTR-96-4-T, para. 482.

[303]   Prosecutor v. Blaskic, Case No. IT-95-14-T, para. 278.

[304]   *Kordić*, Case No. IT-95-14/2-T, para. 387.

[305]   *Id.*

[306]   Prosecutor v. Kvocka, Case No. IT-98-30/1-T, para. 252.

[307]   Prosecutor v. Kordić & Čerkez, Case No. IT-95-14/2-A, Judgment, Appeals Chamber Judgment, para. 27 (Dec. 17, 2004).

[308]   Prosecutor v.Ndindabahizi, Case No. ICTR-2001-71-1, Judgment and Sentence, para. 463 (July 15, 2004); Prosecutor v. Mpambara, Case No. ICTR 2001-65-A, Judgment, para. 18 (Sept. 11, 2006).

[309]   *See* GREGORY S. GORDON, Atrocity Speech Law: Foundation, Fragmentation, Fruition 247-50 (2017) (explaining the problems caused by this confusion).

5.3.4 *Ordering*

As with instigation, we saw that ordering was also inserted into the individual responsibility provisions of the ad hoc Tribunal statutes.[310] And a not insubstantial set of precedents regarding this modality has been generated by the ICTY and ICTR. These decisions establish that the heart of the offense is that a "person in a position of authority uses it to convince another to commit an offence."[311] This subdivides into three separate parts: a circumstance element (superior/subordinate relationship); an *actus reus* element (transmission of an order); and a *mens rea* element (awareness of a substantial likelihood that the crime will be committed in execution of the order).

5.3.4.1 Superior-Subordinate Relationship

The first element is relatively easy to prove. It does not require demonstrating a formal superior-subordinate relationship.[312] Rather, mere evidence of a defendant's authority to compel another to commit a crime in following the order will do.[313] What is more, even "the *implied* existence of a superior-subordinate relationship" will satisfy the requirement.[314] Unlike the doctrine of command responsibility, the superior-subordinate relationship in ordering does not entail showing effective control.[315] Thus, liability can attach in the context of a civilian superior-subordinate relationship.[316]

5.3.4.2 Actus Reus

Per the ad hoc tribunal jurisprudence, prosecutors must prove transmission of an unlawful command to one or more subordinates to satisfy ordering's *actus reus* requirement.[317] The order can be proved via circumstantial evidence.[318] And to be "unlawful," it must violate general international criminal law or international humanitarian law, "even if it is in conformity with the domestic law of the State of

---

[310] ICTR Statute, *supra* note 78, art. 2; ICTY Statute, *supra* note 79, art. 4.

[311] *Akayesu*, Case No. ICTR-96-4-T, para. 483.

[312] Prosecutor v. Kordić and Čerkez, Case No. IT-95-14/2-T, Judgment, para. 28 (Int'l Crim. Trib. for the Former Yugoslavia Feb. 26, 2001).

[313] *Id.*

[314] Prosecutor v. Semanza, Case No. ICTR-97-20-T, Judgment and Sentence, para. 342 (May 15, 2003) (emphasis added).

[315] Prosecutor v. Kamuhanda, Case No. ICTR-99-54A-A, Appeals Chamber Judgment, para. 75 (Sept. 19, 2005).

[316] *See* ILIAS BANTEKAS & SUSAN NASH, INTERNATIONAL CRIMINAL LAW 24 (2007) ("An order is a command for action or omission that is issued by a superior to a subordinate, irrespective of whether the relationship is military or civilian.")

[317] PROSECUTOR V. BRDJANIN, Case No. IT-99-36-T, Judgment, para. 270 (Int'l Crim. Trib. for the Former Yugoslavia Sept. 1, 2004).

[318] *Blaškić* Trial Judgment, Case No. IT-95-14-T, para. 281.

the person who issued it."[319] It may be written or oral, and directed at either a specific individual or individuals or to unknown recipients.[320] And the order itself need not be *prima facie* illegal for liability to attach.[321] It may also be channeled to its intended recipients through a number of intermediaries – and anyone in that chain may be liable.[322]

According to the Appeals Chamber in *Prosecutor v. Galic* (2006), a superior's omission to act is not a basis for ordering liability.[323] That stripe of culpability is covered under Article 7(3) of the ICTY Statute (Article 6(3) of the ICTR Statute and Article 28 of the Rome Statute) under the rubric of superior responsibility.[324]

Ad hoc tribunal jurisprudence establishes that guilt for ordering arises uniquely when the commanded offense is in fact perpetrated.[325] And the order must substantially contribute to the crime's commission (even if not a *sine qua non*). As a result, prosecutors must demonstrate a causal link.[326]

5.3.4.3 Mens Rea

In *Prosecutor v. Blaškić*, the Appeals Chamber articulated the ad hoc tribunal consensus for ordering's *mens rea*: "the awareness of the substantial likelihood that a crime will be committed in the execution of that order."[327] Nevertheless, as alluded to above, an order need not be facially illicit to establish guilt.[328] This is "consonant with the point that a mistake of law that does not affect *mens rea* is not exculpatory, and a mistake about whether certain conduct is criminal does not *per se* affect *mens rea*."[329] Liability is gauged pursuant to the *mens rea* of the person who issued (or passed on) the order, not that of the person who executes it.[330]

---

[319] BANTEKAS & NASH, *supra* note 313, at 24.

[320] *Id.*

[321] Prosecutor v. Blaškić, Case No. IT-95–14-T, Judgment, para. 281, 282 (Int'l Crim. Trib. for the Former Yugoslavia, Mar. 3, 2000) (hereinafter "Blaškić Trial Judgment").

[322] *Id.* para. 282.

[323] Prosecutor v. Galić, Case No. IT-98–29-A, Appeals Chamber Judgment, paras. 90, 103–04 (Nov. 30, 2006).

[324] ICTY Statute, *supra* note 79, art. 7(3); ICTR Statute *supra* note 78, art. 6(3). Blaskic Trial Judgment, *supra* note 318, para. 282.

[325] *Blaškić* Trial Judgment, *id.*

[326] Prosecutor v. Milutinović, Case No. IT-05–87-T, Trial Chamber Judgment, vol. III, para. 1213 (Feb. 26, 2009).

[327] Prosecutor v. Blaškić, Case No. IT-95–14-A, Judgment, para. 42 (Int'l Crim. Trib. for the Former Yugoslavia July 29, 2004).

[328] *Id.*

[329] CRYER, *supra* note 210, AT 376.

[330] *Blaškić* Trial Judgment, para. 282.

5.4 REFLECTIONS ON THE ATROCITY SPEECH LAW LEGACY OF THE AD HOC TRIBUNALS

5.4.1 *The Law's Adolescence as a Growth Phase*

If Nuremberg represented the birth of atrocity speech law,[331] perhaps it can be said that the ad hoc tribunals mark the period of its adolescence. Pioneering American psychologist Granville Stanley Hall once described adolescence as "a new birth" because it is then that "the higher traits" develop.[332] And that may be a fair characterization of the key advances in atrocity speech law since the establishment of the ICTY and ICTR in 1993 and 1994, respectively. Nuremberg's legacy was about beginnings, but it left a jurisprudence that was skeletal and ill-defined. The International Military Tribunal bequeathed us crimes against humanity (persecution) as embodied in a brief clause in a sole subsection of the Nuremberg Charter. Its judgments against Streicher and Fritzsche were not much longer than extended article abstracts. The Nuremberg Military Tribunal's judgment against Dietrich was somewhat lengthier. But apart from its insight that hate speech not explicitly calling for violence can constitute CAH-persecution, it offered very little in terms of doctrinal progress.

And thus, in this sense, the ad hoc tribunals indeed seem like a "new birth," where atrocity speech law comes into its own. For the development of hate speech doctrine within the rubric of crimes against humanity alone, the ICTR/ICTY era was astonishingly transformative. At the outset, the ICTR Statute and ICTY case law helpfully confirmed as permanent the directional shift of Control Council Law No. 10 toward eliminating the armed conflict nexus as a mandatory feature of CAH. ICTY case law was also quick to establish a basic test for CAH-persecution's elements in *Tadić* (discriminatory act/intention and deprivation of fundamental right) that was expanded/elaborated on in terms of *actus reus* in *Kupreškić* (*gross* deprivation of a fundamental right, laid down in international customary or treaty law and of a gravity level comparable to the other CAH offenses). So important groundwork was laid.

And upon that foundation, the hate-speech-as-persecution jurisprudence was built. *Ruggiu* adopted the position that hate speech itself could effect the gross deprivation of fundamental rights. And it stressed that the speaker would be vilifying members of the victim group, aware, and within the context of, a widespread or systematic attack directed against a civilian population, which includes that victim group. The *Media Case* Trial Chamber judgment affirmed this approach and explicitly placed hate-speech-as-persecution at the same gravity level as the other

---

[331] *See* Gregory S. Gordon, *The Propaganda Prosecutions at Nuremberg: The Origin of Atrocity Speech Law and the Touchstone for Normative Evolution*, 39 LOY. L.A. INT'L & COMP. L. REV. 209 (2017) (detailing and contextualizing the cases against the Nuremberg propaganda defendants before the IMT and NMT).

[332] Granville Stanley Hall, Adolescence Vol. 1 xiii (1904).

enumerated CAH offenses. And it demonstrated its status in customary international and treaty law, as evidenced in the hate speech prohibitions of the ICCPR and the CERD, as well as a multitude of domestic jurisdictions. The *Media Case* Trial Chamber judgment also explained the RTLM/*Kangura* resonance with Streicher's hate-journalism in Nazi Germany – both worked as a kind of verbal poison priming the population for the commission of mass murder.

Kordić provided a different perspective and permitted deeper reflection on the offense of hate speech as CAH-persecution. It focused on the hate speech stance of the United States, whose First Amendment abhors restrictions on noxious expression that does not urge imminent violence. Given US resistance to the robust anti-hate-speech provisions in the ICCPR and the CERD, among other human rights instruments, the *Kordić* Trial Chamber found that the anti-hate-speech norm (subsequently relied on by the *Media Case* panel) had not crystalized into customary international law. And, related to this, it concluded that hate-speech-as-persecution did not rise to the same level as the other listed CAH offenses. Consensus may have been lacking, but competing positions were being staked out that would allow the law to take a reflective, reasoned position.

In terms of the law governing the relationship between speech and genocide, the legacy of the ad hoc tribunals is even more impressive. When the Security Council established the ICTY/ICTR in the first part of the 1990s, "direct and public incitement to commit genocide" was merely a small set of words in Article III(c) of the Convention on the Prevention and Punishment of the Crime of Genocide.[333] By midway through the first decade of the new millennium, an entire framework for the offense had been constructed.

The wording itself of Article 2(3)(c) of the ICTR Statute – *direct* and *public* incitement to commit genocide – provides two of the most important elements of the crime. As we have seen, in *Akayesu*, the ICTR found that, for purposes of incitement to genocide, speech could be considered "public" if addressed to "a number of individuals in a public place" or to "members of the general public at large by such means as the mass media, for example, radio or television."[334] And the message could be deemed "direct" if, when viewing the language "in the light of its cultural and linguistic content, the persons for whom the message was intended immediately grasped the implication thereof."[335] *Mens rea* consists of a dual intent: (1) to provoke another to commit genocide; and (2) to commit the underlying genocide itself.[336] Significantly, at least as a matter of legal principle, causation is not an element – in other words, to establish liability, it is not necessary for the advocacy to result in genocide.[337]

---

[333] Genocide Convention, *supra* note 76.
[334] *Akayesu*, Case No. ICTR 96–4-T, para. 556.
[335] *Id.* para. 557.
[336] *Id.* para. 560.
[337] *Id.* para. 553. *See also* Prosecutor v. Nahimana, Barayagwiza, & Ngeze, Case No. ICTR 99–52-T, para. 1015.

The knottiest, and most debated, element of the crime focuses on its chief descriptor – "incitement." In delineating it, the ICTR has had to differentiate between free exercise of legitimate speech (regardless of how repugnant) and corrosion of such discourse into illicit advocacy. As we have seen, the *Media Case* Trial Chamber helpfully identified four analytic criteria to determine whether the rhetoric could be categorized as either lawful expression or criminal advocacy: its purpose[338] (encompassing, on one end of the continuum, patently legitimate objectives, such as historical research or dissemination of news, and, on the other end, clearly criminal ends such as explicit pleas for violence);[339] its text (involving a parsing and exegetical interpretation of the key words in the speech to help divine the speaker's objective);[340] its context (circumstances surrounding the speaker's text – such as contemporaneous large-scale interethnic violence, and the speaker's voice);[341] and the relationship between the speaker and the subject (calling for a more speech-protective analysis when the speaker is part of a minority criticizing either the government or the country's majority population – and less so in other situations).[342]

The ad hoc tribunals have also done a yeoman's job of fleshing out the elements of instigation and ordering. Prosecuting the former entails marshaling evidence of speech that urges violence when the violence actually takes place and the speech can be proved to have contributed to the occurrence of the violence. The crime carries a dual-pronged *mens rea* – the intent to vocalize the speech and the intent for the target crime to be perpetrated. Ordering, for its part, has been characterized by a superior-subordinate relationship between the speaker and the listener, where the latter actually carried out the crime. That the speaker may not have originated the order is of no moment. And the order itself need not be illegal on its surface for a finding of guilt. The *mens rea* consists of the awareness of a substantial likelihood that the offense will be perpetrated in execution of the order.

Overall then, practically out of whole cloth, the ad hoc tribunals have woven together an entire body of jurisprudence with detailed rules and numerous fact patterns to help guide lawyers and judges in gauging culpability for speech fostering or aggravating core international crimes. But that is only a surface assessment of the accomplishments of the ICTY/ICTR in reference to this area of the law. Digging deeper reveals issues created or left unresolved by the ad hoc tribunals. If their statutes and jurisprudence do indeed represent the adolescence of this doctrinal field, it would perhaps be well to observe that this life phase is not merely a flowering.

---

[338] *Id.* paras. 1000–6.

[339] *Id.* paras. 1004–6. The space between these two ends of the spectrum clearly invites contextual analysis. And the Tribunal has proposed certain evaluative factors such as surrounding violence and previous rhetoric. *See Nahimana, id.* at para. 1004 (speaking of massacres taking place surrounding the speaker's utterance); para. 1005 (focusing on previous conduct to reveal purpose of text).

[340] Prosecutor v. Nahimana, Barayagwiza, & Ngeze, Case No. ICTR 99–52-T, para. 1001.

[341] *Id.* para. 1022.

[342] *Id.* para. 1006.

It is also an awkward transition phase. As poet Theodore Roethke eloquently described it: "So much of adolescence is an ill-defined dying, an intolerable waiting, a longing for another place and time, another condition."[343]

5.4.2 *The Law's Adolescence as a Transitional Phase*

Ad hoc tribunal atrocity speech law as doctrinal field in transition, the other view of its adolescence, should be apparent from this paper's exposition of its contributions. The most glaring manifestation in this regard is the law on hate speech as CAH-persecution. We have seen the split between the two tribunals with respect to whether hate speech not calling for action, on its own, can satisfy the *actus reus* requirement for the offense.

In that debate between the ICTR and ICTY, my own position might have been fairly simple to glean from the exposition above. Even if there is ambiguity in the *Streicher* judgment ("poison injected into the minds" [non-advocacy hate-speech] versus "incitement to extermination when Jews in the East were being killed"), the *Dietrich* judgment is clear – nonadvocacy hate speech can be the basis of a CAH-persecution charge. Even without *Dietrich*, that position is better supported. To the extent there are concerns about stifling free speech, consider that the speech is knowingly being uttered as part of a widespread or systematic attack against a civilian population (by necessity, as this is mandated in the CAH chapeau). Such speech in service of an attack on civilians is not deserving of protection.

Moreover, as we have seen, the ICTY position is set forth in the decision of *Prosecutor* v. *Kordić*, a deeply flawed piece of jurisprudence. As pointed out above, it is plagued by internal incoherence and a poor grasp of precedent. Its holding is at odds with the great weight of authority that has taken a flexible approach to qualifying underlying acts of persecution – they need not be physical attacks, and they must be considered in relation to other persecutory acts to better ascertain their contextual significance. The *Kordić* Chamber's abstract exercise of evaluating speech in a vacuum, entirely shorn of context (both with respect to the facts of that particular case and the surrounding jurisprudence), does not make a compelling case for unconditionally shielding such speech from criminal liability.

I treat these issues in much greater detail in my articles *Hate Speech and Persecution: A Contextual Approach*[344] and *The Forgotten Nuremberg Hate Speech Case: Otto Dietrich and the Future of Persecution Law*.[345] As part of that scholarship, I also explain how assessing each hate-speech-as-persecution case should involve a

---

[343] Theodore Roethke, Meditations of an Old Woman, *in* Words for the Wind: The Collected Verse, available at www.goodreads.com/quotes/317936-so-much-of-adolescence-is-an-ill-defined-dying-an-intolerable (last visited Oct. 10, 2017).

[344] Gordon, A Contextual Approach, supra note 254, at 303.

[345] Gregory S. Gordon, *The Forgotten Nuremberg Hate Speech Case: Otto Dietrich and the Future of Persecution Law*, 75 Ohio St. L. J. 571 (2014).

granular approach to fact-finding with a view toward promoting free speech to the greatest extent possible.[346] As atrocity speech law progresses from its ad hoc tribunal "adolescence" to an International Criminal Court "adulthood," it is hoped that future jurisprudence resolves the ICTR/ICTY split as I have suggested in my articles. I believe this will help maximize prevention while protecting invaluable liberty of expression.

The "awkward adolescent" phase is apparent too when looking more closely at the law on incitement. This Chapter has provided hints at the problems lurking beneath the surface. For example, although the judgments consistently state that causation is not an element of the offense, they seem unable to resist the temptation to analyze causation in their factual portions (for example, the *Media Case* judgment devoted a portion of its analysis to establishing the link between broadcasts and the murder of individual Tutsis). And the *Akayesu* Trial Chamber nearly contradicted itself doctrinally by holding that "it is not sufficient to simply establish a possible coincidence between the Gishyeshye meeting and the beginning of the killing of Tutsi in Taba, but that *there must be proof of a possible causal link* between the statement made by the Accused during the said meeting and the beginning of the killings."[347]

This factual preoccupation with causation, along with *Akayesu*'s partially cloaking it in the mantle of quasi-legal element, has invited speculation as to whether it constitutes a *de facto* requirement. Susan Benesch has alluded to this fixation on incitement's catalytic effects as "the ghost of causation."[348] And Richard Wilson observes: "Reviewing the entire corpus of ICTR case law in incitement to commit genocide, one might reasonably ask whether the ICTR judges' attention to causation in adjudicating ICG has elevated it to the level of a requisite element of the crime."[349]

Another troublesome element is the "public" criterion. As was suggested earlier, the nub of the problem was apparent in the ICTR roadblock cases, where speeches were made to gatherings of militia. The inconsistency might have been detected through a casual review of the relevant cases discussed herein – *Bikindi*, *Kalimanzira* and *Ngirabatware*. Certain panels of judges held the roadblocks were "public" places because they were located on "public" roads, with others reaching the opposite conclusion because members of the "public" were not present. In the *Bikindi* case, regardless of all this, the location was found to be public because the defendant's voice was electronically enhanced.

From a policy perspective, there seems to be no principled distinction between or among these decisions. In other words, what was the essence of "public" such that we

---

[346] *See* Gordon, A Contextual Approach, *supra* note 254, at 365–71 (considering various scenarios in which hate speech might be protected against possible CAH-persecution charges).

[347] Prosecutor v. Akayesu, Case No. ICTR 96-4-T, Judgment, para. 349 (Sept. 2, 1998).

[348] Susan Benesch, The Ghost of Causation in International Speech Crime Cases, *in* PROPAGANDA, WAR CRIMES TRIALS AND INTERNATIONAL LAW 262 (Predrag Dojcinovic ed., 2012)(examining the relevance of causation in the ICTR judgments).

[349] Richard Wilson, *Inciting Genocide with Words*, 36 MICH. J. INT'L L. 295–8 (2015).

could define it in a way that justified making it a mandatory element of the crime? Moreover, it is not clear why "private" incitement is not just as capable of stirring listeners to action. If anything, it seems more plausible that close physical proximity to the speaker would arouse more of an emotional response than merely hearing a disembodied voice faintly crackling over the airwaves of a radio broadcast. Why should liability rise or fall pursuant to such a bright-line distinction with such little value?

Other problem areas, whose precise details are beyond the scope of this Chapter, relate to the "direct" and "incitement" elements. Regarding the former, there is a lack of precision regarding its scope. The ICTR's sole direction is to determine if the listener immediately understood the message given its cultural and linguistic content.[350] But there is no guidance as to what kind of speech this might be. For example, could it include predictions of destruction? Could it be phrased conditionally? No insight is given in this regard.

With respect to the "incitement" element, among other problems, the context criterion is wholly underdeveloped. After producing such a large body of case law, it is surprising that the ICTR never set out, in a more systematic way, some of the points of reference in discerning incitement's milieu, for example: international situation of the country where the speech is being uttered (including pressure from external states); outbreak or imminent outbreak of armed conflict; authority of the speaker; and the falsity of the statement, among others.

At the same time, even if parts of it are problematic, the incitement framework set out in the early decisions of *Akayesu* and *Nahimana* offered a basic doctrinal base to which, in theory, future decisions could return as a point of repair and build on as a platform for incitement's normative development. Unfortunately, subsequent ICTR jurisprudence failed to do that. Starting with the *Media Case* appeals judgment, the ICTR's judicial output failed systematically or comprehensively to apply, much less develop, the basic incitement framework.[351]

As the ICC takes the baton from the ad hoc tribunals and further develops the jurisprudence, it is not difficult to see how these problems can be fixed. With respect to causation, future decisions need to reaffirm in very decisive and bold language that causation is not an element of the crime, and they should refrain from analyzing it in the factual portions of the judgments. Regarding the "public" element, it should be eliminated – if the "public" nature of the incitement is relevant, that could be taken into account at sentencing.

As for the direct element, my scholarship has suggested judges create a glossary of incitement techniques that would explicitly identify the following as normatively actionable types of incitement:

---

[350]   *Akayesu*, Case No. ICTR 96-4-T, Judgment, para. 558.
[351]   *See* GORDON, ATROCITY SPEECH LAW, *supra* note 306, at 208–15 (going over the cases that have failed to apply the framework, applied it in a piecemeal fashion or failed to develop it).

(1) direct calls for destruction;
(2) predictions of destruction;
(3) verminization, pathologization, and demonization;
(4) accusation in a mirror;
(5) euphemisms and metaphors;
(6) justification during contemporaneous violence;
(7) condoning and congratulating past violence;
(8) asking questions about violence;
(9) conditional calls for incitement; and
(10) victim-sympathizer conflation (conflating victims-to-be and members of the dominant group who sympathize with them, preparing the audience for the killing of both).[352]

Similarly, regarding the "incitement" element, my scholarship has identified a set of evaluative factors that can help flesh out context (such as political context and audience characteristics).[353] It has also bifurcated context into "internal" (circumstances related to the speaker, including past discourses and tone of voice) and "external" prongs (circumstances surrounding the speech, such as media environment, recent violence, armed conflict).[354]

Of course, for the incitement crime to realize its goals of effective prevention, punishment and expression, its framework must be used systematically and consistently. As I have noted elsewhere:

> [The] most policy-sensible and logically constructed framework will be of little value unless applied by courts ... Whether [future incitement] cases are heard by domestic courts via universal jurisdiction, by new ad hoc international or regional courts, or by the International Criminal Court itself, consistent application of the framework across national and international court systems will be paramount.[355]

Finally, smaller fixes are in order for instigation and ordering. With regard to the former, as to its "contribution" requirement, there has been a confusing array of formulations over the years. I have shown elsewhere how that has arguably saddled the offense with a "but for" causation requirement as suggested in the *Šešelj* Trial Chamber judgment.[356] Thus, in light of other

---

[352] *See id.* at 285–91 (setting these out and explaining them in detail).
[353] *Id.* at 297–9.
[354] *Id.* at 296–7. In my scholarship, I also recommend adding new criteria to the "incitement element" – channel of communication (noting that certain media are more likely to incite effectively than others, such as social media versus print media), temporality and instrumentality (the latter two dealing with situations where the original speech is republished). *See id.* at 299–301.
[355] *Id.* at 303–4.
[356] *Id.* at 250 (showing that by the judgment's own account, Šešelj told militia to remove Croats forcibly and that happened – in light of his well-established influence over the militia, the judgment finding

precedents and sound policy, I recommend adopting a "substantial contribution" requirement.[357]

With regard to the offense of ordering, the problem is that it requires the target crime be actually perpetrated in order for liability to attach to the speaker. But given the required superior-subordinate relationship, which permits a reasonable inference of the substantial likelihood of order execution, I have argued that the crime should carry inchoate liability.[358] This is especially true given that incitement permits prosecuting a stranger *importuning* commission of atrocities based strictly on the speech. A superior *commanding* the same should surely be legally responsible too for the utterance itself.

5.5 CONCLUSION

The time of the ad hoc tribunals is now over. For nearly a quarter of a century, they meted out justice and created an historical record in reference to two bloody end-of-millennium cataclysms in the former Yugoslavia and Rwanda. But their legacy will extend far beyond those two tragedies. For they revived the previously moribund field of international criminal law and left precedents that have irrevocably altered the shape and direction of the jurisprudence. More particularly, they took the sparse judgments handed down at Nuremberg against Nazi propagandists Julius Streicher, Hans Fritzsche and Otto Dietrich, and developed them into a system of principles I call "atrocity speech law."

Direct and public incitement to commit genocide, hate speech as the crime against humanity of persecution, instigation and ordering – each of these modalities was defined and fleshed out by the International Criminal Tribunal for Rwanda and the International Criminal Tribunal for the former Yugoslavia. As this Chapter has argued, if Nuremberg represented the birth of atrocity speech law, the ad hoc tribunals represented their adolescence. Much of that has been good – as indicated in this paper's subtitle. The elements of the crimes have been identified and applied in a plethora of varying fact patterns. Policy rationales have been offered for the normative course taken in respect of each modality. And different panels of judges have weighed in on the contours and nuances of the law governing the relationship between speech and the core international crimes.

Unfortunately, however, the other two descriptors in this Chapter's subtitle – "the bad and the ugly" – also apply to this "adolescent" phase of atrocity speech

there was no "contribution" seems tantamount to imposing a "but for" causation standard). Although discrete portions of the Trial Chamber's judgment were overturned on appeal, the large portion of the judgment that was left undisturbed still leaves us with troubling questions about the scope of the contribution requirement.

[357] In Atrocity Speech Law, I describe other issues related to instigation, including its conflation with incitement and the recently added, and doctrinally unsupported, "different forms of persuasion" requirement). *See id.* at 242–7.

[358] *Id.* at 345–6.

law. I would submit that the "bad" relates to all the confusion, gaps and contradictions in the judgments. For example, we find: (1) the lack of clarity regarding causation in incitement or the contribution requirement for instigation; (2) the polar opposite positions taken by the ICTR and ICTY on the issue of hate speech as the *actus reus* for CAH-persecution; and (3) the lack of inchoate liability for ordering. The "ugly," for its part, has been the complete failure of recent decisions to even apply the framework (or to do so in a very piecemeal and unsystematic fashion). We see this, for example, in *Prosecutor* v. *Muvunyi* in reference to incitement and *Prosecutor* v. *Šešelj* in relation to instigation.

In my recently published book *Atrocity Speech Law: Foundation, Fragmentation, Fruition*,[359] I offer recommendations for how these problems can be fixed (as well as doctrinal and policy rationales supporting the suggested fixes). I submit that these course corrections will yield a more meaningful justice, better able to deliver just desserts, promote deterrence and educate the public. In this way, atrocity speech law can develop significantly toward its full flowering at the International Criminal Court, which is currently trying speech offense charges against former Ivorian politicians Laurent Gbagbo and Charles Blé Goudé (charged with hate-speech-as-persecution and soliciting/ordering CAH/war crimes in connection with post-election violence in Côte d'Ivoire in 2010),[360] and former Lord's Resistance Army Brigadier General Dominic Ongwen (charged with soliciting/inducing CAH/war crimes).[361] Other trials on these crimes potentially await too – of members of ISIS in relation to genocidal speech toward the Yazidis, or extremist Buddhist monks with respect to persecutory discourse against Rohingya Muslims. The law must be prepared to mete out justice fairly and effectively as we anticipate new generations of justice cycles.

Will fixing the individual modalities be enough, however? In *Atrocity Speech Law*, I contend that such "micro-level" repairs will not be sufficient – we need a "macro-level" approach. That approach is captured in my proposed "Unified Liability Theory," which would reconfigure the law such that all of the speech offenses work effectively in conjunction with one another. For instance, why is it that incitement is chargeable only in relation to genocide? Crimes against humanity and war crimes are comparably horrible transgressions. And incitement charges in reference to those crimes would permit early intervention and thus bolster preventive enforcement efforts. Pursuant to the Unified Liability

---

[359] GORDON, ATROCITY SPEECH LAW, *supra* note 306.

[360] Prosecutor v. Gbagbo, Case No. ICC-02/11–01/11–656-Red, Decision on the Confirmation of Charges paras. 167, 226 (June 12, 2014); Prosecutor v. Blé Goudé, Case No. ICC-02/11–02/11–186, Decision on the Confirmation of Charges paras. 192(d), 194 (Dec. 11, 2014).

[361] Open Society Justice Initiative, Briefing Paper, *Dominic Ongwen at the ICC: Confirmation of Charges*, OPEN SOCIETY FOUNDATIONS, January 2016, www.opensocietyfoundations.org/sites/default/files/briefing-ongwen-icc-confirmation-charges%2020160120_0.pdf

Theory, incitement would extend to both crimes against humanity and war crimes.[362]

But that will not be all. The atrocity speech cases before the ad hoc tribunals involved use of the older media – newspapers, radio and television. For speech-related crimes committed in the new media landscape, the law will need to develop further. For example, how will it deal with third-party republication of tweets or potential aiding and abetting liability for social media platforms such as Facebook or Snapchat? At the same time, one can imagine liability being extended to other offenses, such as aggression or potentially even terrorism. Clearly, atrocity speech law will see much growth in the years to come. But its development at the ad hoc tribunals will be looked on by history as likely its most formative phase – the period when atrocity speech law came of age.

---

[362] The Unified Liability Theory proposes many other macro-level fixes, including creation of a new modality, "speech abetting," to cover speech that is synchronous with, but has no causal relation to, atrocity. *See* GORDON, ATROCITY SPEECH LAW, *supra* note 306, at 375–82.

6

The Once and Future Doctrine of Joint Criminal Enterprise

Michael P. Scharf[1]

6.1 INTRODUCTION

During a sabbatical in the fall of 2008, I had the unique privilege of being invited to serve as Special Assistant to the International Prosecutor of the Extraordinary Chambers in the Courts of Cambodia (ECCC). During the time I spent in Phnom Penh, my most important assignment was to draft the prosecutor's brief[2] in reply to the defense motion to exclude "Joint Criminal Enterprise" (JCE), and in particular the extended form of JCE known as JCE III, as a mode of liability from the trial of the five surviving leaders of the Khmer Rouge.[3]

JCE III is a form of liability somewhat similar to the American "felony murder rule," in which a person who willingly participates in a criminal enterprise can be held criminally responsible for the reasonably foreseeable acts of other members of the criminal enterprise. The ICTY Appeals Chamber decision in the 1998 *Tadic*

[1] Michael Scharf is the John Deaver Drinko–BakerHostetler Professor of Law and Director of the Frederick K. Cox International Law Center at Case Western Reserve University School of Law. Portions of this chapter draw directly from the text of the author's draft brief.

[2] *Case of Ieng Sary*, Co-Prosecutors' Supplementary Observations on Joint Criminal Enterprise, Case No. 002/19–09-2007-ECCC/OCIJ, Dec. 31, 2009. A decision of the Trial Chamber is expected in December 2009, but the issue will not be completely settled until after the final decision of the Appeals Chamber.

[3] Pursuant to the co-investigating judges' order of September 16, 2008, the co-prosecutors filed the brief to detail why the extended form of JCE liability, "JCE III," is applicable before the ECCC. The defense motion put forward three main contentions to support the argument that JCE is not applicable at the ECCC. First, it asserts that JCE, as applied in the *Tadic* decision of the International Criminal Tribunal for the former Yugoslavia (ICTY) Appeals Chamber, is a judicial construct that does not exist in customary international law or, alternatively, did not exist in 1975–9. Second, it argues that JCE is not applicable before the ECCC because it is not contained in the ECCC Establishment Law, and customary international law is not applicable in Cambodian courts. Third, it argues that the doctrine of JCE is so broad that its application before this Court would cast "a wide shadow of liability on a variety of distinguished members of Cambodian society and others," thereby unduly staining their reputations. *Case of Ieng Sary*, Ieng Sary's Motion against the Application at the ECCC of the Form of Responsibility Known as Joint Criminal Enterprise, Case No. 002/19–09-2007-ECCC/OCIJ, July 28, 2008, ERN 00208225–00208240, D97.

case was "the first decision of an international tribunal to trace the existence and evolution of the doctrine of JCE in customary international law."[4] Since *Tadic*,[5] dozens of cases before the ICTY,[6] the International Criminal Tribunal for Rwanda (ICTR),[7] the Special Court for Sierra Leone (SCSL),[8] the Iraqi High Tribunal,[9] and the Special Panels for the Trial of Serious Crimes in East Timor[10] have recognized and applied the three forms of JCE liability.[11]

[4] Decision on the Appeals against the Co-Investigative Judges' Order on Joint Criminal Enterprise, Case No. 002/19–19-2007-ECCC/OCIJ, May 20, 2010, at para. 54.

[5] Prosecutor v. Tadic, Judgment, Case No. IT-94–1-A, ICTY Appeals Chamber, July 15, 1999 (hereinafter *Tadic* Appeals Chamber Judgment).

[6] Prosecutor v. Milutinovic, Decision on Dragoljub Ojdanic's Motion Challenging Jurisdiction – Joint Criminal Enterprise Liability, Case No. IT-99–37-AR72, ICTY Appeals Chamber, May 21, 2003 (hereinafter *Milutinovic* Decision); Prosecutor v. Krnojelac, Judgment, Case No. IT-97–25-A, ICTY Appeals Chamber, Sept. 17, 2003, para. 96; Prosecutor v. Simic, Judgment, ICTY Trial Chamber, Case No. IT-95–9-T, Oct. 17, 2003, para. 149; Prosecutor v. Kvocka, Judgment, Case No. IT-98–30/1-A, Feb. 28, 2005, paras. 105, 309; Prosecutor v. Krnojelac, Judgment, Case No. IT-97–25-A, Sept. 17, 2003, paras. 96, 100; Prosecutor v. Brdjanin, Judgment, Case No. IT-99–36-A, Apr. 3, 2007, para. 395; Prosecutor v. Brdjanin, Decision on Interlocutory Appeal, Case No.IT-99–36-A, Mar. 19, 2004; Prosecutor v. Stakic, Case No. IT-97–24-A, Judgment, Mar. 22, 2006, paras. 101–4; Prosecutor v. Krjaisnik, Judgment, Case No. IT-00–39-T, Sept. 27, 2006, para. 1082; Prosecutor v. Milosevic, Decision on Motion for Judgment of Acquittal, Case No. IT-02–54-T, June 16, 2004, para. 291; Prosecutor v. Krstic, Judgment, Case No. IT-98–33-A, ICTY Appeals Chamber, Apr. 19, 2004, para. 144.

[7] Prosecutor v. Ntakirutimana, Judgment, Case Nos. ICTR-96–10-A and ICTR-96–17-A, ICTR Appeals Chamber, Dec. 13, 2004, paras. 461–84; Prosecutor v. Rwamakuba, Decision on Interlocutory Appeal Regarding Application of Joint Criminal Enterprise to the Crime of Genocide, Case No. ICTR-98–44-AR72.4, Oct. 22, 2004, paras. 14–30; Prosecutor v. Kayishema and Ruzindanda, Judgment, Case No. ICTR-95–1-A, ICTR Appeals Chamber, June 1, 2001, para. 193; Prosecutor v. Nchamihigo, Decision on Defence Motion on Defects in the Form of the Indictment, Case No. ICTR-20010630R50, Sept. 27, 2006, paras 14, 21.

[8] Prosecutor v. Brima, Kamara, and Kanue (AFRC Case), Decision on Motions for Judgment of Acquittal Pursuant to Rule 98, Case No. SCSL-04–16-T, Mar. 31, 2006, paras. 308–26; Prosecutor v. Norman, Fofana, and Kondewa (CDF Case), Decision on Motions for Judgment of Acquittal Pursuant to Rule 98, Case No. 04–14-T, Oct. 21, 2005, para. 130.

[9] Al Dujail, Trial Judgment, Nov. 3, 2006, Iraqi High Tribunal, Case No. 1/9 First/2005.

[10] Prosecutor v. Jose Cardoso Fereira, Judgment, Case No.: 04/2001, District Court of Dili, April 5, 2003, paras. 367–76 (finding the accused guilty under JCE theory, applying the *Tadic* Appeals Chamber Judgment and other ICTY judgments in interpreting UNTAET Regulation 2000/15); Prosecutor v. De Deus, Judgment, Case No.: 2a/2004, District Court of Dili, Apr. 12, 2005, 13. (holding that though the accused did not personally beat the victim, he was guilty "as part of a joint criminal enterprise" because he was part of an organized force intent on killing and contributed by carrying a gun, uttering threats, and intimidating unarmed people, thereby strengthening the resolve of the group).

[11] JCE I (basic form) ascribes individual criminal liability when "all co-defendants act . . . pursuant to a common design, [and] possess the same criminal intention . . . even if each co-perpetrator carries out a different role within the [JCE]." The *mens rea* required for this form of JCE is the shared intent of all members to commit a certain crime. JCE II (systemic form) is "characterized by the existence of an organized criminal system, in particular in the case of concentration or detention camps." The *mens rea* required for this form of JCE is the personal knowledge of the system of ill treatment and the intent to further this common concerted system of ill-treatment. JCE III (extended form) ascribes individual criminal liability in situations "involving a common purpose to commit a crime where one of the perpetrators commits an act which, while outside the common plan, is nevertheless a natural and

Under the international law principle of *nullum crimen sine lege* (no crime without law), the Cambodia Tribunal, however, could only apply the substantive law and associated modes of liability that existed as part of customary international law in 1975–1979 – the time of the atrocities committed by the Khmer Rouge regime.[12] Therefore, the question at the heart of the brief I drafted was whether the ICTY was correct in concluding in *Tadic* that Nuremberg and its progeny had established JCE as part of customary international law following World War II.

The Khmer Rouge defendants argued that Nuremberg and its progeny provided too scant a sampling to constitute the widespread state practice and *opinio juris* required to establish JCE as a customary norm as of 1975.[13] In response, the prosecution brief argues that Nuremberg constituted what some commentators call "a Grotian Moment" – an instance in which there is such a fundamental change to the international system that a new principle of customary international law can arise with unusual rapidity.[14] This chapter revisits the question decided by the ICTY Appeals Chamber in *Tadic*, namely whether the Nuremberg and Control Council Law No. 10 cases were sufficient to establish JCE as customary international law by 1975. While this chapter focuses on the concept in the context of the trial of the Khmer Rouge leaders before the Cambodia Tribunal, the analysis has implications far beyond that tribunal, as described in the Conclusion.

6.2 DID THE NUREMBERG PRECEDENT ESTABLISH JCE AS CUSTOMARY INTERNATIONAL LAW?

6.2.1 Application of JCE at Nuremberg

The Nuremberg Charter and Judgment never specifically mention the term "Joint Criminal Enterprise." Yet, a close analysis of the Nuremberg Judgment and the holdings of several Control Council Law No. 10[15] cases reveal that the Nuremberg

---

foreseeable consequence of the effecting of that common purpose." The *mens rea* for this form is either the shared criminal intent of the perpetrators or, at a minimum, the fact that the defendant is aware of the possibility that a crime might be committed as a consequence of the execution of the criminal act and willingly takes the risk. *Tadic* Appeals Chamber Judgment, paras. 196, 202, 228.

[12] The Cambodia Tribunal added that requirement that "the law providing for that form of liability must have been sufficiently accessible at the relevant time to anyone who acted in such a way." Decision on the Appeals against the Co-Investigative Judges' Order on Joint Criminal Enterprise, Case No 002/19–19-2007-ECCC/OCIJ, May 20, 2010, at para. 44.

[13] For the definition of customary international law, see *North Sea Continental Shelf* (Federal Republic of Germany v. Denmark; Federal Republic of Germany v. Netherlands), Merits, Feb. 20, 1969, ICJ Rep. 3, para. 77.

[14] *See* MICHAEL SCHARF, CUSTOMARY INTERNATIONAL LAW IN TIMES OF FUNDAMENTAL CHANGE: RECOGNIZING GROTIAN MOMENTS (Cambridge University Press, 2013).

[15] This Law was based on the Nuremberg Charter and governed subsequent war crimes trials. Control Council Law No. 10, *in Official Gazette of the Control Council for Germany* (1946), vol. 3, at 50.

Tribunal and its progeny applied a concept analogous to JCE, which they called the "common plan" mode of liability.

Prior to Nuremberg, liability for participation in a common plan had existed in some form in the national legislation or jurisprudence of numerous common law and civil law countries since at least the nineteenth century. Indeed, many advanced jurisdictions recognized modes of co-perpetration similar to JCE III; these included conspiracy,[16] the felony murder doctrine,[17] the concept of *association de malfaiteurs*,[18] and numerous other doctrines of co-perpetration.[19]

The drafters of the Nuremberg Charter, like the drafters of the ICTY Statute forty-eight years later, recognized that the unique nature of atrocity crimes justifies and requires a unique mode of liability. This was explained in *Tadic*:

> Most of the time these crimes do not result from the criminal propensity of single individuals but constitute manifestations of collective criminality: the crimes are often carried out by groups of individuals acting in pursuance of a common criminal design. Although only some members of the group may physically perpetrate the criminal act (murder, extermination, wanton destruction of cities, towns or villages, etc.), the participation and contribution of the other members of the group is often vital in facilitating the commission of the offence in question. It follows that the moral gravity of such participation is often no less – or indeed no different – from that of those actually carrying out the acts in question.[20]

Because Control Council Law No. 10 sought to "establish a uniform legal basis in Germany for the prosecution of war criminals," Article I of the law explicitly incorporated the Nuremberg Tribunal Charter as an "integral part" of the Law. Pursuant to Article I, all the military commissions (US, British, Canadian, and Australian) adopted implementing regulations rendering a defendant responsible under the principle of "concerted criminal action" for the crimes of any other member of that "unit or group." UN War Crimes Commission, XV *Law Reports of Trials of War Criminals* 92 (1949).

[16]   *See* Pinkerton v. U.S., 328 US 640 (1946) (establishing the Pinkerton rule, in which a conspirator can be convicted of the reasonably foreseeable consequence of the unlawful agreement).

[17]   The felony murder doctrine, first enunciated by Lord Coke in 1797, has been applied in the United Kingdom, the United States, New Zealand, and Australia. ANTONIO CASSESE, INTERNATIONAL CRIMINAL LAW (2nd edn, 2008), at 202. The rule allows a defendant to be "held accountable for a crime because it was a natural and probable consequence of the crime which that person intended to aid or encourage." WAYNE LAFAVE & AUSTIN SCOTT, CRIMINAL LAW (1972), 515–16.

[18]   Professor van Sliedregt notes that the concept of "association de malfaiteurs," which has been used in France and The Netherlands to deal with mob violence by overcoming causality problems, "inspired the drafters of the Nuremberg Statute to penalize membership of a criminal organization." Eliese van Sliedregt, *Joint Criminal Enterprise as a Pathway to Convicting Individuals for Genocide*, 5 JOURNAL OF INT'L CRIM. J. 184, 199 (2006).

[19]   The Indian Penal Code of 1860 imposed individual liability for unlawful acts committed by several persons in furtherance of a common plan. WALTER MORGAN & A. G. MACPHERSON, INDIAN PENAL CODE (XLV, 1860) (London: GC Hay Co. 1861). Similarly, Section 61(2) of the Canadian Criminal Code of 1893 punishes persons who "form a common intention to prosecute any unlawful purpose," and makes each "a party to every offense committed by any one of them in the prosecution of such common purpose." Section 21(2) of the Criminal Code, RSC 1970, C-34.

[20]   *Tadic* Appeals Chamber Judgment, para. 191.

This passage has been quoted in a number of subsequent judgments of the ICTY,[21] and in *Karemera* the ICTR Trial Chamber articulated a similar rationale for the JCE doctrine:

> To hold criminally liable as a perpetrator only the person who materially performs the criminal act would disregard the role as co-perpetrators of all those who in some way made it possible for the perpetrator physically to carry out that criminal act. At the same time, depending upon the circumstances, to hold the latter liable only as aiders and abettors might understate the degree of their criminal responsibility.[22]

Similarly, Antonio Cassese, the former President of the ICTY, opined:

> International crimes such as war crimes, crimes against humanity, genocide, torture, and terrorism share a common feature: they tend to be expression of collective criminality, in that they are perpetrated by a multitude of persons, military details, paramilitary units or government officials acting in unison or, in most cases, in pursuance of a policy. When such crimes are committed, it is extremely difficult to pinpoint the specific contribution made by each individual participant in the criminal enterprise or collective crime. [...] The notion of joint criminal enterprise denotes a mode of criminal liability that appears particularly fit to cover the criminal liability of all participants in a common criminal plan.[23]

Consistent with the doctrine's historic origins in an international agreement (the 1945 London Charter establishing the Nuremberg Tribunal) and the jurisprudence of international judicial bodies (the Nuremberg and Control Council Law No. 10 Tribunals), Professor van Sliedregt concludes that "JCE is a merger of common law and civil law. JCE in international law is a unique (*sui generis*) concept in that it combines and mixes two legal cultures and systems."[24] Specifically, the major powers sought to create an approach in the Nuremberg Charter that would combine the Anglo-American conspiracy doctrine with the approach in France and the Soviet Union, where conspiracy was not recognized as a crime.[25] Thus, Article 6 of the London Charter implemented a modified form of the initial American proposal to include conspiracy, providing that "leaders, organizers, instigators and accomplices participating in the formulation or *execution of a common plan* or conspiracy to commit any of the foregoing crimes are responsible for all acts performed by any persons in execution of such plan."[26]

---

[21] See, e.g., Prosecutor v. Kvacka et al., Appeal Judgment, Case No. IT-98-30/1-A, Feb. 28, 2005, para. 80; Prosecutor v. Krnojelac, Appeal Judgment, Case No. IT-97-25-A, Sept. 17, 2003, para. 29; Prosecutor v. Blagojevic and Jokic, Trial Judgment, Case. No. IT-02-60-T, Jan. 17, 2005, para. 695.

[22] Prosecutor v. Edourad Karemera, Mathieu Ngirumpatse, Joseph Nzirorera, and Andre Rwamakuba, Decision on the Preliminary Motions by the Defence Challenging Jurisdiction in Relation to Joint Criminal Enterprise, ICTY Trial Chamber III, Case No. ICTR-98-44-T, May 14, 2004, para. 36.

[23] Cassese, *supra* note 17, at 189–91.

[24] van Sliedregt, *supra* note 18, at 199.

[25] Stanislaw Pomorski, *Conspiracy and Criminal Organizations, in* THE NUREMBERG TRIAL AND INTERNATIONAL LAW (George Ginsburgs & V. N. Kudriavtsev eds., 1990), 216.

[26] Agreement for the Prosecution and Punishment of Major German War Criminals of the European Axis, art. 6, 59 Stat. 1544, 82 UNTS 279.

During the Nuremberg Trial, Justice Robert Jackson, the Chief US Negotiator of the Nuremberg Charter and Chief US Prosecutor at Nuremberg explained to the Tribunal the meaning of "common plan," as distinct from the US concept of conspiracy:

> The Charter did not define responsibility for the acts of others in terms of "conspiracy" alone. The crimes were defined in non-technical but inclusive terms, and embraced formulating and executing a "common plan" as well as participating in a "conspiracy." It was feared that to do otherwise might import into the proceedings technical requirements and limitations which have grown up around the term "conspiracy." There are some divergences between the Anglo-American concept of conspiracy and that of either Soviet, French, or German jurisprudence. It was desired that concrete cases be guided by the broader considerations inherent in the nature of the social problem, rather than controlled by refinements of any local law.[27]

In harmony with this statement, the Nuremberg Tribunal[28] and the Control Council Law No. 10 Tribunals accepted their own version of the "common plan" concept, thereby transforming it into what has now become known as the doctrine of JCE. These tribunals found that "the difference between a charge of conspiracy and one of acting in pursuance of a common design is that the first would claim that an agreement to commit offences had been made while the second would allege not only the making of an agreement but the performance of acts pursuant to it."[29] In other words, conspiracy is a crime in its own right, while acting in pursuance of a common design or plan, like JCE, was a mode of liability that attaches to substantive offences. In developing JCE liability from preexisting approaches in domestic jurisdictions, the Nuremberg Tribunal declared that its conclusions were made "in accordance with well-settled legal principles, one of the most important of which is that criminal guilt is personal and that mass punishments should be avoided."[30]

While the Nuremberg Tribunal tried the twenty-two highest ranking surviving members of the Nazi regime, Control Council Law No. 10 was jointly promulgated by the Allied powers to govern subsequent trials of the next level of suspected German war criminals by US, British, Canadian, and Australian military tribunals, as well as German courts, in occupied Germany. Under the authority of Control Council Law No. 10, the tribunals were to follow the Charter and jurisprudence of

---

[27]   Robert H. Jackson, *The Law Under Which Nazi Organizations Are Accused of Being Criminal*, argument by Robert H. Jackson, Feb. 28, 1946, reprinted in THE NURNBERG CASE: AS PRESENTED BY ROBERT JACKSON (1971), 108.

[28]   *See* International Military Tribunal Judgment, *in* Trial of the Major War Criminals Before the International Military Tribunal, Nuremberg, Vol. 1, 1947, 226.

[29]   XV *Law Reports of Trials of War Criminals* 97–98, UN War Crimes Commission, 1948 (summarizing the jurisprudence of the Nuremberg and Control Council Law No. 10 trials).

[30]   International Military Tribunal, Judgment in the Trial of the Major War Criminals Before the International Military Tribunal: Nuremberg, November 14, 1945, October 1, 1947, 256.

the Nuremberg Tribunal.[31] As such, the case law from those tribunals is viewed as an authoritative interpretation of the Nuremberg Charter and Judgment and a reflection of customary international law.[32]

An analysis of several of the Control Council Law No. 10 cases supports the conclusion that the JCE doctrine was in fact employed by those tribunals in 1946–7. In reaching its conclusion about the existence of JCE, the Appeals Chamber of the Yugoslavia Tribunal in *Tadic* relied partly on ten different post-World War II cases – six regarding JCE I,[33] two regarding JCE II,[34] and two regarding JCE III.[35] Most of these cases were published in summary form in the 1949 Report of the UN War Crimes Commission.[36] In addition to these ten, we included in the prosecution's brief another sixteen cases published in the 1949 UN War Crimes Commission Report, and the US Nuremberg War Crimes Tribunal Report, in which the Control Council Law No. 10 tribunals also applied the common plan or design/JCE concept. All of these cases clarified the meaning of Nuremberg's common plan liability – the forerunner of JCE. Summing up this extensive case law and explaining the difference between common design and simple co-perpetration, the UN War Crimes Commission Report states: "the prosecution has the additional task of providing the existence of a common design, [and] once that is proved the prosecution can rely upon the rule which exists in many systems of law that those who take part in a common design to commit an offence which is carried out by one of them are all fully responsible for that offence in the eyes of the criminal law."[37] Consistent

---

[31]   Control Council Law No. 10, in *Official Gazette of the Control Council for Germany*, 1946, vol. 3, 50.

[32]   Prosecutor v. Kupreskic, Judgment, Case No: IT-95–16-A, ICTY Trial Chamber, Jan. 14, 2000, para. 541:

>   It cannot be gainsaid that great value ought to be attached to decisions of such international criminal courts as the international tribunals of Nuremberg and Tokyo, or to national courts operating by virtue, and on the strength, of Control Council Law No. 10, a legislative act jointly passed in 1945 by the four Occupying Powers and thus reflecting international agreement among the Great Powers on the law applicable to international crimes and the jurisdiction of the courts called upon to rule on those crimes. These courts operated under international instruments laying down provisions that were either declaratory of existing law or which had been gradually transformed into customary international law.

[33]   *Trial of Otto Sandrock and three others; Hoelzer and others; Gustav Alfred Jepsen and others; Franz Schonfeld and others; Feurstein and others; Otto Ohlenforf and others.*

[34]   *Dachau Concentration Camp Case (Trial of Martin Gottfried Weiss and thirty-nine others)*; the *Belsen Case (Trial of Josef Kramer and forty-four others).*

[35]   *Essen Lynching Case; Borkum Island Case.* For JCE III, the Appeals Chamber also cited several unpublished Italian decisions.

[36]   Notably, the JCE III *Borkum Island Case* was not included in the Report of the UN War Crimes Commission, but the charging instrument, transcript, and other documents of the case have been publicly available from The United States Archives. See Publication Number M1103, Records of United States Army War Crimes Trials, United States of America v. Goebel, et al., February 6–March 21, 1946. In addition, a detailed account and analysis of the *Borkum Island Case* was published in 1956 in Maximilian Koessler, Borkum Island Tragedy and Trial, 47 JOURNAL OF CRIMINAL LAW 183–96 (1956).

[37]   UN War Crimes Commission, Law Reports of Trials of War Criminals, UNWCC, Vol. XV (1949), 96.

with this explanation, the Appeals Chamber of the Yugoslavia Tribunal in the *Milutinovic* case, after considering extensive filings by the parties on whether JCE is part of customary international law, found that JCE and common plan liability are one and the same.[38]

Given that JCE III is the most controversial type of JCE liability, the three Control Council Law No. 10 cases dealing with that mode of JCE liability are worth examining in some detail. The first is the trial of Erich Heyer and six others – known as the *Essen Lynching Case*. According to the official summary of the trial published in the UN War Crimes Commission Report, this case concerned the lynching of three British prisoners of war by a mob of Germans.[39] Though the case was tried by a British military court, it did so under the authority of Control Council Law No. 10, and it was therefore "not a trial under English law." One of the accused, Captain Heyer, had placed three prisoners under the escort of a German soldier, Koenen, who was to take them for interrogation. As Koenen left, Heyer, within earshot of a waiting crowd, ordered Koenen not to intervene if German civilians molested the prisoners and stated that the prisoners deserved to be and probably would be shot. The prisoners were beaten by the crowd, and one German corporal fired a revolver at a prisoner, wounding him in the head. One died instantly when they were thrown over a bridge, and the remaining two were killed by shots from the bridge and by members of the crowd, who beat them to death. The defence argument that the prosecution needed to prove that each of the accused –Heyer, Koenen, and five civilians – had intended to kill the prisoners was not accepted by the court. The prosecution argued that in order to be convicted the accused had to have been "concerned in the killing" of the prisoner. Both Heyer and Koenen were convicted of committing a war crime in that they were concerned in the killing of the three prisoners, as were three of the five accused civilians. Even though it was not proven which of the civilians delivered the fatal shots or blows, they were convicted because "[f]rom the moment they left those barracks, the men were doomed and the crowd knew they were doomed and every person in that crowd who struck a blow was both morally and criminally responsible for the deaths of the three men."[40]

A second example (surprisingly not cited in *Tadic*), which the UN War Crimes Commission specifically found analogous to the *Essen Lynching Case*, is the *Trial of Hans Renoth and Three Others*.[41] In that case, two policemen (Hans Ronoth and Hans Pelgrim) and two customs officials (Friedrich Grabowski and Paul Nieke) were accused of committing a war crime in that they "were concerned in the killing of an unknown Allied airman, a prisoner of war." According to the allegations, the

---

[38] *Milutinovic* Decision, para. 36.
[39] *Trial of Erich Heyer and Six Others*, British Military Court for the Trial of War Criminals, Essen, December 18–19 and 21–22, 1945, UNWCC, Vol. 1 (1949), 88.
[40] *Id.*, 97.
[41] *Trial of Hans Ronoth and Three Others*, British Military Court, January 9–10, 1946, UNWCC, Vol. XV (1949), 76–7.

pilot crashed on German soil unhurt, and was arrested by Renoth, then attacked and beaten with fists and rifles by a number of people, while the three other defendants witnessed the beating but took no active part to stop it or to help the pilot. Renoth also stood by for a while, and then shot and killed the pilot. "The case for the prosecution was that there was a common design in which all four accused shared to commit a war crime, [and] that all four accused were aware of this common design and that all four accused acted in furtherance of it."[42] All the accused were found guilty, presumably based on the foreseeability that the pilot would eventually be killed during the beating at the hands of the crowd or by one of them.

A third example is the case of *Kurt Goebell et al.* (the *Borkum Island Case*). Although not published in the Report of the UN War Crimes Commission, a detailed record of this case is publicly available through the US National Archives Microfilm Publications.[43] Moreover, a detailed report of the trial (based on trial transcripts) was published in the *Journal of Criminal Law* in 1956.[44] According to that report, the mayor of Borkum and several German military officers and soldiers were convicted of the assault and killing of seven American airmen who had crash-landed. The prosecution argued that the accused were "cogs in the wheel of common design, all equally important, each cog doing the part assigned to it." It further argued that "it is proved beyond a reasonable doubt that each one of the accused played his part in mob violence which led to the unlawful killings" and "therefore, under the law each and every one of the accused is guilty of murder." After deliberating in closed session, the judges rendered an oral verdict in which they convicted the mayor and several officers of the killings and assaults. From the arguments and evidence submitted, it is apparent that the accused were convicted pursuant to a form of common design liability equivalent to JCE III. Essentially, the court decided that though certain defendants had not participated in the murder nor intended for it to be committed, they were nonetheless liable because it was a natural and foreseeable consequence of their treatment of the prisoners.

International judicial decisions, like domestic court cases, can evince state practice and *opinio juris*, establishing customary international law.[45] The Khmer Rouge defendants objected that these Control Council Law No. 10 cases are "unpublished cases" or, in some instances, mere summaries of unwritten verdicts. The suggestion being that the Court could not validly rely on them to glean the substance of

---

42   *Id.*, at 76.
43   The United States Archives, Publication Number M1103, Records of United States Army War Crimes Trials, United States of America v. Goebell, et al., February 6–March 21, 1946. The Appeals Chamber in *Tadic* states that a copy of these case materials are on file in the ICTY's Library. Tadic Appeals Chamber Decision, 93.
44   Koessler, *supra* note 36.
45   In 1950, the International Law Commission listed the following sources as forms of evidence of customary international law: treaties, decisions of national and international courts, national legislation, opinions of national legal advisors, diplomatic correspondence, practice of international organizations. This list, which was not intended to be exhaustive, is useful as a starting point and a basis for discussion ([1950] 2 Y.B. Int'l L. Comm'n 367, UN Doc. A/CN.4/Ser.A/1950/Add.1 [1957]).

customary international law because defendants could not be deemed to have constructive knowledge of unpublished works with respect to the doctrine that ignorance of law is no excuse (*ignorantia juris non excusat*). It is significant, however, that two of the three Control Council Law No. 10 JCE III cases described above were published in summary form in the official UN War Crimes Commission Report in 1949. According to the forward of the collection of case summaries, the "main object of these reports [was] to help to elucidate the law, i.e., that part of International Law which has been called the law of war."[46] This authoritative and widely disseminated multi-volume account of the trials, in which the war crimes tribunals recognized and applied JCE liability, supports the argument that the Khmer Rouge leaders had sufficient constructive notice in 1975–9 that their mass atrocity crimes would attract criminal responsibility under the JCE doctrine.

While the *Borkum Island Case* was not included in the Report of the UN War Crimes Commission, it is significant that the charging instrument, transcript (including oral bench judgment), and other documents of the case have been publicly available from US archives.[47] In addition, as mentioned above a detailed account and analysis of the *Borkum Island Case* was published in 1956 in the *Journal of Criminal Law*.[48] It may be an open question whether a judgment that was the subject of a scholarly article in a widely read, prestigious publication, and which was available in public archives years before the Khmer Rouge launched their genocidal campaign, can be viewed as a published judicial decision for this purpose.

Given the nature of international crimes and mass atrocities, the rationale behind the existence of JCE, and the relative infrequency with which trials for such crimes arise, it is unsurprising that there are few examples of national jurisprudence applying forms of JCE liability in the years after Nuremberg. The most notable example is the Jerusalem District Court and Israeli Supreme Court's decisions in the *Eichmann case*. Those decision demonstrate that, as of 1961, domestic courts recognized JCE as developed by the immediate post-World War II laws and jurisprudence.[49] The Jerusalem District Court's approach to determining Adolf Eichmann's individual responsibility for participating in a common criminal plan to extinguish the Jews in Europe closely resembled that applied by the Control Council Law No. 10 cases cited above (several of which were cited by the Jerusalem District Court). This can be seen clearly in its statement:

---

[46] Foreword, *Law Reports of Trials of War Criminals*, XV UNWCC, p. vii (1949). While the UN War Crimes Commission recognizes that where "there is no reasoned judgment … it is difficult in some cases to specify precisely the grounds on which the courts gave their decision," the Commission goes on to state: "[t]he difficulty is, however, to a large extent surmounted in [such cases] by examining carefully the indictment, the speeches of the counsel on both sides and the judgment."

[47] See Publication Number M1103, Records of United States Army War Crimes Trials, United States of America v. Goebel, et al., February 6–March 21, 1946.

[48] Koessler, *supra* note 36.

[49] Attorney-General of Israel v. Eichmann, 36 ILR 5, December 11, 1961 (hereinafter *Eichmann*) affirmed by Attorney-General of Israel v Eichmann, 36 ILR 277, May 29, 1962 (hereinafter *Eichmann II*).

Hence, everyone who acted in the extermination of Jews, knew about the plan for the Final Solution and its advancement, is to be regarded as an accomplice in the annihilation of the millions who were exterminated during the years 1941–1945, irrespective of the fact of whether his actions spread over the entire front of the extermination, or over only one or more sectors of that front. His responsibility is that of a 'principal offender' who perpetrated the entire crime in co-operation with the others.[50]

The District Court found that Eichmann was made aware of the criminal plan to exterminate the Jews in June 1941; he actively furthered this plan via his central role as Referent for Jewish Affairs in the Office for Reich Security as early as August 1941; and he possessed the requisite intent (specific intent here, because the goal was genocide) to further the plan as evidenced by "the very breadth of the scope of his activities" undertaken to achieve the biological extermination of the Jewish people.[51] On the basis of these findings, Eichmann was held criminally liable for the "general crime" of the Final Solution, which encompassed acts constituting the crime "in which he took an active part in his own sector *and the acts committed by his accomplices to the crime in other sectors* on the same front."[52] In so holding, the District Court ruled that full awareness of the scope of the plan's operations was not necessary noting that many of the principal perpetrators, including the defendant, may have possessed only compartmentalized knowledge.[53] The Israeli Supreme Court also cited the 1946 General Assembly Resolution affirming the Nuremberg principles, stating: "if fifty-eight nations unanimously agree on a statement of existing law, it would seem that such a declaration would be all but conclusive evidence of such a rule, and agreement by a large majority would have great value in determining what is existing law."[54]

6.2.2 Nuremberg As a "Grotian Moment"

The United Nations' International Law Commission (ILC) has recognized that the Nuremberg Charter, Control Council Law No. 10, and the post-World War II war crimes trials gave birth to the entire international paradigm of individual criminal responsibility. The ILC has described the principle of individual responsibility and punishment for crimes under international law recognized at Nuremberg as the "cornerstone of international criminal law" and the "enduring legacy of the Charter and Judgment of the Nuremberg Tribunal."[55]

---

[50] *Eichmann*, para. 194.

[51] *Id.*, para. 182.

[52] *Id.*, para. 197 (emphasis added).

[53] *Id.*, para. 193.

[54] *Eichmann II*, para. 11 (concerning universal jurisdiction for crimes against humanity), para. 14 (concerning rejection of the act of state defence), and para. 15 (concerning rejection of the superior orders defence).

[55] See *Report of the International Law Commission on the Work of its Forty-Eighth Session*, May 6–July 26, 1996, Official Records of the General Assembly, Fifty-First Session, Supplement No. 10, at 19, available at www.un.org/law.ilc/index.htm.

Importantly, on December 11, 1946, in one of the first actions of the newly formed United Nations, its General Assembly unanimously affirmed the principles from the Nuremberg Charter and judgments.[56] This action arguably affirmed as customary international law both the substantive law and the theory of individual criminal liability (including "common plan" liability) codified in the Nuremberg Charter and applied by the Nuremberg Tribunal. As a consequence, a compelling case can be made that common plan (now known as JCE) liability was rendered just as much a part of customary international law as the other fundamental concepts of international criminal liability reflected in the Nuremberg Principles that the ECCC applies. These concepts include: command responsibility, the principle that obeying superior orders is not a defense, the idea that leaders can be held liable for international crimes despite their official position, and the notion that a perpetrator is responsible for an act that constitutes a crime under international law notwithstanding the fact that domestic law does not impose a penalty for this act. Although General Assembly resolutions are by their nature "non-binding," domestic and international courts have long recognized that they are official expressions of the governments concerned and consequently are relevant and entitled to be given weight as evidence of state practice and *opinio juris* – the two components of customary international law.[57]

Subsequently, the International Law Commission (ILC) was directed by the UN General Assembly to formulate the Principles of International Law Recognized in the Charter of the Nuremberg Tribunal and in the Judgment of the Tribunal. In 1950, the ILC submitted the following seven principles to the United Nations:

Principle I: Any person who commits an act which constitutes a crime under international law is responsible therefor and liable to punishment.

Principle II: The fact that internal law does not impose a penalty for an act which constitutes a crime under international law does not relieve the person who committed the act from responsibility under international law.

Principle III: The fact that a person who committed an act which constitutes a crime under international law acted as Head of State or responsible Government official does not relieve him from responsibility under international law.

Principle IV: The fact that a person acted pursuant to order of his Government or of a superior does not relieve him from responsibility under international law, provided a moral choice was in fact possible to him.

[56] Affirmation of the Principles of International Law Recognized by the Charter of the Nuremberg Tribunal, GA Res. 95(I), UN GAOR, 1st Sess., UN Doc A/236 (1946) pt. 2, at 1144.

[57] See Roberts, *Traditional and Modern Approaches to Customary International Law: A Reconciliation*, 95 Am. J. Int'l L. 757 (2001).

Principle V: Any person charged with a crime under international law has the right to a fair trial on the facts and law.

Principle VI: The crimes hereinafter set out are punishable as crimes under international law:

    (a) Crimes against peace: (i) Planning, preparation, initiation or waging of a war of aggression or a war in violation of international treaties, agreements or assurances; (ii) Participation in a common plan or conspiracy for the accomplishment of any of the acts mentioned under (i).

    (b) War crimes: Violations of the laws or customs of war include, but are not limited to, murder, ill-treatment or deportation to slave-labour or for any other purpose of civilian population of or in occupied territory, murder or ill-treatment of prisoners of war, of persons on the seas, killing of hostages, plunder of public or private property, wanton destruction of cities, towns, or villages, or devastation not justified by military necessity.

    (c) Crimes against humanity: Murder, extermination, enslavement, deportation and other inhuman acts done against any civilian population, or persecutions on political, racial or religious grounds, when such acts are done or such persecutions are carried on in execution of or in connexion with any crime against peace or any war crime.

Principle VII: Complicity in the commission of a crime against peace, a war crime, or a crime against humanity as set forth in Principle VI is a crime under international law.[58]

Although the ILC's 1950 formulation neither specifically references nor specifically excludes JCE, it does make clear that anyone who "commits" a crime against peace, a war crime, or crime against humanity, is criminally liable. It is of note in this regard that the ICTY, the ICTR, and the SCSL have all read the word "committed" in their Statutes as including participation in the realization of a common design or purpose.[59]

The UN General Assembly did not pass a resolution endorsing the ILC's 1950 formulation of the Nuremberg Principles, presumably because the General Assembly had four years earlier already confirmed the status of the Nuremberg

---

[58] The ILC's Nuremberg Principles are available at www.icrc.org/ihl.nsf/full/390.

[59] *CDF Case*, Decision on Motions for Judgment of Acquittal Pursuant to Rule 98, Case No. SCSL-04-14-T, October 21, 2005, para. 130: "The Chamber recognizes, as a matter of law, generally, that Article 6(1) of the Statute of the Special Court does not, in its proscriptive reach, limit criminal liability to only those persons who plan, instigate, order, physically commit a crime or otherwise aid and abet in its planning, preparation or execution. Its proscriptive ambit extends beyond that to prohibit the commission of offenses through a joint criminal enterprise, in pursuit of the common plan to commit crimes punishable under the Statute."

Principles as international law. Instead, it directed the International Law Commission to codify them in an "International Code of Offences against the Peace and Security of Mankind." It is noteworthy that the ILC's first draft of the Code in 1956 specifically included "the principle of individual criminal responsibility for formulating a plan or participating in a common plan or conspiracy to commit a crime"[60] – thus indicating that the ILC in fact perceived the common plan concept to be part of the Nuremberg Principles.

In submitting the draft statute for the ICTY to the Security Council in 1993, the United Nations Secretary-General emphasized the customary international law status of the principles and rules emanating from the Nuremberg Trial and other post-World War II jurisprudence. Specifically, he stated that the Statute had been drafted to apply only the "rules of international humanitarian law which are beyond any doubt part of customary international law," which included the substantive law and modes of liability embodied in "the Charter of the International Military Tribunal of 8 August 1945."[61] Logic dictates that this 1993 statement about the content of customary international law also holds true for the time of the crimes in question before the ECCC (1975–9), as there were no relevant major developments in international humanitarian law between 1975 and the establishment of the ICTY in 1993. As Ciara Damgaard documents, "the origins of the JCE Doctrine can be found in the events surrounding the end of World War II."[62]

The Khmer Rouge defendants argued in their brief that even if Nuremberg and a few Control Council Law No. 10 cases recognized the JCE concept, the number of cases was too limited to constitute customary international law. In response, the prosecutor's brief submitted that Nuremberg and its progeny created a so-called "Grotian Moment." Notably, this was the first time in history an organ of an international tribunal used the term.

6.2.3 The Concept of "Grotian Moment"

Hugo Grotius is widely considered to be the "father" of modern international law as the law of nations, and has been recognized for having "recorded the creation of order out of chaos in the great sphere of international relations."[63] In the mid-1600s, at the time that the nation-state was formally recognized as having crystallized into the fundamental political unit of Europe, Grotius "offered a new concept of

---

[60] See *Report of the International Law Commission on the Work of its Forty-Eighth Session*, May 6–July 26, 1996, Official Records of the General Assembly, Fifty-First Session, Supplement No. 10, at 21, available at www.un.org/law.ilc/index.htm.

[61] Report of the Secretary-General Pursuant to Paragraph 2 of Security Council Resolution 808, S/25704, May 3, 1993, paras. 34–5.

[62] Ciara Damgaard, Individual Criminal Responsibility for Core International Crimes (2008), 132, 235.

[63] See Charles S. Edwards, Hugo Grotius, the Miracle of Holland (1981).

international law designed to reflect that new reality."[64] In his masterpiece, *De Jure Belli ac Pacis* (The Law of War and Peace), Grotius addresses questions bearing on just war: who may be a belligerent; what causes of war are just, doubtful, or unjust; and what procedures must be followed in the inception, conduct, and conclusion of war.[65]

Although NYU Professor Benedict Kingsbury has convincingly argued that Grotius' actual contribution has been distorted through the ages, the prevailing view today is that his treatise had an extraordinary impact as the first formulation of a comprehensive legal order of interstate relations based on mutual respect and equality of sovereign states.[66] In "semiotic" terms,[67] the "Grotian tradition" has come to symbolize the advent of the modern international legal regime, characterized by positive law and state consent, which arose from the Peace of Westphalia.[68]

The term "Grotian Moment," on the other hand, is a relatively recent creation, apparently coined by Princeton Professor Richard Falk in 1985.[69] Such a moment is said to occur when there is a transformative development in which new rules and doctrines of customary international law emerge with unusual rapidity and acceptance.[70] Usually this happens during "a period in world history that seems analogous

---

[64] John W. Head, *Throwing Eggs at Windows: Legal and Institutional Globalization in the 21st Century Economy*, 50 KAN. L. REV. 731, 771 (2002).

[65] Hugo Grotius, De Jure Belli ac Pacis (n.p. 1625).

[66] Benedict Kingsbury, *A Grotian Tradition of Theory and Practice? Grotius, Law, and Moral Skepticism in the Thought of Hedley Bull*, 17 QUINNIPIAC L. REV. 3, 10 (1997).

[67] Semiotics is the study of how the meaning of signs, symbols, and language is constructed and understood. Semiotics explains that terms such as "The Peace of Westphalia" or "the Grotian tradition" are not historic artifacts whose meaning remains static over time. Rather, the meaning of such terms changes over time along with the interpretive community or communities. Michael P. Scharf, *International Law in Crisis: A Qualitative Empirical Contribution to the Compliance Debate*, 31 CARDOZO L. REV. 45, 50 (2009)(citing Charles Sanders Peirce, Collected Papers of Charles Sanders Pierce: Pragmatism and Pragmaticism [Charles Hartshorne & Paul Weiss eds., 1935]).

[68] Michael P. Scharf, *Earned Sovereignty: Juridical Underpinnings*, 31 DENVER J. INT'L L. 373, 373 n. 20. The Peace of Westphalia was composed of two separate agreements: (1) the Treaty of Osnabruck concluded between the Protestant Queen of Sweden and her allies on the one side, and the Holy Roman Habsburg Emperor and the German Princes on the other; and (2) the Treaty of Munster concluded between the Catholic King of France and his allies on the one side, and the Holy Roman Habsburg Emperor and the German Princes on the other. The conventional view of the Peace of Westphalia is that by recognizing the German Princes as sovereign, these treaties signaled the beginning of a new era. But in fact, the power to conclude alliances formally recognized at Westphalia was not unqualified, and was in fact a power that the German Princes had already possessed for almost half a century. Furthermore, although the treaties eroded some of the authority of the Habsburg Emperor, the Empire remained a key actor according to the terms of the treaties. For example, the Imperial Diet retained the powers of legislation, warfare, and taxation, and it was through Imperial bodies, such as the Diet and the Courts, that religious safeguards mandated by the Treaty were imposed on the German Princes.

[69] *The Grotian Moment, in* INTERNATIONAL Law: A CONTEMPORARY PERSPECTIVE 7 (Richard Falk, et al. eds., 1985); *see also*, INTERNATIONAL LAW AND WORLD ORDER 1265–86 (Burns H. Weston, Richard A. Falk, Hilary Charlesworth & Andrew K. Strauss eds., Thomson/West 4th edn, 2006).

[70] Saul Mendlovitz & Marev Datan, *Judge Weeramantry's Grotian Quest*, 7 TRANSNATIONAL L. & CONTEP. PROBS. 401, 402 (defining the term "Grotian moment").

at least to the end of European feudalism ... when new norms, procedures, and institutions had to be devised to cope with the then decline of the Church and the emergence of the secular state."[71] Commentators have opined that the creation of the Nuremberg Tribunal at the end of World War II constituted a classic "Grotian Moment," on par with the negotiation of the Peace of Westphalia and the establishment of the UN Charter.[72]

Normally, customary international law crystallizes out of the slow accretion of widespread state practice evincing a sense of legal obligation (*opinio juris*).[73] The process can take decades, or even centuries. The International Court of Justice, however, has made clear that customary norms can sometimes ripen quite rapidly, and that a short period of time is not a bar to finding the existence of a new rule of customary international law, binding on all the countries of the world, save those that persistently objected during its formation.[74] Often this will occur during a so-called "Grotian Moment."

It was thus the paradigm-shifting nature of the Nuremberg precedent, and the universal and unqualified endorsement of the Nuremberg Principles by the nations of the world in 1946, rather than the number of cases applying JCE liability at the time, which crystallized this doctrine into a mode of individual criminal liability under customary international law.[75] As such, in accordance with Article 15(2) of the International Covenant on Civil and Political Rights, the ECCC may try international crimes using internationally recognized modes of liability whether or not such crimes or forms of liability were recognized in the domestic law at the time of their commission.[76]

---

[71] BURNS H. WESTON, INTERNATIONAL LAW AND WORLD ORDER 1369 (3rd edn, 1997).

[72] Ibrahim J. Gassama, *International Law at a Grotian Moment: The Invasion of Iraq in Context*, 18 EMORY INT'L L. REV. 1, 9 (2004) (describing history's Grotian moments, including the Peace of Westphalia, the Nuremberg Charter, and the UN Charter); Leila Nadya Sadat, *The New International Criminal Court: An Uneasy Revolution*, 88 GEORGETOWN L. J. 381, 474 (arguing that the Statute of the International Criminal Court constitutes the most recent Grotian moment).

[73] For the definition of customary international law, see *North Sea Continental Shelf* (Federal Republic of Germany v. Denmark; Federal Republic of Germany v. Netherlands), Merits, February 20, 1969, ICJ Rep. 3, para. 77.

[74] *Id.* at paras 71, 73, 74. While recognizing that some norms can quickly become customary international law, the ICJ held that the equidistance principle contained in Article 6 of the 1958 Convention on the Continental Shelf had not done so as of 1969 because so few States recognized and applied the principle.

[75] See Frank Lawrence, *The Nuremberg Principles: A Defense for Political Protesters*, 40 HASTINGS L. J. 397, (1989), 397 & 408–10 (disputing the argument that "more than a single event is necessary for a proposed principle to be considered part of customary international law"). In 2006, the European Court of Human Rights recognized the "universal validity" of the Nuremberg principles, Kolk and Kislyiy v. Estonia, Decision on Admissibility, Jan. 17, 2006.

[76] ICCPR, Art. 15(2): "Nothing in this article shall prejudice the trial and punishment of any person for any act or omission which, at the time it was committed, was criminal according to the general principles of law recognized by the community of nations." Prosecutor v. Milan Milutinovic, Nikola Sainovic, & Dragoljub Odjanic, Appeals Chamber Decision on Ojdanic's Motion Challenging Jurisdiction – Joint Criminal Enterprise, Case No.: IT-99-37-AR72, May 21, 2003, paras. 41–2

It follows from the above that, in addition to international and hybrid tribunals, domestic courts may legitimately apply the JCE doctrine in criminal prosecutions of war crimes, genocide, and crimes against humanity.

6.3 CONCLUSION

This chapter has demonstrated that, consistent with the ICTY Appeals Chamber's opinion in *Tadic*, JCE liability does in fact have a venerable lineage, anchored securely in the customary international law established during the Grotian Moment of Nuremberg. Nevertheless, JCE III has been widely criticized by commentators and defense counsel as tilting the playing field too far toward the prosecution. In particular, defense counsel decry that the "foreseeability standard" on which JCE III is based introduces a form of guilt by association or strict liability for membership in a criminal organization. By way of concluding observations, I offer a four-part rejoinder to this argument.

First, liability in a JCE is distinguishable from the crime of membership in a criminal organization. The latter was criminalized as a separate offence in Nuremberg and in subsequent trials held under Control Council Law No. 10, where knowing and voluntary membership in an entity deemed to be a criminal organization was sufficient to entail individual criminal responsibility. At Nuremberg, the discrete offence of membership in a criminal organization was adopted to facilitate the later prosecutions of minor offenders.[77] In contrast, criminal liability pursuant to a JCE is not liability for mere membership, but "a form of liability concerned with the participation in the commission of a crime as part of a joint criminal enterprise, a different matter."[78]

Second, the underpinning of the JCE liability is to be found in considerations of public policy. That is, the need to protect society against persons who (1) join together to take part in criminal enterprises, (2) while not sharing the criminal intent of those participants who intend to commit serious crimes outside the common enterprise, nevertheless are aware that such crimes may be committed, and (3) do not oppose or prevent their commission.[79] As the High Court of England and Wales has noted, "[e]xperience has shown that criminal enterprises only too readily escalate into the commission of greater offences."[80] Thus, JCE liability is justified by both the unique threats posed by organized criminality and the unique challenge of prosecuting such perpetrators.

(hereinafter *Ojdanic* JCE Decision) (noting that application of JCE to crimes in Bosnia was legitimate even though the former Yugoslavia did not recognize that mode of liability).

[77] Law Reports of Trials of War Criminals, XV, p. 98–9.
[78] *Ojdanic* JCE Decision, para. 25.
[79] Cassese, *supra* note 17, at 202.
[80] Regina v. Powell and another, Regina v. English, UK House of Lords, Oct. 30, 1997 (Opinion of Lord Steyn) quoted in Cassese, *supra* note 17, at 203.

Third, incidental criminal liability based on foresight and risk is a mode of liability that is dependent on, and incidental to, a common criminal plan. The "incidental crime" is the outgrowth of, rendered possible by, and premised on the existence of prior joint planning to commit the concerted crime or primary criminal acts of the JCE. In other words, there is a causal link between the concerted crime and the incidental crime. Although the secondary offender did not share the intent of the participant that engaged in the incidental crime, his culpability lies in the fact that he could anticipate such conduct, but willingly took the risk that it might occur. He could have prevented the further crime or disassociated himself from its likely commission, and his failure to do so entails that he too must be held responsible for its commission.[81] This is to be distinguished from situations where a crime is committed as an outgrowth of a plan that is, in the first place, legal. Under those circumstances, for example, when a military unit carries out a legitimate military action, and a member commits a subsequent and unanticipated illegal act, the culpability for that act is considered that of the perpetrator alone. Moreover, the Court can take into account the different degrees of culpability of the participants in the JCE at sentencing.[82]

Finally, and most importantly, national and international judges have historically applied a "foreseeability" standard with rigor and fairness in numerous contexts in criminal law. Indeed, an objective "foreseeability" standard is also applicable in the contexts of proving "aiding and abetting" or "command responsibility." Like JCE III, proof of aiding and abetting is based on an objective test, namely whether the defendant was aware that a crime "will probably be committed."[83] And, like JCE III, liability for command responsibility utilizes a "foreseeability" test, namely whether (1) an act or omission incurring criminal responsibility has been committed by other persons than the accused, (2) there existed a superior-subordinate relationship between the accused and the principle perpetrator, (3) the accused as a superior knew or had reason to know that the subordinate was about to commit such crimes or had done so, and (4) the accused as a superior failed to take the necessary and reasonable measures to prevent such crimes or punish the perpetrator thereof.[84] In fact, the command responsibility "had reason to know" standard is an objective test with an even lower *mens rea* requirement than JCE III.

What remains contentious is not that JCE liability exists for crimes under international law, but under what conditions such liability should be applied. The jurisprudence of the ICTY, ICTR, and SCSL have gone a long way toward defining the contours of the JCE III doctrine to the point where it is sufficiently precise. Specifically, this is achieved by requiring that in addition to a defendant's significant contribution to the execution of the criminal plan, he or she also: (a) shares the

---

[81] Cassese, *supra* note 17, at 202.

[82] *Id.*, at 202–5.

[83] Prosecutor v. Furundzjia, Trial Chamber Judgment, Case No. IT-95-17/1-T, Dec. 10, 1998, para. 246.

[84] Prosecutor v. Oric, Judgment, Case No. IT-03-68-T, June 30, 2006, para. 294.

criminal intent or, at a minimum, (b) is aware of the possibility that a crime might be committed as a consequence of the execution of the criminal act and willingly takes the risk. Accordingly, the crime must not only have been a natural and foreseeable consequence of the requisite participation in the plan (which involves an objective test requiring *dolus eventualis*/advertent recklessness); the accused must also have "willingly" taken the risk despite knowing of the foreseeable consequences.[85] Moreover, the ICTY Appeals Chamber has deliberately sought to prevent the JCE doctrine from expanding and becoming amorphous. For example, in *Krnojelac*, it held that using JCE as a mode of liability "requires a strict definition of common purpose," and that the principal perpetrators who physically commit the crime "should be defined as precisely as possible."[86]

In the years since the *Tadic* Appeals Decision, the ICTY, ICTR, SCSL, and other war crimes tribunals have adopted and applied JCE III liability. In contrast, the ECCC appears to have accepted only JCE I and II as "firmly based in customary international law" at the time of the atrocities of the Khmer Rouge in 1975–9.[87] Based on the statutory language of the Rome Statute, the ICC has likewise decided to forego JCE III in favor of the "control of the crime" standard.[88] Meanwhile, in the 2016 *R. v. Jogee* case, the UK Supreme Court held that JCE III required actual intent to assist or encourage the commission of the crime of the primary defendant, and not mere foresight that such a crime might be committed.[89]

Where does that leave the future of JCE III? Whatever its status was in 1975, through the multiple precedents of the several international tribunals, by the twenty-first century JCE III had fully ripened into an accepted customary international law doctrine, and will undoubtedly be applied by many tribunals and domestic courts in the future. But through an evolutionary process, the contours of JCE III have been and will continue to be refined to improve the efficacy and fairness of the mode of liability.

---

[85] *See* Prosecutor v. Babic, Sentencing Judgment, July 18, 2005, ICTY Appeals Chamber, para. 27. (Accused is liable under third-category JCE "so long as the secondary crimes were foreseeable and he willingly undertook the risk that they would be committed, he had the legally required 'intent' with respect to those crimes.")

[86] Prosecutor v. Krnojelac, Judgment, Case No. IT-97-25-A, ICTY Appeals Chamber, Sept. 17, 2003, para. 116.

[87] Decision on the Appeals against the Co-Investigative Judges Order on Joint Criminal Enterprise, Case No 002/19-19-2007-ECCC/OCIJ, May 20, 2010.

[88] Art. 30(1) of the ICC Statute provides that "unless otherwise provided, a person shall be criminally responsible and liable for punishment for a crime within the jurisdiction of the Court only if the material elements are committed with intent and knowledge" (a higher standard than JCE III's "foreseeability"). In *Lubanga*, the ICC Pre-Trial Chamber adopted the "control over the crime theory" of co-perpetration. Prosecutor v. Lubanga, Judgment, International Criminal Court, Trial Chamber 1, Case No ICC-01/04-01/06, Mar. 14, 2012, at 343–8.

[89] R. v. Jogee (2016) 2 WLR 681, 705.

7

The Tribunals' Fact-Finding Legacy

Yvonne McDermott[*]

Over the course of their lifetimes, the ICTY and ICTR issued judgments deciding on the culpability or innocence of 185 defendants.[1] In reaching these judgments, judges assessed the evidence of hundreds of live witnesses and millions of pages of written evidence. In addition, Trial Chambers considered video evidence, maps, sketches, photographs, and judicially noticed facts from other trials admitted into their evidentiary records. From this 'mosaic of evidence',[2] the Tribunals attempted to elucidate what had happened in the former Yugoslavia and Rwanda years, sometimes decades, earlier, and to determine who bore responsibility for those atrocities.

Matters of evidence and proof were at the very core of the Tribunals' *raison d'être*, and were central to many of the established goals of international criminal law, such as contributing to lasting peace and security; fostering the rule of law and the protection of human rights; establishing accountability; and setting a historical record.[3] While 'evidence and proof' are often mentioned together, a distinction can be drawn between the two interrelated concepts. According to Ludes and

[*] Associate Professor of Law, Swansea University. Email: Yvonne.McDermottRees@swansea.ac.uk. An earlier version of this chapter was presented at the Public International Law Discussion Group, Oxford University, in January 2018. I am grateful to Talita de Souza Dias and all present for their helpful comments and questions, which enhanced this chapter significantly.

[1] *Key Figures of the Cases*, INTERNATIONAL CRIMINAL TRIBUNAL FOR THE FORMER YUGOSLAVIA, online at www.icty.org/en/cases/key-figures-cases (last accessed January 2, 2018) (ninety defendants sentenced; nineteen acquitted); *The ICTR in Brief*, International Criminal Tribunal for Rwanda, online at http://unictr.unmict.org/en/tribunal (last accessed January 2, 2018) (fourteen defendants acquitted; sixty-two sentenced).

[2] Prosecutor v. Krstić, Judgment, Case No. IT-98–33-T, 2 August 2001, para. 4.

[3] The goals of the Tribunals were set out in their founding documents: UN Security Council Resolution 827 (1993) May 25, 1993, UN Doc. S/RES/827 (1993), particularly preambular paras 5–7; UN Security Council Resolution 955 (1994) November 8, 1994, UN Doc. S/RES/955 (1994), particularly preambular paras 6–8. Whether these goals are achievable has been questioned in the literature – e.g., Kate Cronin-Furman & Amanda Taub, *Lions and Tigers and Deterrence, Oh My: Evaluating Expectations of International Criminal Justice*, in THE ASHGATE RESEARCH COMPANION TO INTERNATIONAL CRIMINAL LAW: CRITICAL PERSPECTIVES (William A. Schabas, Yvonne McDermott & Niamh Hayes eds., 2013), 435; Immi Tallgren, *The Sense and Sensibility of International Criminal Law*, 13 EJIL 561 (2002); Mirjan R. Damaška, *What Is the Point of International Criminal Justice?*, 83 CHICAGO KENT LR 329 (2008).

Gilbert, 'Proof is the *result* or *effect* of evidence, while "evidence" is the medium or means by which a fact is proved or disproved'.[4]

It is fair to say that the 'evidence' component of evidence and proof in the ICTY and ICTR has received the majority of scholarly attention, with a particular emphasis on the admissibility of evidence before these Tribunals.[5] This is not unusual; the 'law of evidence', as conceived in most Law Schools' curricula and domestic criminal law textbooks worldwide, focuses disproportionately on admissibility rules and related issues of procedure.[6] Much to the chagrin of some of the world's leading evidence scholars, the means of reasoning on and drawing conclusions from that evidence, once admitted, has been traditionally been excluded from teaching and scholarly analysis.[7]

Encouragingly, towards the end of the ad hoc Tribunals' tenures, a number of scholarly works began to examine such issues as the inconsistencies in witnesses' accounts,[8] the link between judgments' legal and factual findings,[9] and the potential use of argumentation schemes[10] in analysing international criminal judgments. Policy briefs also began to examine issues of evidence and proof in greater detail.[11] For example, in 2017, the Case Matrix Network produced a report entitled *Means of Proof for Sexual and Gender-Based Violence Crimes*, which outlines the various types of evidence that have been used to prove particular crimes in twenty key cases on sexual and gender-based violence.[12] These examples illustrate that international

---

[4]   F. J. Ludes & H. J. Gilbert eds., CORPUS JURIS SECUNDUM: A COMPLETE RESTATEMENT OF THE ENTIRE AMERICAN LAW, VOL 31A: EVIDENCE 820 (1964).

[5]   E.g., Peter Murphy, *No Free Lunch, No Free Proof: The Indiscriminate Admission of Evidence Is a Serious Flaw in International Criminal Trials* (2010) 8 JICJ 539–73; Steven Kay, *The Move from Oral Evidence to Written Evidence: 'The Law Is Always Too Short and Too Tight for Growing Humankind'*, 2 JICJ 495–502 (2004); Eugene O'Sullivan & Deirdre Montgomery, *The Erosion of the Right to Confrontation under the Cloak of Fairness at the ICTY*, 8 JICJ 511–38 (2010).

[6]   Paul Roberts, *The Priority of Procedure and the Neglect of Evidence and Proof: Facing Facts in International Criminal Law*, 13 JICJ 479–506, 481 (2015).

[7]   Roberts, *id.*; William Twining, *Taking Facts Seriously*, in RETHINKING EVIDENCE 14 (William Twining ed., 2006); Terence Anderson, David Schum & William Twining, ANALYSIS OF EVIDENCE (2nd edn, 2005) xvii.

[8]   Nancy Combs, *Fact-Finding Without Facts* (2010).

[9]   Marjolein Cupido, *Facing Facts in International Criminal Law: A Casuistic Model of Judicial Reasoning*, 14 JICJ 1–20 (2016).

[10]   Mark Klamberg, *The Alternative Hypothesis Approach, Robustness and International Criminal Justice: A Plea for a 'Combined Approach' to Evaluation of Evidence*, 13 JICJ 535–53 (2015); Roberts, *supra* note 6; Yvonne McDermott, *Inferential Reasoning and Proof in International Criminal Trials* 13 JICJ 507–33 (2015); Yvonne McDermott & Colin Aitken, *Analysis of Evidence in International Criminal Trials using Bayesian Belief Networks*, 16 LAW, PROBABILITY AND RISK 111–29 (2017); Simon De Smet, *Justified Belief in the Unbelievable*, in QUALITY CONTROL IN FACT-FINDING 77–98 (Morten Bergsmo ed., 2013).

[11]   International Bar Association, *Evidence Matters in ICC Trials* (IBA, The Hague, 2016); HUMAN RIGHTS CENTER, DIGITAL FINGERPRINTS: USING ELECTRONIC EVIDENCE TO ADVANCE PROSECUTIONS AT THE INTERNATIONAL CRIMINAL COURT (2014).

[12]   Case Matrix Network, *Means of Proof: Sexual and Gender-Based Violence Crimes* (Centre for International Law Research and Policy, Belgium, 2017)

criminal law scholarship and practice is at the forefront of legal inquiry, and show that the work of the Tribunals has given rise to a growing interdisciplinary scholarship on fact-finding.[13]

In light of this burgeoning literature on proof in international criminal trials, this chapter's modest aim is to elucidate some of the key fact-finding legacies of the ICTY and ICTR. Part I examines the Tribunals' approaches to evaluating the evidence and elucidating the standard of proof. Part II analyses how the Tribunals approached issues of witness testimony, with particular reference to credibility issues. Part III makes some observations on the structure and accessibility of the Tribunals' judgments.

7.1 THE STANDARD OF PROOF AND THE EVALUATION OF EVIDENCE

The ICTY and ICTR Statutes reflected the well-established principle that accused persons are entitled to the presumption of innocence.[14] As a corollary of that principle, the prosecution bears the onus of proving the guilt of the accused beyond reasonable doubt.[15] The Rules of Procedure and Evidence explicitly state that a conviction can be entered only when a majority of the Trial Chamber is satisfied that guilt has been proven beyond reasonable doubt.[16]

While the standard of proof beyond reasonable doubt is notoriously difficult to define,[17] some Chambers of the Tribunals have attempted to provide some clarity as to its meaning. In *Delalić*, for example, the ICTY Trial Chamber drew heavily on common law jurisprudence, quoting Lord Denning's definition that proof beyond reasonable doubt 'need not reach certainty but it must carry a high degree of probability ... [it] does not mean proof beyond the shadow of a doubt'.[18] The Chamber also recalled Australian Chief Justice Barwick's particularised notion of the reasonable doubt standard, which defined a reasonable doubt as any doubt that the jury entertains, which the jury members themselves deem to be reasonable

---

[13] Roberts, *supra* note 6, at 481 (referring to ICL's 'holistic disciplinary vision').

[14] Article 21(3), ICTY Statute; Article 20(3), ICTR Statute.

[15] Prosecutor v. Kayishema and Ruzindana, Judgment, Case No. ICTR-95-1-A, June 1, 2001, para. 107; Prosecutor v. Milošević, Decision on the Prosecution's Interlocutory Appeal against the Trial Chamber's 10 April 2003 Decision on Prosecution Motion for Judicial Notice of Adjudicated Facts, Oct. 28, 2003, Dissenting Opinion of Judge David Hunt, para. 14 (noting that the prosecution 'carries the onus of proof. . . A basic right of the accused enshrined in the Tribunal's Statute is that he or she is innocent until proven guilty by the prosecution.')

[16] Rules 87(A), ICTY RPE and ICTR RPE.

[17] In England and Wales, judges have tried to refrain, insofar as possible, from providing instructions to juries as to its definition: e.g., R v. Yap Chuan Ching (1976) 63 Cr App Rep 7, para. 11. *See also* Federico Picinali, *The Threshold Lies in the Method: Instructing Jurors about Reasoning Beyond Reasonable Doubt*, 19 INT. J. OF EVIDENCE & PROOF 139–53 (2015).

[18] Prosecutor v. Delalić et al., Judgment, Case No. IT-96-21-T, Nov. 16, 1998, para. 600, citing Miller v. Minister of Pensions (1947) 1 All ER 372, 373–4.

in the circumstances.[19] The Chamber added little commentary to these quotes, simply noting that they clearly showed that the burden of proof rested with the prosecution.[20] In *Rutaganda*, the ICTR Appeals Chamber emphasised the need for any doubts, in order to be reasonable, to be founded on solid evidentiary and logical bases, noting that:

> The reasonable doubt standard in criminal law cannot consist in imaginary or frivolous doubt based on empathy or prejudice. It must be based on logic and common sense, and have a rational link to the evidence, lack of evidence or inconsistencies in the evidence.[21]

The ICTR Appeals Chamber in *Ngirabatware* and the ICTY Appeals Chamber in *Mrkšić* took what could be described as the 'alternative hypothesis' approach to the standard of proof.[22] Both noted that the standard of proof required the Chamber to be satisfied that there is no alternative reasonable explanation of the evidence (other than the guilt of the accused) before it can enter a conviction.[23]

Thus, a number of principles on the meaning of the standard of proof can be derived from the case law of the tribunals. First, proof beyond reasonable doubt requires a high degree of probability, although precisely what level of probability is required seems to differ between judges. Judge Antonetti in *Šešelj* opined that proof beyond reasonable doubt requires 'virtual certainty',[24] an approach apparently at odds with that of the Appeals Chamber in *Delalić*, cited above.[25]

Second, if there is an alternative reasonable explanation of the evidence that suggests innocence, the Chamber must acquit the defendant. It need not be convinced of the innocence of the accused beyond reasonable doubt;[26] all that is required is that the judges themselves deem their doubt to be reasonable,[27] and that doubt should be based on common sense, logic, and be linked to the evidence on the record, or the absence thereof.[28]

---

[19] *Delalić et al.* Trial Judgment, *id.*, para. 600, citing Green v. R (1972) 46 AJLR 545.

[20] *Delalić et al.* Trial Judgment, *id.*, para. 601. The Chamber further noted that these principles they established would be borne in mind when examining the culpability of the accused: *id.*, para. 604.

[21] Prosecutor v. Rutaganda, Judgment, Case No. ICTR-96-3-A, 26 May 2003, para. 488.

[22] Peter Lipton, INFERENCE TO THE BEST EXPLANATION 32–8 (1991); De Smet, *supra* note 10, 89–91; Klamberg, *supra* note 10, 535.

[23] Ngirabatware v. Prosecutor, Judgment, Case No. MICT-12-29-A, Dec. 18, 2014, para. 20; Prosecutor v. Mrkšić and Šljivančanin, Judgment, Case No. IT-95-13/1-A, May 5, 2009, para. 220.

[24] Prosecutor v. Šešelj, Judgment, Case No. IT-03-67-T, Mar. 31, 2016, Concurring Opinion of Presiding Judge Jean-Claude Antonetti Attached to the Judgment, 149. The majority in Šešelj (of which Judge Antonetti was a member) appeared to take such an approach at para. 192 of the Judgment, where it noted that it had not received 'sufficient evidence to irrefutably establish the existence of a widespread and systematic attack against the civilian population'. To 'irrefutably establish' a matter is arguably a higher standard of proof than that of proving it 'beyond reasonable doubt'.

[25] *See above*, text to *supra* note 18.

[26] This point is made, in the context of appeals on questions of fact, in Prosecutor v. Akayesu, Judgment, Case No. ICTR-96-4-A, June 1, 2001, para. 178.

[27] *Delalić et al.* Trial Judgment, *supra* note 18, para. 600

[28] *Rutaganda* Judgment, *supra* note 23, para. 488.

In addition, the Tribunals have confirmed that the standard of proof beyond reasonable doubt applies not just to the ultimate issue of the culpability of the accused, but also to 'each and every element of the offences charged'.[29] In *Kupreškić*, the prosecution argued that the Trial Chamber had erred by applying the standard of proof to a particular witness's testimony.[30] The Appeals Chamber dismissed this argument, noting that the conviction of the defendants for persecution hinged on this witness's account, and thus the Trial Chamber was correct in assessing their testimony to the standard of proof beyond reasonable doubt.[31]

Similarly, the ICTR Appeals Chamber dismissed a prosecution argument that the Trial Chamber committed an error of law in employing the standard of proof to assess individual items of testimony.[32] In that case, a witness had testified that he had attended a meeting, where he heard the accused Ntagerura say that 'the fate of the Tutsi will be sealed'.[33] In light of the fact that there were issues with this witness's credibility, and his allegations were uncorroborated, the Trial Chamber concluded that it could not be satisfied beyond reasonable doubt that Ntagerura had taken part in the meeting.[34] The Appeals Chamber found no error in this approach.[35] While it noted that to apply the criminal standard of proof to each piece of evidence would be an error,[36] it drew a distinction between pieces of evidence and the elements of the crimes that those pieces of evidence purport to prove.[37] The standard of proof applies to each fact upon which a conviction is based.[38] Therefore, if there is only one piece of evidence to support a relevant fact, as was the case in *Kupreškić*,[39] the Chamber must assess whether it is convinced of the existence of that fact beyond reasonable doubt.

I have written elsewhere on the two approaches to the evaluation of the evidence – namely, the 'holistic' and 'atomistic' approaches – that judges may choose from in assessing the evidence.[40] An early decision in *Tadić* appeared to argue against a purely atomistic assessment of each piece of evidence:

> [A] tribunal of fact must never look at the evidence of each witness separately, as if it existed in a hermetically sealed compartment; it is the accumulation of all the

[29] Prosecutor v. Gotovina, Judgment, Case No. IT-06-90-T, Apr. 15, 2011, para. 14.
[30] Prosecutor v. Kupreškić et al., Judgment, Case No. IT-95-16-A, Oct. 23, 2001, para. 226
[31] *Id.*
[32] Prosecutor v. Ntagerura et al., Judgment, Case No. ICTR-99-46-A, July 7, 2006, para. 168.
[33] Prosecutor v. Ntagerura, Judgment and Sentence, Case No. ICTR-99-46-T, Feb. 25, 2004, para. 114.
[34] *Id.*, para. 118.
[35] *Ntagerura* Appeal Judgment, *supra* note 32, para. 173.
[36] *Id.*, para. 174.
[37] *Id.*, para. 175.
[38] *Id.* Similar findings were made at paras 195–7, *id.*
[39] *See above*, text to notes 30 and 31.
[40] Yvonne McDermott, *Strengthening the Evaluation of Evidence in International Criminal Trials*, 17 INT'L CRIM. L. REV. 682–702, 687–92 (2017). This distinction borrows heavily from US evidence scholarship, e.g., Michael S. Pardo, *Juridical Proof, Evidence, and Pragmatic Meaning: Toward Evidentiary Holism*, 95 NW. U. L. REV. 399 (2000–2001).

evidence in the case which must be considered. The evidence of one witness, when considered by itself, may appear at first to be of poor quality, but it may gain strength from other evidence in the case. The converse also holds true.[41]

On the other hand, a number of appeals, where one party asserts that the Trial Chamber has taken an insufficiently holistic approach to the evidence 'as a whole', have been unsuccessful.[42] In *Bizimungu*, where defence argued that the Trial Chamber had failed to make the requisite findings to underpin his convictions, the prosecution countered that such findings could be read holistically from the judgment as a whole.[43] The prosecution argument was rejected by the Appeals Chamber, which found that the Trial Chamber's failure to set out its findings amounted 'to a manifest failure to provide a reasoned opinion'.[44]

Both the atomistic and holistic approaches have their critics,[45] and it is clear that neither a purely atomistic evaluation of each piece of evidence, nor a purely holistic approach, is preferable. Thus, a combined approach is needed. To this end, Mark Klamberg has argued that international criminal judges take the following steps in reaching their conclusions: first, they evaluate a single piece of evidence; then, they weigh the totality of evidence in favour of or against the proposition asserted; and then, they make the final determination of whether the combined evidential value is sufficient to establish the proposition.[46]

This may be a rather optimistic view of how evidence is evaluated in practice in international criminal trials. Indeed, one of the very few judicial statements on how the evaluation of evidence works in practice suggests otherwise.[47] The *Ntagerura* Appeals Chamber set out the following three stages that are taken in the evaluation of the evidence.[48] Firstly, an assessment of the credibility of the evidence is undertaken, but the Chamber explicitly said that 'this cannot be undertaken by a piecemeal approach'. Secondly, the Chamber assesses whether the evidence presented by the prosecution 'should be accepted as supporting the existence of the facts alleged', notwithstanding the defence evidence.[49] Thirdly, the Chamber will analyse whether all of the elements of the crimes and modes of liability charged have been proven.[50]

The *Ntagerura* approach to the evaluation of evidence differs from Klamberg's proposed test in two important respects. First, in relation to the first limb, the

---

[41] Prosecutor v. Tadić, Judgment on Allegations of Contempt against Prior Counsel, Milan Vujin, Case No. IT-94-1-A-R77, Jan. 31, 2000, para. 92.

[42] E.g., *Ntagerura* and *Kupreškić*, discussed above, text to notes 30–9.

[43] Prosecutor v. Bizimungu, Judgment, Case No. ICTR-99-50-A, Feb. 4, 2013, paras 14–15.

[44] *Id.*, para. 29.

[45] Outlined in detail in McDermott, *supra* note 40, 687–9.

[46] Klamberg, *supra* note 10, 546–7.

[47] *Ntagerura* Appeal Judgment, *supra* note 32, para. 174.

[48] *Id.*

[49] *Id.*

[50] *Id.*

Chamber's insistence that individual pieces of evidence should only be assessed in light of the rest of the evidentiary record, while broadly correct, misses an important role of the Chamber in analysing the reliability and relevance of each piece of evidence on its own merits. If a piece of evidence is patently lacking in reliability, the fact that another (perhaps equally unreliable) piece of evidence corroborates that evidence is irrelevant. Thus, there is clearly an important need for the 'piecemeal approach' maligned by the Appeals Chamber's exposition of the first stage to be taken, followed by a contextual evaluation of that evidence in the light of other evidence on the record. In the ICTR's stated approach, Klamberg's first two proposed stages are condensed and reduced to a single step of analysing the evidence as a whole. Second, the Chamber's approach adds an important step in its third limb, which sees the application of facts (or, in Klamberg's terms, propositions) to the elements of the crimes and modes of liability charged.

Optimistic though it may be, Klamberg's approach illustrates a good model of how the process of evaluation of evidence *should* work. Combining the differing tests outlined above might lead us to a new, four-stage test for the evaluation of evidence:

1. The examination of a single piece of evidence on a particular fact;
2. The evaluation of that evidence in the context of other evidence on the record;
3. The weighing of the totality of the evidence to determine whether the fact is established. If that fact is an element of the crime or the mode of liability charged, then it must be established beyond reasonable doubt;[51]
4. An examination of whether the fact proven, and other relevant facts established, ensure that all of the elements of the crimes and modes of liability charged have been proven beyond reasonable doubt.

These guidelines on the assessment of evidence, while perhaps incomplete, provide a starting point for future international criminal trials in approaching how they weigh the evidence before them. This would certainly be preferable to the position of the ICTY and ICTR, where it has been argued that 'the absence of clear guidelines on the weighing of evidence… furthers the freedom of assessment; but it achieves this objective at the expense of legal certainty'.[52] The approach proposed above would enable Chambers to incorporate both a thorough scrutiny of each

---

[51] *Id.* Some judgments have used the term 'material fact' to describe those facts that must be proven beyond reasonable doubt: *Delalić et al.* Trial Judgment, *supra* note 18, para. 109; Prosecutor v. Halilović, Judgment, Case No. IT-01-48-A, Oct. 16, 2007, para. 109; Prosecutor v. Martić, Judgment, Case No. IT-95-11-A, Oct. 8, 2008, para. 55; Prosecutor v. Milošević (Dragomir), Judgment, Case No. IT-98-29/1-A, Nov. 12, 2009, para. 20; Prosecutor v. Mladić, Judgment, Case No. IT-09-92-T, Nov. 22, 2017, para. 5250.

[52] Paul Behrens, *Assessment of International Criminal Evidence: The Case of the Unpredictable Génocidaire*, 71 ZEITSCHRIFT FÜR AUSLÄNDISCHES ÖFFENTLICHES RECHT UND VÖLKERRECHT 661–89 (2011).

piece of evidence, and an evaluation of that evidence in the context of the record as a whole.

7.2 EVALUATING WITNESS CREDIBILITY

While the above suggested framework stresses the importance of carrying out an individualised assessment of the evidence presented, the Tribunals' judgments often emphasised a rather more holistic approach. A common statement made in judgments was that the Trial Chamber considered all of the evidence presented before it, and that even if a piece of evidence was not cited in the judgment, the parties could be assured that it had been duly considered and given weight to by the Chamber.[53] This type of statement can give rise to uncertainty as to the precise evidentiary basis of some of the Chamber's conclusions.

Similarly, the manner in which witnesses' credibility or reliability was assessed was not always explicit. On occasion, the Tribunals noted that they adjudged certain witnesses to be unreliable on some points, but reliable on others.[54] For example, in *Gotovina*, the ICTY Trial Chamber noted:

> Some of the witnesses. . . were evasive or not entirely truthful. . . Although aware of this, the Trial Chamber nevertheless sometimes relied on some aspects of these witnesses' testimonies. . . While the Trial Chamber may not always have explicitly stated whether it found a witness's testimony or portions of his or her testimony credible, it consistently took the factors [of credibility, reliability, and demeanour] into account in making findings on the evidence.[55]

In other words, even where the Chamber has not explicitly stated whether or why it found a witness's testimony, or part of that testimony, credible or reliable, it will have made that determination and based its overall judgment on that undisclosed assessment. These 'catch all' provisions made it almost impossible for one of the parties to appeal on the basis that the Trial Chamber made an error of fact.[56]

Nevertheless, while the Tribunals were given the freedom to assess the evidence without constraint to any approach derived from national rules of evidence,[57] a number of preferences and reasonably consistent principles on issues such as

---

53 This statement is found in, *inter alia*, Prosecutor v. Perišić, Judgment, Case No. IT-04-81-T, Sept. 6, 2011, para. 23; *Gotovina* Trial Judgment, *supra* note 29, para. 47; Prosecutor v. Bikindi, Judgment, Case No. ICTR-01-72-T, Dec. 2, 2008, para. 29; Prosecutor v. Stanišić and Simatović, Judgment, Case No. IT-03-69, May 30, 2013, para. 34.

54 *Perišić* Trial Judgment, *id.*, para. 10; Prosecutor v. Ðorđević, Judgment, Case No. IT-05-87/1-T, Feb. 23, 2011, para. 18; Prosecutor v. Strugar, Judgment, Case No. IT-01-42-T, Jan. 31, 2005, para. 10.

55 *Gotovina* Trial Judgment, *supra* note 29, para. 31.

56 Discussed further in Yvonne McDermott, *The ICTR's Fact-Finding Legacy: Lessons for the Future of Proof in International Criminal Trials*, 20 CRIMINAL LAW FORUM 351–72 (2015), where it is argued that apparent alleged errors of fact are often framed as alleged errors of law to further their chance of success on appeal.

57 Rule 89, ICTR RPE.

corroboration, credibility, and reliability emerged in practice. For example, despite the increase over time in rules of evidence that allowed for a greater use of written witness statements in lieu of oral testimony,[58] Trial Chambers continued to express a preference that important evidence be elicited orally from witnesses in court.[59]

In assessing the credibility of witnesses, both the ICTY and ICTR have borne in mind that witnesses' memories may be affected by the passage of time[60] and the trauma suffered.[61] In addition, some Chambers have quite frankly acknowledged that the witnesses who have appeared before them may not have been entirely truthful in their accounts.[62] This may be because of the witness's own involvement in the events at issue, and their attempts to downplay their own culpability.[63] Such 'insider witnesses' are frequently used in international criminal trials; at the Special Court for Sierra Leone, for example, 31 per cent of witnesses were classified as insider witnesses.[64] Other witnesses may have had other underlying motives or affiliations that cast doubt on their credibility or reliability;[65] a number of Chambers noted that issues such as the witnesses' connections with the accused, the prosecution, national governments, or survivors' groups would be noted in the evaluation of their testimony.[66]

The ICTR Trial Chamber in *Akayesu* established some guidelines on assessing the credibility of witnesses. It noted that cultural factors may lead to some witnesses' difficulty in providing specific details on issues such as distances, times, and locations, and that the Chamber did not draw adverse inferences from witnesses'

---

[58] See the references cited above in note 5 for further discussion.

[59] E.g., *Gotovina* Trial Judgment, *supra* note 29, para. 16; Prosecutor v. Akayesu, Judgment, Case No. ICTR-96-4-T, Sept. 2, 1998, para. 137.

[60] *Strugar* Trial Judgment, *supra* note 54, para. 7; *Mladić* Trial Judgment, *supra* note 51, para. 5279; Prosecutor v. Bagilishema, Judgment, Case No. ICTR-95-1A-T, June 7, 2001, para. 24, and *id.*, Separate and Dissenting Opinion of Judge Mehmet Güney, para. 29; Prosecutor v. Bagilishema, Judgment, Case No. ICTR-95-1A-A, July 3, 2002.

[61] *Akayesu* Trial Judgment, *supra* note 59, paras 142–3; *Bagilishema* Trial Judgment, *id.*, Separate and Dissenting Opinion of Judge Güney, para. 30; Prosecutor v. Furundžija, Judgment, Case No. IT-95-17/1-T, Dec. 10, 1998, para. 113; Prosecutor v. Delalić et al., Judgment, Case No. IT-96-21-A, Feb. 20, 2001, para. 497; Prosecutor v. Kunarac, Judgment, Case No. IT-96-23-A, June 12, 2002, para. 324. For further analysis on this point, *see* Robert Cryer, *A Message from Elsewhere: Witnesses before International Criminal Tribunals*, in INNOVATIONS IN EVIDENCE AND PROOF 381–400 (Paul Roberts and Mike Redmayne eds., 2007) and Robert Cryer, *Witness Evidence Before International Criminal Tribunals*, 3 LAW AND PRACTICE OF INTERNATIONAL TRIBUNALS 411–39 (2003).

[62] *Strugar* Trial Judgment, *supra* note 54, para. 7; Prosecutor v. Bizimungu et al., Judgment, Case No. ICTR-99-50-T, Sept. 30, 2011, para. 109; *Perišić* Trial Judgment, *supra* note 53, para. 34.

[63] *Mladić* Trial Judgment, *supra* note 51, para. 5280; *Gotovina* Trial Judgment, *supra* note 29, para. 31.

[64] Special Court for Sierra Leone, *Best Practice Recommendations for the Protection and Support of Witnesses* 11 (2008). A study of ICTY witnesses, *Echoes of Testimonies*, was published in October 2016, but despite gathering information on the ethnicity, age, and gender of witnesses surveyed, the study did not classify the witnesses by background and role in the matters on which they testified.

[65] *Mladić* Trial Judgment, *supra* note 51, para. 5279; Prosecutor v. Limaj, Judgment, Case No. IT-03-66-T, Nov. 30, 2005, para. 15.

[66] *Bizimungu* Trial Judgment, *supra* note 62, para. 109.

'reticence and their circuitous responses to questions'.[67] The Chamber stated that challenges on the credibility of the witness must be individualised to the particular witness – it was insufficient to merely assert that other witnesses for the party had been found to have lied – and that such challenges must be put to the witness themselves, giving them the chance to respond.[68]

In spite of this extrapolation of some of the factors that Chambers will take into account in assessing witness credibility, whether and why a Chamber will deem a witness credible still remains quite uncertain. At times, the ICTY and ICTR Chambers appear to have based these assessments on the judges' own beliefs on how people should normally behave, albeit in the extraordinary circumstances that witnesses have found themselves in. In *Nzabonimana*, for example, the ICTR noted that it was 'unlikely that a group of Tutsis fleeing a violent attack at their place of refuge... would choose to disguise themselves as Hutus and join a group of people gathered in a trading centre for a brief time before continuing on their journey'.[69] In *Gatete*, the fact that a witness 'moved to only metres away from the Accused at the roadblock when *Interahamwe*, who according to her testimony had killed persons with "bladed weapons", were present' led the Chamber to have concerns about the merits of the witness's evidence.[70] These assessments suggest that the ICTR Chambers believed they could accurately predict how people ought to behave when fleeing genocidal attackers, and that any derogation from that norm was to be viewed with suspicion.

This importation of the judges' own expectations of human behaviour in the face of attack seems curious, given the exceptional nature of the atrocities upon which the ICTR adjudged. The ICTY was not immune from making similar cultural transplantations. In *Tadić*, the defence argued that the Trial Chamber had erred by relying on the testimony of a witness who claimed to have seen the events when he returned to his home to check on his pet pigeons.[71] The prosecution had responded by likening his actions to the pet owner who returns to a burning building to rescue their beloved companion.[72] The Appeals Chamber seemingly accepted this argument, noting:

> The Appeals Chamber does not accept as inherently implausible the witness' claim that the reason why he returned to the town where the Serbian paramilitary forces had been attacking, and from which he had escaped, was to feed his pet pigeons. It is conceivable that a person may do such a thing, even though one might think such action to be an irrational risk.[73]

---

[67] *Akayesu* Trial Judgment, *supra* note 59, para. 156. *See also Bagilishema* Trial Judgment, *supra* note 60, Separate and Dissenting Opinion of Judge Güney, para. 28.

[68] *Akayesu* Trial Judgment, *supra* note 59, para. 46.

[69] Prosecutor v. Nzabonimana, Judgment and Sentence, Case No. ICTR-98-44D-T, May 31, 2012, para. 718.

[70] Prosecutor v. Gatete, Judgment and Sentence, Case No. ICTR-2000-61-T, Mar. 31, 2011, para. 232.

[71] Prosecutor v. Tadić, Judgment, Case No. IT-94-1-A, July 15, 1999, para. 58.

[72] Prosecutor v. Tadić, Transcript, Apr. 20, 1999, 419.

[73] *Tadić* Appeals Judgment, *supra* note 71, para. 66.

However, as Paul Roberts has noted, the transcripts reveal that the witness was motivated by other factors than the welfare of his pigeons, including his need to get food and clothes, and to locate his brother.[74] Roberts questions whether the parties, and the Chamber in turn, projected their (perhaps particularly Western) view of the relationship between pets and their owners in evaluating this issue.[75]

The extent to which a witness's account is corroborated is clearly a relevant factor in the Chamber's decision on whether to base its findings on that account. That being said, the Tribunals were not bound by the '*unus testis, nullus testis*' rule – in other words, there was no legal requirement of corroboration for the testimony of a single witness to be accepted as evidence.[76] However, the ICTY and ICTR consistently emphasised that uncorroborated accounts would be treated with caution.[77] Corroboration is particularly important where a witness's statement has been entered in written form in lieu of oral testimony.[78] In *Popović*, the ICTY Appeals Chamber emphasised that findings on material facts could not be based solely or decisively on untested written statements, and that such accounts must be corroborated.[79] Conversely, the fact that many witnesses may corroborate one another does not necessarily prove the credibility of their accounts.[80]

The weight to be placed on the witness's identification of the accused was a contentious issue in both the ICTY and ICTR. In *Tadić*, a distinction was drawn between so-called 'identification witnesses', to whom the accused was previously unknown by sight, and 'recognition witnesses', who knew the accused prior to the relevant events and recognised them as a result.[81] A stricter standard of assessment will apply to the evidence of the former category of witness.[82] However, the distinction between identification witnesses and recognition witnesses can be difficult to draw – in *Lukić*, the ICTY Trial Chamber held that prior knowledge of the accused before the commission of a crime was not a prerequisite to being classified as

---

[74] Paul Roberts, *Why International Criminal Evidence?*, in INNOVATIONS IN EVIDENCE AND PROOF 347, 376 (Paul Roberts and Mike Redmayne eds., 2007).

[75] *Id.*, 377–8.

[76] *Akayesu* Trial Judgment, *supra* note 59, para. 135; Prosecutor v. Aleksovski, Judgment, Case No. IT-95-14/1-A, Mar. 24, 2000, para. 62; Prosecutor v. Seromba, Judgment, Case No. ICTR-2001-66-A, Mar. 12, 2008, paras 91–2; *Delalić et al.* Appeal Judgment, *supra* note 61, para. 506; Prosecutor v. Karadžić, Judgment, Case No. IT-95-5/18-T, Mar. 24, 2016, para. 12.

[77] *Karadžić* Judgment, *id.*, para. 24; *Strugar* Trial Judgment, *supra* note 54, para. 9; *Mladić* Trial Judgment, *supra* note 51, para. 5281; Prosecutor v. Kayishema and Ruzindana, Judgment, Case No. ICTR-95-1-T, May 21, 1999, para. 80. For an illustration of such caution in practice, *see* Bizimungu Trial Judgment, *supra* note 62, paras 203, 207, 229, 233, 248, 252, 259, 306, 493, 544, 549, 555, 658, 712, 764, 779, 1018, 1180, 1181, 1373, 1405, 1406, 1415, 1443, 1450, 1463, 1472, and 1552.

[78] Under Rules 92*bis*, 92*ter*, 92*quater*, or 92*quinquies* ICTY RPE; the ICTR RPE only adopted Rule 92*bis* of these amended Rules on proof of facts other than by means of oral evidence.

[79] Prosecutor v. Popović et al., Judgment, Case No. IT-05-88-A, Jan. 30, 2015, para. 1222. *See also Karadžić* Trial Judgment, *supra* note 76, para. 24.

[80] Prosecutor v. Musema, Judgment and Sentence, Case No. ICTR-96-13-A, Jan. 27, 2000, para. 46.

[81] Prosecutor v. Tadić, Opinion and Judgment, Case No. IT-94-1-T, May 7, 1997, para. 545.

[82] *Tadić* Trial Judgment, *id.*, paras 546–52; *Bagilishema* Trial Judgment, *supra* note 60, Separate and Dissenting Opinion of Judge Güney, para. 27.

a recognition witness; the fact that the witness got to know what the accused looked like over the period of the commission of that crime was sufficient for them to be considered recognition witnesses.[83]

While in-court identification of the accused is generally permissible,[84] little weight should be placed on such evidence; the fact that the defendant will be sitting next to guards in the courtroom will necessarily suggest to the witness that this is the person on trial.[85] However, a witness's inability to identify the accused in court may be relevant in refusing to rely on that witness's identification evidence.[86] In *Kupreškić*, the Trial Chamber placed particular weight on the fact that a witness's 'evidence concerning the identification of the accused was unshaken'.[87] The Appeals Chamber, recalling that a confident demeanour is often a character trait, rather than an indication of truthfulness,[88] found that the Trial Chamber had erred in relying so heavily on this witness's account.[89]

The above analysis shows that the Tribunals' approach to the evaluation of witness testimony was still evolving by the end of their tenures. While some general principles and themes have been identified, practice was generally quite inconsistent on the weight to be given to different types of evidence and the extent to which some Chambers accepted or declined to accept fallibilities in witnesses' accounts.[90] The common statements to be found in Trial Judgments that all evidence, even where not cited, was considered often obfuscated the precise impact of testimonial deficiencies or issues of credibility that the Chambers identified. This observation leads us to examine the structure and layout of judgments and whether they detract from those judgments' clarity and accessibility.

7.3 THE STRUCTURE OF JUDGMENTS

It is a truism that international criminal judgments are exceptionally lengthy, and that is particularly true for the judgments of the *ad hoc* tribunals.[91] Some of the last judgments issued by the ICTY and ICTR before they ceased operations demonstrate

---

[83] Prosecutor v. Lukić and Lukić, Judgment, Case No. IT-98-32/1-T, July 20, 2009, para. 34. Upheld in Prosecutor v. Lukić and Lukić, Judgment, Case No. IT-98-32/1-A, Dec. 4, 2012, para. 119.

[84] Prosecutor v. Kalimanzira, Judgment, Case No. ICTR-05-88-T, June 22, 2009, para. 96; Prosecutor v. Kamuhanda, Judgment, Case No. ICTR-99-54A-A, Sept. 19, 2005, para. 243; Prosecutor v. Limaj et al., Judgment, Case No. IT-03-66-A, Sept. 27, 2007, para. 120.

[85] *Kunarac* Appeal Judgment, *supra* note 61, para. 226; *Kamuhanda* Appeal Judgment, *id.*, para. 27; *Limaj et al.* Appeal Judgment, *id.*, para. 27; *Lukić and Lukić* Trial Judgment, *supra* note 83, para. 32.

[86] *Limaj et al.* Appeal Judgment, *id.*, para. 120; Prosecutor v. Kvočka et al., Judgment, Case No. IT-98-30/1-A, Feb. 28, 2005, para. 473.

[87] Prosecutor v. Kupreškić et al., Judgment, Case No. IT-95-16-T, Jan. 14, 2000, para. 425.

[88] *Kupreškić et al.* Appeal Judgment, *supra* note 30, para. 138.

[89] *Id.*, para. 154.

[90] Combs, *supra* note 8, chapter 7.

[91] This was also true, to some extent, for the Special Court for Sierra Leone – the judgment in Prosecutor v. Taylor, Case No. SCSL-03-01-T, May 18, 2012, was 2,539 pages long.

this fact; the *Mladić* Trial Judgment, issued in November 2017, spans five volumes and is more than 2,500 pages long, plus a confidential annex.[92] Similarly, the *Karadžić* trial judgment has more than 2,600 pages.[93] Even Appeals Chamber judgments can span in excess of 1,000 pages.[94] This length of judgment was not always common; the ICTY's Trial Chamber 1999 judgment in *Aleksovski* was just ninety pages long, although that judgment concerned the accused's responsibility for just three crimes alleged to have been committed over a period of less than six months.[95]

The length of judgments does raise concerns for the accessibility of the Tribunals' findings to the communities affected by the atrocities on trial, as well as to the international and legal community. Assuming an ability to read 200 pages per day of the often highly complex and technical legal language used in judgments, it would take the average reader close to two weeks to read the *Karadžić* judgment alone. The ability to absorb 200 pages in a day would require most people to dedicate themselves solely to the task of reading the judgment, a luxury that many would be unable to afford.

Ironically, perhaps, the huge scope of the judgments could be attributed, at least in part, to the expectation of setting an historical record, or, in the words of Judge Nsereko, establishing 'undisputable findings regarding the atrocities committed'.[96] For example, in reading the *Karadžić* judgment, one aspect that really stands out is the shocking consequences of DutchBat's loss of control, and their role in actually enabling the genocide in Srebrenica.[97] The extensive treatment of this issue is in a sense understandable, given that it forms an important part of the record of how this genocide happened. On the other hand, one could strongly argue that the failings of DutchBat have precisely nothing to do with Karadžić's criminal liability. Given that the DutchBat findings do not appear until 2000 pages into the judgment, one might wonder about the accessibility of these important factual findings. It could be more useful for all concerned if the Chamber released a separate document on 'context of the crimes' for these important factual findings, with the judgment itself limited to the specific elements of the crimes and modes of liability charged, and how the evidence supported those elements.

A more focused judgment may also lead to less repetition; again, in *Karadžić*, one of the key aspects of the case was a phone conversation that the accused had with Deronjić, which was crucial in proving the accused's knowledge that the detainees would be killed. The Trial Chamber judgment includes a full transcript of this

---

[92] *Mladić* Trial Judgment, *supra* note 51.

[93] *Karadžić* Trial Judgment, *supra* note 76.

[94] The Appeals Chamber judgment in Prosecutor v. Prlić et al., Case No. IT-04-74-A, Nov. 29, 2017, spanned over 1,400 pages.

[95] Prosecutor v. Aleksovski, Judgment, Case No. IT-95-14/1-T, June 25, 1999, para. 2.

[96] Daniel David Ntanda Nsereko, *Foreword, in* PRINCIPLES OF EVIDENCE IN INTERNATIONAL CRIMINAL JUSTICE (Karim A. A. Khan, Caroline Buisman & Christopher Gosnell eds., 2010) v–vi, v.

[97] *Karadžić* Trial Judgment, *supra* note 76, paras 4977–5100.

conversation at paragraphs 5311, 5710, and 5772, and it is quoted at length again at paragraph 5805 and 5806.

These issues of accessibility and clarity came to the fore when I wrote, together with a computer scientist colleague with expertise in argumentation theory,[98] an *amicus curiae* brief submitted to the MICT Appeals Chamber in *Karadžić*.[99] As part of a wider project, which examines the potential applicability of argumentation schemes to international criminal judging, we took the Trial Chamber's findings on Karadžić's genocidal intent as a case study.[100] These findings were the subject of an extensive and rather unprecedented level of academic scrutiny.[101] In order to construct a relatively straightforward four-page timeline of relevant events, findings spanning over 600 paragraphs had to be drawn upon.[102] It occurred to us that the inclusion of a timeline or timelines, maps, and an index would make international criminal judgments much more navigable.

More generally, as alluded to in Section 7.2, it might also be useful if judgments could indicate more clearly the probative value of witnesses' testimony and other evidence. One interesting aspect of Judge Antonetti's separate opinion in *Šešelj* was the inclusion of a table on the probative value of witness's evidence and on the exhibits admitted to the record. In these tables, Judge Antonetti assigned levels of probative value on a seven-point scale.[103] The scale adopted bears some similarities to scales familiar in the science of logic – such as the admiralty scale, or 'NATO system', for the evaluation of particular intelligence sources and the level of confidence in the information.[104] Even if this kind of evaluation of evidence using scales and metrics were not included in judgments, they may be useful in the judgment drafting process. Such analyses could in turn feed into charts or tables setting out the elements of each crime and whether they had been proven or not. While some

---

[98] Dr Federico Cerutti, Lecturer, School of Computer Sciences, Cardiff University. This research was funded by CHERISH-DE, the UK's Digital Economy Crucible (http://cherish-de.uk), to which we are very grateful.

[99] Prosecutor v. Karadžić, Proposed *Amicus Curiae* submissions, Case No. MICT-13-55-A, submitted February 2018.

[100] *Karadžić* Trial Judgment, *supra* note 76, paras 5746–831.

[101] E.g., Milena Sterio, *The Karadžić Genocide Conviction: Inferences, Intent, and the Necessity to Redefine Genocide* 31 EMORY INTERNATIONAL LAW REVIEW 271 (2017); Marko Milanovic, *ICTY Convicts Radovan Karadzic*, EJIL: TALK! (Mar. 25, 2016), www.ejiltalk.org/icty-convicts-radovan-karadzic (last accessed Feb. 1, 2018); Kai Ambos, *Karadzic's Genocidal Intent as the 'Only Reasonable Inference'?*, EJIL: TALK! (Apr. 1, 2016), www.ejiltalk.org/karadzics-genocidal-intent-as-the-only-reasonable-inference (last accessed Feb. 1, 2018).

[102] *Amicus Curiae* Brief, *supra* note 99, Appendix A, referring to paras 5157–772. Not all of these 615 paragraphs referred to relevant events, of course, but relevant findings were found in paragraphs within this range, interspersed with other findings that were less relevant to questions of the accused's culpability.

[103] *Šešelj* Trial Judgment, *supra* note 24, Concurring Opinion of Judge Antonetti, 55. The scale placed probative value in one of seven categories: absolute, very strong, strong, fair, poor, very poor, none.

[104] *See further, inter alia*, Jérôme Besombes, Vincent Nimier, and Laurence Cholvy, *Information Evaluation in Fusion Using Information Correlation*, paper presented at the 12th International Conference on Information Fusion, Seattle, USA, July 6–9, 2009, 264–9.

judges would almost certainly object to a more atomistic overview of why the Chamber was brought to its final conclusion, it would clearly be preferable to the Tribunals' approach whereby readers are assured that the decisions were based on the evidentiary records as a whole, and that even where evidence was not explicitly cited, it will have been considered.[105] As one author has argued, 'The courts' judgments do not consistently clarify which facts underlie the decisions, what weight is attached to these facts and how this factual evaluation relates to the legal framework of rules, elements, criteria and precedents.'[106]

A final structural element of the Tribunals' judgments that is worthy of consideration is the not uncommon practice of judges in the majority appending joint concurring opinions or separate opinions to judgments. In other words, the judgment sees two of the three judges (or three out of five judges, for Appeals Chamber decisions) form a majority, with a dissenting opinion from the remaining judge or judges. In addition to that dissenting opinion and majority judgment, one or more of the judges from the majority appends a separate, often lengthy, concurring opinion, emphasizing precisely why they agree with the majority (i.e. their own) judgment.

For example, in *Bagilishema*, Judge Asoka de Z. Gunawardana, who was in the majority, issued a separate opinion that began with the words 'I agree with the Judgment of Judge Møse...'[107] This type of wording may give the impression that the majority judgment was not truly a reflection of the views of the majority, but of one of the judges in that majority. Similarly, in *Šešelj*, as well as the 110-page-long judgment,[108] Judge Niang, who was in the majority, appended a six-page long 'individual statement',[109] while Judge Antonetti, who was also in the majority, issued a 'concurring opinion' spanning almost 500 pages in length.[110] Judge Lattanzi's 'partially dissenting' opinion (although she noted that she disagreed with her colleagues in the majority on 'almost everything'[111]) was forty-nine pages long.[112] This practice of separate majority opinions highlights discord amongst judges, adds further conceptual confusion on the precise basis for the majority judgment, and has the potential to dilute the normative force of the judgment, which is supposed to be the definitive statement of the majority's conclusions. Nevertheless, it is a practice that has permeated into other international criminal jurisdictions, including, most notably, the International Criminal Court.[113]

---

[105] *See above*, Section 7.1.

[106] Cupido, *supra* note 9, 1.

[107] *Bagilishema* Trial Judgment, *supra* note 60, Separate Opinion of Judge Asoka de Z. Gunawardana, para. 1. Judge Guney appended a dissenting opinion to this judgment: *Bagilishema* Trial Judgment, *supra* 60, Separate and Dissenting Opinion of Judge Güney.

[108] Plus annexes totalling twenty-six pages.

[109] *Šešelj* Trial Judgment, *supra* note 24, Individual Statement of Judge Mandiaye Niang.

[110] *Šešelj* Trial Judgment, *supra* note 24, Concurring Opinion of Judge Antonetti.

[111] *Šešelj* Trial Judgment, *supra* note 24, Partially Dissenting Opinion of Judge Flavia Lattanzi – Amended Version, para. 1

[112] *Id.*

[113] Prosecutor v. Katanga, Jugement rendu en application de l'article 74 du Statut, Case No. ICC-01/04-01/07, Mar. 7, 2014, Concurring Opinion of Judges Fatoumata Diarra and Bruno Cotte.

7.4 CONCLUSION

This chapter drew on the rich and varied jurisprudence of the ICTY and ICTR in enunciating some of the key themes that underpinned their fact-finding practices. It provided some suggestions on how the standard of proof could be more clearly articulated, how the evaluation of evidence could be made more explicit, and how international criminal judgments could be made more accessible, drawing on the experience of the ICTY and ICTR. The increased accessibility and clarity that would result would in turn enhance the legal and sociological legitimacy of future international criminal trials.

On the meaning of the standard of proof, Section 7.1 concluded that the standard of proof beyond reasonable doubt applies not just to the Chamber's ultimate conclusion, but also to key facts underpinning the elements of crimes or modes of liability, and that if an alternative reasonable explanation of the evidence exists, the Chamber must acquit the accused. Section 7.1 also noted that there was some uncertainty or apparent differences of opinion between judges on the precise level of certainty required to reach the standard of proof. It also compared the atomistic and holistic approaches to the evaluation of the evidence, and proposed a model of evaluation that would combine both approaches.

Relatedly, Section 7.2 criticised the Chambers' often overly holistic approach to the evaluation of evidence, as illustrated by the common statement found in judgments that says that all of the evidence, even if it was not referred to in the judgment, was duly weighed and considered in reaching judgment. Section 7.2 also extrapolated principles on some of the more contentious issues that arose on the assessment of evidence in practice, such as the role of corroboration, the weight to be given to in-court identifications of the accused, and the factors to be taken into account in deciding whether a witness should be considered credible. Nevertheless, it was noted that the level of credibility a Chamber would attach to a witness's account was rather unpredictable, and the factors relied upon by Chambers in this regard appeared to vary quite significantly between differently constituted Chambers.

Lastly, Section 7.3 discussed the structure of international criminal judgments. It noted that the extreme length of the ICTY and ICTR's judgments could have an impact on their accessibility to the local, international, and legal communities that they serve. It made some suggestions for minor improvements that could have made the Tribunals' judgments much more focused and navigable. Section 7.3 also suggested that the practice of judges appending joint concurring opinions to the majority judgment might detract from the normative force of the original judgment.

Of course, it could be argued, from the point of view of sociological legitimacy, that victims in affected regions are more interested in the outcome of international criminal trials and the sentences given to convicted persons than they are in reading the full judgments and determining the evidentiary underpinnings of the Tribunals' findings. That argument would suggest that judgments only serve prosecution and defence legal teams and the occasional interested academic, and that there is no need for the Tribunals to make their findings more broadly accessible. I would respectfully disagree with such an argument for two reasons. First, practice shows us that affected communities do care about the Tribunals' reasoned judgments. We can see this, for example, by the fact that in some parts of the former Yugoslavia, the *Milošević* Rule 98*bis* decision was published and sold in bookshops.[114] Moreover, even if we were to partially accept the argument that judgments principally serve the parties, and not the affected communities, we might argue, given the preponderance of appeals raised on allegations that the Trial Chamber failed to take relevant evidence into account or gave undue weight to some evidence or facts, that the current structure of judgments does not even live up to that limited promise.

Perhaps one of the more striking conclusions that can be drawn from the above analysis is that proof in international criminal trials is an area that remains beset by uncertainty. In many ways, this is surprising; one might have expected that, by the end of the Tribunals' lifetimes, we would be able to identify reasonably consistent approaches to the evaluation of evidence, a more or less shared understanding of the standard of proof and what it requires, and clear structures for judgments and their scope. However, as illustrated above, these issues were still subject to debate and development, even in the twilight years of the Tribunals.

---

[114]   Muharam Kreso (ed.), *Milošević Guilty of Genocide: Decision on Motion of the Hague Tribunal of 16 June 2004* (in Bosnian as: *Miloševiću Dokazan Genocid u Bosni: Međupresuda Haškog Tribunala od 16 Juna 2004*) (Institute for Research of Crimes against Humanity and International Law, University of Sarajevo, Sarajevo, 2007).

8

The Legacy of the ICTY and ICTR on Sexual and Gender-Based Violence

Valerie Oosterveld

The International Criminal Tribunals for the Former Yugoslavia and Rwanda (ICTY and ICTR, respectively) have played a historic and significant role in the prosecution of sexual and gender-based crimes, and in doing so, have substantially advanced international criminal law in this regard. Through this work, the tribunals have "paved the way for a more robust adjudication of such crimes worldwide,"[1] especially in other international criminal tribunals. The ICTY and ICTR were necessarily pioneering, given the lack of prior attention to sexual and gender-based violence within international criminal law.[2] The dearth of precedent meant that the Tribunals had to establish the meaning and scope of the law applicable to sexual and gender-based violations. They became courts of "firsts." They were the first international tribunals to define the crime against humanity and war crime of rape under international criminal law.[3] The ICTY was the first international tribunal to consider the gendered aspects of the crime against humanity of enslavement and to convict individuals for rape as a form of torture, while the ICTR was the first to consider the link between sexual violence and genocide.[4] The Tribunals were the first to contextualize sexual and gender-based violence within larger, complex patterns of crime.[5] While carrying out this trailblazing work, the Tribunals also grappled with the day-to-day practice of gender-sensitive international criminal law,

[1] Mechanism for International Criminal Tribunals – International Criminal Tribunal for the Former Yugoslavia, *Crimes of Sexual Violence*, www.icty.org/en/features/crimes-sexual-violence (last visited May 20, 2018).

[2] Michelle Jarvis & Kate Vigneswaran, Challenges to Successful Outcomes in Sexual Violence Cases, *in* Prosecuting Conflict-Related Sexual Violence at the ICTY (Serge Brammertz & Michelle Jarvis eds., 2016).

[3] Prosecutor v. Akayesu, Case No. ICTR-96-4-T, Judgment, para. 688 (Sept. 2, 1998) (hereinafter *Akayesu* Trial Judgment).

[4] Prosecutor v. Kunarac et al., Case No. IT-96-23 & 23/T, Judgment (Int'l Crim. Trib. for the Former Yugoslavia Feb. 22, 2001) (hereinafter *Kunarac* Trial Judgment); Prosecutor v. Furundžija, Case No. IT-95-17/T (Int'l Crim. Trib. for the Former Yugoslavia Dec. 10, 1998) (hereinafter *Furundžija* Trial Judgment); *Akayesu* Trial Judgment, *supra* note 3. Each of these cases is discussed in Section 8.1, *infra*.

[5] This is described in: Laurel Baig, Michelle Jarvis, Elena Martin Salgado & Giulia Pinzauti, Contextualizing Sexual Violence: Selection of Crimes, *in* Prosecuting Conflict-Related Sexual Violence at the ICTY 172–219 (Serge Brammertz & Michelle Jarvis eds., 2016); Barbara Goy,

including how best to investigate sexual and gender-based crimes. As a result, they adopted some innovative methods, and learned some lessons due to missteps. These best practices and lessons learned have shaped the techniques and analysis used by subsequent tribunals, and will continue to do so for years to come.[6]

This chapter examines the legacy of the ICTY and ICTR in addressing sexual and gender-based violence. It begins by exploring how the ICTY and ICTR's Trial and Appeals Chambers have influenced the definitions of sexual and gender-based violations within the categories of genocide, crimes against humanity and war crimes. The first section, Section 8.1, considers the far-reaching impact of the Tribunals on the definition of rape, as well as the legal dissonance they created. This section then turns to Tribunal jurisprudence on enslavement through sexual means, gendered forms of persecution, outrages upon personal dignity and other forms of sexual violence. It also assesses the contribution of this jurisprudence to the contextualization of these crimes within the larger picture of mass criminality. In Section 8.2, the chapter explores how the Tribunals' legacy on sexual and gender-based violence expands beyond crime definitions. While this legacy covers procedural and evidentiary matters, victim protection, staffing policies, modes of liability, sentencing, cooperation with national jurisdictions and other topics,[7] this section will focus upon gender-sensitive investigation methods. Such methods provide a useful glimpse into the challenges faced by the tribunals in investigating sexual violence in particular, as well as the solutions implemented that have informed other courts.[8] The chapter concludes with Section 8.3, offering an analysis of the collective legacy of the ICTY and ICTR on the investigation and prosecution of sexual and gender-based violence.

Michelle Jarvis & Guilia Pinzauti, Contextualizing Sexual Violence and Linking it to Senior Officials: Modes of Liability, *in* Prosecuting Conflict-Related Sexual Violence at the ICTY 220–61 (Serge Brammertz & Michelle Jarvis eds., 2016); and Linda Bianchi, The Prosecution of Rape and Sexual Violence: Lessons from the Prosecutions of the ICTR, *in* Sexual Violence as and International Crimes: Interdisciplinary Approaches 123, 135 (Anne-Marie de Brouwer, Charlotte Ku, Renée Römkens & Larissa van den Herik eds., 2013).

[6] For example, best practices and lessons learned from the ICTY and ICTR have been cited in: Office of the Prosecutor, *Policy Paper on Sexual and Gender-Based Crimes* fn 11 (June 2014), www.icc-cpi.int/iccdocs/otp/OTP-Policy-Paper-on-Sexual-and-Gender-Based-Crimes–June-2014.pdf (last visited May 20, 2018) (hereinafter ICC *Policy Paper*).

[7] These legacies are explained in: Serge Brammertz & Michelle Jarvis eds., Prosecuting Conflict-Related Sexual Violence at the ICTY (2016); International Criminal Tribunal for Rwanda, Best Practices Manual for the Investigation and Prosecution of Sexual Violence Crimes in Post-Conflict Regions: Lessons Learned from the Office of the Prosecutor for the International Criminal Tribunal for Rwanda (Jan. 30, 2014), http://unictr.unmict.org/sites/unictr.org/files/legal-library/140130_prosecution_of_sexual_violence.pdf (last visited May 20, 2018) (hereinafter ICTR *Best Practices Manual*).

[8] For example, these practices have informed the International Criminal Court: ICC *Policy Paper*, *supra* note 6, at fn 2, 11, 21, 29, 32, 33, 36 and 65.

8.1 DEVELOPMENT OF CRIME DEFINITIONS

The most recognizable legacy of the ICTY and ICTR in the field of gender-sensitive justice is in the creation of jurisprudence on key violations: rape, enslavement through sexual means, gendered forms of persecution, outrages upon personal dignity and the identification of other forms of sexual violence. This section will therefore consider each of these violations in turn. It will also consider how these violations were contextualized by Tribunal prosecutors into larger pictures of mass criminality through this jurisprudence.

8.1.1 Rape

The ICTY and ICTR have provided foundational jurisprudence on the crime against humanity and war crime of rape, fundamentally shaping the definition, and understanding, of the crime under international criminal law. The ICTY and ICTR Statutes explicitly list rape as a crime against humanity.[9] Rape was also explicitly listed in the ICTR Statute, and implicitly listed in the ICTY Statute, as a violation of the laws and customs of war, including as an outrage upon personal dignity.[10] Rape was also prosecuted at the ICTR as contributing to genocide.[11] Prior to its consideration by the ICTY and ICTR, rape had never before been defined in international criminal law.

The ICTR became the first international criminal tribunal to grapple with the definition of rape. This is reflective of the widespread nature of rape during the genocide:

> Women were raped in every *préfecture* of Rwanda, throughout the genocide, most often in the open in plain view, including at roadblocks, in official and governmental buildings such as military camps, churches, schools and university premises, hospitals, health clinics, stadiums and marketplaces.[12]

While rape was not initially charged in the ICTR's first case, *Prosecutor v. Akayesu*, evidence of rape emerged during trial and charges were added.[13]

A key challenge facing the *Akayesu* Trial Chamber was that international law did not provide guidance on a definition, and national laws varied and did not

---

9   SC res. 827, UN SCOR 48th sess., 3217th mtg., UN Doc. S/Res/827 (1993) at art. 5(g) (May 25, 1993) (hereinafter ICTY Statute); SC res. 955, UN SCOR 49th sess., 3453rd mtg, UN Doc. S/Res/955 (1994) at art. 3(g) (Nov. 8, 1994) (hereinafter ICTR Statute).
10   ICTY Statute, *supra* note 9, at art. 3; ICTR Statute, *supra* note 9, at art. 4(e).
11   This was done through the category of "causing serious bodily or mental harm to members of the group": ICTR Statute, *supra* note 9, at art. 2(b).
12   Bianchi, *supra* note 5, at 126.
13   *Akayesu* Trial Judgment, *supra* note 3, at paras. 416–17. The ICTR's record on the investigation and prosecution of rape has been mixed: Bianchi, *supra* note 5, at 128–49; and Binaifer Nowrojee, "*Your Justice Is Too Slow": Will the ICTR Fail Rwanda's Rape Victims?* (UN Research Institute for Social Development Occasional Paper 10, November 2005), www.unrisd.org/80256B3C005BCCF9/ (httpPublications)/56FE32D5C0F6DCE9C125710F0045D89F (last visited May 20, 2018).

necessarily address the realities of rape occurring during mass atrocity or armed conflict.[14] For example, some national laws define rape as forcible penile penetration of a female vagina, excluding male victims altogether, and excluding rape using objects and fingers.[15] The Trial Chamber reasoned that the international criminal definition of rape required more flexibility: "while rape has been historically defined in national jurisdictions as non-consensual sexual intercourse, variations on the form of rape [as an international crime] may include acts which involve the insertion of objects and/or the use of bodily orifices not considered to be intrinsically sexual."[16] For example, the insertion of a piece of wood into the sexual organs of a woman can constitute rape.[17] Other domestic definitions did not criminalize rape of married women, or they contained discriminatory evidentiary requirements.[18] The Trial Chamber observed that rape can be expressed in a number of ways and can be used for many purposes, such as intimidation, degradation, humiliation, discrimination, punishment, control or destruction of a person.[19] Therefore, the definition of rape as an international crime "cannot be captured in a mechanical description of objects and body parts."[20]

As a result of this reasoning, the *Akayesu* Trial Chamber introduced a broad and gender-neutral definition of the violation: "a physical invasion of a sexual nature, committed on a person under circumstances which are coercive."[21] The Trial Chamber indicated that it followed the example of the Convention against Torture, which "does not catalogue specific acts" but instead creates "a conceptual framework."[22] Some commentators praised this approach because it concentrates on the effect of the act on the victim and more closely resembles the definitions of other crimes.[23]

The definitional approach in *Akayesu* was confirmed in the ICTR's subsequent judgment in *Prosecutor* v. *Musema*.[24] In that case, the Trial Chamber agreed that

---

[14] *Akayesu* Trial Judgment, *supra* note 3, at paras. 596, 686.

[15] *Id.*

[16] *Id.* at para. 686.

[17] *Id.*

[18] *See, for example,* Anne-Marie de Brouwer, Supranational Criminal Prosecution of Sexual Violence: The ICC and the Practice of the ICTY and the ICTR (2005) 107–08.

[19] *Akayesu* Trial Judgment, *supra* note 3, at para. 597.

[20] *Id.* at paras. 597, 687.

[21] *Id.* at para. 688.

[22] *Id.* at paras. 597, 687, referring to the Convention against Torture and Other Cruel, Inhuman or Degrading Treatment or Punishment, Dec. 10, 1984, 1465 UNTS 85.

[23] Kelly Dawn Askin, *Sexual Violence in Decisions and Indictments of the Yugoslav and Rwandan Tribunals: Current Status*, 93 Am. J. Int'l. L. 97 at 109 (1999); UN Special Rapporteur on Violence against Women, Violence against Women Perpetrated and/or Condoned by the State during Times of Armed Conflict (1997–2000), para. 38, UN Doc. E/CN.4/2001/73 (Jan. 23, 2001); de Brouwer, *supra* note 18, at 107–08; Kristen Boon, *Rape and Forced Pregnancy under the ICC Statute: Human Dignity, Autonomy, and Consent*, 32 Colum. Hum. Rts. L. Rev. 625, 649 (2000–1).

[24] Prosecutor v. Musema, Case No. ICTR-96-13-T, Judgment and Sentence (Jan. 27, 2000) (hereinafter *Musema* Trial Judgment).

"the essence of rape is not the particular details of the body parts and objects involved, but rather the aggression that is expressed in a sexual manner under conditions of coercion."[25] The *Musema* judgment expressed the view that "a conceptual definition is preferable to a mechanical definition of rape," because it can "better accommodate evolving norms of criminal justice" and is consistent with certain trends within reform of national legislation.[26]

Shortly after the ICTR introduced a definition of rape in *Akayesu*, the ICTY also decided *Prosecutor v. Furundžija*, a case involving charges of rape. Essentially repudiating the ICTR's conceptual approach in *Akayesu*, the Trial Chamber in *Furundžija* defined rape as:

(i)   The sexual penetration, however slight:
(a)   of the vagina or anus of the victim by the penis of the perpetrator or any other object used by the perpetrator; or
(b)   of the mouth of the victim by the penis of the perpetrator;
(ii) By coercion or force or threat of force against the victim or a third person.[27]

The *Furundžija* Trial Chamber argued that the principle of specificity within international criminal law required it to derive a definition through an examination of national legislation.[28] It implied that the *Akayesu* definition "was not sufficiently specific, and therefore in violation of the legality principle."[29] It therefore refocused the definition on the acts of the perpetrator and on the body parts involved, following the approach in the domestic law of many countries. In so doing, it narrowed the definition to exclude penetration of a victim's vagina by a perpetrator's fingers or tongue.[30]

The ICTY revisited the *Furundžija* approach in the 2001 case of *Prosecutor v. Kunarac*.[31] In that case, the Trial Chamber added an explicit component of nonconsent to the definition, deleting paragraph (ii) from the *Furundžija* definition and adding "where such sexual penetration occurs without the consent of the victim."[32] It also stated: "[c]onsent for this purpose must be given voluntarily, as a result of the victim's free will, assessed in the context of the surrounding circumstances."[33] With this change, the Trial Chamber intended to broaden the application of the definition beyond circumstances involving force or threat of force, in order to capture coercive but nonforcible circumstances.[34] This approach was confirmed by the

---

[25]   *Id.* at para. 226.
[26]   *Id.* at para. 228.
[27]   *Furundžija* Trial Judgment, *supra* note 4, at para. 185.
[28]   *Id.* at para. 178.
[29]   This is de Brouwer's reading of the *Furundžija* Trial Judgment: DE BROUWER, *supra* note 18, at 112.
[30]   As observed by DE BROUWER, *supra* note 18, at 115.
[31]   *Kunarac* Trial Judgment, *supra* note 4.
[32]   *Id.* at para. 460.
[33]   *Id.*
[34]   *Id.* at para. 438.

Appeals Chamber, which explained that a "narrow focus on force or threat of force could permit perpetrators to evade liability for sexual activity to which the other party had not consented by taking advantage of coercive circumstances without relying on physical force."[35] The Appeals Chamber also appeared to try to bridge the gap between the reasoning in *Akayesu* and *Furundžija* by finding that the circumstances of rape "in most cases charged as either war crimes or crimes against humanity will be almost universally coercive. That is to say, true consent will not be possible."[36]

The *Kunarac* approach has been both hailed and critiqued. Those in favor of the approach were of the view that, of the three definitions in *Akayesu*, *Furundžija* and *Kunarac*, the *Kunarac* approach comes closest to avoiding potential over-inclusion of consensual sexual relations or nonrape violations within international criminal prosecutions.[37] Those expressing concern argued that the ICTY improperly imported domestic approaches into the very different and extremely coercive circumstances of crimes against humanity, genocide and war crimes.[38]

This division in the ICTY and ICTR jurisprudence led to some confusion, particularly within the ICTR. Some ICTR judgments endorsed the *Akayesu* approach.[39] Others – such as *Prosecutor v. Semanza*, *Prosecutor v. Kajelijeli*, *Prosecutor v. Kamuhanda*, *Prosecutor v. Ndindiliyimana*, *Prosecutor v. Nyiramasuhuko* and *Prosecutor v. Karemera* – followed the *Kunarac* approach.[40] Some ICTR judgments tried to reconcile the two approaches. For example, the *Muvunyi* Trial Chamber observed the "chequered history of the definition of rape" and focused on the commonality of underlying purpose in both definitions.[41] In time, the Tribunals' jurisprudence became more uniform, as the ICTR jurisprudence acknowledged the

---

[35] Prosecutor v. Kunarac et al., Case No. IT-96-23 & 23/A, Judgment para. 129 (Int'l Crim. Trib. for the Former Yugoslavia June 12, 2002) (hereinafter *Kunarac* Appeal Judgment).

[36] *Id.* at para. 130.

[37] For example, Karen Engle, *Feminism and Its (Dis)Contents: Criminalizing Wartime Rape in Bosnia and Herzegovina*, 99 AM. J. INT'L L. 778, 806 (2005). Note, however, that she expresses concern that the *Kunarac* approach does not completely address the potential for over-inclusiveness.

[38] DE BROUWER, *supra* note 18, at 120–23; Catharine A. MacKinnon, *Defining Rape Internationally: A Comment on Akayesu*, 44 COLUM. J. TRANSNAT'L L. 940, 952 (2005–6).

[39] Prosecutor v. Niyitegeka, Case No. ICTR-96-14-T, Judgment and Sentence, para. 456 (May 16, 2003); Prosecutor v. Delalić et al., Case No. IT-96-21-T, Judgment, paras. 478–9 (Int'l Crim. Trib. for the Former Yugoslavia Nov. 16, 1998) (hereinafter *Delalić* Trial Judgment). Due to insufficient evidence, Niyitegeka was acquitted of the charge of rape as a crime against humanity. The *Akayesu*, *Musema* and *Niyitegeka* cases were all decided by Trial Chamber I, which may explain their consistent approach.

[40] Prosecutor v. Semanza, Case No. ICTR-97-20-T, Judgment, para. 345 (May 15, 2003); Prosecutor v. Kajelijeli, Case No. ICTR-98-44A-T, Judgment and Sentence, para. 915 (Dec. 1, 2003) (hereinafter *Kajelijeli* Trial Judgment); Prosecutor v. Kamuhanda, Case No. ICTR-99-54A-T, para. 709 (Jan. 22, 2004); Prosecutor v. Ndindiliyimana et al., Case No. ICTR-00-56-T, Judgment, paras. 2121–2 (May 17, 2011) (hereinafter *Ndindiliyimana* Trial Judgment); Prosecutor v. Nyiramasuhuko et al., Case No. ICTR-98-42-T, Judgment, para. 6075 (June 24, 2011); Prosecutor v. Karemera et al., Case No. ICTR-98-44-T, Judgment, paras. 1676–7 (Feb. 2, 2012).

[41] Prosecutor v. Muvunyi, Case No. ICTR-00-55-T, Judgment, paras. 517, 521 (Dec. 12, 2006).

Akayesu definition but adopted the *Kunarac* approach, while acknowledging that the prosecution can prove nonconsent through evidence of coercive circumstances.[42] The *Kunarac* definition influenced subsequent tribunals, such as the Special Court for Sierra Leone.[43] However, the International Criminal Court has a different definition, which was adopted prior to the issuance of *Kunarac* and therefore was derived from the *Akayesu* and *Furundžija* definitions.[44]

Another Tribunal legacy relates to the relationship between rape and genocide. The ICTR has examined rape within the genocide definition through the art. 2(b) category of "causing serious bodily or mental harm to members of the group."[45] In considering this category of harm, the *Akayesu* Trial Chamber noted that "rapes resulted in physical and psychological destruction of Tutsi women, their families and their communities," and therefore contributed to genocide.[46] The Trial Chamber also noted the link between the media portrayal of Tutsi women and rape during genocide: the "sexualized representation of ethnic identity graphically illustrates that Tutsi women were subjected to sexual violence because they were Tutsi. Sexual violence was a step in the process of destruction of the Tutsi group – destruction of the spirit, of the will to live, and of life itself."[47] Therefore, the *Akayesu* judgment "was instrumental in bringing about the recognition that acts of sexual violence can be a means to achieve genocide" and was a "breakthrough interpretation."[48] The link between rape and genocide has been confirmed in other ICTR judgments, including *Prosecutor v. Rutaganda* and others.[49] The ICTR's pronouncements on the link between rape and genocide influenced the

---

[42] For example, Prosecutor v. Gacumbitsi, Case No. ICTR-2001–64-A, Judgment, paras. 152–5 (July 7, 2006) (hereinafter *Gacumbitsi* Trial Judgment).

[43] For example, Prosecutor v. Taylor, SCSL-03–01-T, Judgment, para. 415 (May 18, 2012) hereinafter *Taylor* Trial Judgment); Prosecutor v. Brima, Kamara and Kanu, SCSL-04–16-T, Judgment, para. 693 (June 20, 2007).

[44] Elements of Crimes of the International Criminal Court, UN Doc. PCNICC/2000/1/Add.2 (2000), listing these common elements for arts. 7(1)(g)-1, 8(2)(b)(xxii)-1 and 8(2)(e)(vi)-1:

   1. The perpetrator invaded the body of a person by conduct resulting in penetration, however slight, of any part of the body of the victim or of the perpetrator with a sexual organ, or of the anal or genital opening of the victim with any object or any other part of the body.

   2. The invasion was committed by force, or by threat of force or coercion, such as that caused by fear of violence, duress, detention, psychological oppression or abuse of power, against such person or another person, or by taking advantage of a coercive environment, or the invasion was committed against a person incapable of giving genuine consent (hereinafter ICC Elements of Crimes).

[45] The findings of the ICTR were confirmed in the ICTY. For example, in Prosecutor v. Krstić, the Trial Chamber listed rape and sexual abuse among acts that may cause serious bodily or mental injury: Prosecutor v. Krstić, Case No. IT-98–33-T, Judgment, para. 513 (Int'l. Crim. Trib. for the Former Yugoslavia Aug. 2, 2001) (hereinafter *Krstić* Trial Judgment). The *Akayesu* Trial Judgment also opined that other forms of sexual violence may also satisfy this same category of harm, and may also satisfy the offence of "imposing measures to prevent births within the group": *Akayesu* Trial Judgment, *supra* note 3, at paras. 507–9.

[46] *Akayesu* Trial Judgment, *supra* note 3, at paras. 731–2.

[47] *Id.* at para. 732.

[48] DE BROUWER, *supra* note 18, at 80; Bianchi, *supra* note 5, at 141.

[49] For example, Prosecutor v Rutaganda, Case No. ICTR-96–3-T, Judgment and Sentence, para. 51 (Dec. 6, 1999); Prosecutor v. Kayishema and Ruzindana, Case No. ICTR-95–1-T, Judgment, paras.

inclusion of a footnote in the International Criminal Court's Elements of Crimes document stating that serious bodily or mental harm "may include, but is not necessarily restricted to, acts of torture, rape, sexual violence or inhuman or degrading treatment."[50]

Another way in which the Tribunals have established their legacy is through the link between rape and torture. The ICTY's Prosecutor charged some individuals with torture committed through rape or threatened rape.[51] The court found that these actions amounted to the infliction of severe physical and/or mental pain or suffering committed for a prohibited purpose.[52] The *Furundžija* Trial and Appeals Chambers identified humiliation as one prohibited purpose,[53] thereby giving "legal recognition to one of the key strategic reasons for using sexual violence – to humiliate and dehumanize."[54] Other prohibited purposes recognized by the ICTY included discrimination, for example in the targeting for rape of non-Serb detained women.[55] The ICTY also recognized that the prohibited purpose is not affected even when it is accompanied by a sexual motive.[56] The ICTY's cases linking rape and torture additionally demonstrated that a "single act of sexual violence may be used 'strategically' for one of the prohibited purposes of torture, underscoring that low frequency sexual violence can nevertheless reflect a strategic use."[57] Finally, it should be noted that the ICTY also established that sexual violence other than rape can "satisfy the severity of physical or mental pain or suffering threshold for torture," including threatened rape, attempted rape, touching of sexual organs, being forced to

---

108–9 (May 21, 1999); Prosecutor v. Bagilishema, Case No. ICTR-95-1A-T, Judgment, para. 59 (June 7, 2001); *Musema* Trial Judgment, *supra* note 24, at para. 156; *Kajelijeli* Trial Judgment, *supra* note 40, at paras. 815–16; Gacumbitsi Trial Judgment, *supra* note 42, at paras. 291–3. For the ICTY, *see: Krstić* Trial Judgment, *supra* note 45, at para. 513; Prosecutor v. Stakić, Case No. IT-97-24-T, Judgment, para. 516 (Int'l Crim. Trib. for the Former Yugoslavia July 31, 2003) (hereinafter *Stakić* Trial Judgment).

[50] ICC Elements of Crimes, *supra* note 44, at art. 6(b), fn 3. *See also* Charles Garraway, *Elements of the Specific Forms of Genocide, in* THE INTERNATIONAL CRIMINAL COURT: ELEMENTS OF CRIMES AND RULES OF PROCEDURE AND EVIDENCE 49, 50–51 (Roy S. Lee ed., 2001).

[51] For example, *Delalić* Trial Judgment, *supra* note 39, paras. 495–6; Prosecutor v. Stanišić and Župljanin, Case No. ICTY-08-91-T, Judgment, vol. 1, para. 48 (Int'l Crim. Trib. for the Former Yugoslavia Mar. 27, 2013); Prosecutor v. Brđanin, Case No. IT-99-36-T, Judgment, para. 485 (Int'l Crim. Trib. for the Former Yugoslavia Sept. 1, 2004).

[52] For example, *Kunarac* Trial Judgment, *supra* note 4, at para. 150.

[53] *Furundžija* Trial Judgment, *supra* note 4, at para. 182; Prosecutor v. Furundžija, Case No. ICTY-95-17/1, Judgment, para. 111 (Int'l Crim. Trib. for the Former Yugoslavia July 21, 2000).

[54] Baig et al., *supra* note 5, at 190.

[55] Prosecutor v. Kvočka et al., Case No. IT-98-30/1-T, Judgment, para. 560 (Int'l Crim. Trib. for the Former Yugoslavia Nov. 2, 2011) (hereinafter *Kvočka* Trial Judgment).

[56] *See* discussion in Baig et al., *supra* note 5, at 188, noting that this "point has been clearly understood and applied in torture cases," but not necessarily in persecution and genocide cases. *See also, id.*, at 205, 208–9, 211–12.

[57] *Id.* at 188.

watch sexual attacks on an acquaintance or family member, forced mutual masturbation and genital beatings.[58]

From a gender perspective, the ICTY and ICTR are best known for their contributions to the international criminal law of rape, by positing definitions and considering the links between rape and genocide, and rape and torture. However, the legacy of the tribunals with respect to the prosecution of sexual and gender-based violence extends further: the ICTY and ICTR also significantly developed the international criminal law on enslavement through sexual means, gendered forms of persecution, outrages upon personal dignity and other forms of sexual violence. The following subsections will explore each of these categories.

8.1.2 Enslavement through Sexual Means

Another legacy of the ICTY relates to its jurisprudence on enslavement carried out through sexual means. In the *Kunarac* case, the Prosecutor laid charges relating to enslavement of women and girls achieved through sexual violence and forced labor. Two accused were charged and convicted with enslaving five girls and one young women: two victims were kept in an abandoned house by Kunarac and four were kept by a co-accused, Kovać, in his apartment.[59] They were physically and psychologically unable to leave "as they would have had nowhere to go had they attempted to flee," and were aware of the treatment they would be subjected to if recaptured.[60] While in captivity, the victims were frequently raped, sexually assaulted in other ways, threatened, beaten, forced to dance naked for entertainment and forced to do household chores.[61] Some were offered to others for sexual exploitation and sold for monetary gain.[62]

This case represented the first time enslavement carried out through sexual means was prosecuted in an international criminal tribunal, and therefore the ICTY's consideration of this type of enslavement was groundbreaking. The judges noted that enslavement based on sexual exploitation constitutes "a distinct offence from that of rape."[63] Rather, it is a violation predicated on "the quality of the relationship" between the accused and the victim,[64] because the prosecution must prove that the accused intentionally exercised "any or all of the powers attaching to a right of ownership" over the victim.[65]

---

[58] *Kvočka* Trial Judgment, *supra* note 55, at paras. 560–61; *Furundžija* Trial Judgment, *supra* note 4, at paras. 267–8; *Brđanin* Trial Judgment, *supra* note 51, at paras. 498, 500; Prosecutor v. Martić, Case No. IT-95-11-T, Judgment, paras. 288, 413, fn 899 (Int'l Crim. Trib. for the Former Yugoslavia June 12, 2007).

[59] Kunarac Trial Judgment, *supra* note 4, at paras. 742, 780–3.

[60] *Id.* at para. 750.

[61] *Id.* at paras. 739–42, 749–52, 757–9, 772, 779–81.

[62] *Id.* at paras. 739–41, 759, 761–5, 742, 754–6.

[63] *Kunarac* Appeal Judgment, *supra* note 35, at para. 186.

[64] *Id.* at para. 121.

[65] *Kunarac* Trial Judgment, *supra* note 4, at paras. 539–40.

In order to consider the relationship between the perpetrators and the victims, the Trial Chamber adopted a list of indicia of enslavement: "control of someone's movement, control of physical environment, psychological control, measures taken to prevent or deter escape, force, threat of force or coercion... assertion of exclusivity, subjection to cruel treatment and abuse, control of sexuality and forced labour."[66] This list was further elaborated:

> [I]ndications of enslavement include elements of control and ownership; the restriction or control of an individual's autonomy, freedom of choice or freedom of movement; and, often, the accruing of some gain to the perpetrator. The consent or free will of the victim is absent. It is often rendered impossible or irrelevant by, for example, the threat or use of force or other forms of coercion; the fear of violence, deception or false promises; the abuse of power; the victim's position of vulnerability; detention or captivity, psychological oppression or socio-economic conditions. Further indications of enslavement include exploitation; the exaction of forced or compulsory labour or service, often without remuneration and often, though not necessarily, involving physical hardship; sex; prostitution; and human trafficking.[67]

These indicia have been extremely influential within international criminal law. They have been cited by the Special Court for Sierra Leone and the Extraordinary Chambers in the Courts of Cambodia, among others, when considering enslavement and sexual slavery charges.[68] They are viewed as foundational, and will continue to be cited in international and other courts for years to come.

8.1.3 Gendered Forms of Persecution

The ICTY and ICTR have also created a jurisprudential legacy through their consideration of the crime against humanity of persecution. The Statutes of both Tribunals listed persecution as a crime against humanity.[69] Persecution has been defined by the ICTY as

> an act or omission which discriminates in fact and which: denies or infringes upon a fundamental right laid down in international customary or treaty law (the *actus reus*); and was carried out deliberately with the intention to discriminate on one of the listed grounds, specifically race, religion or politics (the *mens rea*).[70]

---

[66] *Id.* at para. 543.

[67] *Id.* at para. 542.

[68] *Taylor* Trial Judgment, *supra* note 43, at para. 420; Prosecutor v. Sesay, Kallon and Gbao, SCSL-04-15-T, Judgment, para. 160 (Mar. 2, 2009); Prosecutor v. Kaing Guek Eav alias "Duch," 001/18-07-2007-ECCC/SC, Judgment, para.342 (July 26, 2010).

[69] ICTY Statute, *supra* note 9, at art. 5(h); ICTR Statute, *supra* note 9, at art. 4(h).

[70] Prosecutor v. Krnojelac, Case No. IT-97-25-A, Judgment, para. 185 (Int'l Crim. Trib. for the Former Yugoslavia Sept. 17, 2003). This was confirmed in other cases, including Prosecutor v. Popović et al., Case No. IT-05-88-T, Judgment, para. 964 (Int'l Crim. Trib. for the Former Yugoslavia June 10, 2010).

As this definition indicates, gender is not enumerated as a prohibited ground of persecution in the Statutes, which only recognize political, racial and religious grounds. Only the later-adopted Rome Statute of the International Criminal Court itemizes gender as a specific discriminatory ground of persecution.[71] Despite this gap in the Tribunals' Statutes, the ICTY and ICTR have developed important case law on persecution carried out though gendered means.

At the ICTY, the most frequent charge for sexual violence was persecution as a crime against humanity, especially in leadership cases.[72] This charge was used to highlight the broader context within which the sexual violence occurred – a context that often included killings, torture and other human rights violations.[73] The ICTY therefore developed international criminal law jurisprudence on gendered forms of persecution in two ways. First, it considered the types of gender-based acts that can amount to persecution. Both the ICTY Trial and Appeals Chambers found that rape can constitute a persecutory act.[74] Additionally, sexual assault could also be a persecutory act, which it defined as "all serious abuses of a sexual nature inflicted upon the physical and moral integrity of a person by means of coercion, threat of force or intimidation in a way that is humiliating and degrading for the victim's dignity."[75] In one example, the ICTY found that orders given to detained men to perform fellatio on each other resulted in persecution.[76] Other examples of persecutory acts of a sexual nature included a Bosnian Croat woman forced to undress in front of cheering male Bosnian Serb police and soldiers, and a Bosnian Muslim women who had a knife run along her breast.[77]

Second, the ICTY's jurisprudence demonstrated that sexual violence could be successfully linked to discrimination on political, racial and/or religious grounds.[78] In doing this, ICTY prosecutors had to overcome the perception that small-scale sexual violence was "not an integral component of a criminal campaign," and therefore that leaders could not be connected to that sexual violence.[79] This

---

[71]   Rome Statute of the International Criminal Court, art. 7(1)(h), July 17, 1998, UN Doc. A/CONF. 183/9; 2187 UNTS 90 (hereinafter Rome Statute of the ICC).

[72]   Baig et al., *supra* note 5, at 202. Leadership cases involved individuals who may not have been physically present at the scene of the individual violations alleged in the indictment, but who exercised some kind of command, control or influence over those violations.

[73]   *Id.*

[74]   *Brđanin* Trial Judgment, *supra* note 51, at para. 1008; Prosecutor v. Ðorđević, Case No. IT-05–87/1-A, Judgment, paras. 877, 886, 891–3, 895, 897, 901 (Int'l Crim. Trib. for the Former Yugoslavia Jan. 27, 2014) (hereinafter Ðorđević Appeal Judgment); Prosecutor v. Šainović et al., Case No. IT-05–87-A, Judgment, paras. 580, 584–5, 591, 593, 597, 599 (Int'l Crim. Trib. for the Former Yugoslavia Jan. 23, 2014) (hereinafter Šainović Appeal Judgment).

[75]   *Brđanin* Trial Judgment, *supra* note 51, at para. 1012. *See also* Ðorđević Appeal Judgment, *supra* note 74, at para. 850; Prosecutor v. Milutinović et al., Case No. IT-05–87, Judgment, para. 201 (Int'l Crim. Trib. for the Former Yugoslavia Feb. 26, 2009).

[76]   Prosecutor v. Todorović et al., Case No. IT-95–9/1-S, Sentencing Judgment, paras. 9, 12, 38–40 (Int'l Crim. Trib. for the Former Yugoslavia July 31, 2001).

[77]   *Brđanin* Trial Judgment, *supra* note 51, at para. 1013.

[78]   *See* cases in fn 74–77 above.

[79]   Baig et al., *supra* note 5, at 202.

assumption stems from a historical myth that sexual violence is "personal in nature and separate from the main activity of war."[80] Two trial judgments – in *Prosecutor v. Đorđević* and *Prosecutor v. Šainović* – highlighted this assumption, and the appeals judgments demonstrate the prosecutors' efforts to overcome the perception that sexual violence is somehow different from other violations.

Đorđević was originally acquitted at trial of persecution carried out through sexual violence on the grounds that, while sexual assaults against two Kosovo Albanian victims by Serbian forces were proven, the limited number of incidents did not permit the court to conclude that the ethnicity of the victims was the basis of their targeting.[81] The Appeals Chamber reversed this decision: "the Trial Chamber failed to evaluate the surrounding circumstances of . . . [the] sexual assaults . . . [that is,] that these crimes occurred in the course of the forcible displacement of the Kosovo Albanian populations."[82] Considering the broader context, the Appeals Chamber found that the only reasonable inference that could be drawn from the evidence was that the sexual assaults were committed with discriminatory intent, thus satisfying the requirements of the crime of persecution.[83] In the *Šainović* case, the ICTY Appeals Chamber similarly overturned acquittals of persecution committed through sexual violence.[84] The Appeals Chamber found that the "inescapable conclusion" had to be that the accused were aware of sexual assaults carried out in an "atmosphere of aggression and violence that prevailed" in which "Kosovo Albanian women forced out of their homes were rendered particularly vulnerable."[85] Thus, the Appeals Chamber found in both cases that evidence relating to both the surrounding circumstances of the rape and the broader context in which the rapes occurred may be used to infer the required discriminatory intent of the perpetrators.[86] Additionally, the Appeals Chamber recognized the need to differentiate between motive and intent: "a perpetrator may be motivated by sexual desire but at the same time possess the intent to discriminate against his or her victim" on prohibited grounds.[87]

Through these findings, the ICTY significantly advanced international criminal law's understanding of the crucial link between gendered violations, including sexual violence, and other forms of discriminatory conduct amounting to

---

[80] Michelle Jarvis & Elena Martin Salgado, Future Challenges to Prosecuting Sexual Violence Under International Law: Insights from ICTY Practice, *in* Sexual Violence as an International Crime: Interdisciplinary Approaches 101, 102 (Anne-Marie de Brouwer, Charlotte Ku, Renée Römkens & Larissa van den Herik eds., 2013).

[81] Prosecutor v. Đorđević, Case No. IT-05–87/1-T, Judgment, para. 1796 (Int'l Crim. Trib. for the Former Yugoslavia Feb. 23, 2011).

[82] *Đorđević* Appeal Judgment, *supra* note 74, at para. 877.

[83] *Id.* at para. 901.

[84] *Šainović* Appeal Judgment, *supra* note 74, at para. 1847.

[85] *Id.* at paras. 1581–2, 1592, 1602–3.

[86] *Đorđević* Appeal Judgment, *supra* note 74, at paras. 877, 886, 891–3, 895, 897, 901; *Šainović* Appeal Judgment, *supra* note 74, at paras. 580, 584–5, 591, 593, 597, 599.

[87] *Đorđević* Appeal Judgment, *supra* note 74, at para. 887. *See also* Baig et al., *supra* note 5, at 203.

persecution. The Tribunal also contributed to disproving myths about the "personal" nature of sexual violence in armed conflict.

The ICTR also influenced the development of international criminal law on persecution. For example, the ICTR found that the rape of Tutsi women at roadblocks in Kigali and in two religious buildings amounted to persecution.[88] Perhaps more groundbreaking is the ICTR's consideration of the use of gendered language in the role of persecution. In *Prosecutor v. Nahimana*, the Trial Chamber considered how Tutsi women were portrayed in the media as "seductive agents of the enemy" and were "vilified."[89] These media depictions "articulated a framework that made the sexual attack of Tutsi women a foreseeable consequence of the role attributed to them" and set the stage for persecution.[90] This jurisprudence helped to identify the role of media in creating the broader context in which persecutory sexual violence may occur.

8.1.4 *Outrages upon Personal Dignity*

The two Tribunals have also established a somewhat less-recognized legacy in the category of outrages upon personal dignity. The 1949 Geneva Conventions and their 1977 Additional Protocols prohibit outrages upon personal dignity.[91] This type of violation was explicitly included as a war crime in the ICTR Statute and deemed by the ICTY judges to be implicitly included in the ICTY Statute.[92] The ICTY defined outrages upon personal dignity as "any act or omission which would be generally considered to cause serious humiliation, degradation or otherwise be a serious attack on human dignity."[93] The act need not cause lasting suffering.[94]

The ICTY and ICTR identified a range of gendered actions as amounting to outrages upon personal dignity, such as forced nudity (including forced public nudity), threats of sexual mutilation, rape, sexual violence, sexual exploitation (including the sale of victims to others as sexual slaves) and the constant fear of

---

[88]   Prosecutor v. Bagosora et al., ICTR 98–41-T, Judgment and Sentence, para. 2210 (Dec. 18, 2008).

[89]   Prosecutor v. Nahimana et al., ICTR-99–52-T, Judgment and Sentence, para. 1079 (Dec. 3, 2003).

[90]   *Id.*

[91]   Geneva Convention for the Amelioration of the Condition of the Wounded and Sick in Armed Forces in the Field art. 3, Aug. 12, 1949, 75 UNTS 31; Geneva Convention for the Amelioration of the Condition of Wounded, Sick and Shipwrecked Members of Armed Forces at Sea art. 3, Aug. 12, 1949, 75 UNTS 85; Geneva Convention Relative to the Treatment of Prisoners of War art. 3, Aug. 12, 1949, 75 UNTS 135; Geneva Convention Relative to the Protection of Civilian Persons in Time of War art. 3, Aug. 12, 1949, 75 UNTS 287; Protocol Additional to the Geneva Conventions of 12 August 1949, and Relating to the Protection of Victims of International Armed Conflicts arts. 75(2)(b), 85(4), June 8, 1977, 1125 UNTS 3; Protocol Additional to the Geneva Conventions of 12 August 1949, and Relating to the Protection of Victims of Non-International Armed Conflicts art. 4(2)(e), June 8, 1977, 1125 UNTS 609.

[92]   ICTR Statute, *supra* note 9, at art. 4(e); included implicitly in ICTY Statute, *supra* note 9, at art. 3; *Kunarac* Trial Judgment, *supra* note 4, at para. 498

[93]   *Kunarac* Trial Judgment, *supra* note 4, at para. 507.

[94]   *Id.* at para. 501; *Kvočka* Trial Judgment, *supra* note 55, at para. 168.

being subjected to sexual violence.[95] The Tribunals helped to broaden the understanding of outrages upon personal dignity to include forms of violence not previously acknowledged as violations in international criminal law, such as forced nudity. The development of the law in this manner by the ICTY and ICTR was helpful for the Special Court for Sierra Leone, which relied upon ICTY and ICTR case law when considering acts associated with the "bush wife" phenomena as outrages upon personal dignity.[96]

Note, however, that the Tribunals' legacy on this crime will not cross over to the International Criminal Court. The Rome Statute of the International Criminal Court separates outrages upon personal dignity from sexual and gender-based violations and places them into separate provisions.[97] The negotiators did this deliberately because of the concern that characterizing rape solely as a violation of dignity was outdated because it downplayed the fact that rape is a crime of physical and psychological violence.[98] That said, the Tribunals' jurisprudence on outrages upon personal dignity will continue to influence the interpretation of customary international humanitarian law.

8.1.5 *Identification of Other Forms of Sexual Violence*

Another important legacy of the ICTY and ICTR is that both tribunals expanded the discussion of violations that amount to sexual violence beyond consideration of rape. In defining sexual violence, the ICTY Appeals Chamber noted that

> [o]ften the parts of the body commonly associated with sexuality are targeted or involved. Physical contact is, however, not required for an act to be qualified as sexual in nature. Forcing a person to perform or witness certain acts may be sufficient, so long as the acts humiliate and/or degrade the victim in a sexual manner.[99]

In other words, sexual violence need not look like rape. This was an important advance, given the lack of explicit recognition of other forms of sexual violence within the Tribunals' Statutes and other international criminal law documents extant at the time of the creation of the ICTY and ICTR.

Many different forms of sexual violence have been identified in Tribunal case law set out in Sections 8.1.1 to 8.4.4. The ICTY's Trial Chamber in *Prosecutor* v. *Kvočka*

---

95 *Kunarac* Trial Judgment, *supra* note 4, at paras. 436, 756, 773; *Kunarac* Appeal Judgment, *supra* note 35, at para. 16; *Furundžija* Trial Judgment, *supra* note 4, at paras. 40, 270–5, 436; *Ndindiliyimana* Trial Judgment, *supra* note 40, at para. 2158; *Kvočka* Trial Judgment, *supra* note 55, at para. 173.

96 *Taylor* Trial Judgment, *supra* note 43, at para. 432.

97 Rome Statute of the ICC, *supra* note 71, at arts. 8(2)(b)(xxi) and (xxii).

98 Cate Steains, Gender Issues, *in* THE INTERNATIONAL CRIMINAL COURT: THE MAKING OF THE ROME STATUTE – ISSUES, NEGOTIATIONS, RESULTS 357, 363 (Roy S. Lee ed., 1999). On this concern, *see* JUDITH G. GARDAM & MICHELLE JARVIS, Women, Armed Conflict and International Law 102 (2001).

99 *Đorđević* Appeal Judgment, *supra* note 74, at para. 852.

also listed sexual molestation, sexual mutilation, forced marriage,[100] forced abortion, forced pregnancy and enforced sterilization as other forms of sexual violence.[101] The ICTR Trial Chamber provided an example of sexual violence in which "the Accused ordered the Interahamwe to undress a student and force her to do gymnastics naked in the public courtyard of the bureau communal, in front of a crowd."[102] These examples have helped to inform the content of the International Criminal Court's open-ended crimes against humanity and war crimes provisions referring to other forms of sexual violence.[103]

8.1.6 *Contextualization of Gendered Crimes*

A final legacy evident within the ICTY and ICTR jurisprudence relates to how the prosecutors contextualized gender-based violence – in particular, sexual violence against women, girls, men and boys – within larger crime patterns. One of the ICTY's "key insights" was that it was necessary to focus "on accurately and powerfully reflecting connections between sexual violence and the context in which it is committed" in the same way as for any other crime.[104] As one example, in the case of *Prosecutor* v. *Brđanin*, the prosecution successfully contextualized the rapes of Bosnian Muslim women by Bosnian Serb soldiers and police as occurring as part of a widespread or systematic attack against the civilian population.[105] The sexual violence occurred during searches for weapons and alongside the detention and beating of Bosnian Muslim men, the destruction of mosques and the damaging of Bosnian Muslim businesses.[106] Thus, the sexual violence occurred within, and was intimately connected to, the larger context of violence targeted against Bosnian Muslim civilians.[107]

The Tribunals have contextualized sexual violence crimes in three main ways: through the selection and charging of the crimes (e.g., rape, enslavement, torture, and persecution as described above), in the identification of the modes of liability and by presenting the connections between the sexual violence and other crimes.[108]

---

[100] But see the jurisprudence of the Special Court for Sierra Leone rejecting this classification of forced marriage as solely sexual, and reclassifying it as gendered instead (with both sexual and nonsexual aspects): Prosecutor v. Brima, Kamara and Kanu, SCSL-04-16-A, Judgment, paras. 195, 201–3 (Feb. 22, 2008).

[101] *Kvočka* Trial Judgment, *supra* note 55, at paras. 179–80 and fn 343.

[102] *Id.*

[103] Rome Statute of the ICC, *supra* note 71, at arts. 7(1)(g), 8(2)(b)(xxii), 8(2)(e)(vi). *See also* the ICC *Policy Paper, supra* note 6, at 3, which defines sexual violence as "not limited to physical violence, and may not involve any physical contact – for example, forced nudity. Sexual crimes, therefore, cover both physical and non-physical acts with a sexual element."

[104] Baig et al., *supra* note 5, at 173.

[105] *Prosecutor* v. *Brđanin*, Case No. IT-99-36-A, Judgment, paras. 253, 256–7 (Int'l Crim. Trib. for the Former Yugoslavia Apr. 3, 2007).

[106] *Id.* at paras. 256–7.

[107] *Id.* at paras. 253, 256–7.

[108] Baig et al., *supra* note 5, at 173.

Done well, contextualizing sexual violence ensures that the victim's experience is not artificially compartmentalized by focusing on only one aspects of their suffering. It enables prosecutors to fairly and accurately label both the intent of the perpetrators and the particular form that sexual violence took in any given case and... it creates an essential foundation for linking sexual violence to senior officials in appropriate cases.[109]

In other words, presenting the sexual violence violations as part of the larger context of criminality helps to provide a more complete picture of the experiences of the victims and of the interlinked nature of the perpetrator's acts. This approach was also taken in other tribunals,[110] and logically should be the standard approach at all international criminal justice mechanisms.

The ICTY prosecutors found that contextualization was straightforward in cases involving direct, relatively low-level perpetrators of sexual violence.[111] This was because such cases resembled cases the investigators, prosecutors and judges "were familiar with from their national jurisdictions."[112] However, this conceptualization became more difficult over time for both Tribunals as they moved to the prosecution of mid- and senior-level officials who were "removed from criminal conduct on the ground and/or who were charged with crimes requiring proof of links between sexual conduct and a campaign of other violence crimes."[113]

Both the ICTY and ICTR found it more difficult to contextualize sexual violence within more complex crime categories and link sexual violence to higher level individuals, because these cases were very different from national prosecution models.[114] Such cases "necessarily depend on prosecutors and fact-finders seeing connections between sexual violence and other violent crimes, being alert to patterns of sexual violence in the broader context of the conflict and understanding the indicators of sexual violence that make its occurrence foreseeable to higher-level officials."[115] There have been successes in this contextualization, for example in *Prosecutor v. Stakić*, in which the accused was convicted of persecution through sexual violence, which was found to be an important part of ethnic cleansing operations.[116] There have also been failures.[117]

---

[109]   *Id.* at 177.
[110]   The Special Court for Sierra Leone contextualized sexual and gender-based violence within the war crime of committing acts of terror, described in: Valerie Oosterveld, *The Gender Jurisprudence of the Special Court for Sierra Leone: Progress in the Revolutionary United Front Judgments*, 44 CORNELL INT'L L. J. 49, 68–71 (2011).
[111]   Baig et al., *supra* note 5, at 174.
[112]   *Id.*
[113]   Jarvis & Salgado, *supra* note 80, at 103, 107–17; Bianchi, *supra* note 5, at 134–7.
[114]   Baig et al., *supra* note 5, at 174.
[115]   Jarvis & Salgado, *supra* note 80, at 103; *see also* Bianchi, *supra* note 5, at 134–7.
[116]   *Stakić* Trial Judgment, *supra* note 49, at paras. 234–6, 240–1, 244, 757, 791–806, 818–26, 872, 881–2.
[117]   *See,* for example, the Đorđević and Sainović cases described at notes 81–87 above.

In the cases involving senior officials, the prosecutors often relied upon joint criminal enterprise as the mode of liability to contextualize the sexual violence within a common criminal purpose.[118] In practice, this meant proving that sexual violence was one of the means used to discriminate against certain groups of civilians, a method to destroy an ethnic group, a tool to drive people from a territory, or part of a system of ill-treatment.[119] The most difficult challenge was proving that sexual violence crimes were a foreseeable outcome of the common purpose. Sexual violence has been treated differently and more restrictively in certain cases due to misconceptions, including assumptions that sexual violence is simply an incidental by-product of conflict.[120] As described in Section 8.1.3 on persecution, the *Đordević* and *Sainović* Trial Judgments are examples of this restrictive interpretation of foreseeability.

In sum, the Tribunals have substantially developed the modes of contextualization of sexual violence within larger patterns of crime. This is a valuable legacy which is central to all future international investigations and prosecutions of sexual violence.[121]

8.2 LEGACY STEMMING FROM THE PRACTICE OF THE TRIBUNALS: INVESTIGATION OF SEXUAL VIOLENCE

This chapter has discussed the legacy of the ICTY and ICTR with respect to their significant jurisprudential development of the definitions of sexual and gender-based violence within international criminal law. It is also essential to highlight that the legacy of both tribunals extends beyond the jurisprudence. This section will discuss one example of this type of legacy: the impact of the Tribunals on how international courts and tribunals investigate sexual violence.

When they began, the ICTY and ICTR were the first institutions to investigate sexual violence as an international crime, and "[t]here were no precedents or examples to follow."[122] This meant that both Tribunals had to establish their policies and procedures on investigation without previous guidance, and the staff soon realized that "it would be difficult to dismantle centuries of inaction concerning war-time sexual violence and to travel a new more visionary path."[123]

---

[118]   Goy et al., *supra* note 5, at 220–1, 223.

[119]   *Id.* at 223.

[120]   Baig et al., *supra* note 5, at 173; Goy et al., *supra* note 5, at 226.

[121]   For example, this will be important for the International, Impartial and Independent Mechanism on International Crimes committed in the Syrian Arab Republic, as it works to "collect, consolidate, preserve and analyse evidence of violations of international humanitarian law and human rights violations and abuses and to prepare files in order to facilitate and expedite fair and independent criminal proceedings . . . in national, regional or international courts or tribunals that have or may in the future have jurisdiction over these crimes": GA Res. 71/248 para. 4 (Dec. 21, 2016).

[122]   Bianchi, *supra* note 5, at 130.

[123]   Jarvis & Salgado, *supra* note 80, at 102.

The ICTR's positive jurisprudential legacy outlined above conceals a less successful legacy on investigations. This investigations legacy is very uneven for four main
interrelated reasons. First, many individuals within the Office of the Prosecutor did
not have the "understanding, know-how and training to elicit the necessary evidence
that would support a conviction."[124] This was particularly acute in the early days of
the ICTR, when "investigators received little or no training with respect to the
methodology of investigating crimes of sexual violence in the context of the
Rwandan genocide and crimes against humanity."[125] Many of the investigators
had not studied international humanitarian or criminal law, and had no prior
experience in the investigation of sexual violence.[126] They therefore were often
unaware of the legal elements that must be proven in order for the case to be proven
beyond a reasonable doubt.[127]

Second, this lack of training and experience was compounded by the absence of
an overarching investigation strategy for sexual violence (despite having an overarching policy to prosecute rape and sexual violence).[128] The ICTR's investigators
prioritized the collection of evidence of murder and extermination over evidence of
other kinds.[129] Only after individuals were identified for prosecution based on these
crimes did the investigators then try to determine whether they could also locate
evidence of sexual violence.[130] "The target-based manner in which the [Office of the
Prosecutor] set of naming a target then finding an actual woman who had been
raped by that target, was equivalent to looking for a needle in a haystack."[131] This
meant that evidence of sexual violence committed by other individuals was not
collected, "yet these rapes were numerous."[132] The drawback of this after-the-fact
method of incorporating sexual violence crimes was clear: "[t]he strategy seemed to
perceive and portray sexual violence as crimes being committed by individual
persons on a random basis, as opposed to it being viewed holistically" as part of
the genocide.[133] This affected how the judges perceived the evidence. One troubling
example occurred in *Prosecutor v. Rukundo*.[134]

Rukundo was an ordained priest and military chaplain for the Rwandan Armed
Forces. He was convicted at trial of, *inter alia*, committing genocide by sexually
assaulting a young Tutsi woman in May 1994 at the Saint Léon Minor Seminary in

---

[124] Bianchi, *supra* note 5, at 131.
[125] *Id.* at 131.
[126] *Id.* at Bianchi 132.
[127] *Id.*
[128] *Id.* at 129.
[129] *Id.* at 131.
[130] *Id.*
[131] *Id.*
[132] *Id.*
[133] *Id.*
[134] Prosecutor v. Rukundo, Case No. ICTR-2001–70-T, Judgment (Feb. 27, 2009) (hereinafter *Rukundo*
         Trial Judgment); Prosecutor v. Rukundo, Case No. ICTR-2001–70-A, Judgment (Oct. 20, 2010)
         (hereinafter *Rukundo* Appeal Judgment).

Gitarama Prefecture.[135] The woman testified that, when Rukundo arrived at the seminary, she asked if he could hide her because she feared for her life.[136] He responded that he could not help her because her entire family had to be killed.[137] She helped him carry some items to his room in the hope that he would change his mind and hide her, but once at the room, he locked the door and sexually assaulted her.[138] Given the totality of the circumstances, from the general context of mass violence against Tutsis in the area and the specifics of Rukundo's words prior to assaulting the young woman (that her entire family had to be killed), a majority of the Trial Chamber convicted Rukundo of committing genocide through the sexual assault.[139] A majority of the Appeals Chamber then reversed this conviction, reasoning that "genocidal intent is not the only reasonable inference to be drawn from Rukundo's assertion that the young woman's family had to be killed because one of her relatives was assisting the *Inyenzi*."[140] Instead, the majority found that "Rukundo's language can plausibly be interpreted as expressing anger that a former friend was affiliated with the '*Inyenzi*,' without signifying a personal desire to destroy Tutsis."[141] As well, even though the young woman and her family were Tutsis seeking refuge from death in the seminary, the Appeals Chamber majority found that the act committed against the young woman was "qualitatively different from the other acts of genocide perpetrated by Rukundo."[142] They considered the sexual assault of the young woman by Rukundo to be "unplanned and spontaneous," and therefore "an opportunistic crime that was not accompanied by the specific intent to commit genocide."[143] As noted by one commentator, the "Majority reasoning in this case poignantly illustrates the major obstacles still faced in prosecuting these crimes ... these crimes can be easily mistakenly viewed as falling outside the sphere of the core crimes committed during these types of mass atrocities."[144]

---

[135] *Rukundo* Trial Judgment, *supra* note 134, at paras. 4, 574–6.
[136] *Id.* at paras. 373, 384.
[137] *Id.* at para. 373.
[138] *Id.*
[139] *Id.* at para. 576.
[140] Rukundo Appeals Judgment, *supra* note 134 at para. 235.
[141] *Id.* at para. 235.
[142] *Id.*
[143] *Id.* Note that Judge Pocar issued a strong and convincing partial dissent, arguing that the sexual assault was not qualitatively different from Rukundo's other acts (para. 4), and that the surrounding context was instrumental in understanding the seriousness of the crime: the young woman was a Tutsi refugee "fleeing violence in the surrounding area in which Tutsis were being hunted down. She was dirty and hungry and her place of refuge was not safe"; she knew and trusted Rukundo; Rukundo was armed; and Rukundo used force against her to hold her down and to commit a sexual act (paras. 5–8). Judge Pocar also made a key distinction between motive and intent – in response to the majority's reference to the sexual assault as "opportunistic" – stating that, even if the perpetrator's motivation is entirely sexual, it does not follow that he does not have the requisite genocidal intent or that his conduct does not cause severe pain and suffering (para. 10).
[144] Bianchi, *supra* note 4, at 143.

A third reason for the ICTR's very uneven investigations record is that many early investigators used inappropriate interviewing methodology.[145] In addition, they were not necessarily culturally sensitive.[146] Investigators were often unaware of how best to elicit evidence of sexual violence and missed the euphemisms victims used to describe rape, such as "he made me sit down" or "he married me."[147] A majority of investigators in the early days were male, and many female Rwandan victims "had great difficulty in relaying their experiences to men," and consequently did not reveal that they had been raped.[148]

A final reason for the ICTR's relative lack of success in the prosecution of sexual violence is lack of leadership over time – with some variation – from the highest levels of the Office of the Prosecutor.[149] A failure by the chief Prosecutor and senior management to establish a clear prosecution, and therefore investigation, strategy at the outset had ramifications throughout the life of the Tribunal.[150] While certain Prosecutors attempted to address these shortcomings, and there were improvements under those chief Prosecutors, the original deficiencies were never entirely over-come.[151] The result was a low rate of conviction at the ICTR for crimes of sexual violence,[152] which prompted the final chief Prosecutor to create a Committee for the Review of the Investigation and Prosecution of Sexual Violence in 2007.[153] That Committee looked at all of the ICTR's cases, "as well as the experiences of the Office of the Prosecutor, to identify the successes and failures of the office, and the reasons attributable to these successes and failures."[154] The Committee first reviewed all completed and ongoing cases by interviewing trial lawyers and examining the case files. It then created the lengthy *Best Practices Manual for the Investigation and Prosecution of Sexual Violence in Post-Conflict Regions: Lessons Learned from the Office of the Prosecutor for the International Criminal Tribunal for Rwanda*, which was posted on the ICTR's website (now hosted by the Mechanism) and distributed at numerous conferences.[155] This Manual is a helpful legacy document which has already informed other efforts to improve investigation strategies for international and domestic criminal tribunals.[156]

---

[145]   Nowrojee, *supra* note 13, at 9.
[146]   Bianchi, *supra* note 4, at 132.
[147]   *Id.*
[148]   *Id.*
[149]   *Id.* at 130–131; Nowrojee, *supra* note 13, at 9–11.
[150]   This seems to be Bianchi's conclusion, *supra* note 5, at 131.
[151]   Nowrojee, *supra* note 13, at 9–11; Bianchi, *supra* note 5, at 131.
[152]   Bianchi outlines a 36 percent success rate at the time of writing her chapter: *supra* note 5, at 128.
[153]   *Id.* at 129.
[154]   *Id.*
[155]   ICTR *Best Practices Manual, supra* note 7.
[156]   ICC *Policy Paper, supra* note 6, at fn 11; Sara Ferro Ribeiro & Danaé van der Straten Ponthoz, *International Protocol on the Documentation and Investigation of Sexual Violence in Conflict: Best Practice on the Documentation of Sexual Violence as a Crime or Violation of International Law*, 2nd edn. 29, 48, 53, 59, 60, 73, 145, 245 (2017) (hereinafter International Protocol on Documentation of Sexual Violence).

The ICTY's investigation legacy is somewhat more positive than that ICTR's legacy described above. The conviction rate for the sexual violence charges is somewhat higher, and the acquittal rate is lower for the ICTY than for the ICTR.[157] This appears to be related to the comparatively higher levels of political will, internal investigations expertise and more comprehensive investigations strategy from the outset of the tribunal through to its conclusion, each of which will be discussed in turn. However, there were also obstacles within each of these developments which affected the ICTY's success rate.

The ICTY's first Prosecutor, Richard Goldstone, took crucial initial steps that ultimately laid a foundation for the integration of sexual and gender-based violence into the Tribunal's investigations. One of these steps was the appointment of a Legal Advisor for Gender Issues as a member of his Secretariat,[158] having recognized gender bias within his Office.[159] The work of the Gender Advisor was crucial in the early days, as it "provided an essential foundation upon which the [Office of the Prosecutor] could begin to build successful outcomes" in law and policy directions.[160] The impact of this advisor ultimately led the drafters of the Rome Statute to include a provision requiring the International Criminal Court's Prosecutor to "appoint advisers with legal expertise on specific issues, including, but not limited to, sexual and gender violence."[161] Another step taken by Goldstone was to voice support for policy changes, such as increased training of investigators in sexual violence interviewing skills.[162] Over time, other Prosecutors, such as Louise Arbour and Serge Brammertz, also helped to shape the legacy of the ICTY by demonstrating similarly focused political will to advance the prosecution of sexual and gender-based crimes.[163]

The second aspect of the ICTY's relative success was its level of internal investigations expertise developed over time. The ICTY faced some of the same initial

---

[157] Based on September 2016 numbers posted on the website of the Mechanism for International Criminal Tribunals, 32 out of 78 (41 percent) individuals charged with sexual violence were convicted and 14 out of 78 were acquitted (18 percent), with the remaining cases ongoing or withdrawn: Mechanism for International Criminal Tribunals, *supra* note 1. Bianchi indicates that 12 of 33 individuals charged with sexual violence were convicted (36 percent), while 22 accused were acquitted: Bianchi, *supra* note 5, at 128.

[158] Patricia Viseur Sellers, *Gender Strategy Is Not a Luxury for International Courts*, 17 AM. U. J. GENDER, SOC. POL'Y & L. 301, 307 (2009); Richard J. Goldstone & Estelle A. Dehon, *Engendering Accountability: Gender Crimes Under International Criminal Law*, 19 NEW ENG J PUB. POL'Y 121, 123 (2003).

[159] Richard J. Goldstone, *Prosecuting Rape as a War Crime*, 34 CASE W. RES. J. INT'L L. 277, 280 (2002).

[160] Michelle Jarvis & Najwa Nabti, Policies and Institutional Strategies for Successful Sexual Violence Prosecutions, *in* PROSECUTING CONFLICT-RELATED SEXUAL VIOLENCE AT THE ICTY 73, 75 (Serge Brammertz & Michelle Jarvis eds., 2016). This is despite the limitations – such as lack of a dedicated budget and managerial influence over the investigators and trial lawyers – built into the role: *id.* at 75.

[161] Rome Statute of the ICC, *supra* note 71, at art. 42(9).

[162] These policy steps were helpful, but not all of them were uniformly implemented: Jarvis and Nabti, *supra* note 160, at 80.

[163] For example, *id.* at 78, 84.

challenges with respect to sexual violence investigations expertise as the ICTR. Initially, there were few female investigators.[164] Prosecutors Goldstone and Arbour implemented proactive measures to recruit female investigators, which assisted in increasing the numbers, though there was still a gender imbalance in staffing levels.[165] Additionally, in the first few years, most of the male investigators came from a police or military background, which led to the transfer of certain assumptions and approaches from those settings to the ICTY.[166] For example, some of the male investigators intentionally avoided investigating sexual and gender-based crimes.[167] Others only conducted inadequate or cursory interviews of sexual violence victims, and some dismissed the severity of these crimes or viewed sexual violence as a lower priority than killings.[168] A number of these individuals "held the perception that working on sexual violence cases was a 'soft' or less prestigious assignment, reflecting hierarchies imported from domestic criminal law offices."[169]

Another challenge was that some investigators and prosecutors within the Office of the Prosecutor viewed rape entirely as an opportunistic crime, reflecting a "disproportionate tendency to assume that sexual violence is an isolated act."[170] They "had difficulty seeing sexual violence as integral to the expulsion campaigns unleashed during the conflicts."[171] "As a result, evidentiary leads were not always followed up on the basis that they were insufficiently connected to the case theory."[172] In order to address these issues, the Office of the Prosecutor implemented training sessions for investigators and prosecutors, thematic prosecution of sexual violence in the *Kunarac* case, and a recruitment policy aimed at decreasing the Office's gender bias.[173] One of the most fundamental lessons learned at the Office was that dismantling gender-insensitive misconceptions was "the key to improving accountability outcomes" for sexual violence crimes.[174]

The third aspect of the ICTY's relative success in investigating sexual and gender-based violence was in its adoption of a comprehensive investigations strategy. Unlike

[164]   *Id.* at 84.

[165]   *Id.*

[166]   Goldstone, *supra* note 159, at 280.

[167]   *Id.*; Peggy Kuo, *Prosecuting Crimes of Sexual Violence in an International Tribunals*, 34 CASE W. RES. J. INT'L L. 305, 310–11 (2002).

[168]   Michelle Jarvis & Kate Vigneswaran, Challenges to Successful Outcomes in Sexual Violence Cases, in PROSECUTING CONFLICT-RELATED SEXUAL VIOLENCE AT THE ICTY, 33, 37 (Serge Brammertz & Michelle Jarvis eds., 2016); Kuo, *supra* note 167, at 310–11; Xabier Agirre Aranbaru, Beyond Dogma and Taboo: Criteria for the Effective Investigation of Sexual Violence, in UNDERSTANDING AND PROVING INTERNATIONAL SEX CRIMES 267, 269 (Morten Bergsmo, Alf Butenschøn Skyre & Elisabeth J. Wood eds., 2012); John Hagan, Justice in the Balkans: Prosecuting War Crimes in The Hague Tribunal 52 (2003).

[169]   Jarvis & Vigneswaran, *supra* note 168, at 37.

[170]   *Id.* at 39.

[171]   *Id.* at 38.

[172]   *Id.*

[173]   Jarvis & Nabti, *supra* note 160, at 81, 85–7, 96.

[174]   Jarvis & Vigneswaran, *supra* note 168, at 35.

the ICTR, the ICTY's Prosecutor made all investigation teams responsible for investigating sexual violence.[175] This led to the creation of gender-integrated investigation teams with both male and female investigators, so as to be able to meet witness preferences.[176] Both of these steps helped to establish the crime base through successful prosecution of lower-level perpetrators that would later assist in linking sexual violence to higher-level accused.[177]

This section has examined the lessons learned within the ICTR and ICTY with respect to the investigation of sexual violence crimes. This example is used as an illustration of challenges faced, and solutions adopted, by the Tribunals as they broke new ground in their investigations. They encountered failures, as well as successes, and both are part of their legacy insofar as subsequent tribunals (and capacity-building projects)[178] followed their best practices and attempted to avoid their mistakes.[179] It should be noted that, although this section concentrated on the ICTY and ICTR's investigations record, the legacy of the Tribunals also extends into procedural and evidentiary matters, victim protection, staffing policies, modes of liability, sentencing, cooperation with national jurisdictions and other topics.[180]

8.3 CONCLUSION

The ICTY has defined legacy as "that which the Tribunal will hand down to successors and others."[181] The ICTY and ICTR have already handed down significant, trailblazing jurisprudence on sexual and gender-based crimes. Most obviously, both Tribunals have made substantial contributions to the development of international criminal law's understanding of rape and other forms of sexual and gender-based violence, enslavement carried out through sexual means and gendered forms of persecution. Less often recognized is the crucial work both Tribunals did in demonstrating that sexual violence must be contextualized in a number of ways in order for the court to understand its import and modalities. This work is evidenced in the most gender-sensitive jurisprudence, which explains the role played by sexual violence in perpetuating genocide, crimes against humanity and war crimes. This

---

[175] Jarvis & Nabti, *supra* note 160, at 83.

[176] *Id.*

[177] *Id.*

[178] For example, the *International Protocol on Documentation of Sexual Violence, supra* note 156.

[179] For example, learning from the mistakes of the ICTR in particular, the Special Court for Sierra Leone's first Prosecutor hired highly experienced investigators with expertise in gender-based violence and human rights violations among his very first staff: Valerie Oosterveld, *The Special Court for Sierra Leone: Initial Structural and Procedural Decisions on Sexual and Gender-Based Violence*, 46 Cambrian L. Rev. 131, 137–8 (2015–16).

[180] These topics are covered in Serge Brammertz & Michelle Jarvis eds., Prosecuting Conflict-Related Sexual Violence at the ICTY (2016), and in the ICTR *Best Practices Manual, supra* note 7.

[181] International Criminal Tribunal for the Former Yugoslavia, *Assessing the Legacy of the ICTY – 2010 Conference*, www.icty.org/sid/10293 (last visited May 20, 2018).

body of jurisprudence has influenced other international criminal courts,[182] domestic prosecutions[183] and discussions of women, peace and security within the UN Security Council.[184] As well, the Tribunals will continue to influence international criminal practice due to their investigation strategies, producing both best practices and lessons learned from gender-insensitive mistakes that should be avoided in the future.

[182] As mentioned earlier in this chapter, the Tribunal's jurisprudence has influenced, among others, the Special Court for Sierra Leone and the International Criminal Court.

[183] For example, R. v. Munyaneza, 2009 QCCS 2201, cited to ICTR case law in paras. 94–5 in its consideration of sexual violence.

[184] For example, United Nations Secretary General, *Report of the Secretary-General on Women, Peace and Security*, paras. 94–5, UN Doc S/2002/1154 (Oct. 16, 2002).

9

The Defense of Duress to Killing Innocents: Assessing the Mixed Legacy of the ICTY and the ICTR

Jonathan Witmer-Rich[*]

The audacious goal of international humanitarian law is to bring the rule of law into the anarchy of war. Nowhere is the audacity of this project more evident than in the context of duress – a soldier commanded to commit atrocities on pain of his own death. Rosa Ehrenreich Brooks writes, "[h]uman rights law is premised upon the idea that even the almost unimaginable extremes of human emotion and behavior can be made subject to the law's rationalizing power; that law can reach into the very heart of darkness, and make us better than we have so far proven to be."[1] Duress tests the extreme edge of the law's reach and poses a deep moral-legal dilemma involving the conflict between the protection of innocent life versus the prerequisite of moral culpability for the imposition of criminal punishment.

In Section 9.1, this chapter first assesses the legacy of the International Criminal Tribunal for the Former Yugoslavia (ICTY) and the International Criminal Tribunal for Rwanda (ICTR) with respect to duress as a defense to war crimes and crimes against humanity. Later, in Section 9.2 this chapter uses the ICTY's *Erdemović* decision to re-evaluate how defenses should be approached in international criminal law.

The Legacy of the ICTY and the ICTR on Duress

The decisions of the ICTY and ICTR pushed international criminal law toward the categorical rejection of duress as a defense to the killing of innocents, elevating the protection of innocent life over doubts about a defendant's personal moral culpability. Yet the seeds of the contrary view – insisting on individual moral culpability as a prerequisite to criminal conviction – appear powerfully in the dissenting opinions in the ITCY, which were effectively adopted by the Rome Statute of the International Criminal Court (ICC).

[*] Joseph C. Hostetler – Baker Hostetler Professor of Law, Cleveland-Marshall College of Law, Cleveland State University.
[1] Rosa Ehrenreich Brooks, *Law in the Heart of Darkness: Atrocity & Duress*, 43 VA. J. INT'L L. 861, 862 (2003).

In the period beginning with World War II and leading up to the ICTR and the ICTY, tribunals applying international criminal law had a mixed record as to whether duress could serve as a defense to homicide offenses. In the landmark *Erdemović* case, the ICTY Appeals Chamber in a divided 3–2 decision held that duress could not serve as a defense for a soldier charged with a crime against humanity involving the killing of an innocent person.[2] In four separate opinions, the judges offered detailed and thoughtful analyses of the cases both for and against the recognition of the defense of duress in this context.

The ICTR adopted the *Erdemović* approach and likewise rejected duress as a defense in this context.[3] The ICTY and the ICTR thus moved international criminal law toward rejecting duress as a defense to homicide offenses.

At the same time, the learned and considered views of the *Erdemović* dissenters laid a strong foundation for the contrary view.

The drafters of the Rome Statute settled upon a definition of "duress" that does not exclude homicide offenses from its ambit.[4] The Rome Statute definition does require, among other things, that "the person does not intend to cause a greater harm than the one sought to be avoided."[5] While the Rome Statute does not categorically exclude homicide offenses from this defense, it will remain a disputed question whether and when an offense involving the killing of an innocent person can be said to involve the intent not "to cause a greater harm than the one sought to be avoided." On that difficult question, the majority and dissenting opinions in *Erdemović* will no doubt have continuing relevance.

In Section 9.1, this chapter first sketches the evolution, within international criminal law, of duress as a defense to war crimes or crimes against humanity involving the killing of innocents, from the post-World War II tribunals, through the ICTY and ICTR, to the Rome Statute of the ICC. The chapter then describes in Section 9.2 the landmark *Erdemović* decision, highlighting the different disagreements embedded within the various opinions: disagreement about past precedents, moral disagreement, and disagreement about the process of formulating international law. The chapter further analyzes this final disagreement in Section 9.3 – about how to conceptualize defenses within international criminal law.

Defenses in International Criminal Law: Seeking Consensus on Condemnation

The chapter uses the *Erdemović* decision to argue a more general point about when defenses should be recognized in international criminal law. International criminal law is a tool to reflect and carry out a consensus among nations that

---

[2] Erdemović v. Prosecutor, Case No. IT-06–22-A, Appeals Judgment (Int'l Crim. Trib. for the Former Yugoslavia Oct. 7, 1997).

[3] Prosecutor v. Rutaganira, Case No. ICTR-95-IC-T, para. 161 (Mar. 14, 2005).

[4] Rome Statute of the International Criminal Court art. 31(1)(d), July 17, 1998, 2187 UNTS 90.

[5] *Id.*

particular types of conduct should be condemned and punished (and punished not just as domestic offenses but international offenses). When nations disagree significantly about the availability of a defense in a particular set of circumstances – such as duress as a defense to homicide offenses – this indicates a lack of consensus among nations for condemning the defendant in those particular circumstances. Accordingly, the lack of consensus as to the defense should lead jurists to recognize that defense under international criminal law – at least until such time as nations can come to agreement through a treaty or through the process of customary international law.

Thus the split in authority on the availability of the defense of duress to homicide offenses should have led the ICTY in *Erdemović* to the opposite conclusion reached by the majority. The division of legal authority should have led the court to conclude that duress was a valid defense under international criminal law, including as a defense to homicide offenses.

9.1 THE HISTORY OF DURESS AS A DEFENSE IN INTERNATIONAL CRIMINAL LAW

9.1.1 *Inconsistencies among Post-World War II Tribunals*

Discussions of duress in international criminal law typically begin with the various tribunals that operated in the wake of World War II. The charter for the International Military Tribunal at Nuremburg (IMT) expressly rejected two possible defenses – superior orders and official capacity – but otherwise left the substantive law of any possible defenses up to the tribunal to decide.[6] Evaluating the case law, Cherif Bassiouni observes that as to duress as a defense to crimes against humanity, the post-World War II tribunals operating under Allied Control Council Law No. 10 were "inconsistent on these points to say the least."[7]

The mixed precedents of these post-World War II tribunals is described and debated extensively by the various opinions in the *Erdemović* case of the ICTY Appeals Chamber. Judges MacDonald and Vohrah claimed that the predominant view among these post-World War II tribunals was "that duress may not be pleaded as a defence to a war crime involving the killing of innocent persons generally, regardless of whether the accused was or was not a soldier."[8] They cited rejections of duress for the killing of innocents in cases such as *Stalag Luft III* and *Feurstein*

---

[6] *See* WILLIAM A. SCHABAS, The International Criminal Court: A Commentary on the Rome Statute (hereinafter Schabas, The International Criminal Court) 481 (2010).

[7] M. CHERIF BASSIOUNI, Crimes against Humanity: Historical Evolution and Contemporary Application 618 (2011) (hereinafter BASSIOUNI, CRIMES AGAINST HUMANITY). *See id.* at 620–1 (discussing various decisions from post-World War II tribunals showing mixed approaches to the question of duress).

[8] *Erdemović*, Joint Separate Opinion of Judge MacDonald and Judge Vohrah, para. 42, para. 44.

before British military tribunals, the *Hölzer* case before a Canadian military tribunal, as well as earlier American cases.[9]

At the same time, these judges acknowledged authority to the contrary. In the *Einsatzgruppen* case, before a United States military tribunal, the court stated:

> Let it be said at once that there is no law which requires that an innocent man must forfeit his life or suffer serious harm in order to avoid committing a crime which he condemns. The threat, however, must be imminent, real and inevitable. No court will punish a man who, with a loaded pistol at his head, is compelled to pull a lethal lever.[10]

In addition, the IMT articulated what scholars have come to call the "moral choice" test for duress:

> That a soldier was ordered to kill or torture in violation of the international laws of war has never been recognised as a valid defence to such acts of brutality, though, as the Charter here provides, the order may be urged in mitigation of the punishment. The true test, which is found in varying degrees in the criminal law of most nations, is not the existence of the order, but whether moral choice was in fact possible.[11]

Cherif Bassiouni notes that this "moral choice" test has been called "cryptic" and "not easy to fathom."[12] Judge MacDonald and Judge Vohrah minimized the importance of the IMT's statement, arguing that "[t]his unelaborated statement, in our view, makes no significant contribution to the jurisprudence on this issue."[13]

Judge Cassese, dissenting, disputed the majority's characterization of these post-World War II tribunal decisions.[14] He found considerably more ambiguity in these cases, stating there was not sufficient uniformity to conclude "that a customary rule excepting murder-type offences from the ambit of duress has evolved in international criminal law."[15] Judge Stephen, also dissenting, agreed: "it cannot be said that,

---

[9]   *Id.* at paras. 42–3 (citing Trial of Max Wielen and 17 Others (*Stalag Luft III* case)), Law Reports, vol. XI, 33; Trial of Valentine Feurstein and Others (*Feurstein* case), Proceedings of a Military Court held at Hamburg (Aug. 4–24, 1948), Public Record Office, Kew, Richmond, file no. 235/525; Law Reports, vol. XV, 173; Trial of Robert Hölzer and Two Others (*Hölzer* case), Record of Proceedings of the Trial by Canadian Military Court of Robert Hölzer and Walter Weigel and Wilhelm Ossenbach held at Aurich, Germany, 25 Mar.–6 Apr. 1946, vol. 1; Arp v. State, 97 Ala. 5, 12 So. 201 (1893); State v. Nargashian, 26 R.I. 299, 58 A. 953 (1904)).

[10] *Id.* at para. 43 (citing Trial of Otto Ohlendorf et al. (*Einsatzgruppen* case), Trials of War Criminals, vol. IV, 480). *See also* the acceptance of duress in the Jepsen case before a British military tribunal. *Id.* at para. 42 (citing Trial of Gustav Alfred Jepsen and Others (*Jepsen* case), Proceedings of a War Crimes Trial held at Luneberg, Aug. 13–23, 1946, judgment of Aug. 24, 1946 (original transcripts in Public Record Office, Kew, Richmond), Law Reports, vol. XV, 172).

[11] *Id.* at para. 45 (quoting Trial of the German Major War Criminals (Proceedings of the International Military Tribunal Sitting at Nuremberg, Germany), H. M. Stationery Office, London, 1950, Part 22, 447).

[12] Bassiouni, Crimes Against Humanity 618 (quoting commentators).

[13] *Erdemović*, Joint Separate Opinion of Judge MacDonald and Judge Vohrah, para. 45.

[14] *Id.*, Separate and Dissenting Opinion of Judge Cassese, paras. 20–30.

[15] *Id.* para. 29.

in applying one principle or another to particular cases, the necessary *opinio iuris sine necessitatis* was present so as to establish any rule of customary international law" on the issue of duress as a defense to the killing of innocent persons.[16]

9.1.2 *The Civil Law Approach versus the Common Law Approach*

A division likewise exists among national legal systems on the viability of duress as a defense to the killing of innocents. Most civil law countries permit duress to serve as a defense to any crime, including the killing of innocents, albeit according to relatively strict proof requirements. In contrast, common law countries categorically limit the defense of duress to nonhomicide offenses.

The five judges in *Erdemović* all agreed on this basic description of the civil law-common law divide. Judge MacDonald and Judge Vohrah observed that "[t]he penal codes of civil law systems, with some exceptions, consistently recognise duress as a complete defence to all crimes."[17] They noted that duress is available as a defense to all crimes, including homicide offenses, in France, Belgium, the Netherlands, Spain, Germany, Italy, Norway, Sweden, Finland, Venezuela, Nicaragua, Chile, Panama, Mexico, and the former Yugoslavia.[18] Many of these jurisdictions contain some version of a proportionality requirement – that the harm caused does not exceed (or is not disproportionate to) the harm avoided.[19] This proportionality requirement has led some civil law courts to reject the defense of duress in particular cases – that the killing of innocent persons was disproportionate to the defendant's own threatened death.[20] But even these courts do not categorically reject duress as a possible defense to homicide charges.

Cases from other civil law jurisdictions have permitted the defense of duress to homicide offenses, in particular in cases similar to *Erdemović* – in which the victims would have been killed regardless of the defendant's actions. For example, in the *Masetti* case, the Italian Court of Assize upheld the defendant's claim of duress for the shooting of two captured partisans during World War II.[21] The *Masetti* court reasoned that "the possible sacrifice by Masetti and his men would have been in any case to no avail and without any effect in that it would have had no impact whatsoever on the plight of the persons to be shot, who would have been executed anyway even without him."[22]

---

[16] *Id.*, Separate and Dissenting Opinion of Judge Stephen, para. 24.
[17] *Id.*, Joint Separate Opinion of Judge MacDonald and Judge Vohrah, para. 59.
[18] *Id.*
[19] *Id.* para. 68 (noting Italy, Norway, Sweden, Nicaragua, Japan, and the former Yugoslavia).
[20] *Id.* para. 68 (discussing case law of Norway).
[21] *Id.* para. 79 (citing Decision of the Court of Assize of L'Aquila, June 15, 1948 (unpublished; President Cassese's personal translation of the copy of the hand-written original was kindly provided by the Registry of the Court of Appeal of L'Aquila)).
[22] *Id.*

In contrast to the civil law approach, "[t]raditional common law rejects the defence of duress in respect of murder and treason."[23] The defense of duress is categorically unavailable for homicide offenses (as well as additional offenses, in particular jurisdictions) in England, most jurisdictions in the United States, Australia, Canada, India, Malaysia, and Nigeria.[24]

After this extensive survey of national legal authorities, Judge MacDonald and Judge Vohrah concluded:

> It is clear from the differing positions of the principal legal systems of the world that there is no consistent concrete rule which answers the question whether or not duress is a defence to the killing of innocent persons. It is not possible to reconcile the opposing positions and, indeed, we do not believe that the issue should be reduced to a contest between common law and civil law.[25]

The dissenting judges in *Erdemović* agreed as to the basic contours of this division between civil law and common law jurisdictions, even while they perhaps disagreed on some particulars.[26]

9.1.3 *The ICTY, ICTR, and the Rome Statute*

While the Rome Statute was finalized after the creation of the ICTY and the ICTR, preparatory work on a statute for an international criminal court began well before the creation of the ad hoc tribunals.[27] In 1991, the International Law Commission (ILC) released a draft ICC statute describing the court and defining offenses. That draft did not set forth any defenses, but provided that "[t]he competent court shall determine the admissibility of defences under the general principles of law, in light of the character of each crime."[28] The commentary noted that the Commission regarded defenses "as very important concepts," but was unable to draft specific provisions "on which all members could agree."[29] Some members took the view that "defences could never be invoked in connection with certain categories of crimes,

---

[23]   *Id.* para. 63.

[24]   *Id.* para. 60.

[25]   *Id.* para. 72.

[26]   *Id.*, Separate and Dissenting Opinion of Judge Stephen, para. 25 (agreeing generally with the description by Judge MacDonald and Judge Vohrah that duress is available for homicide offenses in most civil law countries, with some qualifications, while it is not available for homicide offenses in most common law countries, at least in some circumstances); Separate and Dissenting Opinion of Judge Cassese, paras. 29–30 and notes 60 and 63.

[27]   Cherif Bassiouni observes that "[t]he efforts to establish a permanent ICC started with the League of Nations" in 1937. M. Cherif Bassiouni, The Making of the International Criminal Court, 117 & n.1, *in* 3 International Criminal Law (M. Cherif Bassiouni ed., 3rd edn. 2008) (hereinafter 3 International Criminal Law).

[28]   *See* Schabas, The International Criminal Court 482 (quoting Yearbook of the International Law Commission, 1991, Volume 2, UN Doc. A/CN.4/SER.A/1001/Add.1 (Part 2), at 2).

[29]   *Id.* at 482 (quoting Yearbook . . . 1991, at 100).

such as crimes against humanity."[30] The final draft code from the ILC, issued in 1996, likewise left possible defenses unarticulated.[31]

During this same period, the United Nations Security Council, responding to atrocities in the former Yugoslavia as well as in Rwanda, created the two ad hoc criminal tribunals: the International Criminal Tribunal for the Former Yugoslavia, created in May 1993, and the International Criminal Tribunal for Rwanda, created in November 1994.[32]

On the question of defenses, the statutes of the ICTY and the ICTR took the same approach as the IMT, rejecting a few defenses (such as superior orders) but otherwise leaving the tribunals with the task of determining what defenses might apply, and what the substance of those defenses would be.[33]

In 1994, the UN General Assembly convened an Ad hoc Committee for the Establishment of an International Criminal Court, and in December 1995 established a Preparatory Committee.[34] The Preparatory Committee was charged with "draft[ing] texts with a view to preparing a widely acceptable consolidated text that could be considered by a diplomatic conference of plenipotentiaries."[35]

The sessions of the Preparatory Committee featured considerable debate and disagreement over the type and content of potential defenses, including the issues of whether any defenses could exist for crimes against humanity, and whether the statute should exhaustively list all available defenses or leave the court with residual authority to consider additional defenses.[36]

The report of the 1997–98 Preparatory Committee articulated defenses as well as offenses. For many provisions, the draft text offered alternative versions, reflecting different approaches that might be taken.[37] Article 31, titled "Grounds for excluding criminal responsibility," included a provision on duress. William Schabas observes

[30] Yearbook . . . 1991, at 101.

[31] SCHABAS, THE INTERNATIONAL CRIMINAL COURT 482 (citing Yearbook . . . 1996, UN Doc. A/CN/3/SER. A/1996/Add.1 (Part 2), 39).

[32] *See* Roy S. Lee, Introduction: The Rome Conference and Its Contributions to International Law, *in* The International Criminal Court: The Making of the Rome Statute 6 and n. 12 (Roy S. Lee ed. 2002); SC Res. 827, UN Doc. S/RES/827 (May 25, 1993) (ICTY); SC Res. 955, UN Doc. S/RES/955 (Nov. 8, 1994) (ICTR). On the creation of the ICTY, *see* Bartram S. Brown, The International Criminal Tribunal for the Former Yugoslavia, *in* 69–101 3 International Criminal Law. On the creation of the ICTR, *see* Roman Boed, The International Criminal Tribunal for Rwanda, *in* 103–16 3 International Criminal Law.

[33] *See* SCHABAS, THE INTERNATIONAL CRIMINAL COURT 481; Statute of the International Criminal Tribunal for the Former Yugoslavia art. 7, May 25, 1993, SC Res. 827, UN SCOR, 48th Sess., 3217th mtg., at 1–2, U.N. Doc. S/RES/827 (1993), 32 ILM 1159; Statute of the International Criminal Tribunal for Rwanda art. 6, November 8, 1994, SC Res. 955, UN SCOR, 49th Sess., 3453th mtg., UN Doc. S/RES/955 (1994), 33 ILM 1598.

[34] *See* SCHABAS, THE INTERNATIONAL CRIMINAL COURT 19; M. Cherif Bassiouni, The Making of the International Criminal Court 124, *in* 3 International Criminal Law.

[35] SCHABAS, THE INTERNATIONAL CRIMINAL COURT 19–20.

[36] *See id.* at 483.

[37] Report of the Preparatory Commission on the Establishment of an International Criminal Court, Art. 31, at 34–5, available at http://legal.un.org/icc/rome/proceedings/E/Rome%20Proceedings_v3_e.pdf.

that this draft Article 31 "resembles the first two paragraphs of article 31 [of the ICC], although it contains many options and footnotes related to specific defences."[38]

For present purposes, what is particularly notable is that this draft did not purport to resolve the divide between civil law and common law approaches to duress, but effectively included both as alternatives. In particular, Article 31.1(d) provided that duress could serve as a defense, "provided that the person's action [causes] [was not intended to cause] [n]either death [n]or a greater harm than the one sought to be avoided."[39] In addition, two alternatives to this clause were mentioned in footnotes to the draft. One alternative: duress would be available so long as the person's action "is under the circumstances not reasonably more excessive than the threat or perceived threat."[40] A second alternative: duress would be available so long as the person was "employing means which are not disproportionate to the risk faced."[41]

Thus while duress was included as a possible defense in this draft, it was unclear whether the common law limitation – excluding the defense in cases involving death – would be included in the definition.

This Preparatory Committee report was completed on April 3, 1998, just two months before the Rome Conference began in June 1998.[42]

The previous year, in October 1997, the Appeals Chamber of the ICTY issued its landmark decision, *Erdemović*, holding by a 3–2 vote that duress was not available as a defense for a soldier charged with killing innocent persons in a crime against humanity (discussed at greater length below).[43]

The Rome Conference was held in June and July of 1998, culminating in the signing of the Rome Statute establishing the International Criminal Court.[44] In contrast to the categorical limitation on duress in *Erdemović*, the Rome Statute includes a definition of duress that does not, on its face, categorically exclude offenses involving the killing of innocents. Article 31, "Grounds for excluding criminal responsibility," provides in relevant part:

1. In addition to other grounds for excluding criminal responsibility provided for in this Statute, a person shall not be criminally responsible if, at the time of that person's conduct: ...

   (d) The conduct which is alleged to constitute a crime within the jurisdiction of the Court has been caused by duress resulting from a threat of imminent death or of

---

[38] Schabas, The International Criminal Court 483.
[39] Report of the Preparatory Commission on the Establishment of an International Criminal Court, Art. 31, at 34–5 (brackets in original).
[40] *Id.* at 34 note 95.
[41] *Id.* at 35 note 96.
[42] M. Cherif Bassiouni, The Making of the International Criminal Court 130, *in* 3 International Criminal Law.
[43] Erdemović v. Prosecutor, Case No. IT-06–22-A, Appeals Judgment (Int'l Crim. Trib. for the Former Yugoslavia Oct. 7, 1997).
[44] *See* Roy S. Lee, Introduction: The Rome Conference and Its Contributions to International Law, 10-12, *in* The International Criminal Court: The Making of the Rome Statute (Roy S. Lee ed. 2002).

continuing or imminent serious bodily harm against that person or another person, and the person acts necessarily and reasonably to avoid this threat, provided that the person does not intend to cause a greater harm than the one sought to be avoided. Such a threat may either be:

(i) Made by other persons; or
(ii) Constituted by other circumstances beyond that person's control.[45]

There is little record of why the members of the Rome Conference settled on this language rather than the more limited option excluding homicide offenses. William Schabas states that "[t]he Diplomatic Conference spent little time on the matter," and observes simply that "[t]he drafters of the Rome Statute preferred the post-Second World War [*Einsatzgruppen*] version, and effectively adopted the views of the minority of the [ICTY] Appeals Chamber" in *Erdemović*.[46] Alexander K. A. Greenawalt states that the dissenting views in *Erdemović* "received subsequent vindication" in the Rome Statute.[47]

The ICTR Trial Chamber did not decide the legal question of duress as a defense to killing innocents until its decision in *Rutaganira* in March 2005, well after the Rome Statute was signed.[48] Vincent Rutaganira was charged with extermination as a crime against humanity "for having by omission, aided and abetted the massacre of thousands of Tutsi civilians who had taken refuge at Mubugu Church."[49] Rutaganira was the "*conseiller communal* of Mubuga *secteur* ... and was as such responsible for the economic, social and cultural development of his *secteur*."[50] In that role, Rutaganira knew that "thousands of Tutsi civilians sought shelter in Mubuga church," that those civilians were attacked, and that before the attack, he "had observed the attackers, including the *bourgmestre*, armed Hutu civilians, *commune* policemen and members of the national *gendarmerie* assembling."[51] The court concluded that "[d]espite his position and of his having knowledge of the above-mentioned events, [Rutaganira] failed to act to protect the Tutsi."[52]

---

[45] Rome Statute of the International Criminal Court art. 31(1)(d), July 17, 1998, 2187 UNTS 90. The other subparts of Article 31.1 set forth the terms of the insanity defense (31.1(a)), the intoxication defense (31.1(b)), and self-defense and defense of others (31.1(c)). This list is not exclusive, for Article 31.3 contains a residual defense clause, providing that the court "may consider a ground for excluding criminal responsibility other than those referred to in paragraph 1 where such ground is derived from applicable law as set forth in Article 21." *Id.*, Article 31.3.

[46] SCHABAS, THE INTERNATIONAL CRIMINAL COURT 490.

[47] Alexander K. A. Greenawalt, *The Pluralism of International Criminal Law*, 86 IND. L.J. 1063, 1119 (2011). *See also* Luis E. Chiesa, *Duress, Demanding Heroism, and Proportionality*, 41 VAND J. TRANSNAT'L L. 741, 750 (2008) ("the drafters of the Rome Statute of the International Criminal Court seemed to follow Cassese's position regarding duress").

[48] Prosecutor v. Rutaganira, Case No. ICTR-95-IC-T, para. 169 (Mar. 14, 2005).

[49] *Rutaganira*, para. 169.

[50] *Id.* para. 31.

[51] *Id.* para. 32.

[52] *Id.* para. 33.

In response to a plea of duress, the ICTR Trial Chamber announced that it "fully endorses the finding by the Appeals Chamber of the ICTY that 'duress does not afford a complete defence to a soldier charged with a crime against humanity and/or war crime involving the killing of innocent human beings.'"[53] The ICTR Trial Chamber, like the *Erdemović* majority, agreed that duress could serve as a mitigating factor at sentencing.[54]

Notably, the ICTR Trial Chamber in *Rutaganira* did not cite or discuss the contrary position contained in Article 31 of the Rome Statute. Of course, the Rome Statute governs the ICC, not the ICTR, which predates the adoption of the Rome Statute. At the same time, a good argument can be made that a defendant should be permitted to make use of any change in international law that insures to his or her benefit. This principle is reflected in the Rome Statute, which provides:

> In the event of a change in the law applicable to a given case prior to a final judgement, the law more favourable to the person being investigated, prosecuted or convicted shall apply.[55]

Accordingly, it might be argued that to the extent that the Rome Statute establishes the availability of a defense for a person for whom, at the time of the conduct, the defense was not available, that defendant should be permitted to invoke the defense under the terms set forth in the Rome Statute. In particular, while the 1997 *Erdemović* decision represented a rejection, in international criminal law, of the defense of duress for the killing of innocents, the 1998 Rome Statute could be invoked by a person whose conduct pre-dated its adoption in support of the availability of the defense of duress under international criminal law.

As noted above, however, the ICTR Trial Chamber did not discuss the defense of duress under the Rome Statute or explain why it did not apply. The Court simply adopted, with little discussion, the majority holding in *Erdemović*. Moreover, at least one judge on the ICTY Appeals chamber likewise remarked, in 2004, on the continued validity of *Erdemović* as a precedent – again, without reference to the contrary approach adopted in the Rome Statute in 1998.[56]

It might be surprising that the ICTR did not address the issue of duress as a defense until 2005, many years into its work, when as a factual matter it might be expected that many participants in the Rwandan genocide could at least plausibly claim duress as a defense for their participation. On this point, it is worth

---

[53] *Id.* para. 161.

[54] *Id.* The ICTR Appeals Chamber mentioned the defense of duress in a 2014 opinion, Ndahimana v. Prosecutor, but only to explain that the defendant failed to properly raise the defense and thus the court would not rule on its applicability. Ndahimana v. Prosecutor, Case No. ICTR-01-68-A, Judgment, paras. 172–5, December 16, 2013, www.unmict.org/sites/default/files/acclrt/judgements/2013/Ndahimana%20AJ.pdf.

[55] Rome Statute, Article 24.2.

[56] *See* SCHABAS, THE INTERNATIONAL CRIMINAL COURT 490 (citing Basiljevic (IT-98-32-A), Separate and Dissenting Opinion of Judge Shahabuddeen, Feb. 25, 2004, para. 41).

emphasizing that international criminal tribunals often use their limited resources to prosecute primarily political and military leaders rather than many of the low-level participants for whom duress would be a plausible defense. The ICTY and the ICTR largely focused on high-level political and military leaders who were believed to have participated extensively in the planning of atrocities, and thus who could not plausibly claim duress.[57] In Rwanda, many lower-level participants were processed by the *gacaca* courts – "a modified version of traditional community based justice mechanism" – established by the Rwandan government.[58]

The *Erdemović* prosecution thus is notable in part because of how unusual it is for an international criminal tribunal to prosecute a low-level soldier rather than a political or military leader. *Erdemović* "was ... the first time a truly international tribunal has concluded the trial of a minor war criminal, as opposed to a senior military commander or political leader."[59] Erdemović's prosecution came about because Erdemović himself first told his story to a European journalist, making his story an international sensation and eventually leading to his prosecution.[60]

In summary, the legacy of the ICTY and the ICTR with respect to the defense of duress is somewhat fractured. On the one hand, both courts categorically rejected duress as a defense to the killing of innocents. On the other hand, only the ICTY analyzed the issue at any length in writing, and that decision was a 3–2 split opinion that contained two strong dissents advocating in favor of the possibility of duress, at least in some limited, extreme cases. Moreover, the Rome Statute effectively adopted the approach of the *Erdemović* dissenters.

---

[57]   *See* Bartram S. Brown, The International Criminal Tribunal for the Former Yugoslavia, 100 (explaining that the Security Council "completion strategy" for the ICTY called "for the ICTY to focus on trying the most senior leaders while referring those accused who are of intermediate and lower rank to national courts"), *in* 3 International Criminal Law; UN Secretary-General, Letter dated Oct. 3, 2003, from the UN Secretary General addressed to the President of the Security Council, Annex: Completion Strategy of the International Criminal Tribunal for Rwanda P 6, U.N. Doc. S/2003/946 (Oct. 6, 2003), www.unictr.org/Portals/o/English*FactSheets*Completion_St*s-2003–946.pdf (http://perma.cc/SFH-2ZQE) ("The Prosecutor's strategy is to prosecute before the ICTR, those persons bearing the highest responsibility for the crimes committed in Rwanda in 1994."); Alex Odora-Obote, Investigations and *Case Selection* 252 ("To prosecute those most responsible, the [ICTR] prosecutor adopted a policy of selecting cases that involved participation of senior political and military leaders. Also included were individual perpetrators, regardless of their rank, provided their actions involved incidents and offenses that were considered serious."), *in* THE ELGAR COMPANION TO THE INTERNATIONAL CRIMINAL TRIBUNAL FOR RWANDA (Anne-Marie de Brouwer & Alette Smeulers eds., 2016).
[58]   *See* Barbora Holá & Alette Smeulers, Rwanda and the ICTR: Facts and Figures 70 ("Other Prosecutions"), *in* The Elgar Companion to the International Criminal Tribunal for Rwanda. While evaluating the *gacaca* courts is well beyond the scope of this chapter, it is worth noting that according to Lars Waldorf, "the gacaca law makes no provision for defenses and justifications, even though some perpetrators and accomplices may have colorable claims of duress." Lars Waldorf, *Mass Justice for Mass Atrocity: Rethinking Local Justice as Transitional Justice*, 79 TEMP. L. REV. 1, 33 (2006).
[59]   David Turns, *The International Criminal Tribunal for the Former Yugoslavia: The Erdemović Case*, 47 INT'L & COMP. L.Q. 461, 461 (1998).
[60]   *See* Brooks, *supra* note 1, at 865–6.

9.2 *ERDEMOVIĆ*: FACTS, OPINIONS, SOURCES OF DISAGREEMENT

The ICTY Appeals Chamber *Erdemović* decision has been called a "milestone ... in the development of international criminal law generally."[61] Because the ICTR likewise adopted the majority approach from *Erdemović*, any assessment of the legacy of the ICTY and ICTR on this legal issue must necessarily focus substantially on the *Erdemović* opinions, and on the various disagreements therein.

9.2.1 *Factual and Procedural History*

Drazen Erdemović was charged with a crime against humanity, and a violation of the laws of war, "for his participation in the execution of approximately 1,200 unarmed civilian Muslim men at the Branjevo farm near the town of Pilica in eastern Bosnia on 16 July 1995."[62]

The broader socio-military context, as recounted in the Indictment against Erdemović, begins with a UN Security Council resolution in April 1993 "demanding that all parties to the conflict in the Republic of Bosnia and Herzegovina treat Srebrenica and its surroundings as a safe area which should be free from any armed attack or any other hostile acts."[63]

Notwithstanding this resolution, around July 6, 1993, the Bosnian Serb army began an attack on this safe area, entering the city on July 11.[64] Thousands of Bosnian Muslim civilians sought refuge in and around the UN compound in Potocari.[65] Around July 12–13, the Bosnian men who had sought refuge were separated from the women and children.[66] Another group of approximately 15,000 Bosnians fled Srebrenica and went through the woods toward Tuzla.[67] A large number of Bosnian men in this group were captured by Bosnian Serb army or police personnel.[68]

Thousands of the men from these two groups "were sent to various collection sites outside of Srebrenica."[69] Between July 13 and July 22, "thousands of Bosnian Muslim men were summarily executed by members of the Bosnian Serb army and Bosnian Serb police at diverse locations" in this area.[70]

---

[61] Turns, *supra* note 59, at 462.
[62] *Erdemović*, Judgment para. 1. For other descriptions of the facts in *Erdemović*, *see* Brooks, *supra* note 1, at 863–9; Turns, *supra* note 59.
[63] Judgment para. 3 (quoting Indictment para. 1).
[64] Judgment para. 3 (quoting Indictment para. 2).
[65] Judgment para. 3 (quoting Indictment para. 3).
[66] Judgment para. 3 (quoting Indictment para. 5).
[67] Judgment para. 3 (quoting Indictment para. 6).
[68] Judgment para. 3 (quoting Indictment para. 6).
[69] Judgment para. 3 (quoting Indictment para. 7).
[70] Judgment para. 3 (quoting Indictment para. 8).

The defendant, Drazen Erdemović, was a 23-year-old member of the 10th Sabotage Detachment of the Bosnian Serb army.[71] According to Erdemović's own testimony at his sentencing hearings, which was consistent with the allegations in the Indictment, his participation in the killing occurred as follows:

> On the morning of 16 July 1995, Drazen Erdemović and seven members of the 10th Sabotage Unit of the Bosnian Serb army were ordered to leave their base at Vlasenica and go to the Pilica farm north-west of Zvornik. When they arrived there, they were informed by their superiors that buses from Srebrenica carrying Bosnian Muslim civilians between 17 and 60 years of age who had surrendered to the members of the Bosnian Serb police or army would be arriving throughout the day.
>
> Starting at 10 o'clock in the morning, members of the military police made the civilians in the first buses, all men, get off in groups of ten. The men were escorted to a field adjacent to the farm buildings where they were lined up with their backs to the firing squad. The members of the 10th Sabotage Unit, including Drazen Erdemović, who composed the firing squad then killed them. Drazen Erdemović carried out the work with an automatic weapon. The executions continued until about 3 o'clock in the afternoon. The accused estimated that there were about 20 buses in all, each carrying approximately 60 men and boys. He believes that he personally killed about seventy people.
>
> Drazen Erdemović claims that he received the order from Brano Gojkovic, commander of the operations at the Branjevo farm at Pilica, to prepare himself along with seven members of his unit for a mission the purpose of which they had absolutely no knowledge. He claimed it was only when they arrived on-site that the members of the unit were informed that they were to massacre hundreds of Muslims. He asserted his immediate refusal to do this but was threatened with instant death and told "If you don't wish to do it, stand in the line with the rest of them and give others your rifle so that they can shoot you." He declared that had he not carried out the order, he is sure he would have been killed or that his wife or child would have been directly threatened. Regarding this, he claimed to have seen Milorad Pelemis ordering someone to be killed because he had refused to obey. He reported that despite this, he attempted to spare a man between 50 and 60 years of age who said that he had saved Serbs from Srebrenica. Brano Gojkovic then told him that he did not want any surviving witness to the crime.
>
> Drazen Erdemović asserted that he then opposed the order of a lieutenant colonel to participate in the execution of five hundred Muslim men being detained in the Pilica public building. He was able not to commit this further crime because three of his comrades supported him when he refused to obey.[72]

It is worth noting, as emphasized by Judge Stephen in his dissenting opinion, that the evidence against Erdemović had come from his own confessions – his

---

[71] Judgment para. 10.

[72] Judgment para. 8 (quoting Trial Chamber); *See also* Judgment para. 3 (quoting Indictment paras. 9–12).

indictment was "based exclusively upon statements made by the Appellant to investigators from the Office of the Prosecutor of the International Tribunal but that the Trial Chamber had before it no evidence of the events forming the basis of the charges other than the Appellant's own testimony, which he gave at length on more than one occasion."[73]

At his initial appearance on May 31, 1996, Erdemović pleaded guilty to one count of a crime against humanity, explaining during his plea colloquy that he had been forced to participate in the killings on pain of death:

> Your Honour, I had to do this. If I had refused, I would have been killed together with the victims. When I refused, they told me: "If you are sorry for them, stand up, line up with them and we will kill you too." I am not sorry for myself but for my family, my wife and son who then had nine months, and I could not refuse because then they would have killed me. That is all I wish to add.[74]

The Trial Chamber sentenced Erdemović to ten years of imprisonment.[75] On appeal, Erdemović's counsel argued, among other things, that the Trial Court erred by sentencing Erdemović to ten years and by refusing to recognize the duress under which he suffered.

The Appeals Chamber requested that the parties address, among other things, the following question: "In law, may duress afford a complete defence to a charge of crimes against humanity and/or war crimes such that, if the defence is proved at trial, the accused is entitled to an acquittal?"[76] This ultimately led to the Appeals Chamber split decision, by a 3–2 vote with four separate written opinions, rejecting duress as a defense to the killing of innocents by a soldier.

The Appeals Chamber did, however, reverse Erdemović's guilty plea on the ground that it was not sufficiently informed.[77] Ultimately, Erdemović again pleaded guilty and was sentenced to five years in prison.[78]

9.2.2 *Appeals Chamber Decision in* Erdemović

At the time the Appeals Chamber decision was announced, Presiding Judge Cassese explained that the judges had "deliberated for many months in this matter" because Erdemović's case "raises issues of the greatest importance for law and morality."[79]

---

[73] *Id.*, Separate and Dissenting Opinion of Judge Stephen, para. 3.
[74] Judgment para. 4.
[75] Judgment para. 10.
[76] Judgment para. 16.
[77] Judgment para. 20.
[78] Prosecutor v. Erdemović, Case No. IT-96–22-Tbis, Sentencing Judgement, March 5, 1998, at Disposition.
[79] *Erdemović*, Press Release, Summary (Comments addressed to Mr. Erdemović by the Presiding Judge).

The Appeals Chamber consisted of five judges. Three judges – Judge McDonald, Judge Vohrah, and Judge Li – concluded "that duress does not afford a complete defence to a soldier charged with a crime against humanity and/or a war crime involving the killing of innocent human beings."[80] Two judges – Judge Stephen and Judge Cassese – disagreed and dissented on this point.[81]

The judges all agreed that the question of duress was distinct from the defense of "superior orders." It was no defense that the defendant killed simply because he was following the orders of a military superior. The judges emphasized that "[s]uperior orders and duress are conceptually distinct and separate issues," and rejecting the former as a defense does not resolve the viability of the latter.[82]

The judges also agreed that apart from whether duress could constitute a complete defense, it could serve as a proper ground for mitigation of any sentence.[83]

Turning to the validity of duress as a complete defense, the judges disagreed in at least three significant respects: disagreement about how best to characterize past precedents, disagreement about the fundamental moral questions presented, and disagreement about the process of formulating international criminal law.

9.2.2.1 Disagreement about Legal Precedent

First, there was some disagreement about how best to describe the state of international law on the question of duress as a defense to crimes involving the killing of innocents. The different opinions disagreed about the force and precedential value of certain prior decisions. For example, Judges MacDonald and Vohrah claimed that the "preponderant view of international authorities" was that duress could not be used as a defense to the killing of innocents.[84] The dissenters, Judge Stephen and Judge Cassese, disagreed with that characterization.[85]

These disagreements were substantial, but ultimately this doctrinal disagreement was not at the root of the conflict between the majority and dissenting judges. That is because all five judges recognized that there was a substantial division of opinion among the relevant legal precedents.[86] For example, notwithstanding the claim by Judge MacDonald and Judge Vohrah about the "preponderant view" of

---

[80]   *Erdemović* Judgment para. 19.
[81]   *Id.*
[82]   *Erdemović*, Joint Separate Opinion of Judge MacDonald and Judge Vohrah, paras. 34–36. *See also* Separate and Dissenting Opinion of Judge Cassese, in agreement on this point, para. 15.
[83]   *See* Erdemović, Joint Separate Opinion of Judge MacDonald and Judge Vohrah, para. 66; Separate and Dissenting Opinion of Judge Li, para. 12; Separate and Dissenting Opinion of Judge Cassese, para. 12.
[84]   *Id.*, Joint Separate Opinion of Judge MacDonald and Judge Vohrah, para. 44.
[85]   *Id.*, Separate and Dissenting Opinion of Judge Stephen, para. 24; Separate and Dissenting Opinion of Judge Cassese, paras. 20–30.
[86]   Compare Joint Separate Opinion of Judge MacDonald and Judge Vohrah, para. 32; Separate and Dissenting Opinion of Judge Li, paras. 2–3; Separate and Dissenting Opinion of Judge Stephen, para. 24; Separate and Dissenting Opinion of Judge Cassese, para. 29.

international authorities, they fundamentally concluded that "[n]o customary international law rule can be derived on the question of duress as a defence to the killing of innocent persons."[87]

Thus, no judge in *Erdemović* claimed that relevant precedent uniformly supported his or her view. While they disagreed in various respects about how best to characterize past case law, they agreed on the fundamental premise that there existed substantial support – both in international and domestic courts – for both sides of the legal issue. They all recognized that there was no uniformly settled position in international criminal law.[88]

9.2.2.2 Disagreement about Moral Principles

A second and more significant source of disagreement involved the basic moral question presented. While the moral debate on this issue is complex, the basic motivating principles can perhaps be briefly summarized as follows. On the one hand is the fundamental moral value of protecting innocent life, which mitigates against allowing for the defense of duress in this context. The defense, if permitted, excuses defendants who knowingly kill innocent persons. On the other hand is the defendant's moral guilt or culpability. If most reasonable persons would likewise choose, in the defendant's extraordinary circumstance, to kill another rather than sacrifice himself or herself, then perhaps the defendant cannot be blamed for having done so. This mitigates in favor of allowing the defense.

The majority and dissenting opinions differed in part in how they chose to resolve that moral dilemma. The judges in the majority all chose to elevate the protection of innocent life as the most fundamental value, leaving questions of the defendant's moral blameworthiness to be dealt with as a possible mitigating ground at sentencing. Judge MacDonald and Judge Vohrah explained this explicitly: "Thus, our rejection of duress as a defence to the killing of innocent human beings does not depend upon what the reasonable person is expected to do. We would assert an absolute moral postulate which is clear and unmistakable for the implementation of international humanitarian law."[89] Judge Li noted that "the main aim of international humanitarian law is the protection of innocent civilians, prisoners of war and other persons *hors de combat*."[90] Given the split of legal authority on the question presented, Judge Li concluded that "this International Tribunal cannot but opt for the solution best suited for the protection of innocent persons."[91]

---

[87]   *Id.*, Joint Separate Opinion of Judge MacDonald and Judge Vohrah, heading III.B.1.

[88]   *Id.*, Joint Separate Opinion of Judge MacDonald and Judge Vohrah, para. 32; Separate and Dissenting Opinion of Judge Li, paras. 2–3; Separate and Dissenting Opinion of Judge Stephen, para. 24; Separate and Dissenting Opinion of Judge Cassese, para. 29.

[89]   *Id.*, Joint Separate Opinion of Judge MacDonald and Judge Vohrah, para. 83.

[90]   *Id.*, Separate and Dissenting Opinion of Judge Li, para. 8.

[91]   *Id.* para. 8.

In contrast, the dissenting judges argued that there exist some cases in which the defendant cannot properly be blamed for making a choice which most other persons would likewise make. Judge Stephen distinguished Erdemović's case from that of a defendant who could have saved the victim by sacrificing his own life. "However [Erdemović] chose," Judge Stephen noted, "the lives of the innocent would be lost and he had no power to avert that consequence."[92] Erdemović's only choice was "whether or not to lay down his life for the sake of the highest of ethical principles."[93] Judge Stephen argued, "that is not the sort of choice the making of which criminal laws should enforce with penal sanctions."[94]

Judge Stephen noted that he was "alive to the concerns expressed by other members of this Appeals Chamber of the need to protect innocent life in conflicts such as that in the former Yugoslavia which involve so great a threat to innocent life."[95] But he was unwilling to enforce that principle against one who had no moral choice: "to my mind, that aim is not achieved by the denial of a just defence to one who is in no position to effect by his own will the protection of innocent life."[96]

Judge Cassese, also dissenting, argued that "Law is based on what society can reasonably expect of its members. It should not set intractable standards of behaviour which require mankind to perform acts of martyrdom, and brand as criminal any behaviour falling below those standards."[97]

Much of the scholarly commentary on *Erdemović* focuses on this difficult moral problem.[98]

---

[92] *Id.*, Separate and Dissenting Opinion of Judge Stephen, para. 54.
[93] *Id.* para. 54.
[94] *Id.*
[95] *Id.* para. 65.
[96] *Id.* para. 65.
[97] *Id.*, Separate and Dissenting Opinion of Judge Cassese, para. 47.
[98] For commentators defending the conclusion of the majority, *see* Brooks, *supra* note 1, at 880 ("Although I have been sympathetic in this essay to the views of Cassese and the Model Penal Code drafters ... I tend to think that if I had been in the Appeals Chamber at the Hague, I would ultimately have joined the plurality decision ... As the plurality says, when push comes to shove there seems to be an 'absolute moral postulate' that says that killing innocent people in order to save ones [sic] own life is always wrong."); Saira Mohamed, *Deviance, Aspiration, and the Stories We Tell: Reconciling Mass Atrocity and the Criminal Law*, 124 YALE L.J. 1628, 1680 (2015) (criticizing the majority for insisting that Erdemović could have behaved differently from the ordinary person because he was a soldier, but defending the view that the law should be aspirational, both in "reinforcing clear prohibitions against killing" as well as "voicing that the law operates in horrific situations"). For commentators defending the view of the dissenting judges, *see, e.g.*, Chiesa, *supra* note 47, at 773 ("Erdemović should have prevailed on a plea of duress. Because he could not have prevented the deaths of his victims even if he had resisted coercion, it is unfair to punish him for choosing to yield to the coercion in order to save his own life. Hence, although the fact that he lacked the capacity to prevent the death of the civilians should not be considered a sufficient reason to justify his conduct, it offers compelling grounds for excusing his admittedly wrongful act."); Noam Wiener, *Excuses, Justifications, and Duress at the International Criminal Tribunals*, 26 PACE INT'L L. REV. 88, 128–9, 131 (2014)("If the judges at the ICC wish to bolster the legitimacy of the organization by acting

9.2.2.3 Disagreement about the Process of Formulating International Criminal Law

The third disagreement – which has received less scholarly attention – relates to the process of formulating international criminal law. In particular, how should an international tribunal assess the validity of a defense when the weight of international and domestic authorities is deeply divided as to the validity of the defense? Does the division indicate that the defense is not part of international criminal law? Or should the tribunal resolve such a difference in favor of the defendant?[99]

Entirely apart from the moral disagreement noted above, the majority and dissenting opinions charted out distinctly different approaches to this process question. Because this feature of *Erdemović* has not received much scholarly attention, and because it represents a significant puzzle for international criminal law, this chapter focuses most of its attention on assessing the merits of the majority and dissenting approaches to this question: how to formulate international criminal law, in particular with respect to defenses, in the face of significant disagreement among national and international precedent.

9.3 FORMULATING DEFENSES IN INTERNATIONAL CRIMINAL LAW: SEEKING CONSENSUS ON CONDEMNATION

The defense of duress as discussed in *Erdemović* raises a complex question as to how international criminal law should recognize defenses in general, in particular for defenses which enjoy partial but not universal recognition among states.

International instruments do not explain precisely how courts should formulate defenses – they generally instruct courts to look to general principles of law. The UN Secretary-General, in a report on the responsibilities of the ICTY, stated the following: "The International Tribunal [the ICTY] itself will have to decide on various personal defences which may relieve a person of individual criminal responsibility, such as minimum age or mental incapacity, drawing upon general principles of law recognised by all nations."[100] The International Law Commission's Draft Code of Crimes against the Peace and Security of Mankind likewise states that a tribunal "shall determine the admissibility of defences in accordance with the general principles of law, in the light of the character of each crime."[101] The Commentary

---

> towards the perpetrators as ends rather than as means, thereby claiming the moral high-ground and refusing to treat them as they treated their victims, they will follow in the footsteps of the NMTs and refuse to hold responsible individuals who are inculpable because they had no choice but to commit the crimes because of duress.")

99   Alexander Greenawalt argues that in the face of disagreement, an international tribunal should apply the law of the domestic jurisdiction in which the crime took place. *See* Greenawalt, *supra* note 47.

100 Report of the Secretary-General pursuant to paragraph 2 of Security Council resolution 808 (1993), UN Doc. S/25704, para. 58.

101 Report of the International Law Commission on the Work of its Forty-eighth Session, May 6–July 26, 1996, GAOR, 51st Sess., Supp. No.10, UN Doc. A/51/10, Article 14, 39.

further explains that a court assessing a defense "must consider the validity of the defence raised by the accused under general principles of law," limiting possible defenses "to those defences that are well-established and widely recognized as admissible with respect to similarly serious crimes under national or international law."[102]

Cherif Bassiouni states that "[i]ncreasingly, comparative criminal law and procedure furnishes international law through 'general principles of law,' which are identified from national laws with norms of the 'general part' and the 'procedural part' of domestic criminal law."[103] With respect to defenses, "[t]he 'general part' of ICL, which includes elements of criminal responsibility and factors exonerating from criminal responsibility, are established by 'general principles of law,' which are a source of international law, but which are derived from national legal systems."[104]

Bassiouni identifies major questions yet to be resolved:

> How do the various defenses or exonerating conditions arise in ICL? If their legal source is "general principles of law," how are these principles identified, and by what method? What is the influence of the jurisprudence of the international tribunals on the evolution of these questions?[105]

This chapter makes two contributions toward resolving some of those questions, using the opinions in *Erdemović* to illustrate the choices to be made. The first contribution is to show how courts, when assessing whether a particular defense is available under international criminal law, can manipulate the outcome by either combining or separating the legal questions presented. This process, illustrated by the opinions in *Erdemović*, raises the obvious concern that courts can manipulate international criminal law toward desired ends.

The second contribution is an attempt to resolve this problem and to articulate a principled general approach that international tribunals should use when evaluating a defense that is accepted by some nations and rejected by others. In formulating international criminal law, courts should ask whether most nations would criminally condemn the defendant in the circumstances described – considering both offenses and defenses at the same time. Jurists should not disaggregate the offense from the defense – that is, should not separately evaluate international consensus for offenses and international consensus for defenses. When there is significant division among national legal authorities over the availability of the defense, this means that the defense should presumptively be available under international law. This is because a division over the availability of a defense indicates that there is not consensus among

---

[102] *Id.*, Commentary to Article 14, para. 3, 39.
[103] M. Cherif Bassiouni, The Discipline of International Criminal Law 6 (*in* 1 INTERNATIONAL CRIMINAL LAW (M. Cherif Bassiouni ed., 3rd edn. 2008).
[104] *Id.* at 8.
[105] BASSIOUNI, CRIMES AGAINST HUMANITY 583.

the international community to criminally condemn the defendant in the particular circumstances present.

9.3.1 The Process of Formulating International Criminal Law: Aggregation and Disaggregation

When evaluating whether a particular defense is part of international criminal law through wide acceptance in state practice, jurists must choose whether to consider different legal issues separately – for example, to disaggregate the offense from the defense in question – or whether to aggregate the legal issues and consider them all together.

To "disaggregate" is to take the approach of considering a particular offense (say, crimes against humanity) separately from the particular defense (say, duress). Indeed, one could disaggregate the legal issues even further, separately considering whether different parts of a defense (or offense) are each independently supported by international agreement.

To "aggregate" is to ask this same question about state practice, but to apply it to the offense and applicable defense all together (not separately).

The aggregation/disaggregation decision, and its implications, are illustrated by the defense of duress to a homicide crime against humanity, and by the different discussions of state practice in the *Erdemović* opinions.

As discussed above, Erdemović sought to plead duress as a defense to the offense of crimes against humanity – the killing of about 70 civilians. He argued that he attempted to refuse the order to participate in the killings, and participated only after he had been informed, credibly, that if he did not participate he would also be killed.

In effect, the majority in *Erdemović* framed its analysis as follows:

A. Under international criminal law, does the intentional killing of civilians during wartime constitute a crime against humanity?
B. Under international criminal law, is duress available as a legal defense for a soldier who kills innocent persons and would otherwise be guilty of a crime against humanity?

The answer to the first question, not in dispute in *Erdemović*, is yes – this is evident from longstanding state practice and international authorities, as well as the statute of the ICTY.[106] The answer to the second question was not so simple, as the ICTY statute neither adopted nor rejected duress as a defense. Thus the court had to turn to both customary international law and general principles of law. Surveying the law of both international tribunals and domestic courts, the majority found that that there was not sufficient consensus in international or domestic law to support statement

---

[106] *See* Bassiouni, Crimes Against Humanity 361–5; ICTY Statute art. 5, *supra* note 33.

(B) either as a matter of customary international law or based on general principles of law.

Judge Cassese dissented, arguing that duress should be recognized as a defense in a case like Erdemović's. In part, his dissent was based on disaggregating parts of the defense of duress, and framing the relevant questions as follows:

A. Under international criminal law, does the intentional killing of civilians during wartime constitute a crime against humanity?
B. Duress
    i.   Under international criminal law, is duress is generally available as a defense to criminal charges?
    ii. Under international criminal law, is there an exception that denies the defense of duress for offenses involving the killing of an innocent person?

Thus, Judge Cassese separated, or disaggregated, the international law question for the defense of duress into two questions rather than one. In so doing – and even acknowledging the same general trends in the law recognized by the majority – he came to the opposite conclusion from the *Erdemović* majority.

In Judge Cassese's disaggregated inquiry, the answers are [A] "Yes," [B.i] "Yes," and [B.ii] "No." That is, international law (on Judge Cassese's view) can be said to reflect the following: [A] this conduct is an offense under international criminal law; and [B.i] duress is generally recognized as a defense. In contrast, international law does not support [B.ii] – that homicide offenses should be excluded from duress. By framing the questions in this manner, Judge Cassese concluded that Erdemović should be entitled to invoke the duress defense, unencumbered by the limitation that excludes it from homicide offenses – a limitation not part of customary international law or general principles of law.

In part, then, the dispute between the majority and the dissent turned on the question of whether to aggregate or disaggregate the legal issues involved when assessing the state of international law. While Judge Cassese disaggregated the duress question into two separate issues, he did not offer a general theoretical account of why that move would be appropriate. The majority implicitly rejected that disaggregation – by refusing to engage in it – but also did not explain why disaggregation is or is not appropriate.

The aggregation/disaggregation question presents even more options than those illustrated by the majority and Judge Cassese – and different formulations produce different results. The legal issues can be broken down in various ways, from fully aggregated to very disaggregated, as shown below:

1. Fully aggregating all legal issues:
    A. Under international criminal law, is the defendant in this case, if he committed the conduct as alleged, guilty of the offense charged (taking into account possible defenses as well as the elements of the offense)?

2. Disaggregating the offense and the defense (*Erdemović* majority approach):
   A. Under international criminal law, does the intentional killing of civilians during wartime constitute a crime against humanity?
   B. Under international criminal law, is duress available as a legal defense for a soldier who kills innocent persons and would otherwise be guilty of a crime against humanity?
3. Disaggregating the offense and the defense, and sub-parts of the defense (*Erdemović* Judge Cassese approach):
   A. Under international criminal law, does the intentional killing of civilians during wartime constitute a crime against humanity?
   B. Duress
      i. Under international criminal law, is duress is generally available as a defense to criminal charges?
      ii. Under international criminal law, is there an exception that denies the defense of duress for offenses involving the killing of an innocent person?

A creative lawyer or jurist could no doubt disaggregate questions further into sub-issues raised by the offense and sub-issues raised by the defense. With the right mix of aggregation and disaggregation, a court could presumably reach any conclusion it desired.

As explained above, the second approach (disaggregating the offense and the defense) leads to the conclusion that the defense of duress is not available to Erdemović. The third approach (further disaggregating sub-parts of the defense of duress) leads to the conclusion that the defense of duress is available to Erdemović.

The first approach above – full aggregation of the offense and defense – likewise leads to the conclusion that the defense of duress should be available to Erdemović. Rather than separately asking whether the offense is supported by international law and whether the defense is supported by international law, the first approach consolidates all legal issues in the case into one question – whether international law supports the conclusion that the defendant is guilty of an offense.

9.3.2 *Seeking Consensus on Condemnation*

In the context of international criminal law, courts should seek a consensus of condemnation: broad agreement from national legal systems that the defendant's conduct, in the circumstances in which it occurred, is deserving of criminal conviction and punishment. Neha Jain notes that "[i]nternational criminal tribunals represent the exercise of coercive power by the international community, where the tribunals claim the authority to try and punish individuals alleged to have violated fundamental norms of humanity."[107] To properly claim this authority, it should be

---

[107] Neha Jain, *Judicial Lawmaking and General Principles of Law in International Criminal Law*, 57 HARV. INT'L L.J. 111, 115 (2016).

the case that – whether through the mechanism of a written treaty, customary international law, or general principles of law – most nations agree that a defendant's conduct does violate a fundamental norm of humanity.

In the context of offenses, seeking a consensus of condemnation means that courts should look for broad agreement as to the offense: if all nations agree that a defendant who commits Offense X is a proper subject of criminal condemnation, then Offense X may be a proper basis for international criminal liability.

In the context of possible defenses, seeking a consensus of condemnation leads to a different analysis. Courts should look for broad agreement that the defense is not available to this defendant. If all nations agree that Defense Y is no defense to Offense X, then the defense should be rejected as a matter of international criminal law, because all nations agree that the defendant who commits Offense X under the circumstances of Defense Y is nonetheless a proper subject for conviction and punishment. But if there is broad disagreement as to Defense Z, then Defense Z should be available under international criminal law. This is because, if some nations recognize Defense Z as a defense to Offense X, there is no consensus of condemnation: no broad agreement in the community of nations that a defendant who commits Offense X in the circumstances of Defense Z should be properly punished and convicted.

Viewed this way, Erdemović (assuming he could prove the facts of his defense) should have been found not guilty under international criminal law. About half of jurisdictions would deem him guilty, and about half would deem him not guilty. All jurisdictions recognize that the killing of innocents is a grave offense. Common law jurisdictions – which generally reject the duress defense for homicide crimes – would thus find him guilty of that grave offense. In contrast, civil law countries – which generally allow duress as a potential defense to all crimes – would find him not guilty.

Fundamentally, then, the defense might frame the issue as follows: would most jurisdictions deem Erdemović to be guilty of the offense charged? The answer is no – about half of jurisdictions would recognize his duress defense and thus find him not guilty, notwithstanding the fact that he committed the elements of an offense.

I now turn to criticize both the majority and Judge Cassese's dissent in *Erdemović* and then further explain why the proper approach is to seek a consensus on condemnation.

9.3.2.1 Majority Approach: Separately Evaluate the Offense and the Defense

The *Erdemović* majority takes what appear to be the two questions most directly presented, and addresses each in turn: first, whether the offense charged is recognized under international criminal law, and second, whether the defense claimed is likewise recognized. Judge Cassese, in contrast, might be accused of manipulating matters by separating the "duress" question into two sub-parts, so as to achieve the result he desires.

Jurists and commentators are accustomed to considering offenses and defenses as conceptually distinct, and evaluating them on their own terms. Certainly in the realm of international criminal law, it is easy to see the separation between offenses and defenses. Offenses are often codified and are the subject of much discussion. Both in codes and treatises, defenses typically occupy a separate section.[108] In some instances – such as in the IMT and in the ad hoc tribunals – defenses were left partly or entirely unarticulated, left to the court to determine, whereas offenses are set out expressly.[109]

At the same time, it is not clear what fundamental principles, if any, are reflected by this conventional separation and taxonomy of offenses versus defenses. It may simply reflect convenience and ease of use to consider them separately. In particular, there is no theoretical reason that a particular jurisdiction might not incorporate certain defenses into the definition of the offense itself. Cherif Bassiouni observes that "[l]egal systems differ as to how they characterize" defenses, broadly thought of as those "questions of law that stand in the way of finding criminal responsibility or applying a criminal sanction to a person charged with a crime."[110] Not all legal systems agree as to which factors relating to criminal responsibility are (1) an element of the offense charged versus (2) aspects of a defense that might be raised to defeat the charge. "For example, sanity may be deemed a foundational condition for criminal responsibility, whereas insanity may be deemed an exonerating factor, a legal excuse, or a legal defense."[111]

Accordingly, the conventional separation of factors as relating to "elements of an offense" versus "defenses" may not reflect any deep conceptual principle. It may be the case that different states all recognize that some minimum legal of mental sanity is a prerequisite for criminal blameworthiness of the defendant, even though some states view that mental sanity as an element of the offense while others view a lack of sanity as a defense to the charge.

In *Erdemović*, the majority does not provide any foundational principle justifying its decision to separately evaluate (1) the existence of the offense under international law and (2) the existence of the defense under international law.

---

[108]   *See, e.g.*, Rome Statute of the International Criminal Court, Articles 5–9 (crimes and elements) versus Articles 31–33 (grounds for excluding criminal responsibility and other defenses); BASSIOUNI, CRIMES AGAINST HUMANITY, Chapters 1–6 (discussing the history and nature of the offense of crimes against humanity) versus Chapter 8 ("Defenses and Exonerations"); SCHABAS, THE INTERNATIONAL CRIMINAL COURT; M. Cherif BASSIOUNI, A Draft International Criminal Code and a Draft Statute for an International Criminal Tribunal (1987).

[109]   *See infra* note 33.

[110]   M. CHERIF BASSIOUNI, CRIMES AGAINST HUMANITY: HISTORICAL EVOLUTION AND CONTEMPORARY APPLICATION 581 (2011).

[111]   *Id.*

Moreover, the majority fails to grapple with the fundamental notion that condemnation through an international criminal tribunal should reflect an international consensus that a defendant in these circumstances should be convicted and punished. When a large number of jurisdictions would afford the defendant a valid defense in the circumstances, then this fundamental principle is not satisfied and the defense should be available.

9.3.2.2 Judge Cassese: Dividing Duress into "General Approach" versus "Exceptions"

Judge Cassese reached the opposite conclusion from the majority judges. In part, his conclusion reflected his disagreement on the basic moral question presented – balancing the protection of innocent life against the arguable lack of culpability of one who operates under true duress.

In part, however, Judge Cassese himself justified his conclusion by framing the relevant questions of international law in a manner different from the majority. Rather than first considering the status of the offense under ICL, and then second considering the status of the defense of duress under ICL, Judge Cassese further subdivided the relevant analysis as related to duress.

Judge Cassese accused the majority of drawing the wrong conclusion from its detailed analysis of international and domestic precedents:

> [A]fter finding that no specific international rule has evolved on the question of whether duress affords a complete defence to the killing of innocent persons, the majority should have drawn the only conclusion imposed by law and logic, namely that the general rule on duress should apply – subject, of course, to the necessary requirements.[112]

According to Judge Cassese, this was a simple failure of logic: "In logic, if no exception to a general rule be proved, then the general rule prevails."[113]

Judge Cassese argued that the "manifest inconsistency of State practice warrants the dismissal of the Prosecution's contention: no special customary rule has evolved in international law on whether or not duress can be admitted as a defence in case of crimes involving the killing of persons."[114] Judge Cassese further explained that "the Appeals Chamber majority does not draw from the absence of that special rule the only conclusion logically warranted: that one must apply, on a case-by-case basis, the general rule on duress to all categories of crime, whether or not they involve killing."[115]

---

[112] *Erdemović*, Separate and Dissenting Opinion of Judge Cassese, para. 11.
[113] *Id.* para. 11.
[114] *Id.* para. 40.
[115] *Id.* para. 41.

Judge Cassese thus contrasts the "general rule" of duress from the "special rule" prohibiting duress as a defense to homicide offenses. In his view, the "general rule" of duress is part of customary international law, whereas the "special rule" rejecting it for homicide offense is not part of customary international law.

Accordingly, Judge Cassese did not believe that he was left with the intractable conflict faced by the majority: "[w]hat I have argued so far leads me to the conclusion that international criminal law on duress is not ambiguous or uncertain."[116]

Judge Cassese's approach is based on the following premises:

1. The "general rule": As a general matter, duress is recognized as a defense by all legal systems, and thus is a rule of ICL.
2. The "special rule": Some jurisdictions (predominantly common law systems) have adopted an exclusion or limitation on this general rule of duress, precluding the defense categorically in cases involving the killing of an innocent person. This "special rule" (exclusion or limitation) is rejected by a substantial number of international and domestic authorities, and thus is not a part of ICL.

While I will soon defend Judge Cassese's ultimate conclusion, this form of analysis is itself logically flawed. The flaw comes at step one, in which Judge Cassese purports to articulate a "general rule" accepted by all nations. A common law judge could properly object that Statement 1 is false – it is not correct to say that all nations recognize duress as a defense *in general*. Rather, it would be correct to state that all nations recognize duress as a defense *to nonhomicide offenses*.

It is thus not clear why duress can be called the "general rule" and the common law limitation a "special rule." Instead, the "general rule," properly formulated to reflect the actual acceptance of duress among domestic legal systems, would reflect the fact that duress is generally accepted as a defense by all legal systems to nonhomicide offenses.

So formulated, the "general rule" of duress does not resolve Erdemović's case. Judge Cassese is left in the same difficult position as the majority: with a "general rule" that does not apply to Erdemović, and a deeply divided set of precedents on the defense that might apply to Erdemović.

9.3.2.3 A Principled Approach: Seeking a Consensus on Condemnation

Cherif Bassiouni identifies international criminal law not as a unitary doctrine, but a discipline of various components "bound by their functional relationship in the pursuit of its value-oriented goals."[117] He identifies those goals as including "the prevention and suppression of international criminality, enhancement of accountability and reduction of impunity, and the establishment of international criminal justice."[118] Bassiouni

---

[116] *Id.* para. 49.
[117] M. Cherif Bassiouni, The Discipline of International Criminal Law 3, *in* 1 International Criminal Law.
[118] *Id.*

argues that ICL's "functional goals of prevention and suppression of international criminality" are fundamentally "an extension of the same goals of national criminal law in the prevention and suppression of national criminality."[119]

Bassiouni identifies four factors driving the "values and policies of ICL":

> (1) the mutual interests of states in cooperating to prevent and suppress international and domestic criminality, (2) the demands of national sovereignty, (3) the impulse for humanistic and humanitarian values, and (4) the needs of the world order.[120]

The twin concerns reflected in these purposes are first, the coordination and cooperation of separate and nations of the world, and second, the prevention and suppression of criminality as an expression of humanistic and humanitarian values.

In formulating a principled approach to aggregation/disaggregation, then, jurists should consider both the substantive goals of preventing and suppressing international criminality and the cooperative goal of adequately mediating potentially competing interests and values among different sovereign nations.

One approach toward achieving both of these goals – punishing international criminality while mediating disagreements among nations – is to compare various approaches among different states, and to accept residual points of agreement about imposition of criminal liability, rejecting it in cases in which a substantial number of states would not impose criminal liability.

The lodestar of formulating rules of international criminal law should not be simply whether one isolated legal rule or sub-rule enjoys broad acceptance and endorsement among states. Rather, the fundamental principle is that international criminal law should coalesce around those circumstances in which a broad number of states together stand willing to condemn a defendant as guilty of a particular offense. If most state legal systems stand willing to condemn a particular defendant, in a particular set of circumstances, then the underlying purposes of international criminal law are served: the punishment of international criminality and the mediation of differences among nations. Only when there is a consensus on condemnation can it be said that the defendant has "violated fundamental norms of humanity."[121]

This suggests that courts must recognize the different implications of state disagreement as to *offenses* versus state disagreement as to *defenses*.

When considering offenses, or modes of imposing criminal liability (such as conspiracy or aiding and abetting), a split in state authority and practice indicates that the offense should be *rejected* as part of international criminal law. This is because the split of authority for defining offenses indicates that some significant portion of states would not stand willing to criminally condemn a defendant in the

---

[119] *Id.* at 9–10.
[120] *Id.* at 17.
[121] Neha Jain, *Judicial Lawmaking and General Principles of Law in International Criminal Law*, 57 HARV. INT'L L.J. 111, 115 (2016).

given circumstances. Thus a rule of international law providing for criminal conviction in those circumstances does not enjoy the broad support of state practice.

In contrast, when considering defenses, or modes of rejecting criminal liability, a
substantial split in state authority and practice indicates that the defense should be
accepted as part of international criminal law. This is because the split of authority for
defining defenses indicates that some significant portion of states would not stand
willing to criminally condemn a defendant in the given circumstances – the presence
of the defense accepted by some but not all states. Thus a rule of international law
rejecting this type of defense would result in convictions of persons in circumstances
in which a broad swath of state practice would not support conviction.

9.4 CONCLUSION

The case law of the ICTY and ICTR, in particular the *Erdemović* decision, contributed significantly toward the evolution of duress as a defense to war crimes and crimes
against humanity in international criminal law. The four opinions in *Erdemović*
provide fertile ground for both proponents and opponents of the defense of duress.

In *Erdemović*, Judge Cassese and Judge Stephen were right to conclude that under
the principles of customary international law, Erdemović should have been entitled
to raise the defense of duress. Judge Cassese's reasoning was flawed, however,
because he falsely claimed the existence of a "general rule" of duress that encompassed all offenses, when no such "general rule" in fact exists under international law.

The majority was wrong to reject Erdemović's possible duress defense. While it
recognized the significant split of authority within international, military, and
domestic legal authorities on this question, it drew the wrong conclusion from
that divergence.

For an offense, substantial disagreement among state authorities indicates that the
offense is not part of ICL. This is because the disagreement indicates that a
substantial number of nations do not stand willing to condemn the defendant
under the circumstances – there is not an international law consensus to support
the existence of the offense. But for a defense, substantial disagreement among state
authorities indicates that the defense should be viewed as available under ICL. That
is because the disagreement among states indicates that a substantial number of
nations do not stand willing to condemn the defendant under the circumstances –
and thus there is not an international law consensus to prohibit the defense and thus
condemn the defendant. This approach correctly reflects the fundamental principles of international criminal law of punishing international criminality while
appropriately mediating the legal differences among nations.

10

Sentencing Policies of the Ad Hoc Tribunals

Yvonne M. Dutton

This chapter examines the legacy that the ICTY and ICTR have produced through their sentencing policies, practices, and decisions. Together, the two ad hoc tribunals have sentenced more than 140 defendants for their involvement in genocide, crimes against humanity, and war crimes during conflicts in the former Yugoslavia and Rwanda.[1] Although both tribunals have imposed life sentences, the Rwandan tribunal has sentenced far more defendants to life terms than has the ICTY. Further, the ICTY's sentences appear to be relatively lenient overall as compared to the ICTR's sentences.[2] Scholars have noted these apparently divergent outcomes, and a significant body of literature has addressed the question of whether the tribunals' sentencing practice is inconsistent.[3]

This chapter also addresses the issue of the consistency of the tribunals' sentencing practice. It acknowledges that consistency is a fundamental principle of criminal justice in that like cases should be treated similarly in approach and outcome.[4] On the other hand, fairness also dictates that sentences be individualized to reflect the particular circumstances of the crime, as well as the defendant's circumstances. This chapter's review of the empirical literature examining the tribunals' sentencing decisions shows that sentencing outcomes are comparable when one considers the gravity of the crime for which the sentence was imposed, as well as relevant aggravating and mitigating factors. Brief case studies of some of the tribunals' sentencing decisions further bolsters this conclusion.

---

[1] The ICTY sentenced eighty-three defendants and the ICTR sentenced sixty-two.

[2] *See* Margaret M. deGuzman, *Harsh Justice for International Crimes?*, 39 YALE J. INT'L L. 1, 8 (2006).

[3] *See, e.g.,* Barbora Hola, Catrien Bijleveld, & Alette Smeulers, *Consistency of International Sentencing: ICTY and ICTR case study*, 9 EUR. J. OF CRIMINOLOGY 539, 540 (2012); Barbora Hola, *Sentencing of International Crimes at the ICTY and ICTR: Consistency of Sentencing Case Law*, 4 AMSTERDAM LAW FORUM 3, 4 (2012); Mirko Bagaric & John Morss, *International Sentencing Law: In Search of a Justification and Coherent Framework*, 6 INT'L. CRIM. L. REV. 191 (2006); Mark A. Drumbl, *Collective Violence and Individual Punishment: The Criminality of Mass Atrocity*, 99 Nw. U. L. REV. 539, 592 (2005).

[4] *See* Hola, Bijleveld & Smeulers, *supra* note 3, at 540; James Meernick & Kimi King, *The Sentencing Determinants of the International Criminal Tribunal for the Former Yugoslavia: An Empirical and Doctrinal Analysis*, 16 LEIDEN J. INT'L L. 717, 717–18 (2003).

The chapter concludes that the ad hoc tribunals have contributed a legacy toward a uniform and coherent sentencing approach in the field of international criminal law. As noted in other chapters, for the purposes of this book, "legacy" is defined as the enduring influence of the tribunals' work and processes on the ideals, conceptions, and instrumentalities of international criminal law, justice, and human rights. The Trial Chambers have not always been as transparent as they might be in their sentencing decisions. Nor have they employed or adhered to a uniform set of sentencing guidelines. Nevertheless, the evidence demonstrates that the tribunals have developed and consistently employed sentencing principles that tie sentencing severity to both the gravity of the crime and relevant aggravating and mitigating factors. Moreover, reviewing some of the ICC's sentencing policies and practices shows that the tribunals' work has already been emulated, thus ensuring the enduring influence of the tribunals' work as regards sentencing in international criminal law.

10.1 TRIBUNAL SENTENCING LAW AND PROCEDURE

The tribunal statutes are nearly identical in vesting Trial Chamber judges with wide discretion in sentencing convicted defendants.[5] Both counsel judges to "take into account such factors as the gravity of the offence and the individual circumstances of the convicted person."[6] The tribunals' Rules of Procedure and Evidence (RPE) contain some additional sentencing guidance. RPE Rule 101 limits the maximum prison sentence to life.[7] That same rule also instructs judges to consider any aggravating circumstances and "any mitigating circumstances including the substantial cooperation with the Prosecutor by the convicted person before or after conviction."[8] The statutes permit the tribunal judges to refer to national laws and principles when deciding on what sentence to impose, though there is little evidence that they have done so.[9] With these few restrictions, tribunal judges have otherwise been free to develop their own sentencing jurisprudence, including how to assess gravity and the factors that will increase or decrease sentence length.

10.1.1 *Gravity and Individual Circumstances*

The tribunals' jurisprudence shows that judges have heeded the instruction to consider gravity, individual circumstances, and aggravating and mitigating factors when making sentencing determinations. As to gravity, the judges often state that it

---

[5]   Three-judge Trial Chamber panels determine sentences in the first instance. Both the prosecution and the defense may appeal any sentence to a shared five-judge Appeals Chamber.
[6]   ICTY Statute, UN Doc. S/Res/827, Art. 24; ICTR Statute, UN Doc. S/Res/955, Art. 23.
[7]   ICTY/ICTR Rules of Procedure and Evidence, Rule 101 (A).
[8]   ICTY/ICTR Rules of Procedure and Evidence, Rule 101 (B).
[9]   *See* Hola, Bijleveld, & Smeulers, *supra* note 3, at 540–1.

is the most important sentence determinant.[10] The case law tends to emphasize gravity *in concreto*, rather than *in abstracto*. Instead of assessing gravity based solely on the subjective and objective elements of the crimes, the judges look to the facts of the particular case. Judges generally consider gravity *in concreto* to encompass (1) the particular circumstances of the crime, including the amount of harm caused, the scale of the crime, the number of victims, and the amount of victim suffering; in addition to (2) the offender's culpability, including the form and degree of the accused's participation in the crime.[11] One caveat is that the Trial Chambers have not always been consistent in what factors they include in their gravity calculus. For example, some include the number of victims in their gravity calculation, while some consider the number of victims as an aggravating factor. Although this inconsistency in practice is in some ways unfortunate, judges are not permitted to "double count": if the chamber included a factor in the gravity analysis, the chamber may not include it as an aggravating factor.[12] Further, the Appeals Chamber has indicated that it is not troubled by the different practices employed, stating that although gravity and aggravating circumstances are distinct concepts, the Trial Chambers have discretion "as to the rubric under which they treat particular factors."[13]

Given the limited sentencing guidance in the tribunal statutes and the RPE, judges are vested with wide discretion in determining what individual circumstances will increase or decrease sentence length, as well as the weight to be accorded any particular circumstance. The prosecution has the burden of proving any aggravating factors to the Trial Chamber beyond a reasonable doubt. Aggravating factors must relate specifically to the conduct underlying the crimes the defendant is charged with committing. For mitigating factors, the burden is lower. The defense need only prove these by a preponderance of the evidence. Further, mitigating factors need not be tied to the offense conduct.[14]

The ICTY and the ICTR have found that many different individual circumstances may aggravate or mitigate a sentence.[15] Frequently cited aggravating factors include (1) abuse of one's superior or authoritative position; (2) the cruelty of the attack; (3) the defendant's active participation in the attack; (4) the large number of

[10] *See, e.g., Prosecutor* v. *Mucic et al.*, Judgment, Case No. IT-96-21, Trial Chamber, Nov. 16, 1998, para. 1182; *Prosecutor* v. *Akeyesu*, Judgment, Case No. ICTR-96-4-A, Appeals Chamber, June 1, 2001, para. 131.

[11] *See* Barbora Hola, Alette Smeulers & Catrien Bijleveld, *International Sentencing Facts and Figures: Sentencing Practice at the ICTY and ICTR*, 9 J. INT'L CRIM. JUST. 411, 415 (2011).

[12] *See* Joseph W. Doherty & Richard H. Steinberg, *Punishment and Policy in International Criminal Sentencing: An Empirical Study*, 110 AM. J. INT'L L. 49, 54 (2016). *See also* Prosecutor v. Deronjic, Judgment on Sentencing Appeal, Case No. IT-02-61-A, Appeals Chamber, July 20, 2005, paras. 106–7.

[13] Prosecutor v. Hadzihasaovic & Kubura, Judgment, Case No. IT-01-47-A, Appeals Chamber, Apr. 22, 2008, para. 317.

[14] *See* Hola, *supra* note 3, at 10; Hola, Smeulers, & Bijleveld, *supra* note 11, at 419–20.

[15] *See, e.g.*, William R. Pruitt, *Aggravating and Mitigating Sentencing Factors at the ICTR – An Exploratory Analysis*, 14 INT'L CRIM. L. REV. 148, 153 (2014) (referencing the point about discretion in the ICTR context).

victims harmed; and (5) the extra suffering of victims.[16] Frequently cited mitigating factors include (1) providing assistance to victims; (2) the defendant's otherwise good character; (3) the defendant's family circumstances; (4) the defendant's decision to plead guilty; and (5) the defendant's cooperation with the prosecution.[17] In general, research reveals no significant differences between the ICTY and the ICTR in the types of circumstances the Trial Chambers cite as aggravating or mitigating factors.[18] On the other hand, research also reveals that some types of individual circumstances can be either aggravating or mitigating factors depending on the specific facts of the case. For instance, in some cases, the judges treated the defendant's education or respected status as an aggravating factor, while in other cases, judges accepted those factors in mitigation.[19]

10.1.2 *Sentencing Procedures and Decisions*

Since 1998, the RPE require the prosecution and defense to submit evidence relevant to sentencing at the conclusion of the trial, instead of at a separate sentencing hearing after the Trial Chamber has made a decision on guilt. The judges modified the RPE to abandon the two-phase common law approach in favor of the civil law approach where guilt and punishment are addressed concurrently.[20] Accordingly, after evidence of guilt has been submitted, the prosecution and defense immediately present any evidence regarding aggravating and mitigating factors.[21] The Trial Chambers thereafter announce the counts of conviction and the sentence in the same judgment.[22] As one might expect, this practice has not been without criticism. Combining the guilt and sentencing phase necessarily has the benefit of efficiency: it saves time and money associated with holding a separate hearing. Yet critics charge that the procedure is unfair to defendants and undermines their right to be presumed innocent until proven otherwise. The procedure requires a defendant present evidence to mitigate their guilt *before* any final determination as to guilt.[23] As a result, some defense counsel refuse to present mitigating evidence prior to the final verdict because they believe it would constitute an admission of guilt on their client's behalf.[24]

---

[16] *See* Hola, Smeulers, & Bijleveld, *supra* note 11, at 435.

[17] *See id.* at 433.

[18] *Id.* at 433, 435.

[19] *See* Hola, *supra* note 3, at 14 and n. 30.

[20] *See* Andrew N. Keller, *Punishment for Violations of International Criminal Law: An Analysis of Sentencing at the ICTY and ICTR*, 12 Ind. Int'l & Comp. L. Rev. 53, 67–8 (2001).

[21] *See, e.g.*, Jennifer J. Clark, *Zero to Life: Sentencing Appeals at the International Criminal Tribunals for the Former Yugoslavia and Rwanda*, 96 Georgetown L. J. 1685, 1688 (2008). *See also* Pruitt, *supra* note 15, at 154 (noting the requirement of presenting evidence on mitigating factors prior to a final verdict on guilt).

[22] *See* RPE Rule 87 (requiring the Trial Chamber to impose sentences if it finds the accused guilty of the charges).

[23] Keller, *supra* note 20, at 68–9.

[24] Pruitt, *supra* note 15, at 154.

The Trial Chamber's final sentence is supposed to reflect the totality of the criminal conduct for which the defendant was convicted. At the ICTY and ICTR, most defendants are convicted of multiple counts, and since 2000, tribunal judges have typically handed down one global sentence.[25] This practice of global sentencing is reflected in RPE Rule 87(C), which offers judges the option to "impose a single sentence reflecting the totality of the criminal conduct of the accused,"[26] instead of imposing a sentence for each of the offenses separately. As some have pointed out, this practice of issuing global sentences provides less transparency. Although the Trial Chambers generally state that the sentence imposed reflects the totality of the defendant's criminal behavior, often the chambers do not indicate what portion of the sentence is attributable to what conduct or crime.[27]

Further, although the judges always reference the aggravating and mitigating circumstances that influenced their sentence determination, they do not always explain in detail how precisely those factors affect the sentence.[28] Prosecutors and defense counsel have many times appealed sentences arguing that the Trial Chamber failed to properly weigh aggravating and mitigating circumstances – pointing out the lack of transparency and clarity in sentencing decisions.[29] The Appeals Chamber, however, has concluded that the Trial Chambers' wide discretion over sentencing matters includes the discretion not to indicate the precise weight each factor contributes to the judgment.[30] In fact, the Appeals Chamber has rejected most appeals lodged complaining about the Trial Chambers' improper weighting of factors – again noting the wide discretion the judges enjoy over sentencing matters.[31]

One additional "transparency and clarity" criticism is that the Trial Chambers have not adopted and applied a uniform underlying rationale for imposing punishment, nor consistently linked any such rationale to the specific sentence they impose.[32] Scholars acknowledge that the judges often refer to retribution and

---

[25] See Hola, *supra* note 3, at 8.

[26] ICTY Rules of Procedure and Evidence, Rule 87(C) (amended 2000). The ICTR did not amend its Rules of Procedure and Evidence, but the judges similarly have assumed the power to issue global sentences. See also Hola, *supra* note 3, at 8.

[27] See Hola, *supra* note 3, at 9.

[28] See, e.g., Hola, *supra* note 3, at 14–15. See also Pruitt, *supra* note 15, at 174 (stating that the ICTR judges "rarely explained why a factor was aggravating or mitigating" and "rarely explained how much weight these factors carried in determining the final sentence").

[29] See Hola, *supra* note 3, at 14–15.

[30] See id. at 15 (citing Prosecutor v. Seromba, Judgment, Case No. ICTR-2001–66-A, Appeals Chamber, March 12, 2008, para. 235).

[31] See Hola, *supra* note 3, at 15.

[32] See, e.g., Sharam Dana, *The Sentencing Legacy of the Special Court for Sierra Leone*, 42 GA. J. INT'L L. 615, 670 (2014) (stating that in their sentencing decisions, the ICTY and the ICTR typically point to retribution and deterrence, but have also referenced "reconciliation, rehabilitation, general affirmative, expressivism," among other rationales for punishment); Hola, *supra* note 3, at 6 (referencing the confusion resulting from the absence of a uniform approach regarding the underlying rationale for sentences, the weight to be ascribed to particular rationales, and how particular rationales inform sentence severity).

deterrence – at least briefly – in their sentencing decisions.[33] But the judges do not confine themselves to these rationales, nor are they consistent in stating whether retribution or deterrence is the most important factor in determining the appropriate sentence.[34] As Barbara Hola notes, though, even without a consistently stated rationale, the tribunals still could be consistently meting out aggravating and mitigating factors in a consistent manner.[35] No doubt the tribunals could have avoided some of the criticisms leveled at them had they clearly stated the underlying punishment rationale that informed their sentencing determination and linked that to sentence severity.

10.2 THE "INCONSISTENCY" CRITIQUE AND THE "INDIVIDUALIZATION" REPLY

The above description of the tribunals' sentencing policies shows that the ICTY and ICTR developed and applied a general set of sentencing policies and practices. The tribunals gave meaning to the term "gravity," and used it to principally guide their sentencing determinations. They created and employed a process by which the prosecution and defense prove aggravating and mitigating circumstances. They referenced and applied a large number of aggravating and mitigating factors to increase or decrease sentence severity. They also rendered sentences they concluded reflect the totality of the defendant's criminal conduct.

On the other hand, by failing to always overtly and clearly explain precisely how various factors and crimes influenced the term of imprisonment, the Trial Chambers rendered themselves vulnerable to the critique that their sentencing determinations are not consistent. The reason is because when one looks only at sentencing outcomes, the ICTR sentences tend to be longer than those typically imposed by the ICTY. Proving that those sentences are nonetheless consistent is more challenging when one is lacking details about the weights assigned to factors or crimes.[36] Arguably, the Trial Chambers could have been more transparent and

---

[33] James Meernik, *Sentencing Rationales and Judicial Decision Making at the International Criminal Tribunals*, 92 Soc. Sci. Q. 588, 590 (2011) (noting that the tribunal judges usually briefly make reference to the need to impose a sentence that reflects the gravity of the crimes and to deter others); Hola, *supra* note 3, at 6–7 (stating that the Trial Chambers typically state that deterrence and retribution are the main aims of international sentencing, but that the judges have also advanced other rationales).

[34] Hola, *supra* note 3, at 7.

[35] *Id.* at 7. One empirical study, in fact, finds that the judges have been consistent in sentencing based on retribution and deterrence, even though the decisions themselves may not make that clear. James Meernick concludes that the "tribunal judges' sentences are informed by the traditional punishment rationales of retribution and deterrence" – the rationales that lead a judge to impose punishment that "reflects the gravity of the crime and the culpability of the accused." Meernick, *supra* note 33, at 589, 605.

[36] *See* Hola, *supra* note 3, at 23 (stating that the judges' practices of not indicating the weight assigned to sentencing factors and how each crime relates to total sentence severity makes it "difficult to identify patterns as to the sentencing ranges applicable to individual offences or the contribution of individual sentencing factors to sentence length").

clearer in describing precisely how they arrived at the sentence of imprisonment for each convicted defendant, and better explained the rationale behind the sentence imposed. Instead of sometimes listing applicable aggravating and mitigating factors, they could have assigned a precise weight to each factor. They also could have explained how the various crimes for which the defendant was convicted contributed to the total sentence imposed.

Commentators have noted the tribunals' lack of transparency and the apparently disparate sentencing outcomes, and many have called for reforms.[37] Some have even suggested that the tribunals should be required to abide by a set of sentencing guidelines to insure greater uniformity in sentencing practices.[38] For example, one could circumscribe judges' discretion with regard to aggravating and mitigating factors, perhaps by limiting relevant factors or assigning some suggested weights to factors.[39] Those calling for reforms and less discretion emphasize that justice requires like cases to be treated alike. As one scholar puts it, the apparently differing outcomes "favors the perception of sentences as 'unjust,' as opposed to ideal 'just sentences' characterized by the consistent application of legitimate influential factors in all cases."[40] Sentencing policies and practices should be consistent and uniform so that justice is not only dispensed fairly, but also so that the public *perceives* that justice is being dispensed fairly.[41]

This chapter does not disagree that consistency in sentencing practices is relevant to whether justice is dispensed fairly, and whether the public also perceives that judges are acting impartially and treating like cases similarly. The tribunals, though, are also charged with individualizing sentences to reflect the particular circumstances of the case, as well as the defendant's unique personal circumstances.[42] The

---

[37] See, e.g., Clark, *supra* note 21, at 1687 (noting that commentators have criticized the tribunals for rendering inconsistent sentences); Andrew K. Woods, *Moral Judgments and International Crimes: The Disutility of Desert*, 52 VA. J. INT'L L. 633, 657, 672 (2012) (referencing the calls for greater consistency in international sentencing practices).

[38] See, e.g., Woods, *supra* note 37, at 657, 672; Keller, *supra* note 20, at 66.

[39] See Meernick & King, *supra* note 4, at 730 (stating that some of the strongest criticisms levelled at the ICTY relate to the broad discretion judges have to render sentences based on a great number of different aggravating and mitigating circumstances); *see id.* at 748 (suggesting that guidelines might include a list of factors relevant to sentencing).

[40] Silvia d'Ascoli, SENTENCING IN INTERNATIONAL CRIMINAL LAW 204 (2011).

[41] See Clark, *supra* note 21, at 1789–90 (citing to a quote from an opinion by the Appeals Chamber). *See also* Allison Marston Danner, Constructing a Hierarchy of Crimes in International Criminal Law Sentencing, 87 VA. L. REV. 415, 440 (2001) (arguing that to be perceived as distributing impartial justice, the tribunals need consistency in their jurisprudence, including sentencing practices).

[42] See, e.g., Prosecutor v. Babic, Case No. IT-03–72-A, Judgment on Sentencing Appeal, July 18, 2005, para. 7 (stating that Trial Chambers have broad discretion to determine sentences because they are obligated to individualize punishment based on the gravity of the crime and the circumstances of the accused); Prosecutor v. Galic, Case No. IT-98–29-A, Judgment, Nov. 30, 2006, para. 392 (stating that Trial Chambers have broad discretion in determining sentences because they must individualize penalties to address the gravity of the crime and the circumstances of the accused); Prosecutor v. Nikolic, Case No. IT-02–60/1-A, Judgment on Sentencing Appeal, March 8, 2006, para. 8 (noting that Trial Chambers have broad discretion due to their obligation to make penalties fit the circumstances of the accused and the gravity of the crime).

tribunal statutes specifically state as much. As Meernick and King eloquently argue, individualization means that judges should be able to consider all factors relevant to the defendant's sentence, and one may not be able to formulate sentencing guidelines that would "enumerate exhaustively all manner of human cruelty, or all forms of human decency."[43] Permitting (and perhaps even encouraging) judges to consider all relevant individual circumstances allows them to render independent and individual sentences.[44] Moreover, that the judges consider a host of factors may have the beneficial effect of causing defendants to feel they have been heard, and that they have received a sentence tailored to their situation.[45] In other words, individualized sentences may also be, and appear to be, fair and just sentences.

Of course, the result of individualizing sentences is that one may not be able to predict with certainty the precise sentence a defendant will receive.[46] Two defendants charged with similar crimes should in theory receive similar sentences. Yet as the Appeals Chamber has noted, "often the differences are more significant than the similarities, and the mitigating and aggravating factors dictate different results."[47] Thus, two defendants charged with committing the same crime – such as genocide – may receive different sentences because of their role in the offense, how many victims they harmed, how viciously they acted, or because they pled guilty, cooperated with the prosecutor, and demonstrated remorse. On the face of it, the sentences for these two defendants charged with the same crime may appear inconsistent. One cannot necessarily say from looking at the term of imprisonment alone, however, that the Trial Chambers approached sentencing in an inconsistent manner or treated either of the defendants unfairly.

In short, one cannot judge the consistency of the tribunals' sentencing practices by looking only at sentencing outcomes. Those outcomes may be consistent when one considers the crime charged, its gravity, the circumstances surrounding the commission of the crime, and the defendant's individual circumstances. To explore this point, the chapter first turns to the studies that have empirically examined the tribunals' sentencing outcomes in an effort to assess their underlying consistency. After discussing some of the findings from the empirical studies, the chapter examines some of the ICTY and ICTR sentencing decisions to further explore the consistency issue.

---

[43] Meernick & King, *supra* note 4, at 749.
[44] *See* Pruitt, *supra* note 15, at 173.
[45] *Id.*
[46] *See, e.g.*, Hola, Bijleveld, & Smeulers, *supra* note 3, at 548 ("Theoretically, sentencing should never be 100 percent predictable. In order to be fair, sentences should be not only predictable but also individualized, reflecting the particularities of each case.")
[47] Prosecutor v. Celebici, Case No. IT-96–21-T, Judgment on Sentencing Appeal, Feb. 20, 2001, para. 719.

10.3 THE EMPIRICAL LITERATURE EXAMINING CONSISTENCY IN SENTENCING DETERMINATIONS

The empirical studies examining the sentencing decisions of the ICTY and ICTR generally find that when one looks beyond the sentencing outcomes, the sentences imposed by the tribunal judges can be attributed to the consistent application of sentencing policies and procedures.[48] The number of empirical studies is not large,[49] and they were conducted at different time periods.[50] Also, the studies do not always reach the same precise conclusions about whether and to what extent a particular factor influences sentencing severity.[51] Still, they reveal several factors or groups of factors consistently influencing ICTY and ICTR sentencing decisions.[52]

---

[48] *See, e.g.*, Doherty & Steinberg, *supra* note 12, at 51, 72 (finding that the factors relating to the gravity of the crime and aggravating factors regularly affect sentence length at the ICTY and ICTR); D'Ascoli, *supra* note 40, at 259–60 (finding "general patterns of consistency" between the ICTY and ICTR Trial Chamber in terms of sentence length and the influence of aggravating and mitigating factors); Hola, Bijleveld, & Smeulers, *supra* note 3, at 541, 549 (finding from a study of 111 defendants sentenced by the ICTY and ICTR that "[e]mpirically consistent (and legally relevant) patterns have emerged in the sentencing practice of both tribunals"); Meernik, *supra* note 33 (concluding from a study of 131 defendants sentenced at the ICTY, the ICTR, and the SCSL that defendants are sentenced "according to the severity of their crimes and level of responsibility"); Hola, Smeulers, & Bijleveld, *supra* note 11, at 422–3, 434 (showing that the ICTY and ICTR approached sentencing consistently by, for example, sentencing persons convicted of genocide to more severe sentences and persons who plead guilty to lesser sentences). However, the article does not consider a handful of empirical studies that were issued earlier in the tribunals' existence

[49] This chapter addresses only the studies of ICTY and ICTR sentencing consistency produced from 2011 forward for several reasons. First, space limitations do not allow a survey of all studies. Second, the later studies have the benefit of more observations. Finally, the point of analyzing the empirical studies is not to prove absolutely that any one study is correct, but rather to explore how outcomes might be "consistent" even though the sentences imposed might vary greatly.

[50] The earlier studies obviously have fewer observable cases from which to draw conclusions about judges' sentencing practices. By contrast, the most recent study addressed in this chapter includes sentencing data on 131 defendants – eighty from the ICTY and fifty-one from the ICTR. *See* Doherty & Steinberg, *supra* note 12, at 69.

[51] That the studies would not reach the same precise conclusions should be expected given that they also employ different methodologies. For example, Doherty and Steinberg create categories of sentences to test their hypotheses: sentences are either short, medium, long, or life. Doherty & Steinberg, *supra* note 12, at 69. Hola, Bijleveld, and Smeulers, by contrast, tested their hypothesis against a dependent variable of sentences at the level of a defendant measured in precise years of imprisonment, with life counting as fifty-five years. Hola, Bijleveld, & Smeulers, *supra* note 3, at 542. Those same scholars tested the influence of aggravating and mitigating factors on sentence length using a "count" of such factors, rather than trying to determine which precise aggravating or mitigating factors led to increases or decreases in sentence length across tribunal decisions. *Id.* at 542. Doherty and Steinberg, however, looked at the impact of various aggravating and mitigating factors. Doherty & Steinberg, *supra* note 12, at 69–71.

[52] The authors acknowledge other limitations of their studies. For example, Hola, Bijleveld, & Smeulers note that because of the many factors legally relevant to the tribunals' sentencing determinations, in practice one cannot examine them all at the same time in "multivariate analysis with a dataset that is small in a statistical sense – even though it comprises the entire 'population' of decided cases." Hola, Bijleveld, & Smeulers, *supra* note 3, at 549.

First, although the tribunals have rejected the notion of a hierarchy of crimes,[53] the evidence indicates that the judges consider defendants convicted of genocide to have committed the gravest offenses, such that they deserve more severe sentences. Hola, Bijleveld, and Smeulers found that defendants convicted of genocide received significantly greater sentences than those convicted of crimes against humanity. Also, compared with individuals "convicted solely of war crimes, those convicted of crimes against humanity receive 5.3 years extra and those convicted of genocide are sentenced to an extra 20.1 years."[54] Doherty and Steinberg reached a similar conclusion, finding "with high statistical confidence" that, all other things being equal, genocide yields the longest sentence, followed by crimes against humanity, grave breaches of the Geneva Conventions, and war crimes."[55] These scholars concluded that although the ICTR sentences are on average longer than the ICTY sentences, the fact that the ICTR had far more convictions for genocide helps to explain this difference in outcomes. Almost all of the ICTR's cases involved genocide, while only a handful of the ICTY's cases involved such charges.[56]

One's rank and position also appear to influence sentence length. At both tribunals, high-ranking organizers of criminal activity received the longest sentences.[57] Indeed, the impact of this factor helps to explain the longer sentences imposed at the ICTR, because the majority of the accused convicted at that tribunal abused their positions of power and "exercised authority over others and their criminal conduct."[58] With this said, the studies also show that the tribunals mete out severe sentences to lower-ranked defendants if those defendants were active and zealous participants in the criminal behavior.[59] In other words, "zeal" is an aggravating factor that can greatly increase sentence length. One scholar reports that at the ICTR, out of eight cases where the judges cited zeal as an aggravating factor, five of the defendants received life sentences.[60] By contrast, the tribunals are willing to

---

[53] Hola, *supra* note 3, at 11 (referencing the tribunals' statements to the effect that there is no set hierarchy of crimes); Dana, *supra* note 32, at 671 (noting that the ad hoc tribunals refused to embrace a hierarchy of crimes in their sentencing practice).

[54] Hola, Bijleveld, & Smeulers, *supra* note 3, at 546. Hola, Bijleveld, and Smeulers have similarly pointed out that one reason the ICTR's sentences are more severe is because that tribunal had more genocide cases, while the ICTY had more cases charging the defendants with committing crimes against humanity and war crimes. Hola, Bijleveld, & Smeulers, *supra* note 3, at 549.

[55] Doherty & Steinberg, *supra* note 12, at 72.

[56] *Id.* at 74 (noting that of the ICTR's fifty-one convictions, forty-four were for genocide, while of the ICTY's eighty convictions, five were for genocide). *See also* Pruitt, *supra* note 15, at 154 (noting that of sixty defendants before the ICTR, fifty-three were charged with genocide).

[57] Hola, Smeulers, & Bijleveld, *supra* note 11, at 431. *See also* Doherty & Steinberg, *supra* note 12, at 72 (finding that defendants who directly ordered crimes received longer sentences and that "the higher the rank, the longer the term").

[58] Hola, Smeulers, & Bijleveld, *supra* note 11, at 436–7.

[59] Hola, Smeulers, & Bijleveld, *supra* note 11, at 431. *See also* Doherty & Steinberg, *supra* note 12, at 72 (stating that sentences increased greatly if the tribunal judges found "that the accused acted with sadism"); Pruitt, *supra* note 15, at 165 (noting that the ICTR judges have said that defendants who acted zealously deserved a higher sentence due to their fervor).

[60] Pruitt, *supra* note 15, at 165.

consider a sentence reduction when the facts suggest the defendant only participated in the offense reluctantly and under duress.

In addition, evidence from the empirical studies indicates that the tribunals tend to increase sentence severity if a defendant directly and actively participated in the offense. One study determined that sentences of imprisonment were greater when the accused personally inflicted pain on the victims. By contrast, the tribunals tended to treat more leniently those defendants who participated more indirectly, such that they were charged using the doctrine of superior responsibility or as accomplices. One illustration: among the lower sentences imposed by the tribunals, ten involved defendants who were convicted "as superiors for their omissions to supervise subordinates or as facilitators for only ancillary activities."[61] The authors of the study further opined that the influence of the mode of liability could help to explain the facially different sentencing outcomes between the two tribunals. They observed that in the majority of cases the ICTR defendants were convicted of several modes of liability such as perpetration and ordering, in addition to being convicted on the grounds of superior responsibility.[62]

Finally, the studies also find evidence suggesting that the tribunals will significantly decrease sentence severity for those defendants who have in some way shown that they accept responsibility for their actions. Specifically, defendants who plead guilty, cooperate, and express remorse generally receive more lenient sentences, as do defendants who surrender themselves.[63] Meernik, for instance, found that the judges sentenced those who pled guilty to approximately fifty-six months fewer on average, and those who surrender to approximately forty-three months fewer on average, *ceteris paribus*.[64] Hola, Bijleveld, and Smeulers found that pleading guilty "resulted in lower sentences at both Tribunals (ICTY median sentence of guilty plea cases is 12.5 years versus 15.0 years for cases with no guilty plea; ICTR: 11.0 versus 45.0)." Pruitt's study of the sentences imposed by the ICTR produced comparable findings. He found that pleading guilty appeared to mitigate the defendant's sentence, noting that only one of eight defendants who pled guilty received a life sentence, while the others received sentences of fifteen years or lower.[65] And fewer defendants pled guilty at the ICTR than at the ICTY, a fact which scholars have

---

[61] Hola, Smeulers, & Bijleveld, *supra* note 11, at 426.

[62] *Id.* at 429.

[63] The results of Doherty and Steinberg's study on the impact of pleading guilty on tribunal sentences differed from the several other studies discussed in this section. Those scholars found that "[w]hile pleading guilty, showing remorse, and proving familial duress are highly correlated with shorter sentences in the bivariate analysis, none of these purported mitigating factors is significantly related to sentence length in the multivariate model." Doherty & Steinberg, *supra* note 12, at 75.

[64] Meernik, *supra* note 33, at 602–3.

[65] Pruitt, *supra* note 15, at 171. Pruitt also found that selective assistance to Tutsis was associated with a lower sentence length. Only five of the sixteen defendants found to have aided Tutsis received life sentences, while the remaining defendants received sentences of between six and thirty years. *Id.* at 166. Further, remorse played a role in reducing sentence length, with nine of thirteen defendants who expressed remorse receiving sentences at the ICTR of between six and thirty years. *Id.*

suggested may help explain why ICTR sentences on average appear to be longer than the sentences imposed by the ICTY.[66]

In sum, the empirical studies provide some evidence suggesting the ICTY and ICTR are not as inconsistent as one might think if one looks only at the term of sentence imposed. Instead, disparities in sentence lengths can be attributed to the unique facts of each case and each uniquely situated defendant. More particularly, the evidence shows that tribunal judges tend to increase sentence severity for defendants (1) convicted of genocide; (2) in leadership positions or who otherwise abuse their authority; and/or (3) who participate actively or zealously in the offenses. By contrast, the tribunals tend to decrease sentence severity for defendants (1) convicted based on actions committed by others (modes of liability such as superior responsibility and accomplice liability); and (2) who commit their acts under duress, plead guilty, cooperate with the prosecutor, turn themselves in, or otherwise show less of a guilty intent or remorse.

10.4 CASE STUDIES: COMPARING SENTENCING DECISIONS OF THE ICTY AND ICTR

To further examine consistency in the tribunals' sentencing practices, this chapter turns to some brief case studies.[67] These brief case studies do not, and cannot, unequivocally demonstrate that the ICTY and ICTR consistently sentenced like defendants to like sentences. One reason is because, as noted above, the tribunals' sentencing decisions do not always assign precise weights to the factors deemed relevant to sentence severity, nor do the tribunals always indicate the portion of the total sentence attributable to a particular crime for which the defendant was convicted.[68]

Nevertheless, the cases do illustrate and bolster the findings from the empirical studies about consistency in sentencing approaches. As noted above, some systemic underlying differences in the cases before the tribunals help to explain why, as a general matter, the sentences imposed by the ICTR appear to be harsher than those imposed by the ICTY. For example, more cases at the ICTR involved genocide and defendants who were leaders and abused their positions of authority. More cases at the ICTY involved guilty pleas. However, when one looks behind the sentences imposed to the facts of the cases, sentencing outcomes become more comparable. The sentencing approach is consistent in that the tribunals increase sentence severity for the gravest crimes and for defendants who actively participate in crimes as leaders or with great zeal. The tribunals decrease sentence severity for defendants

---

[66] Hola, Smeulers, & Bijleveld, *supra* note 11, at 434.

[67] Space constraints dictate that the chapter focus only on a select number of cases – generally some of the tribunals' more high-profile cases.

[68] *See* Hola, Smeulers & Bijleveld, *supra* note 11, at 413 (noting that one complication is that the tribunals typically state the total sentence, but do not say what amount pertains to each crime of conviction).

who are not direct participants in the crime and who show that they accept responsibility for their actions.

Consider the facts of some of the cases in which the ICTR imposed a life sentence. They involve the crime of genocide, as well as defendants in leadership positions who also participated in some of the offenses. Jean Paul Akayesu was sentenced to life[69] following his conviction on nine counts of genocide and crimes against humanity.[70] Akayesu was the Mayor of the Taba commune from April 1993 until June 1994 – a commune where a great number of Tutsis were killed or subjected to violence. As Mayor, Akayesu was responsible for protection of the public, yet he personally supervised the murder of some Tutsis and did nothing to stop others from being killed. In addition, he gave death lists to other Hutus and ordered them to search for Tutsis so they could be murdered.[71] He led groups of communal police in a door-to-door search for Tutsis and ordered police to torture and kill civilians.[72] Tutsi women seeking shelter were raped by communal police with Akayesu's knowledge and support.[73] Akayesu gave a speech calling for the mass killing of Tutsis, knowing that people would respond by exterminating Tutsis.[74]

Other ICTR cases imposing life imprisonment reflect the presence of these same aggravating factors. The ICTR sentenced Alfred Musema to life imprisonment for his leadership role in the extermination of Tutsi refugees in Kibuye district.[75] The Trial Chamber unanimously found Musema guilty of one count of genocide, one count of extermination as a crime against humanity, and one count of rape as a crime against humanity.[76] The crimes were sufficiently grave as they involved killing thousands of Tutsis between April and June 1994.[77] Musema personally participated in the attacks against Tutsis on several different occasions, firing with his rifle into the crowd.[78] As the director of a tea factory, Musema was a major employer in the area and had political connections.[79] He used his authority to transport Hutus to groups of Tutsis and encouraged the massacres of the Tutsis.[80]

---

[69] Prosecutor v. Akayesu, Case No. ICTR-96-4-T, Sentence, 13 (Int'l Crim. Trib. for Rwanda Oct. 2, 1998).

[70] *Id.* 293.

[71] Prosecutor v. Akayesu, Case No. ICTR-96-4-T, Judgment para. 382 (Int'l Crim. Trib. for Rwanda Sep. 2, 1998).

[72] *Id.* para. 409.

[73] *Id.* para. 452.

[74] *Id.* para. 674.

[75] Prosecutor v. Musema, Case No. ICTR-96-13-A, Judgment and Sentence (Int'l Crim. Trib. for Rwanda Jan. 27, 2000); Musema v. Prosecutor, Case No. ICTR-96-13-A, Judgment (Int'l Crim. Trib. for Rwanda Nov. 16, 2001).

[76] Trial Judgment page 269. The Appeals Chamber reversed the rape conviction but affirmed the sentence.

[77] Trial Judgment para. 1002.

[78] *Id.*

[79] *Id.* para. 874.

[80] *Id.* para. 890.

Sylvestre Gacumbitsi also received a life sentence after the Appeals Chamber revised his initial sentence of thirty years' imprisonment upwards.[81] Gacumbitsi was convicted of genocide, as well as "extermination as a crime against humanity" and "rape as a crime against humanity."[82] Here, too, Gacumbitsi committed the crimes while in a leadership position.[83] As the Mayor of the commune of Rusumo,[84] Gacumbitsi issued an order to the sector councillors to organize meetings aimed at inciting the Hutus to massacre any persons who were accomplices to the Tutsis.[85] To help carry out the massacre, Gacumbitsi also took delivery of weapons and then distributed them to Hutus in the Rusumo commune.[86] The Trial Chamber particularly noted that Gacumbitsi's leadership position, active participation in plans for genocide, and transporting attackers were aggravating circumstances.

The facts of the *Karadzic* case demonstrate that the ICTY, like the ICTR, considers these same factors – gravity and leadership – as warranting an increase in sentence severity. That case involved genocide charges based on the killing of about 8,000 Bosnian Muslim men and boys in the town of Srebrenica. The defendant, Radovan Karadzic, was the President of Republika Srpska during the Bosnian War.[87] He received the relatively severe sentence of forty years in prison[88] for his role in organizing the Srebrenica genocide that aimed to kill every male in town and exterminate the Bosnian Muslim community. In addition to being President of the Republika Srpska, Karadzic was Supreme Commander of the Army of the Republika Srpska and had full strategic and, at times, operational control of the armed forces that committed genocide and war crimes.[89]

Both the ICTR and the ICTY mitigated sentence severity for defendants who did not participate directly in committing the crimes for which they were convicted. For instance, the ICTR sentenced Anto Furundzija to only ten years' imprisonment. The evidence showed that Furundzija interrogated a civilian Bosnian Muslim woman who was made to be nude in front of about forty soldiers, while one threatened her with genital mutilation if she did not tell the truth.[90] Thereafter, the woman was taken to

---

[81] Prosecutor v. Gacumbitsi, Case No. ICTR-2001–64-T, Judgment para. 356 (Int'l Crim. Trib. for Rwanda June 17, 2004) (*Gacumbitsi* Trial Judgment); Gacumbitsi v. Prosecutor, Case No. ICTR-2001–64-A, Judgment para. 207 (Int'l Crim. Trib. for Rwanda July 7, 2006) (*Gacumbitsi* Appeal Judgment).

[82] *Gacumbitsi* Trial Judgment para. 334.

[83] *Id.* para. 345.

[84] *Id.* para. 6.

[85] *Id.* para. 51.

[86] *Id.* para. 102.

[87] *Id.* para. 6052.

[88] Prosecutor v. Karadzic, Case No. IT-95–5/18-T, Public Redacted Version of Judgment issued on March 24, 2016, para. 6070 (Int'l Crim. Trib. for the Former Yugoslavia Mar. 24, 2016).

[89] *Karadzic* Judgment, *supra* note 88, para.para.paras. 3142, 3157.

[90] Prosecutor v. Furundzija, Case No. IT-95–17/1-T, Judgment, para. 82 (Int'l Crim. Trib. for the Former Yugoslavia Dec. 10, 1998).

another room holding a Bosnian Croat man who had obviously been badly beaten. Furundzija interrogated both victims while one soldier beat the man and another soldier forced the woman to perform oral and vaginal sex acts with the other victim. Furundzija was present the entire time and did not try to stop the beating or sexual violence.[91] In its sentencing decision, the Trial Chamber acknowledged that the crimes were grave in how they were committed. On the other hand, the number of victims was two.[92] In terms of mitigating factors, however, the judges emphasized that Furundzija committed these crimes by aiding and abetting.[93]

"Mode of liability" also played a role in the ICTY's decision to sentence Rasim Delic to only three years' imprisonment. The judges found Delic guilty of one count of committing war crimes based on his role as a superior.[94] The defendant did not harm anyone himself, but was convicted of failing to prevent or punish individuals under his effective control who cruelly treated twelve Serb soldiers who were captured during the fighting in the former Yugoslavia.[95] The soldiers were subjected to humiliating abuse, beaten, deprived of water, and tied in painful positions for long periods of time. One of the captives was murdered by a guard and then decapitated. The captives were then forced to see and hold the severed head.[96] In justifying the relatively lenient sentence, the judges noted the evidence showed that Delic could not have known about the murders in time to stop them, such that his knowledge of the cruel treatment was only imputed.[97]

Other relatively light ICTY sentences evidence how a defendant's acceptance of responsibility acts to mitigate sentence length – even in cases where the defendant's crimes are grave and committed while in a leadership position. For example, the ICTY sentenced Miroslav Deronjic to ten years' imprisonment despite the gravity of his crimes.[98] Deronjic, a Bosnian Serb, was convicted of crimes against humanity based on persecution for his actions that led to the massacre of sixty-four victims in the Bosnian village of Glogova.[99] Deronjic also ordered the forcible displacement of Bosnian Muslims from Bratunac.[100] Aggravating factors included that Deronjic had a leadership role and also ordered the massacre.[101] In mitigation,

---

[91] *Id.* paras. 84–7.

[92] *Id.* paras. 264–75.

[93] *Id.* para. 282.

[94] Prosecutor v. Delic, Case No. IT-04-83-T, Judgment, para. 557 (Int'l Crim. Trib. for the Former Yugoslavia Sept. 15, 2008).

[95] *Id.* para. 82.

[96] *Id.* paras. 255–69.

[97] *Id.* para. 564. Also, in mitigation, the judges mentioned that Delic surrendered voluntarily to the ICTY. *Id.* para. 573.

[98] Prosecutor v. Deronjic, Case No. IT-02-61-S, Sentencing Judgment, at 77 (Int'l Crim. Trib. for the Former Yugoslavia Mar. 30, 2004).

[99] *Id.* para. 97.

[100] *Id.* para. 100.

[101] *Id.* para. 98.

the tribunal noted that the defendant eventually pleaded guilty and cooperated with the prosecutor.[102]

The ICTY sentenced former president of the Republika Srpska, Biljana Plavsic, to only eleven years' imprisonment[103] after she plead guilty to one count of crimes against humanity.[104] Plavsic was one of five members of the Presidency of the Bosnian Serb government. While she was not the most powerful member, she supported the government's actions and made public statements that the Serb forces were justified in their actions, and denied that atrocities were being committed.[105] The evidence essentially showed that she used her platform during the Bosnian War to create impossible conditions, and used terror tactics and persecution to encourage non-Serbs to leave and to deport or liquidate those who refused.[106] In its sentencing decision, the Trial Chamber recognized the gravity of the crimes committed and the defendant's leadership role.[107] It was persuaded to impose a relatively light sentence, however, because of the facts showing that Plavsic accepted responsibility for her actions: she pled guilty and expressed remorse.[108]

The very low sentence the ICTY imposed upon Drazen Erdemovic reflects mitigation for acceptance of responsibility, as well as for duress. Erdemovic, an ethnic Bosnian Croat, participated in shooting 1,200 persons in 1995 during the Srebrenica genocide. Clearly, the crimes committed were of significant gravity. Yet the evidence showed that Erdemovic tried to refuse, but was told by General Ratko Mladic that if he did not kill, then he himself would be shot. In 1996, Erdemovic confessed to a reporter his participation in the genocide, and was thereafter arrested and taken to the ICTY. After he entered a guilty plea to the crime of genocide, the Trial Chamber sentenced Erdemovic to ten years' imprisonment.[109] The Appeals Chamber, however, reduced Erdemovic's sentence to five years, emphasizing that the defendant committed the crime under duress.[110]

These case study illustrations do not prove that the ICTY and the ICTR assigned precisely the same weight to any given factor when deciding what sentences to impose. Creating and demonstrating a sentencing legacy, however, does not require that the tribunals act in lock step. Sentencing is something of an art, because judges must consider the unique facts of the case and the uniqueness of the defendant's

[102] *Id.* paras. 227, 242.
[103] Prosecutor v. Plavsic, Case No. IT-00–39&40/1-S, Sentencing Judgment, para. 10 (Int'l Crim. Trib. for the Former Yugoslavia Feb. 27, 2003).
[104] *Id.* para. 5.
[105] *Id.* paras. 14, 18.
[106] *Id.*
[107] *Id.* para. 54, 57, 60.
[108] *Id.* paras. 61–110.
[109] Prosecutor v. Erdemovic, Case No. IT-96–22-T, Sentencing Judgment, (Int'l Crim. Trib. for the Former Yugoslavia Nov. 29, 1996).
[110] Prosecutor v. Erdemovic, Case No. IT-96–22-A, Judgment, para. 19 (Int'l Crim. Trib. for the Former Yugoslavia Oct. 7, 1997); Prosecutor v. Erdemovic, No. IT-96–22-T*bis*, Sentencing Judgment, para. 23 (Int'l Crim. Trib. for the Former Yugoslavia Mar. 5, 1998).

circumstances. The case study illustrations show not only that the cases before the tribunals are unique, but also that the judges of both tribunals made sentence determinations based on the gravity of the offense and the defendant's individual circumstances, as well as applying certain aggravating and mitigating factors consistently to either increase or decrease sentence severity.

10.5 THE AD HOC TRIBUNALS' SENTENCING LEGACY: EVIDENCE FROM THE ICC

A final way to assess the sentencing legacy of the ICTY and the ICTR as relates to informing international criminal law is by examining the sentencing rules, policies, and practices of the International Criminal Court (ICC). As Professor Meg deGuzman states in her chapter assessing the sentencing legacy of the SCSL, whether and to what extent the ICC follows the hybrid tribunal's sentencing practices and policies is an important part of the SCSL's legacy.[111] That legacy includes sentencing jurisprudence successes that future courts, like the ICC, decide to emulate.[112] Although the ICC is a relatively new court and has only sentenced a few defendants,[113] the evidence thus far indicates that ad hoc tribunals' sentencing decisions have produced a positive sentencing legacy that has influenced the future of international criminal law.

Indeed, the ICC's overarching approach to sentencing mirrors that of the ad hoc tribunals. The ICC follows the ad hoc tribunals in (1) emphasizing the importance of determining sentences based on the gravity of the crime and the defendant's individual circumstances, and (2) granting great discretion to the judges to individualize sentences based not only on gravity and individual circumstances, but also based on the application of an unlimited number of aggravating and mitigating circumstances.[114] In other words, sentencing at the ICC, like sentencing at the

---

[111] Margaret deGuzman, *The Sentencing Legacy of the Special Court for Sierra Leone* 379, *in* THE SIERRA LEONE SPECIAL COURT AND ITS LEGACY: THE IMPACT FOR AFRICA AND INTERNATIONAL CRIMINAL LAW (Charles Jalloh ed., 2013).

[112] A sentencing legacy can also include "lessons learned" from any failures or criticized practices or policies. *Id.* This chapter focuses only on the positive contributions because they are the practices and policies that have survived and continue to shape the future of international criminal law.

[113] As of December 2017, the ICC has sentenced four defendants: Thomas Lubanga Dyilo, Germain Katanga, Jean-Pierre Bemba Gombo, and Ahmad Al-Faqi Al-Mahdi. *See* Prosecutor v. Dyilo, Decision on Sentence pursuant to Article 76 of the Statute, Case No. ICC-01/04-01/06, July 10, 2012; Prosecutor v. Katanga, Decision on Sentence pursuant to article 76 of the Statute, Case No. ICC-01/04-01/17, May 23, 2014; Prosecutor v. Bemba Bombo, Decision on Sentence pursuant to article 76 of the Statute, Case No. ICC-01/05-01/08, June 21, 2016; Prosecutor v. Al-Mahdi, Judgment and Sentence, Case No. ICC-01/12-01/15, Sept. 27, 2016.

[114] Because of space constraints, this chapter focuses on the evidence showing how the ad hoc tribunals influenced the more overarching sentencing policies of the ICC. One can, however, also see evidence of the ad hoc tribunals' positive sentencing legacy on a smaller, less global, level. A couple of examples will suffice. The ICC follows the ad hoc tribunals in requiring the prosecution to prove aggravating factors beyond a reasonable doubt, and requiring that the defense prove mitigating factors

tribunals, is not constrained by any sentencing guidelines. Unlike the ICTY and the ICTR, however, the ICC did not have to begin from a blank slate in creating a list of factors relevant to individualizing sentences.

Regarding the first point, Article 78 of the Rome Statute states that in determining the sentence, "the Court shall ... take into account such factors as the gravity of the crime and the individual circumstances of the convicted person."[115] The ICC's Rules of Procedure and Evidence (ICC RPE) similarly highlight the need to consider these matters when imposing a sentence. ICC RPE 145(1)(b) requires the court to issue a sentence that reflects the circumstances of the crime and of the convicted person.[116] Rule 145(1)(a) requires the sentence to reflect the "culpability of the convicted person."[117] Rule 145(1)(c) sets out a nonexhaustive list of factors the judges must consider when assessing the gravity of the crime and the convicted person's individual circumstances. As to gravity, judges must consider "the extent of the damage caused, in particular the harm caused to the victims and their families, the nature of the unlawful behaviour and the means employed to execute the crime." As to individual circumstances, judges must consider "the degree of participation of the convicted person; the degree of intent; the circumstances of manner, time and location; and the age, education, social and economic condition of the convicted person."[118]

Regarding the second point above, the ICC sentencing policies and principles emulate those of the ad hoc tribunals by vesting judges with wide discretion over sentencing matters, so that they can individualize sentences to reflect the unique facts of the case and the uniqueness of the defendant's situation.[119] ICC RPE 145 contains a long, but nonexhaustive, list of potentially applicable aggravating and mitigating factors ICC judges may consider when making sentencing determinations. Among the many factors are those the ICTY and ICTR consistently applied to increase or decrease sentence severity. Aggravating factors include that the defendant abused a position of authority, was particularly cruel in the commission of

---

by a balance of the probabilities. *See Lubanga* Decision, *supra* note 113, at paras. 33–4; *Katanga* Decision, *supra* note 113, at para. 34; *Bemba* Decision, *supra* note 113, at paras. 18–19; *Al Madhi* Decision, *supra* note 113, at paras. 73–4. The ICC also follows the ad hoc tribunals in not permitting judges to double-count factors – e.g., toward gravity and toward aggravating circumstances. *See Lubanga* Decision, *supra* note 113 at para. 35; *Katanga* Decision, *supra* note 113, at para. 35; *Bemba* Decision, *supra* note 113, at para. 14; *Al Madhi* Decision, *supra* note 113, at para. 70.

[115] Rome Statute of the International Criminal Court, July 17, 1998, UN Doc. A/CONF 183/9 (1998) (hereinafter Rome Statute), at Art. 78(1).

[116] ICC RP & Evid. 145(1)(b), Assembly of States Parties, 1st Sess., Sept. 3–10, 2002, ICC-ASP/1/3 (Sept. 9, 2002), www.icc cpi.int/en_menus/icc/legal%20texts%20and%20tools/official%20journal/Documents/RulesProcedureEvidenceEng.pdf (hereinafter ICC RPE).

[117] ICC RPE 145(1)(a).

[118] ICC RPE 145(1)(c).

[119] ICC RPE 145(1)(b) requires the judges to "[b]alance all the relevant factors, including any mitigating and aggravating factors and consider the circumstances both of the convicted person and of the crime." Rome Statute, Art. 78(1) requires the judges to "take into account such factors as the gravity of the crime and the individual circumstances of the convicted person."

crimes, or that many victims suffered.[120] Mitigating factors listed include that the defendant acted under duress or took steps to compensate victims or cooperate.[121]

The ICC's few sentencing decisions show that judges are considering gravity, individual circumstances, and aggravating and mitigating factors when reaching their decisions on sentence length. For example, on May 23, 2014, Trial Chamber II sentenced defendant Katanga to twelve years of imprisonment[122] after he was found guilty as an "accessory to the crime of murder as a crime against humanity and as a war crime; the crime of attacks against a civilian population as such or against individual civilians not taking direct part in hostilities as a war crime; the crime of destruction of enemy property as a war crime; and the crime of pillaging as a war crime."[123] As to gravity, the judges noted, among other things, that the crimes involved intentionally killing civilians with machetes and guns, and that the attacks were committed even as the victims begged to be spared.[124] As to the defendant's circumstances, the judges found that Katanga was in a position of authority and sufficiently influenced the commission of the crimes by arming the attackers.[125] Although the prosecution proffered some aggravating circumstances, the judges did not find the presence of any beyond a reasonable doubt.[126] On the other hand, the judges found the presence of several mitigating factors, including that Katanga played a positive role in the process of disarming and demobilizing child soldiers.[127]

On June 21, 2016, Trial Chamber III sentenced defendant Bemba to eighteen years in prison. He was convicted under Rome Statute Art. 28(a) for his role as a military commander and charged with crimes against humanity and war crimes, with underlying acts including murder, rape, and pillaging.[128] In the sentencing decision, the judges considered the gravity of each of the crimes for which Bemba was convicted. By way of example, it concluded that the crimes involving rape were of the utmost gravity, having harmed many victims and occurred over much territory.[129] As to Bemba himself, the judges found that he was an educated, high-level commander who not only tolerated the commission of crimes, but by failing to take action instead encouraged and contributed to them.[130] Aggravating circumstances included that the victims of the rapes were particularly young and vulnerable, and that the crimes were committed with particular cruelty.[131] The earlier *Lubanga* sentencing decision and the later *Al Madhi* sentencing decision similarly

---

[120] ICC RPE 145(2)(b).
[121] ICC RPE 145(2)(a).
[122] *Katanga* Decision, *supra* note 113, at paras. 146–7.
[123] *Id.* at para. 1.
[124] *Id.* at 46–9, 53.
[125] *Id.* at paras. 61–9.
[126] *Id.* at para. 75.
[127] *Id.* at para. 115.
[128] *Bemba* Decision, *supra* note 113, at paras. 2, 21, 95.
[129] *Id.* at para. 40.
[130] *Id.* at paras. 59–67.
[131] *Id.* at paras. 41–7.

demonstrate that the judges individualized sentences after considering the gravity of the offense, the defendant's individual circumstances, and any relevant aggravating and mitigating factors presented by the prosecution and defense.[132]

The above illustrations do not prove, and do not seek to prove, that the ICC judges reached the "correct" sentence in each of the cases discussed. In every case, reasonable people might evaluate the very same facts and impose different sentences. Again, sentencing is something of an art, not a science. Still, the sentencing decisions show that the ICC judges are doing just what the judges at the ad hoc tribunals did: individualizing sentences after grappling with and considering gravity, individual circumstances, and relevant aggravating and mitigating circumstances. This alone is evidence of the enduring influence of the ad hoc tribunals' work as regards sentencing in international criminal law.

---

[132] Trial Chamber I sentenced defendant Lubanga to fourteen years' imprisonment as a co-perpetrator for conscripting child soldiers and using them to participate actively in hostilities in the Ituri region of the Democratic Republic of the Congo. *See Lubanga* Decision, *supra* note 113, at para. 1. As to gravity, conscripting children causes particular and severe harm to them, and in this case the offense was committed on a large scale. *Id.* at paras. 37–44, 45–50. As to the defendant's circumstances, the judges emphasized Lubanga's relatively high level of education showed he knew what he was doing was wrong. *Id.* at para. 56. The judges found no aggravating factors, though they concluded that Lubanga's cooperation with the court, among other things, warranted a mitigation of his sentence. *Id.* at paras. 91, 96. Trial Chamber VIII sentenced defendant Al Madhi to nine years in prison after Al Madhi pled guilty to war crimes for intentionally directing attacks against religious and historical buildings in Timbuktu, Mali during 2012. *See Al Madhi* Decision, *supra* note 113, at paras. 7, 10, 11, 30, 109. The judges found that Al Madhi participated in the attacks both by supervising other perpetrators, distributing tools to carry out the attacks, and also by personally participating in the attack against at least five of the religious and historical sites. *Id.* at para. 40. As to gravity, the judges noted the religious, emotional, and cultural value of the buildings attacked, and that they were attacked for a religious motive. *Id.* at paras. 79–81. They found no aggravating factors, but did credit the defendant with five mitigating factors, including that he cooperated and showed remorse. *Id.* at para. 109.

11

Mixed Messages: The Sentencing Legacies of the Ad Hoc Tribunals

Margaret M. deGuzman[*]

INTRODUCTION

The ad hoc tribunals have left important legacies through the sentences they imposed and the decisions they rendered in support of those sentences. The concept of legacy is complex and multifaceted.[1] I use the term in both a normative sense, to refer to the legal and moral norms reflected in the tribunals' sentencing practices, and a sociological one, connoting the impact of the tribunals' sentencing practices on perceptions of the value of their work among relevant audiences. As the first modern international criminal tribunals, the ad hoc tribunals have had a substantial influence on other international courts, including through their sentencing practices. Courts such as the International Criminal Court (ICC), the Extraordinary Chambers in the Courts of Cambodia, and the Special Tribunal for Lebanon have adopted sentencing norms developed at the ad hoc tribunals.[2] Additionally, the ad hoc tribunals' sentencing practices greatly influenced perceptions of the tribunals' legitimacy among important audiences, particularly at the local level. In this chapter, I argue that a particular aspect of the tribunals' sentencing practices undermined their normative and sociological legacies: their failure to clarify whether and when the tribunals apply and ought to apply global sentencing

---

[*] Professor of Law, Temple University Beasley School of Law. I am grateful to Connor Brooks and Danielle DerOhannesian for their excellent research assistance.

[1] *See* Carsten Stahn, Legacy in International Criminal Justice, *in* Arcs of Global Justice: Essays in Honour of William A. Schabas 271, 276 (Margaret M. deGuzman & Diane Marie Amann eds., 2018).

[2] *See, e.g.*, Prosecutor v. Al Mahdi, Case No. ICC-01/12–01/15, para. 100 (Sept. 27, 2016) (citing case law of ICTY in support of holding that an admission of guilt is a mitigating factor); Prosecutor v. Bemba Gombo, Case No. ICC-01/05–01/08, paras. 15, 19 (June 21, 2016) (citing ICTY and ICTR cases regarding gravity and aggravating and mitigating factors); Akhbar Beirut S.A.L, Reasons for Sentencing Judgment, Case No. STL-14–06/S/CJ, para.15 (Sept. 5, 2016) (agreeing "with the ICTY's case-law that the most important factors in determining the appropriate penalty in a contempt case are the gravity of the conduct and the need to deter repetition and similar conduct by others"); Co-Prosecutors v. Nuon Chea and Khieu Samphan, Case No. 002/19–09-2007/ECCC/TC, Judgment, para. 1071 fn. 3127 (Aug. 7, 2014) (citing Prosecutor v. Blaškić, Case No. IT-95–14-T, Appeals Chamber Judgment, para. 687 (July 29, 2004) (guidance on whether remaining silent at times was considered an aggravating factor).

norms, and when the application of local norms is more appropriate. The tribunals' creators hoped they would promote both global and local justice, and enshrined in their statutes a requirement of consulting local norms in determining sentences. But those sentencing norms were sometimes in tension with global norms. Rather than addressing that tension and explaining when and why they chose to adopt one or the other, the tribunals left the question unaddressed. This both detracted from the tribunals' ability to promote their own normative legitimacy, as well as that of the international criminal law regime generally, and promoted perceptions of illegitimacy among some local audiences.[3]

The chapter begins by explaining the relationship between legacy and legitimacy to provide the foundation for the argument that follows. It then surfaces the global-local tension and shows how it played out in the tribunals' sentencing practices.[4] Next, it argues that the ambiguity about whether the tribunals pursued global or local sentencing norms detracted from their normative legacies, including their ability to contribute positively to the legitimacy of the international criminal law regime. Finally, it shows the negative effects of the global-local tension in sentencing on perceptions of the tribunals' legitimacy.

11.1 LEGACY AND LEGITIMACY

One of the most important questions to ask about an institution's legacy is whether it contributes positively to the institution's legitimacy and, in the case of institutions embedded in a broader regime, to the legitimacy of the regime as a whole. Legitimacy, like legacy, is not absolute or static, but exists on a continuum and evolves over time. Also, like legacy, legitimacy can be understood in normative or sociological terms.[5] An institution's legacy contributes positively to its normative legitimacy when the institution adhered to appropriate moral and legal norms and promoted appropriate goals and priorities. In the sentencing context, relevant norms include those related to the nature and quantity of punishment, and relevant goals may include the infliction of deserved punishment and the promotion of social goods such as general and individual deterrence, incapacitation, and rehabilitation.

Which sentencing norms and goals are appropriate for a given court depends on the community the institution is intended to serve. Courts are generally established

---

[3] I made similar arguments with respect to the sentencing legacy of the Special Court for Sierra Leone in Margaret M. deGuzman, *The Sentencing Legacy of the Special Court for Sierra Leone, in* The Sierra Leone Special Court and Its Legacy (Charles Chernor Jalloh ed., 2014).

[4] I have examined the global-local tension in relation to the work of the International Criminal Court in Margaret M. deGuzman, The Global-Local Dilemma and the ICC's Legitimacy, *in* Legitimacy and International Courts (Harlan Grant Cohen et al. eds., forthcoming 2018), https://papers.ssrn.com/sol3/papers.cfm?abstract_id=3078123.

[5] For a discussion of the legal, moral, and sociological aspects of legitimacy, *see* Margaret M. deGuzman, *Gravity and the Legitimacy of the International Criminal Court*, 32 Fordham Int'l L. J. 1400 (2009) (hereinafter *Gravity and Legitimacy*).

by particular communities to accomplish the goals and enforce the norms of those communities.[6] The strength of a tribunal's normative legacy thus largely depends on the extent to which it enforced that community's norms and served its objectives. But there is an important exception to this rule: because some moral norms are universal, an institution's normative legacy is strongest when it enforces such norms, even in the face of contrary local norms.[7] In light of their universal validity, no community's institutions ought to violate universal moral norms; and this is particularly important for institutions that include participation by the international community, whether through significant funding, contribution of personnel, or by virtue of their establishment under international law.[8] When such institutions violate universal moral norms they not only contribute to immoral outcomes in particular cases, they also undermine the strength of the norm, potentially leading to further violations elsewhere.

A tribunal's legacy contributes positively to its sociological legitimacy when important audiences perceive its work as highly valuable. Sociological legacy thus relates to normative legacy in that relevant audiences are more likely to view a tribunal's work positively when the tribunal adhered to appropriate moral and legal norms. However, perceptions of a tribunal's work may be more or less positive than the work itself merits for all of the many reasons that perceptions often fail to reflect reality, including, for instance, confirmation and implicit biases.[9] Moreover, as noted above, a community's norms may conflict with universal moral norms, causing the community to perceive the institution's work more negatively than is normatively warranted. Finally, a tribunal's sociological legacy depends significantly on its ability to communicate effectively with relevant audiences. If an audience is unaware of, or misunderstands, the successes of an institution, its sociological legacy may also be weaker than is normatively warranted.

In light of the importance of community norms to an institution's legacy, ambiguities about the relevance of particular community norms tend to weaken the ability of that legacy to contribute positively to the institution's legitimacy, both actual and perceived. This chapter argues that such ambiguities, particularly about the relevance of, and priorities among, global and local norms, have undermined the legacies of the ad hoc tribunals and their ability to promote the legitimacy of the international criminal law regime. On the one hand, the tribunals were established

---

[6] *See* Nancy A. Combs, *Seeking Inconsistency: Advancing Pluralism in International Criminal Sentencing*, 41 YALE J. INT'L L. 1, 34–5 (2016)(asserting that "[d]omestic sentencing laws are understood to reflect and incorporate community norms" and explaining that this is because the legislators who create the sentencing laws are elected officials, "who are expected to represent local constituencies").

[7] Jack Donnelly, *Cultural Relativism and Human Rights*, 6 HUM. RTS. Q. 400 (1985).

[8] William A. Schabas, *Sentencing by International Tribunals: A Human Rights Approach*, 7 DUKE J. COMP. & INT'L L. 461, 467 (1997).

[9] Laurie A. Rudman, *Social Justice in Our Homes, Minds, and Society: The Nature, Causes, and Consequences of Implicit Bias*, 17 SOC. JUST. RES. 129, 130 (2004); Raymond S. Nickerson, *Confirmation Bias: A Ubiquitous Phenomenon in Many Guises*, 2 REV. GEN. PSYCHOL. 175, 175 (1998).

by an international organization, acting under international law, for the ostensible purpose of promoting international peace and security. Accordingly, an orientation toward the goals and norms of the global community would seem appropriate. On the other hand, the means by which the tribunals were to advance international peace and security was by promoting peace and security *in the former Yugoslavia and Rwanda*, a task that they could presumably accomplish, if at all, by centering the goals of those communities. Rather than address this global-local tension in their sentencing decisions and explain when they were giving priority to global and local goals, the judges of the ad hoc tribunals left ambiguous the extent to which each community's goals guided their decisions. This ambiguity undermined the tribunals' normative and sociological legacies and their ability to promote the legitimacy of international criminal law more broadly.

11.2 THE GLOBAL-LOCAL TENSION IN SENTENCING AT THE AD HOC TRIBUNALS

Although the tribunals' Statutes and Rules of Procedure and Evidence required the judges to "have recourse to the general practice regarding prison sentences" in the former Yugoslavia and Rwanda respectively, in determining sentences,[10] the rules did not clarify which practices were relevant[11] or how those practices ought to impact upon the judges' decision-making. The judges interpreted "have recourse" to mean they should consider national practice but were not bound to follow it.[12] With respect to the goals of sentencing, the tribunals' Statutes were essentially silent, stating merely that "the Trial Chambers should take into account such factors as the gravity of the offence and the individual circumstances of the convicted person."[13]

[10]   Statute of the International Criminal Tribunal for the former Yugoslavia, Art. 24(1), in Report of the Secretary General Pursuant to Paragraph 2 of UN Sec. Council Res. 808, UN Doc. S/25704 (1993) (hereinafter ICTY Statute); Statute of the International Criminal Court for Rwanda, Article 23(1), in UN Sec. Council Res. 955, UN SCOR, 49th Year, Res. And Dec., at 15, UN Doc. S/INF/50 (1994) (hereinafter ICTR Statute); International Criminal Tribunal for the former Yugoslavia Rules and Procedure of Evidence, IT/32/Rev.50, *as amended* July 8, 2015, Art. 101 (B); International Criminal Tribunal for Rwanda Rules and Procedure of Evidence, UN Doc. ITR/3/REV.1, *entered into force* July 5, 1995, *as amended* May 13, 2015, Art. 101(B).

[11]   As William Schabas notes, it was not "evident whether the Statutes contemplated the actual practice of the courts in sentencing offenders, or simply the legislation in force." *See* William A. Schabas, Perverse Effects of the *Nulla Poena* Principle: National Practice and the Ad Hoc Tribunals, 11 EUR. J. INT'L L. 521, 526 (2000) (hereinafter Schabas, *Perverse Effects*).

[12]   Prosecutor v. Kambanda, Case No. ICTR-97–23-S, Judgment and Sentence, paras. 11, 41 (Sept. 4, 1998) ("Reference to the Rwandan sentencing practice is intended as a guide to determining an appropriate sentence and does not fetter the discretion of the judges of the Trial Chamber to determine the sentence."); Prosecutor v. Mucić, Case No. IT-96–21-A, Appeal Judgment, paras. 813, 816 (Int'l Crim. Trib. for the Former Yugoslavia Feb. 20, 2001) ("It is now settled practice that, although a Trial Chamber should 'have recourse to' and should 'take into account' this general practice regarding prison sentences in the courts of the former Yugoslavia, this does not oblige the Trial Chambers to conform to that practice; it only obliges the Trial Chambers to take account of that practice.")

[13]   ICTY Statute, *supra* note 10, at Art. 24(2); ICTR Statute, *supra* note 10, at Art. 23(2).

This provision begs the question whether factors like gravity and individual circumstances ought to be evaluated from a local or global perspective; and it fails entirely to guide the judges in terms of how to conceptualize the goals of sentencing, such as retribution and deterrence.

Consequently, although the sentencing judgments of the ad hoc tribunals often open with an acknowledgment of the judges' obligation to consider national sentencing practice, they also affirm the judges' ultimate discretion in determining sentences. The following statement from the sentencing judgment in the ICTY's *Delic* case is typical:

> The Trial Chamber is required to take into account the general practice regarding prison sentences in the courts of the former Yugoslavia, although it is not obligated to conform to such practice in making its sentencing determination. While review of such practice serves as an aid in determining the appropriate penalty, the Trial Chamber may, if the interests of justice so merit, impose a sentence less than or in excess of that which would be applicable under the relevant law of the former Yugoslavia.[14]

Despite the assertion that divergences should occur only the "if the interests of justice so merit," the judges generally failed to explain the basis for diverging from national sentencing practice in particular cases.[15] Instead, their method was to conduct a review of relevant factors, including the gravity of the crime, the role of the convicted person, and any aggravating and mitigating circumstances, and announce a number of years in prison.[16]

With regard to the purposes of punishment, the judgments frequently invoke such goals as deterrence and retribution, but rarely specified whether such objectives ought to be interpreted in terms of local or global norms. In many of the judgments, the tribunals seem focused on international community values. For instance, a trial chamber of the ICTY considered "one of the essential functions of a prison sentence for a crime against humanity," to be "public reprobation and stigmatisation by the international community, which would thereby express its indignation over heinous crimes and denounce the perpetrators."[17] This idea that sentencing ought to be viewed as a vehicle for the international community's expression of moral

---

[14] Prosecutor v. Delić, Case No. IT-04-83-T, Judgment, para. 592 (Int'l Crim. Trib. for the Former Yugoslavia Sept. 15, 2008).

[15] *But see* Prosecutor v. Erdemović, Case No. IT-96-22-T, Sentencing Judgment, para. 37 (Int'l Crim. Trib. for the Former Yugoslavia Nov. 29, 1996) (explaining that the Trial Chamber could not reference domestic sentencing practices for the Former Yugoslavia because the Trial Chamber "was unable to obtain the factual elements which characterised the specific cases which came before the national courts of the former Yugoslavia and which the [national courts] took into consideration when determining the length of prison sentences").

[16] *See* Barbora Hola, *Sentencing of International Crimes at the ICTY and ICTR: Consistency of Sentencing Case Law*, 4 AMSTERDAM L. F. 3, 8 (2012).

[17] Prosecutor v. Erdemović, Case No. IT-96-22-T, Sentencing Judgment, para. 65 (Int'l Crim. Trib. for the Former Yugoslavia Nov. 29, 1996).

condemnation reflects the rationale that is often cited for prosecuting these crimes in a supra-national forum. For instance, when the ICTY convicted a defendant of willfully destroying or damaging "institutions dedicated to religion, charity, education, and the arts and sciences, and to historic monuments and works of art and science," it asserted that "[t]his crime represents a violation of values *especially protected* by the international community."[18]

While many judgments reflect this emphasis on global values, some are more ambiguous about whether they aim to promote global or local sentencing goals. In the *Babic* case, an ICTY Trial Chamber explained the aims of punishment thus:

> As a form of retribution, punishment expresses society's condemnation of the criminal act and of the person who committed it. It should be proportional to the seriousness of the crime. The Tribunal's punishment thus conveys the indignation of humanity for the serious violations of international humanitarian law of which a person is found guilty. Punishment may in this way reduce the anger and sense of injustice caused by the commission of the crimes among victims and in their wider community.[19]

This statement seems to reflect several perspectives: the Trial Chamber first invoked an unidentified "society" as the audience for which condemnation is intended, then identified "humanity" as the entity expressing condemnation, before finally asserting that the victims and their wider community are the ultimate beneficiaries of punishment. Similarly, in the *Nikolić* judgment, the ICTY Trial Chamber seemed to take a view of retribution focused on the international community when it stated: "retribution is better understood as the expression of condemnation and outrage of *the international community* at such grave violations of, and disregard for, fundamental human rights at a time that people may be at their most vulnerable, namely during armed conflict."[20] But it then expressed a more local community sentiment, asserting: "It is also recognition of the harm and suffering caused to the victims."[21] In one judgment, the ICTY specifically referenced the tension between global and local norms, stating:

> [A] trial chamber must consider its obligations to the individual accused in light of its responsibility to ensure that it is upholding the purposes and principles of international criminal law. This task becomes particularly difficult in relation to punishment. A review of the history of punishment reveals that the forms of punishment reflect norms and values of a particular society at a given time. The Trial

---

[18] Prosecutor v. Jokić, Case No. IT-01-42/1-S, Sentencing Judgment, para. 46, 67 (Int'l Crim. Trib. for the Former Yugoslavia Mar. 18, 2004) (emphasis added).

[19] Prosecutor v. Babić, Case No. IT-03-72-S, Sentencing Judgment, para. 44 (Int'l Crim. Trib. for the Former Yugoslavia June 29, 2004); *see also* Prosecutor v. Jokić, Case No. IT-01-42/1-S, Sentencing Judgment, para. 31 (Int'l Crim. Trib. for the Former Yugoslavia Mar. 18, 2004).

[20] Prosecutor v. Nikolić, Case No. IT-02-60/1, Judgment, para. 86 (Int'l Crim. Trib. For the Former Yugoslavia Dec. 2, 2003).

[21] *Id.*

Chamber must therefore discern and apply the underlying principles and rationale for punishment that respond to both the needs of the society of the former Yugoslavia and the international community.[22]

Commentary on the sentencing practices of the ad hoc tribunals reflects divergent views about the extent to which the tribunals took account of global and local norms and goals. According to Kai Ambos, references to local sentencing practice were "mere lip service,"[23] and Barbora Hola and Catrien Bijleveld note that: "judges cite applicable domestic provisions mostly as a formality."[24] An insightful student note that examines the extent to which the ad hoc tribunals considered national sentencing practice provides a more nuanced view, showing that the tribunals focused on local practice more in some regards than in others.[25] For instance, the tribunals generally complied with national practices regarding minimum and maximum prison terms and time served,[26] but also valued the promotion of uniform international sentencing norms.[27]

The uncertainty about the appropriate role of national and global norms in the sentencing decisions of the ad hoc tribunals reflects a tension in the tribunals' founding documents between global and local objectives more generally. The ICTY and ICTR were each created by a Security Council resolution issued pursuant to the Council's Chapter VII mandate to maintain and restore peace and security.[28] In establishing the ICTY, the Security Council stated that "in the particular circumstances of the former Yugoslavia," the establishment of an ad hoc international tribunal would help end the serious crimes that were threatening international peace and security, and would bring to justice those responsible.[29] These statements suggest that the tribunal was intended to serve the international community's goal of promoting global peace and security. However, the mechanism

---

[22] Prosecutor v. Obrenović, Case No. IT-02-60/2-S, Sentencing Judgment, para. 47 (Int'l Crim. Trib. for the Former Yugoslavia Dec. 10, 2003).

[23] Kai Ambos, 2 Treatise on International Criminal Law: The Crimes and Sentencing 282 (2013).

[24] Barbora et al., Consistency of International Sentencing: ICTY and ICTR Case Study, 9 Eur. J. Criminology 539, 541 (2012). *See also* William R. Pruitt, *Aggravating and Mitigating Sentencing Factors at the ICTR – An Exploratory Analysis*, 14 INT'L CRIM. L. REV. 148, 151 (2014) (noting that sentencing focused on "international outrage").

[25] Jessica Leinwand, *Punishing Horrific Crime: Reconciling International Prosecution with National Sentencing Practices*, 40 COLUM. HUM. RTS. L. REV. 799, 816–23 (2009).

[26] *Id.* at 802–3.

[27] *Id.* at 803; Prosecutor v. Obrenović, Case No. IT-02-60/2-S, Sentencing Judgment, para. 47 (Int'l Crim. Trib. for the Former Yugoslavia Dec. 10, 2003) ("As the Tribunal is applying international law, it must have due regard for the impact of its application of internationally recognised norms and principles on the global level. Thus, a trial chamber must consider its obligations to the individual accused in light of its responsibility to ensure that it is upholding the purposes and principles of international criminal law.")

[28] UN Sec. Council Res. 827, UN SCOR, 48th Sess., 3217th mtg., UN Doc. S/RES/827 (1993) (hereinafter UN Sec. Council Res. 827); UN Sec. Council Res. 955, UN SCOR, 49th Sess., 3453rd mtg., UN Doc. S/RES/955 (1994) (hereinafter UN Sec. Council Res. 955).

[29] UN Sec. Council Res. 827, *supra* note 27.

through which this goal was to be achieved required the promotion of goals with great local importance – stopping crimes and holding people responsible for crimes already committed. The Council used similar language in establishing the ICTR, but also included a more explicit emphasis on local goals, stating that the tribunal "would contribute to the process of national reconciliation and to the restoration and maintenance of peace."[30] The purpose of each institution thus included both promoting global peace and security and contributing to the well-being of the national populations most affected by the crimes the institutions adjudicated.

Although the statutes required the tribunals to consult local sentencing practice as explained above, they also limited the judges' ability to follow local norms in important respects. First, in both the former Yugoslavia and Rwanda the death penalty was permitted at the time the tribunals were established, but unavailable at the tribunals.[31] Second, in the former Yugoslavia, the maximum term of imprisonment was set at fifteen years for most crimes, or twenty-four years for genocide when death was not imposed.[32] This seems to reflect a social norm that life imprisonment may actually be worse than death.[33] In contrast, the ICTR had unfettered discretion to impose prison terms up to life. The tribunals' statutes thus sent mixed messages: the tribunals were established to promote international peace and security, but to do so through individual accountability and reconciliation; and the judges were to consult local practices in determining sentences, but were restricted in the extent they could follow them.

A further ambiguity arose at the appellate level. The statutes were silent as to whether appellate review included compliance with local sentencing practices. Given that the tribunals shared an Appeals Chamber, it is perhaps unsurprising that the judges at that level did not assume *sua sponte* the responsibility of conducting such review. Instead, appellate review of sentencing decisions at the ad hoc tribunals focused on the extent to which a sentence was consistent with sentences handed down by international tribunals in similar cases.[34] As such, despite the statutes' requirements that local practice be considered at sentencing, the appellate

---

[30]   UN Sec. Council Res. 955, *supra* note 27.

[31]   This has since changed. The countries that emerged from the former Yugoslavia do not permit imposition of the death penalty, and Rwanda abolished the death penalty in response to pressure from the ICTR. *Abolitionist and Retentionist Countries*, Death Penalty Information Center (Dec. 31, 2016), https:// deathpenaltyinfo.org/abolitionist-and-retentionist-countries (providing a list of countries who currently do not provide for the death penalty for any crime); Sigall Horovitz, *International Criminal Courts in Action: The ICTR's Effect on Death Penalty and Reconciliation in Rwanda*, 48 Geo. Wash. Int'l L. Rev. 505, 507 (2016) ("Rwanda abolished the death penalty in mid-2007 as part of a larger set of legal reforms intended to satisfy the ICTR's requirement for referring cases to national courts.")

[32]   Crim. Code Socialist Fed. Rep. Yugoslavia, ch. 16, arts. 141–56 (1976) (hereinafter Former Yugoslavia Crim. Code), available at www.eulexkosovo.eu/training/justice/docs/ Criminal_Code_of_SFRY_1976.pdf.

[33]   *See* John R. W. D. Jones, The Practice of the International Criminal Tribunals for the former Yugoslavia and Rwanda 43 (2nd edn. 1999).

[34]   Mark A. Drumbl & Kenneth S. Gallant, *Appeals in the Ad Hoc International Criminal Tribunals: Structure, Procedure, and Recent Cases*, 3 J. App. Prac. & Process 582, 621 (2001)(citing Prosecutor v. Aleksovski, Case No. IT-95-14/1-A, Appeal Judgment, para. 107 (Int'l Crim. Trib. for the Former

standard drew explicitly on international sentencing norms. Appeals judgments were sometimes clear about their international orientations. For instance, in the *Aleksovski* judgment, the Appeals Chamber asserted that retribution "[should not] be understood as fulfilling a desire for revenge but as duly *expressing the outrage of the international community* at these crimes."[35]

The extent to which the ad hoc tribunals' trial chambers actually adhered to local sentencing norms is difficult to gauge in light of the sparsity of justifying language in the judgments. Although the norms of the former Yugoslavia – particularly the twenty-year maximum term of imprisonment – may help to explain the relatively low imprisonment terms the ICTY imposed on many defendants, this rationale is generally not made explicit in the sentencing judgments.[36] Likewise, when the ICTY diverged from the twenty-year maximum, as it did in many cases,[37] it generally did not clarify the basis for the divergence. At the ICTR, the major difference in sentencing compared to local courts was the rejection of the death penalty, but some commentators have also noted that sentences were lenient compared to local norms.[38] As Jessica Leinwand has pointed out, ICTR judgments sometimes provided extensive references to Rwandan procedure, "only to substitute that analysis with an independent determination."[39] The tribunals also at times adhered to national practice regarding aggravating and mitigating circumstances, and at other times diverged from it.[40]

Yugoslavia Mar. 24, 2000) ("The Appeals Chamber, therefore, concludes that a proper construction of the Statute, taking due account of its text and purpose, yields the conclusion that in the interests of certainty and predictability, the Appeals Chamber should follow its previous decisions, but should be free to depart from them for cogent reasons in the interests of justice.")

[35] Prosecutor v. Aleksovski, Case No. IT-95-14/1-A, Appeal Judgment, para. 185 (Int'l Crim. Trib. for the Former Yugoslavia Mar. 24, 2000) (emphasis added); *see also* Prosecutor v. Tolimir, Case No. IT-05-88/2-T, Judgment, para. 1209 (Int'l Crim. Trib. for the Former Yugoslavia Dec. 12, 2012); Prosecutor v. Nikolić, Case No. IT-94-S, Sentencing Judgment, para. 140 (Int'l Crim. Trib. for the Former Yugoslavia Dec. 18, 2003).

[36] Jessica Leinwand, *Punishing Horrific Crime: Reconciling International Prosecution With International Sentencing Practices*, 40 COLUM. HUM. RTS. L. REV. 799, 815 (2009); *but see* Prosecutor v. Delalić, Case No. IT-96-21-T, Judgment, paras. 1194–6 (Int'l Crim. Trib. for the Former Yugoslavia Nov. 16, 1998) (asserting that because no international standard for sentencing exists, the court must rely on domestic guidance).

[37] *See, e.g.*, Prosecutor v. Karadzić, Case No. IT-95-5/18-T, Judgment, para. 6070 (Int'l Crim. Trib. for the Former Yugoslavia Mar. 24, 2016) (imposing a forty-year sentence); Prosecutor v. Tolimir, Case No. IT-05-88/2-A, Appeal Judgment, para. 648 (Int'l Crim. Trib. for the Former Yugoslavia Apr. 8, 2015) (life sentence); Prosecutor v. Martić, Case No. IT-95-11-A, Appeal Judgment, para. 355 (Int'l Crim. Trib. for the Former Yugoslavia Oct. 8, 2008) (thirty-five-year sentence); Prosecutor v. Krstić, Case No. IT-98-33-A, Appeal Judgment, para. 275 (Int'l Crim Trib. for the Former Yugoslavia Apr. 19, 2004) (thirty-five-year sentence).

[38] Sam Szoke-Burke, *Avoiding Belittlement of Human Suffering: A Retributivist Critique of ICTR Sentencing Practices*, 10 J. INT'L CRIM. JUST. 561, 562 (2012) ("The lack of proportionality between sentences at the ICTR and domestic courts risks belittling the suffering of victims of the Rwandan genocide.")

[39] Leinwand, *supra* note 24, at 827.

[40] *Id.* at 833.

In an empirical study of the sentencing practices of the ad hoc tribunals, Joseph Doherty and Richard Steinberg examined the extent to which the sentences the tribunals imposed reflect the factors they embraced in their sentencing doctrines, including consideration of local sentencing norms.[41] Interestingly, they found that the length of sentences the tribunals imposed did not depend on which institution handled the case. This was surprising given the significantly harsher sentencing practices in Rwanda compared to the former Yugoslavia and suggests that local sentencing practice did not have a substantial effect on sentencing outcomes.[42]

In sum, although the tribunals purported to consider local sentencing practices and, to a lesser extent, local goals in their sentencing judgments, the degree to which such practices and goals influenced sentencing outcomes remains unclear.

11.3 THE GLOBAL-LOCAL TENSION AND THE TRIBUNALS' NORMATIVE SENTENCING LEGACY

An important criterion of an institution's legitimacy is effectiveness: achieving the goals for which the institution was established.[43] Because it is unclear whether the ad hoc tribunals were established for, or indeed, strived to, promote global or local goals, it is hard to determine the extent to which their sentencing practices were effective. Commentators take different views on the subject. Some scholars argue that the tribunals ought to have given greater deference to local norms and goals. According to Sam Szoke-Burke, the ICTR's failure to impose sentences matching those of national courts undermined the goal of retribution, and "risks belittling the suffering of victims of the Rwandan genocide."[44] Christina Carroll urged the tribunals to do more to contribute to the development of national justice systems.[45] Ralph Henham suggested they adopt restorative approaches to sentencing, centering on the needs of local populations.[46] Nancy Combs asserted that "domestic sentencing norms remain vitally relevant to international sentencing largely because a key constituency of the international criminal courts–local communities–considers them vitally relevant."[47] Finally, Yuval Shany expressed concern about international tribunals failing to adhere to local norms because

---

[41] Joseph W. Doherty & Richard H. Steinberg, *Punishment and Policy in International Criminal Sentencing: An Empirical Study*, 110 AM. J. INT'L L. 49 (2016).

[42] *Id.* at 75.

[43] Yuval Shany, Assessing the Effectiveness of International Courts 14 (2014).

[44] Szoke-Burke, *supra* note 37, at 562.

[45] Christina M. Carroll, *An Assessment of the Role and Effectiveness of the International Criminal Tribunal for Rwanda and the Rwandan National Justice System in Dealing with the Mass Atrocities of 1994*, 18 B.U. INT'L L. J. 163, 194–6 (2000).

[46] Ralph Henham, *The Philosophical Foundations of International Sentencing*, 1 J. INT'L CRIM. JUST. 64, 81 (2003).

[47] Combs, *supra* note 6, at 38.

"judgments that run contrary to important state interests could lead states to try and challenge their legitimacy."[48]

In contrast, other commentators supported a more global orientation for the ad hoc tribunals' sentencing practice. Mirjan Damaška asserted that such international criminal courts "should aim their denunciatory judgments at strengthening a sense of accountability for international crimes."[49] He believes that international judges should focus on developing the normative content of international criminal law, rather than paying close attention to "local customs and sensibilities."[50] William Schabas criticized the statutory provisions requiring the ad hoc tribunals to have recourse to national sentencing practice as "unnecessary," "virtually unworkable," and an unsuccessful attempt to "appease a spirit of zealous positivism."[51] Mary Penrose lamented that such provisions "undermine ... the true 'international' character of war crimes and crimes against humanity."[52] Others, including Michael Dafel, advocate for the adoption of international sentencing guidelines.[53]

The unresolved global-local tension thus inhibits evaluation of their effectiveness, and the extent to which their sentencing practices promoted their legitimacy or that of the international criminal justice regime. As noted above, many of the legal norms that comprise the tribunals' normative legacy reflect a global orientation. These include, in particular, the central place awarded in many of the judgments to the goal of global condemnation, and the development of a rough hierarchy of international crimes.[54] They also include holdings about the importance of leadership

---

[48] Yuval Shany, *Seeking Domestic Help: The Role of Domestic Criminal Law in Legitimizing the Work of International Criminal Tribunals*, 11 J. INT'L CRIM. JUST. 5 (2013).

[49] Mirjan R. Damaška, *What Is the Point of International Criminal Justice?*, 83 CHI.-KENT L. REV. 329, 345 (2008).

[50] *Id.* at 335.

[51] Schabas, *Perverse Effects, supra* note 11, at 538.

[52] Mary Margaret Penrose, *Lest We Fail: The Importance of Enforcement in International Criminal Law*, 15 AM. U. INT'L L. REV. 321, 375 (1999).

[53] Michael Dafel, Legitimacy, Judicial Legislating, and the Sentencing Practices of the ICTR, AFRICAN Y.B. INT'L HUMANITARIAN L. (African Found. for Int'l L.) 110 (2013), at 2; *see also* Jens David Ohlin, *Towards a Unique Theory of International Criminal Sentencing*, CORNELL LAW FACULTY PUBLICATIONS 392–7 (2009) (proposing an International Sentencing Commission "to guide judges in exercising their discretion" as one of at least three procedural changes the author suggests to "promote the institutional development of a *sui generis* system of international sentencing"). *But see* Barbora Holá, *Consistency and Pluralism in International Sentencing: An Empirical Assessment of the ICTY and ICTR Practice*, in PLURALISM IN INTERNATIONAL CRIMINAL LAW 202–3 (Elies van Sliedregt and Sergey Vasiliev eds., 2014) ("Consequently, despite the lack of sentencing guidelines and great discretionary powers of judges at the international level, the ICTY and ICTR sentences appear to be at least as statistically predictable as sentences in domestic legal systems ... [Thus,] [t]his finding could have implications for the validity of recent calls to limit judicial sentencing discretion at the international level and to enact international sentencing guidelines.")

[54] Doherty & Steinberg, *supra* note 41, at 72.

position,[55] brutality,[56] cooperation,[57] good deeds,[58] and other aggravating and mitigating circumstances.[59] But whether or not the global emphasis in many of the legal rules the tribunals developed around sentencing was appropriate depends on one's view of the tribunals' goals.

A related question is whether the ICTY's imposition of sentences longer than those that would have been permitted under national law contributed positively or negatively to its normative legitimacy. One could argue that this practice violated universal moral norms of fairness, notice, and due process. Alternatively, as Beth Van Schaack suggests, perhaps perpetrators ought to have known they could be subjected to high penalties in light of the gravity of the crimes they committed.[60] Again, the appropriateness of this aspect of the tribunals' legacy depends on resolution of the global-local tension. If the tribunals were primarily intended to vindicate particularly important global norms, it may be plausible to resolve issues of notice by reference to the particular nature of international crimes. If, on the other hand, the tribunals' most important focus was local, they ought to have more closely hewn to local norms, including those concerning sentence length.

There is at least one aspect of the tribunals' normative legacy that deserves unqualified praise, however: the rejection of the death penalty. While the claim

[55] *See e.g.*, Prosecutor v. Bagosora et al., Case No. ICTR-98-41-T, Judgment and Sentence, para. 2272 (Dec. 18, 2008) ("In aggravation, the Chamber has considered Bagosora's role as a superior in connection with Kigali area roadblocks and Nsengiyumva's role as a superior with respect to the targeted killings in Gisenyi town, including Alphonse Kabiligi, and the massacres at Mudende University and Nyundo Parish."); Prosecutor v. Plavsić, Case No. IT-00-39&40/1-S, Sentencing Judgment, para. 57 (Int'l Crim. Trib. for the Former Yugoslavia Feb. 27, 2003) ("The Trial Chamber accepts that the superior position of the accused is an aggravating factor in the case."); Prosecutor v. Kamuhanda, Case No. ICTR-99-54-A, Judgment, para. 764 (Jan. 22, 2004) ("The Chamber finds that the high position Kamuhanda held as a civil servant can be considered as an aggravating factor.")

[56] *See e.g.*, Prosecutor v. Mrškić et al., Case No. IT-95-13/1-A, Appeal Judgment, para. 400 (Int'l Crim. Trib. for the Former Yugoslavia May 5, 2009) ("Indeed factors to be considered when assessing the gravity of the offence include . . . the scale and brutality of the crime.")

[57] *See, e.g.*, Prosecutor v. Serugendo, Case No. ICTR-2005-84-I, Judgment, para.62 (June 12, 2006) ("Based on the submissions of the parties, it is clear that Serugendo's co-operation with the Prosecution has been substantial. The Chamber finds this factor to be a significant mitigating circumstance.")

[58] Jean Galbraith, *The Good Deeds of International Criminal Defendants*, 25 LEIDEN J. INT'L L. 799, 800 (2012) (discussing holdings regarding good deeds).

[59] *See, e.g.*, Prosecutor v. Blaškić, Case No. IT-95-14-T, Trial Chamber Judgment, para. 790 (Mar. 3, 2000) ("Direct participation in the crime is accordingly an aggravating circumstance which will more often than not be held against the actual perpetrators rather than against the commanders."); Prosecutor v. Hadžihasanović & Kubura, Case No. IT-01-47-A, Appeal Judgment, para. 329 (Int'l Crim. Trib. for the Former Yugoslavia Apr. 22, 2008) ("Thus, the Appeals Chamber finds that the Prosecution failed to demonstrate that the Trial Chamber erred by taking into account Hadžihasanović's intelligence and good education as mitigating factors."); Prosecutor v. Kayishema & Ruzindana, Case No. ICTR-95-1-A, Judgment, para. 351 (June 1, 2001) ("The zeal with which a crime is committed may be viewed as an aggravating factor.")

[60] Beth Van Schaack, *Crimen Sine Lege: Judicial Lawmaking at the Intersection of Law and Morals*, 97 GEO. L.J. 119, 156 (2008).

that the death penalty violates universal moral values remains controversial, many commentators recognize the importance of its progressive abolition and assert that new institutions, particularly those with international credentials, should avoid it.[61] Other commentators, most notably Jens Ohlin, argue that international crimes are so grave that the death penalty ought to be available to international courts.[62] As I have argued elsewhere, however, the gravity-based argument for the death penalty is problematic due to the absence of agreed content to the concept of gravity.[63] More importantly, imposition of the death penalty is simply morally wrong, so its rejection is always a positive contribution to normative legitimacy.[64]

In sum, the extent to which the sentencing practices of the ad hoc tribunals promoted the legitimacy of the institutions depends on one's view of the central goals of those institutions. Those who consider them primarily vehicles of global justice can count many successes in the norms they developed, whereas commentators who take a more local justice perspective will be more critical. Regardless of one's perspective, however, it seems fair to conclude that the ambiguity surrounding the tribunals' sentencing goals undermined their effectiveness and legitimacy. This in turn detracted from their ability to promote the legitimacy of the international criminal law regime more broadly. The legitimacy of that regime suffers from similar ambiguity surrounding the goals of many of its other institutions.[65] The ad hoc tribunals missed an opportunity to clarify the appropriate roles of global and local norms in sentencing, at least for other ad hoc tribunals. Only one other ad hoc tribunal is currently operating – the Special Tribunal for Lebanon, which applies exclusively national law. However, there has been talk of establishing new ad hoc tribunals,[66] and any such institutions will have little guidance from the ICTY or ICTR as to how to address the global-local tension.

---

[61] United Nations Human Rights Office of the High Commissioner, *Death Penalty*, UNITED NATIONS, www.ohchr.org/EN/Issues/DeathPenalty/Pages/DPIndex.aspx (accessed Jan. 26, 2018) ("More and more Member States from all regions acknowledge that the death penalty undermines human dignity, and that its abolition, or at least a moratorium on its use, contributes to the enhancement and progressive development of human rights.")

[62] Jens David Ohlin, *Applying the Death Penalty to Crimes of Genocide*, 99 AM. J. INT'L L. 747, 768–9 (2005).

[63] Margaret M. deGuzman, *Harsh Justice for International Crimes?*, 39 YALE J. INT'L L. 1 (2014).

[64] William Schabas, International Sentencing: From Leipzig (1923) to Arusha (1996), *in* 3 INTERNATIONAL CRIMINAL LAW 171 (M. Cherif Bassiouni ed., 2nd edn., 1999) (arguing that the refusal of international tribunals such as the ICTY and ICTR to impose the death penalty is "a significant benchmark in its progressive abolition, which has been a theme of both criminal and human rights law since the end of World War Two").

[65] As noted above, I have written about this issue in regard to the International Criminal Court. *See* deGuzman, *Gravity and Legitimacy, supra* note 5.

[66] Beth Van Schaack, *The Building Blocks of Hybrid Justice*, 44 DENV. J. INT'L L. & POL'Y 101,102 (2015).

11.4 THE GLOBAL-LOCAL TENSION AND THE TRIBUNALS' SOCIOLOGICAL LEGITIMACY

The tribunals' failure to address the global-local tension in their sentencing practices has also contributed to weak sociological legitimacy among important local audiences. This aspect of the tribunals' work is certainly not the only source of challenges to their legitimacy. Numerous social, political, and historic forces account for these negative perceptions; but the failure to sentence according to local norms and expectations, or to provide convincing explanations for decisions not to do so, has been a contributing factor.[67]

Comparative analyses of the ad hoc tribunal sentences and those imposed in the relevant national contexts have shown that the tribunals' sentences tended to be more lenient.[68] In Rwanda before abolition of the death penalty, numerous people convicted of genocide were sentenced to death. In fact, some of those sentenced to death in national courts are considered less responsible than those who received prison sentences from the ICTR.[69] The ICTY also imposed sentences that are at least arguably more lenient that they would have been in national courts. For instance, Biljana Plavsic, who served in a key government position and participated in the planning of crimes against humanity, received an eleven-year sentence after she cooperated with the tribunal. According to a Bosnian observer "'you could get more years for killing someone in traffic' than the ICTY imposes for war crimes."[70]

More important than any actual sentencing discrepancies for purposes of sociological legitimacy, however, are perceptions regarding the appropriateness of sentences. On this front, both tribunals scored rather poorly, with important local audiences judging the sentences to be inappropriately lenient.[71] Some high-profile sentences were particularly unpopular. Radovan Karadzić, former President of Republika Srpska, was sentenced to forty years in prison for genocide. Many Bosnian Muslims and Croats felt he should have received a life sentence or even death.[72] Radislav Krstić was sentenced to thirty-five years for aiding and abetting genocide, among other charges, provoking the President of the Srebrenica Women's Association to remark:

---

[67] Frédéric Mégret, *The Legacy of the ICTY as Seen Through Some of Its Actors and Observers*, 3 GOETTINGEN J. INT'L L. 101 (2011) (Sentences more lenient than those typically handed out in domestic courts in the former Yugoslavia seen as "confusing" and "a mockery of justice."); Hola, *supra* note 16, at 9.

[68] *See e.g.*, Mark B. Harmon & Fergal Gaynor, *Ordinary Sentences for Extraordinary Crimes*, 5 J. INT'L CRIM. JUST. 683 (2007).

[69] Mark A. Drumbl & Kenneth S. Gallant, *Sentencing Policies and Practices in the International Criminal Tribunals*, 15 FED. SENT'G REP. 140 (2002).

[70] Diane F. Orentlicher, That Someone Guilty Be Punished: The Impact of the ICTY in Bosnia 51 (Open Society Justice Initiative 2010) (quoting Senad Pećanin, editor of Dani, Sarajevo).

[71] Combs, *supra* note 6, at 33.

[72] *"Is the tribunal Not ashamed?" Karadžić sentence angers victims*, THE GUARDIAN (Mar. 24, 2016), www .theguardian.com/world/2016/mar/24/radovan-karadzic-hague-tribunal-sentence-survivors-victims-reaction.

Any sentence shorter than a life sentence for a criminal such as Krstic is unacceptable for us. Of course, no-one listens to us. We are so disappointed with the Hague Tribunal and unhappy with their sentences. If a criminal who is being tried just admits that he committed crimes, he is forgiven for half [of what he did] and gets a minimum sentence. Thus, we really do not expect justice from them.[73]

Likewise, many Serbs were dissatisfied with the sentence imposed on Naser Oric, a Bosnian Muslim military police commander found guilty based on superior liability for murders and cruel treatment of prisoners and sentenced to two years in prison.[74] According to one commentator, most victims were dissatisfied with the sentences the ICTY imposed.[75] Indeed, interviews with over one hundred witnesses before the ICTY revealed that the Tribunal's sentencing practices had "embittered" many of them.[76] According to Frédéric Mégret, lenient sentences were perceived as "a mockery of justice."[77] ICTY victims were also unhappy with the Tribunal's early release policy.[78]

Many Rwandans likewise perceive the sentences imposed by the ICTR as unduly lenient.[79] Not only did lower-level defendants receive harsher punishments in national courts, including the death penalty as noted above, but the facilities in which they served their sentences were considered luxurious compared to Rwandan prisons, and even to the living conditions for many Rwandans.[80] As Mark Drumbl has noted, the quality of health care provided to ICTR prisoners exceeded that in Rwandan prisons, and even that provided to victims.[81]

Some commentators blame the negative perceptions of the ad hoc tribunals' sentences on inconsistencies among sentences and a lack of transparency regarding

---

[73]   Dan Saxon, *Exporting Justice: Perceptions of the ICTY among the Serbian, Croatian, and Muslim Communities in the Former Yugoslavia*, 4 J. Hum. Rts. 559, 564 (2005).

[74]   Diane F. Orentlicher, Shrinking the Space for Denial: The Impact of the ICTY in Serbia 80-81 (Open Society Justice Initiative 2008).

[75]   Janine Natalya Clark, *Judging the ICTY: Has It Achieved Its Objectives?*, 9 Se. Eur. & Black Sea Stud. 123, 130 (2009).

[76]   Eric Stover, The Witnesses: War Crimes and the Promise of Justice in The Hague 142 (University of Pennsylvania Press 2005).

[77]   Frédéric Mégret, *The Legacy of the ICTY as Seen through Some of Its Actors and Observers*, 3 Goettingen J. Int'l L. 1011, 1034 (2011).

[78]   Edin Ramulic, *Victims' Perspectives, in* Assessing the Legacy of the ICTY 104 (Richard H. Steinberg ed., 2011).

[79]   *See* Klaus Bachmann & Aleksandar Fatić, The U.N. Criminal Tribunals: Transition Without Justice? 93 (2015); *Rwanda Unhappy with Ruggiu Sentence*, Hirondelle News Agency (June 1, 2000), www.justiceinfo.net/en/component/k2/15783-en-en-rwanda-unhappy-with-ruggiu-sentence65496549.html; *Criticise ICTR, but Not for Lack of Setting Critical Legal Precedents*, The East African (Dec. 27, 2014), www.theeastafrican.co.ke/Rwanda/Opinion/1433246-2569914-logqsj/index.html).

[80]   Madeline H. Morris, *The Trials of Concurrent Jurisdiction: The Case of Rwanda*, 7 Duke J. Comp. & Int'l L. 349, 363-4 (1997); Okechukwu Oko, *The Challenges of International Criminal Prosecutions in Africa*, 31 Fordham Int'l L.J. 343, 385 (2008).

[81]   Mark A. Drumbl, *Law and Atrocity: Settling Accounts in Rwanda*, 31 Ohio N.U. L. Rev. 41, 47-8 (2005).

the bases for sentencing decisions.[82] Silvia D'Ascoli cites the discrepancy between the twenty-year sentence awarded to Dusko Tadić, a prison guard who acted under duress, and the eleven years Plavsić received as an example of the Tribunal's sentencing inconsistency.[83] According to Allison Danner, such sentencing inconsistencies decreased the Tribunals' legitimacy.[84] Likewise, Steven Glickman asserts that the lack of uniformity among sentences "undermines the legitimacy of those tribunals, particularly among the victims and the communities affected most acutely by the war crimes in question."[85] Sam Szoke-Burke blames this lack of consistency on unresolved conflicts among sentencing goals.[86] Barbora Hola also highlights the lack of transparency in tribunal decision-making processes as part of the problem.[87]

Interestingly, some recent empirical studies suggest the tribunals' sentences were not as inconsistent as many believe. Doherty and Steinberg's study of 131 cases found a high level of consistency among the tribunals' sentences in relation to factors affecting the gravity of the crimes.[88] Moreover, it is far from clear that more consistency or even additional transparency would have promoted more positive perceptions of the tribunals' sentences among local populations. The major criticisms of the tribunals' sentences did not focus on inconsistency, but rather on largely consistent leniency. Indeed, additional transparency regarding the bases for sentences might actually have further harmed local perceptions by revealing reasoning that was less, rather than more, convincing to local populations.

CONCLUSION

The ad hoc tribunals were not endowed by their creators with clear goals, but instead were mandated to both promote global justice and pursue local objectives such as peace and reconciliation. The sentencing provisions in their statutes reflected this ambitious yet ambiguous mandate by requiring them to take account of local sentencing practices, but failing to provide any guidance on how such practice should affect their decisions. The judges did not take up the challenge of articulating clearly the roles that global and local considerations played in their decisions. The result is a sentencing legacy that contributes less than it could have to the

---

[82]   *See, e.g.*, Steven Glickman, *Victims' Justice: Legitimizing the Sentencing Regime of the International Criminal Court*, 43 Colum. J. Transnat'l L. 229, 237 (2004).

[83]   Silvia D'Ascoli, Sentencing in International Criminal Law: The UN ad hoc Tribunals and Future Perspectives for the ICC 196 n.363 (2011).

[84]   Allison Marston Danner, *Constructing a Hierarchy of Crimes in International Criminal Law Sentencing*, 87 Va. L. Rev. 415, 441 (2001).

[85]   Glickman, *supra* note 88, at 237; *see also* Michael Dafel, Legitimacy, Judicial Legislating, and the Sentencing Practices of the ICTR, African Y.B. Int'l Humanitarian L. (African Found. for Int'l L.) 110 (2013), at 8.

[86]   Szoke-Burke, *supra* note 37, at 568.

[87]   Barbora Hola, *Sentencing of International Crimes at the ICTY and ICTR: Consistency of Sentencing Case Law*, 4 Amsterdam L. F. 3, 4 (2012).

[88]   Doherty and Steinberg, *supra* note 40, at 69–75 (discussing methodology and results of study).

normative legitimacy of the tribunals or to the broader international criminal law regime, and is widely criticized by some local audiences, undermining perceptions of the tribunals' legitimacy.

In the future, those establishing international tribunals should strive to provide greater clarity regarding the appropriate mix of global and local considerations for sentencing, and judges should seek to articulate more fully the relationships between such considerations and the sentences they impose. Such clarity regarding an institution's goals will promote the tribunals' normative legitimacy, and will also likely support more positive perceptions among important audiences of the institutions and of the global criminal justice system generally.

Combatting Chaos in the Courtroom

Lessons from the ICTY and ICTR for the Control of Future War Crimes Trials

Michael P. Scharf[*]

12.1 INTRODUCTION

International criminal trials are often messy affairs. Maintaining control of the courtroom in such trials presents unique challenges to the presiding judges, especially when the defendant decides to take advantage of the right to self-representation.[1] Because of the political context and widespread publicity, former leaders on trial are more likely than ordinary defendants to have concluded that they do not stand a chance of obtaining an acquittal by playing by the judicial rules. Instead, they may engage in a range of disruptive conduct, hoping to transform themselves through political speeches into martyrs in the eyes of their followers and to discredit the tribunal by provoking the judges into inappropriately harsh responses which will make the process appear unfair.

Disruptive conduct may be defined as any intentional actions by the defendant or defense counsel in the courtroom "that substantially interferes with the dignity, order, and decorum of judicial proceedings."[2] Such conduct can be broken down into six main types:

(1) passive disrespect, for example, the refusal to address the judge as "Your Honor," refusal to stand when the judge enters the courtroom, or sitting with one's back to the judges;

---

[*] Joseph C. Hostetler – BakerHostetler Professor of Law and Dean of the Law School, Case Western Reserve University School of Law. The author thanks Cox Center Fellows Harry Quast and Adriana Velazquez-Martinez for their invaluable research assistance.

[1] In common law jurisdictions, self-representation has been interpreted as permitting the accused to act on his own behalf before a court rather than being represented by a lawyer. Civil law jurisdictions, in contrast, require that in serious criminal cases an accused must not appear in court without the assistance of defense counsel. The accused in such circumstances is generally allowed to speak at his trial, but so is the appointed lawyer. A. Cassese ET AL., THE OXFORD COMPANION TO INTERNATIONAL CRIMINAL JUSTICE 508 (2009).

[2] NORMAN DORSEN ET AL., DISORDER IN THE COURT: REPORT OF THE ASSOCIATION OF THE BAR OF THE CITY OF NEW YORK, Special Committee on Courtroom Conduct 91 (1973).

(2) refusal to cooperate with the essential ground rules of the judicial proceedings, for example by constantly insisting on making political speeches instead of asking questions during cross-examination;

(3) boycotting the proceedings and/or engaging in hunger strikes in an attempt to shut down the trial;

(4) repeated in-court interruptions, ranging from insulting remarks to loud shouting or cursing;

(5) attempting to incite acts of mass violence or publicly disclosing the identities of protected witnesses; and

(6) resorting to physical violence in the courtroom, including attempts to injure oneself or commit suicide.[3]

As Robert Jackson, the Chief Prosecutor at the Nuremberg trial, observed seventy years ago, war crimes trials, whether before international tribunals or domestic courts, seek to establish a credible historic record of abuses and elevate the rule of law over the force of might, thereby facilitating the restoration of peace and the transition to democracy.[4] While tolerating dissent is a healthy manifestation of a democratic government, "a courtroom is not an arena in which dissension, particularly of a disruptive nature, may supplant, or even take precedence over, the task of administering justice."[5] This is especially true in an international war crimes trial.

Unlike other forms of acceptable political expression, a disruptive defendant or defense lawyer who interferes with the "grandeur of court procedure" (as Hannah Arendt once described the judicial process)[6] threatens the proper administration of criminal justice in several fundamental ways. First, disruptive conduct renders it more difficult for the defendant and any co-defendants to obtain a fair trial. Second, it hampers the court's ability to facilitate the testimony of victims and other witnesses, and thereby create a historic record. Third, it undermines the public's confidence in and respect for the legal process.

There are those who would argue that a defendant has a right, through his own (or through his lawyer's) disruptive and obstructionist conduct, to an unfair trial, but modern war crimes tribunals have held that the defendant's right to employ disruptive tactics which seek to discredit the judicial process must give way to the tribunal's obligation to protect "the integrity of the proceedings" and "to ensure that the administration of justice is not brought into disrepute."[7] The duty of a war crimes

---

[3] *Id.* at 91.

[4] Robert H. Jackson, Report to the President, June 7, 1945, *quoted in* Michael P. Scharf, Balkan Justice 37 (1997) ("We must establish incredible events by credible evidence."); *see also* Robert H. Jackson, Opening Speech for the Prosecution at Nuremberg, Nov. 21, 1945 *quoted in* Trial of the Major War Criminals Before the International Military Tribunal Nuremberg, Vol. II 98–9 (1946).

[5] United States v. Dougherty, 473 F.2d 1113 (D.C. Cir. 1972) (Aams, J., concurring and dissenting).

[6] Hannah Arendt, Civil Disobedience, *in* Is Law Dead? 212 (Eugene V. Rostow ed., 1971).

[7] *See e.g.*, Prosecutor v. Norman et al., Decision on the Application of Samuel Hinga Norman for Self-Representation under Article 17(4)(d) of the Statute of the Special Court, Case No. SCSL-04-14-T, para. 28 (Jan. 17, 2005).

tribunal to ensure that a trial is fair has been interpreted as including concerns that go beyond just those of the accused.

This chapter examines how the ICTY, ICTR, and other modern war crimes trials have grappled with the challenges of maintaining control of the courtroom, especially in the context of self-represented defendants. It discloses an evolution in the responses of the tribunals and the emergence of a set of best practices that may inform the future of war crimes trials.

12.2 HISTORY'S MOST TUMULTUOUS TRIALS

12.2.1 *From the Chicago Seven to Zacarias Moussaoui*

Chaos in the courtroom is not unique to international trials. The administration of justice has always endured a degree of disorder and there have been many notable occasions when trial participants have been particularly unruly and disrespectful to judicial authority. A list of history's most disruptive defendants would include Sir Walter Raleigh (tried in Britain for high treason in 1603), William Penn (tried in Britain for unlawful assembly in 1670), Auguste Vaillant (tried in France for blowing up the Chamber of Deputies in 1894), Michele Angiolillo (tried in Spain for assassinating the Spanish premier in 1897), and Gaetano Bresci (tried in Italy for killing Italian King Humbert in 1899).[8] But by far the most notorious disorderly domestic trial in modern history was the US Chicago Seven conspiracy trial of 1969–70.

In the Chicago Seven case, the leaders of the anti-Vietnam war movement – Bobby Seale, David Dellinger, Abbie Hoffman, Jerry Rubin, Rennie Davis, Tom Hayden, Lee Weiner, and John Froines – were charged with conspiring, organizing, and inciting riots during the 1968 Democratic National Convention in Chicago.[9] The trial drew considerable public notice because of the defendants' notoriety and their courtroom antics.

On the first day of the trial, when the presiding judge, Julius Hoffman, refused to issue a postponement so that Bobby Seale's attorney would have time to recover from a gall bladder operation,[10] Seale said to the judge, "If I am consistently denied this right of legal defense counsel of my choice who is effective by the judge of this Court, then I can only see the judge as a blatant racist of the United States Court."[11] This brought a strong rebuke from Judge Hoffman.[12] That same day, Judge Hoffman reprimanded Tom Hayden for giving a clenched fist salute to the jury

---

[8] NORMAN DORSEN ET AL., DISORDER IN THE COURT: REPORT OF THE ASSOCIATION OF THE BAR OF THE CITY OF NEW YORK, Special Committee on Courtroom Conduct 91 (1973).

[9] Although there were initially eight defendants, Bobby Seale was severed from the case before it went to the jury.

[10] *See* United States v. Seale, 461 F.2d 345, 358 (7th Cir. 1972).

[11] *Id.* at 374.

[12] *Id.*

and Abbie Hoffman for blowing kisses at the jurors.[13] A few days later, the defendants tried to drape the counsel table with a North Vietnamese flag in celebration of Vietnam Moratorium Day, drawing another round of sharp words from the judge.[14]

Throughout the trial, the defendants refused to rise at the beginning or close of court sessions.[15] On two occasions, defendants Abbie Hoffman and Jerry Rubin wore judicial robes in court onto which were pinned a Jewish yellow star, meant to imply that Judge Hoffman was running his courtroom like the courts of Nazi Germany.[16] The defendants frequently called Judge Hoffman derogatory names, accused him of racism and prejudice, and made sarcastic comments to him, such as asking "How is your war stock doing?" The most serious disorder occurred two weeks into the trial, when Judge Hoffman learned that a few minutes before the commencement of the court session, Bobby Seale had addressed the audience of his supporters in the courtroom, telling them that if he were attacked "they know what to do."[17] Judge Hoffman responded by having Seale bound and gagged. Defense counsel William Kunstler then scolded the Court, saying "This is no longer a court of order, your Honor; this is a medieval torture chamber. It is a disgrace."[18]

At the conclusion of the trial, Judge Hoffman issued a total of 159 citations to the defendants and their lawyers for contempt in response to these incidents of disruption and disrespect. The Seventh Circuit Court of Appeals, however, reversed the contempt convictions on the ground that the judge cannot wait until the end of the trial to punish the defendants and their lawyers for misconduct. It also reversed the convictions on the substantive charges, in part due to the prejudicial remarks and actions of the trial judge and inflammatory statements by the prosecutor during the trial.[19] It should come as no surprise that the Chicago Seven trial is universally seen as a low point in American courtroom management. Rather than viewing Judge Hoffman as a brave hero fighting anarchy, history remembers him more as an accomplice who unwittingly fanned the flames of disorder. Many of the defendants before the ICTY and other international criminal tribunals set out to do the same thing to the international judges presiding over their trials.

Just a few months after the Chicago Seven trial, the US Supreme Court held in *Illinois* v. *Allen* that an unruly defendant could be excluded from the courtroom during his trial if his disruptive behavior threatened to make orderly and proper

---

[13]   See Pnina Lahav, *Theater in the Courtroom: The Chicago Conspiracy Trial*, 16 CARDOZO STUD. L. & LIT. 381, 387 (2004).

[14]   *See id.*

[15]   461 F.2d at 382, 386.

[16]   Lahav, *supra* note 13, at 430.

[17]   *Id.*

[18]   *Id.*

[19]   United States v. Seale, 461 F.2d 345 (7th Cir. 1972); United States v. Dillinger, 472 F.2d 340 (7th Cir. 1972).

proceedings difficult or wholly impossible.[20] Allen had been tried in a state court in 1957 for armed robbery of a tavern owner. During his trial, Allan threatened the judge's life, made abusive remarks to the court, and announced that under no circumstances would he allow his trial to proceed. The court responded by removing him from the courtroom, after appropriate warning, and Allen was convicted in his absence.

The Supreme Court affirmed Allen's conviction, ruling that removal after a warning was permissible and far less objectionable than use of restraints. In a passage that was obviously inspired by the publicity surrounding the Chicago Seven trial, the Supreme Court stated:

> Trying a defendant for a crime while he sits bound and gagged before the judges and jury would to an extent comply with that part of the Sixth Amendment's purposes that accords the defendant an opportunity to confront the witnesses at the trial. But even to contemplate such a technique, much less see it, arouses a feeling that no person should be tried while shackled and gagged except as a last resort. Not only is it possible that the sight of shackles and gags might have a significant effect on the jury's feelings about the defendant, but the use of this technique is itself something of an affront to the very dignity and decorum of judicial proceedings that the judge is seeking to uphold.[21]

Yet the Court declined to rule that physical restraints may never be used, saying: "However, in some situations which we need not attempt to foresee, binding and gagging might possibly be the fairest and most reasonable way to handle a defendant who acted as Allen did here."[22]

The first major chaotic trial to arise after the Supreme Court's *Allen* decision was that of Charles Manson who, along with three female members of his cult, was tried from June 1970 to March 1971 for the gruesome murder of movie actress Sharon Tate and five others. During the trial, Manson constantly interrupted proceedings by shouting, chanting, turning his back on the judge, assuming a crucifixion pose, and singing (actions often parroted by the three women co-defendants).[23] The court responded by repeatedly having the defendants removed from the courtroom. In one instance, the judge removed Manson after he leaped over the defense table to attack the judge with a pencil, shouting "In the name of Christian justice, someone should cut your head off."[24]

---

[20] Illinois v. Allen, 397 U.S. 337 (1970). The Court explained that it was "essential to the proper administration of criminal justice that dignity, order, and decorum be the hallmark of all court proceedings in our country." *Id.* at 343.

[21] *Id.* at 344.

[22] *Id.*

[23] Robert Dardenne, The Case of Charles Manson, *in* THE PRESS ON TRIAL 159, 167 (Lloyd Chiasson Jr. ed., 1991).

[24] *Id.*

More recently, in February 2006, accused al-Qaeda terrorist Zacarias Moussaoui, was thrown out of the courtroom by US District Judge Leonie Brinkema, and then temporarily banned from returning to court, due to his disruptive and belligerent outbursts. "This trial is a circus... God curse you and America," Moussaoui shouted at the judge as he was led away. "You are the biggest enemy of yourself," Judge Brinkema replied, ordering that Moussaoui watch the remainder of the proceedings via closed-circuit feed from a jail cell inside the courthouse. Media outlets reported that most legal scholars agreed that Judge Brinkema acted appropriately.[25]

12.3 THE RIGHT OF SELF-REPRESENTATION: THE CASE LAW OF THE ICTR, SCSL, ICTY, AND IHT

12.3.1 *The ICTR*

The ICTR was the first international tribunal to face the question of a defendant's right to self-representation, holding in the case of Jean-Bosco Barayagwiza that defense counsel could be assigned over the objection of the accused.[26] Barayagwiza, like Slobodan Milosevic (discussed below), was a lawyer by training and a former high-level government official. The ICTR Trial Chamber took the right to self-representation as articulated in the Statute as a starting point, but noted that according to international (and some national) jurisprudence, this right is not absolute.

The Registrar declined Barayagwiza's request on January 5, 2000, for the withdrawal of his counsel, J. P. L. Nyaberi. Barayagwiza sought the withdrawal citing reasons of "lack of competence, honesty, loyalty, diligence, and interest."[27] The Registrar's decision was confirmed by the President of the ICTR on January 19, 2000, but on January 31, 2000, the Appeals Chamber ordered the withdrawal of Barayagwiza's defense counsel, J. P. L. Nyaberi, and ordered the assignment of new counsel and co-counsel for Barayagwiza.[28] Barayagwiza declined to accept the assigned counsel, and instructed them not to represent him at the trial. The ICTR Trial Chamber ordered counsel to continue representing Barayagwiza. Counsel filed a motion to withdraw on October 26, 2000, given their client's instructions not

---

[25] Michael P. Scharf, Did the Dujail Trial Meet International Standards of Due Process, *in* SADDAM ON TRIAL: UNDERSTANDING AND DEBATING THE IRAQI HIGH TRIBUNAL 162, 163 (Michael P. Scharf & Gregory S. McNeal eds., 2006); *see generally* Neil A. Lewis, *Judge Ejects 9/11 Suspect after Outburst*, N.Y. TIMES, Feb. 15, 2006, at A20; Kelli Arena & Kevin Bohn, *Al Qaeda Conspirator Barred from Court*, CNN.COM, Feb. 14, 2006, www.cnn.com/2006/LAW/02/14/moussaoui.trial/index.html/.

[26] ICTR, Prosecutor v. Barayagwiza, Decision on Defense Counsel Motion to Withdraw, Case No. ICTR-97–19-T, Nov. 2, 2000.

[27] ICTR, Prosecutor v. Barayagwiza, Decision on Defense Counsel Motion to Withdraw, Case No. ICTR-97–19-T, Nov. 2, 2000.

[28] ICTR, Prosecutor v. Barayagwiza, Decision on Defense Counsel Motion to Withdraw, Case No. ICTR-97–19-T, Nov. 2, 2000.

to represent him at trial, which was denied on November 2, 2000, on the basis that the ICTR Trial Chamber had to ensure the rights of Barayagwiza.[29]

The ICTR Trial Chamber held Barayagwiza's behavior to be "an attempt to obstruct proceedings. In such a situation, it cannot reasonably be argued that Counsel is under an obligation to follow them, and that [sic] not do so would constitute grounds for withdrawal."[30] It referred to the "well established principle in human rights law that the judiciary must ensure the rights of the accused, taking into account what is at stake for him."[31] The ICTR Trial Chamber further noted that assigned counsel "represents the interest of the Tribunal to ensure that the Accused receives a fair trial. The aim is to obtain efficient representation and adversarial proceedings."[32] In a separate concurring opinion, Judge Gunawardana stressed the effect a decision to grant the withdrawal of counsel would have on the administration of justice of the trial. He submitted that Article 20(4)(d), the provision founded on ICCPR Article 14(3)(d), is "an enabling provision for the appointment of a 'standby counsel'," and in such circumstances the ICTR should make use of court-appointed standby counsel.[33]

12.3.2 *The SCSL*

In one of its first cases, the Special Court for Sierra Leone (SCSL) held that the defendant Samuel Hinga Norman could not represent himself without the assistance of standby counsel.[34] Norman, who, like Barayagwiza and Milosevic, was a lawyer by training and a former high-level government official, indicated in a letter of June 3, 2004, after the opening statement of the prosecutor, that he wished to represent himself and that he was dispensing of his defense counsel that had been acting on his behalf since March 2003.

In requiring the appointment of standby counsel, the SCSL Trial Chamber sought to distinguish Norman's situation from that of the ICTY *Milosevic* case (discussed in Section 12.3.3) in two respects: First, the SCSL noted that Norman was being tried with two co-defendants. Second, Norman had not signaled his intention to represent himself from the outset. The SCSL Trial Chamber then

---

[29] ICTR, Prosecutor v. Barayagwiza, Decision on Defense Counsel Motion to Withdraw, Case No. ICTR-97–19-T, Nov. 2, 2000.

[30] ICTR, Prosecutor v. Barayagwiza, Decision on Defense Counsel Motion to Withdraw, Case No. ICTR-97–19-T, Nov. 2, 2000.

[31] ICTR, Prosecutor v. Barayagwiza, Decision on Defense Counsel Motion to Withdraw, Case No. ICTR-97–19-T, Nov. 2, 2000.

[32] ICTR, Prosecutor v. Barayagwiza, Decision on Defense Counsel Motion to Withdraw, Case No. ICTR-97–19-T, Nov. 2, 2000.

[33] ICTR, Prosecutor v. Barayagwiza, Decision on Defense Counsel Motion to Withdraw, Case No. ICTR-97–19-T, Nov. 2, 2000.

[34] Prosecutor v. Norman et al., Decision on the Application of Samuel Hinga Norman for Self-Representation under Article 17(4)(d) of the Statute of the Special Court, Case No. SCSL-04-14-0T, June 8, 2004.

turned to the characteristics of the trial that made it impossible for Norman to represent himself. According to the SCSL Trial Chamber, the right of counsel is an essential and necessary component of a fair trial. Without counsel, the judges are forced to be a proactive participant in the proceedings instead of the arbiter, which is one of the greatest characteristics of an adversarial proceeding. The SCSL Trial Chamber turned to the complexity of the case and the intricacies of international criminal law, as well as the national and international interest in the "expeditious completion of the trial." The trial judges were also concerned with the impact on the court's timetable.[35]

12.3.3 *The ICTY: Milosevic, Seselj, and Karadzic*

Slobodan Milosevic was the first former head of state to be tried in an international war crimes trial. Although assisted by an army of defense counsel, Milosevic asserted his right to act as his own lawyer in the televised proceedings before the Yugoslavia Tribunal, as this would enable him to make lengthy opening and closing statements and turn cross-examinations into opportunities for unfettered political diatribes. The presiding judge, Richard May, concluded that Milosevic had an absolute right of self-representation, which could not be revoked no matter Milosevic's antics.[36] As the trial unfolded, Milosevic exploited his right of self-representation to treat the witnesses, prosecutors, and the judges in a manner that would earn ordinary defense counsel expulsion from the courtroom. He often strayed from the forensic case into long vitriolic speeches and he was frequently strategically disruptive.[37]

---

[35] Prosecutor v. Norman et al., Decision on the Application of Samuel Hinga Norman for Self-Representation under Article 17(4)(d) of the Statute of the Special Court, Case No. SCSL-04-14-T, June 8, 2004, at para. 26.

[36] Prosecutor v. Milosevic, Case No.: IT-99-37-PT, Transcript, Aug. 30, 2001, at 18 ("Status Conference").

> We have to act in accordance with the Statute and our Rules which, in any event, reflect the position under customary international law, which is that the [defendant] has a right to counsel, but he also has a right not to have counsel. He has a right to defend himself, and it is quite clear that he has chosen to defend himself. He has made that abundantly clear. The strategy that the Chamber has employed of appointing an amicus curiae will take care of the problems that you have outlined, but I stress that it would be wrong for the Chamber to impose counsel on the [defendant], because that would be in breach of the position under customary international law. *Id.*

[37] For references by the Tribunal of Milosevic misusing hearings and cross examinations as a platform for making political speeches, see Prosecutor v. Milosevic, Case No. IT-02-54-T, Initial Appearance (July 3, 2001); Prosecutor v. Milosevic, Case No. IT-02-54-T, Status Conference, (Oct. 30, 2001); Prosecutor v. Milosevic, Case No. IT-02-54-T, Open Session, (Nov. 10, 2004); Prosecutor v. Milosevic, Case No. IT-02-54-T, Hearing, (Nov. 10, 2004); Prosecutor v. Milosevic, Case No. IT-02-54-T Pre-Defense Conference, (June 17, 2004); *see also* Jerrold M. Post & Lara K. Panis, *Tyranny on Trial: Personality and Courtroom Conduct of Defendants Slobodan Milosevic and Saddam Hussein,* 38 Cornell Int'l L. J. 823, 832 (2005).

On numerous occasions, the presiding judge, Richard May, tried to reign in Milosevic with little success. A defendant who is represented by a lawyer is ordinarily able to address the court only when he takes the stand to give testimony during the defense's case-in-chief. And in the usual case, the defendant is limited to giving evidence that is relevant to the charges, and he is subject to cross-examination by the prosecution. While a judge can control an unruly lawyer by threatening fines, jail time, suspension, or disbarment, there is much less a judge can do to effectively regulate a disruptive defendant who is acting as his own counsel.

While Milosevic's antics did not win him points with the judges, they had a significant impact on public opinion back home in Serbia. Rather than discredit his nationalistic policies, the trial had the opposite effect. His approval rating in Serbia doubled during the first weeks of the trial, and two years into the trial he easily won a seat in the Serb parliament in a nationwide election. In addition, opinion polls indicated that a majority of Serbs felt that he was not getting a fair trial, and that he was not actually guilty of any war crimes.[38]

On September 22, 2004, with the Milosevic trial about to begin the defense phase, the Trial Chamber (now composed of Patrick Robinson, O-Gon Kwon, and Iain Bonomy who replaced the deceased Richard May) decided to revisit Judge May's ruling that Slobodan Milosevic had an unfettered right to represent himself in the courtroom. As authority for his position, Judge May had cited the US Supreme Court's 1975 ruling in *Faretta* v. *California*, which held that there was a fundamental right to self-representation in US courts. But the US high court also added a caveat, which Judge May overlooked, stating that "the right of self-representation is not a license to abuse the dignity of the courtroom." US appellate courts have subsequently held that the right of self-representation is subject to exceptions – such as when the defendant acts in a disruptive manner or when self-representation interferes with the dignity or integrity of the proceedings.

However, the Trial Chamber did not focus on Milosevic's disruptive behavior, but rather on his deteriorating health. In its ruling on September 22, the Trial Chamber determined that Milosevic's high blood pressure and heart condition, which repeatedly required pauses in the trial, justified appointment of counsel to represent him in court for the remainder of the proceedings. In its view:

> If at any stage of a trial there is a real prospect that it will be disrupted and the integrity of the trial undermined with the risk that it will not be conducted fairly, then the Trial Chamber has a duty to put in place a regime which will avoid that. Should self-representation have that impact, we conclude that it is open to the Trial Chamber to assign counsel to conduct the defense case, if the Accused will not appoint his own counsel.[39]

---

[38] Michael P. Scharf & Christopher M. Rassi, *Do Former Leaders Have an International Right to Self-Representation in War Crimes Trials?*, 20 OHIO ST. J. DISPUTE RESOLUTION 3, 6 (2005).

[39] Prosecutor v. Milosevic, Case No.: IT-99-37-PT, Order on the Modalities to be Followed by Court Assigned Counsel, Sept. 3, 2004, *at* www.un.org/icty/milosevic/trialc/order-e/040903.htm (last visited Oct. 10, 2017).

Following the Trial Chamber's decision of September 22, Milosevic refused to cooperate in any way with assigned counsel. Believing that they could not adequately represent the defendant without such cooperation, assigned counsel brought an interlocutory appeal to the ICTY Appeals Chamber (consisting of Theodor Meron, Fausto Pocar, Florence Mumba, Mehmet Guney, and Innes Monica Weinberg de Roca).

The Appeals Chamber decision, which was authored by Judge Meron, represented an obvious attempt at compromise. The Appeals chamber agreed with the Trial Chamber that defendants have "a presumptive right to represent themselves before the Tribunal" but that this right was subject to limitations. According to the Appeals Chamber, the test to be applied is that "the right may be curtailed on the grounds that a defendant's self-representation is substantially and persistently obstructing the proper and expeditious conduct of his trial." Applying this test, the Appeals Chamber concluded that the Trial Chamber had not abused its discretion in deciding to restrict Milosevic's right to self-representation.[40]

However, the Appeals Chamber felt that the Trial Chamber's order requiring Milosevic to act through appointed counsel went too far, and that the proportionality principle required that a more "carefully calibrated set of restrictions" be imposed on Milosevic's trial participation.[41] Under these, when he is physically able to do so, Milosevic must be permitted to take the lead in presenting his case – choosing which witnesses to present, questioning those witnesses, giving the closing statement, and making the basic strategic decisions about the presentation of his defense. "If Milosevic's health problems resurface with sufficient gravity, however, the presence of Assigned Counsel will enable the trial to continue even if Milosevic is temporarily unable to participate."[42] Milosevic's health problems did indeed resurface, and the former Serb leader died just before the conclusion of his trial.

Six months after Milosevic's death, another former Serb leader, Vojislav Seselj, decided that he, too, would utilize the right of self-representation as a means of disrupting his trial before the ICTY. Seselj made his unruly intentions clear on the eve of trial when he published three books in Serbia entitled *Genocidal Israeli Diplomat Theordor Meron* (about the President of the ICTY), *In the Jaws of the Whore Del Ponte* (about the Chief Prosecutor of the Tribunal), and *The Lying Hague Homosexual, Geoffrey Nice* (about the lead trial prosecutor).[43] Seselj tried repeatedly to provoke the judges at pretrial hearings and made numerous obscene and improper statements in his pretrial motions, including one submission which

---

[40] Decision on Interlocutory Appeal of the Trial Chamber's Decision on the Assignment of Defense Counsel, Milosevic (IT-02–54-AR73.7), Appeals Chamber, 1 November 2004.

[41] Decision on Interlocutory Appeal of the Trial Chamber's Decision on the Assignment of Defense Counsel, Milosevic (IT-02–54-AR73.7), Appeals Chamber, 1 November 2004.

[42] Decision on Interlocutory Appeal of the Trial Chamber's Decision on the Assignment of Defense Counsel, Milosevic (IT-02–54-AR73.7), Appeals Chamber, 1 November 2004.

[43] Prosecutor v. Seselj, Case No. IT-03–67-PT, Decision on Assignment of Counsel, para. 30 (Aug. 21, 2006).

stated, "You, all you members of The Hague Tribunal Registry, can only accept to suck my cock."[44]

On the eve of trial in August 2006, the Trial Chamber revoked Seselj's right to self-representation, stating:

> While it is clear that the conduct of the Accused brings into question his willingness to follow the "ground rules" of the proceedings and to respect the decorum of the Court, more fundamentally, in the Chamber's view, this behavior compromises the dignity of the tribunal and jeopardizes the very foundations upon which its proper functioning is based.[45]

The Appeals Chamber agreed that the Trial Chamber could revoke the right to self-representation where the Trial Chamber found "that appropriate circumstances, rising to the level of substantial and persistent obstruction to the proper and expeditious conduct of the trial exist."[46] The Appeals Chamber, however, held that the Trial Chamber had to first give the defendant an explicit warning. The Trial Chamber subsequently did so, and in light of Seselj's continuing disruptive behavior, appointed counsel over his objection to represent him for the trial.

Seselj immediately launched a hunger strike, while simultaneously appealing the Trial Chamber's appointment of counsel. As Seselj's health deteriorated, the Appeals Chamber became increasingly concerned of a repeat of what happened to Milosevic, so it decided that Seselj should be entitled to continue to represent himself.[47] In so doing, the Appeals Chamber wrote that its decision should "in no way be construed as evidence... rewarding Seselj's behavior," but there really is no other way to view the holding than as "a betrayal of the Trial Chambers' sincere efforts to achieve optimal trial management."[48]

One of the last defendants to be tried by the ICTY was Radovan Karadzic, the Bosnian Serb political leader accused, and ultimately convicted of, genocide. At his first appearance on July 31, 2008, Karadzic made clear that he intended to exercise his right to represent himself, but that he had no intention of obstructing the proceedings or abusing the court as Seselj had done.[49] However, in protest of the Trial Chamber's refusal to grant him more time before the start of the trial, when the Trial Chamber called the case to start on October 26, 2009, Karadzic refused to attend. Two days later, the Trial Chamber ruled that Karadzic's boycott

---

[44] *Id.* para. 48.

[45] *Id.* para. 77.

[46] Prosecutor v. Seselj, Decision on Appeal against the Trial Chamber's Decision on Assignment of Counsel, IT-03-67-AR73.3, Oct. 20, 2006, at para. 21.

[47] ICTY, Prosecutor v. Vojislav Seselj, Decision on Appeal against the Trial Chamber's Decision (No. 2) on Assignment of Counsel, Case No. IT-03-67-AR73.4, December 8, 2006, paras. 22–3.

[48] Richard Harvey, Who Needs A Lawyer Anyway? Self-Representation And Standby Counsel in International Criminal Trials, in Defense Perspectives On International Criminal Justice 95 (2017), https://www.amazon.com/Defense-Perspectives-International-Criminal-Justice/dp/1107086671

[49] ICTY, Prosecutor v. Radovan Karadzic, Status Conference – Transcript, Case No. IT-95-5/18-PT, Sept. 17, 2008, at 43.

had "substantially and persistently obstructed the proper and expeditious conduct of his trial" and appointed Richard Harvey to serve as standby counsel to represent him in his absence.[50] The Trial Chamber gave stand by counsel four months to familiarize himself with the case before the trial would commence.

The Trial Chamber defined the role of Karadzic's standby counsel to include the following functions: (1) receipt of all court documents, filings, and disclosed materials generated by or sent to Karadzic; (2) to be present in the courtroom during all proceedings; (3) to actively engage in preparation of the case so as to be prepared to question witnesses on Karadzic's behalf or to represent Karadzic's interests at any time should the Chamber find that to be necessary; and (4) to address the Chamber whenever so requested by the Chamber.[51] In the end, Karadzic terminated his boycott, participated as his own counsel throughout his trial, and there was no need for standby counsel to supplant Karadzic or his chief legal adviser, Peter Robinson. On March 24, 2016, Karadzic was convicted of genocide and sentenced to forty years.[52] A week later, Vojislav Seselj was acquitted of all counts against him,[53] but Seselj's acquittal was overturned on appeal, and he was ultimately sentenced to time served.[54]

12.3.4 *The IHT: Disarray in the Dujail Trial*

On August 11, 2005, the democratically elected Iraqi National Assembly adopted the Statute of the Iraqi High Tribunal with some modifications. Notably, the Assembly replaced the clause providing for a right of self-representation with a clause that said that all defendants before the Tribunal had to be represented by Iraqi counsel, who could be assisted by foreign lawyers.[55] The judges, however, decided to follow the unique Iraqi legal tradition of permitting a defendant to cross-examine each witness after his lawyer had done so.[56] This made it extremely difficult for the judges to

---

[50] ICTY, Prosecutor v. Karadzic, Decision on Appointment of Counsel and Order on Further Trial Proceedings, Case No. IT-95–5/18-T, Nov. 5, 2009, at paras. 21–6.

[51] ICTY, Prosecutor v. Karadzic, Decision on Appointment of Counsel and Order on Further Trial Proceedings, Case No. IT-95–5/18-T, Nov. 5, 2009, at para. 9.

[52] ICTY, Prosecutor v Radovan Karadzic, Judgment, Case No. IT-95–5/18-T, March 24, 2016.

[53] ICTY, Prosecutor v. Vojislav Seselj, Judgment, Case No. IT-03–67-T, March 31, 2016.

[54] ICTY, Prosecutor v. Vojislav Seselj, Appeals Chamber Judgment, Case No. MICT-16-99-A, April 11, 2018.

[55] Qanoon Al-Mahkamat Al-Jeena'eyyat Al-Eraqiyyat Al-Mukhtas [Statute of the Iraqi High Tribunal] art. 19 (d), Oct. 18, 2005, *available at* www.law.case.edu/saddamtrial/documents/IST_statute_official_english.pdf (Iraq), *reproduced in* MICHAEL P. SCHARF & GREGORY S. MCNEAL, Saddam on Trial: Understanding and Debating the Iraqi High Tribunal 283 (2006); English Translation of the Iraqi High Tribunal Rules of Procedure and Evidence (2005), Rule 29, *id.* at 313.

[56] There is also some international tribunal precedent for the approach of the IHT. After assigning counsel over the accused's objection, the ICTY permitted the accused Krajisnic "as an exception to the usual regime, to supplement counsel's cross-examination with his own questions." Prosecutor v. Krajisnic, Reasons for Oral Decision Denying Mr. Krajisnik's Request to Proceed Unrepresented by Counsel, Case No. IT-00–39-T, Aug. 18, 2005, para. 3.

maintain control of the courtroom during the trial of Saddam Hussein and other leaders of the Ba'athist Regime.

During their trial, Saddam Hussein and the other defendants were constantly disruptive and prone to political theater. Hussein's disruptive conduct often coincided with the most emotionally compelling testimony of victims. He engaged in frequent angry outbursts. He yelled at the judge to "go to hell" and called the judge a homosexual, a dog, and a whore-monger. He made wild accusations of mistreatment by his American jailers. He insisted on prayer breaks in the middle of witness testimony, went on hunger strikes, and repeatedly refused to attend trial sessions. Most troubling, he took advantage of his right as a defendant to cross-examine witnesses after his lawyer had finished doing so by making frequent political speeches and impelling his followers – who were watching the television broadcasts of the proceedings – to kill American occupiers and Iraqi government collaborators.

Meanwhile, Hussein's co-defendant, Barzan al-Tikriti, who served as head of the Internal Security Agency, competed with Hussein for the most offensive insults directed at the bench. On one occasion, he appeared in court wearing only his pajamas,[57] and another time, he insisted on sitting on the courtroom floor with his back to the judge.[58]

For their part, Saddam Hussein's retained lawyers, in particular Lebanese defense attorney Bushra al-Khalil and Jordanian lawyer Salah al-Armouti, frequently made outrageous political speeches and acted in outright contempt of the Iraqi High Tribunal. They engaged in tactics such as insulting Judge Ra'ouf, holding up photos of US prison abuses at Abu Ghraib,[59] and on one occasion pulling off their defense counsel robes and hurling them at the bench.[60] Saddam Hussein's retained lawyers also staged a walkout in the middle of a trial session and boycotted the majority of the trial sessions, including the closing arguments.[61] These acts violated Iraqi law and the Iraqi Code of Legal Professional Ethics, which provide that lawyers practicing in Iraqi courts must be respectful toward the court, must appear in court on the set dates, should not try to delay the resolution of a case, and must facilitate the task of the judge.[62]

The first presiding judge, Rizgar Amin, attempted to deal with such disruptive behavior by ignoring it.[63] Although human rights groups applauded Judge Rizgar's

57   Edward Wong, *The Reach of War: The Trial; Hussein, Gleeful, Badgers the Judge and Declares a Hunger Strike Over His Treatment*, N.Y. TIMES, Feb. 15, 2006, at A10.

58   Robert F. Worth, *Prosecutors of Hussein Press Charges of Execution*, N.Y. TIMES, Feb. 14, 2006, at A8.

59   Edward Wong, *Saddam Admits He Swiftly Doomed 148 Villagers*, INT'L HERALD TRIB., April 2006.

60   Hussan M. Fatah, *For a Shiite, Defending Hussein Is a Labor of Love*, N.Y. TIMES, June 24, 2006, at A4.

61   *See* Nehal Bhuta, Judging Dujail: The First Trial Before the Iraqi High Tribunal 71 (Human Rights Watch, 2006) (discussing the role of Defense Office lawyers after privately retained defense counsel began boycotting the Dujail trial in February of 2006).

62   Law of the Legal Profession, No. 173 of 1965, art. 50; Lawyer's Professional Code of Conduct, June 16, 1987 (annexed to the Law of the Legal Profession), art. 9, *cited in* Bhuta, *supra* note 38, at 70.

63   *See* Michael Scharf, Who Won the Battle of Wills in the December Proceedings of the Saddam Trial?, *in* SADDAM ON TRIAL: UNDERSTANDING AND DEBATING THE IRAQI HIGH TRIBUNAL 129, 130 (Michael P. Scharf & Gregory S. McNeal eds., 2006).

calm demeanor in conducting the trial, the Iraqi population felt that he was losing the "battle of the wills" against the former dictator, and he resigned under the weight of mass public criticism.[64] The new presiding judge, Ra'ouf Abdul Rahman, employed a number of tactics in an attempt to regain control of his courtroom.[65]

Judge Ra'ouf began his first day as presiding judge by sternly warning defendants and counsel that outbursts and insults would not be tolerated. A few minutes later, he demonstrated his resolve by evicting defendant Barzan al-Tikriti and defense counsel Bushra al-Khalil when they failed to heed to his admonishment. When the retained defense counsel responded by boycotting the trial *en masse*, Judge Ra'ouf appointed public defenders to replace them. Notably, when the retained defense counsel later asked to return, Judge Ra'ouf permitted them to do so. He never imposed fines or other sanctions on them for their misbehavior, despite the fact that they resorted to such tactics again and again throughout the trial. Nor did he revoke the defendants' right to question the witnesses or to address the court, despite the fact that it was frequently abused.

12.4 REMEDIES FOR DISRUPTION

12.4.1 *Limiting Self-Representation*

As the various cases discussed above indicate, permitting a former leader to assert the right of self-representation in a war crimes trial is a virtual license for abuse. In contrast to the United States, many countries of the world require that defendants be represented by counsel in all cases involving serious charges.[66] The Iraqi National Assembly was prudent to require that defendants before the Iraqi High Tribunal be represented by Iraqi lead counsel, whom the Tribunal could control through various sanctions available under Iraqi law.

It was a mistake, however, for the presiding judges of the Iraqi High Tribunal to allow the defendants to question witnesses following their lawyers' cross-examinations, as this completely undermined the objective of the National Assembly's revisions to the IHT Statute. Instead, the judges should have recognized that departures from the traditional civil law practice are warranted in an extraordinary trial of this nature, especially as the traditional practice was neither required by Iraqi nor international law.

[64] *See* Michael Scharf, A Changing of the Guard at the Iraqi High Tribunal, *in* SADDAM ON TRIAL: UNDERSTANDING AND DEBATING THE IRAQI HIGH TRIBUNAL 136, 136–7 (Michael P. Scharf & Gregory S. McNeal eds., 2006).

[65] *See* Michael Scharf, *The Battle of the Wills – Part Two*, *in* SADDAM ON TRIAL: UNDERSTANDING AND DEBATING THE IRAQI HIGH TRIBUNAL 143, 143–4 (Michael P. Scharf & Gregory S. McNeal eds., 2006).

[66] Michael P. Scharf & Christopher M. Rassi, *Do Former Leaders Have an International Right to Self-Representation in War Crimes Trials?*, 20 OHIO ST. J. DISPUTE RESOLUTION 3, 13–15 (2005).

Even in a tribunal such as the ICTY, whose statute provides for the right of self-representation, the Appeals Chamber decisions in the *Milosevic, Seselj,* and *Karadzic* cases recognize that such a right is a qualified one. Abuse it and you lose it.[67] Drawing from international tribunal precedent, standby defense counsel should be imposed on a defendant who seeks to represent himself where: (1) the defendant attempts to boycott his trial;[68] (2) the defendant's self-representation would prejudice the fair trial rights of co-defendants;[69] (3) the defendant is being persistently disruptive or obstructionist;[70] or (4) self-representation would unreasonably prolong the trial.[71]

While some commentators advocate for a hybrid approach where the self-represented defendant can act as co-counsel with standby counsel,[72] this author believes the better approach is that of the common law countries. In the United States, for example, courts have held that a defendant who is represented by a lawyer has no right to act as co-counsel by, for example, cross-examining witnesses, addressing the bench, or making opening or closing arguments. The rule limiting the defendant's participation is necessary "to maintain order, prevent unnecessary consumption of time or other undue delay, to maintain the dignity and decorum of the court and to accomplish a variety of other ends essential to the due administration of justice."[73]

Since most war crimes tribunal courtrooms are partitioned by soundproof glass, and televising the proceedings are subject to a thirty-second delay, a judge may effectively deal with minor disruptions by simply turning off the defendant's microphone. In the case of major or persistent disruptions, the judge must give a specific warning before revoking the right of self-representation, and the revocation must meet the standard of proportionality. In addition, the defendant should be accorded at least a chance to reclaim the right if he manifests a willingness to conduct himself consistently with the decorum and respect inherent in the concept of courts and judicial proceedings.

---

[67] *See* Prosecutor v. Seselj, Case No. IT-03–67-AR73.4, Decision on Appeal against the Trial Chamber's Decision on Assignment of Counsel, para. 21 (Oct. 20, 2006).

[68] Prosecutor v. Barayagwiza, Case No. ICTR-07–19-T Decision on Defense Counsel Motion to Withdraw, para. 24 (Nov. 2, 2000); *see also* Diaz v. United States, 223 U.S. 442, 458 (1912) (holding that a trial could continue where the defendant refused to appear in the courtroom ... to hold otherwise would enable the defendant to "paralyze the proceedings of courts and juries and turn them into a solemn farce").

[69] Prosecutor v. Norman et al., Case No. SCSL-4–14-T, Decision on the Application of Samuel Hinga Norman for Self-Representation under Article 17(4)(d) of the Statute of the Special Court, para. 14 (Jan. 17, 2005).

[70] Prosecutor v. Seselj, Case No. IT-03–67-AR73.4, Decision on Appeal against the Trial Chamber's Decision on Assignment of Counsel, para. 21 (Oct. 20, 2006).

[71] Prosecutor v. Milosevic, Case No. IT-02–54-AR73.7, Decision on Interlocutory Appeal of the Trial Chamber's Decision on the Assignment of Defense Counsel, para. 17 (Nov. 1, 2004).

[72] Richard Harvey, *Who Needs a Lawyer Anyway? Self-Representation and Standby Counsel in International Criminal Trials,* in Defense Perspectives On International Criminal Justice 107 (2017), https://www.amazon.com/Defense-Perspectives-International-Criminal-Justice/dp/1107086671

[73] United States v. Foster, 9 F.R.D. 367, 372 (S.D.N.Y. 1949).

12.4.2 *Standby Public Defenders*

In cases of self-representation, a war crimes tribunal should have standby counsel ready to step in when needed.[74] Such occasions would include situations where a self-represented defendant engages in persistently disruptive or obstructionist behavior, or where they stage a walkout or a boycott of the proceedings

Just as a war crimes tribunal should appoint at least one alternate judge who observes the trial from its commencement in case one of the judges should need to be replaced for health or other reasons, so too should standby public defenders be present from the beginning of a trial involving a self-represented defendant. Such counsel should be highly qualified, receive the same international training as prosecutors and judges, and be assisted by international experts. The very presence of standby public defenders can have a deterrent effect on misconduct by a self-represented defendant because they will recognize that their disruptive actions will not successfully derail the trial, which can proceed without pause with standby counsel.

Ironically, the Iraqi High Tribunal did, in fact, appoint standby public defenders, but failed to provide timely notice to the media of their appointment, to describe their credentials, or to explain their function. Consequently, several print and broadcast media outlets erroneously reported that Saddam Hussein was not represented by any counsel during those periods in which his retained counsel were boycotting the proceedings. Similarly, human rights organizations, which were publicly critical of the skills and experience of the public defenders, failed to recognize that they were, in fact, being assisted by international experts obtained and paid by the International Bar Association.[75]

12.4.3 *Expulsion and Other Sanctions*

The ICTY Appeals Chamber indicated in the *Milosevic* case that the principle of proportionality must always be taken into account in crafting an appropriate response to disruption or delay.[76] With this admonition in mind, a war crimes tribunal should deal with the six categories of defendant misconduct identified above as follows:

> First, passive disrespect should generally be ignored unless it substantially interferes with the proceedings. The essential dignity and decorum of a courtroom does not turn on whether the defendant stands or addresses the judge as "Your Honor."

---

[74] The concept of standby counsel refers to an attorney who is appointed to assist a self-represented defendant. Daniel Klein, *Annotation*, Right, under Federal Constitution, of accused to represent himself or herself in criminal proceeding—Supreme Court cases, 145 L.Ed. 2d 1177 (2004).

[75] *See* Eric Blinderman, *Judging Human Rights Watch*, 39 Case W. Res. J. Int'l L. (2007).

[76] *See* Prosecutor v. Milosevic, Case No. IT-02-54-AR73.7, Decision on Interlocutory Appeal of the Trial Chamber's Decision on the Assignment of Defense Counsel, paras. 17–18 (Nov. 1, 2004).

Second, a judge should inquire as to why a defendant is refusing to cooperate with the fundamental ground rules of court proceedings. Often such behavior is in response to perceived unfair decisions by the bench.[77] The defendant should be assured that his rights will be protected, and warned that he faces exclusion from the courtroom or other appropriate and proportional actions.

Third, a single obscenity or outburst should be met with a warning that continued disruptions of this kind will lead to sanctions, including expulsion from the courtroom.

Fourth, repeated interruptions of a trial may be dealt with by expulsion after appropriate warnings have been given. Where the defendant is excluded from his trial the court should make reasonable efforts to enable him to keep apprised of the progress of the trial and to communicate with his attorney.

Fifth, since a televised trial gives the defendant the opportunity to communicate directly with the population at large, the judge must be particularly vigilant not to permit the defendant to use the courtroom as a stage to incite mass violence or to threaten witnesses.[78]

Sixth, physical violence in the courtroom cannot be tolerated and a court may deal with it by immediate expulsion or use of physical restraints.

Following the first incident of disruption, the judge should issue a warning, explicitly describing the sanction that will be imposed if the disruptive conduct continues. The warning should explain that the defendant's conduct is disruptive and will not be tolerated. It should also alert the defendant that future occurrences will result in expulsion from the trial for as long as his disruptive posture is maintained and that the trial will continue in his absence. The warning should explain that in addition to exclusion, the judge may impose other sanctions on the defendant, such as relocating him to a smaller cell, decreasing the time he gets for recreation, or reducing his access to other prisoners and family.

While the judicial process may well proceed more smoothly without the defendant in the courtroom, his absence may diminish the educative function of the trial. During Saddam Hussein's boycott of the Dujail trial, for example, print and broadcast media attention quickly dwindled, denying the public a chance to learn about some of the most important documents and testimony admitted into evidence. Thus, there are good reasons to avoid the sanction of expulsion if possible. Consequently, if disruptive conduct persists despite the initial warning, the judge should issue a firmer warning, recess to discuss the matter with the defendant and his lawyer, or briefly adjourn the proceedings to allow for a cooling-off period. Further

[77]   In the case of the Saddam Hussein trial, this perception was in part caused by the judges' ill-conceived decision to defer pronouncement of most pretrial motions until after the trial's conclusion.

[78]   Most war crimes tribunals have employed a twenty-minute delay in the broadcast of the trial proceedings to enable them to edit out such dangerous outbursts, but the judge should firmly communicate that such statements will be met with the sanction of exclusion. In the Dujail trial, the judge reportedly told Saddam Hussein it was one thing to encourage supporters to kill Americans, but it was utterly unacceptable for him to encourage the killing of Iraqis.

disruption should result in temporary exclusion, followed by a calibrated response proportionate to the degree and persistence of disruption.

12.4.4 *Responding to Contumacious Counsel*

With respect to disorderly defense counsel, the judge should clearly set the ground rules of the trial from the beginning, warning that disruptive conduct will not be tolerated and describing the sanctions that will be imposed in response to such transgressions. Although the demeanor and conduct of counsel that is deemed acceptable may vary somewhat from country to country, most of the world's legal professions follow the basic principle that a lawyer must be "respectful, courteous and above-board in his relations with a judge" before whom he appears.[79] Especially in a major war crimes trial, deferential courtroom behavior is necessary to ensure that the judge's decisions are not perceived to be based on emotional reactions to insult.

Following the lead of the Special Court for Sierra Leone, all war crimes tribunals should adopt a Code of Professional Conduct, which spells out the rules of courtroom decorum applicable to both the prosecution and defense counsel. Consistent with such a code, after an appropriate warning, persistent insults and disrespectful comments should be met with sanctions, including fines, jail time, suspension, and even disbarment. Because a judge has inherent power to remove a disruptive defendant from the courtroom, he also possesses the inherent power to deal with a disruptive lawyer in the same way and to temporarily or permanently replace him with standby counsel.

It is important in this regard to stress that the obligations of a defense counsel are not just to his client, but also to the court and to the larger interests of justice that the court is serving. Defense counsel are not merely agents of their client, permitted and perhaps even obliged to do for the accused everything he would do for himself were he trying his own case. As the American Bar Association has explained, "[i]t would be difficult to imagine anything which would more gravely demean the advocate or undermine the integrity of our system of justice than the idea that a defense lawyer should be simply a conduit for his client's desires."[80] If a client insists on his attorney asking improper questions, making irrelevant speeches, insulting the bench, or staging walkouts or boycotts, the lawyer must reject those instructions, for he cannot excuse his own professional misconduct on the ground that his client demanded it.

Moreover, the defense counsel should seek to dissuade his client from improper courtroom behavior, including explaining to him the sanctions that may be imposed by the judge and the probable prejudice to his case if he disrupts the proceedings. A defense counsel who encourages courtroom misconduct may be punished under the

---

[79] *E.g.*, MODEL CODE OF PROF'L RESPONSIBILITY, EC 7–36 (1980).

[80] STANDARDS RELATING TO THE PROSECUTION FUNCTION AND THE DEFENSE FUNCTION 146 (ABA Project on Standards for Criminal Justice, 1971).

rules that establish his own responsibility for maintaining courtroom decorum. If he advises a client to act disruptively (or suggests methods for doing so), the court has authority to discipline counsel.

12.5 CONCLUSION: FAIR TRIAL VERSUS INTEREST OF JUSTICE

Revoking the right of self-representation, replacing retained counsel with standby public defenders, or expelling the defendant or defense lawyer from the courtroom may initiate a number of practical difficulties. After the revocation of Slobodan Milosevic's right of self-representation, for example, the defendant refused to cooperate with the assigned counsel, and witnesses for the defendant refused to appear in court or to answer questions until the defendant's control of his case was restored.[81] Similarly, Saddam Hussein not only refused to cooperate with the public defenders during the boycott of his retained counsel, but he attempted (without success) to prevent the public defenders from delivering a closing argument on his behalf.[82] And Vojislav Seselj not only refused to cooperate with standby counsel, but nearly died from a hunger strike in protest of their appointment.

Such a situation obviously impacts negatively on the defendant's fair trial rights, but the international tribunals have interpreted the duty to ensure that a trial is fair to include concerns that go beyond just those of the defendant. While prudent compromises may sometimes be necessary, the narrow fair trial rights of the defendant must be considered in the context of broader interests of justice which require "that the trial proceeds in a timely manner without interruptions, adjournments or disruptions."[83] As Judge Schomburg wisely observed in his dissent in *Prosecutor v. Krajisnik*, when self-representation conflicts with the overarching right to a fair, public and expeditious trial, the right to self-representation must yield.[84]

---

[81] *See generally* Prosecutor v. Milosevic, Case No. IT-02–54-T, Open Session (Nov. 10, 2004) (submissions by the prosecution, referring to the accused being implicated in refusal of witnesses to testify).

[82] *See* Eric Blinderman, *Judging Human Rights Watch*, 39 CASE W. RES. J. INT'L L. (2007).

[83] Prosecutor v. Seselj, Case No. IT-03–67-PT, Decision on Prosecution's Motion for Order Appointing Counsel to Assist Vojislav Seselj with His Defense, para. 21 (May 9, 2003).

[84] Prosecutor v. Kraisnik, Case No. IT-00–39-A (May 11, 2007)(Appeals Chamber), at 56–62.

PART III

Impact of the Yugoslavia and Rwanda Tribunals on the Future of International Criminal Law and Global Peace and Justice

13

The Impact of the Ad Hoc Tribunals on the International Criminal Court

Stuart Ford[*]

13.1 INTRODUCTION

The idea of a permanent international criminal court has a long history.[1] Most people probably think of the International Criminal Court (ICC) as being a product of the 1990s. But, while it is true that the Rome Statute[2] was negotiated during the 1990s,[3] the origins of the ICC go back much farther. In fact, they stretch all the way back to World War I.

At the end of World War I, the Commission on the Responsibility of the Authors of the War and on Enforcement of Penalties proposed the creation of a "high tribunal" composed of jurists from many different states that would use international law to judge the actions of individuals accused of violations of the laws of war.[4] The Allies rejected this proposal and eventually consented to having the trials conducted in Germany by a German court.[5] The trials were a failure,[6] which led

---

[*] Professor of Law at the John Marshall Law School in Chicago, Illinois.

[1] See M. Cherif Bassiouni, *The Time Has Come for an International Criminal Court*, 1 IND. INT'L & COMP. L. REV. 1, 2–11 (1991) (describing the history of proposals to establish an international criminal court).

[2] The Rome Statute of the International Criminal Court (*hereinafter* Rome Statute) is the constitutive document of the ICC. It is called the Rome Statute because it achieved its final form at the Rome Diplomatic Conference in the summer of 1998. The Rome Statute is available from the website of the ICC at www.icc-cpi.int/resource-library#legal-texts.

[3] See generally Fanny Benedetti & John Washburn, Drafting the International Criminal Court Treaty: Two Years to Rome and an Afterword on the Rome Diplomatic Conference, 5 Global Governance 1 (1999); Philippe Kirsch & John T. Holmes, *The Birth of the International Criminal Court: The 1998 Rome Conference*, 36 CAN. Y.B. INT'L L. 3 (1998).

[4] See Commission on the Responsibility of the Authors of the War and on Enforcement of Penalties, Report Presented to the Preliminary Peace Conference, 14 AM. J. INT'L L. 95, 122–4 (1920).

[5] See Hugh H. L. Bellot, A *Permanent International Criminal Court*, 31 INT'L L. ASS'N REP. CONF. 63, 72–3 (1922).

[6] Bellot, *supra* note 5, at 73; Vespasian V. Pella, *Towards an International Criminal Court*, 44 AM. J. INT'L L. 37 at n. 4 (1950). See also Stuart Ford, *Crimes against Humanity at the Extraordinary Chambers in the Courts of Cambodia: Is a Connection with Armed Conflict Required?*, 24 UCLA PAC. BASIN L. J. 125, 138 (2007).

Professor Bellot to call for the establishment of a permanent international criminal court in 1922.[7] Throughout the decades that followed, there were periodic calls for the establishment of an international criminal court.[8]

While there was considerable academic support for such a court almost from the beginning, states were not interested in creating a permanent international criminal court and it lay dormant for many years.[9] As late as 1991, Professor Bassiouni lamented that "the political will of the world's major powers has been lacking" and that progress toward the goal of a permanent international criminal court was "slow."[10] And then, suddenly, during the early 1990s the idea of a permanent international criminal court changed from seeming virtually impossible to eminently achievable.[11] This change was largely the result of two related events: 1) the end of the Cold War; and 2) the creation of the International Criminal Tribunal for the former Yugoslavia (ICTY) and the International Criminal Tribunal for Rwanda (ICTR). Collectively, the ICTR and ICTY are known as the ad hoc tribunals.[12]

The end of the Cold War led to a brief period of cooperation between East and West. One result of this cooperation was the creation of the ICTY and the ICTR by the United Nations Security Council. This marked the beginning of a period of court-building, and other international criminal tribunals were subsequently created.[13] But the ICTR and ICTY were the first courts created after the Cold War, and they had an enormous impact on those that came later. In particular, the

---

[7]   See Bellot, *supra* note 5, at 75–80.

[8]   See Pella, *supra* note 6; Bienvenido C. Ambion, *Organization of a Court of International Criminal Jurisdiction*, 29 PHIL. L.J. 345 (1954); John W. Bridge, *The Case for an International Court of Criminal Justice and the Formulation of International Criminal Law*, 13 INT'L & COMP. L. QUARTERLY 1255 (1964); M. Cherif Bassiouni & Daniel H. Derby, *Final Report on the Establishment of an International Criminal Court for the Implementation of the Apartheid Convention and Other Relevant International Instruments*, 9 HOFSTRA L. REV. 523 (1980).

[9]   See, e.g., Richard I. Miller, *Far Beyond Nuremberg: Steps toward International Criminal Jurisdiction*, 61 KY. L.J. 925, 925 (1973) (noting that "the goal of creating a [permanent international criminal court] is as remote today as when it was first proposed more than half a century ago"). See also Leo Gross, *International Terrorism and International Criminal Jurisdiction*, 67 AM. J. INT'L L. 508 (1973) (noting the failure of various proposals for the creation of an international criminal court).

[10] See Bassiouni, *supra* note 1, at 11.

[11] See Benedetti & Washburn, *supra* note 3, at 3–4 (describing how momentum for the creation of the ICC built rapidly during the early 1990s in ways that "surprised" many of those who had hoped to delay or prevent the creation of the court).

[12] They are called ad hoc tribunals because they were created by the Security Council as an ad hoc response to the atrocities committed in the Balkans and in Rwanda. See, e.g., Jonathan I. Charney, *The Impact on the International Legal System of the Growth of International Courts and Tribunals*, 31 INT'L L. & POLITICS 697, 697–8 (1999) ("Prior to the establishment of the Permanent International Court of Justice after World War I, many ad hoc tribunals had been used.") The term "ad hoc" thus distinguishes the ICTR and the ICTY from their successor the ICC, which is a permanent court. While the term can be used to refer to any tribunal created in response to a particular crisis, in this chapter the phrase "ad hoc tribunal" refers only to the ICTY and ICTR.

[13] See Stuart Ford, *How Leadership in International Criminal Law is Shifting from the United States to Europe and Asia: An Analysis of Spending on and Contributions to International Criminal Courts*, 55 St. Louis Univ. L.J. 953, 957–60 (2011). See also *infra* text accompanying note 40.

early experiences at the ICTR and ICTY demonstrated two things that drove the creation of the ICC. First, they demonstrated that international criminal justice was possible, even if it would not be easy.[14] Second, they demonstrated that creating ad hoc tribunals in response to atrocities was not a sustainable solution.[15] This led to renewed interest in establishing a permanent international criminal court.[16] The end result of that interest was the Rome Diplomatic Conference in 1998, which hammered out the details of the new International Criminal Court.

The ad hoc tribunals played an important role in catalyzing the creation of the ICC. They also influenced the shape of the Rome Statute, and the drafters of the Rome Statute incorporated many of the features of the ad hocs into it. At the same time, however, the ICC was also a reaction to the ad hoc tribunals, and the drafters of the Rome Statute sought to remedy what they perceived as the ad hocs' flaws. The rest of this chapter will explore these two ideas: 1) how the ICC is indebted to the ad hocs; and 2) how the ICC is a reaction to them.

13.2 THE END OF THE COLD WAR, THE AD HOC TRIBUNALS, AND THE CREATION OF THE ICC

The idea of a permanent international criminal court has been around since the end of World War I,[17] but it languished for decades because states were unwilling to concede sovereignty over their nationals to an international court.[18] That changed with the end of the Cold War. During the 1990s, there was a brief period when cooperation between East and West was possible.[19] At the same time, the collapse of the Soviet Union sparked a number of violent ethnic conflicts, including the conflict in the former Yugoslavia.[20] The conflict in the Balkans, in particular, was marked by widespread ethnic cleansing and violence against civilians as well as a breakdown in

---

[14] *See* Benedetti & Washburn, *supra* note 3, at 3 ("Now the ad hoc tribunals were concrete proof that international criminal courts could exist and function.")

[15] *See* M. Cherif Bassiouni, *Establishing an International Criminal Court: Historical Survey*, 149 Military L. Rev. 49, 57 (1995).

[16] *Id.* at 57.

[17] *See supra* text accompanying notes 4–8.

[18] *See, e.g.*, Pella, *supra* note 6, at 37–39 (noting that while many scholars and organizations had called for the creation of an international criminal court, states had generally refused to consider it because of concerns that creating such a court would infringe on their sovereignty). This view remained the dominant one of states right up until the end of the Cold War. *See* Bassiouni, *supra* note 1, at 11 (noting in 1991 that the principal objection to the creation of a permanent international criminal court was state concerns about losing sovereignty over their nationals).

[19] Antonio Cassese, *On the Current Trends towards Criminal Prosecution and Punishment of Breaches of International Humanitarian Law*, 9 Eur. J. Int'l L. 2, 7 (1998); Bassiouni, *supra* note 1, at 1 ("The end of the 'Cold War' presents an historic opportunity to advance the international rule of law by establishing an international criminal court to preserve peace, advance the protection of human rights and reduce international and transnational criminality.")

[20] *See* Cassese, *supra*, note 19 at 8.

the rule of law.[21] Attempts to end the violence in the former Yugoslavia with economic sanctions and political initiatives proved fruitless, however, and calls grew for the international community to do more to end the fighting and address the atrocities that had been committed.[22] The end of the Cold War thus both spawned the conflicts that demonstrated the need for a stronger response to mass atrocities and made possible the cooperation necessary to create new international criminal justice institutions.[23]

In response to the violence in the former Yugoslavia, the Security Council created the ICTY in 1993.[24] A year later, the Security Council acted again, in response to the genocide in Rwanda, to create the ICTR.[25] These were extraordinary actions.[26] Never before had the Security Council created new international institutions through the exercise of its powers under Chapter VII of the United Nations Charter.[27] The resulting courts were far from perfect,[28] but the creation of the ad hoc tribunals demonstrated that international criminal justice was possible.[29]

The result was a rapid change in how people (and states) viewed international criminal courts. For example, Ralph Zacklin, looking back at the establishment of the ICTY and ICTR, noted:

> Within one decade, the notion that crimes such as genocide, war crimes, crimes against humanity and grave breaches of the Geneva Conventions can forever remain beyond the reach of international law has been severely challenged. A new culture of human rights and human responsibility, in which there can be no impunity for such crimes, has gradually taken root and the link between an established system of individual accountability and the maintenance of international peace and security has been confirmed.[30]

---

[21] *See* Graham T. Blewitt, *Ad Hoc Tribunals Half a Century after Nuremberg*, 149 MIL. L. REV. 101, 103–4 (1995)(noting that the widespread ethnic cleansing in the former Yugoslavia gave rise to fears that Europe was seeing another Holocaust); Allison Marston Danner, *When Courts Make Law: How the International Criminal Tribunals Recast the Laws of War*, 59 VAND. L. REV. 1, 18 (2006).

[22] *See* Danner, *supra* note 21, at 18–19.

[23] *See* Philippe Kirsch, *The International Criminal Court: Current Issues an Perspectives*, 64 L. & CONTEMP. PROBLS. 3, 4 (2001); Kirsch & Holmes, *supra* note 3, at 5.

[24] *See* David Tolbert, *International Criminal Law: Past and Future*, 30 U. PA. J. INT'L L. 1281, 1285–6 (2009)(describing the creation of the ICTY).

[25] *See* Tolbert, *supra* note 24, at 1286; Danner, *supra* note 21, at 22–3.

[26] *See* Blewitt, *supra* note 21, at 103–4 (noting that the establishment of the ICTY and ICTR was a "remarkable and perhaps drastic step" and that it "took most of the world by surprise").

[27] *See* Prosecutor v. Tadić, Decision on the Defence Motion for Interlocutory Appeal on Jurisdiction, ICTY Appeals Chamber, dated Oct. 2, 1995, at paras. 26–48, *reprinted at* 35 ILM 35 (1996).

[28] *See generally* Ralph Zacklin, *The Failings of Ad Hoc International Tribunals*, 2 J. INT'L CRIM. JUST. 541 (2004).

[29] *See* Benedetti & Washburn, *supra* note 3, at 3 ("Now the ad hoc tribunals were concrete proof that international criminal courts could exist and function."); Claude Jorda, *The Major Hurdles and Accomplishments of the ICTY*, 2 J. INT'L CRIM. J. 572, 578 (2004) ("They [the ad hoc tribunals] have proven that international justice is feasible.")

[30] *See* Zacklin, *supra* note 28, at 541.

Other writers who witnessed the establishment of the ad hoc tribunals have similarly observed that the ICTY and ICTR quickly changed perceptions about whether international criminal justice was possible.[31]

At the same time that they demonstrated the viability of international criminal justice, the ICTR and ICTY also demonstrated the limitations of the Security Council's ad hoc approach.[32] The ad hoc tribunals were extremely expensive and took up a sizable chunk of the United Nations' budget.[33] This quickly led to "tribunal fatigue."[34] More importantly, the ad hocs were limited in their jurisdiction. Having been created in response to particular atrocities, they could only investigate and prosecute crimes associated with those atrocities.[35] If the ad hoc model were followed, this would mean that whenever a new atrocity occurred that warranted international prosecutions, a new ad hoc tribunal would have to be established. Given widespread "tribunal fatigue" it seemed unlikely that the international community would have the political will to create a new tribunal every time it was warranted.[36] Moreover, if the international community were to rely on the Security Council to create new tribunals, it seemed likely that the permanent members of the Security Council would utilize their veto powers to block the creation of tribunals that might threaten their interests.[37] The result would be selective and biased access to justice.[38] A more permanent and equitable solution was required. This led to renewed calls for the creation of a permanent international criminal court.[39] In this way, the ad hoc tribunals demonstrated both the viability of and the need for the ICC.

Of course, the ICC was not the only result of the court-building that followed the end of the Cold War. Several other international courts were created in the aftermath of the ad hoc tribunals, including the Special Court for Sierra Leone (SCSL)

---

[31] *See* Benedetti & Washburn, *supra* note 3, at 2–3 (arguing that the establishment of the ad hoc tribunals "constituted a psychological, political and legal breakthrough for the international criminal court proposal and for the concept of the international accountability of individuals for gross and massive crimes"); Frédéric Mégret, *The Legacy of the ICTY as Seen Through Some of Its Actors and Observers*, 3 GOETTINGEN J. INT'L L. 1011, 1021–2 (2011).

[32] *See* Danner, *supra* note 21, at 56.

[33] *See* Zacklin, *supra* note 28, at 543.

[34] *See* Bassiouni, *supra* note 15, at 57; Zacklin, *supra* note 28, at 545 (arguing that "it is impossible today to envisage the establishment of an ICTY-type tribunal in new situations, however egregious the violations of international criminal law may be").

[35] *See* Updated Statute of the International Criminal Tribunal for the former Yugoslavia (*hereinafter* ICTY Statute), Art. 1 (limiting the ICTY to prosecuting crimes committed on the territory of the former Yugoslavia); Statute of the International Criminal Tribunal for Rwanda (*hereinafter* ICTR Statute), Art. 1 (limiting the ICTR to prosecuting crimes committed in the territory of Rwanda).

[36] *See* Benedetti & Washburn, *supra* note 3, at 4.

[37] *See* Kirsch, *supra* note 23, at 4 (noting that the creation of the ICC was a result of both tribunal fatigue and a concern that it was unwise to rely on the Security Council to create additional courts).

[38] *See* Bartram S. Brown, *Primacy of Complementarity: Reconciling the Jurisdiction of National Courts and International Criminal Tribunals*, 23 YALE J. INT'L L. 383, 386 (1998); Kirsch & Holmes, *supra* note 3, at 8–9; Benedetti & Washburn, *supra* note 3, at 18.

[39] *See* Benedetti & Washburn, *supra* note 3, at 4; Brown, *supra* note 38, at 416.

and the Extraordinary Chambers in the Courts of Cambodia (ECCC).[40] The SCSL
and ECCC were attempts to address the high cost and slow pace of the ad hoc
tribunals by creating smaller, cheaper, and hopefully quicker international courts.[41]
These became known as the hybrid courts because they combined elements of
international and domestic law.[42] But, like the ICTY and ICTR, the SCSL and
ECCC were created in response to a particular set of atrocities and had limited
mandates.[43] As a result, they suffered from many of the same drawbacks as the ad
hocs.[44] None of them could provide a permanent and global forum for prosecuting
serious violations of international criminal law. In the end, the most lasting result of
this decade of court-building was the establishment of the ICC.

The creation of the ICC required an unusual confluence of events. The 1990s
were preceded by decades of gridlock at the highest levels of the international
community.[45] Somewhat unexpectedly given the high hopes of the 1990s, the period
since then has also been marked by mistrust and a lack of cooperation between the
great powers. Today, the Security Council is once again divided on matters of
international criminal justice.[46] Only in the period between 1990 and 2000 was
the window open for the creation of the ICC.[47] Thus, the end of the Cold War was
an important factor in the establishment of the ICC. If the Rome Statute had not
been completed in 1998, it might have had to wait for another period when
cooperation at a global level was possible. It could be decades before such
a window opens again.[48]

The creation of the ICC also depended on the example set by the ad hocs.
The ICTY and ICTR, simply by virtue of existing, rapidly changed conceptions of
what was possible in international criminal justice.[49] In the space of four or five
years, a permanent international criminal court went from seeming impossible to
the triumphant adoption of the text of the Rome Statute at the conclusion of the

---

[40]   *See* Zacklin, *supra* note 28, at 541.
[41]   *See generally* Laura A. Dickinson, *The Promise of Hybrid Courts*, 97 AM. J. INT'L L. 295 (2003).
[42]   *Id.*
[43]   *See* Statute of the Special Court for Sierra Leone, Art. 1 (limiting the SCSL to the investigation of
       crimes committed in the territory of Sierra Leone); Law on the Establishment of Extraordinary
       Chambers in the Courts of Cambodia for the Prosecution of Crimes Committed during the Period of
       Democratic Kampuchea, Art. 2 (limiting the court to prosecuting crimes committed between April 17,
       1975 and January 6, 1979).
[44]   *See infra* text accompanying notes 34–37.
[45]   *See* Blewitt, *supra* note 21, at 102 (noting that the Cold War prevented any further cooperation on
       a permanent international criminal court after World War II); Kirsch & Holmes, *supra* note 3, at 4–5.
[46]   *See* Stuart Ford, *The ICC and the Security Council: How Much Support Is There for Ending
       Impunity?*, 26 IND. INT'L & COMP. L. Rev. 33 (2016).
[47]   *See* Tolbert, *supra* note 24, at 1288 (noting that it is unlikely the ICC could have been created after
       2001).
[48]   *Cf.* Benedetti & Washburn, *supra* note 3, at 20 (noting that many countries believed in the 1990s that if
       a permanent international criminal court was not agreed upon quickly that the entire process could
       unravel, and that another opportunity might not appear for decades).
[49]   *See supra* text accompanying notes 30–31.

Rome Diplomatic Conference. But it was not the example of the ad hocs alone that made the ICC possible. The International Military Tribunal (IMT) at Nuremburg provided an example that could have led to the establishment of a permanent international court in the years following World War II, but it did not do so because the Cold War prevented cooperation between the East and West.[50] This suggests that the establishment of the ICC required both the period of global cooperation that followed the end of the Cold War and the precedent set by the establishment of the ad hoc tribunals. At the same time, the ICC is also a reaction to the limitations of the ICTY and ICTR, particularly their ad hoc nature.[51]

13.3 THE INFLUENCE OF THE AD HOC TRIBUNALS ON THE ROME STATUTE

While the ad hocs were instrumental in renewing interest in a permanent international criminal court, that was not their only effect on the ICC. At the time of the Rome Diplomatic Conference, both ad hoc courts were fully operational and producing extensive jurisprudence[52] and the work of the ad hocs clearly influenced the final form of the Rome Statute. For example, the definitions of the crimes in the Rome Statute owe a lot to both the statutes of the ad hoc tribunals and to their growing jurisprudence. Of course, the experience of the ad hoc tribunals was not the only one that informed the creation of the ICC. Nevertheless, many elements of the Rome Statute were influenced by or simply borrowed from the ICTR and ICTY.

At the same time that the Rome Statute adopted many of the elements of the ad hocs, however, it also represented an opportunity for the drafters to incorporate lessons they had learned from the experience of the ad hocs. Thus, the drafters used the Rome Statute to fix a number of perceived flaws in the ad hoc tribunals. So, for example, they felt that the ICTY's judges had been too activist, and incorporated several provisions within the Rome Statute intended to limit the ability of the ICC's judges to create new international obligations for states and their nationals. In addition, various women's groups argued that the statutes of the ad hoc tribunals had failed to give sufficient consideration to crimes of sexual violence, and successfully lobbied the drafters of the Rome Statute to further develop international law on this subject. This section will explore the most important ways in which the Rome Statute was both influenced by and a reaction to the ad hoc tribunals.

---

[50] *See* Blewitt, *supra* note 21, at 102–3.
[51] *See supra* text accompanying notes 32–39.
[52] *See* Sean D. Murphy, *Progress and Jurisprudence of the International Criminal Tribunal for the Former Yugoslavia*, 93 Am. J. Int'l L. 57 (1999) (describing the operations of the ICTY in 1998); Third annual report of the International Criminal Tribunal for the Prosecution of Persons Responsible for Genocide and Other Serious Violations of International Humanitarian Law Committed in the Territory of Rwanda, UN Doc. No. A/53/429, Sept. 23, 1998 (describing the operations of the ICTR in 1998).

13.3.1 *The Definitions of the Crimes*

Despite proposals to expand the ICC's jurisdiction to include a variety of new crimes,[53] the Court's initial jurisdiction ended up being quite similar to that of the ad hocs: war crimes, crimes against humanity and genocide.[54] The crimes themselves were also defined in similar ways. Genocide, in particular, is defined almost identically across all three courts.[55] The definitions are so similar because all three courts closely follow the definition of genocide in the Genocide Convention.[56] It appears, however, that the requirement in the ICC's Elements of Crimes that genocide take place in the "context of a manifest pattern of similar conduct"[57] was added in response to decisions by the ICTY holding that genocide could be committed by an individual acting alone.[58]

The Rome Statute's definition of crimes against humanity is not exactly like either the ICTY's definition or the ICTR's definition, although it is closer to that of the ICTR. The ICTY's Statute required a connection with an armed conflict for the prosecution of crimes against humanity, and it did not include any reference to a widespread or systematic attack.[59] The ICTY subsequently held, however, that the nexus with armed conflict, while a requirement of the ICTY Statute, was not part of the customary definition of a crime against humanity.[60] It also held that the customary definition of crimes against humanity required that the enumerated acts be committed as part of a widespread or systematic attack.[61]

The ICTR Statute did away with the armed conflict requirement that was present in the ICTY Statute and required instead that crimes against humanity be committed as "part of a widespread or systematic attack against any civilian population."[62] But the ICTR Statute also added a requirement that all crimes against humanity be committed with a discriminatory motive.[63] The ICTR

---

[53] See Kirsch & Holmes, *supra* note 3, at 22; Andreas Zimmerman, Article 5: Crimes within the Jurisdiction of the Court, at 130–2 *in* Commentary on the Rome Statute of the International Criminal Court (Otto Triffterer ed., 2nd edn. 2008).

[54] See Rome Statute, Arts. 6–8. It was intended that the Rome Statute would eventually have jurisdiction over the crime of aggression. *See* Rome Statute, Art. 5(d). No definition of aggression was included in the Rome Statute as it was initially adopted, however, because of deep disagreements about how it should be defined. *See* Zimmerman, *supra* note 53, at 135–41. A definition has subsequently been agreed upon, but it had not yet entered into force at the time of writing. *See* Rome Statute, Arts. 8*bis*, 15*bis*.

[55] *Compare* Rome Statute, Art. 6 *with* ICTY Statute, Art. 4 *and* ICTR Statute, Art. 2.

[56] See Convention on the Prevention and Punishment of the Crime of Genocide, Art. II. *See also* William A. Schabas, Article 6: Genocide at 143–4 *in* Commentary on the Rome Statute of the International Criminal Court (Otto Triffterer ed., 2nd edn. 2008).

[57] *See, e.g.,* Elements of Crimes, Art. 6(a)(4).

[58] See Schabas, *supra* note 56, at 146.

[59] See ICTY Statute, Art. 5.

[60] See Machteld Boot et al., Article 7: Crimes against Humanity at 173 *in* Otto Triffterer ed. Commentary on the Rome Statute of the International Criminal Court (Otto Triffterer ed., 2nd edn. 2008).

[61] Id.

[62] See ICTR Statute, Art. 3.

[63] See Boot et al., *supra* note 59, at 173.

subsequently held that this motive requirement, while required for prosecutions under the ICTR Statute, was not part of the customary definition of crimes against humanity.[64]

The Rome Statute adopted the "widespread or systematic attack" requirement of the ICTR Statute,[65] but it omitted both the requirement of a discriminatory motive and the nexus with armed conflict. This definitively resolved the lingering question of whether a crime against humanity could only occur in connection with an armed conflict.[66] While the Rome Statute definition of crimes against humanity is not identical to that contained in the statutes of the ad hoc tribunals, it is quite similar to what the ICTY and ICTR arrived at in their jurisprudence.[67] In this way, the ad hocs' decisions appear to have influenced the final definition of crimes against humanity in the Rome Statute.[68]

There are also ways in which the definition of crimes against humanity at the ICC is a reaction to the legacy of the ad hocs. For example, the Rome Statute requires that an attack upon a civilian population be done "pursuant to or in furtherance of a State or organizational policy."[69] The ad hoc tribunals had rejected a policy requirement as a component of crimes against humanity.[70] It appears the drafters of the Rome Statute added the policy requirement to mollify states concerned that the ad hocs' definition of crimes against humanity was too expansive.[71] The Rome Statute also expanded upon the list of enumerated acts. While the ICTY and ICTR Statutes contain the same list of enumerated acts, the Rome Statute significantly expands the list of enumerated acts. In particular, it includes a much broader provision on crimes of sexual violence.[72] This was done partly to fill perceived gaps in the ad hocs' definitions.

The Rome Statute's definition of war crimes was also influenced by the work of the ad hoc tribunals. Prior to the 1990s, it had generally been thought that there was no individual criminal responsibility under international law for war crimes committed in noninternational armed conflicts.[73] The ICTR challenged this view in

---

[64] *Id.*

[65] *See* Rome Statute, Art. 7.

[66] *See* generally Stuart Ford, *Crimes against Humanity at the Extraordinary Chambers in the Courts of Cambodia: Is a Connection with Armed Conflict Required?*, 24 UCLA PAC. BASIN L.J. 125 (2007).

[67] *See supra* notes 59–64 (noting that the ICTY and ICTR both held that the customary definition of crimes against humanity was different from the definition contained in their respective statutes).

[68] *See* Darryl Robinson, *Defining "Crimes against Humanity" at the Rome Conference*, 93 AM. J. INT'L L. 43 (1999).

[69] *See* Rome Statute, Art. 7(2)(a).

[70] *See* Boot et al., *supra* note 59, at 235–6; Antonio Cassese, Crimes against Humanity 375–6, *in* THE ROME STATUTE OF THE INTERNATIONAL CRIMINAL COURT: A COMMENTARY (Antonio Cassese et al. eds., 2002). *But see* WILLIAM A. SCHABAS, The International Criminal Court: A Commentary on the Rome Statute 149–52 (2010).

[71] *See* SCHABAS, *supra* note 70, at 151–2 (arguing that without the policy limitation, "many States will be reluctant to join the Court").

[72] This development is discussed in more detail in Section 13.3.2.

[73] *See* Roberta Arnold et al., Article 8: War Crimes at 286 *in* COMMENTARY ON THE ROME STATUTE OF THE INTERNATIONAL CRIMINAL COURT (Otto Triffterer ed., 2nd edn. 2008).

1994 when it was given jurisdiction over "violations of Article 3 common to the Geneva Conventions."[74] The protections of Common Article 3 only apply in noninternational armed conflicts.[75] Shortly thereafter, the ICTY held that it too had jurisdiction to prosecute war crimes committed in noninternational conflicts.[76] The Rome Statute adopted this position and provided for criminal penalties for war crimes committed during noninternational armed conflicts.[77] This effectively resolved the question of whether there is criminal liability for war crimes committed in noninternational armed conflicts.

While the definitions of war crimes, crimes against humanity and genocide in the Rome Statute are not identical to those same crimes in the statutes of the ICTY and ICTR, they were influenced by them. Whether it was adopting criminal penalties for war crimes committed in noninternational crimes, or adopting the requirement of a widespread or systematic attack as part of the definition of crimes against humanity, the Rome Statute was influenced by both the ICTR and ICTY Statutes and by the decisions of the ad hoc tribunals. At the same time, it was also a reaction to their work. This can be seen in the expanded list of enumerated acts that constitute a crime against humanity, the decision to impose a policy requirement on crimes against humanity and the decision to impose a "manifest pattern of similar conduct" requirement on genocide.

13.3.2 *Crimes of Sexual Violence*

The definitions of the crimes in the Rome Statute were influenced by the ad hoc tribunals, but the Rome Statute was also used to fill perceived gaps in the crimes prosecuted at the ad hocs. This is particularly true with respect to crimes of sexual violence. When the Rome Statute was drafted, there was a widely held belief that the ad hocs had not given enough consideration to crimes of sexual violence.[78] For example, the only crime of sexual violence contained in the ICTY statute was rape as a crime against humanity or war crime.[79] The ICTR Statute was similarly limited.[80]

Both the ICTY and ICTR eventually prosecuted individuals for rape and used their case law to expand the meaning of rape in international law,[81] but many women's organizations argued that the Rome Statute should explicitly incorporate

---

[74] ICTR Statute, Art. 4.

[75] *See, e.g.*, Geneva Convention for the Amelioration of the Condition of the Wounded and Sick in Armed Forces in the Field of 12 August 1949, Art. 3 (noting that Common Article 3 shall apply "[i]n case of armed conflict not of an international character occurring in the territory of one of the High Contracting Parties").

[76] *See* Arnold et al., *supra* note 73, at 286.

[77] *See* Rome Statute, Arts. 8(2)(c) and 8(2)(e).

[78] *See* Benedetti et al., *supra* note 146, at 12–13.

[79] *Id.*

[80] *See, e.g.*, ICTR Statute, Art. 3(g).

[81] *See* Rana Lehr-Lehnardt, *One Small Step for Women: Female-Friendly Provisions in the Rome Statute of the International*, 16 B.Y.U. J. Pub. L. 317, 324–36 (2002).

a larger range of crimes, and they organized to push for changes to the Statute.[82] They were largely successful, and the Rome Statute contains much broader provisions related to crimes of sexual violence than the statutes of the ad hocs.[83] As a result, the Rome Statute prohibits rape, but it also prohibits "sexual slavery, enforced prostitution, forced pregnancy, enforced sterilization, or any other form of sexual violence of comparable gravity."[84] This expansion of crimes of sexual violence has been claimed as "one of the greatest achievements of the Rome Statute."[85] Women's organizations were also successful in including other "female friendly" provisions in the Rome Statute, including specific provisions for the protection of victims of sexual violence and a provision that calls for "fair representation of female" judges at the ICC.[86] Ultimately, the inclusion of much more detailed provisions related to crimes of sexual violence was the result of a concerted effort to fill a gap in the statutes of the ad hoc tribunals.

13.3.3 Modes of Liability

One of the most significant contributions of the ad hoc tribunals was their jurisprudence on modes of liability. The ICTY, in particular, developed a complex theory of liability called joint criminal enterprise (JCE).[87] A joint criminal enterprise was held to exist when a plurality of persons intentionally participated in a common purpose or plan, which amounted to or involved the commission of a crime.[88] Joint criminal enterprise was used extensively at the ICTY,[89] but it was also repeatedly criticized.[90] When it came time to draft the Rome Statute, the provision on individual criminal responsibility – Article 25 – was not based on the jurisprudence of the ad hoc tribunals. Rather, it was based on a proposal jointly submitted by Canada, Germany, the Netherlands, and the United Kingdom that was said to represent "various legal systems."[91]

---

[82] See BENEDETTI ET AL., *supra* note 146, at 149–51; Lehr-Lehnardt, *supra* note 81, at 318, 338–9.

[83] See BENEDETTI ET AL., *supra* note 146, at 150–1; Lehr-Lehnardt, *supra* note 81, at 318, 340–2.

[84] See Rome Statute, Art. 7(1)(g). *See also* Rome Statute, Arts. 8(2)(b)(xxii); 8(2)(e)(vi).

[85] See BENEDETTI ET AL., *supra* note 146, at 148. *See also* Lehr-Lehnardt, *supra* note 81, at 318.

[86] See Lehr-Lehnardt, *supra* note 81, at 342–5. *See also* Rome Statute, Arts. 36(8), 68(1).

[87] See Kai Ambos, Article 25: Individual Criminal Responsibility at 748–50 *in* COMMENTARY ON THE ROME STATUTE OF THE INTERNATIONAL CRIMINAL COURT (Otto Triffterer ed., 2nd edn. 2008).

[88] See Giulia Bigi, Joint Criminal Enterprise in the Jurisprudence of the International Criminal Tribunal for the Former Yugoslavia and the Prosecution of Senior *Political and Military Leaders*, 14 Max Planck Yearbook of United Nations Law 51, 56 (2010).

[89] See Stuart Ford, Fairness and Politics at the ICTY: Evidence from the Indictments, 39 NORTH CAROLINA J. INT'L L. & COMM. REG. 45, 81 (2013) (noting that JCE was used in sixty-four indictments at the ICTY).

[90] See Antonio Cassese, *The Proper Limits of Individual Responsibility under the Doctrine of Joint Criminal Enterprise*, 5 J. INT'L CRIM. JUST. 109, 114–23 (2007); Steven Powles, *Joint Criminal Liability: Criminal Liability by Prosecutorial Ingenuity and Judicial Creativity?*, 2 J. INT'L CRIM. JUST. 606 (2004); Jenia Iontcheva Turner, *Defense Perspectives on Law and Politics in International Criminal Trials*, 48 VA. J. INT'L L. 529, 560–63 (2008).

[91] See SCHABAS, *supra* note 70, at 423–4.

While Article 25(3)(d) of the Rome Statute contains a provision that looks super-ficially like JCE,[92] the ICC has been adamant that the theory of joint criminal enterprise developed at the ICTY will not be used by the court.[93] Instead, the ICC has focused on the concept of co-perpetration, which it finds in Article 25(3)(a) of the Rome Statute.[94] The court's doctrine of co-perpetration has been the subject of criticism and appears to be in flux,[95] and it may be some time before we fully understand the contours of individual criminal responsibility at the ICC. Nevertheless, it is relatively certain that JCE will not play a major role at the International Criminal Court.[96] In this sense, the judges at the ICC appear to have rejected one of the ad hoc tribunals' most important contributions to interna-tional criminal law.

13.3.4 *States vs. Judges as Sources of International Law*

A question that is central to the Rome Statute is: who makes international law? The judges at the ICTY had expanded the boundaries of international law, particu-larly with respect to war crimes.[97] This made states uncomfortable because it represented a diminution of their sovereignty without their consent. The negotiations over the creation of the ICC thus represented an opportunity to reassert control over the process of defining international criminal law. Thus, one way to view the Rome Statute is as an attempt by states to ensure that the content of international criminal law is determined first and foremost by states.

While states had expressed a belief at their creation that the ad hoc tribunals would not have the ability to create new international law,[98] the reality was slightly different. The text of the ICTY Statute was, for political reasons, quite vague about the details of the crimes within the jurisdiction of the court.[99] This gave the judges considerable latitude to interpret the text.[100] And interpret it they did. For example, in one of its earliest decisions, the ICTY Appeals Chamber held that the court had jurisdiction over crimes committed in noninternational conflicts, and that there was individual criminal responsibility for violations committed during noninternational

---

92 *See* Rome Statute, Art. 25(3)(d) (referring to commission of a crime by a "group of persons acting with a common purpose").
93 *See* SCHABAS, *supra* note 70, at 428.
94 *Id.*
95 *See* Alicia Gil & Elena Maculan, *Current Trends in the Definition of 'Perpetrator' by the International Criminal Court: From the Decision on the Confirmation of Charges in the Lubanga case to the Katanga judgment*, 28 LEIDEN J. INT'L L. 349 (2015); Jens David Ohlin et al., *Assessing the Control-Theory*, 26 LEIDEN J. INT'L L. 725 (2013).
96 *See* Schabas, *supra* note 93, at 436.
97 *See infra* text accompanying notes 101–5.
98 *See* Danner, *supra* note 21, at 21.
99 *Id.*
100 *Id.* at 46 (describing the ICTY Statute as "the bold outlines of a coloring book: much remained for the judges to fill in").

conflicts.[101] This was arguably inconsistent with the most straightforward reading of the Statute[102] and contrary to the position taken by many states when these issues were debated during the negotiation of Additional Protocol II to the Geneva Conventions.[103] Moreover, the ICTY Appeals Chamber justified this decision, in part, on the grounds that international law had moved away from a "State-sovereignty-oriented approach," and had moved toward a "human-being-oriented approach."[104] In the same decision, the court went on to adopt a definition of "armed conflict" that was broader than that which states had accepted in the Additional Protocols.[105] The decision "stunned" international lawyers with its breadth.[106] And states were probably not happy to hear judges at the ICTY declare that state sovereignty was no longer at the center of international law.

While the Rome Statute ended up incorporating most of the changes to the laws of war that were pioneered by the judges at the ICTR and ICTY,[107] states were concerned that the judges had gone too far in expanding the scope of international law. This made states nervous, particularly as many of the accused at international criminal tribunals are agents of a state. Thus, the drafters of the Rome Statute did several things designed to limit the ability of the judges at the ICC to create new international law.

One thing the drafters did was to define the crimes within the jurisdiction of the ICC in great detail.[108] While the crime of genocide is laid out quite briefly in the Rome Statute,[109] the definition of crimes against humanity has more than twenty sub-parts, and that of war crimes has more than fifty sub-parts.[110] These crimes are then further expanded upon in the Elements of Crimes. Contrast this with the Statute of the ICTY, which is far less detailed. For example, the ICTY Statute simply lists "persecutions on political, racial and religious grounds" as a crime against humanity.[111] The Rome Statute has a much longer and more detailed definition of persecution.[112] It is then further defined in a separate definitions section.[113] The components of the crime are then also explained in the Elements of Crimes.[114] The difference is even more striking for war crimes. The Statute of the ICTY granted the court jurisdiction over violations of

---

[101]   *See* Danner, *supra* note 21, at 27–9; Arnold et al., *supra* note 73, at 286.
[102]   *See* Danner, *supra* note 21, at 28.
[103]   *Id.* at 13–17.
[104]   *See* Prosecutor v. Tadić, *supra* note 27, at para. 97.
[105]   *See* Danner, *supra* note 21, at 30.
[106]   *See* Wiliam Schabas, An Introduction to the International Criminal Court 42 (2001).
[107]   *See* Danner, *supra* note 21, at 34–6. *See also supra* text accompanying notes 73–77.
[108]   *See* Bruce Broomhall, Article 22: Nullum crimen sine lege at 714 *in* COMMENTARY ON THE ROME STATUTE OF THE INTERNATIONAL CRIMINAL COURT (Otto Triffterer ed., 2nd edn. 2008) ("The result was a move towards the vision, finally affirmed in the Rome Statute, of a Court the subject-matter jurisdiction of which is exhaustively defined in its constitutive document.")
[109]   *See* Rome Statute, Art. 6.
[110]   *Id.*, Arts. 7–8.
[111]   *See* ICTY Statute, Art. 5(h).
[112]   *See* Rome Statute, Art. 7(1)(h).
[113]   *Id.*, Art. 7(2)(g).
[114]   *See* Elements of Crimes, Art. 7(1)(h).

"the laws and customs of war."[115] It then provided a nonexhaustive list of such violations.[116] The Rome Statute takes a completely different approach. It grants the court jurisdiction over war crimes,[117] but it provides the judges with an extremely detailed definition of war crimes.[118] There is no provision in Article 8 of the Rome Statute like the open-ended "including but not limited to" language in Article 3 of the ICTY Statute. The effect is to constrain the ability of judges to expand the scope of international criminal law through their decisions.

Another way that states sought to rein in the judges was through the imposition of a very strict principle of legality. Article 22 of the Rome Statute states that "[a] person shall not be criminally responsible under this Statute unless the conduct in question constitutes, at the time it takes place, a crime within the jurisdiction of the Court."[119] Article 22(2) goes on to say that "[t]he definition of a crime shall be strictly construed and shall not be extended by analogy."[120] While the principle of legality is a well-accepted part of international law, the specific formulation of the principle in the Rome Statute is stricter than necessary.[121] In particular, the prohibition on the extension of the crimes by analogy is probably not required by customary international law.[122] This provision was inserted by states in reaction to "the perceived willingness of the ICTY to engage in liberal reasoning-by-analogy."[123] States wanted to make sure that the authority to expand the scope of the court's jurisdiction rested with them rather than with the judges.[124] So one legacy of the ad hocs is that, after a brief period when international judges were at the forefront of developing and expanding the scope of international criminal law, the Rome Statute has reined in judges and put states once again at the center of deciding the content of international law.

13.3.5 *Primacy vs. Complementarity*

An important feature of both the ICTR and the ICTY was the principle of primacy.[125] The ad hoc tribunals had primacy over national systems, meaning that national systems in the former Yugoslavia and Rwanda had to give way to them.[126]

---

[115] *See* ICTY Statute, Art. 3.

[116] *Id.* (noting that "[s]uch violations shall include, but not be limited to" a list of violations).

[117] *See* Rome Statute, Art. 8(1).

[118] *Id.*, Art. 8(2).

[119] *See* Rome Statute, Art. 22(1).

[120] *Id.*, Art. 22(2).

[121] *See* Broomhall, *supra* note 108, at 717–18.

[122] *Id.* at 718 (noting that some use of analogy is ordinarily permitted in international law despite the principle of legality).

[123] *Id.* at 725.

[124] *Id.*

[125] *See* Jorda, *supra* note 29, at 581.

[126] *See* ICTY Statute, Art. 9(2) ("The International Tribunal shall have primacy over national courts."); ICTR Statute, Art. 8(2) ("The International Tribunal for Rwanda shall have the primacy over the national courts of all States.")

If the ICTY or the ICTR wished to investigate or prosecute someone, then national systems had to defer to them. This was a key feature of the ad hoc tribunals and one that was deemed necessary to their functioning by the Security Council,[127] but it was also subject to criticism.[128]

Over time, the ad hocs learned to work with national systems.[129] For example, the ICTY began a process of transferring cases back to national jurisdictions in the former Yugoslavia.[130] The ICTR did something similar in Rwanda.[131] The end result was a situation quite different from the one that existed when the ad hocs were created. Although they still had primacy over national jurisdictions, procedures were put in place to ensure that only the most serious cases came before them while cases of lower gravity or involving less responsible accused would be referred back to national systems.[132] In this sense, the ICTY and ICTR eventually developed a division of labor with national systems.

The question of the relationship between the ICC and national systems was an important one during the negotiation of the Rome Statute.[133] States were very reluctant to create a permanent international criminal court that would have primacy over their national systems.[134] During negotiations, there was support for a court that was "complementary to national criminal justice systems" rather than one that had primacy over them.[135] This gave rise to the doctrine of complementarity, which is central to the structure of the International Criminal Court.[136] Under Article 17 of the Rome Statute, the ICC may not exercise jurisdiction over a case if that case is already being investigated or prosecuted by a state, unless that state is "unwilling or unable" to genuinely carry out the investigation or prosecution.[137] Thus, states have the primary responsibility to investigate and prosecute international crimes, and the ICC only steps in when states are unable or unwilling to do so.

---

[127] See Mohamed M. El Zeidy, *From Primacy to Complementarity and Backwards: (Re)-Visiting Rule 11 bis of the Ad Hoc Tribunals*, 57 INT'L & COMP. L. Q. 403, 403 (2008); Brown, *supra* note 38, at 387.

[128] See Jorda, *supra* note 29, at 575 (noting that the ICTY was unable to prosecute all of the individuals involved in the crimes committed in the former Yugoslavia and that it was essential to involve national systems in the process and arguing that "involving national courts . . . will contribute to re-establishing the rule of law in the countries of the former Yugoslavia"); David Schwendiman, *Primacy and the Accountability Gap: A View from Bosnia and Herzegovina*, 103 ASIL PROCEEDINGS 207 (2009); Brown, *supra* note 38, at 398–9 (noting that several states questioned the desirability and binding nature of the principle of primacy).

[129] See Zeidy, *supra* note 127, at 405–8.

[130] See Jorda, *supra* note 29, at 575–6, 581–2.

[131] See Zeidy, *supra* note 127, at 408.

[132] Id. at 409–10 (discussing Rule 11bis of the Rules of Procedure and Evidence at both the ICTR and ICTY).

[133] See Brown, *supra* note 38, at 417 ("The question of how to reconcile the jurisdiction of an ICC with state sovereignty has been a central question [during negotiations].")

[134] See Sharon A. Williams & William A. Schabas, Article 17: Issues of Admissibility 609 in COMMENTARY ON THE ROME STATUTE OF THE INTERNATIONAL CRIMINAL COURT (Otto Triffterer ed., 2nd edn. 2008).

[135] See Brown, *supra* note 38, at 417. See also Kirsch & Holmes, *supra* note 3, at 6–7.

[136] See Williams and Schabas, *supra* note 134, at 606.

[137] See Rome Statute, Art. 17(1).

Unlike the ad hocs, the ICC does not have primacy over national systems. Rather, the ICC's jurisdiction is carefully circumscribed to ensure that states bear the primary responsibility for investigating and prosecuting violations of international criminal law. The ICC may only exercise jurisdiction if very specific criteria are met, and states will almost always be in a position to block ICC jurisdiction if they are willing to meet those criteria. This is almost the opposite of the situation at the ad hoc tribunals. In most cases, it is national systems that will have primacy over the ICC.[138]

In practice, however, the ICC may operate in a similar fashion to the ad hocs. Like the ad hocs, the ICC does not have the capacity to take on every case that it could exercise jurisdiction over.[139] Rather, it will have to pick and choose. Thus, it seems quite likely that there will emerge a cooperative division of labor between the ICC and states where the ICC takes on cases involving the most serious violations or those most responsible, while simultaneously promoting and supporting national systems in their efforts to investigate and prosecute the many perpetrators who will never appear before the ICC.[140] This would, in essence, be quite similar to the system that the ad hocs eventually arrived at,[141] although it would be based on a very different legal relationship.

13.3.6 *Common Law vs. Civil Law*

The rules of evidence and procedure at the ICTY, in particular, were heavily influenced by the common law system, and the ICTY ended up adopting what was essentially an adversarial approach to the trials.[142] There was criticism of this approach. For example, Claude Jorda, who was a judge at the ICTY from 1994 until 2002, described the judges as "singularly powerless to guide the proceedings" and lamented the extremely adversarial nature of the trials.[143] Over time, the ICTY's procedural rules were amended in ways that incorporated some features associated with civil law systems.[144] Nevertheless, during the drafting of the Rome Statute,

---

[138] *See* Brown, *supra* note 38, at 386 ("In effect, complementarity would replace the primacy of international tribunals with priority for national courts."); Tolbert, *supra* note 24, at 1289 ("[T]he ICC is the reverse of the situation of the ICTY and ICTR which have primacy over local jurisdictions.")

[139] *See* William W. Burke-White, *Proactive Complementarity: The International Criminal Court and National Courts in the Rome System of International Justice*, 49 HARV. J. INT'L L. 53, 53–4 (2008) (noting the contrast between the high expectations of the ICC and the reality that the ICC has limited resources and modest capabilities); *id.* at 64–67.

[140] *See generally id.*

[141] *See supra* text accompanying notes 129–31.

[142] *See* Alphons Orie, Accusatorial v. Inquisitorial Approach in International Criminal Proceedings Prior to the Establishment of the ICC and in the Proceedings Before the ICC 1463–4 *in* THE ROME STATUTE OF THE INTERNATIONAL CRIMINAL COURT: A COMMENTARY (Antonio Cassese et al. eds., 2002).

[143] *See* Jorda, *supra* note 29, at 578.

[144] *See* Orie, *supra* note 142, at 1464 ("Since the adoption of the original Rules, the judges of the ICTY have amended them more than twenty times. These amendments tend towards an inquisitorial direction."); Jorda, *supra* note 29, at 582–3.

a group of civil law countries, led by France, argued that the ad hocs had gone too far in adopting a common law approach and that the ICC should include more elements of civil law systems.[145]

During the negotiations, France even produced its own proposed statute for an international criminal court based on civil law.[146] The French proposal was not adopted, but thereafter the drafters attempted to incorporate more features of the civil law system into the Rome Statute.[147] One result is that trial judges at the ICC have greater powers to manage the trial than judges in common law systems typically possess.[148] For example, the Pre-Trial Chamber has considerable control over whether particular cases go forward.[149] It also has a veto over attempts by the Prosecutor to initiate an investigation on her own.[150] The Pre-Trial Chamber has the ability to move, on its own initiative, to preserve evidence necessary for the defense.[151] Similarly, the Trial Chamber has the right to request the introduction of evidence that it believes is "necessary for the determination of the truth."[152] It may also require the attendance of witnesses and the production of documents.[153] Of course, the ICC is not a purely civil-law system. Rather, it is a hybrid of elements of both the civil and common law systems.[154] Nevertheless, the more balanced approach at the ICC is, in part, a response to concerns about the ICTY's fundamentally common law approach.

13.4 CONCLUSION

The ICC has both been influenced by the ad hoc tribunals and is a reaction to them. In particular, the example of the ICTY and ICTR made the creation of the ICC possible. Academics had called for the creation of a permanent international criminal court since the end of World War I, but nothing happened for decades.[155] It was only in the early 1990s that support really began to build for the creation of the ICC. And

---

[145] *See* Benedetti & Washburn, *supra* note 3, at 16.

[146] *See* FANNY BENEDETTI ET AL., Negotiating the International Criminal Court: New York to Rome 1994–1998 (2014) at 41–2; Orie, *supra* note 142, at 1493.

[147] *See* BENEDETTI ET AL., *supra* note 146, at 42; Jorda, *supra* note 29, at 578 (noting that the French delegation had worked hard to secure the creation of the Pre-Trial Chambers).

[148] *See* BENEDETTI ET AL., *supra* note 146, at 42; Orie, *supra* note 142, at 1475–7. *See also* Jorda, *supra* note 29, at 578–9 (arguing that unless the judges at the ICC are given more power to control the proceedings, the ICC will end up having many of the same problems that plagued the ICTY).

[149] *See* Rome Statute, Art. 61 (describing the confirmation of charges hearing); *id.* at Arts. 17, 19(6) (describing challenges to admissibility).

[150] *Id.*, Art. 15(4).

[151] *Id.*, Art. 56(3).

[152] *Id.*, Art. 69(3).

[153] *Id.*, Art. 64(6).

[154] *See* Orie, *supra* note 142, at 1494–5. *See also id.* at 1442 (arguing that a permanent international criminal court "should in its law of procedure be as universal as possible" and that it should "be balanced in the degree to which it reflects each one of the major criminal justice model systems").

[155] *See supra* Section I.

this was due in no small part to the example of the ad hoc tribunals. They demonstrated to a skeptical world that international criminal justice was possible. Of course,
the ICTY and ICTR were not the sole causes of the ICC,[156] but they played an
important role in catalyzing support for the creation of the ICC, and it is unlikely that
the ICC would have been created without the example they provided.[157] This outcome was a fortuitous accident,[158] but that does not lessen the importance of the role
played by the ad hoc tribunals. In the long run, the ad hocs' influence on the ICC may
be their most important legacy, as the ICC will continue operating long after the
ICTY and ICTR have become footnotes in history, much as the IMT is today.

At the same time that the experience of the ad hoc tribunals catalyzed support for
the ICC, the ICC was also fundamentally a reaction to those very same courts,
particularly their ad hoc nature. The ICTR and ICTY demonstrated both that
international criminal justice was possible and that an ad hoc approach to court
building was not sustainable. It became apparent that the international community
would quickly run out of the political will to build new ad hoc courts, and that the
essentially political nature of their creation made it very likely that an ad hoc
approach would result in selective and biased access to justice.[159] Thus, support
grew for the establishment of a permanent global International Criminal Court.

The ad hocs also heavily influenced the shape of the Rome Statute. For one thing,
the ICC and the ad hoc tribunals have quite similar subject matter jurisdiction and
personal jurisdiction. While today that seems unremarkable, this was not a foregone
conclusion. There were proposals during the drafting of the Rome Statute to
significantly expand or alter the personal and subject matter jurisdiction of the
ICC. For example, there were many proposals to greatly expand the scope of the
ICC's jurisdiction to include crimes like terrorism and drug trafficking.[160] There was
also a proposal by the French delegation to include organizations within the
jurisdiction of the ICC.[161] Instead, while the court's subject matter jurisdiction
provisions were updated by the drafters of the Rome Statute, they remained largely
based on that of the ad hocs.[162] And the personal jurisdiction of the Rome Statue

---

[156] *See supra* Section II (arguing that the creation of the ICC required both the example of the ad hoc
       tribunals and the period of global cooperation that followed the end of the Cold War).
[157] *Id.*
[158] *See* Zacklin, *supra* note 28, at 542 (arguing that the ad hoc tribunals were not established "as part of
       a deliberate policy [of] promoting international justice" but rather they were "acts of political
       contrition, because of egregious failures to swiftly confront the situations in the former Yugoslavia
       and Rwanda").
[159] *See supra* Section II.
[160] *See* Kirsch & Holmes, *supra* note 3, at 22.
[161] *See* Kai Ambos, Article 25: Individual Criminal Responsibility at 745 *in* COMMENTARY ON THE ROME
       STATUTE OF THE INTERNATIONAL CRIMINAL COURT (Otto Triffterer ed., 2nd edn. 2008); William
       A. Schabas, The International Criminal Court: A Commentary on the Rome Statute 425–7 (2010).
[162] *See supra* Section III(A) (noting that the ICC's definitions of the crimes are not identical to those of
       the ad hoc tribunals but were heavily influenced by both the Statutes of the ICTY and ICTR and by
       their jurisprudence).

remained limited to individuals, just like at the ICTR and ICTY.[163] Ultimately, the final form of the Rome Statute owes a lot to the influence of the ad hoc tribunals.[164]

At the same time, the ICC was also an opportunity for the drafters to fix some of the perceived flaws in the ad hoc tribunals. Thus, for example, the drafters took the opportunity to greatly expand crimes of sexual violence.[165] They also tweaked the definitions of the crimes to try and narrow some crimes that were perceived as too broad,[166] and they added some features of civil law systems.[167] But perhaps the most important "fix" was to re-establish the centrality of states and state sovereignty at the ICC. The ad hocs were created unilaterally by the Security Council, and the judges used the vagueness of their founding documents to create new international criminal law.[168] In many ways, the Rome Statute was a reaction to both of these developments. By creating a permanent international criminal court by multilateral treaty, states largely took control over international criminal justice away from the Security Council.[169] By exhaustively defining the crimes and including a strict ban on extending the crimes by analogy, states sought to take control of the process of creating new international criminal law away from the judges.[170] The doctrine of complementarity, which is central to the Rome Statute, is also an acknowledgment of the importance of state sovereignty.[171] The result was a narrower and more circumscribed court.[172] Of course, there was also disagreement between states on certain issues,[173] but there appears to have been general agreement that states and state sovereignty should be central to the creation of a permanent international criminal court. In this way, the ICC is a rejection of Antonio Cassese's declaration in *Tadić* that a "State-sovereignty-oriented-approach has been gradually supplanted by a human-being-oriented-approach."[174]

---

[163]   *Compare* ICTR Statute, Art. 1, *and* ICTY Statute, Art. 1, *with* Rome Statute, Art. 25(1).

[164]   On the other hand, the ICC has rejected most of the ad hocs' innovations with respect to modes of liability. *See supra* Section III(C).

[165]   *See supra* Section III(B).

[166]   *See supra* Section III(A) (noting that the drafters of the Rome Statute added a policy requirement to crimes against humanity and a manifest pattern of conduct requirement to genocide).

[167]   *See supra* Section III(F).

[168]   *See supra* Section III(D).

[169]   *But see* Rome Statute, Art. 16 (granting the Security Council the right to defer investigations and prosecutions).

[170]   *See supra* Section III(D).

[171]   *See supra* Section III(E).

[172]   *See* Tolbert, *supra* note 24, at 1288 ("In many respects, the Rome Statute is a conservative document, and the powers of the court and the prosecutor are much more circumscribed than in the ad hoc Tribunals.")

[173]   *See, e.g., supra* Section III(F) (noting disagreements between civil law and common law countries over matters of procedure).

[174]   *See* Prosecutor v. Tadić, *supra* note 27, at para. 97.

14

Twenty-Four Years On: The Yugoslavia and Rwanda Tribunals' Contributions to Durable Peace

Paul R. Williams* and Kimberly Larkin**

14.1 INTRODUCTION

As discussed in earlier chapters, the International Criminal Tribunal for the former Yugoslavia ("Yugoslavia Tribunal") had a profound impact on the development of international criminal law. The effects of this groundbreaking international criminal tribunal, however, went beyond courtrooms in The Hague. This chapter explores the ways in which the work of the Yugoslavia Tribunal influenced social and political dynamics during and after the conflict in the former Yugoslavia. We argue that while the Yugoslavia Tribunal's work was often timid and tardy, it shaped peace processes, geopolitical dynamics, and historical memory creation in the former Yugoslavia while also contributing to a renaissance of international criminal accountability for atrocity crimes.

The chapter first considers how the Yugoslavia Tribunal helped to remove and neutralize destabilizing actors during peace negotiations and post-conflict state-building in the former Yugoslavia. Next, it considers how Yugoslavia Tribunal indictments influenced NATO decision-makers' choice to use force during the Kosovo conflict and helped them to justify that choice to their constituents. Thirdly, this chapter considers how the Yugoslavia Tribunal's documentation of atrocity crimes established a historical record that has generally provided catharsis to victims while countering false moral equivalencies put forward by regional ethno-nationalist groups. Finally, it addresses how the Yugoslavia Tribunal initiated a culture of international criminal justice that has profoundly influenced subsequent international criminal tribunals, shaped victim and perpetrator expectations of justice in "The Hague," and birthed a class of international criminal justice professionals.

*   Paul R. Williams is the Rebecca Grazier Professor of Law and International Relations, American University. Co-Founder, Public International Law & Policy Group.
** Kimberly Larkin is an Associate, Three Crowns, LLP; formerly Legal Consultant, Public International Law & Policy Group.

Throughout, the chapter compares the Yugoslavia Tribunal's impact on geopolitics, social transition, and professional development with that of the International Criminal Tribunal for Rwanda ("Rwanda Tribunal"). It concludes that, like the Yugoslavia Tribunal, the Rwanda Tribunal contributed to peacebuilding by removing certain destabilizing actors from the country's post-genocide unity government. Notably, however, the Rwanda Tribunal's one-sided prosecutions may have limited its contributions to historical memory and weakened its effectiveness as a tool for reconciliation.

14.2 NEUTRALIZING SPOILERS

The Yugoslavia Tribunal's first major contribution to peace in the former Yugoslavia came from its ability to neutralize and remove war criminals from peace talks and post-conflict nation-building. Earlier peace talks had created false moral equivalencies among Bosniaks,[1] Croats, and Serbs and had enabled Serbian hardliners to derail talks with increasingly unreasonable demands. When the Yugoslavia Tribunal indicted these hardliners prior to the Dayton talks, it drastically reduced their ability to spoil peace negotiations. The indictments also gave the Dayton negotiators greater moral clarity about Serbian ethnic cleansing, which led the Dayton drafters to ban individuals indicted by the Yugoslavia Tribunal from holding elected office in the new nation states that formed out of the former Yugoslavia. Banning accused war criminals from elected leadership generally provided increased stability for these fledgling post-conflict societies.

14.2.1 *Neutralizing Spoilers during the Peace Negotiations*

Yugoslavia Tribunal indictments promoted peace by removing spoilers – individuals or groups empowered by the conflict that seek to maintain their position by undermining the peace process[2] – from the peace process in the former Yugoslavia. For example, the indictment of Republika Srpska political and military leaders Radovan Karadžić and Ratko Mladić was crucial to the success of the Dayton talks. Prior to Dayton, a series of talks led by the United Nations and European Union from 1990 to 1993 had attempted to balance Bosniak, Croat, and Serbian interests by partitioning

---

[1] This paper uses the term "Bosniaks" to refer to the group of people characterized by traditional adherence to Islam, historic ties to the territory of Bosnia, and use of the Bosnian language. The authors have chosen this term, rather than the term "Bosnian Muslims," because it includes not only members of the group who are current adherents of Islam but also group members of other faiths. This term also addresses the fact that Bosniaks were targeted for both their religion and their ethnic identity. The Dayton Agreement also uses this term to refer to this group (with the less-standard spelling "Bosniac").

[2] Stephen John Stedman, Spoiler Problems in Peace Processes, 178–224, *in* INTERNATIONAL CONFLICT RESOLUTION AFTER THE COLD WAR (Paul C. Stern & Daniel Druckman eds., 2000) www.nap.edu/read/9897/chapter/6

Bosniak territory into roughly equal parts divided along ethnic lines. These efforts alienated Bosniak negotiators, who felt that an equal partition would unjustly reward the Republika Srpska for its war crimes. UN and EU negotiators argued that overlooking these war crimes in the name of peace would prevent further civilian deaths.

Negotiators' appeasement of Serbian hardline positions emboldened Karadžić and Mladić to act as spoilers for early peace accord attempts. From 1991 to 1994, the two hardliners rejected a series of proposed peace agreements despite the fact that those agreements increasingly accommodated Serbian demands. The two Serbian leaders also stepped up their ethnic cleansing campaign during this time, further expanding Serbian territory and strengthening their position as spoilers who could gain more from continued war than from a negotiated peace. This strategy ultimately led US Secretary of State Lawrence Eagleburger to "name and shame" Karadžić and Mladić for their role in Serbian atrocity crimes during the Vance-Owen talks in December 1992.[3] While Eagleburger intended for this to undermine the hardliners' ability to derail peace talks, the Serbian delegation neutralized the United States' accusations by calling them politically motivated and overblown.[4] As a result, Karadžić and Mladić continued to push the Serbian delegation at the Vance-Owen talks toward increasingly extreme positions, leading Serbian delegates Momčilo Krajišnik and Biljana Plavšić to say that "six million Serbian casualties [was] not too high a price for the Bosnian Serbs to pay for their goals."[5] Ultimately, the Vance-Owen peace talks failed, causing more, not fewer, civilian deaths in the years that followed.

The fact that the Dayton negotiations succeeded where the Vance-Owen talks failed was due in part to Yugoslavia Tribunal prosecutor Richard Goldstone's decision to indict Karadžić and Mladić for genocide on July 24, 1995, before the Dayton talks began, and reconfirm their indictments on November 16, 1995, during the Dayton negotiations.[6] Goldstone worried that the two Bosnian Serbs might continue to commit war crimes with impunity unless he brought criminal charges against them. He also feared that amnesty might be used as a bargaining chip at Dayton, and therefore "added the second indictments as if to remind the mediators of the horrific crimes for which [Karadžić and Mladić] were accused."[7]

---

[3] Elaine Sciolino, *US Names Figures It Wants Charged with War Crimes*, NEW YORK TIMES (Dec. 16, 1992), www.nytimes.com/1992/12/17/world/us-names-figures-it-wants-charged-with-war-crimes.html?pagewanted=all

[4] *See* Michael Scharf quote in Nikolas M. RAJKOVIC, The Politics of International Law and Compliance: Serbia, CROATIA, and the Hague Tribunal 25 (2012) (stating that Eagleburger's "naming names" speech had been carefully crafted in advance as part of US negotiating strategy).

[5] Raymond Bonner, *In Reversal, Serbs of Bosnia Accept Peace Agreement*, NEW YORK TIMES (Nov. 24, 1995), www.nytimes.com/1995/11/24/world/in-reversal-serbs-of-bosnia-accept-peace-agreement.html.

[6] PAUL WILLIAMS & MICHAEL SCHARF, Peace with Justice? 157 (2002)

[7] Joyce Neu, Pursuing Justice in the Midst of War: The International Criminal Tribunal for the Former Yugoslavia, 83–4, Negotiation and Conflict Management Research (Feb. 2012), http://onlinelibrary.wiley.com/woh/doi/10.1111/j.1750-4716.2011.00091.x/full

These charges helped make accountability a priority during the Dayton talks and allowed negotiating parties to successfully cut Karadžić and Mladić out of the formal negotiation process. During earlier peace processes, EU and UN negotiators had opposed US efforts to exclude Karadžić and Mladić, arguing that the two hardliners would use their substantial sway over Republika Srpska forces to undermine any peace agreement that they did not help negotiate. Once the Yugoslavia Tribunal indicted them in July 1995, these negotiators were much more open to sidelining them. After Karadžić and Mladić were accused war criminals, the United States, United Kingdom, and European Union had valid reasons to publicly refuse to meet with them. The parties increasingly negotiated with Serbian political leader Slobodan Milošević as the sole Serbian representative. Like Karadžić and Mladić, Milošević was a hardline Serbian leader responsible for ethnic cleansing both in Bosnia and, later, in Kosovo. Nevertheless, at Dayton, he portrayed himself as a moderating force, more open to a negotiated settlement than his two colleagues and capable of convincing the Bosnian Serb delegation to sign the final agreement. As US representative Richard Holbrooke noted, "even though [Milošević] was one of the gorillas, he could also be the zookeeper."[8]

These dynamics ultimately sidelined Karadžić's and Mladić's hardliner rhetoric within the Bosnian Serb delegation during the Dayton negotiations. Given their exclusion from the negotiating table, Karadžić and Mladić tried to channel their uncompromising stance toward Bosniaks and Croats through Serb political leader Momčilo Krajišnik, whom the Yugoslavia Tribunal had not indicted and who was present at Dayton. Indeed, Krajišnik's stubborn, uncompromising attitude at Dayton led Holbrook to christen him "Dr. No."[9] Fortunately, Dr. No did not win the day. With his two indicted colleagues removed from negotiations, Krajišnik could not overpower Milošević's moderate Bosnian Serbs. Ultimately, Milošević and other moderate-acting Bosnian Serbs were able to consolidate control over the Serbian delegation and work with other parties to negotiate a peace agreement after more than three bitter years of failed peace talks and continued fighting.[10] This cooperation was not disinterested: while the resulting agreement required the newly formed republics of Croatia, Serbia, and Bosnia-Herzegovina to cooperate with the Yugoslavia Tribunal, it also reduced international sanctions on the former Yugoslavia that threatened to undercut these leaders' authority over their respective groups.

While many factors contributed to the ultimate success of the Dayton talks, the Yugoslavia indictments had a major impact on power dynamics at Dayton and, therefore, on the outcome of the negotiations. The indictments provided an objective reason for excluding the two spoilers, Mladić and Karadžić, enabling Holbrooke to persuade the United Nations, United Kingdom, and other negotiating parties to

---

[8] Quoted in Joyce Neu, *supra* note 6.
[9] Richard Holbrooke, To End a War, 255 (1998).
[10] Williams & Scharf, *supra* note 5, at 160–1.

refuse to include a faction helmed by two accused war criminals. As Professor Juan Mendez notes, "the object lesson [of the Yugoslavia indictments] is that sometimes the true spoilers of a peace accord have to be removed from the negotiating table, and removing them on the basis of an objective standard like a judicial indictment provides the whole peace process with credibility and likelihood of success."[11]

14.2.2 *Neutralizing Spoilers during the Postconflict Political Process*

Yugoslavia Tribunal indictments also promoted peace by shaping the substance of the Dayton Accords. In order to issue its indictments in July 1995, the Tribunal had thoroughly documented ethnic cleansing, forced deportation, and other atrocity crimes committed by Karadžić, Mladić, and other political and military leaders. This work was painstaking, slow, and led to timid and tardy indictments that failed to prevent some of the worst atrocities of the Yugoslav conflict. Nevertheless, this extensive documentation meant that by the time of the Dayton talks in November 1995, negotiators were well aware that much of the Croat leadership and Bosnian Serb leadership – and thus many potential post-conflict elected officials – had been directly or indirectly involved in committing atrocity crimes during the conflict.

Dayton negotiators feared that if these leaders were elected to post-conflict leadership positions, they would enflame ethnic tensions and bring further conflict to the fledgling multicultural state of Bosnia. Negotiators relied on the Tribunal's documentation of atrocities committed by key military figures to argue that the Dayton Accords should categorically ban all Tribunal indictees from post-conflict leadership. As Holbrooke noted, "the [Yugoslavia] tribunal emerged as a valuable instrument of policy that allowed us ... to bar Karadžić and all other indicted war criminals from public office."[12]

At first, the Yugoslavia Tribunal was timid and tardy in issuing indictments against war criminals in the former Yugoslavia. The Tribunal indicted only a handful of individuals in the years immediately following Dayton, and many of those indicted – including Mladić and Karadžić – continued to live freely in the Yugoslav state.[13] However, as the Dayton Accords were implemented and the Tribunal uncovered more evidence of atrocity crimes, Tribunal indictments became an important way to limit the political power of those responsible. While some individuals indicted by the Tribunal continued to influence regional politics informally, the Dayton Accords prevented them from seeking formal political positions, which had the positive by-product of opening up elections to non-combatants, political moderates,

---

[11] Juan Mendez, *The Arrest of Ratko Mladić and Its Impact on International Justice and Prevention of Genocide and Other International Crimes, in* 17 The Holocaust and the United Nations Outreach Programme Discussion Papers, 94–5 (2013), www.un.org/en/holocaustremembrance/docs/pdf/chapter8.pdf.

[12] Quoted in Joyce Neu, *supra* note 6.

[13] Paul Williams & Michael Scharf, *supra* note 5, 168.

and other democratic actors. Moreover, as Tribunal investigations and prosecutions increased, regional and international actors regarded indicted individuals with an "almost indelible impression of shame," and were reluctant to continue negotiating or contracting with them.[14] As arrests increased, the indictments themselves began to serve as "significant retribution," limiting indictees' ability to travel, run for and hold public office, and live as private citizens under their own names.[15] Finally, arrest warrants issued by the Tribunal ultimately caused many destabilizing actors to be physically removed from the fragile post-conflict states in the Balkans. Their arrest warrants were often carried out in dramatic fashion via manhunts spearheaded by NATO forces. Once captured, accused war criminals were transported out of their countries of origin to The Hague for trial. This limited their physical and media access – and thus their political and social impact – within the Balkans.

Physically removing destabilizing actors from post-conflict Yugoslavia was one of the Yugoslavia Tribunal's most obvious – and perhaps most effective – contributions to peace. As former Tribunal prosecutor Payam Akhavan noted:

> One of the immediate effects of the tribunal, which has little to do with subtle and long term shifts of people's perception of history, is the removal of certain individuals from the political space. And that is a very immediate and tangible effect: you take someone, who is a demagogical leader, who is responsible for violence, who cannot be trusted to conduct politics in any way except to incite hatred, and you remove that person. In criminological terms, it is a form of incapacitation, which in itself is extremely valuable.[16]

International criminal law scholar David Luban concurs, stating that removal of destabilizing actors may be "the most obvious contribution of the Tribunal to peace and security."[17]

One illustrative example of this contribution can be found in the Yugoslavia Tribunal's indictment and arrest of Bosnian Serb leader Biljana Plavšić. Plavšić, a genetic biologist, rose in the ranks of the Serbian Democratic Party, serving as president of the self-proclaimed Serbian Republic of Bosnia-Herzegovina and as a member of the Supreme Command of the Republika Srpska forces, as well as a member of the Republika Srpska delegation during the Vance-Owen negotiations. She was perhaps best known for her inflammatory rhetoric about Serbian ethnic superiority, which blended white supremacist and xenophobic ideas with pseudoscientific theories of genetic hierarchies derived from her former career as a biologist.

---

[14] *Id.* at 159.

[15] Paul C. Szasz & Theodor Meron, *The Bosnian Constitution: The Road to Dayton and Beyond*, 90 AM. SOC'Y INT'L L. PROC. 1, at 479–85 (1996), www.jstor.org/stable/25659064.

[16] Frédéric Mégret, *The Legacy of the ICTY as Seen Through Some of Its Actors and Observers*, GOETTINGEN J. OF INT'L L. 3, 1011–52 (2011), www.gojil.eu/issues/33/33_article_megret.pdf.

[17] David Luban, Symposium on the International Criminal Tribunals for the Former Yugoslavia and Rwanda: Broadening the Debate, Demystifying Political Violence: Some Bequests of ICTY and ICTR, AM. J. OF INT'L L. Unbound 251, 256, www.asil.org/sites/default/files/Luban,%20Some%20Bequests%20of%20ICTY%20and%20ICTR.pdf.

For example, in 1994, she declared that the Republika Srpska could not negotiate or govern alongside Bosniaks because of their genetic inferiority, arguing that it was "genetically deformed material that embraced Islam." [18] She claimed, "With each successive generation it simply becomes concentrated. It gets worse and worse. It simply expresses itself and dictates their style of thinking, which is rooted in their genes. And through the centuries, the genes degraded further."[19]

Plavšić's uncompromising stances on ethnicity sometimes placed her to the extreme of other Serbian hardliners on questions of power-sharing and reconciliation with Bosniaks. After Milošević expressed support for the Vance-Owen power-sharing agreement in 1992, she refused to shake the Serbian leader's hand, feeling that he had betrayed his genetically superior ethnicity.[20] Karadžić was so impressed with her unbending hatred toward Bosniaks that he nominated her to run for the Republika Srpska presidency. He was later described as believing she was "more extreme than him in every way."[21]

In the years following Dayton, Plavšić substantially moderated her positions to maintain her influence in the Republika Srpska as it became increasingly dependent on international support. Nevertheless, she continued to derail reconciliation efforts between Serbia and Bosnia-Herzegovina due to her ongoing hostility toward Bosniaks and her status as a symbol of extreme Serbian ethno-nationalist ideology. In 2001, she voluntarily surrendered to the Yugoslavia Tribunal, which had indicted her the year before for genocide and crimes against humanity. The Tribunal agreed to an eleven-year prison sentence in exchange for her guilty plea, ending her Serbian political career and physically removing her from the former Yugoslavia. While fringe extremist Serbian groups viewed Plavšić as an unjustly accused martyr, her indictment and prison sentence helped to discredit her extreme, pseudoscientific ethnocentrism in the eyes of most Serbians.[22] It also left the Serbian supremacist movement without a figurehead, hampering its ability to affect politics in the new Serbian state.

Similarly, while Slobodan Milošević was not as extreme as his colleague Plavšić in his anti-Bosniak rhetoric, his indictment by the Yugoslavia Tribunal and arrest by Yugoslav authorities may have undermined hardline Serbian rhetoric even more effectively. Indicted in 1999, Milošević had managed to avoid arrest for three years, until the United States threatened to eliminate $50 million in aid to Serbia if he was

---

[18] Quoted in Michael Sells, Islam in Serbian Religious Mythology, *in* ISLAM AND BOSNIA: CONFLICT RESOLUTION AND FOREIGN POLICY IN MULTI-ETHNIC STATES 58 (Maya Shatzmiller ed., 2002).

[19] Quoted in Michael Sells, Islam in Serbian Religious Mythology, *in* ISLAM AND BOSNIA: CONFLICT RESOLUTION AND FOREIGN POLICY IN MULTI-ETHNIC STATES 58 (Maya Shatzmiller ed., 2002).

[20] Ian Black, *The Iron Lady of the Balkans*, THE GUARDIAN (Sept. 9, 2001), www.theguardian.com/world/2001/sep/10/gender.uk1.

[21] Judgment, Prosecutor v. Milošević, Case No. IT-02–54 (Int'l Crim. Trib. for the Former Yugoslavia, Aug. 30, 1995), www.icty.org/x/cases/slobodan_Milošević/trans/en/050830IT.htm.

[22] Jelena Subotić, The Cruelty of False Remorse: Biljana Plavsic at the Hague, 36 J. OF SOUTHWESTERN EUROPE 39 (2012).

not arrested by March 31, 2001.[23] As a consequence, Yugoslav authorities cornered Milošević along with his family and twenty bodyguards in his Belgrade estate for thirty-six hours.[24] Throughout the standoff, Milošević boasted that he "would not go to jail alive," and attempted to escape the estate undetected multiple times.[25] After hours of painstaking negotiations, the standoff came to an end in the early hours of April 1, 2001, with Milošević carted away to a high-security Belgrade prison, and then to The Hague.[26] Aid money from the United States, the European Union, and the World Bank flowed into the Serbian government shortly thereafter.[27] Milošević's hollow bravado toward state authorities and the Tribunal, along with the heavy financial incentives Serbian authorities received to separate themselves from the former Republika Srpska leader, helped cement his irrelevance to the future of Serbia.

While political dynamics had already forced him to the fringes of Serbian politics, Milošević's marginalization may not have happened to the same extent without the Tribunal's indictment. As Professor Luban notes, "Had Milošević not been extradited to The Hague, he might have been able to work further mischief in Serbian politics notwithstanding his downfall."[28] Furthermore, while Serbian hardliners continue to claim that Milošević was a martyr killed by authorities in The Hague rather than by heart failure, his indictment for war crimes and genocide served to make him a controversial, contested figure in the former Yugoslavia today.

The Yugoslavia Tribunal, however, did not discredit only Serbian hardliners. While the first two Tribunal prosecutors, Louise Arbour and Richard Goldstone, never issued a formal indictment against Croatian leader Franjo Tuđman, their successor Carla del Ponte noted that she had sufficient evidence to indict Tuđman had he not died in 1999.[29] In addition, the *Gotovina* and *Prlić* cases before the Yugoslavia Tribunal presented serious allegations of Tuđman's involvement in a joint criminal enterprise of ethnic cleansing against Serbians and non-Croats in the Krajina region of Serbia and throughout Bosnia-Herzegovina.[30] While Tuđman remains a revered "father of modern Croatia" today, these allegations helped weaken political support for his ethnocentric, isolationist approach to regional politics and Croatian history.[31] This in turn paved the way for democratically minded leaders like

---

[23] *Milošević Arrested*, BBC NEWS (Apr. 1, 2001), http://news.bbc.co.uk/2/hi/europe/1254263.stm

[24] *Id.*

[25] *Id.*

[26] *Milošević Extradited*, BBC NEWS (Apr. 2, 2001), http://news.bbc.co.uk/2/hi/europe/1412828.stm.

[27] *Milošević Extradition Unlocks Aid Coffers*, BBC NEWS (June 29, 2001), http://news.bbc.co.uk/2/hi/europe/1413144.stm.

[28] David Luban, *supra* note 12, at 256.

[29] Christiane Amanpour, *Del Ponte Urges War Crimes Arrests*, CNN (Apr. 27, 2001), http://edition.cnn.com/2001/WORLD/europe/04/27/delponte.amanp/index.html.

[30] Marlise Simons, *U.N. Court Convicts Two Croatian Generals of War Crimes and Frees a Third*, NEW YORK TIMES (Apr. 15, 2011), www.nytimes.com/2011/04/16/world/europe/16hague.html.

[31] Steven Erlanger, *Croatia Elects a Moderate to Follow the Tuđman Era*, NEW YORK TIMES (Feb. 8, 2000), www.nytimes.com/2000/02/08/world/croatia-elects-a-moderate-to-follow-the-Tuđman-era.html.

Stjepan Mesić and Ivo Josipović to lead Croatia away from Tuđman's ethnocentric ideology, toward a more cosmopolitan outlook that would ultimately usher Croatia into relative economic prosperity, peace, and both NATO and EU membership several years later.

Admittedly, the limited sentences that the Tribunal handed down tempered its ability to neutralize these destabilizing actors. Most Yugoslavia Tribunal sentences were not life sentences, so many convicted war criminals have been released back into their still-fragile home countries. When Plavšić was released in 2009, she was shocked to discover that she had become a folk hero for ethnic nationalists in Serbia, many of whom continue to reference her and her speeches in their current anti-Muslim hate speech.[32] Similarly, Krajišnik was stunned that a large crowd and local band greeted him when he returned to Serbia at the end of his prison term in 2013, because, as he noted, "after all, I am a war criminal."[33] Serbian nationalist groups have also martyrized Slobodan Milošević, who died of a heart attack while awaiting trial in The Hague, with many current Serbian nationalists believing that Western powers killed him to undermine the Serbian state.[34] These instances indicate that international criminal tribunals may be more effective at promoting peacebuilding by removing destabilizing actors in countries like Croatia, where democratic, cosmopolitan systems have replaced toxic political structures, rather than in states like Serbia, where underlying, ethnically charged political hierarchies and rhetoric have remained largely unchanged.

14.2.3 *Jurisdictional Limitiatons on Removing Spoilers*

The Rwanda Tribunal similarly contributed to the post-genocide peace process by removing destabilizing actors from the state. The Rwanda Tribunal's arrest, prosecution, and incarceration of hardline Hutus reduced the social and political influence of extremist Rwandan politicians and private citizens who remained loyal to charismatic *genocidaires* such as Jean-Paul Akeyesu.[35] The Tribunal also diluted the influence of anti-Tutsi hate rhetoric by criminalizing genocidal ideology and incarcerating its chief proponents. The landmark *Nahimana* case sentenced the leading Hutu extremist propagandists to life imprisonment and silenced their *Radio Television Libre des Milles Collines* broadcasts, which had spread fear, distrust,

---

[32] Anes Alic, *Walking and Baking for War Criminals* (ETH Zurich Ctr. for Sec. Studies, Working Paper, 2017), www.css.ethz.ch/en/services/digital-library/articles/article.html/109375/pdf; *see also* Bojana Barlovac, *Dodik Says Had Moral Reasons to Welcome Plavšić, Balkans Transitional Justice*, BALKAN TRANSITIONAL JUSTICE (Oct. 28, 2009), www.balkaninsight.com/en/article/dodik-says-had-moral-reasons-to-welcome-Plavšić.

[33] *Bosnian Serbs welcome freed war criminal*, AL JAZEERA (Aug. 30, 2013), www.aljazeera.com/news/europe/2013/08/2013830203137245488.html.

[34] Peter Mass, *What Slobodan Milošević Taught Me About Donald Trump*, THE INTERCEPT (Feb. 7, 2017), https://theintercept.com/2017/02/07/what-slobodan-Milošević-taught-me-about-donald-trump/.

[35] Matthew Piper, *Rape as a War Crime: SLC Lawyer Recalls Rwandan Genocide Trial*, SALT LAKE TRIBUNE (Nov. 17, 2016), www.sltrib.com/home/4594324-155/two-decades-after-the-rwandan-genocide.

and hatred of Tutsis and moderate Hutus among rural Hutu populations leading up to the genocide in April 1994.[36]

However, the Rwanda Tribunal was less effective than the Yugoslavia Tribunal at neutralizing destabilizing actors. First, the conflict in Rwanda ended in a decisive military victory for the Rwandan Patriotic Front (RPF) rather than a negotiated settlement between warring parties. As a result, many of the destabilizing actors in the Rwandan Genocide had already fled the country by the time the Rwanda Tribunal began issuing indictments and were unlikely to return after its work began.[37] Consequently, the Rwanda Tribunal played a less direct role in the political transformation of post-genocide Rwanda than its Yugoslavian counterpart played in the Balkans.

Secondly, the Rwanda Tribunal's narrow focus on prosecuting those responsible for the genocide reduced its ability to remove non-*genocidaire* destabilizing actors from the country. This narrow focus had two primary causes. First, Rwanda Tribunal prosecutors believed that despite its broader jurisdictional mandate, its main purpose was to investigate and prosecute only those directly responsible for the genocide. The Rwanda Tribunal had been given jurisdiction over "serious violations of international humanitarian law committed in the territory of Rwanda and Rwandan citizens responsible for such violations committed in the territory of neighbouring States between 1 January 1994 and 31 December 1994."[38] Nevertheless, Rwanda Tribunal prosecutor Richard Goldstone noted that he had neither the financial nor the diplomatic support necessary to go after perpetrators of violence on both sides. "My attitude was to give priority in investigations and prosecutions to the most guilty," he noted, stating that "we didn't have enough resources to investigate all the nines and tens ... and the RPF, who acted in revenge, were at ones and twos and maybe even fours and fives at worst."[39]

Prosecuting the RPF was also politically toxic. The Rwandan government exercised much greater control over the Rwanda Tribunal's actions than former Yugoslavian states did over the Yugoslavia Tribunal. For example, when the Appeals Chamber released accused *genocidaire* Jean-Bosco Barayagwiza in 1999, the government suspended its cooperation with the Tribunal. It blocked prosecutors from traveling to Rwanda for two weeks and refused to cooperate until the Appeals Chamber reversed its decision.[40] Similarly, when the Rwanda Tribunal considered

---

[36] Sophia Kagan, *The "Media case" before the Rwanda Tribunal: The Nahimana et al. Appeal Judgment*, THE HAGUE JUSTICE PORTAL (Apr. 24, 2008), www.haguejusticeportal.net/index.php?Id=9166.

[37] Lilian Barria & Steven Roper, How Effective Are International Criminal Tribunals? An Analysis of the ICTY and the ICTR, 9 THE INTERNATIONAL JOURNAL OF HUMAN RIGHTS 3, 360, http://stevendroper .com/ICTY.pdf.

[38] Statute of the International Criminal Tribunal for Rwanda, art. 1 (2009) http://legal.un.org/avl/pdf/ha/ ictr_EF.pdf.

[39] Quoted in Victor Peskin, *Beyond Victor's Justice? The Challenge of Prosecuting the Winners at the International Criminal Tribunals for the Former Yugoslavia and Rwanda*, 222–24, https://web.law.asu .edu/Portals/25/Files/Facutly%20Scholarship/Peksin_beyound.pdf.

[40] *Id.* at 223.

bringing charges against RPF members in 2002, Rwandan president and former RPF commander Paul Kagame refused to permit any witnesses to travel to Arusha to testify in front of the Rwanda Tribunal and prevented Tribunal staff from accessing key documents. Ultimately, Rwanda Tribunal prosecutors gave in, transferring these cases to the Rwandan domestic court system for prosecution.[41]

This limitation curbed the Rwanda Tribunal's ability to promote peace in Rwanda by neutralizing destabilizing actors. In failing to prosecute RPF troops for their looting of moderate Hutu homes or their raiding of refugee camps in eastern DRC and Tanzania, the Rwanda Tribunal failed to neutralize RPF hardliner commanders' influence on Rwandan politics. Moreover, the Tribunal's failure to address these violations fueled exiled Hutu extremists, who decried the Tribunal as victors' justice and denounced the current government for systematically discriminating against the Rwandan Hutu population. The Tribunal's behavior has also obscured the fact that moderate Hutu allies were harmed alongside Tutsis during the genocide, which curbed community reconciliation efforts in ethnically diverse regions of Rwanda.[42] Thus, while the Rwanda Tribunal did help minimize anti-Tutsi genocide ideology in post-conflict Rwanda, its one-sided prosecutions limited its effectiveness.

14.3 JUSTICE AND HUMANITARIAN INTERVENTION

During the Kosovo conflict, the Yugoslavia Tribunal not only limited the influence of destabilizing actors, but also encouraged and enhanced the ability of other actors to protect civilians, prevent further atrocities, and bring the conflict to a swifter end. By providing NATO decision-makers with more information about who was a victim and who was a perpetrator in the Kosovo conflict, the Yugoslavia Tribunal brought moral clarity to NATO's choice to use force against Serbian targets in Kosovo. In addition, heads of NATO member states relied on Yugoslavia Tribunal indictments to justify their use of force in Kosovo to their own citizens.

14.3.1 *Moral Clarity*

Misinformed claims of moral equivalence complicated debates between Western powers on whether to intervene in the Bosnian War. For example, the United States, the United Kingdom, and the United Nations often fell prey to Serbian campaigns of deliberate misinformation about atrocities during the Bosnian conflict, leading them to mistakenly conclude that both sides had equally dirty hands. As a result, there was almost no humanitarian intervention on behalf of Bosniaks trapped in Sarajevo or executed at Srebrenica. By the time that fighting broke out in Kosovo in

---

[41] HUMAN RIGHTS WATCH, RWANDA: JUSTICE AFTER GENOCIDE – 20 YEARS ON (Mar. 28, 2014), www.hrw .org/news/2014/03/28/rwanda-justice-after-genocide-20-years.

[42] David Luban, *supra* note 16.

1998, however, the Yugoslavia Tribunal's investigation into Serbian regime atrocities in Bosnia had revealed that the international community had done far too little, far too late to protect innocent human lives during the Bosnian War. The world's inaction in the face of the 1994 Rwandan genocide further reinforced the need to investigate and intervene during humanitarian crises. Nevertheless, the international community still needed reliable, fact-based, morally clear justifications for intervening on behalf of one side, particularly in secession-based civil wars, like the conflict in Kosovo, where supporting a secessionist movement could set a dangerous precedent for secessionist groups in other countries.

The Yugoslavia Tribunal indictments provided the fact-based moral clarity that the NATO powers needed. For example, former Yugoslavia Tribunal prosecutor Louise Arbour discussed Goldstone's indictment of Mladić, noting that the "evidence upon which this indictment was confirmed raise[d] serious questions about [Yugoslavian leaders'] suitability to be guarantors of any deal let alone a peace agreement."[43] As Milošević began rounding up Kosovo Albanian men into concentration camps, a senior NATO diplomat observed that "we allowed Milošević to hoodwink us into thinking he would scale back the violence in Kosovo, but it has only gotten worse."[44] Yugoslavia Tribunal Judge McDonald sent repeated reports about mounting Yugoslav atrocities against Kosovar Albanians, provoking outrage from US and UK leaders. US Secretary of Defense Casper Weinberger noted that the practice of making "all kinds of strong statements that grave consequences will be faced by Mr. Milošević and then nothing ever happens, is the worst way to go about dealing with aggression and terrorism ... the more you let the people involved know it is not going to be punished, the more you are going to have of it."[45]

By April 1999, NATO member states realized that their attempts to negotiate, appease, and coerce Milošević into a negotiated settlement had failed. As they considered whether to use military force against Milošević's troops, they increasingly relied on justice-based norms and the work of the Yugoslavia Tribunal. While NATO's motives were not purely humanitarian – several NATO commanders pointed out that airstrikes alone would likely not end the ethnic cleansing campaign – NATO member states' rhetoric became increasingly focused on atrocity prevention. British Prime Minister Tony Blair noted, "This is not a battle for NATO. This is not a battle for territory. This is a battle for humanity... allowing people the security and peace which is the right of any decent human being in the civilized world."[46] Former Prime Minister Margaret Thatcher concurred, stating that "Milošević's regime and the genocidal ideology that sustains it represent... a

---

[43] Edward S. Herman & David Peterson, *The Dismantling of Yugoslavia* (Part II), MONTHLY REVIEW (October 2005), https://monthlyreview.org/2007/10/01/the-dismantling-of-yugoslavia-part-ii/#en57.

[44] Quoted in Paul Williams & Michael Scharf, *supra* note 5 at 184.

[45] *Id.* at 186.

[46] Chris Bird & Lucy Ward, *Blair Pledge to Refugees*, THE GUARDIAN (May 3, 1999) www.theguardian.com/world/1999/may/04/lucywardBritish prime minister.

truly monstrous evil… and the only victory worth having now is one that prevents Serbia from ever again having the means to attack its neighbors and terrorize non-Serb inhabitants."[47]

Around this time, the US State Department began pressuring Yugoslavia Tribunal prosecutor Louise Arbour to indict Milošević as a way of bolstering the prevalent humanitarian argument for NATO air strikes. The indictment also helped quell some NATO member states' concerns that a NATO intervention on behalf of the Kosovars would legitimate further destabilization of other states in the region. As Williams and Scharf note, "the indictment had the positive effect of strengthening the resolve of America's European partners in the NATO air campaign … and provided a legitimate basis for the peace builders to call for a regime change, something they had previously been reluctant to do because it would be perceived as a violation of [Yugoslav] sovereignty."[48]

Thus, after Milošević's indictment, NATO leaders showed a clear willingness to use NATO power to force Milošević and others to surrender themselves to the Tribunal and conduct further investigations. For example, US State Department spokesman James P. Rubin said "US has long held Milošević personally and politically responsible for the crimes considered by the indictment. He's got to surrender."[49] NATO Spokesman Jamie Shea concurred, saying "The alliance is ready to help bring indicted war crimes suspects to trial. The NATO countries will also help provide the U.N. war crimes tribunal with evidence to support its indictments."[50]

14.3.2 *Justifying the Use of Force*

Once they were convinced that military intervention in Kosovo was the correct course of action, NATO member states' leaders had to convince their citizens to support their decision. This was not always easy: military interventions are often costly in terms of both money and lives. Plus, Western constituents had not forgotten how Dutch peacekeepers were humiliated in Srebrenica, how Belgian blue helmets were massacred in Kigali, or how US Rangers were attacked in Mogadishu.[51] Indeed, by 1999 many felt that Western humanitarian interventions were useless at best, and often did more harm than good. Foreign policy analysts also worried that NATO strikes against Serbian military targets in Kosovo could drive Serbian forces to target Kosovar Albanians more explicitly, worsening the humanitarian suffering in the

---

[47]   Margaret Thatcher, Former British Prime Minister, Speech at the International Free Enterprise Dinner (Apr. 20, 1999), www.margaretthatcher.org/document/108381.

[48]   Paul Williams & Michael Scharf, *supra* note 5 at 207.

[49]   Walter Gicardi, *The Charge of a King: Slobodan Milošević Indicted*, DIRITTO.IT, www.diritto.it/ articoli/transnazionale/giacardi4.html.

[50]   *Id.*

[51]   Benjamin Schwarz & Christopher Layne, *The Case against Intervention in Kosovo*, THE NATION (Apr. 1, 1999), www.thenation.com/article/case-against-intervention-kosovo/.

region.[52] Others felt that characterizing Serbian actions as genocide "trivialize[d] truly genocidal campaigns" and felt that both Serbian leaders and the KLA were responsible for civilian tragedies in the "particularly brutal and hellish" Kosovo civil war.[53]

To counter this, NATO leaders needed to clearly and factually describe the atrocities being committed in Kosovo and needed to link them to Serbian leadership. They then needed to transform that link into a moral imperative to act. Fortunately, this work had already been done for them through the Yugoslavia Tribunal's investigations and indictments, which continued throughout the NATO intervention. NATO leaders ultimately relied heavily on the Yugoslavia Tribunal's findings regarding ethnic cleansing of Kosovar Albanians when justifying NATO interventions to their constituents.

Though he rarely directly discussed the Tribunal's work, US President Bill Clinton often cited the language in reports by the Yugoslavia Tribunal to explain why intervening in Kosovo was a moral imperative. For example, during a press conference in late April 1999, Clinton relied on the Tribunal's preliminary findings of ethnic cleansing in Kosovo, calling the Serbian army's actions "a meticulously planned campaign, organized by the government of Belgrade for a specific political purpose – to maintain its grip over Kosovo by ridding the land of its people" and reminding the American people that NATO was countering that campaign "both against military targets in Kosovo and against the infrastructure of political and military power in Belgrade."[54]

During a speech justifying US support for NATO military intervention in Kosovo less than a week later in May 1999, Clinton again echoed the Tribunal's indictment against Milošević, stating, "You do not have systematic slaughter in an effort to eradicate the religion, the culture, the heritage, the very record of presence of a people in any area unless some politician thinks it is in his interest to foment that sort of hatred."[55] In the case of Kosovo, Clinton reminded his countrymen, that leader was Slobodan Milošević: "Even now, Mr. Milošević is being investigated by the International War Crimes Tribunal for alleged war crimes, including mass killing and ethnic cleansing."[56] Clinton alluded to the Tribunal's preliminary findings that "[ethnic cleansing was] carried out according to a plan carefully designed months earlier in Belgrade. Serb officials pre-positioned forces, tanks and fuel and mapped

---

[52] Francis X. Clines, *Crisis in the Balkans, The Overview; NATO Hunting for Serb Forces; US Reports Signs of "Genocide,"* THE NEW YORK TIMES (Mar. 30, 1999), www.nytimes.com/1999/03/30/world/crisis-balkans-overview-nato-hunting-for-serb-forces-us-reports-signs-genocide.html.

[53] Benjamin Schwarz & Christopher Layne, *supra* note 49.

[54] *Transcript: President Bill Clinton Speaks on Kosovo,* CNN (Apr. 28, 1999), www.cnn.com/ALLPOLITICS/stories/1999/04/28/kosovo/transcript.html.

[55] *Clinton: NATO Must Stop Milosevic's Atrocities against Kosovo,* CNN (May 13, 1999), www.cnn.com/ALLPOLITICS/stories/1999/05/13/clinton.kosovo/.

[56] Bill Clinton, Former US President, Remarks to the Veterans of Foreign Wars of the United States at Fort McNair, Maryland (May 13, 1999), www.presidency.ucsb.edu/ws/?pid=57561.

out the sequence of attacks," and reassured Americans that NATO intervention was an attempt to "grind down [Serbia's] war machine" by "striking at strategic targets in Serbia and directly at Serb forces in Kosovo, making it harder for them to obtain supplies, protect themselves, and attack the ethnic Albanians who are still there."[57]

UK authorities also relied on Yugoslavia Tribunal findings to call out Serbian authorities and solidify British support for continued NATO intervention in Kosovo. British Prime Minister Tony Blair relied on the Tribunal's indictment to call for airstrikes that would lead to regime change, stating that "the world cannot help you [Serbs] rebuild your country while Mr. Milošević is at its head. And nor will the world understand, as the full extent of these atrocities is revealed, if you just turn a blind eye to the truth and pretend it is nothing to do with you ... this evil was carried out by your soldiers and by your leaders."[58] During a March 1999 press conference, UK Foreign Secretary Robin Cook noted reports of Serbian concentration camps with dismay, citing the Tribunal's previous work: "[w]e remember the way in which many refugees were herded together and executed by the Serb forces during the civil war in Bosnia" before angrily telling Serbian leadership that "this is your responsibility... [w]e know the chain of command back to the political leadership in Belgrade."[59] Faced with doubts from the British public, Cook reminded them that "[i]f we had not acted, all of you would now be asking why we stood by while this ethnic cleansing took place."[60] He later told reporters that in light of these atrocities "there would be no reasons that would allow Milošević to escape prosecution," assuring them that "Britain will work to see that those indicted would stand trial."[61]

NATO likewise relied on the Yugoslavia Tribunal's findings to justify its intervention to member states and their populations. NATO Secretary-General Lord George Robertson's remarks one year after the intervention demonstrate the role that atrocities revealed by Tribunal investigations played in NATO's decision to intervene. "Consider for a moment what would have happened had NATO not acted? Milošević would have continued his policy of violent expulsion – systematically organised and ruthlessly executed. Hundreds of thousands of Kosovar Albanians would today be stranded in refugee camps throughout the region and beyond it, with no hope of return. An already unstable region would have been thrown into further massive political and economic turmoil. The barbaric policy of Belgrade would have succeeded and the credibility, not only of NATO but of western democracy itself and its values, would have been seriously damaged."[62]

During its 1999 meeting, NATO officials similarly cited the Yugoslavia Tribunal's findings as justification for their support for NATO's intervention and its continuing

57   Id.
58   Williams & Scharf, *supra* note 5 at 207.
59   Francis X. Clines, *supra* note 50.
60   Id.
61   Gicardi, *supra* note 47.
62   Lord George Robertson, NATO Chief, Speech on Kosovo (Mar. 21, 2000), http://bit.ly/2u8sag3.

support of the Tribunal, including investigations into Serbian war crimes. NATO members noted that "Atrocities against the people of Kosovo by FRY military, police and paramilitary forces represent a flagrant violation of international law" and pledged that "[o]ur governments will co-operate with the International Criminal Tribunal for the former Yugoslavia (ICTY) to support investigation of all those, including at the highest levels, responsible for war crimes and crimes against humanity."[63] The Council concluded by reminding its constituents that "[t]here can be no lasting peace without justice."[64]

While humanitarian intervention remains controversial, many believe the NATO air strikes in Kosovo were a qualified success. After seventy days of the air campaign, Milošević's Serbian army agreed to peace on the terms set out in UN Resolution 1244. This ended Milošević's ethnic cleansing campaign and led to his political downfall, culminating in his arrest and deportation to The Hague for trial. This ultimately stabilized the region, allowing Kosovar Albanian refugees to return to their homes and paving the way for an independent Kosovar state.

NATO might have conducted airstrikes without the Yugoslavia Tribunal, as NATO member states may have found it strategically desirable to stabilize the Kosovo region. But the Tribunal's regular reporting of Serbian atrocities within Kosovo and its indictment of Milošević for repeated incidents of ethnic cleansing, genocide, and war crimes during both the Bosnian and Kosovo conflicts likely catalyzed NATO member states' decision to engage militarily. The Tribunal's work may have also led NATO member states to focus their military engagement on preventing further atrocities via regime change in the region, rather than simply on curbing Milošević's power. That Kosovar peace has been largely durable is due in significant part to the humanitarian focus of the NATO intervention, which in turn owes much to the documentation and indictments provided by the Yugoslavia Tribunal.

14.4 THE ROLE OF JUSTICE

14.4.1 *Victim Catharsis*

Victims from Bosnia-Herzegovina, Croatia, and Serbia have expressed varying levels of satisfaction with the Yugoslavia Tribunal. While many victims acknowledge the Tribunal's important work in documenting atrocities and ending impunity, most feel that the Tribunal did not provide adequate space for victim testimony. Many are also disappointed that the Tribunal had no accompanying compensation mechanism for victims and focused exclusively on the rights of the accused. Some also

---

[63] Press Release, Heads of State and Government Participating in the meeting of the North Atlantic Council, Statement on Kosovo, NATO Press Release 2-1(99) 062 (Apr. 23, 1999), www.nato.int/cps/en/natohq/official_texts_27441.htm?selectedLocale=en.

[64] *Id.*

expressed concern that plea bargains and reduced sentences for perpetrators might enable those perpetrators to threaten victims again in the future.

The Yugoslavia Tribunal has provided limited space for victims to have their suffering acknowledged. In Bosnia, some victims' advocates have critiqued the Tribunal for focusing on the rights of the accused to the exclusion of victims' rights, noting that the Tribunal often relied on a small handful of witnesses rather than identifying and interviewing a greater number of victims, and it did not provide for any form of victim compensation.[65] Others have noted that they are partially satisfied with the Yugoslavia Tribunal as its work definitively proved that, for example, "[g]enocide was committed in Srebrenica, as proven before the ICTY, which is very important for Bosnia and Herzegovina in general."[66] However, the Yugoslavia Tribunal's leniency toward perpetrators, such as Plavšić, concerns Bosniak victims, as they find her remorse insincere and her release a threat to their continued safety and stability.[67]

Vice-President of the Yugoslavia Tribunal Judge Carmel Agius has noted that many in Croatia feel that the Tribunal communicated "that the days of impunity are over."[68] Though not everyone could participate, the trials offered some Croatian victims the opportunity to testify and to have their dead recognized for what happened to them.[69] This sentiment is not always shared by Serb-majority areas of Croatia, however. Croatian Serb victims often complained about the lack of any indictments for crimes committed against Serbs in Vukovar, describing how that denied them recognition of their suffering and reinforced Croats' ability to dismiss all Serbians as atrocity-committing perpetrators.[70] Many Croatian Serbs also feel that the Tribunal's sentences are too lenient given the magnitude of the atrocities committed. For example, many expressed frustration that Yugoslav Serbian commander Vesilin Šljivančanin, a convicted war criminal who murdered 194 Croatian Serb prisoners during the conflict, was released from his Tribunal-mandated sentence of seventeen years after serving only ten years.[71]

Serbian victims expressed a wide range of opinions toward the Yugoslavia Tribunal. During a year-long study in 2015, Professor Diane Orentlicher noted that many victims felt the Tribunal failed as a deterrent since some of the worst

---

[65] Edin Ramulić, Activist of Izvor NGO, Prijedor, BiH, quoted in *Legacy of the ICTY in the Former Yugoslavia: Conference Proceedings* (Nov. 6, 2012), www.icty.org/x/file/Outreach/conferences_pub/naslijedje_mksj_sa-zg_en.pdf.

[66] Kada Hotić, Association of Mothers of Srebrenica and Žepa Enclaves, quoted in *Legacy of the ICTY in the Former Yugoslavia, supra* note 63, at 32.

[67] *Id.*

[68] Judge Carmel Agius, Vice-President of the ICTY, *Legacy of the ICTY in the Former Yugoslavia, supra* note 63, at 128.

[69] *Id.*

[70] Janine Natalya Clark, The ICTY and Reconciliation in Croatia: A Case Study of Vukovar, JOURNAL OF INTERNATIONAL CRIMINAL JUSTICE (2012), www.researchgate.net/publication/277379861_The_ICTY_and_Reconciliation_in_Croatia_A_Case_Study_of_Vukovar.

[71] *Id.*

atrocities occurred after its creation.[72] However, many victims agreed that this was due to the Tribunal's timid, tardy beginnings. Often, victims agreed that as the number of arrests and transfers increased, so did the deterrence of possible future atrocities.[73] Furthermore, many interviewees shared the perception that without the Yugoslavia Tribunal there would have been "wholesale impunity."[74] Serbian victims also credit the Tribunal with removing Milošević, which helped Serbia transition to democracy. However, many Serbian victims feel that "the past" as defined by the Yugoslavia Tribunal is not yet over, and they resist its attempts to encourage victims and perpetrators alike to "mediate something through narrative."[75]

While less openly opposed to the Yugoslavia Tribunal than their Serbian counterparts, Bosniak and Kosovar victims expressed mixed reactions toward its work. Many victims believed the Tribunal's sentences were too lenient, calling them "insignificant or small"[76] and "basically nothing."[77] Some were also frustrated with the fact that Milošević, who died while awaiting judgment, was never officially sentenced by the Tribunal.[78] In addition, some Bosniak and Kosovar victims critiqued the Tribunal's sluggish, selective prosecutions. One Srebrenica survivor noted, "[t]he men who raped me are still at large, I've found some of them on social networks. They walk around freely… After 20 years, many victims have already died. They didn't live long enough to see justice being done."[79]

Other Bosniak and Kosovar victims were more optimistic about the Tribunal. Kosovar survivor Dren Kaka explained that he testified before the Tribunal during the Milošević trial because he wanted "to show people that I haven't forgotten. I will never, I will never forget. I am more than glad to go and testify and get these guys locked up."[80] Bosniak survivor Munira Subasic concurred, noting that "a verdict [in the Radovan Karadžić case] is very important to show new generations… what really happened in Bosnia."[81] Similarly, Bosniak civil society leader Dobrila Govdarica found that "[c]larifying that Srebrenica was a genocide was the most important

---

[72] Diane Orentlicher, *International Justice Marks its Fifteenth Anniversary: A Preliminary Assessment of the ICTY's Impact in Serbia*, AMERICAN UNIVERSITY – WASHINGTON COLLEGE OF LAW HUMAN RIGHTS Brief 16 (2009), www.wcl.american.edu/hrbrief/16/20rentlicher.pdf.

[73] *Id.* at 19.

[74] *Id.*

[75] Jelena Obradovic-Wochnik, *Serbian Civil Society as an Exclusionary Space: NGOs, the Public and "Coming to Terms with the Past,"* Civil Society and Transitions in the Western Balkans 210 (2013), https://link.springer.com/chapter/10.1057%2F9781137296252_13#page-1.

[76] Diane F. Orentlicher, *That Somebody Guilty Be Punished*, 51 (2010).

[77] *Id.*

[78] *Id.*

[79] Stuart Hughes, *Bosnia's Wartime Rape Survivors Losing Hope of Justice*, BBC (Apr. 1, 2014) www.bbc.com/news/world-europe-26833510.

[80] Neil Tweedie, *Kosovo War Massacre: Sole Survivor Found by Telegraph Ten Years On*, THE TELEGRAPH (Mar. 31, 2009).

[81] *Serb Leader Guilty of Genocide, Jailed for 40 Years*. CNBC (Mar. 24, 2016), www.cnbc.com/2016/03/24/Karadžić-guilty-of-bosnia-genocide-jailed-for-40-years.html.

achievement and without the [Yugoslavia Tribunal] it wouldn't be possible."[82] Sasa Madacki, another Bosniak civil society leader, agreed, saying, "I hate the Tribunal but I need the Tribunal."[83]

Yugoslavia Tribunal officials have emphasized that the Tribunal cannot address each individual victim's story of suffering. As Yugoslavia Tribunal Judge Fausto Pocar stated, "[i]nevitably, a number of victims are not mentioned individually, and their specific case is not taken up. If the case is to be kept manageable, this is, unfortunately, unavoidable in these mass crimes trials. I understand the frustration."[84] Others have noted that the Tribunal lacks the resources necessary to provide victims with compensation for their losses, noting that victims' expectations for the Tribunal were "high and perhaps unreasonable."[85] Yet, Tribunal officials have noted that "[t]he Statute of the ICTY is not exactly the ideal statute when it comes to victims' compensation in particular," even while nevertheless emphasizing that the Tribunal is "a platform that otherwise would not have existed, that gave the opportunity to victims to travel to The Hague and tell their story. It is fundamentally important and it is part of our legacy... [w]e have helped, in our small way, to give them the opportunity to be heard."[86]

The Rwanda Tribunal has also had limited impact on reconciliation and victim catharsis within its post-conflict context. Victims have expressed frustration that the Rwanda Tribunal prosecuted the most-guilty destabilizing actors, while leaving mid- and lower-level actors to domestic courts and local tribunals like the *gacaca* system.[87] Some victims may also perceive the Rwanda Tribunal as meting out more lenient "international justice" to the chief *genocidaires*, while giving lower-level perpetrators harsher sentences that they had to serve in domestic Rwandan prisons with much more poorly equipped cells than those in Scheveningen.[88] Furthermore, the Tribunal's limited focus on Hutu crimes against Tutsis may have helped to further entrench the post-genocide ethnic divide, leaving Rwanda vulnerable to renewed ethnic violence in the future.[89] Thus, while the Rwanda Tribunal made some substantial contributions to Rwanda's remarkable twenty-eight years of conflict-free existence, its one-sided prosecutions may have contributed to Rwandans' skepticism about "international justice" and continued ethnic divisions within the country.

---

[82] ORENTLICHER, *supra* note 63, at 66.

[83] *Id.* at 85.

[84] Judge Fausto Pocar, *Legacy of the ICTY in the Former Yugoslavia*, *supra* note 63, at 83.

[85] Martin Petrov, Chief of Immediate Office of the Registrar, ICTY, *Legacy of the ICTY in the Former Yugoslavia*, *supra* note 63, at 56.

[86] Judge Carmel Agius, Vice-President of ICTY, *Legacy of the ICTY in the Former Yugoslavia*, *supra* note 63, at 22.

[87] Barria & Roper, *supra* note 35, at 363.

[88] *Id.* at 368.

[89] HUMAN RIGHTS WATCH, *supra* note 39; Peskin, *supra* note 37, at 216–17.

14.4.2 *Comprehensive Historical Record*

The Yugoslavia Tribunal was effective at creating fact-based historical records of major atrocity crimes. These records contradicted Serbian disinformation campaigns focused on minimizing or dismissing allegations of Serbian atrocities committed during the Bosnian War. These historical records also helped dispel false moral equivalencies between Bosnian Serb and Bosniak forces regarding atrocity crimes committed during the conflict.

For example, during the siege of Sarajevo from April 1992 to February 1996, Serbian leaders claimed that Bosniaks fired on themselves during what came to be known as the "breadline massacre," in which Serbian mortar shells killed ninety-four Bosniak civilians in Sarajevo in 1992. Serbian officials unequivocally denied their involvement in the attack, leading many Western media outlets to conclude that the city's mainly Muslim defenders had fired on their own civilians as a propaganda ploy to win world sympathy and military intervention.[90] A UN official who investigated the incident at the time noted that he thought Bosniak forces loyal to President Alija Izetbegovic may have detonated a bomb, claiming, "We believe it was a command-detonated explosion, probably in a can. The impact which is there now is not necessarily similar or anywhere near as large as we came to expect with a mortar round landing on a paved surface."[91] Even media sources from the time that did not blame Bosniaks for the attack seemed to indicate that the truth was unknown and perhaps both sides were to blame. For example, shortly following the breadline massacre, a *New York Times* article reported that the mortars were launched by Serbian units in hills south of Sarajevo, but went on to report sources blaming Bosniaks, Bosnian Serbs, and Yugoslav national forces for the attack.[92]

Similarly, local Serbian politicians denied that Serbian units had anything to do with the 1994 and 1995 market attacks, which killed sixty-six and sixteen Sarajevo residents respectively.[93] Again, they implied that Bosniak forces shelled the market themselves.[94] After the 1994 attack, Miroslav Toholj, "information minister" of the self-styled Bosnian Serb republic, said that the Bosniaks were responsible for the attack, arguing that "Serbs don't kill civilians."[95] Bosnian Serb militias threatened to halt relief flights to Sarajevo unless they were "exonerated" by the United

---

[90] Leonard Doyle, *Muslims "Slaughter Their Own People": Bosnia Bread Queue Massacre Was Propaganda Ploy*, U.N. *Told*, THE INDEPENDENT (Aug. 21, 1992), www.independent.co.uk/news/muslims-slaughter-their-own-people-bosnia-bread-queue-massacre-was-propaganda-ploy-un-told-1541801.html.

[91] *Id* (quoting an unnamed senior U.N. official who investigated the attack).

[92] John Burns, *Mortar Attack on Civilians Leaves 16 Dead in Bosnia*, THE NEW YORK TIMES (May 28, 1992), www.nytimes.com/1992/05/28/world/mortar-attack-on-civilians-leaves-16-dead-in-bosnia.html.

[93] *Id.*

[94] John Kifner, *66 Die as Shell Wrecks Sarajevo Market*, THE NEW YORK TIMES (Feb. 6, 1994), www.nytimes.com/1994/02/06/world/66-die-as-shell-wrecks-sarajevo-market.html?pagewanted=all.

[95] Mark Heinrich & Robert Block, *Sarajevo Atrocity Turns Market into Bloodbath*, THE INDEPENDENT (Feb. 6, 1994), www.independent.co.uk/news/sarajevo-atrocity-turns-market-into-bloodbath-1392207.html.

Nations.[96] While the United Nations confirmed that the mortar had been fired from northeast of the market, it could not determine the mortar's exact origin and, as with the breadline massacre, threw up its hands, concluding that the ultimate truth of who was responsible for the attack was unknowable.

The truth of these massacres remained unknown until the Yugoslavia Tribunal investigated them and presented the facts found by those investigations during the Galić, Karadžić, Mladić, and Milošević cases. During trial proceedings in the Galić case, Tribunal prosecutors established that the 1994 market massacre was committed by Serb forces around Sarajevo.[97] The Chamber concluded that the mortars used in the attack came from Serbian-controlled territory and were fired deliberately at non-military objects.[98] Similarly, the Trial Chamber for Milošević established that the 1995 market attack came from a mortar fired by Serbian forces located on Serbian-controlled territory.[99] While the Appeals Chamber ultimately found that Milošević could not be held liable for these attacks, it concluded that his deputy commander – not Bosniak forces – was responsible for it.[100]

Bosnian Serbs also tried to spread disinformation about the Srebrenica genocide. As the conflict ended, many Serbs denied the extent of the acts committed by the Bosnia Serb military, police, and other forces, arguing that "only" 2,000 people died, and that most of the dead were Bosniak soldiers killed in battle.[101] Still others claimed that it was a "crime of passion," as Serbian troops sought revenge for the many Serbs killed in the villages around Srebrenica.[102] Others, including the defense counsel in the Krstić case, claimed that what happened in Srebrenica may have been mass killing, but was not ethnically motivated and thus should not be considered a genocide.[103]

Yugoslavia Tribunal investigations and prosecutions of the Srebrenica atrocities proved these claims false. As noted in the Krstić case, the Tribunal established beyond a reasonable doubt that the number of dead was around 7,000; that the victims were civilians, not armed combatants; that the mass killings were a planned operation, not a crime of passion; and that the atrocities in Srebrenica were ethnically motivated acts of genocide.[104]

[96]   Kifner, *supra* note 92.
[97]   Prosecutor v. Stanislav Galić, Case No. IT-98–54, paras. 439–96 (Int'l Crim. Trib. for the Former Yugoslavia, Dec. 5, 2003).
[98]   *Id.* at paras. 494–96.
[99]   Judgment, Prosecutor, v. Milošević, *supra* note 19, at paras. 714–24.
[100] Appeals Judgment, Prosecutor v. Milošević, Case No. IT-02–54, paras. 291–94 (Int'l Crim. Trib. for the Former Yugoslavia, Nov. 12, 2009).
[101] *Facts about Srebrenica*, ICTY, www.icty.org/x/file/Outreach/view_from_hague/jit_srebrenica_en.pdf.
[102] *Id.*
[103] Judgment, Prosecutor v. Radislav Krstić, Case No. IT-98–33, para. 593 (Int'l Crim. Trib. for the Former Yugoslavia, Nov. 12, 2009).
[104] *Facts about Srebrenica, supra* note 87.

To prove this, the Tribunal uncovered, investigated, catalogued, and publicly presented substantial evidence. To establish the number of people killed at Srebrenica, the Trial Chamber in the Krstić case interviewed a demographics expert who researched and reported the total number of missing persons at Srebrenica and conservatively estimated that number at 7,475 people.[105] The Chamber also examined authenticated Serbian military documentation that stated that Bosnian Serb forces had captured around 6,000 people,[106] and that "of the 10,000 military aged men who were in Srebrenica, 4,000–5,000 have certainly kicked the bucket."[107] Trial testimony by Serbian officer Erdemović further confirmed that he and other members of the Bosnian Serb forces killed between 1,000 and 1,200 Bosniak men in one day in one location.[108]

To establish that victims at Srebrenica were civilians, not combatants, the Tribunal considered further information from the exhumed graves. This revealed that victims had been blindfolded and handcuffed with wire, cloth, or string.[109] Several of them were handicapped, indicating that they were not likely to have been combatants.[110] VRS Deputy Commander for Security and Intelligence Momir Nikolić's oral testimony confirmed this, stating, "Do you really think that in an operation where 7,000 people were set aside, captured, and killed that somebody was adhering to the Geneva Conventions? Do you really believe that somebody adhered to the law, rules and regulations in an operation where so many were killed?... Because had they, then the consequences of that particular operation would not have been a total of 7,000 people dead."[111]

To establish that these killings were premeditated and organized, rather than crimes of passion, the Tribunal considered evidence from twenty-one "primary" and "secondary" mass graves.[112] The Tribunal found that Bosnian Serbs used the secondary graves to cover up their actions, using heavy machinery to exhume and rebury the bodies.[113] This showed a deliberate, planned operation, not a crime of passion. Further intercepts showed that local Serbian commanders had requested additional men to help with the executions and additional fuel for the bulldozers used to dig the mass graves - requests that the Serbian central command fulfilled.[114] This was supported by testimony that Mladić had issued specific orders to kill and capture Bosniaks that "everyone knew

---

[105] Prosecutor v. Krstić, *supra* note 101 at para. 81.
[106] *Id.* at para. 83.
[107] *Id.*
[108] Prosecutor v. Krstić, *supra* note 101 at paras. 234, 239–40.
[109] Prosecutor v. Krstić, *supra* note 101 at para. 75.
[110] *Id.*
[111] Testimony of Momir Nikolić, T 1959, in Prosecutor v. Vidoje Blagojević and Dragan Jokić, Case No.: IT-02-60, (Int'l Crim. Trib. for the Former Yugoslavia, Sept. 25, 2003).
[112] Prosecutor v. Krstić, *supra* note 101 at para. 71.
[113] *Id.* at para. 80.
[114] *Id.* at para. 116.

about."[115] Genocidal intent was further established through Serbian forces' destruction of Bosniak homes and the principal mosque in Srebrenica.[116]

Through its investigation, documentation, and prosecution of atrocity crimes, the Yugoslavia Tribunal created a comprehensive record of events like the Srebrenica genocide and the Sarajevo attacks that formed the basis for the criminal convictions of several Serb leaders. Most members of the international community would concur with the Yugoslavia Tribunal's own assessment that "the detail in which the ICTY's judgements describe the crimes and the involvement of those convicted make it impossible for anyone to dispute the reality of the horrors that took place in and around Bratunac, Brčko, Čelebići, Dubrovnik, Foča, Prijedor, Sarajevo, Srebrenica and Zvornik, to name but a few."[117]

Nevertheless, Serbian counter-narratives continue to hold sway over many in Serbia today. In 2008, Diane Orentlicher noted that while the Yugoslavia Tribunal was effectively "shrinking the space for denial" of atrocities within Serbia, many Serbians still echo Milošević's critique of the Yugoslavia Tribunal as fundamentally "an instrument of [anti-Serb] power" rather than as an impartial court of justice.[118] More recently, Marko Milanovic has noted that public opinion surveys conducted in Serbia, Croatia, Bosnia-Herzegovina, and Kosovo in 2016 show that "[b]arely one-fifth of the Bosnian Serb population believe that any crime (let alone genocide) happened in Srebrenica, while two-fifths say that they never even heard of any such crime."[119] Thus while the Yugoslavia Tribunal has been largely successful at establishing a global record of atrocities, it has struggled to communicate that record to local populations in a persuasive, lasting way.

14.4.3 Limitations of Justice

While the Rwanda Tribunal has also helped construct a narrative of the 1994 genocide, its restricted prosecutions limited its ability to provide victim catharsis, dispel disinformation, and heal cultural divisions within the country. As discussed earlier in this chapter, unlike its Yugoslavian counterpart, the Rwandan government prevented the Rwanda Tribunal from investigating allegations of RPF war crimes. This resulted in judicial decisions that communicated a binary vision of the events of 1994 in which Hutus were the only perpetrators of atrocity crimes. This may have contributed to Rwandans' perception of the Hutu population's collective guilt for

---

[115] Judgment, Prosecutor v. Dragan Obrenović, Case No. Case No. IT-02-60/2-S, Annex B (Int'l Crim. Trib. for the Former Yugoslavia, Nov. 12, 2009).

[116] Prosecutor v. Krstić, *supra* note 101 at paras. 594–99.

[117] *Achievements*, ICTY, www.icty.org/sid/324#establishing. This language has existed in several iterations for more than a decade on the Tribunal's website.

[118] Diane Orentlicher, Shrinking the Space for Denial: The Impact of the ICTY in Serbia 17 (2008), www.opensocietyfoundations.org/sites/default/files/serbia_20080501.pdf

[119] Marko Milanovic, *The Impact of the ICTY on the Former Yugoslavia: An Anticipatory Post-Mortem*, AM. J. OF INT'L L. (Mar. 28, 2016), https://ssrn.com/abstract=2755505.

the genocide and may have marginalized stories of moderate Hutu victims who were also targeted by Hutu extremists in April 1994.[120] In addition, as with the Yugoslavia Tribunal, the Rwanda Tribunal provided limited opportunities for witness testimony and did not provide a victim compensation program. This meant that even Tutsi victims who participated in the Tribunal's work left feeling only partially satisfied. Consequently, the Rwandan population has tended to express skepticism about the Rwanda Tribunal's work.[121]

Restrictions on the Rwanda Tribunal's work also limited its ability to provide a comprehensive historical record of the genocide and its context. Along with many human rights advocates, Rwandan scholar Dibussi Tandé notes that the Rwanda Tribunal was a vital part of post-genocide accountability efforts, stating that the Tribunal "was a necessary legal instrument, given the need to bring the architects of the Rwandan genocide to justice… [and] demonstrate how the quest for political power and ethnic hegemony… can easily slide into crimes against humanity and genocide."[122] Nevertheless, as Human Rights Watch has noted, the Tribunal's inability to investigate RPF war crimes, including a massacre at the Kibeho refugee camp on the Rwandan-Tanzanian border, has led many to regard its decisions as one-sided.[123] This limitation has also prevented the Tribunal from dispelling the moral equivalency created by extremists' anti-RPF allegations, such as the accusation that RPF forces, not genocidal extremists, shot down President Habyarimana's plane in April 1994 and precipitated the genocide.[124]

Finally, the Rwanda Tribunal's restrictions may have undermined reconciliation efforts within the country. The Rwandan government's restrictions on Tribunal investigations and prosecutions has limited the Tribunal's ability to address the harm caused to moderate Hutus from the genocidal campaign of extremist Hutus. This undermined Hutu cultural identity and ensured that within Rwanda, "Hutus are forbidden any collective mourning."[125] It also contributed to Rwandans' perception that all Hutus are former or future *genocidaires*, which further deepened latent ethnic divisions in Rwanda.[126] As a result, the Rwanda Tribunal has produced an important factual account of the genocide which provides incomplete catharsis to the many victims of Hutu extremists' 1994 campaign.

---

[120]   See Helen Hintjens, *Post-Genocide Identity Politics in Rwanda*, ETHNICITIES 8 22 (2008), https://hal .archives-ouvertes.fr/hal-00571890/document.

[121]   Timothy Longman, *Trying Times for Rwanda*, HARVARD INT'L REV. (Aug. 2010) http://hir.harvard.edu/ article/?a=2686.

[122]   Dibussi Tande, Assessing the International Criminal Tribunal for Rwanda, Institute for Policy Studies (Oct. 2010) www.ips-dc.org/assessing_the_international_criminal_tribunal_for_rwanda_ictr/

[123]   Rwanda: Tribunal Risks Supporting 'Victor's Justice', HUMAN RIGHTS WATCH (Jun. 1, 2009) www.hrw .org/news/2009/06/01/rwanda-tribunal-risks-supporting-victors-justice.

[124]   See Helen Hintjens, *supra* note 119, at 24–25.

[125]   Jean-Philippe Rémy, *Hanté par le génocide, le Rwanda organise une difficile commémoration*, LE MONDE, (Apr. 7, 2004), www.lemonde.fr/archives/article/2004/04/06/hante-par-le-genocide-le-rwanda-organise-une-difficile-commemoration_360118_1819218.html?xtmc=hante_par_le_genocide&xtcr=46.

[126]   Hintjens, *supra* note 119, at 31.

14.5 LAUNCHING A CULTURE OF INTERNATIONAL CRIMINAL JUSTICE

In addition to impacts on their respective conflict areas, the Yugoslavia and Rwanda Tribunals profoundly affected how people throughout the world think about impunity, accountability for atrocities, and international criminal law. The fight against impunity, begun at Nuremburg, lay dormant during the Cold War. As the first major post-Cold War effort to seek accountability for atrocity crimes, the Yugoslavia Tribunal reawakened this fight and inspired a renaissance of international criminal justice. As this renaissance grew worldwide, the work of the Yugoslavia and Rwanda Tribunals began to influence victims' and perpetrators' expectations that justice would be handed down in "The Hague." And as justice has increasingly taken place in The Hague and Arusha, the Yugoslavia and Rwanda Tribunals have recruited, employed, and mentored accountability-minded individuals, creating an international criminal justice professional class that largely leads the fight against impunity today.

14.5.1 Post-Cold War Renaissance of International Criminal Justice

The International Military Tribunal at Nuremburg ("Nuremburg Tribunal"), which operated from 1945 to 1946 in the wake of World War II, contributed substantially to ending impunity for atrocity crimes. The Nuremburg Tribunal produced a "flurry of normative developments," including the principle of individual criminal responsibility for war crimes, the definition of crimes against humanity, and the concept of criminal accountability provided by the international community.[127]

Unfortunately, these groundbreaking developments stagnated in the postwar period. After Nuremburg, many argued for the creation of a permanent international criminal body with jurisdiction over war crimes and crimes against humanity in order to solidify the international community's commitment to ending impunity. As the postwar period crystallized into the Cold War, however, the international community – and, more notably, the UN Security Council – was too bitterly divided to reach a consensus on whether and how to create such an international criminal tribunal. Such a tribunal could have addressed the many global atrocity crimes committed between 1949 and 1990. Instead, those responsible for these violations escaped accountability for decades and, in many cases, were never forced to answer for their crimes.

As the Berlin Wall fell and ushered in the "Pax Americana" of the 1990s, new possibilities for international consensus on accountability for atrocity crimes emerged. The United States no longer solely regarded efforts to end impunity as a liability in its Cold War rivalry. Instead, as discussed above, it gradually regarded international criminal justice as a tool to build stability in post-Soviet states like the former Yugoslavia. This strategic recalculation led the United States to support

---

[127] Jelena Pejic, *Accountability for International Crimes: From Conjecture to Reality*, 84 INT'L REV. OF THE RED CROSS (Mar. 2002) at 14, www.loc.gov/rr/frd/Military_Law/pdf/RC_Mar-2002.pdf.

international criminal accountability and facilitated the international community's return to the fight against impunity.

Founded three years after the end of the Cold War and forty-seven years after the end of the Nuremburg Tribunal, the Yugoslavia Tribunal was the first major international effort to end impunity since the Nazi war crime trials. The Yugoslavia Tribunal renewed Nuremburg's effort to ensure that individuals who committed war crimes and crimes against humanity should be punished, not pardoned. For the first time since World War II, world leaders seriously considered – and created – peace agreements that acknowledged, and to some extent adopted, norms of justice and accountability, thanks in part to the work of the Yugoslavia Tribunal. While the Tribunal has been rightly critiqued for being incomplete in delivering justice in the former Yugoslavia, it nevertheless reestablished accountability as an essential element in peace talks, constitution drafting, and post-conflict peacebuilding.

By reestablishing accountability for atrocities as an international norm, the Yugoslavia and Rwanda Tribunals helped launch a renaissance of international criminal justice. Judicial and quasi-judicial bodies addressing violations of international law have featured in peace agreements for most conflicts after 1993. These bodies, including the Special Court for Sierra Leone, the Special Tribunal for Lebanon, and the Extraordinary Chambers in the Courts of Cambodia ("Cambodia Tribunal"), as well as the permanent International Criminal Court ("ICC"), have accountability-focused missions and jurisdiction that reflects these two tribunals' approach of ending impunity by prosecuting the highest-level individuals responsible for these crimes. As discussed elsewhere in this book, these courts' jurisprudence also reflects legal principles first established by the Yugoslavia and Rwanda Tribunals.

These tribunals also profoundly influenced other international criminal courts' organizational structures. Founded not long after the Yugoslavia Tribunal, the Rwanda Tribunal was largely modeled on its immediate predecessor, adopting the Yugoslavia Tribunal's model of three trial chambers overseen by sixteen judges of different nationalities.[128] The two tribunals also shared a registry and appeals chamber for most of their existences.[129] The Special Court for Sierra Leone adopted the Yugoslavia Tribunal's organizational structure as well, creating three trial chambers and one appeal chamber, although as a hybrid tribunal, more Sierra Leonean judges than international judges presided there.[130] Additionally, while its organizational structure and jurisdiction varied greatly from the Yugoslavia Tribunal's, the Special

---

[128] Statute of the International Criminal Tribunal for the Former Yugoslavia, arts. 12, 13bis (2009), www.icty.org/x/file/Legal%20Library/Statute/statute_sept09_en.pdf; Statute of the International Criminal Tribunal for Rwanda, arts. 11, 12bis (2009), http://legal.un.org/avl/pdf/ha/ictr_EF.pdf.

[129] *Organisation of the International Criminal Tribunal for the Former Yugoslavia*, ICTY, www.icty.org/en/about/tribunal/organisational-chart; *Detention*, ICTY, www.icty.org/en/about/detention; *Chambers*, ICTR http://unictr.unmict.org/en/tribunal/chambers; *Registry*, ICTR, http://unictr.unmict.org/en/tribunal/registry; *Defense and detention*, ICTR http://unictr.unmict.org/en/tribunal/defence.

[130] Statute of the Special Court for Sierra Leone Statute, arts. 1 and 11 (2000), www.rscsl.org/Documents/scsl-statute.pdf.

Tribunal for Lebanon adopted the Yugoslavia Tribunal's requirement that all judges be of different nationalities and modeled their Office of the Prosecutor on that of the Yugoslavia Tribunal.[131]

14.5.2 *Global Expectations of Justice*

The renaissance of international criminal justice ushered in by the Yugoslavia and Rwanda Tribunals helped foster a growing expectation among both perpetrators and victims of atrocity crimes that those crimes could and would be accounted for in The Hague. The Dutch capital city, which has been home to the Yugoslavia Tribunal, the Rwanda Tribunal's Appeals Chamber, and later the International Criminal Court, has often been used as shorthand for international criminal accountability efforts. As international criminal law has developed since the Yugoslavia Tribunal's creation in 1993, victims' and perpetrators' perceptions of justice "in The Hague" have evolved, reflecting concern, skepticism, but also hope about accountability efforts and international criminal institutions' enforcement capabilities. Nevertheless, the fact that victims and perpetrators continue to seriously grapple with international criminal justice institutions reflects the continued impact and legacy of the Yugoslavia Tribunal, the original source of atrocity accountability in The Hague.

Perpetrators have increasingly expected and taken seriously the threat of arrest, prosecution, and detention in The Hague. Since the Yugoslavia Tribunal's first indictments, perpetrators have responded vehemently to international criminal justice efforts, indicating not only their opposition to these judicial bodies, but also their fear that those bodies could hold them accountable for their actions. The fact that perpetrators publicly criticize, react to, and resist international criminal warrants and investigations indicates that the accountability efforts begun by the Yugoslavia Tribunal are taken seriously by those who have committed atrocity crimes.

Yugoslavia Tribunal defendants often addressed the idea of international criminal accountability in The Hague. Croat defendant Franjo Tuđman noted the Tribunal's wide jurisdictional reach on tapes privately recorded during his presidency, on which he noted, "I haven't mentioned another argument, The Hague tribunal. It is clear our generals and all of you who are sitting here now with me could end up there, too."[132] Similarly, Slobodan Milošević addressed the Tribunal as a "farce of a trial" but nevertheless saw it as enough of a threat that he "must struggle here to topple this tribunal... and the masterminds behind it who are using it against people who are fighting for freedom in the world."[133]

---

[131] Statute of the Special Tribunal for Lebanon, art. 1 (2007), www.stl-tsl.org/index.php?option=com_k2 &Id=70_36819111552cbe394c8efcf0586eo81c&lang=en&task=download&view=item.

[132] Philip Sherwell & Alina Petric, *Tuđman Tapes Reveal Plans to Divide Bosnia and Hide War Crimes,* THE TELEGRAPH (June 18, 2000), www.telegraph.co.uk/news/worldnews/europe/bosnia/1343702/ Tuđman-tapes-reveal-plans-to-divide-Bosnia-and-hide-war-crimes.html.

[133] *Slobodan Milošević: Key Quotes,* CNN (Feb. 11, 2002), http://edition.cnn.com/2002/WORLD/eur ope/o2/11/Milošević.quotes/index.html.

ICC indictees and defendants have reacted to its accountability efforts with similar vehemence. Sudanese leader Omar al-Bashir responded to the ICC warrant against him by saying, "They will issue their decision tomorrow... this coming decision, they can prepare right now: they can eat it."[134] Similarly, when the ICC issued a warrant against Muammar Qaddafi and his two sons, Libyan justice minister Mohammed al-Qamoodi stated that "Libya... does not accept the decision of the ICC which is a tool of the Western world to prosecute leaders in the Third World."[135] During his ICC trial, Congolese general Jean-Pierre Bemba noted that "we should aspire to something more than a forced confession, a secret trial and a punishment meted out by a beating or a bullet" before arguing that the ICC was not a "court of unfettered jurisdiction" that could judge wartime atrocities that did not rise to the level of war crimes.[136]

Current-day victims of atrocity crimes have also indicated growing expectations – and critiques – of international accountability "in The Hague" for the perpetrators that have harmed them. International criminal justice remains too limited for some victims. For example, witnesses in recent ICC cases felt "the [ICC] hears the voices of the people who perpetrated this violence, not the victims."[137]

Nevertheless, victims' awareness of and expectation that justice will be delivered "in The Hague" has increased substantially since the Yugoslavia and Rwanda Tribunals were founded. Victims of the Cambodia genocide expressed hope about the Cambodia Tribunal's ability to "find justice for the people who suffered in that evil regime" and wanted the court "to be able to finally provide and support people who are sick... because of forced labor during the regime."[138] Ugandan victims described the ICC as "a universal court... [that] has the power to prosecute leaders of states and rebel groups... like [Lord's Resistance Army commander Joseph] Kony, who keep moving from state to state. Since the ICC is universal, it has the mandate to get those who are committing atrocities, no matter where they go."[139] Victims in the ICC case against former Ivory Coast president Laurent Gbagbo similarly stated that "we are expecting the truth from the court because on the day of the killings they – I am talking

---

[134] Mike Pflanz, *Sudan's Omar al-Bashir Says ICC Can "Eat" His Arrest Warrant*, THE TELEGRAPH (Mar. 2, 2009), www.telegraph.co.uk/news/worldnews/africaandindianocean/sudan/4933329/Sudans-Omar-al-Bashir-says-ICC-can-eat-his-arrest-warrant.html.

[135] *Libya Rejects International Court Warrant for Gaddafi*, REUTERS (Jun. 27, 2011) www.reuters.com/article/libya-icc-idUSLDE75Q1LT20110627.

[136] Transcripts from Trial Chamber proceedings, The Prosecutor v. Jean-Pierre Bemba Gombo, Case No. ICC-01/05-01/08-T (International Criminal Court, Jan. 15, 2016), www.icc-cpi.int/Transcripts/CR2016_00332.PDF.

[137] Quoted in Berkeley Human Rights Center, The Victim's Court? A Study of 622 Victim Participants at the International Criminal Court (2015), www.law.berkeley.edu/wp-content/uploads/2015/04/VP_report_2015_final_full2.pdf.

[138] Quoted in Elisa Hoven & Saskia Schiebel, *Justice for Victims' in Trials of Mass Crimes: Symbolism or Substance?*, INT'L REV. OF VICTIMOLOGY (Apr. 2015), www.researchgate.net/publication/276084308_'Justice_for_victims'_in_trials_of_mass_crimes_Symbolism_or_substance.

[139] Quoted in THE VICTIM'S COURT?, *supra* note 136.

about those who did it, those in power at the time – said there was no murders; they said it was untrue. We were shocked…. It is the denial that pushes me to want the truth… If there is a verdict, the truth will be revealed."[140]

While international criminal justice mechanisms may not always satisfy victims' transitional justice needs, they are now an integral part of many victims' expectations for post-conflict accountability. And while current mechanisms differ somewhat substantially from the Yugoslavia and Rwanda Tribunals, they still feature a focus on high-level, individual perpetrators; a multinational panel of judicial decision-makers; and a strong reliance on international human rights conventions and international criminal law precedent, much of it inherited from these two ad-hoc tribunals. Thus, the Yugoslavia and Rwanda Tribunals have helped create a belief that the international community will use some kind of judicial mechanism to address mass atrocity crimes – with varying levels of success.

14.5.3 *The Creation of an International Criminal Justice Professional Class*

The Yugoslavia and Rwanda Tribunals also recruited, trained, and prepared a group of practitioners that have formalized and professionalized the field of international criminal law. After their time at the Yugoslavia and/or Rwanda Tribunals, many judges, attorneys, investigators, documenters, and administrative professionals have led other international human rights bodies, including hybrid and international tribunals. Others have founded accountability-oriented organizations, including advocacy institutes, documentation initiatives, and support groups for tribunals. Others have taught and mentored the next generation of international criminal justice professionals.

Many Yugoslavia and Rwanda Tribunal alumni went on to work at other international human rights organizations. Antonio Cassese, former president and judge at the Yugoslavia Tribunal, became the chairman of the International Commission of Inquiry on Darfur in 2004, investigating reports of violations of international humanitarian and human rights law. In 2009, he was elected president of the Special Tribunal for Lebanon. Richard Goldstone, who served as prosecutor at both the Yugoslavia and Rwanda Tribunals, later served as chairman of the International Independent Inquiry on Kosovo. Similarly, Louise Arbour became the UN High Commissioner for Human Rights after her tenure as a prosecutor at the Yugoslavia and Rwanda Tribunals.

Yugoslavia and Rwanda Tribunal alumni have also become integral members of the international criminal law academy. Alex Whiting, a trial attorney at the Yugoslavia Tribunal, went on to serve as prosecutions coordinator at the ICC and now teaches international practice at Harvard Law School. Former Yugoslavia and Rwanda Tribunal legal officer Bin Bing Jia now teaches law at Tsinghua University

---

[140] Quoted in THE VICTIM'S COURT?, *supra* note 136.

in Beijing. Hannah Garry, legal officer at both the Yugoslavia and Rwanda Tribunals' Appeals Chambers, served as legal adviser at the Cambodia Tribunal and ICC before founding the University of Southern California Law School's international human rights clinic. Georges Abi-Saab, former judge for the Yugoslavia and Rwanda Tribunals' Appeals Chambers, now teaches international law at NYU Law School, Cairo University, and the Graduate Institute of International Studies in Geneva. In addition, numerous courses in international criminal law and accountability have been created in response to the Yugoslavia and Rwanda Tribunals and their progeny.

Finally, the Yugoslavia Tribunal in particular inspired numerous documentation and accountability initiatives. American University Washington College of Law's War Crimes Research Office began in 1995 in response to a request for assistance from the prosecutor of the Yugoslavia and Rwanda Tribunals. Similarly, the War Crimes Evidence Library at Chicago-Kent Law School began in 1996 in response to the Dayton Accords' documentation needs. And the Belgrade Centre for Human Rights, the Humanitarian Law Center in Belgrade, the Centre for Human Rights in Serbia, and the Croatian Association for Promoting Inclusion were all founded in the former Yugoslavia to serve the Yugoslavia Tribunal's documentation needs as well as reconciliation needs in their respective countries.

14.6 CONCLUSION

The Yugoslavia and Rwanda Tribunals had profound impacts on international criminal law, but, as this chapter shows, their effects went beyond international criminal jurisprudence. While their work was often timid and tardy, these Tribunals ultimately helped to shape peace processes, geopolitical dynamics, and historical memory creation in their respective regions, while also contributing to a renaissance of international criminal accountability for atrocity crimes.

Both the Yugoslavia and Rwanda Tribunals helped neutralize destabilizing actors during key points in the peacebuilding process in their respective regions. Yugoslavia Tribunal indictments helped to remove and neutralize destabilizing actors during peace negotiations at Dayton. Similarly, the Rwanda Tribunal helped neutralize the influence of *genocidaires* in the ethnically divided post-conflict state, although its inability to prosecute RPF members prevented it from removing all potential war criminals from political office.

In addition to neutralizing bad political and military actors in Serbia and Croatia, Yugoslavia Tribunal indictments also helped shaped the outcome of the Kosovo conflict. The Tribunal's indictment of Milošević and documentation of Serbian-perpetrated ethnic cleansing of Kosovars contributed to NATO leaders' decision to intervene during the Kosovo conflict. The moral clarity provided by the Tribunal's evidence-gathering and indictments also helped NATO leaders justify this intervention to their citizens.

The Yugoslavia and Rwanda Tribunals' documentation of atrocity crimes also helped to establish a comprehensive historical record of those crimes within their respective regions. While victims in both Rwanda and the former Yugoslavia have critiqued their respective tribunals' portrayals of atrocity crimes they suffered, many victims in both regions have found tribunal-established historical records to be important factors in their healing and catharsis. These records have also helped to contradict false narratives of moral equivalency between victims and perpetrators put forward by ethno-nationalist groups in both Rwanda and the former Yugoslavia and to counteract the effects of the Serbian campaign to eradicate Bosniak memory and culture from the Balkan region.

The Yugoslavia and Rwanda Tribunals profoundly impacted international criminal law. These two tribunals' structures and operations have influenced the organization and management of other hybrid and international criminal tribunals. In addition, the work of the Yugoslavia Tribunal, the Rwanda Tribunal, and the ICC has led both perpetrators and victims of atrocity crimes to expect that "The Hague," and the international jurists that work there, will provide some form of accountability for atrocity crimes committed in the future. Finally, the two tribunals fostered a new class of international criminal law professionals who now work at other hybrid and international tribunals; spearhead new international human rights initiatives; and teach and mentor the next generation of international criminal lawyers. This enables future hybrid, regional, and international criminal tribunals to address atrocity crimes more agilely and aggressively than their predecessors.

Conclusion

Michael P. Scharf and Milena Sterio

After an inauspicious start where only a handful of low-level perpetrators were surrendered to and tried by the ICTY in its early years, the tribunal ultimately convicted eighty-three individuals of war crimes, crimes against humanity and genocide; acquitted nineteen accused; and referred thirteen accused to national jurisdictions for trial. Those tried included Slobodan Milosevic, the President of the Federal Republic of Yugoslavia; Ratko Mladic, the top Serb general involved in the conflict; and Radovan Karadzic, the political leader of the Bosnian Serb Republic; as well as other politicians, military officers, and detention camp commanders. Seven defendants, including Milosevic, died in the custody of the ICTY prior to judgment.[1]

The ICTR demonstrated similar results. A total of sixty-two defendants were convicted of war crimes, crimes against humanity, and genocide, while fourteen accused were acquitted or released and two indictees died before judgment.[2] Among those convicted were the former Prime Minister of Rwanda, Jean Kambanda; the former army chief of staff, General Augustin Bizimungu; and the former Defense Ministry chief of staff, Colonel Théoneste Bagosora; as well as other political, military, and paramilitary leaders, and corporate and media figures.

The total price tag of the two ad hoc tribunals was $3.8 billion, covered by UN assessments to all member states, 22 percent of which was paid for by the United States (not including its voluntary contributions). But, while international justice has not come cheaply, these costs are a fraction of the costs of a peacekeeping mission or military operation. At the Pentagon, the cost for one B-2 stealth bomber is $3 billion, the cost for a Virginia-class attack submarine is $2.7 billion, and one Arleigh Burke-class guided missile destroyer costs American taxpayers $1.7 billion.[3] In 2017, the United States was spending $3.1 billion per month to wage war in

---

[1] ICTY, *Key Figures of the Cases*, www.icty.org/en/cases/key-figures-cases (last visited Apr. 16, 2017).

[2] ICTR, *Key Figures of Cases*, http://unictr.unmict.org/en/cases/key-figures-cases (last visited Apr. 16, 2017).

[3] David Axe, *Why Can't the Air Force Build an Affordable Plane?*, The Atlantic (Mar. 26, 2012), www .theatlantic.com/national/archive/2012/03/why-cant-the-air-force-build-an-affordable-plane/254998/; Ronald O'Rourke, *Navy Virginia (SSN-774) Class Attack Submarine Procurement: Background and Issues for Congress* 3 (Apr. 6, 2017), https://fas.org/sgp/crs/weapons/RL32418.pdf; Congressional Budget

Afghanistan.[4] It is noteworthy that in the two and a half decades since the creation of the ad hoc tribunals, neither war nor genocide has returned to the former Yugoslavia or Rwanda.

But the significance of the ICTY and ICTR should not be measured in the numbers of convictions and acquittals or its price tag. Gregory Gordon has argued in Chapter 5 of this book that the Nuremberg trials constituted the "birth" of atrocity speech law, but that the International Criminal Tribunal for Yugoslavia (ICTY) and the International Criminal Tribunal for Rwanda (ICTR) represent its "adolescence."[5] Similarly, it may be argued that Nuremberg "birthed" the concept of individual criminal responsibility for international crimes before an international tribunal, and that the ICTY and the ICTR extended this concept to its "adolescence." While the tribunals did not create an entirely novel idea – that international criminal justice should be imposed on individuals who commit particularly heinous crimes – they resurrected accountability at the international level, which had been dormant since Nuremberg. The tribunals thus represent an enormous development in the field of international criminal justice, and their legacy will likely continue to shape the future of international criminal law.

It has been this book's aim to discuss the ICTY's and the ICTR's legacy through the lens of international criminal law, and to assess the tribunals' impact on this field on a general level, but also on a more specific normative and operational level. While it would be inaccurate to claim that the tribunals' entire legacy is positive, and many of the trials have been particularly messy, as Michael Scharf documented in Chapter 10, it is this book's conclusion that overall, the tribunals have contributed significantly to the development of international criminal law and international humanitarian law, and that they will continue to influence future prosecutions at the International Criminal Court, as well as future efforts to instill international justice.

Throughout the chapters above, five major themes and conclusions emerge. First, as Chapters 1 and 2 argue, it is important to use appropriate benchmarks when assessing the ad hoc tribunals' legacy. On the one hand, the ICTY and the ICTR have contributed significantly to the development of international criminal law and have thus created a significant legacy within this field. The tribunals have successfully prosecuted several defendants of genocide and other genocidal offenses; they have prosecuted defendants and developed important case law regarding crimes of sexual violence; they have fine-tuned various modes of liability useful toward the prosecution of various defendants, such as superior responsibility and joint criminal

Office, *An Analysis of the Navy's Fiscal Year 2016 Shipbuilding Plan* 22 (Feb. 2017) www.cbo.gov/sites/default/files/115th-congress-2017–2018/reports/52324-shipbuildingreport.pdf.

4   Mark Lander & Eric Schmitt, *Trump Administration Is Split on Adding Troops to Afghanistan*, N.Y. Times, May 23, 2017, www.nytimes.com/2017/05/23/world/europe/saudi-arabia-arms-deal-nato.html ?_r=0.

5   Gregory S. Gordon, Atrocity Speech Law Comes of Age: The Good, the Bad and the Ugly of the International Speech Crimes Jurisprudence at the Ad Hoc Tribunals [104].

enterprise liability; they have established a legacy of cooperation with national prosecutorial authorities and an operational legacy regarding complex case management; they have developed a procedural legacy regarding international criminal proceedings, through the elaboration of sophisticated rules of procedure and evidence; and they have established a legacy of defense rights, applicable to all defendants, including those accused of the most heinous violations of international criminal law. On the other hand, the ICTY and the ICTR have been far less successful in achieving national reconciliation and goals of societal transformation. This may be an important lesson for future tribunals: while it may be appropriate to ask such future international criminal courts to render justice and develop international criminal law, it may be futile to demand that such courts accomplish extrajudicial goals of societal change and reconciliation. As Jennifer Trahan argued in Chapter 2 above, "perhaps the international community should not claim tribunals will achieve reconciliation; this may simply not be an appropriate goal to foist on the shoulders of a judicial institution."[6]

Second, it is clear that the ICTY and the ICTR have contributed significantly to the development of international criminal law in both the normative as well as the operational sense. As Chapters 3 through 10 demonstrate, the tribunals have, through their extensive case law, developed and fine-tuned various doctrines and norms of international criminal law. The ICTY and the ICTR have established that the same principles of individual liability apply to international as well as to internal armed conflict; in addition, they have successfully convicted defendants of genocidal offenses, and thereby confirmed the importance of imposing genocide liability on particular defendants within particular conflicts. Moreover, the ICTY and the ICTR have developed case law on the prosecution of speech crimes, by imposing additional liability on defendants for inciting the commission of serious crimes within international criminal law. The tribunals have elaborated on various modes of liability, including superior responsibility and advanced modes of joint criminal enterprise, which have enabled the prosecution of nondirect perpetrators of international crimes. The ICTY and the ICTR have also focused on defense rights, by establishing that duress can be a mitigating factor in the imposition of a criminal sentence, and both tribunals have contributed to a sentencing legacy, by establishing a uniform and coherent sentencing approach in the field of international criminal law. In addition, the tribunals have created an operational legacy, by creating specific case management procedures and courtroom management techniques which ensure that international criminal trials proceed in a fair and just manner. Despite some shortcomings, particularly in the field of defense rights, as Chapter 7 argues, and regarding sentencing, as Chapter 10 discusses, it is unquestionable that

---

[6] Jennifer Trahan, *Examining the Benchmarks by Which to Evaluate the ICTY's Legacy* [25].

the ICTY and the ICTR have left behind a tremendous legacy and significant contributions to the field of international criminal law.

Third, it is evident that the ICTY and the ICTR will continue to influence future international criminal prosecutions, including those at the International Criminal Court, as well as future global peace and justice efforts. The International Criminal Court's creation has surely been influenced by the existence of the ICTY and the ICTR, which have sparked a rebirth of the field of international criminal law and contributed to the international community's awareness that international criminal justice matters. In addition, the International Criminal Court will undoubtedly continue to refine the ICTY's and ICTR's case law and procedures, in order to further enhance them and correct any ad hoc tribunals' shortcomings Moreover, the ICTY and the ICTR will have a meaningful impact on future peace and justice efforts. As Paul Williams and Kimberly Larkin have argued in Chapter 10, "these Tribunals ultimately helped to shape peace processes, geopolitical dynamics, and historical memory creation in their respective regions, while also contributing to a renaissance of international criminal accountability for atrocity crimes."[7] Future tribunals and peace builders will likely look back on the ICTY and on the ICTR as models and guidance, and the two ad hoc tribunals' legacy in terms of peace-building will likely shape future efforts toward societal reconciliation. Although the ICTY and the ICTR may have had a relatively small impact on their respective regions, as argued in Chapter 2, they certainly influenced some actors, produced some desirable societal outcomes, and created models for future peace-building efforts.

Fourth, although the ICTY and the ICTR have prosecuted different defendants and have grappled with slightly different issues, it may be argued that the two tribunals have contributed toward the development of international criminal law in a substantially similar manner, and that they have left behind similar general, normative, and operational legacies. Although some of the chapters in this volume have discussed certain issues in the context of one of the two tribunals only, on a more general level it may be concluded that the tribunals' achievements and contribution to the field of international criminal law are comparable and complementary.

Last, as both the ICTY and the ICTR have closed, one might wonder about the future of international criminal justice. The two ad hoc tribunals have successfully completed all their prosecutions and have transferred additional cases to national authorities for prosecution at the national level. It may be argued that their work has been completed, and that international justice has been adequately imposed on the former Yugoslavia and on Rwanda. However, it is uncertain how future conflicts and crimes will be addressed, and whether appropriate accountability at the

---

7 Paul R. Williams & Kimberly Larkin, Twenty-Four Years On: The Yugoslavia and Rwanda Tribunals' Contributions to Durable Peace [326].

international level will continue to be imposed on future perpetrators of heinous crimes. The International Criminal Court may fill a small gap and may be able to impose individual criminal responsibility on a small number of perpetrators, but, as we have witnessed regarding Syria, the accountability gap remains wide and international justice does not reach many conflicts. An important aspect of the ICTY's and the ICTR's legacy may be the very idea that international justice matters, and that international criminal law plays an important role in the imposition of individual accountability, as well as in societal transformation and reconciliation. The ICTY and the ICTR "experience" may persuade actors in the international community to create future accountability mechanisms, so that international justice reaches many. This would constitute the tribunals' most significant achievement.

Index

CPSIA information can be obtained
at www.ICGtesting.com
Printed in the USA
LVHW021654190319
611166LV00015B/270/P